Lecture Notes in Artificial Intelligence 3040

Edited by J. G. Carbonell and J. Siekmann

Subseries of Lecture Notes in Computer Science

T0180379

Springer
Berlin
Heidelberg
New York
Hong Kong
London
Milan
Paris
Tokyo

Ricardo Conejo
Maite Urretavizcaya
José-Luis Pérez-de-la-Cruz (Eds.)

Current Topics in Artificial Intelligence

**10th Conference of the Spanish Association for
Artificial Intelligence, CAEPIA 2003, and
5th Conference on Technology Transfer, TTIA 2003
San Sebastian, Spain, November 12-14, 2003
Revised Selected Papers**

 Springer

Series Editors

Jaime G. Carbonell, Carnegie Mellon University, Pittsburgh, PA, USA
Jörg Siekmann, University of Saarland, Saarbrücken, Germany

Volume Editors

Ricardo Conejo
José-Luis Pérez-de-la-Cruz
Universidad de Málaga, ETSI Informática
Dpto. Lenguajes y Ciencias de la Computación
Boulevard Louis Pasteur, 35, 29071 Málaga, Spain
E-mail: {conejo,perez}@lcc.uma.es

Maite Urretavizcaya
EPV/EHU, Facultad de Informática
Dept. Lenguajes y Sistemas Informáticos
Código Postal 649, 20080 San Sebastián, Spain
E-mail: jipurlom@sc.ehu.es

Library of Congress Control Number: 2004107012

CR Subject Classification (1998): I.2, F.4.1, F.1

ISSN 0302-9743
ISBN 3-540-22218-9 Springer-Verlag Berlin Heidelberg New York

Springer-Verlag is a part of Springer Science+Business Media

springeronline.com

© Springer-Verlag Berlin Heidelberg 2004
Printed in Germany

Typesetting: Camera-ready by author, data conversion by Olgun Computergrafik
Printed on acid-free paper   SPIN: 11014201   06/3142   5 4 3 2 1 0

Preface

The Spanish Association for Artificial Intelligence (AEPIA) was founded in 1983 aiming to encourage the development of artificial intelligence in Spain. AEPIA is a member of the ECCAI (European Co-ordinating Committee for Artificial Intelligence) and a founder member of IBERAMIA, the Iberoamerican Conference on Artificial Intelligence. Under the succesive presidencies of José Cuena, Francisco Garijo and Federico Barber, the association grew to its present healthy state. Since 1985, AEPIA has held a conference (CAEPIA) every second year. Since 1995 a Workshop on Technology Transfer of Artificial Intelligence (TTIA) has taken place together with CAEPIA.

The CAEPIA-TTIA conferences were traditionally held mostly in Spanish and the proceedings were also published in our language. However, in order to promote an even more fruitful exchange of experiences with the international scientific community, the decision was made to publish a postproceedings English volume with the best contributions to CAEPIA-TTIA 2003.

In fact, 214 papers were submitted from 19 countries and 137 were presented at the conference. From these, 66 were selected and were published in this book; that also includes an invited talk paper. We must express our gratitude to all the authors who submitted their papers to our conference.

The papers were reviewed by an international committee formed by 80 members from 13 countries. Each paper was reviewed by two or three referees, with an average of 2.7 reviews per paper. The papers included in this volume were submitted to a second review process. We must also express our deepest gratitude to all the researchers whose invaluable contributions guaranteed a high scientific level for the conference.

The conference was organized by the GALAN group of the Department of Computer Science, University of the Basque Country (EHU-UPV). We must mention that the Organizing Committee provided a really charming environment where researchers and practitioners could concentrate on the task of presenting and commenting on contributions.

The conference was supported by the liberal sponsorship of the Spanish Ministerio de Ciencia y Tecnologia, the Basque Government, the University of the Basque Country (Vicerrectorado del Campus de Gipuzkoa) and the Caja de Ahorros de Guipuzcoa-Kutxa. We thank them for the generous funding that allowed the presence of invited speakers and granted students.

March 2004

Ricardo Conejo
Maite Urretavizcaya
José Luis Pérez de la Cruz

Organization

The 10th Conference of the Spanish Association for Artificial Intelligence and the 5th Sessions on Technology Transfer of Artificial Intelligence (CAEPIA-TTIA 2003) were organized by the Universidad del País Vasco - Euskal Herriko Unibertsitatea - in Donostia-San Sebastián, Spain, in November, 12–14, 2003.

Program Committee Chair

Ricardo Conejo (Universidad de Málaga, Spain)

Program Committee

Enrique Alba (Universidad de Málaga, Spain)
Carlos Alonso González (Universidad de Valladolid, Spain)
Analia Amandi (Universidad Nac. Centro de Buenos Aires, Argentina)
José Luis Ambite (University of Southern California, USA)
Antonio Bahamonde (Universidad de Oviedo, Spain)
José Ángel Bañares (Universidad de Zaragoza, Spain)
Federico Barber (Universidad Politécnica de Valencia, Spain)
Senen Barro (Universidad Santiago de Compostela, Spain)
Beatriz Barros (UNED, Spain)
Vicent Botti (Universidad Politécnica de Valencia, Spain)
Ivan Bratko (Jozef Stefan Institute, Slovenia)
Pavel Brazdil (LIACC/Porto, Portugal)
Osvaldo Cairo (ITAM, Mexico)
Nuria Castell (Universidad Politécnica de Cataluña, Spain)
María José Castro Bleda (Universidad Politécnica de Valencia, Spain)
Stefano A. Cerri (Université de Montpellier II & CNRS, France)
Cristina Conati (University of British Columbia, Canada)
Juan M. Corchado (Universidad de Salamanca, Spain)
Ulises Cortés (Universidad Politécnica de Cataluña, Spain)
Alicia D'Anjou (Universidad del País Vasco, Spain)
Miguel Delgado (Universidad de Granada, Spain)
Yves Demazeau (LEIBNIZ-IMAGCNRS, France)
Arantza Díaz de Ilarraza (Universidad del País Vasco, Spain)
Ed Durfee (University of Michigan, USA)
Luis Fariñas (Université de Toulouse, France)
Isabel Fernández-de-Castro (Universidad del País Vasco (UPV/EHU), Spain)
Alfredo Fernández-Valmayor (Universidad Complutense de Madrid, Spain)
Antonio Ferrandez (Universidad de Alicante, Spain)

Maite Urretavizcaya (Universidad del País Vasco (UPV/EHU), Spain)
Álvaro del Val (Universidad Autónoma de Madrid, Spain)
Felisa Verdejo (UNED, Spain)
José M. Vidal (University of South Carolina, USA)
Lluis Vila (Universidad Politécnica Cataluña, Spain)
Beverly Park Woolf (University of Massachusetts, USA)

External Reviewers

Eneko Agirre-Bengoa
Eduardo Alonso
Mercedes Amor
Olatz Arregi-Uriarte
Paulo Azevedo
Holger Billhardt
David Bueno
Alberto-José Bugarín-Diz
Alfredo Burrieza
César Cáceres
Xavier Carreras
Javier De Lope
Carmelo Del-Valle-Sevillano
Jon-Ander Elorriaga-Arandia
Gerard Escudero
Marc Esteva Vivanco
Nerea Ezeiza-Ramos
Alberto Fernández
Maríano Fernández-López
Juan-Antonio Fernández-Madrigal
Cesar Ferri
Inmaculada Fortes
Francisco-José Galán-Morillo
Ana García-Sipols
R.M. Gasca
Adriana Giret-Boggino
Daniela Godoy
Manuel Graña-Romay
Eduardo Guzmán-de-los-Riscos
Josefa Hernández
José Hernández-Orallo
Elena Lazkano-Ortega
Javier López-Muñoz
David Losada-Carril
Huget Marc-Philippe

J. Marques de Sa
Paloma Martínez
José María Martínez-Montiel
Patricio Martínez-Barco
Ignacio Mayorga
Eva Millán
Andrés Montoyo-Guijarro
Llanos Mora
J. Marcos Moreno-Vega
Manuel Mucientes-Molina
Marlon Nuñez
Manuel Ojeda-Aciego
Abraham Otero-Quintana
Lluís Padró
José Palma
Juan-Manuel Pikatza-Atxa
Enric Plaza
Jorge Puente
José M. Puerta
Gonzalo Ramos
Iñaki Rañó
Oscar Reinoso
Horacio Rodríguez
Juan-Antonio Rodríguez
Juan-José Rodríguez-Díez
Jordi Sabater-Mir
Miguel A. Salido
Silvia Schiaffino
José María Sebastian-y-Zuñiga
Juan Manuel Serrano
Mónica Trella
José-Luis Triviño
Oswaldo Vélez-Langs
Francisco Villatoro

Table of Contents

Invited Talk

Selected Papers from the 10th Conference of the Spanish Association for Artificial Intelligence (CAEPIA03)

Selected Papers from the 5th Sessions on Technology Transfer of Artificial Intelligence (TTIA03)

Reasoning about Teaching and Learning

Beverly Park Woolf

Computer Science Department,
University of Massachusetts, Amherst, MA, USA
Bev@cs.umass.edu

Abstract. Artificial Intelligence (AI) technology has been extended for use in tutoring systems to dynamically customize material for individual students. These techniques model and reason about the student, the domain and teaching strategies, and communicate with the student in real time. Evaluation results show increased learning, reduced costs, and improved grades.

We will demonstrate intelligent and distributed technology that makes education available anytime and anyplace. At the grade school level, a mathematics tutor positively influences students' confidence and image of their mathematics ability. Machine learning was used to model student performance and to derive a teaching policy to meet a desired educational goal. At the college level, an inquiry tutor moves students towards more active and problem-based learning. We will also discuss other tutors that introduce new pedagogy and address inequities in the classroom.

1 Artificial Intelligence in Education

The field of Artificial Intelligence in Education (AIED) is relatively new, being less than thirty years. Broadly defined, AIED addresses issues of knowledge and learning and is not limited solely to production of functional intelligent tutors. Issues and questions addressed by this field include:

What is the nature of knowledge? How is knowledge represented?
How can an individual student be helped to learn?
What styles of teaching interactions are effective and when?
What misconceptions do learners have?

The field has developed answers to some of these questions, and artificial intelligence (AI) techniques have enabled intelligent tutors to adapt both content and navigation of material to a student's learning needs. The goal of AI in Education is not to reproduce existing classroom teaching methods. In fact, in some cases the goal is to remove the traditional education mold altogether. As working and learning become increasingly the same activity, the demand for lifelong learning creates a demand for education that will exceed the capability of traditional institutions and methods. This creates an opportunity for new intermediaries and learning agents that are not part of the traditional, formal education system. Such opportunities are likely to be supported by computer technology.

R. Conejo et al. (Eds.): CAEPIA-TTIA 2003, LNAI 3040, pp. 1–15, 2004.

Ample evidence exists that intelligent tutors produce a substantial improvement in learning and productivity in industry and the military. Formal evaluations show that intelligent tutors produce the same improvements as one-on-one human tutoring, which increases performance to around the 98 percentile in a standard

Please click on the animal you wish to learn about

Fig. 1. Real World Context: In AnimalWatch, the student chooses an endangered species from among the Right Whale, Giant Panda and Takhi Wild Horse.

classroom [1]. These tutors effectively reduce by one-third to one-half the time required for learning [2], increase effectiveness by 30% as compared to traditional instruction [3, 2, 4], and networked versions reduce the need for training support personnel by about 70% and operating costs by about 92%.

The term "intelligent tutor" designates technology-based instruction that contains one or more of the following features: generativity, student modeling, expert modeling, mixed initiative, interactive learning, instructional modeling and self-improving. The key feature is generativity – the system's ability to generate customized problems, hints or help – as opposed to the presentation of prepared "canned" instruction. Generativity relies on models of the subject matter, the student and tutoring, which enable the tutor to generate customized instruction as needed by an individual student. Advanced instructional features, such as mixed-initiative (a tutor that both initiates interactions and responds usefully to student actions) and self-improving (a tutor that evaluates and improves its performance as a result of experience), set tutors apart from earlier computer-aided instructional systems. No agreement exists on which features are absolutely necessary and it is more accurate to think of teaching systems as lying along a continuum that runs from simple frame-oriented systems to very sophisticated intelligent tutoring. The most sophisticated systems include, to varying degrees, the features listed above.

Fig. 2. Interface of AnimalWatch for a simple addition of whole numbers problem.

For example, the Arithmetic Tutor described below was *generative* since all math problems, hints and help were generated on the fly based on student learning needs (Figs. 1-3). The tutor *modmodeled expert knowledge* of arithmetic as a topic network, with nodes such as "subtract fractions" or "multiply whole numbers" which were resolved into child nodes such as "find least common denominator" and "subtract numerators," Fig. 4. The tutor modeled *student knowledge*, recording each sub-task learned or needed based on student action and the tutor was *self-improving* in that it used machine-learning techniques to predict a student's ability to correctly solve a problem.

2   Customizing Help by Gender and Cognitive Development

The first example tutor, AnimalWatch, used AI techniques to adapt its tutoring of basic arithmetic and fractions, Figs. 1-3. It helped students learn fractions and whole numbers at a 4th-6th grade level. The tutor used student characteristics including gender and cognitive development, and an overlay student model which made inferences about the student's knowledge as he/she solved problems. The tutor adjusted its problem selection to provide appropriate problems and hints. For example, students unable to handle abstract thinking (according to a Piagetian pre-evaluation) benefited from concrete representations and concrete objects to manipulate instead of formal approaches, equations, or symbols and textual explanations, Figs. 5-6. Students moved through the curriculum only if their performance for each topic was acceptable. Thus problems generated by the tutor were an indication of the student's mathematics proficiency and the tutor's efficiency as described below.

Results indicated that girls were more sensitive to the amounts of help than to the level of abstraction (e.g., the use of concrete objects to manipulate, Fig. 7, vs. equations and procedures, Fig. 6) and performed better in problems when the help was highly interactive. Boys, affected by the level of abstraction, were more prone to ignore help and to improve more when help had low levels of interactivity.

AnimalWatch tutored arithmetic using word problems about endangered species, thus integrating mathematics, narrative and biology. Math problems were designed to motivate students to use mathematics in the context of practical problem solving, embedded in an engaging narrative, Figs. 1 and 2. Students "worked" with scientists as they explored environmental issues around saving endangered animals. Animal-Watch maintained a *student model* and made inferences about the

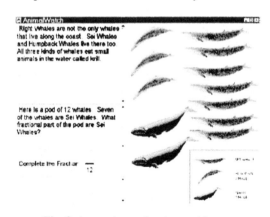

Fig. 3. A sample pre-fraction problem.

student's knowledge as s/he solved problems. It increased the difficulty of the problems depending on the student's progress and provided mathematics instruction for each student based on a dynamically updated probabilistic *student model*. Problems were dynamically generated based on inferences about the student's knowledge, progressing from simple one-digit whole-number addition problems to complex problems that involve fractions with different denominators.

The student's cognitive level was determined via an on-line pretest [5] based on Piaget's theory of development and a series of questions on topics such as combinatorics, proportions, conservation of volume and other elements that determine student ability to reason abstractly.

Several evaluation studies with 10 and 11-year-old students totaling 313 children indicate that AnimalWatch provided effective individualized math instruction and had a positive impact on students' own mathematics self concept and belief in the value of learning mathematics [6, 7]. When a student encountered a difficult pro-

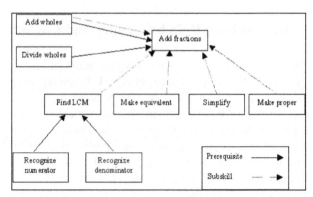

Fig. 4. A Portion of the AnimalWatch topic network.

blem, AnimalWatch provided hints classified along two dimensions, symbolism and interactivity. The first hints provided little information, but if the student kept entering wrong answers, AnimalWatch provided hints that ultimately guided the student through the whole problem-solving process.

Expert Model. The expert model was arranged as a topic network where nodes represented skills to be taught, Fig. 4. The links between nodes frequently represented a prerequisite relationship. For instance, the ability to add is a prerequisite to learning how to multiply. *Topics* were major components of the curriculum, e.g., "add fractions" or "divide wholes", while *skills* referred to any curriculum elements (including topics), e.g., "recognize numeration" or "recognize denominator." *Subskills* were steps within a topic that the student performs in order to accomplish a task. For example, the topic "adding fractions" had the subskills of finding a least common denominator (LCM), converting the fractions to an equivalent form with a new numerator, adding the numerators, simplifying the result, and making the result proper.

Table 1. Three sample add-fraction problems and the subskills required for each.

Subskill	Problem 1 $\frac{1}{3}+\frac{1}{3}$	Problem 2 $\frac{1}{3}+\frac{1}{4}$	Problem 3 $\frac{2}{3}+\frac{5}{8}$
Find LCM	No	Yes	Yes
Equivalent fractions	No	Yes	Yes
Add numerators	Yes	Yes	Yes
Make proper	No	No	Yes

Note that a topic such as "add wholes" was both a prerequisite and a subskill for "add fractions." For a given problem, not all these subskills were required. Table 1 shows the subskills required for some sample add-fraction problems.

Fig. 2 is an example of a simple problem for addition of whole numbers and Fig. 3 an example of a topic generated from the "pre-fractions" area of the curriculum. Generating the topic customized to learning needs was one way the tutor adapted the curriculum to the

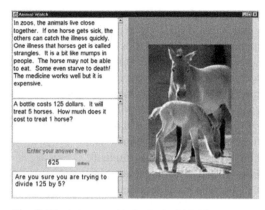

Fig. 5. The tutor provided a textual hint in response to the student's incorrect answer. It later provided a symbolic or a manipulative hint, Figs. 6 and 7.

learning needs of the student. Students moved through the curriculum only if their performance for each topic was acceptable.

Student Model. The *student model* continually updated an estimate of each student's ability and understanding of the mathematics domain and generated problems of appropriate difficulty. Students were given hints with little information first and richer explanations later if the former were not effective. The *student model* adjusted the difficulty of each problem and constructed each hint dynamically based on presumed student learning needs. For example, addition of fraction problems vary widely in their degree of difficulty, Table 1. The more subskills required, the harder the problem. Similarly, larger numbers also increased the tutor's rating of the problem's difficulty: it is harder to find the least common multiple of 13 and 21 than it is to find the least common multiple of 3 and 6.

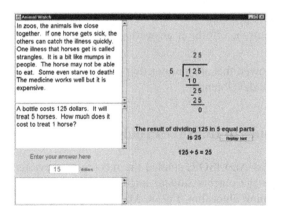

Fig. 6. The tutor provided a symbolic hint demonstrating the processes involved in long division.

Subskills referred to steps necessary to solve a problem. For example $\frac{1}{3}+\frac{1}{3}$ involves fewer subskills than $\frac{2}{3}+\frac{5}{8}$ which also requires finding a common multiple, making the result proper, etc. Problem difficulty was calculated via a heuristic that took into account the subskills used and the difficulty in applying these subskills.

AnimalWatch adjusted problems based on individual learning needs, as suggested in the *student model* and selected a hint template, perhaps describing procedural rules, Fig. 6 or requiring manipulation of small rods on the screen, Fig. 7. The machine learner (described in Section 3) recorded the effectiveness of each hint and the results of using specific problems in a database used to generate problems and hints for subsequent students. Figs. 5 and 6 demonstrate hints that provide varying amounts of information. The hint in Fig. 5, bottom left, is brief and text based, while the hint in Fig. 6 is symbolic and the hint in Fig. 7 is

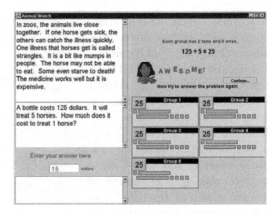

Fig. 7. Finally the tutor provided a interactive hint, in which the student moved five groups of rods, each containing 25 units.

interactive, requiring manipulation of rods. If the student continued to make mistakes, more and more specific hints were provided until the question was answered correctly.

The *student model* noted how long the student took to generate a response, both after the initial problem presentation and (in the event of an incorrect response), the delay in responding after a hint was presented. The student's level of cognitive development [5], according to Piaget's theory of intellectual development [8], correlated with the student's math performance and was used to further customize the tutor's teaching [9].

When the student was presented with an opportunity to provide an answer, the system took a "snap shot" of her current state, consisting of information from four main areas:

Student: The student's level of proficiency and level of cognitive development
Topic: How hard the current topic is and the type of operand/operators
Problem: How complex is the current problem
Context: Describes the student's current efforts at answering this question, and hints he has seen.

Empirical evaluation, Section 4, showed that student reaction to each class of hint was dependent on gender and cognitive development.

3   Machine Learning Techniques to Improve Problem Choice

A machine learning component, named ADVISOR, studied the records of previous users an$d predicted how much time the current student might require to solve a problem by using a "two-phase" learning algorithm, Fig. 8. Machine learning automatically computed an optimal teaching policy, such as reducing the amount of mistakes made or time spent on each problem. The architecture included two learning agents: one responsible for modeling how a student interacted with tutor (the population student model, PSM) and the other responsible for constructing a teaching policy (the pedagogical agent, PA). The population student model was trained to understand student behavior by observing hundreds of students using the tutor and was capable of predicting an individual student's reaction to teaching actions, such as presentation of specific problem type.

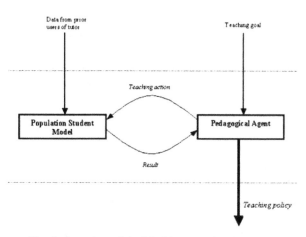

Fig. 8. Overview of the Machine Learning Component.

The PSM took the current state, proposed teaching action and then acted as a simulation of the future actions of the current student. It predicted the probable response of the current student in terms of time taken and correctness of solution. This information updated the state description which, along with another proposed action, was fed back into the PSM for the next iteration of the simulation. This process continued until the PSM predicted that the student would give a correct response.

The PSM and PA worked together to enable the tutor to learn a good teaching policy directly from observing previous students using the tutor. The architecture was evaluated by comparing it to a "classical" tutor that taught via heuristics without the aid of machine learning agent, Section 4. The metrics used to assess student performance included subjective measures, (e.g., mathematics self-confidence and enjoyment) as well as objective measures (e.g., mathematics performance).

The learning component modeled student behavior at a coarse level of granularity. Rather than focusing on whether the student knew a particular piece of knowledge, the learning agent determined how likely the student was to answer a question correctly and how much time was needed to generate this correct response. The learning mechanisms predicted whether the student's response would be correct or incorrect and how long the student would take to respond. This model was contextualized on the current state of the world or the problem being solved.

State Information Recorded. To make predictions, data about an entire population of users was gathered. Logs gathered from prior deployments of AnimalWatch were used as training data for the PSM. Over 10,000 data points and 48 predictor variables were used. These logs provided the training instances for a supervised learning agent. Approximately 120 students used the tutor (a medium sized study) for a brief period of time, only 3 hours. The goal of the induction techniques was to construct two prediction functions: one for the amount of time a student required to respond and the second for the probability that the response was correct. Rather than making predictions about an "average student," the model made predictions about "an average student with a proficiency of X who has made Y mistakes so far on the problem." The PMS was a student model since it differentially predicted student performance.

The PSM recorded information from a variety of sources, including information about the student, the current problem being worked on, feedback presented to the student and context or the student's current efforts at solving the problem. Information about the student included data about the student's abilities, such as the tutor's knowledge about both the student's proficiency in this particular area and the student's overall capabilities. Student data also included proficiency on current topic, scores on individual cognitive development test items, and gender. Current problem information included were: number of *subskills* tested, type of problem (operator and operand types), and problem difficulty.

Feedback Information. When AnimalWatch selected a hint, it based its decision on a set of hint features that provided information along several hint dimensions. These features described hints at a pedagogical level and were generalized among all hints in the system, i.e. the PSM learned about the impact of "highly interactive" hints, not specifically about "hint #12." The pedagogical features of each hint included:

- interactivity
- procedural information contained in the hint
- information about the result conveyed by the hint (e.g. "try again" versus telling the student to "divide 125 by 5")
- information about the context
- data about the context of the problem representing information about the student's current effort while solving the problem.

There were two regression models. The first had 48 input features and determined the probability the student's next response would be correct. The second had the same 48 features as input, and also used the first model's output (i.e. whether the response was correct or incorrect). The second model was responsible for predicting the amount of time the student would take until his next response. Note that the model did not try to predict the student's longer term performance on the current problem, only his/her immediate action.

4   Evaluations of the Machine Learner

AnimalWatch was evaluated in classrooms numerous times, with different versions of the tutor, deployed in both rural and urban schools, and evaluated with and without the machine learning component. Students were randomly assigned to one of two conditions: the experimental condition used the ADVISOR and machine learning to direct its reasoning; the control condition used the classic AnimalWatch tutor. The only difference between the two conditions was that in the experimental group artificial intelligence methods were used to make the selection of topics, problems, and feedback. The AnimalWatch story-line, word problems, etc. were identical in both groups.

ADVISOR was given the goal of minimizing the amount of time students spent per problem. Evidence of ADVISOR's ability to adapt instruction can be seen in Table 2. The percentage field refers to the proportion of problems of a specified type students in each condition saw. For example, in the control condition 7.2%

Table 2. Summary of student performance by topic area. The experimental group used ADVISOR, the machine learner tutor; the control group used the heuristic tutor. Percentage refers to the proportion of problems seen and time refers to the time needed to solve a problem.

		Control	Experimental
Whole	Percentage	73.6%	60%
	Time	43.4 sec	28.1 sec
Prefraction	Percentage	19.3%	27.3%
	Time	22.7 sec	21.7 sec
Fraction	Percentage	7.2%	12.7%
	Time	44.5 sec	38.5 sec

of the problems solved were fraction problems. The time field refers to the mean time needed to solve a problem. Students using ADVISOR averaged 27.7 seconds to solve a problem, while students using the classic version of AnimalWatch averaged 39.7 seconds. This difference was significant at P<0.001. Just as important, the difference was meaningful: reducing average times by 30% is a large reduction. Thus, the agent made noticeable progress in its goal of reducing the amount of time students spent per problem.

Equivalent students did perform differently when using ADVISOR as compared with those using the classic version, without the learning component. Again, this was evidence that the architecture can adapt, not that it caused 30% more "learning" to occur.

Students in the experimental group solved whole (P<0.001) and fraction problems (P<0.02) significantly faster than students in the control group. Students in the experimental group finished the whole number and prefraction topics relatively quickly, so worked more on fraction problems.

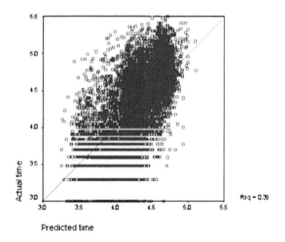

Fig. 9. PSM's accuracy for predicting response time. The PSM's predictions correlated at 0.63 ($R^2=0.40$) with actual student performance.

Fig. 9 shows the PSM's accuracy for predicting how long students required to generate a response. In this graph, both the predicted and actual response times are measured in milliseconds, and then the $\log_{10}$ is taken[1]. The PSM's predictions correlated at 0.63 ($R^2=0.40$) with actual performance.

5   Empirical Evaluation of AnimalWatch

AnimalWatch, with or without the learning component, was effective at teaching arithmetic. Additionally, it enabled researchers to evaluate the behavior of students with respect to solving math problems based on gender and cognitive development. The behavior of girls and boys of same cognitive development was quite opposite in terms of their response to hints. In general, the best help types for one gender were the worst for the other gender. The tutor pushed students forward, going from simple whole number addition problems to others that involved fractions with different de-nominators, based in part on the tutor's ability to correct student mistakes through help provided. The tutor recorded the effectiveness of hints and the results of using specific problems. The number of mistakes a student made on problems of a similar type continued to reduce, showing that they learned the topic.

Fig. 10 illustrates the number of errors (Y axis) measured against the problems of a given type (X axis). The problem types are listed on the right of Fig. 10. Clearly students learned each topic, as errors were reduced from greater than 2 to less than 1. For more difficult topics, e.g. hard division, the learning curve was slower and in-volved making more errors.

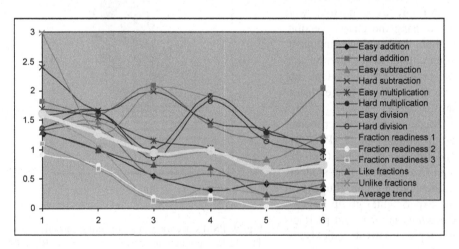

Fig. 10. Teaching effectiveness of AnimalWatch. Mistake reduction over problems of simi-lar type.

---

[1] Since the granularity of record keeping was at the second level, this explains the horizontal level of seconds "bands" at the bottom of the graph. The bottom band is one second, the next is two seconds, etc (1 second = 1,000 milliseconds, $log_{10}1000=3$).

Formal help was significantly worse than other kinds of help for low cognitive development boys. Also, formal help was significantly worse for low than for high cognitive development boys. Formal help produced significantly worse mistake change rates for boys of low cognitive development than for girls of the same cognitive development. Low cognitive development girls improved significantly less with reduced help than girls of high cognitive development with reduced help. Also, girls of high cognitive development improved most with reduced help.

While girls' math value and self-confidence was affected positively by the existence of intense help, boys' math value was harmed. Some boys may have felt bothered by structured help, especially when we consider they spent 25% less time at each hint than girls. Too much help when they didn't need it slowed them down, probably they went through all the help while they could have figured it out by themselves.

High cognitive development boys behaved opposite to high cognitive development girls: girls profited from different amounts of help depending on the topic, while boys profited from intense help all over. Gender differences were apparent in the time that students spent on hints (independent samples t-test, $p<0.05$). On average, girls stayed 25% more time than boys within hints. Overall, girls mastered similar amount of topics compared with boys. Boys ignored help more (specially high cognitive development boys) and appeared to be more selective about the help provided to them.

6   Implementing Difficult Pedagogy: Inquiry Learning

The previous tutor supported a teaching strategy used in most classrooms; present a problem to a student and then support him/her to solve the problem by providing hints as needed. One advantage to AnimalWatch is that, unlike a human teacher with 30 students, the tutor was able to individualize problems and hints for each student.

The next tutor we discuss implements a tutoring strategy that is extremely difficult to implement in any classroom.

The inquiry tutor helps students ask their own questions and refine them so they can be answered through gathering data in a laboratory or library situation. During inquiry, students are presented with a case, situation and goals. They are guided to observe and synthesize their observations. Inquiry teaching is very expensive in terms of time and resources. It requires that a teacher track, analyze and then comment on each

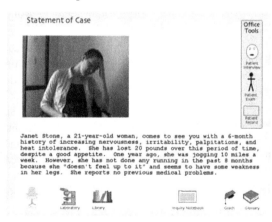

Fig. 11. Rashi presents a medical case to the student. Navigation icons (bottom and right) and are always available, providing access to the *Inquiry Notebook*, coach and glossary. Icons on the top right represent data collection tools.

student's selection of data and creation of hypotheses and inferences. Since student groups might pursue dissimilar questions and require distinct data, supporting inquiry in the traditional classroom is very difficult.

Rashi[2], the inquiry tutor, helps students generate hypotheses and select data. It encourages students to support or refute hypotheses with sufficient evidence. Coaches advise students about illogical statements and inconsistent reasoning and help them organize and qualify their know-

Fig. 12. Interview Tool. The student interviews the patient though free text, by typing "diet" into the tool. The patient answers in audio, video and transcript.

ledge. The tutor understands (to some extent) the reasoning behind students' hypotheses. Prototype inquiry tutors exist in human biology, forestry, civil engineering and geology [10, 11].

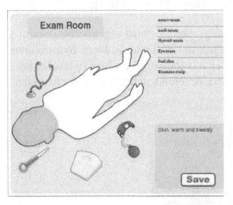

Fig. 13. Patient Examination Tool enables students to measure weight, pulse, blood pressure, etc. In this example the student has selected the head and is given choices of viewing exam results for eyes, ears, neck, etc.

In the human biology inquiry tutor, a patient presents with symptoms, Fig. 11, including fatigue, weight loss, anxiety, and sweaty palms. Students try to diagnose the cause of these symptoms by extracting pertinent information and trying to recognize the difference between pure observation and inference. The patient's complaints form an initial set of data from which the student begins the diagnostic process.

Students brainstorm and list predictions or subgoals that might resolve some aspect of the problem. They type in causes for the observed phenomena and later predict data that will either support or weaken the hypotheses. An

---

[2] Rashi was a biblical scholar who introduced inquiry methods in the eleventh century. He wrote extensive commentaries, produced queries, explanations, interpretations and discussions of each phrase and verse of the bible. Rashi's written commentary on the bible made it more comprehensible for everyday scholars. Today, these and other commentaries, assembled in the Talmud, have been extended to nearly 40 volumes and continue as a source of biblical law [12].

initial hypothesis might be vague: "She sounds like she might have an anxiety disorder." Hypotheses of this sort require further refinement.

Rashi provides several data collection tools to enable students to confirm or refute their hypothesis and resolve open questions. For example, students might interview the patient about symptoms, Fig. 12, perform an examination, Fig. 13, and request medical history or lab tests. Data helps students to eliminate or support hypothesis and assess evidence that bears on their hypothesis independent of a teacher's input.

The *Inquiry Notebook* supports student data collection and helps record open questions and hypotheses, Fig. 14. Data reveals flaws in hypotheses, students revise hypotheses and change their opinions of how strongly data supports or refutes hypotheses. Once the student is oriented to the goal of the case and uses data gathering tools, she records meaningful units of data or *propositions,* keeping track of where propositions come from (i.e., citing the

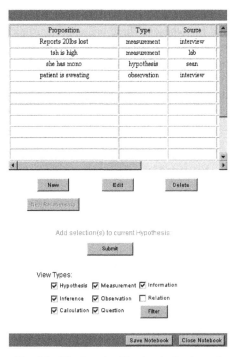

Fig. 14. The Inquiry Notebook. Student observations in the exam and the interview are automatically recorded in the inquiry notebook. The student indicated type (observations, inferences and hypothesis).

sources) and indicating relationships between propositions by linking them with *supports/refutes* links. Finally, these chains of relationships terminate in hypothesis.

Students ask the electronic Coach for an assessment of their work and their argument supporting or eliminating a hypothesis. The Coach analyzes the student's *Inquiry Notebook* and history of activities and gives feedback about how best to proceed. A Bayesian Belief Network (BBN), the basis of the Coach's performance, comments about the *syntactic structure* of the student's argument (Does the student understand the difference between data and hypotheses?) and its *semantic content* (Are inferences and conclusions supported by data and medical knowledge?).

As each student moves through the inquiry cycle, the tutor follows her reasoning by matching it with an expert's assessment of the medical case. As an example, consider a student who interviewed the patient, recorded important symptoms, "performed" a medical exam and identified salient symptoms and lab results. The student isolated data that supported, refuted, or had no bearing on a given hypothesis. The student read medical source documents and studied the patient's signs and symptoms. The tutor tracked student activities and issued prompts through the expert system if the student failed to explore some range of information. Rashi responded to the student with carefully crafted questions, never revealing directly the solution to the case.

Finally, students type in their reports, including all the selected data, inferences and hypotheses. These are sent electronically to the human teacher for evaluation. In some cases, a sequential review of all observations, hypotheses, data, and explanations is presented graphically, and can be edited and re-ordered to look for patterns. At some point each student makes a final submission which involves designating one hypothesis as the "best." Then they turn in the *Inquiry Notebook* complete with all the competing hypotheses and their arguments for eliminating them. Rashi is being evaluated in both small colleges and large universities.

7 Summary

Artificial intelligence provides an opportunity to explore teaching methods that might be difficult to produce in traditional classrooms or that require excessive teacher time and resources. This paper suggested using intelligent tutors to generate individualized problems and hints and also to build support for inquiry learning. AI offers a way to test teaching methods by bringing a specific strategy (such as problem solving or inquiry learning) into a classroom and regulating its components, e.g., problem/hint selection, student performance and the interaction of performance with gender or cognitive development. The learning strategies are assessed by tracking student behavior as a function of student characteristics, e.g., background and cognitive development.

In sum, AI technology, along with cognitive science and web-technology, are the large poles in the tent, or the key components in a coming revolution in education. They help push the frontier of intelligent tutors toward new pedagogy and address inequities in the classroom. These systems use a model of the student to customize feedback and engage students. They explore the effectiveness of help for students of different genders and cognitive developments, and in one case, concluded that girls were more sensitive to the amounts of help while boys were affected by the level of abstraction.

AI technology also facilitates development of an inquiry system that tracks, analyzes and then comments on a student's selection of data and creation of hypotheses and inferences. We expect to identify the strategies students use to generate hypotheses and explore data. Intelligent tutor technology is almost at the point where we could say that the computer system is teaching a student to think!

Acknowledgements

Research described in this paper was funded in part by the National Science Foundation under grant no. DUE-0127183, "Inquiry Tools for Case-based Courses in Human Biology," M. Bruno, PI. and partly by the U.S. Department of Education, "Expanding a General Model of Inquiry Learning," Fund for the Improvement of Post Secondary Education, Comprehensive Program, #P116B010483, B. Woolf, P.I. AnimalWatch research was also supported in part by grants from NSF's Program for Gender Equity, HRD-9555737 and HRD-9714757 to C. Beal.

References

1. Bloom, B.: The 2 sigma problem: The search for methods of group instruction as effective as one-to-one tutoring. *Educational Researcher*, Vol. 13. (1984) 3-16
2. Regian, J.W. : Functional area analysis of intelligent computer-assisted instruction (Report of TAPSTEM ICAI-FAA Committee), Brooks AFB, TX (1997)
3. Fletcher, J.D.: Does this stuff work? Some findings from applications of technology to education and training. In: Proceedings of conference on teacher education and the use of technology based learning systems. Warrenton, VA: Society for Applied Learning Technology (1996)
4. Fletcher, J.D.: Intelligent training systems in the military. In: S.J. Andriole & G.W. Hopple (Eds.), Defense applications of artificial intelligence: Progress and prospects. Lexington, MA: Lexington Books (1988)
5. Arroyo, I., Beck, J. E., Schultz, K. & Woolf, B.: Piagetian psychology in intelligent tutoring systems. In: Proceedings of the 9th International Conference on Artificial Intelligence in Education. Lemans, France (1999)
6. Beck, J., Arroyo, I., Woolf, B.P., Beal, C.R.: Affecting self-confidence with an ITS. *Ninth International Conference on Artificial Intelligence in Education*, Paris (1999) 611-613
7. Beal, C.R., Beck, J.E., Woolf, B.P., Rae-Ramirez, M.A.: WhaleWatch: An intelligent model-based mathematics tutoring system. *Fifteenth IFIP World Computer Congress, 1998*. J. Cuena (Ed.) (1998)
8. Piaget, J. (1954) The Construction of Reality in the Child. New York: Ballentine Books (1954)
9. Arroyo, I., Beck, J., Woolf, B., Beal, C., Schultz, K.: Macroadapting AnimalWatch to gender and cognitive differences with respect to hint interactivity and symbolism. *Fifth International Conference on Intelligent Tutoring Systems, 2000*. Montreal (2000) 574-583
10. Woolf, B.P., Reid, J., Stillings, N., Bruno, M., Murray, D., Reese, P., Peterfreund, A., Rath, K.: A General Platform for Inquiry Learning. *International Conference on Intelligent Tutoring Systems, 2001*. France (2001)
11. Woolf, B.P., Marshall, D., Mattingly, M., Lewis, J., Wright, S., Jellison, M., Murray, T.: Tracking Student Propositions in an Inquiry System. *Artificial Intelligence in Education, 2003*, Sydney, Australia (2003)
12. Steinsaltz, Adin: The Essential Talmud. Perseus Books, Basic Books (1976)

A Document-Oriented Approach
to the Development of Knowledge Based Systems[*]

José L. Sierra, Baltasar Fernández-Manjón,
Alfredo Fernández-Valmayor, and Antonio Navarro

Dpto. Sistemas Informáticos y Programación, Fac. Informática, Universidad Complutense
28040 Madrid, Spain
{jlsierra,balta,alfredo,anavarro}@sip.ucm.es

Abstract. ADDS (Approach to Document-based Development of Software) is
an approach to the development of applications based on a *document-oriented
paradigm*. According to this paradigm, applications are described by means of
documents that are marked up using descriptive domain-specific markup languages. Afterwards, applications are produced processing these marked up
documents. Formulation of domain-specific markup languages in ADDS is a
dynamic and eminently pragmatic activity since these languages evolve in accordance with the authoring needs of the main actors that participate in the development process (i.e. *domain experts* and *developers*). OADDS (Operationalization in ADDS) is a processing model that promotes the construction of
modular language processors and their incremental evolution. Thus, OADDS is
specifically designed to cope with the evolutionary nature of the domain-
specific markup languages encouraged by ADDS. ADDS and OADDS have
successfully been applied to the development of applications in knowledge-
intensive domains (i.e. transport networks and educational hypermedias). This
paper also describes the advantages (incremental development and maintenance
improvement) that this approach supposes for the development of knowledge-
based systems.

1 Introduction

The development of applications in general, and of Knowledge-based Systems
(KBSs) in particular, can be considered as a linguistic activity arising from the collaboration between the clients that have a problem to be solved, the domain experts
with the knowledge required to solve that problem, the developers building the application, and the final users. Indeed, looking for ways to facilitate the communication
between all the actors in this process is essential in order to guarantee a successful
development. This is particularly true in the development of KBSs, where communication between clients, knowledge engineers and developers has always been considered to be critical.

This paper describes our approach for application development, which we called
document-oriented paradigm, and its specialization in the development of KBSs.

---

[*] The Spanish Commitee of Science and Technology (TIC2000-0737-C03-01, TIC2001-1462
and TIC2002-04067-C03-02) has supported this work.

R. Conejo et al. (Eds.): CAEPIA-TTIA 2003, LNAI 3040, pp. 16–25, 2004.

According to this paradigm, the building of an application begins by describing the application using one or more documents, marking up these documents using a domain-specific markup language, and finally, producing the application using a suitable processor for this language. Thus, the development of a KBS using this paradigm implies the provision of a document written in a natural language subset. This document contains the knowledge that is going to be managed by the system. Then, tags and attributes are pragmatically added to this document in accordance with a previously defined markup language. These tags and attributes make the data and knowledge structures relevant to the inference engine explicit. Finally, the inference engine for the KBS is conceived as a processor driven by the markup.

The ADDS approach (Approach to Document-based Development of Software) is an implementation of the document-oriented paradigm where the document types and the languages used to markup them up evolve incrementally according to the needs of domain experts and developers. OADDS (Operationalization in ADDS) is a processing model for ADDS documents that introduces mechanisms used in the production of modular processors to adapt to the evolutionary nature of languages in ADDS.

The rest of this paper is structured as follows. Section 2 describes the development of KBSs according to the document-oriented paradigm. Section 3 describes ADDS, the approach that implements this paradigm. Section 4 describes OADDS, the operationalization model of ADDS. Section 5 describes some related work. Finally, section 6 presents the conclusions and gives some ideas for future work.

2   The Development of KBSs
Using the Document-Oriented Paradigm

Documents play an important role in human communication. Therefore, the adoption of a *document-oriented paradigm* for the development of applications must be seen as a plausible alternative that could alleviate the communication problems arising among the different actors engaged in the software development process.

The development and maintenance of KBSs is particularly sensible to these communication problems. Indeed, the knowledge acquisition problem is a critical aspect of this type of system. The model-based approaches that arose during the nineties (see [16] for a survey) conceive the solution to this problem as the explicit formulation of a *knowledge model* capable of identifying and structuring the different types of knowledge required to solve a problem, together with the roles played by these types of knowledge in the reasoning process. Nevertheless, these approaches usually distinguish between the model and its subsequent implementation. This means that for the participants either an initially complete model is provided (and this is not realistic even for little toy domains), or they must cope with the maintenance problems derived from the translation of model changes into the implementation. This scenario is similar to that arising in the domain of educational applications [5].

The document-oriented paradigm gives a pragmatic solution to the maintenance problem in the construction of model-based KBSs. Indeed, according to this paradigm:

(a)

> Jam Problem in Incorporation to M30.
> The speed registered by the sensor S1 is low,
> the speed registered by S2 also is low,
> but the speed registered by S3 is normal.

(b)

```
<pattern>
  <name>Jam Problem in Incorporation to M30.<name>
  <body>
<and><measure>The <type>speed</type> registered by the sensor <sensor>S1</sensor> is <value>low</value></measure>,
<measure>the <type>speed</type> registered by <sensor>S2</sensor> also is <value>low</value></measure>,
but <measure>the <type>speed</type> registered by <sensor>S3</sensor> is <value>normal</value></measure>.</and>
  <body>
</pattern>
```

Fig. 1. (a) Knowledge about an anomalous situation pattern in a traffic network, (b) markup of the knowledge expressed in (a).

- The model leads to different domain-specific languages for describing the different types of knowledge. Actually, these languages are suitable subsets of the natural language similar to those used by the domain experts (see Fig.1a). This similarity facilitates the experts' elicitation of knowledge as documents in natural language.
- Then, using descriptive domain-specific markup languages the structure of this knowledge is made explicit. Thus, documents marked using these languages are prepared for their automatic processing (see Fig.1b). This initial markup can be performed by the developers. But because of the simplicity and legibility of the descriptive markup, domain experts can *understand* these documents, and they can directly modify the knowledge described in them (the *contents* of such documents), and with the help or supervision of the developers, they could even extend the language by adding new tags (either directly or using a specific edition tool).
- The developers, in turn, can include additional *operational contents* oriented to make the final processing of the knowledge possible. Examples of this situation are problem – solving methods written in some suitable formal language or knowledge transformations given as document transformations.
- Finally, the implementation of the KBS is obtained building a suitable processor for the markup language used in the pragmatic markup of the document.

With the document-oriented paradigm, the *implementation-model* duality disappears, collapsing into documents where the knowledge provided by the experts and other additional knowledge mix together. Tags, attributes and structure are added by the developers and domain experts to make document processing possible. In addition, the use of descriptive markup facilitates the incremental evolution of the languages and documents. These domain-specific markup languages are not static, unmovable entities, but they can evolve according to changes in the needs of experts and/or developers, or when new markup needs are discovered as a consequence of model evolution.

Fig. 2 sketches the structure of a KBS according to the document-oriented paradigm. Such a structure is a generalization of the one arising in the arena of electronic document processing based on descriptive markup technologies [6].

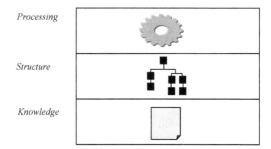

Fig. 2. Organization of a KBS according to the document-oriented paradigm.

The next sections analyze how to adapt the pragmatic nature of the document-oriented paradigm, either in the formulation of markup languages, or in the construction of the processors for such languages.

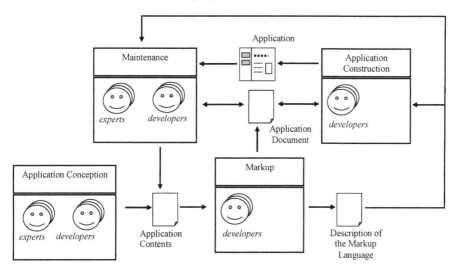

Fig. 3. Participants, activities and products in ADDS.

3   The ADDS Approach

ADDS [13] is an implementation of the document-oriented paradigm that is mainly driven by the authoring needs of the people involved in the process of documenting the applications (domain experts and developers). Fig. 3 sketches the different products, participants and activities involved in ADDS. The next subsections detail each of these aspects.

3.1   Participants

ADDS distinguishes two types of participants in the application development:

- *Domain experts.* They are responsible for the provision and maintenance of the application contents. In the KBS domain, they are the experts that provide the different types of knowledge that will finally be included in the system.
- *Developers.* They are responsible for building the final application. In the KBS domain, the range of developers includes, from knowledge engineers that design the knowledge models, to programmers developing the inference engine and other software needed to produce the executable application.

According to the document-oriented paradigm, the interaction between these participants is mediated by the final document to be produced (*application document*). For instance, during the initial stages of the development, developers interact with domain experts to decide the type and the form of the contents to be included in the application documentation. In addition, developers mark up these contents and assist the domain experts during the maintenance of the marked up document.

3.2 Products

According to ADDS, application construction involves the following types of products:

- The *contents* integrated in the application document.
- The *application document* produced by marking up such contents with tags and attributes.
- The *description of the specific markup language* used for the markup process of such contents.
- The final *application* produced by processing the application document.

3.3 Activities

ADDS identifies the following activities in the application production:

- *Initial application conception.* In this activity, the domain experts, assisted by the developers, conceive and produce an initial description of the application to be built. In the KBS construction, the developers help the experts to informally define the set of documents required to describe all the knowledge needed by the system.
- *Markup.* In this activity, the developers decide how to mark up the application contents documents to obtain the application document. As a result, an explicit description of the markup language (given by an schema or DTD) is produced, together with the application document marked up with this language. Note that because the iterative nature of ADDS, the markup language can evolve to accommodate newly identified markup needs.
- *Application construction.* In this activity, the developers produce the application from the application document. During this activity, developers can add new operational contents to the document and mark up such contents. Finally, they produce the application following the OADDS model introduced in the next section.
- *Maintenance.* In this activity, the experts, assisted by the developers, perform suitable modifications on the marked contents. These modifications are driven by the evaluation of the application produced at previous stages. The domain experts

can even master the markup language, thus being able to use this language to add new markup. This situation is promoted by the use of descriptive markup, focused on content structure, and providing domain significant tag names and attributes. In addition, during this activity the need for introducing new contents may arise (in the case of a KBS, to introduce new knowledge as a consequence of an evolution in the model). Therefore, this will mean an evolution in the markup language used. This evolution will be done by developers and approved by domain experts.

4   The OADDS Operationalization Model

OADDS is the operationalization model used in ADDS to produce applications from marked documents. OADDS is based on the classical techniques of construction of language processors based on syntax-directed translation [1]. Thus, OADDS conceives operationalization as the processing of the application document with an appropriate language processor, that is, a processor specifically built for the markup language used to mark up the application document. But, because of the evolutionary nature of the markup languages used in ADDS, OADDS establishes mechanisms to obtain *modular* processors from components. These components can be extended and combined according to the markup language evolution. Despite being independent from specific implementation technologies, OADDS is naturally implemented as an object-oriented framework. Finally, the document-oriented paradigm itself can be applied in the construction of OADDS processors. So, it is possible to describe processors as a collection of marked documents. The contents of these documents will be the code associated with the basic *semantic actions* required during the processing of the application documents, while the markup will establish how to combine these actions to produce the final processor (in this point of view, OADDS extends and combines similar approaches used in languages such as YACC and XSL [19]). Thus, the complete documentation of an application could include not only the document describing it, but also the documentation of the processor used to process the application document.

Fig. 4 sketches the different products and activities involved in OADDS. All these activities are carried out by the developers (their presence is omitted). The following subsections detail each one of the aspects depicted in Fig. 4.

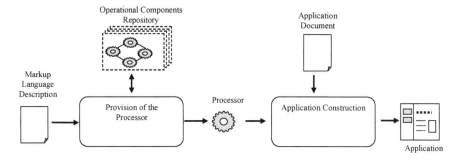

Fig. 4. Products and activities in OADDS.

4.1 Products

In addition to the application document and the description of the language used to mark up this document, OADDS introduces the processor of this language, together with a repository of *operational components* that facilitates the modular construction and the evolution of this processor.

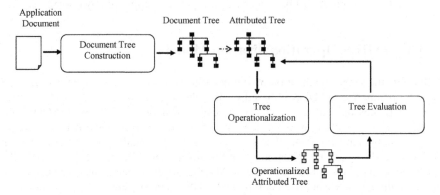

Fig. 5. Outline of the information flow in OADDS processors.

Fig. 5 sketches the information flow (that can be implemented in a modular way using the appropriated operational components) inside the OADDS processors. The key object of such processing is the *attributed tree*. Each node of this tree is associated with a set of attributes, each one having a value. The processing starts building the tree representing the application document. The construction of this tree can be carried out using any of the usual parsing frameworks for structured documents [3]. Next, the processing proceeds with the iteration of the attributed tree over a *tree operationalization* stage, followed by a *tree evaluation* stage. During the tree operationalization step, each node in the tree is decorated with (i) a *controller*, which is a procedure determining the evaluation order for the neighbours of the node, and (ii) an *initializer*, an *advancer* and a *finalizer*, which are the procedures organizing the local processing of this node. During the evaluation stage, the procedures decorating the tree are applied in the right order. Basically, this stage consists of a tree traversal commanded by the controllers. In this traversal, the processing procedures are applied in the right order. The modularity of the model is obtained thanks to the possibility for extending these procedures. The extensions will be devoted to propagating new attribute values in the tree, and to interrupting the evaluation when errors or other abnormal conditions are discovered. These adaptation and extension capabilities are essential in order to simplify the development and maintenance of complex systems, such as KBSs.

4.2 Activities

OADDS introduces the following two activities into the application development:

- *Provision of the processor.* In this activity the processor used to execute the application documented by the application document is provided. Usually such a processor has been previously constructed for a similar application, so it will be re-used on the new application document. In case the new application document uses new markup structures, the old processor will be adequately extended by adding new operational components for dealing with the new structures and with the extensions of existing ones. Only at the initial stages of the development of a new type of applications will the implementation of a new processor from scratch be mandatory, and, even in this case, the provision of operational components that can be reused in the construction of new processors will pay off in the long run

- *Application construction.* The application arises as the result of processing the application document with its processor.

5   Related Work

Descriptive markup languages were introduced as a convenience for the processing of electronic documents [6]. HyTime [9], an SGML [6] extension devised to deal with the design and construction of hypermedia applications, demonstrated that in some domains, these kinds of languages could be used for describing applications in terms of documents that, in turn, could be processed for building the final application. Moreover, proposals like DSSSL [8] proved that this document-oriented paradigm could be used not only for the applications, but also for describing the processors used to produce the applications. XML [19] and its related technologies have generalized the use of descriptive markup languages as a standard way for information inter-change between applications and for many other uses. Indeed, there are several pro-posals for applying markup languages to the KBSs domain (see [2]). Note that most of these approaches conceive markup languages as *static* entities. ADDS takes a more pragmatic position because markup languages are considered as *dynamic* objects that evolve when the contents or the markup needs of these contents change. OADDS gives an operational solution to this dynamic nature of the languages, encouraging the construction of modular processors from components that can be extended and adapted according to markup language evolution.

ADDS shares many features with the approach to software development based on *Domain-Specific Languages* (DSLs [17]). The main difference is that, while these kinds of languages are, in essence, specific purpose programming languages, ADDS follows a document-oriented paradigm, more suitable for content intensive applica-tions, such as KBSs, where there is a clear distinction between contents and the lan-guages used to structure such contents.

Modular language processor construction has been popularized by the functional programming community, where the main approach is based on *monads* and *monads transformers* [7], although proposals in the object-oriented paradigm (based on the use of *mixins* [4]), and in the attribute grammar approach to the construction of lan-guage processors can also be found [18]. OADDS semantic modularity mechanisms are inspired by these proposals, and also resemble the extension mechanisms of meth-ods in CLOS [15]. Indeed, the extensions of initializers, advancers and finalizers are similar to the definition of *before*, *around* and *after* methods in CLOS. In this sense controllers are analogous to primary methods.

ADDS generalizes the methods for the construction of educational applications for foreign language text compression presented in [5]. ADDS also generalizes the approach for the generation of hypermedia prototypes from XML documents describing the hypermedia contents and navigation presented in [10]. Work in [12][13][14] shows the evolution of ADDS. Initially, in [12][14] this approach was called DTC (structured Documents, document Transformations and software Components). The use of this approach for the construction of applications in the transport networks domain (more precisely, subway networks) is described in [12]. Work in [11] explores its use in the educational hypermedia domain.

6   Conclusions and Future Work

This paper outlines the development of KBSs using a document-oriented paradigm. According to this paradigm, knowledge is initially described using documents formulated in the same language used by the domain experts: a subset of the natural language. Afterwards, domain-specific descriptive markup languages are used to make the structure of the knowledge described in these documents explicit. This makes its automatic processing possible. The ADDS approach, together with the OADDS operationalization model, provides for an implementation of this paradigm. The pragmatic nature of ADDS supposes the evolutionary nature of these markup languages, as a response to the dynamic process of determining all the knowledge needed by KBSs. The modularity and extensibility of the inference engines promoted by OADDS simplifies the maintenance and the updating of the final application. Moreover, it also simplifies the development of application families, because, once all the basic components are made available, it is very simple to produce new related applications.

As future work it seems interesting to perform a more systematic study about the markup process applied to knowledge documentation and the cooperation between domain experts and developers in this process. Also, a study of the viability of knowledge acquisition tools based on ADDS / OADDS is needed. These tools will facilitate the edition and the markup processes of knowledge documents.

References

1. Aho, A. Sethi, R. Ullman, J. D. Compilers: Principles, Techniques and Tools. Adisson-Wesley. 1986.
2. Antonoiou,G.; van Harmelen,F. Web Ontology Language: OWL. In Staab,S.; Studer,R. Handbook on Ontologies in Information Systems. Springer-Verlag. 2003.
3. Birbeck,M et al. Professional XML 2nd Edition. WROX Press. 2001.
4. Duggan, D. A Mixin-Based Semantic-Based Approach to Reusing Domain-Specific Programming Languages. 14th European Conference on Object-Oriented Programming ECOOP'2000. Cannes. France. June12-16 2000.
5. Fernández-Valmayor, A.; López Alonso, C. Sèrè A. Fernández-Manjón,B. Integrating an Interactive Learning Paradigm for Foreign Language Text Comprehension into a Flexible Hypermedia system. IFIP WG3.2-WG3.6 Conference Building University Electronic Educational Environments. University of California Irvine, California, USA August. 4-6 1999.
6. Goldfard, C. F. The SGML Handbook. Oxford University Press. 1990.

7. Hudak,P. Domain-Specific Languages. Handbook of Programming Languages V. III: Little Languages. And Tools. Macmillan Tech. Publishing. 1998.
8. International Standards Organization. Document Style Semantics and Specification Language (DSSSL). ISO/IEC 10179. 1996.
9. International Standards Organization. Hypermedia/Time-based Structuring Language (HyTime) – 2d Edition. ISO/IEC 10744 . 1997.
10. Navarro, A., Fernández-Manjón, B., Fernández-Valmayor, A., Sierra, J.L. Formal-Driven Conceptualization and Prototyping of Hypermedia Applications. Fundamental Approaches to Software Engineering FASE 2002. ETAPS 2002. Grenoble. France. April 8-12. 2002.
11. Navarro,A.; Sierra, JL.; Fernández-Manjón, B.; Fernández-Valmayor, A. XML-based Integration of Hypermedia Design and Component-Based Techniques in the Production of Educational Applications. In M. Ortega and J. Bravo (Eds). Computers and Education in the 21st Century. Kluwer Publisher. 2000.
12. Sierra, J. L. Fernández-Manjón, B. Fernández-Valmayor, A. Navarro, A. Integration of Markup Languages, Document Transformations and Software Components in the Development of Applications: the DTC Approach. International Conference on Software ICS 2000. 16th IFIP World Computer Congress. Beijing - China. August 21-25. 2000.
13. Sierra, J. L. Fernández-Valmayor, A. Fernández-Manjón, B. Navarro, A. Building Applications with Domain-Specific Markup Languages: A Systematic Approach to the Development of XML-based Software. Third International Conference on Web Engineering ICWE 2003. Oviedo. July 14-18. 2003.
14. Sierra, J. L. Fernández-Valmayor, A. Fernández-Manjón, B. Navarro, A. Operationalizing Application Descriptions with DTC: Building Applications with Generalized Markup Technologies. 13th International Conference on Software Engineering & Knowledge Engineering SEKE'01. Buenos Aires. Argentina. June 13-15. 2001.
15. Steele JR, G.L. Common LISP: The Language (Second Edition). Digital Press. 1990.
16. Studer, R.; Fensel, D.;Decker,S.;Benjamins,V.R: Knowledge Engineering: Survey and Future Directions. In: F. Puppe (ed.): Knowledge-based Systems: Survey and Future Directions. Lecture Notes in Artificial Intelligence (LNAI), vol. 1570, Springer-Verlag, 1999.
17. Van Deursen, A. Klint, P.Visser, J. Domain-Specific Languages: An Annotated Bibliography. ACM SIGPLAN Notices. 35(6). 2000.
18. Van Wyk,E. de Moor, O. Backhouse, K. Kwiatkowski,P. Forwarding in Attribute Grammars for Modular Language Design. Compiler Construction CC 2002. ETAPS 2002. Grenoble France. April 8-12. 2002.
19. www.w3.org/TR.

A Flexible Approach to the Multidimensional Model: The Fuzzy Datacube

Miguel Delgado[1], Carlos Molina[1], Daniel Sánchez[1],
Lázaro Rodriguez Ariza[2], and M. Amparo Vila[1]

[1] Universidad de Granada, Dpto. de Ciencias de la Computación e I.A., E.T.S.I. de Informática
C/ Periodista Daniel Saucedo Aranda s/n
18071 Granada, Spain
{mdelgado,carlosmo,daniel,vila}@decsai.ugr.es
[2] Universidad de Granada, Depto. Economía Financiera y Contabilidad,
Faculty of Economics and Business Sciences
Campus Universitario de la Cartuja, 18071 Granada, Spain
lazaro@ugr.es

Abstract. As a result of the use of OLAP technology in new fields of knowledge and the merge of data from different sources, it has become necessary for models to support this technology. In this paper, we propose a new multidimensional model that can manage imprecision both in dimensions and facts. Consequently, the multidimensional structure is able to model data imprecision resulting from the integration of data from different sources or even information from experts, which it does by means of fuzzy logic.

1 Introduction

Ever since the appearance of the OLAP technology ([5]), there have been various proposals to support its special needs, and in particular, two different approaches have been documented. The first of these extends the relational model to support the structures and operations which are typical of OLAP, and the first proposal of such a type can be found in [9]. Since then, there have been other proposals (e.g. [10]), and most of the present relational systems include extensions to represent datacubes and operate on them. The second approach is to develop new models using a multidimensional view of the data. Many authors have proposed models in this way ([1, 3, 4, 12]).

In the early 70s, the need for flexible models and query languages to manage the ill-defined nature of information in DSS was identified ([8]). Nowadays, the application of the OLAP technology to other knowledge fields (e.g. medical data) and the use of semi-structured sources (e.g. XML) and non-structured sources (e.g. plain text) has made these requirements on the models even more important. The systems now need to manage imprecision in the data, and more flexible structures are needed to represent the analysis domain. New models have appeared to manage incomplete datacubes ([7]), imprecision in the facts ([11]), and the definition of facts using different levels in the dimensions ([13]). In addition, these models continue to use rigid hierarchies and this makes it extremely difficult for certain domains to be modelled. Consequently, this could result in the loss of information when we need to merge data from different sources with incompatibilities in their schemata.

R. Conejo et al. (Eds.): CAEPIA-TTIA 2003, LNAI 3040, pp. 26–36, 2004.

In this paper, we propose a new multidimensional model which is able to handle imprecision in hierarchies and facts by using fuzzy logic. The use of fuzzy hierarchies enables the structures of the dimensions to be defined to the final user more intuitively, thereby allowing a more intuitive use of the system. Furthermore, this allows information to be merged from different sources with incompatibilities in their structures, or even information given by experts to be used in order to improve the multidimensional schema. In the next section, we shall introduce classical multidimensional models as an introduction to presenting our approach. Then, in the third section we shall include an example of the structure proposed to show how to apply the operations on the multidimensional structure. The final section presents the main conclusions and future work.

2   Multidimensional Model

In this section, we shall present our proposed multidimensional model. Firstly, we shall introduce what we have called the classical models (these being the first documented models). Secondly, we shall define the multidimensional structure for managing imprecision. We shall then include the basic operations on the multidimensional models (roll-up, drill-down, dice, slice and pivot), and show how these are applied on the fuzzy structure.

2.1   Classical Multidimensional Models

In classical multidimensional models, we can distinguish two different types of data: on one hand, we have the facts being analysed, and on the other, the dimensions are the context for the facts. Hierarchies may be defined in the dimensions. The different levels of the dimensions allow us to access the facts at different levels of granularity. In order to do so, classical aggregation operators are needed (maximum, minimum, average, etc).

The defined hierarchies use many-to-one relations, so one element in a level can only be grouped by a single value of each upper level in the hierarchy. This makes the final structure of a datacube rigid and well defined in the sense that given two values of the same level in a dimension, the set of facts relating to these values have empty intersection.

The normal operations (roll-up, drill-down, dice, slice and pivot) are defined on this structure.

2.2   Multidimensional Structure

Definition 1. A dimension is a tuple $d=(l,\leq_d,l_\perp,l_\top)$ where $l=\{l_i, i=1,...,n\}$ such that each l_i is a set of values and $l_i \cap l_j = \emptyset$ if $i \neq j$, and $\leq_d$ is a partial order relation between the elements of l. $l_\perp$ and $l_\top$ are two elements in l such that $\forall l_i \in l \ \ l_\perp \leq_d l_i$ and $l_i \leq_d l_\top$.

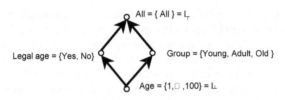

Fig. 1. Example of an age hierarchy.

Each element l_i is called a level. In order to identify level l of dimension d, we shall use $d.l$. The two special levels $l_\perp$ and $l_\top$ shall be called the *base level* and *top level*, respectively. The partial order relation in a dimension gives the hierarchical relation between the levels.

In Figure 1, you can see a definition of an age hierarchy. The definition of the dimension as we have presented it would be $Age = (\{Age, Group, legal\ age, All\}, \leq_{Age}, Age, All)$, and the relation $Age \leq_{Age} Age$, $Group \leq_{Age} Group$, $Legal\ age \leq_{Age} Legal\ age$, $All \leq_{Age} All$, $Age \leq_{Age} Group$, $Age \leq_{Age} Legal\ age$, $Age \leq_{Age} All$, $Group \leq_{Age} All$ and $Legal\ age \leq_{Age} All$.

Definition 2. For each dimension d, the domain is $dom(d) = \bigcup l_i$.

In the above example, the domain of the dimension Age is $dom(Age) = \{1, ..., 100, Young, Adult, Old, Yes, No, All\}$.

Definition 3. For each l_i, the set

$$H_{l_i} = \{l_j / l_j \neq l_i \wedge l_j \leq_d l_i \wedge \neg \exists l_k \quad l_j \leq_d l_k \leq_d l_i\}, \tag{1}$$

and we call this the *set of children of level l_i*.

Using the same example of the dimension on the ages, the set of children of the level *All* is $H_{All} = \{Group, Legal\ age\}$. In all the dimensions we define, for the *base level*, this set will be always the empty set, as you can see from the definition.

Definition 4. For each l_i, the set

$$P_{l_i} = \{l_j / l_j \neq l_i \wedge l_i \leq_d l_j \wedge \neg \exists l_k \quad l_i \leq_d l_k \leq_d l_j\}, \tag{2}$$

and we call this the *set of parents of level l_i*.

On the hierarchy we have defined, the set of parents of level Age is $P_{Age} = \{Legal\ age, Group\}$. In the case of the *top level* of a dimension, this set will always be the empty set.

Definition 5. For each pair of levels l_i and l_j such that $l_j \in H_{l_i}$, we have the relation $\mu_{ij} : l_i \times l_j \rightarrow [0,1]$, and we call this the *kinship relation*.

The degree of inclusion of the elements of a level in the elements of their parent levels can be defined using this relation. If we only use the values 0 and 1 and one element is only included with degree 1 for a single element of its parent levels, this relation represents a crisp hierarchy. Following the example, the relation between the levels *Legal age* and *Age* is of this type. The parent relation in this situation is

$$\mu_{LegalAge,Age}(Yes,x) = \begin{cases} 1 & \text{if } x \in [18,100] \\ 0 & \text{in other case} \end{cases} \qquad \mu_{LegalAge,Age}(No,x) = \begin{cases} 1 & \text{if } x \in [1,17] \\ 0 & \text{in other case} \end{cases}. \qquad (3)$$

If we relax these conditions and allow values to be used in the interval [0,1] without any other limitation, we have a fuzzy hierarchical relation. This allows several hierarchical relations to be represented more intuitively. An example can be seen in Figure 2 where we present the group of ages according to linguistic labels. Furthermore, this fuzzy relation allows hierarchies to be defined in which there is imprecision in the relationship between elements in different levels. In this situation, the value in the interval shows the degree of confidence in the relation.

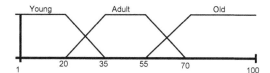

Fig. 2. Kinship relation between levels *Group* and *Age*.

Definition 6. For each pair of levels l_i y l_j of the dimension d such that $l_j \leq_d l_i \wedge l_j \neq l_i$, the relation $\eta_{ij} : l_i \times l_j \to [0,1]$ is defined as

$$\eta_{ij}(a,b) = \begin{cases} \mu_{ij}(a,b) & \text{if } l_j \in H_{l_i} \\ \displaystyle\bigoplus_{l_k \in H_{l_i}} \bigoplus_{c \in l_k} (\mu_{ik}(a,c) \otimes \eta_{kj}(c,b)) & \text{in other case} \end{cases}, \qquad (4)$$

where $\oplus$ y $\otimes$ are a t-conorm and a t-norm, respectively, or operators from the families MOM or MAM defined by Yager ([15]), which include the t-conorms and t-norms, respectively. This relation is called the *extended kinship relation*.

This relation gives us information about the degree of relation between two values in different levels in the same dimension. In order to obtain this value, it considers all the possible paths between the elements in the hierarchy. Each one is calculated by aggregating the *kinship relation* between elements in two consecutive levels using a t-norm. The final value is then the aggregation of the result of each path using a t-conorm. By way of example, we will show how to calculate the value of $\eta_{All, Age}(All,25)$. In this situation, we have two different paths. Let us look at each:

- *All – Legal age – Age*. In Figure 3.a, you can see the two ways to get to 25 from *All* passing the level *legal age*. The result of this path is $(1 \otimes 1) \oplus (1 \otimes 0)$.

- *All – Group – Age*. This situation is very similar to the previous one. In Figure 3.b, you can see the three different paths going through the level *Group*. The result of this path is $(1 \otimes 0.7) \oplus (1 \otimes 0.3) \oplus (1 \otimes 0)$.

We must now aggregate these two values using a t-conorm in order to obtain the result. If we use the *maximum* as the t-conorm and the *minimum* as the t-norm, the result is $((1 \otimes 1) \oplus (1 \otimes 0)) \oplus ((1 \otimes 0.7) \oplus (1 \otimes 0.3) \oplus (1 \otimes 0)) = (1 \oplus 0) \oplus (0.7 \oplus 0.3 \oplus 0) = 1 \oplus 0.7 = 1$, so the value of $\eta_{All,Age}(All,25)$ is 1, which means that the age 25 is grouped by *All* in the level *All* with grade 1.

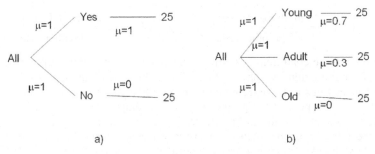

Fig. 3. Example of the calculation of the extended kinship relation. a) path *All – Legal age – Age* b) path *All – Group – Age*.

Definition 7. We say that any pair *(h, α)* is a fact when *h* is an m-tuple on the attributes domain we want to analyze, and $\alpha \in [0,1]$.

The management of uncertainty in the facts is carried out using a degree of certainty with each one. This degree of certainty allows us to use values in analysis that might be interesting to the decisor but which imply imprecision. The value α of each pair controls the influence of the fact in the analysis.

Definition 8. An object of type *history* is the recursive structure

$$H = \overset{\#}{\underset{!}{(A,l_b,F,G,H')}} \overset{\Omega}{,} \tag{5}$$

where Ω is the recursivity clause, F is the fact set, l_b is a set of levels $(l_{1b},...,l_{nb})$, A is an application from l_b to F, G is an aggregation operator, and H' is a structure of type *history*.

The role of this structure will be clear after the operations have been defined in the next section.

Definition 9. A datacube is a tuple $C=(D,l_b,F,A,H)$ such that $D=(d_1,...,d_n)$ is a set of dimensions, $l_b=(l_{1b},...,l_{nb})$ is a set of levels such that l_{ib} belongs to d_i, $F = R \cup \emptyset$ where R is the set of facts and $\emptyset$ is a special symbol, H is an object of type *history*, and A is an application defined as $A : l_{1b} \times...\times l_{nb} \rightarrow F$, giving the relation between the dimensions and the facts defined.

If for $\vec{a} = (a_1,...,a_n)$, $A(\vec{a}) = \emptyset$, this means that no fact is defined for this combination of values.

Definition 10. We say that a datacube is *basic* if $l_b = (l_{11},...,l_{n\perp})$ and $H = \Omega$.

Having defined the structure, we shall now show how to translate a multidimensional schema into our model. An example of a multidimensional model is shown in Figure 4. In this schema, we want to analyze the sales in a company. The broken lines represent the fuzzy relation between the levels, i.e. the relations take values in the entire interval [0,1]. It is possible to see how three dimensions are considered: *Time*, *Product* and *Customer*. This schema translated into our model corresponds to $C_{sales}=(\{customer, product, time\}, \{(price, amount)\} \cup \emptyset, A, \Omega)$. In order to complete the definition, we need the dimension structures: *Customer = (\{Age, Legal Age,*

Group, All}, $\leq_{Customer}$, Age, All), Product = ({Product, Category, Provider, Quality, All}, $\leq_{Product}$, Product, All), Time = ({Date, Month, Holiday, All},$\leq_{Time}$, Date, All) and the application *A* that gives the relation between the dimensions and the facts: *A: Age x Product x Date → {(price, amount)}UØ* .

2.3 Operations

Once we have defined the multidimensional structure, we need the basic operations to work with it. In this section, we shall define the operations to change the level in the hierarchies (roll-up and drill-down) as well as the selection (dice), projection (slice) and pivot. First, two preliminary concepts are needed.

Definition 11. An aggregation operator is a function $G(B)$ where $B = \{(h,\alpha)/(h,\alpha) \in F\}$ and the result is a tuple *(h', α')*.

The parameter of an aggregation operator can be seen as a fuzzy bag ([6]) since it concerns a collection of elements (the facts) which can be repeated, with each having a value in the [0,1] interval (the α defined in the tuples).

Definition 12. For each value *a* in a level l_i, we have the set

$$F_a = \begin{matrix} \# & \bigcup_{l_j \in H_{l_i}} F_b / b \in l_j \wedge \mu_{ij}(a,b) > 0 & if & l_i \neq l_b \\ ! & \{h / h \in H \wedge \exists a_1,...,a_n A(a_1,..,a,...,a_n) = h\} & if & l_i = l_b \end{matrix} \qquad (6)$$

This set includes all the facts that are in any way related to value *a*, and this is all we need to introduce the operations and to apply them on the fuzzy multidimensional structure proposed.

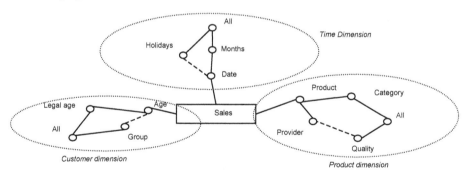

Fig. 4. Example of multidimensional schema.

Definition 13. The result of applying *roll-up* on dimension d_i, level l_r $(l_r \neq l_s)$, using the aggregation operator G on a datacube $C=(D,l_b,F,A,H)$ is another datacube $C'=(D,l'_b,F',A',H')$ where $l'_b=(l_{1b},...,l_r,...,l_{nb})$, $A'(a_1,...,a,...,a_n) = G(\{(b,\alpha \otimes \eta_{rb}(a,c))/(b,\alpha) \in F_a \wedge A(a_1,...,c,...,a_n) = (b,\alpha)\})$, F' is the range of A', and $H'=(A, l_b, F, G, H)$.

Definition 14. The result of applying *drill-down* on a datacube $C=(D,l_b,F,A,H)$ having $H=(A',l'_b,F'.H')$ is another datacube $C'=(D,l'_b,F',A',H')$.

After the definition of the *drill-down* operation, we can see the role of the structure *history* inside our proposal. This recursive structure enables us to return at any time to the previous state before the *roll-up* was applied. Consequently, loss of information is prevented as you progress up the hierarchy.

Definition 15. The result of applying *dice* with the condition β on level l_r of dimension d_i in a datacube $C=(D,l_b,F,A,H)$ is another datacube $C'=(D',l'_b,F',A',\Omega)$ where $D'=\{d_1,...,d'_i,...,d_n\}$ where $d'_i=(l_i',\leq_{d_i},l_b,l_T)$ having $l'=\{l/l_b\leq_{d_i}l'_j\}$ and

$$d'_i.l'_j = \begin{cases} \{v/v\in l_j \wedge \beta(v)\} & if \quad l'_j=l_r \\ \{v/v\in d_i.l_j \wedge \exists x\in l_r\beta(x)\wedge \eta_{r_j}(x,v)>0\} & if \quad l'_j\leq_d l_r, \\ \{v/v\in d_i.l_j \wedge \exists x\in l_r\beta(x)\wedge \eta_{j_r}(v,x)>0\} & if \quad l_r\leq_d l'_j \end{cases}$$

$A'(a_1,...,a_i,...,a_n)=(h,\alpha\otimes\mu_\beta)/a_1\in d'_1.l'_b \wedge...a_n\in d'_n.l'_b \wedge A(a_1,...,a_n)=(h,\alpha)$ where $\mu_\beta=\bigoplus_{c\in d'_i.l'_r}\eta_{rb}(c,a_i)$, and F' is the range of A'.

Definition 16. The result of applying *slice* on dimension d_i using the aggregation operator G in a datacube $C=(D,l_b,F,A,H)$ is another datacube $C'=(D',l_b',F',A',\Omega)$ where $D'=(d_1,...,d_{i-1},d_{i+1},...,d_n)$, $l_b'=(l_{1b},...,l_{i-1b},l_{i+1b},...,l_{nb})$, $A'(a_1,...,a_{i-1},a_{i+1}...,a_n)$ $=G(\{h,a)/\exists xA(a_1,...,a_{i-1},x,a_{i+1}...,a_n)=(h,a)\})$, and F' is the range of A'.

Definition 17. The result of applying pivot on dimensions d_i and d_j in a datacube $C=(D,l_b,F,A,H)$ is another datacube $C'=(D',l_b',F,A',\Omega)$ where $D'=(d_1,...,d_{i-1},d_j,d_{i+1},...,d_{j-1},d_i,d_{j+1},...,d_n)$, $l_b'=(l_{1b},...,l_{i-1b},l_{jb},l_{i+1b},...,l_{j-1b},l_{ib},l_{j+1b},...,l_{nb})$, and $A'(a_1,...,a_{i-1},a_i,a_{i+1},...,a_{j-1},a_j,a_{j+1},...,a_n)=A(a_1,...,a_{i-1},a_i,a_{i+1},...,a_{j-1},a_i,a_{j+1},...,a_n)$.

Although we now have the operations to work with the structure proposed, this structure can represent objects that are not suitable for the operations defined above. We must therefore say when a datacube is valid to work with it.

Definition 18. A datacube is *valid* if it is *basic* or has been obtained by applying a finite number of operations on a *basic datacube*.

2.4 User View

We have presented a structure that manages imprecision by means of fuzzy logic. We need to use aggregation operators on fuzzy bags in order to apply some of the operations presented. Most of the methods previously documented give a fuzzy set as a result. As this situation can make the result difficult to understand and use in a decision process, we propose a two-layer model: one of the layers is the structure presented in the previous section; and the other is defined on this, and its main objective is to hide the complexity of the model and provide the user with a more understandable result. In order to do so, we propose the use of a fuzzy summary operator that gives a more intuitive result but which keeps as much information as possible. Using this type of operator, we shall define the *user view*.

Definition 19. Given a summary operator M, we define the *user view* of a datacube $C=(D,l_b,F,A,H)$ using M as the structure $C_M=(D,l_b,F_M,A_M)$ where $A_M(a_1,...,a_n)$ $=M(A(a_1,...,a_n))$ and F_M is the range of A_M.

We can define as many user views of a datacube as the number of summary operators used. Therefore, each user can have their own *user view* with the most intuitive view of data according to their preferences by using a datacube. As an example of this type of operator, we can use the one proposed in [2]. This operator proposes the use of the fuzzy number that best fits, in the sense of fuzziness, the fuzzy set or fuzzy bag.

3   Example

Once we have defined the fuzzy structure and the operations on it, we shall present an example of a simple multidimensional schema in order to show the application of operations on it. This example will be modelled using the classical multidimensional or crisp model to show the differences between both approaches. We will use the schema in Figure 4.

In the fuzzy case, the dimension *Customer* is the fuzzy hierarchy on ages which we have used previously. The remaining elements in both the fuzzy and the crisp case are shown in Figure 5, with the exception of the partial order relations which are clear in the schema. Here we see the first differences between both approaches when we model the levels *group* and *holiday*. In the crisp case, these concepts are modelled using intervals on the ages and dates, respectively. In our approach, we use linguistic labels. The facts used in the example and their relation with the values in the dimension are shown in Table 1. If the user wants to know *"the average amount of sales at Christmas for the different age groups and the quality of the provider"*, the sequence of operations to apply is:

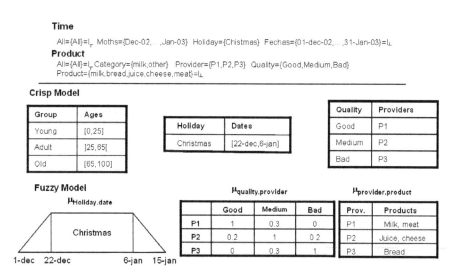

Fig. 5. Dimension structures for the multidimensional schema.

1. dice on the dimension *time*, in the level *holiday* with the condition $(x)=$ "*x is Christmas*".
2. roll-up in the dimension *time* and level *holiday*, dimension *product* and level *quality* and dimension *customer* and level *group*, using the aggregation operator *average* on the *amount*.

In order to apply the roll-up operation, we need the average aggregation operator. Although we can use the classical operator in the crisp case, in the fuzzy model we need an operator that works with fuzzy bags. In the example, we have used the operators proposed by Rundensteiner ([14]) for a fuzzy relational model. The adaptation of these operators to our approach is simple: if R is an aggregation operator defined by Rundensteiner, the operator G_R for our approach is defined as $G_R(h)=(R(h),1)$.

We need another operator to show the results in the fuzzy case. We have used the linguistic summary ([2]) as the summary operator. The results in both approaches are shown in the Tables 2-4. When analyzing the results, we need to bear in mind the differences between both approaches. Therefore, when the user gets the result in the crisp case, for example for the group *young*, the results correspond to the query "*the average amount of sales in the interval [22-dic,6-jan] by the customer with ages in the interval [0,25] and the quality of the provider*". In the fuzzy case, the user gets a result which is closer to his/her concept of Christmas and youth.

If we want to refine the results in order to obtain "*the maximum average amounts sold by age groups*", we need to apply *slice* on the dimensions *Products* and *Time*, using the *maximum* aggregation operator. The result is shown in Table 5.

The results obtained in each case are different. This occurs because the values involved in each calculation and their importance are different in both approaches. In the crisp case, all the values inside the intervals have the same weight in the aggregation process. In the fuzzy model, on the other hand, the values at the edges of the concepts do not have the same importance as the values in the kernel in the final result. We can also see the role of the user view in the fuzzy model. The multidimensional structure proposed is based on fuzzy logic and the results shown to the user are fuzzy sets which are difficult to understand. The user view helps to interpret the results, showing the information obtained in a more expressive and understandable way to the user (using a fuzzy number and the associated linguistic expression in each case).

Table 1. Data in the datacube example.

Fact No.	product	Date	Age	Price	Amount	α	Fact No.	product	Date	Age	Price	Amount	α
1	milk	23-dec	19	10	1	1	13	bread	6-jan	17	3	2	1
2	meat	7-jan	40	18	3	1	14	meat	22-dec	65	6	3	1
3	bread	10-jan	45	1	5	1	15	cheese	2-jan	52	10	2	1
4	juice	28-dec	75	2	2	1	16	bread	27-dec	66	5	2	1
5	cheese	3-jan	20	5	1	1	17	cheese	04-jan	70	5	3	1
6	milk	10-jan	20	1	5	1	18	bread	24-dec	60	3	6	1
7	bread	25-dec	22	3	1	1	19	bread	10-jan	65	4	4	1
8	bread	1-jan	55	5	2	1	20	milk	03-jan	64	5	2	1
9	juice	28-dec	23	4	3	1	21	cheese	10-jan	15	5	5	1
10	bread	6-jan	75	6	4	1	22	cheese	28-dec	40	3	5	1
11	milk	23-dec	78	3	3	1	23	bread	02-jan	65	4	5	1
12	meat	29-dec	40	18	2	1	24	milk	26-dec	23	5	5	1

4 Conclusions

In this paper, we have presented a new multidimensional model. The main contribution of this new model is that it is able to operate on data with imprecise facts and hierarchies. Classical models impose a rigid structure that makes it difficult for information from different sources to be merged if there are incompatibilities in the schemata. Our model can handle these problems by means of fuzzy logic which allows our proposal to carry out the integration, relaxing the schemata in order to obtain a new one that covers the others and attempting to preserve as much information as possible. In addition, our model can manage information given by experts which is often imprecise. This data can be used to improve the multidimensional schema so that it may be used by the final user in the decision process. Another advantage is that it can model situations to users more naturally so that they can access the information more intuitively.

Table 2. Result of applying dice on the dimension *Time*, on the level *Holiday* with the condition $\beta(x)$= "*x is Christmas*" over C. In the fuzzy case, the value shown is the new α of the fact. In the crisp case, X means that this fact satisfies the condition.

Fact	1	2	3	4	5	6	7	8	9	10	11	12
Fuzzy	1	0.9	0.6	1	1	0.6	1	1	1	1	1	1
Crisp	X	-	-	X	X	-	X	X	X	X	X	X
Fact	13	14	15	16	17	18	19	20	21	22	23	24
Fuzzy	1	1	1	1	1	1	0.6	1	0.6	1	1	1
Crisp	X	X	X	X	X	-	X	X	-	X	X	X

Table 3. Result of applying roll-up in the dimension *Time* on the level *Holidays*, dimension *Product* and level *Quality* and dimension *Customer* and level *Group* in the datacube C' in the fuzzy case. *Time* dimension is not shown due to the fact that there is only one value.

Customer	Product					
	Good		Medium		Bad	
	C"	C"$_M$	C"	C"$_M$	C"	C"$_M$
Young	{1/1 0.6/3, 0.4/3.67, 0.2/3.33},1	(1,1,0,1.5) "greater than 1"	{1/1, 0.6/3, 0.3/2.88},1	(1,1,0,1.45) "greater than 1"	{1/2, 0.6/1.5, 0.2/2.4},1	(2,2,0.5,0.39) "around 2"
Adult	{1/2, 0.9/2.5, 0.6/3.4, 0.5/3.33, 0.2/3.3},1	(2,2,0,1.19) "greater than 2"	{1/3.5, 0.6/3.33, 0.3/3.44},1	(3.5,3.5,0.17,0) "a bit less than 3.5"	{1/2, 0.8/4, 0.5/3.8, 0.4/3.33, 0.2/3.3},1	(2,2,0,1.6) "grater than 2"
Old	{1/3, 0.5/2.67, 0.2/2.6},1	(3,3,0.4,0) "a bit less than 3"	{1/2, 0.8/2.5, 0.3/3.22},1	(2,2,0,1.22) "greater than 2"	{1/4, 0.6/3, 0.5/3.75, 0.3/4.2, 0.2/3.71},1	(4,4,0.29, 0.19) "around 4"

Table 4. Result of applying roll-up in the dimension *Time* on the level *Holiday*, dimension *Product* and level *Quality* and dimension *Customer* and level *Group* in the datacube C' in the crisp case.

Customer (Age group)	Product		
	Good	Medium	Bad
Young	3	2	1.5
Adult	2	3.5	4
Old	3	2.5	3.7

Table 5. Result of applying slice on the dimensions *Product* and *Time* in the datacube C".

Customer	Fuzzy		Crisp
	C'''	C'''$_M$	Fact
Young	{1/2, 0.6/1.5, 0.2/2.4, 0.6/3, 0.3/2.88, 0.4/3.67, 0.2/3.33},1	(2,2,0.5,1.3) "around 2"	3
Adult	{1/3.5, 0.8/4, 0.6/3.8, 0.6/3.33, 0.3/3.44, 0.5/3.67},1	(3.5,3.5,0.17,0.5) "around 3.5"	4
Old	{1/4, 0.6/3, 0.5/3.75, 0.3/4.2, 0.2/3.71, 0.3/3.22},1	(4,4,0.99,0.2) "around 4"	3,7

In order to complete the model, we need to study the properties of the operations on the structure. Another line is to develop a graphical means of representing the results of the operations so that the information obtained may be read more intuitively. To finish the decision process, we need to study the integration process so as to obtain a formal way to merge data from different sources, including experts' knowledge.

References

1. Agrawal, R. Gupta, A., Sarawagi, S.: Modeling Multidimensional Databases. IBM Research Report, IBM Almaden Research Center, September 1995
2. Blanco, I., Sánchez, D., Serrano, J.M., Vila, M.A.: A New Proposal of Aggregation Functions: the Linguistic Summary. Proceedings of IFSA'2003 Istanbul (Turkey) 2003
3. Cabibbo, L., Torlone, R.: A Logical Approach to Multidimensional Databases. Advances in Databases Technology (EDTB'98) No. 1337 in LNCS pp. 183-197 Springer 1998
4. Cabibbo, L., Torlone, R..: Querying Multidimensional Databases. Proceedings of the 6th Int. Workshop on databases programming languages (DBPL6) Estes Pork (U.S.A.) 1997
5. Codd, E.F.: Providing OLAP (On-line Analytical Processing) to User-Analysts: An IT Mandate. Technical report, E.F. Codd and Associates, 1993
6. Delgado, M., Martín-Bautista, M.J., Sánchez, D., Vila, M.A.: On A Characterization of Fuzzy Bags. Proceedings of IFSA'2003 Istanbul (Turkey) 2003
7. Dyreson, C.: Information Retrieval from an Incomplete Data Cube. Proceedings of the 22nd Int. Conf. on VLDB pp. 532-543. Morgan Kaufman Publishers, 1996
8. Gorry, G.A., Scott Morton, M.S.: A Framework for Management Information Systems. Sloan Management Review 13 (1) (1971) 50-70
9. Gray, J., Chaudhuri, S., Bosworth, A., Layman, A., Reichart, D., Venkatrao, M.: Data Cube: A Relational Aggregation Operator Generalizing Group-By, Cross-Tab, and Sub-Totals. Data Mining and Knowledge Discovery 1 (1997) 29-53
10. Kimball, R.: The Data Warehouse Toolkit. Wiley, New York, 1996
11. Laurent, A., Bouchon-Meunier, B., Doucet, A.: Flexible Unary Multidimensional Queries and their Combinations. Proceedings of IPMU 2002, Annecy (France) 2002
12. Li, C., Wang, X.S.: A Data Model for Supporting On-Line Analytical Processing. Proceedings of the 5th Int. Conf. on Information and Knowledge Management (CIKM) 1996
13. Pedersen, T.B., Jensen, C.S., Dyreson, C.E.: A Foundation for Capturing and Querying Complex Multidimensional Data. Information Systems 26 (2001) 383-423
14. Rundensteiner, E.A., Bic, L.: Aggregates in Possibilistic Databases. Proceedings of the 15th Conf. on Very Large Databases (VLDB'98), Amsterdam (Holland), 287-295, 1989
15. Yager, R.R.: Aggregation Operators and Fuzzy Systems Modelling. Fuzzy Sets and Systems 67 (1994) 129-145

A Framework for Ontology Reuse
and Persistence Integrating UML and Sesame

Carlos Pedrinaci, Amaia Bernaras, Tim Smithers,
Jessica Aguado, and Manuel Cendoya

San Sebastian Tecnology Park, Paseo Mikeletegi 53,
20009 San Sebastian, Spain
{carlos,amaia,tsmithers,jessica}@miramon.net
mcendoya@miramon.es

Abstract. Nowadays there is a great effort underway to improve the World
Wide Web. A better content organisation, allowing automatic processing, leading to the Semantic Web is one of the main goals. In the light of bringing this
technology closer to the Software Engineering community we propose an architecture allowing an easier development for ontology-based applications. Thus,
we first present a methodology for ontology creation and automatic code generation using the widely adopted CASE UML tools. And based on a study of
the art of the different RDF storage and querying systems, we couple this methodology with the Sesame system for providing a framework able to deal with
large knowledge bases.

1 Introduction

The huge amount of information available in the World Wide Web has led researchers
to work towards improving its organisation, by providing machine-understandable
data. *"The Semantic Web is an extension of the current web in which information is
given well-defined meaning, better enabling computers and people to work in cooperation."*[1]. It is obvious that the Semantic Web will offer new possibilities for the
web but as Mark Frauenfelder suggests *"There is a big question as to whether people
will think the benefits are worth the extra effort of adding metadata to their content in
the first place. One reason the Web became so wildly successful, after all, was its
sublime ease of creation."*[2].

This paper presents some of the results obtained in the ongoing EU project OBE-
LIX (IST-2001-33144) during the creation of an ontology-based online events design
application [3],[4]. We propose a framework for the development of Semantic Web
applications development so as to bring this technology closer to the Software
Engineering community. Bearing that purpose in mind, the proposed framework focuses on the ease of creation and use. The same way web designers don't have to be
aware of HTTP protocol's details (and very often even of HTML details), it would be
interesting to obtain the same level of independency from the implementation details
surrounding the Semantic Web which are much more complex. Obtaining such facilities for creating Semantic Web applications is difficult due to its inherent complexity,
but we should however try to fill the gap between AI community and the Software
Engineering community, by providing an easy and suitable framework. Moreover,
software agents will need to interact with other systems, usually based on different

R. Conejo et al. (Eds.): CAEPIA-TTIA 2003, LNAI 3040, pp. 37–46, 2004.

ontologies, supported by different architectures and adequately supporting the interaction with humans. Semantic Web applications are complex systems, thus, maintaining and/or improving them is a hard task. Software Engineering has proven that in such cases, and in general for every system, a clear, well defined and powerful methodology is a must. Such methodologies facilitate the creation and minimize the problems raised when improving and modifying a system.

In this paper, we first present the use of the Unified Modelling Language (UML) [5] for knowledge representation, along with a procedure for generating from a UML class diagram a specialised RDF schema [6],[7] and a set of Java classes corresponding to the classes in the model. Afterwards we compare the different RDF storage and querying systems, and justify the selection of Sesame for ensuring persistence for large RDF knowledge bases [8]. Next, we present and explain Sesame. In section five, we propose an architecture for developing ontology-based applications, using UML for knowledge representation and relying on Sesame for data persistance. Finally, we conclude and present some directions for future research.

2   UML for Knowledge Representation and Exchange

The Unified Modeling Language (UML) is a standard language from the Object Management Group (OMG) [9] with an associated graphical notation for object-oriented analysis and design. It is widely adopted in industry, and several CASE tools are already available to facilitate software engineers' work. The benefits of using UML for ontology development have been extensively argued in [10], [11], [12] and [13]. Some of these benefits are: (i) UML is a standard language; (ii) UML is a graphical notation based on many years of experience in software analysis and design, which is currently suported by widely-adopted CASE tools that are more accessible to software practitioners than current ontology tools; (iii) agent-based systems will need to interact with legacy enterprise systems, which often have UML models; (iv) knowledge expressed using UML is directly accessible for human comprehension and for machine processing; (v) thanks to the modular nature of object-oriented modelling, the knowledge in a UML model can be changed without affecting other features.

In [11] and [13] Stephen Cranfield proposes an implementation for object-oriented knowledge representation, using UML for defining ontologies and domain knowledge in the Semantic Web. Fig. 1 shows a pictorial description of this proposal. The proposed methodology is as follows. First, a domain expert designs the ontology graphically with one of the available CASE tools supporting UML (e.g. Rational Rose, Poseidon, ArgoUML, etc). The ontology is then saved in the standard format XML Model Interchange (XMI) [14]. Using a pair of XSLT stylesheets the XMI representation of the ontology is transformed into a set of Java classes and interfaces corresponding to the concepts present in the ontology, and into an RDF schema. The java classes allow an application to represent knowledge about the domain as in-memory data structures. The RDF schema, defines the concepts that an application can reference when serializing the knowledge in RDF/XML. For performing the marshalling and unmarshalling of objects to and from RDF/XML documents, a marshalling package is also provided. This feature is provided via two classes: MarshalHelper and UnmarshalHelper. These delegate to the generated Java classes decisions about the names and types for each field, and are then called back to perform the un/marshalling from/to RDF, using the Stanford RDF API [15].

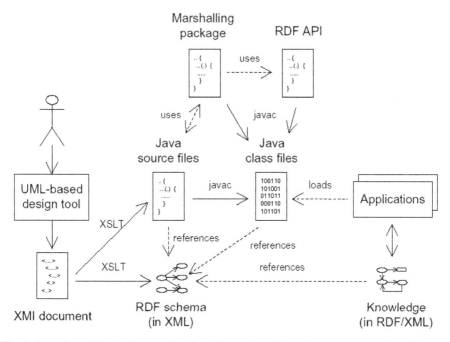

Fig. 1. Overview of the implementation for object-oriented knowledge representation. (Taken from [13]).

It is important to note that the generated RDF schema does not contain all the information from the designed UML model. Its purpose is to define resources corresponding to all the classes, interfaces, attributes and associations in the ontology in order to allow serialisation of in-memory objects in the standard language RDF. Thus, for accessing all the ontology information one of the available Java APIs for XMI can be used: [16] and [17].

The system does also allow modelling incomplete knowledge. Therefore, the generated Java classes include extra boolean fields for each attribute that record whether the value is known or not. Also, when marshalling incomplete information, a non-standard RDF property, *notClosedFor,* is used and associates a property with a resource, meaning that the information is incomplete.

Obtaining an instance from the RDF/XML representation involves parsing the whole file, which is not a problem for small knowledge bases. However, when dealing with large knowledge bases, there are more efficient approaches: RDF storage and querying systems.

3   Comparison of the RDF Storage and Querying Systems

To adapt Cranefield's approach to large knowledge bases, we have studied the different RDF storage and querying facilities available. The state of the art of the different systems is based on [18], with updated information.

Table 1 presents an analysis of the different storage systems currently available. The main criteria that were kept in mind for determining the RDF storage and querying system that suits better to our needs are:

- Storage: The method/architecture used for ensuring the data persistance.
- Platform: List of all the different platforms supported. It includes the Operating Systems but also the need for any other components like a Perl interpreter or a Java Virtual Machine.
- API: The possible ways for interacting with the system. It includes protocols and APIs provided for different programming languages.
- Querying: The languages the system allows to be used for querying a data repository.
- Inferencing: The capability of the system to infer new knowledge, that is to generate new statements based on the existing knowledge. For the majority of the systems only class subsumption is provided. However, some systems allow more powerful inferencing by providing mecanisms for defining user rules.
- Extras: Whether the system has other functional elements associated or prepared for interacting with it.

From the analysis and comparison performed, and shown in , Sesame was chosen for the following reasons:

Sesame allows inferencing over RDF(s) thanks to its query language RQL [19], [20]. Moreover, the system can be deployed in any platform with a Java Virtual Machine. It provides several ways for interacting with it such as RMI, SOAP or HTTP. It has been installed on top of many DBMS like Oracle, MySQL or PostgreSQL and has a generic implementation for SQL92 compliant DBMS. In addition to all these characteristics, support for DAML+OIL [21] has been added, improving its capabilities but also showing Sesame's modularity and the possibility to adapt the system to new languages. Finally, the new versionning and access control features implemented, turn Sesame into a suitable system for developing and maintaining knowledge bases providing the same control level as CVS does for programmers.

It is worth noting that, although KAON [22] and Cerebra [23] are good candidates for their interesting features, Sesame is superior to KAON for its support for DAML+OIL. Concerning Cerebra the fact it is not Open Source was determinant.

4   Sesame

Sesame is a system for efficient storage and expressive querying of large quantities of metadata in RDF and RDF Schema. It was initially developed by Aidministrator Nederland b.v. as part of the European IST project On-To-Knowledge [24] and is currently been extended and improved by Aidministrator Nederland b.v., the "Sesame community" and NLNet [25].

"Sesame's design and implementation are independent from any specific storage device. Thus, Sesame can be deployed on top of a variety of storage devices, such as relational databases, triple stores, or object-oriented databases, without having to change the query engine or other functional modules" [8]. This independence is granted by the Storage And Inference Layer (SAIL) (see Fig. 2). SAIL is an Applica-

Table 1. RDF storage and querying systems comparison.

	Querying	Platform	API	Storage	Inference	Extras
ICS-RDFSuite	RQL	Solaris - Linux	Java - C++ - SQL	O-RDBMS	Yes	
Sesame	RQL*, RDQL	Any (JVM)	Java - HTTP RMI - SOAP	O-RDBMS	Yes	OMM, BOR
Inkling	SquishQL	Any (JVM)	Java	Memory - JDBC	No	
RDFDB	SquishQL*	Solaris - Linux - FreeBSD	C - Perl	SleepyCat	Yes	
RDFSTORE	SquishQL	Any (Perl)	Perl	Memory - BerkeleyDB	Yes	
EOR	Triple-matching	Any (JVM)	Java - HTTP SQL	SQL DB	No	
Redland	Triple-matching	Solaris - Linux - MacOS X FreeBSD - OSF/1	C - Java - Perl Python - Tcl	Memory - SleepyCat BerkeleyDB	No	
Jena	RDQL	Any (JVM)	Java	Memory - BerkeleyDB PostgreSQL	No	
RDF Gateway	RDFQL	Windows NT/2000	ADO - JDBC	RDBMS	Yes (+ user-defined)	
TRIPLE	TRIPLE	Any (JVM)	Java	Memory	Yes (+ user-defined)	RACER
KAON	F-Logic	Any (JVM)	Java	Memory - RDBMS	Yes (+ user-defined)	KAON TOOL SUITE
CEREBRA	DL-based	Any (JVM)	Java - SOAP	Distributed data (CORBA)	Yes (+ user-defined)	Cerebra Suite

tion Programming Interface (API) that offers specific methods for accessing RDF information. It defines a basic interface for storing, retrieving and deleting RDF and RDFS from repositories while it abstracts from the particular storage mechanism. It was designed to support low end hardware like PDAs and to be extendable to other RDF-based languages. Several implementations of SAIL are distributed with Sesame like SQL92SAIL, which is a generic implementation for SQL92 compliant DBMS, SyncSAIL for supporting concurrent reads as well as implementations for specific DBMS like MySQL, OracleDB and PostgreSQL.

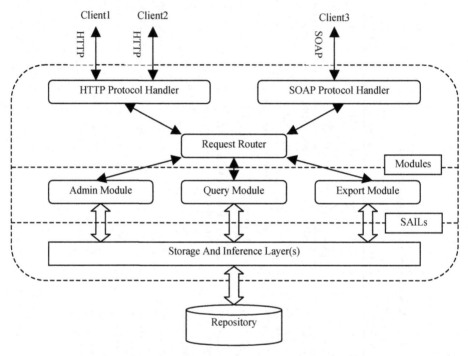

Fig. 2. Sesame's architecture. Taken from [8].

Sesame implements the Resource Query Language (RQL) a declarative language for querying both RDF descriptions and RDF schemas, as well as RDQL [26] which is derived from SquishQL [27]. These functions are provided by the *Query Module* which performs the queries on a repository. Any query is first parsed to build a tree model representation, which is afterwards optimised. The majority of the query is evaluated in this module, the access to the repository is handled by SAIL. It is important to note that Sesame implements a slightly modified version of the RQL language proposed in [20]. Sesame's version of RQL includes support for domain and range restrictions as well as multiple domain and range restrictions, but it does not feature support for datatyping.

For the metadata administration, another module is provided, the *Admin Module*. Its purpose is to manage the insertion and deletion of RDF and RDF Schema information into/from a repository.

The extraction of any information from a Sesame repository is handled by the *Export Module*. This module allows to selectively export the schema, the data or both from a repository, facilitating the integration and interaction with other RDF tools.

Concerning the interaction with external applications Sesame currently offers three methods: HTTP, SOAP and RMI. Each protocol has its associated handler, which translates and redirects any query received into an intermediate module: the *Request Router*. This intermediate module abstracts Sesame's core from any protocol specificity leaving the possibility to add a new handler without having to modify the rest of the system.

For making the results of the On-To-Knowledge project easier for integration in real-world applications an "administrative" software infraestructure was created: The Ontology Middleware (OMM). *"The central issue is to make the methodology and modules available to the society in a shape that allows easier development, management, maintenance, and use of middle-size and big knowledge bases"*[28]. In particular the OMM supports versionning, access control and meta-information for knowledge bases forming the Knowledge Control System (KCS). In addition to the administrative modules, BOR extends the reasoning capabilities of Sesame by providing support for DAML+OIL. This new reasoning module implements the SAIL API, thus it can perfectly interact with the rest of the modules of Sesame.

5 Architecture Proposal

We have seen previously that in Stephen Cranefield's approach a marshalling package is used for mashalling and unmarshalling object-oriented information between in-memory data structures and RDF serialisations of that information. This solution is not efficient enough for managing large RDF files. Thus, the available RDF storage and querying tools have been studied, and Sesame was choosen based on its characteristics.

In order to support large knowledge bases (more than five thousand triples), Fig. 3 shows an adaptation of Stephen Cranefield's approach by replacing the marshalling elements by calls to the Sesame API. Any serialisation or deserialisation of knowledge is performed over an RDF repository in Sesame. The generation of ontology-based applications remains, from the developer point of view, unchanged and transparent. The process still involves editing the ontology in a CASE environment supporting UML and XMI. Afterwards Java classes and the RDF Schema file are generated and their usage, during the creation of an ontology-based application, remains unmodified. However, the architecture gains greatly in versatility and power due to the new mechanisms that grant the persistence and access of the knowledge base provided by Sesame. The RDF/RDF Schema is stored in a Sesame repository. Thus, applications interact with Sesame for retrieving and/or storing knowledge and at the same time they have all the Sesame's features available like, for example, the querying language RQL.

There is however an important difference concerning the generation of the Java classes. The proposed architecture maintains the XSLT for generating the RDF schema file, whereas the generation of the Java classes is not performed using XSLT. We are developing a Java Code Generator that benefits from Sesame's features by accessing the ontology stored in a Sesame repository where the associated RDF schema has been stored. Thanks to the SAIL API Sesame offers, our program can browse the whole ontology in a more confortable way. Thus, the difficulties associated to the use of a stylesheets processor are avoided. Moreover, the code generation gains in modularity, and ease of maintenance, so that future improvements can be easily added.

We are also investigating another important aspect, which is the possibility of adapting the whole system to a more powerful language like DAML+OIL. Several projects are already using UML and DAML+OIL together. The UML Based Ontology Tool-set (UBOT) project [29] is working on an UML to DAML mapping [30]. In this project UML is also used as a front-end for visualizing and editing DAML ontologies. Also, the Components for Ontology Driven Information Push (CODIP) project [31] is using UML to build and map DAML ontologies. This project is creating the DAML-UML Enhanced Tool (DUET) which provides a UML visualization and authoring environment for DAML. Core DAML concepts are being mapped into UML through a UML profile for DAML. DUET is currently available as a plug-in for Rational Rose [32] and ArgoUML [33]. The results of both projects could be applied to the proposed architecture for obtaining a "DAML+OIL version".

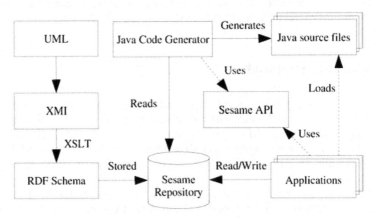

Fig. 3. Architecture proposal.

Finally, in addition of the persistance related benefits, Sesame comes with a Web interface, that can be installed on a web server like Tomcat. This is a step forward for publishing the ontologies along with the instances in the World Wide Web, so that external applications like agents, can also retrieve the information and process it.

6   Conclusions and Future Research

In the previous sections we have described an architecture for creating ontology-based applications in a more suitable way for Software Engineers than the currently available tools like OilED, Ontoedit or Protégé. This architecture integrates the UML to RDF mapping based on the approach presented in [11] and [13], with Sesame as the RDF storage and querying system. This integration is also improved by the addition of our Java Code Generator which makes use of the best of the two integrated approaches. The result is a framework for developing ontology-based applications in an easy and scalable way, with an automatic code generation to facilitate the use of object diagrams as internal knowledge representation structures. However, the majority of the ontology-based applications that have been developed, have shown that an ontology expressed in RDF or DAML+OIL is not enough for obtaining all the needed functionality. They still need the capability to define rules and constraints, so as to provide more powerful inferencing over the knowledge base. Unfortunately there is no standard language for defining rules. This has been solved by different developers with ad hoc methods: choosing the most appropriate and convenient inferencing engine or directly with hard-wired code. In our case, there is no mechanism provided for defining inferencing rules, thus it would be desirable to cover also that aspect. UML's definition includes the Object Constraint Language (OCL), however it lacks a formal definition. Currently the precise UML group [34] is addressing this issue.

With a formal specification, the code generation could also integrate automatic rules generation based on the OCL rules definition. This kind of code generation has already been undertaken by Frank Finger in [35]. Further research is needed in that respect.

Finally, we are also investigating dynamic code generation over evolving ontologies so as to provide a better adaptability to the dynamism of the Web.

References

1. T. Berners-Lee, J. Hendler and O. Lassila: The Semantic Web. Scientific American (2001)
2. M. Frauenfelder: A Smarter Web. Technology Review (2001)
3. M. Cendoya, A. Bernaras, T. Smithers, J. Aguado, C. Pedrinaci, I. Laresgoiti, E. García, A. Gómez, N. Peña, A. Z. Morch, H. Sæle, B. I. Langdal, J. Gordijn, H. Akkermans, B. Omelayenko, E. Schulten, J. Gordijn, B. Hazelaar, P. Sweet, H.-P.Schnurr, H. Oppermann, and H. Trost: D3 Business needs, Applications and Tools Requirements (2002)
4. A. Maier, J. Aguado, A. Bernaras, I. Laresgoiti, C. Pedinaci, N. Peña,T. Smithers: Integration with Ontologies. 2nd Conference on knowledge management (WM2003) (2003)
5. OMG: Unified Modelling Language Specification version 1.5 (2003)
6. D. Brickley, R.V. Guha: Resource Description Framework(RDF) Schema Specification 1.0. http://www.w3.org/TR/2000/CR-rdf-schema-20000327 (2000)
7. O. Lassila, R. R. Swick: Resource Description Framework(RDF) Model and Syntax Specification. http://www.w3.org/TR/REC-rdf-syntax/ (1999)
8. J. Broekstra, A. Kampman, and F. van Harmelen: Sesame: A Generic Architecture for Storing and Querying RDF and RDF Schema. International Semantic Web Conference (ISWC) (2002)
9. Object Management Group web page. http://www.omg.org. (Last visited: June 2003)
10. S. Cranefield and M. Purvis: UML as an Ontology Modelling Language. In Proceedings of the Workshop on Intelligent Information Integration, 16th International Joint Conference on Artificial Intelligence (IJCAI-99) (1999)
11. S. Cranefield: Networked Knowledge Representation and Exchange using UML and RDF. Journal of Digital Information (2001)
12. P. Kogut, S. Cranefield, L. Hart, M. Dutra, K. Baclawski, M. Kokar, J. Smith. UML for Ontology Development. Knowledge Engineering Review Journal Special Issue on Ontologies in Agent Systems (2002)
13. S. Cranefield: UML and the Semantic Web. Proceedings of the International Semantic Web Working Symposium (2001)

14. Object Management Group: OMG XML Metadata Interchange (XMI) Specification (2002)
15. Sergey Melnik: RDF API. http://www-db.stanford.edu/~melnik/rdf/api.html. (Last visited: June 2003)
16. Unisys Corporation: Java Metadata Interface (JMI) specification (2002)
17. Novosoft: Novosoft metadata framework and UML library (2002)
18. A. Magkanaraki, G. Karvounarakis, T. T. Anh, V. Christophides, D. Plexousakis: Ontology storage and querying. Technical Report 308, ICS-FORTH (2002)
19. G. Karvounarakis, V. Christophides: The RQL v1.5 User Manual. http://139.91.183.30:9090/RDF/RQL/Manual.html . (Last visited: June 2003)
20. G. Karvounarakis, S. Alexaki, V. Christophides, D. Plexousakis, and M. Scholl: RQL: A Declarative Query Language for RDF. 11th International World Wide Web Conference (WWW2002) (2002)
21. Joint United States / European Union ad hoc Agent Markup Language Committee: DAML+OIL (March 2001) release (2001)
22. KAON web page. http://kaon.semanticweb.org/ . (Last visited: June 2003)
23. Cerebra home page. http://www.networkinference.com/. (Last visited: June 2003)
24. On-To-Knowledge (IST-1999-10132) web page. http://www.ontoknowledge.org/ .(Last visited: June 2003)
25. Sesame Project web page. http://sourceforge.net/projects/sesame/. (Last visited: June 2003)
26. RDF Data Query Language (RDQL). http://www.hpl.hp.com/semweb/rdql.htm. (Last visited: June 2003)
27. L. Miller: RDF Squish query language and Java implementation. http://www.ilrt.bris.ac.uk/discovery/2001/02/squish/. (Last visited: June 2003)
28. A. Kiryakov, K. Simov, D. Ognyanov: Ontology Middleware: Analysis and Design. IST Project IST-1999-10132 On-To-Knowledge Deliverable 38 (2002)
29. UBOT web page. http://ubot.lockheedmartin.com/. (Last visited: June 2003)
30. K. Baclawski, M. Kokar, P. Kogut, L. Hart, J. Smith, W. Holmes, J. Letkowski, M. Aronson: Extending UML to Support Ontology Engineering for the Semantic Web. 4th International Conference on UML (2001)
31. DARPA, AT&T: Components for Ontology Driven Information Push (CODIP) Home Page. http://codip.grci.com/. (Last visited: June 2003)
32. Rational UML software home page. http://www.rational.com/uml/index.jsp. (Last visited: June 2003)
33. ArgoUML web page. http://argouml.tigris.org/. (Last visited: June 2003)
34. Precise UML group home page. http://www.puml.org/. (Last visited: June 2003)
35. Frank Finger: Design and Implementation of a Modular OCL Compiler. Diploma Thesis (2000)

A Method to Adaptively Propagate the Set of Samples Used by Particle Filters

Alvaro Soto

Pontificia Universidad Catolica de Chile
asoto@ing.puc.cl

Abstract. In recent years, particle filters have emerged as a useful tool that enables the application of Bayesian reasoning to problems requiring dynamic state estimation. The efficiency and accuracy of these type of filters are highly dependent on an appropriate propagation of the particles in time. In this paper we present a new method to improve the propagation step of the regular particle filter. Using results from the theory of importance sampling, our method adaptively propagates the set of samples without adding a significant computational load to the normal operation of the filter. Compared to existing techniques, our approach introduces two important enhancements: 1) An adaptive method to improve the propagation function, 2) A mechanism to identify when the use of adaptation is beneficial. We show the advantages of our method by applying the resulting filter to the visual tracking of targets in a real video sequence.

1 Introduction

The particle filter is a highly general tool used to perform dynamic state estimation via Bayesian inference. Over the last years, this tool has been successfully applied in diverse engineering fields to solve a variety of problems. The key idea is to represent a posterior distribution by samples (particles) that are constantly re-allocated after each new estimation of the state.

The re-allocation or propagation of the samples in time plays a key role in the efficiency and accuracy of the particle filter. As a Monte Carlo (MC) technique the effectiveness of the filter depends on allocating the samples in key areas of the hypotheses space. The traditional implementation of the particle filter uses a combination of the current estimation of the posterior and the dynamics of the process to allocate the samples to the next iteration. Therefore the efficiency of the filter is highly dependent on how this combination or dynamic prior can resemble the new posterior distribution.

The main limitation of using the dynamic prior as the importance function is that it does not consider the most recent observations. This can be highly inefficient in cases where the current observations do not support relevant areas under the prior, or in Bayesian terms, when there is a disagreement between the prior distribution and the likelihood function.

Previous works [4] [7] presented methods to improve the propagation step of the particle filter by incorporating in the predictions the most recent evidence available. In this paper we exploit the same idea, but our method provides two important and complementary advantages: 1) There is an generic and mathematically founded mechanism

R. Conejo et al. (Eds.): CAEPIA-TTIA 2003, LNAI 3040, pp. 47–56, 2004.

to improve the propagation function, 2) There is a mechanism to decide when it is worth to improve the propagation function. To our current knowledge, this last point has not been addressed before.

2   Background

2.1   Particle Filter

The main goal of a particle filter is to keep track of a posterior distribution. In the dynamic case, the posterior distribution can be expressed through Bayes' rule by:

$$P(x_t/\boldsymbol{y}_t) = \beta\, P(y_t/x_t)\, P(x_t/\boldsymbol{y}_{t-1}) \tag{1}$$

where β is a normalization factor; x_t represents the state of the system at time t; and $\boldsymbol{y}_t$ represents all the information collected until time t. Equation (1) assumes that x_t totally explains the current observation y_t.

The particle filter estimates the posterior in Equation (1) by a discrete distribution given by a set of weighted samples. The estimation is achieved in three main steps: sampling, weighting, and re-sampling. The sampling step assumes that the dynamics of the system follows a first order Markov process. Then the dynamic prior in Equation (1) can be expressed by:

$$P(x_t/\boldsymbol{y}_{t-1}) = \sum_{i=1}^{N} P(x_t/x_{t-1}^i)\, P(x_{t-1}^i/\boldsymbol{y}_{t-1}) \tag{2}$$

Equation (2) provides a recursive implementation of the filter, which is one of the key points that explains its efficiency. Equation (2) allows the filter to use the last estimation $P(x_{t-1}/\boldsymbol{y}_{t-1})$ to select the particles for the next iteration. These particles are then propagated by the dynamics of the process $P(x_t/x_{t-1}^i)$ to complete the sampling step. Next, in the weighting step, the resulting particles are weighted by a likelihood term. Finally, a re-sampling step is usually applied to avoid the degeneracy of the particle set [2].

Recently, independent works by Doucet [1] and Liu et al. [3] present an interesting alternative view of the filter in terms of the statistical principle of importance sampling [6]. Importance sampling provides an efficient way to obtain samples from a density $p(x)$, that we call the true distribution, in cases where the function can be evaluated, but it is not convenient or possible to sample directly from it. The basic idea is to use a proposal distribution $q(x)$ (also called importance function) to obtain the samples, and then weigh each sample x_i by a compensatory term given by $p(x_i)/q(x_i)$. It is possible to show [6] that under mild assumptions the set of weighted-samples can be used to represent $p(x)$.

In terms of importance sampling, it is possible to view the sampling and weighting steps of the particle filter as the basic steps of an importance sampling process. In this case, given that the true posterior $p(x_t/\boldsymbol{y}_t)$ is not known, the samples are drawn from an importance function that corresponds to the dynamic prior $P(x_t/\boldsymbol{y}_{t-1})$. Using this importance function, the compensatory terms are exactly the un-normalized weights used in the weighting step of the particle filter.

The interpretation of the particle filter in terms of importance sampling provides a more general setting. In particular the theory of importance sampling suggests that one can use alternative proposal distributions that can achieve a better allocation of the samples. Unfortunately, the use of an arbitrary importance function can significantly increase the computational load in the calculation of the weights. To see this clearly, consider the use of an arbitrary importance function $g(x_t/x_{(\cdot)}, y_{(\cdot)})$. Using an MC approximation of the dynamic prior $p(x_t/\boldsymbol{y}_{t-1})$, the un-normalized weight w_t^j corresponding to the sample x_t^j is given by:

$$w_t^j = \frac{p(y_t/x_t^j) \sum_{k=1}^{M} p(x_t^j/x_{t-1}^k)}{g(x_t^j/x_{(\cdot)}, y_{(\cdot)})} \qquad (3)$$

where each x_{t-1}^k is a fair sample from $p(x_{t-1}/\boldsymbol{y}_{t-1})$. In this case, as opposed to the standard particle filter, the estimation of each weight requires the evaluation of the dynamic prior. This increases the computational complexity of the resulting filter to $O(M \cdot N)$, where M is the number of samples used for the MC approximation of the dynamic prior and N is the number of particles. Giving that M and N are generally very large, the use of an arbitrary importance function takes away the computational efficiency of the particle filter, which is one of its main strengths. In this paper we show a new method to build a suitable importance function that takes into account old estimates of the state and current observations. One of the advantages of this new approach is that the complexity of the resulting filter is still $O(N)$.

2.2   Previous Work

In the literature about particle filters and importance sampling, it is possible to find several techniques that help to allocate the samples in areas of high likelihood under the target distribution. The most basic technique is rejection sampling [6]. The idea of rejection sampling is to accept only the samples with an importance weight above a suitable value. The drawback is efficiency: there is a high rejection rate in cases where the proposal density does not match closely the target distribution.

In [8], West presents a method to adaptively build a suitable importance function using a kernel-based approximation (mixture approximation). The basic idea is to apply consecutive refinements to the mixture representation until it resembles the posterior with a desired accuracy. This approach is simple and general, but the computational complexity is $O(R \cdot M \cdot N)$; where R is the number of refinements, M the number of components in the mixture, and N the number of particles.

Pitt and Shephard propose the auxiliary particle filter [4]. They argue that the computational complexity of the particle filter can be reduced by performing the sampling step in a higher dimension. To achieve this, they augment the state representation with an auxiliary variable k that corresponds to the index in the sum to calculate the dynamic prior in Equation (3). To sample from the resulting joint density, Pitt and Shephard use a generic importance function that produces a sampling scheme that is $O(N)$. The gain in efficiency comes from using an importance function that is proportional to the probability that a particle x_{t-1}^{kj} evolves to a particle x_t^j with a high probability under the likelihood function. The disadvantage of the method is the additional complexity of finding such a convenient importance function. Pitt and Sheppard give just some general intuitions about the form of a possible function, and in this paper we improve on this point by presenting a new method to find a suitable importance function.

In the context of mobile robot localization, Thrun et al. [7] notice that in cases where the likelihood function consists of a high peak, meaning a low level of noise in the observations, the particle filter suffers a degradation of performance. This suggests that the particle filter performs worse with accurate sensors. The explanation for this counter-intuitive observation comes from the fact that for a peaked likelihood a slightly inaccurate prior can produce a significative mismatch between these distributions. To solve this problem they propose using a mixture proposal distribution consisting of the prior and the likelihood function as an importance function. The problem of this approach is the need to sample directly from the likelihood function, which in many applications is not feasible or prohibitive.

3   Our Approach: Adaptive Propagation of the Samples

The regular implementation of the particle filter uses the dynamic prior as the importance function. Although this simplifies the calculation of the importance weights, allowing a computational complexity of $O(N)$, it has the limitation of allocating the samples without considering the most recent observation y_t. This section shows a new algorithm that improves this situation by incorporating the current observation in the generation of the samples, and also keeping the computational complexity of $O(N)$.

Consider the following expression for the dynamic prior:

$$p(x_t/\boldsymbol{y}_{t-1}) = \int p(x_t/x_{t-1})\, p(x_{t-1}/\boldsymbol{y}_{t-1})dx_{t-1}. \qquad (4)$$

Using the particle filter and MC integration, this integral can be approximated by:

$$p(x_t/\boldsymbol{y}_{t-1}) \approx \sum_{k=1}^{n} \beta_k\, p(x_t/x_{t-1}^k) \qquad (5)$$

where the set of weighted samples $\{x_{t-1}^k, \beta_k\}_{k=1}^n$ corresponds to the approximation of the posterior given by the particle filter at time $t-1$. Using this approximation, it is possible to generate samples from the dynamic prior by sampling from a set of densities $p(x_t/x_{t-1}^k)$ with mixture coefficients β_k.

The previous sampling scheme is analogous to the re-sampling and sampling steps of the regular particle filter. Under this scheme the selection of each propagation density depends on the mixture coefficients β_k's, which do not incorporate the most recent observation y_t. From an MC perspective, it is possible to achieve a more efficient allocation of the samples by including y_t in the generation of the coefficients. The intuition is that the incorporation of y_t increases the number of samples drawn from mixture components $p(x_t/x_{t-1}^k)$ associated with areas of high probability under the likelihood function.

Under the importance sampling approach, it is possible to generate a new set of coefficients β_k^* by sampling from the desired importance function $p(x_{t-1}/\boldsymbol{y}_t)$ and then adding appropriate weighting factors. In this way, the set of samples x_t^i from the dynamic prior $p(x_t/\boldsymbol{y}_{t-1})$ is generated by sampling from the mixture,

$$\sum_{k=1}^{n} \beta_k^* \, p(x_t/x_{t-1}^k) \tag{6}$$

and then adding to each particle x_t^i a correcting weight given by,

$$w_t^i = \frac{p(x_{t-1}^k/\boldsymbol{y}_{t-1})}{p(x_{t-1}^k/\boldsymbol{y}_t)}, \quad \text{with } x_t^i \sim p(x_t/x_{t-1}^k) \tag{7}$$

The resulting set of weighted samples $\{x_t^i, w_t^i\}_{i=1}^n$ still comes from the dynamic prior, so the computational complexity of the resulting filter is still $O(N)$. The extra complexity of this operation comes from the need to evaluate and to draw samples from the importance function $p(x_{t-1}^i/\boldsymbol{y}_t)$. Fortunately, the calculation of this function can be obtained directly from the operation of the regular particle filter. To see this clearly, consider the following:

$$\begin{aligned} p(x_t, x_{t-1}/\boldsymbol{y}_t) &\propto p(y_t/x_t, x_{t-1}, \boldsymbol{y}_{t-1}) \, p(x_t, x_{t-1}/\boldsymbol{y}_{t-1}) \\ &\propto p(y_t/x_t) \, p(x_t/x_{t-1}, \boldsymbol{y}_{t-1}) p(x_{t-1}/\boldsymbol{y}_{t-1}) \\ &\propto p(y_t/x_t) p(x_t/x_{t-1}) p(x_{t-1}/\boldsymbol{y}_{t-1}) \end{aligned} \tag{8}$$

Equation (8) shows that, indeed, the regular steps of the particle filter generate an approximation of the joint density $p(x_t, x_{t-1}/\boldsymbol{y}_t)$. After re-sampling from $p(x_{t-1}/\boldsymbol{y}_{t-1})$, propagating these samples with $p(x_t/x_{t-1})$, and calculating the weights $p(y_t/x_t)$, the set of resulting sample pairs (x_t^i, x_{t-1}^i) with correcting weights $p(y_t/x_t^i)$ forms a valid set of samples from the joint density $p(x_t, x_{t-1}/\boldsymbol{y}_t)$. Considering that $p(x_{t-1}/\boldsymbol{y}_t)$ is just a marginal of this joint distribution, the set of weighted-samples x_{t-1}^i are valid samples from it.

The previous description suggests that an adaptive version of the particle filter that uses y_t in the allocation of the samples can be constructed with a $O(2N)$ algorithm. First, N particles are used to generate the importance function $p(x_{t-1}/\boldsymbol{y}_t)$. Then, starting from this importance function, another N particles are used to generate the desired posterior $p(x_t/\boldsymbol{y}_t)$. Figure 1 uses a 2-D tracking example to illustrate the main steps involved in this adaptive version of the particle filter. In this example, each hypothesis about the position of a target is given by a bounding box defined by height, width, and the coordinates of its center.

Figure 1a) shows the initial set of weighted hypotheses used to estimate a hypothetical posterior distribution at time $t - 1$. This hypothetical posterior consists of three main clusters of bounding boxes, which are labeled with identification numbers to facilitate their reference within the text. For each of the rectangular hypotheses, its gray level intensity is proportional to its probability, and its thickness is proportional to the number of times that the hypothesis is repeated in the sample set.

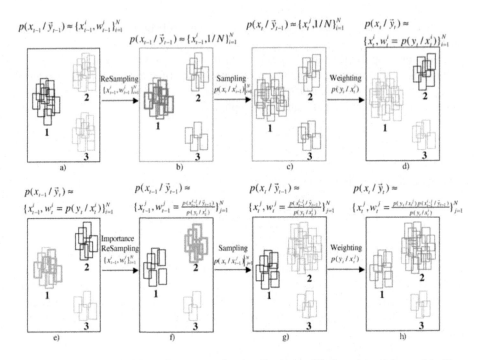

Fig. 1. Schematic view of the different steps involved in the modified version of the particle filter that includes an updated version of the dynamic prior using the current observation y_t. For each rectangular hypothesis, its gray level intensity is proportional to its probability, and its thickness is proportional to the number of times that the hypothesis is repeated in the sample set. The algorithm is equivalent to the application of two iterations of the particle filter. The first iteration is shown in Figures a)-d). It provides an estimate of $p(x_{t-1}/y_t)$, which corresponds to an updated version of the prior $p(x_{t-1}/y_{t-1})$ including the last observation y_t. Next, Figures e)-h) show the second iteration of the filter. This corresponds to a modified version of the regular particle filter using the updated version of the prior to run the re-sampling step that determines the allocation of the samples to estimate $p(x_t/y_t)$.

In the upper part, Figures 1a)-d) sketch the first three steps of the algorithm. These correspond to the regular steps of the particle filter. First, the transition between Figures 1a) and b) shows the re-sampling step. Because the particles in cluster 1 have higher probability, they are re-sampled many times. In contrast, only a few of the particles in clusters 2 and 3 survive the re-sampling.

The transition between Figures 1b) and c) shows the sampling step. The example assumes a stationary and isotropic motion model, such as a Gaussian model of zero mean and low variance. Using this type of motion model, the resulting predictive function or dynamic prior $p(x_t/y_{t-1})$ is characterized by a massive exploration of the state space around cluster 1.

The transition between Figures 1c) and d) shows the weighting step. To illustrate the relevance of the algorithm proposed here, the example assumes a mismatch between the dynamic prior and the likelihood function. In this way, while the prior mainly supports the exploration of the area around cluster 1, the likelihood function gives a higher support to the particles in cluster 2. Figure 1d) shows the resulting representation of the posterior at time t. The representation is highly inefficient: while many unlikely particles are allocated around cluster 1, just a few highly likely particles are allocated in the critical area around cluster 2.

Figures 1e)-h) sketch the novel steps of the algorithm. These are similar to the regular steps of a particle filter with the important modification that the original prior at time $t-1$ is enhanced including information about the most recent observation y_t. Using the estimate of the joint conditional density $p(x_t, x_{t-1}/y_t)$ built by the regular steps of the particle filter, the algorithm discards the samples x_t^i, leaving an estimate of $p(x_{t-1}/y_t)$. This density is the starting point to the next step of the algorithm denoted as importance re-sampling.

The transition between Figures 1e) and f) shows the importance re-sampling step. This step provides the re-allocation of the particles towards areas associated to high probability under the likelihood function. Using importance sampling, the new samples from $p(x_{t-1}/y_{t-1})$ are drawn from the estimate of $p(x_{t-1}/y_t)$. Each new sample x_{t-1}^j is weighted by the correction term $p(x_{t-1}^{i,j}/y_{t-1})/p(y_t/x_t^i)$. The notation $x_{t-1}^{i,j}$ denotes that the new particle x_{t-1}^j is a re-sampled version of a particle x_{t-1}^i from the set $\{x_{t-1}^i, w_t^i\}_{i=1}^n$ used to estimate $p(x_{t-1}/y_t)$.

In contrast to the representation of the prior shown in Figure 1b), the new representation shown in Figure 1f) has shifted the allocation of the samples toward cluster 2. It is important to note that, although these representations allocate the samples in a different way, they represent the same pdf. The difference lays in the way that they exploit the duality between number of samples and weights to represent a density function.

The transitions between Figures 1f) and g) and between Figures 1g) and h) show the final two steps of the algorithm. These are equivalent to the sampling and weighting steps of the regular particle filter, but carrying the weights obtained in the importance re-sampling step. Figure 1h) shows the final estimate of the posterior at time t. In contrast to the representation of the posterior given by the regular particle filter (Figure 1d)), the reallocation of the samples toward cluster 2 increases the efficiency of the representation. This is observed by the even distribution of the gray level intensities of the importance weights.

In the previous algorithm, the overlapping with the first three steps of the regular particle filter provides a convenient way to perform an online evaluation of the benefits of updating the dynamic prior with the last observation. Even though in cases of a poor match between the dynamic prior and the posterior distribution the updating of the dynamic prior can be beneficial, in cases where these distributions agree, the extra processing of updating the dynamic prior does not offer a real advantage, and should thus be avoided. To our current knowledge, this issue has not been addressed before.

The basic idea is to run the regular particle filter, evaluating at the same time the efficiency in the allocation of the samples. If the efficiency is low, the algorithm uses the estimate of $p(x_{t-1}/y_t)$ given by the regular particle filter as the importance function to update the dynamic prior. The intuition behind this idea is to quantify at each iteration of the particle filter the trade-off between continuing to draw samples from a known but potentially inefficient importance function versus incurring the cost of building a

Fig. 2. Tracking results for the ball and the left side child for frame 1, 5, and 14. The bounding boxes correspond to the most probable hypotheses in the sample set used to estimate the posterior distributions.

new importance function that provides a better allocation of the samples. The important observation is that, once the regular particle filter reaches an adequate estimate, it can be used to estimate both the posterior distribution $p(x_t/y_t)$ and the updated importance function $p(x_{t-1}/y_t)$, which is the key to avoid adding a significant computational load.

Considering that the efficiency of the sample allocation depends on how well the dynamic prior resembles the posterior distribution, an estimation of the distance between these two distributions is a suitable index to quantify the effectiveness of the propagation step. We found [5] a convenient way to estimate the Kullback-Leibler divergence (KL-divergence) between these distributions, and in general between a target distribution $p(x)$ and an importance function $q(x)$:

$$KL(p(x), q(x)) \approx \log(N) - H(\hat{w}_i). \tag{9}$$

Equation (9) has a intuitive interpretation. It states that for a large number of particles, the KL-divergence between the dynamic prior and the posterior distributions measures how distant the entropy of the distribution of the weights, $H(\hat{w}_i)$, is from being uniform.

4   Application

To illustrate the advantages of our method we use a set of frames of a video sequence consisting of two children playing with a ball. In this case, the goal is to keep track of the positions of the ball and the left side child. Each hypothesis about the position of a target is given by a bounding box defined by height, width, and the coordinates of its center. The motion model used for the implementation of the particle filter corresponds to a Gaussian function of zero mean and standard deviations of 20 for the center of each hypothesis and 0.5 for its width and height.

Figure 2 shows the results of tracking the targets using a regular version of the particle filter that includes an adaptive selection of the number of particles needed to achieve a successful tracking with a specified confidence level [5]. The labels over the bounding boxes correspond to the visual algorithms used to track the targets (see [5] for more details).

The results of the tracking show that to track the child the algorithm needs a roughly constant number of particles during the entire sequence. This is explained because the child has only a small and slow motion around a center position during the entire sequence. Therefore the stationary Gaussian motion model is highly accurate and there is not a real advantage of improving the propagation function.

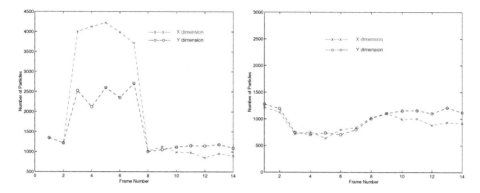

Fig. 3. Number of particles used at each iteration to track the ball. Left: without adapting the importance function. Right: Adapting the importance function.

In the case of the ball, the situation is different, since the number of particles needed to achieve the desired error level has a large increment during the period that the ball travels from one child to the other (Frames 3 to 7). During this period the ball has a large and fast motion, therefore the Gaussian motion model is a poor approximation of the real motion. As a consequence there is a large mismatch between the dynamic prior and the posterior distribution. This produces an inefficient allocation of the samples and the estimate needs a larger set of samples to populate the relevant parts of the posterior. Figure 3-left shows the number of particles needed to estimate the posterior distribution of the ball at each frame, to achieve a certain predefined level of accuracy [5].

Applying the modified version of the particle filter and setting a suitable value for the threshold on the KL-divergence, the tracking engine decides to adapt the importance function at all the frames where the ball travels from one child to the other (Frames 3-7). Figure 3-right shows the number of particles needed to achieve a successful tracking of the ball with the same specified confidence level used before, but adapting the importance function. Comparing with the non-adaptive case, during Frames 3 to 7 it is possible to observe a significant reduction in the number of samples due to a better allocation of them.

Figure 4 compares the location of the resulting set of samples to estimate the posterior distribution of the position of the ball at Frame 5. For clarity only the (x, y) coordinates of the center of each hypothesis are shown in the graphs. In the case of no adaptation the mismatch between the dynamic prior and the likelihood produces many wasted particles allocated in the tails of the posterior distribution. In contrast, in the adaptive case the use of the current observation produces a re-allocation of the samples towards areas of high likelihood, reducing the number of wasted samples.

5   Conclusions

In this paper we presented a method to adaptively propagate the set of samples used by the particle filter. The method can be added to the regular particle filter as an extra

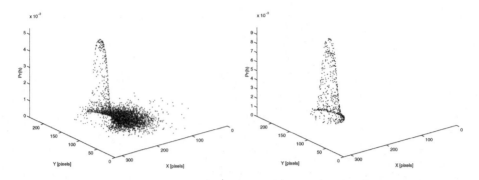

Fig. 4. Estimate of the posterior distribution of the position of the center of the ball at Frame 5. Left: without adapting the importance function. Right: adapting the importance function.

step without significant computational overload. In contrast to previous algorithms, our method includes the construction of a suitable importance function and a mechanism to identify when the adaptation of the importance function may be beneficial. To achieve this last goal, we use an estimation of the KL-divergence between the dynamic prior and the posterior distribution. The results of testing the new method for tracking targets in real video sequences shows the advantages of the adaptive version with respect to the regular particle filter. Using the adaptive version it was possible to efficiently track targets with different motions using a highly general motion model.

References

1. A. Doucet. On sequential simulation-based methods for Bayesian filtering. Tech report CUED/F-INFEG/TR 310, Cambridge University, 1998.
2. N. Gordon, D. Salmon, and A. Smith. A novel approach to nonlinear/non Gaussian Bayesian state estimation. In *IEE Proc. on Radar and Signal Processing*, pages 107–113, 1993.
3. J. Liu and R. Chen. Monte Carlo methods for dynamics systems. *Journal of American Statistical Association*, 93:1032–1044, 1998.
4. M. Pitt and N. Shephard. Filtering via simulation: Auxiliary particle filters. *Journal of the American Statistical Association*, 94(446):590–599, June 1999.
5. A. Soto. A probabilistic approach for the adaptive integration of multiple visual cues using an agent framework. Tech report CMU-RI-TR-02-30, Carnegie Mellon University, 2002.
6. M. Tanner. *Tools for Statistical Inference*. Springer-Verlag, 3nd edition, 1996.
7. S. Thrun, D. Fox, and W. Burgard. Monte Carlo localization with mixture proposal distribution. In *AAAI National Conf. on Artificial Intelligence*, pages 859–865, Austin, Tx, 2000.
8. M. West. Approximating posterior distributions by mixtures. *Journal of the Royal Statistical Society, Serie B*, 55(2):409–422, 1993.

A Model for Fuzzy Temporal Reasoning on a Database*

Manuel Campos, José Palma, Roque Marín,
B. Llamas, and A. González

Artificial Intelligence and Knowledge Engineering Group
University of Murcia, Campus de Espinardo, Murcia 30071, Spain
mcampos@dif.um.es

Abstract. In decision support systems for Intensive Care Units (ICU), the data management subsystem plays an essential role since the data have a heterogeneous origin. The temporal dimension of the data is also very important in capturing the intrinsic dynamism in patients' evolution data. This situation requires the integration of data in a unique platform in which time representation and management techniques should be considered. The selection of a data model that simplifies the expression of (complex) queries relies on an efficient internal representation of data for processing updates and queries on temporal data. On the other hand, due to the large amount of data regarding patient evolution a DataBase Management Systems (DBMS) is required. Therefore, the integration of a DBMS with a temporal reasoner is required if temporal reasoning capabilities on patients' evolution data are to be provided. This paper presents the integration of a DBMS with a generic fuzzy temporal reasoning (FuzzyTIME).

1 Introduction

In recent years, static consultation systems in medical domains have been replaced by systems that can deal with the temporal dimension needed to capture the patient's evolution over time, as in the area of decision support systems in Intensive Care Units (ICU) [1]. Therefore, the inclusion of modules which make temporal reasoning on patients' evolution data possible is essential. An example of this modules is FuzzyTIME [2] a generic temporal reasoner based on Fuzzy Temporal Constraint Network (FTCN) formalism [3], which can be easily integrated into any application that requires managing temporal information.

From the temporal reasoning perspective, temporal knowledge, usually captured by a constraint network, can be represented more effectively if the network is complemented by a database for storing the information typically associated to label the nodes of the network [4].

A decision support systems for the ICU domain has to deal with a large amount of data provided by both the signals monitored and clinical history data. In such a context, the integration of databases in these systems is essential.

There have been several approaches to the problem of integrating temporal information and databases, from the point of view of both artificial intelligence and databases.

---

* This work was supported by the Spanish MCyT, under project TIC2000-0873-C02-02, and by Seneca Foundation under project PB/46/FS/02.

R. Conejo et al. (Eds.): CAEPIA-TTIA 2003, LNAI 3040, pp. 57–65, 2004.

From the point of view of database technology, the introduction of time information into a database can be carried out in several ways, although the most usual is the introduction of a time stamp attribute with some fixed granularity [5]. This attribute can be managed explicitly by the database management system, so the database becomes a temporal database, defined as a collection of facts associated with one or more temporal contexts. In this line of work, TSQL2 [6] has an implicit time model in which the time for the tuples is not specified and temporal consistency is guaranteed. The main problem with this approach lies in how to solve queries in which the exact absolute time is not specified in the database [7]. In decision support systems for ICU in diagnosis it is necessary to deal explicitly with qualitative and quantitative temporal constraints and this kind of solution is not, therefore, well adapted to the problem.

It is not unusual to find information systems in which absolute time is managed, but what is unusual is to find systems that manage qualitative and quantitative constraints. Some attemps are currently being made to apply qualitative temporal constraints to databases in constraint and relational database [8, 9]. This kind of reasoning is essential, for example, in a temporal abstraction process (an important task in medical domains) like the one described in [10], where there is an explicit treatment of qualitative relations and time is considered to be a variable. A temporal reasoner must be able to infer temporal relations, that is, deal with date arithmetic, temporal relations and temporal granularities.

Brusoni, in LATER [5], gives a solution to this problem, but he deals with it from the database perspective: he proposes a redefinition of the relational algebra operators for managing qualitative temporal constraints between tuples. In this work, we present a model for the integration of a database with a general purpose temporal reasoner, Fuzzy-TIME, in order to enable mechanisms of temporal reasoning on the elements stored in a database. The module resulting from this integration is the core subsystem of ACUDES [11], a general purpose architecture for decision support systems for ICUs which provides temporal reasoning capabilities. Moreover, FuzzyTIME uses Possibility Theory for solving queries about necessity and possibility, by means of a fuzzy extension of classic modal operators MAY and MUST, which allows us to obtain a value between 0 and 1 as the answer for a temporal query. In our proposal, the temporal reasoning module is plugged on top of the DataBase Management Systems (DBMS), contributing thus to the treatment of imprecision and uncertainty (since temporal constraints used in the reasoner are fuzzy).

The rest of the paper is structured as follow: A concise description of FuzyTIME temporal reasoner is given in section 2. The structure of the database as well as the different type of temporal information considered is put forward in section 3. In the same section, the integration of FuzzyTIME with the database is introduced, where special attention is placed on the kind of queries than can be solved by the system. Finally, some conclusions and discussion are presented.

2   Temporal Reasoning Module: FuzzyTIME

FuzzyTIME is based on a three-layered architecture, which allows us to separate the interface for querying and updating temporal information (interface layer) from the layer where temporal entities and relations are managed (temporal world layer), and from their low level representation (FTCN layer). An expressive language which allows the formulation of complex queries involving disjunctions of relations is provided in the upper layer. The proposed language is an extension of the one presented in [12].

The second layer is called temporal world and contains a high level representation of temporal entities and relations. In FuzzyTIME two kinds of temporal entities have been considered: time instants and intervals (a time interval is decomposed into a ordered pair of two points). Time entities can be related to each other by means of both qualitative and quantitative relations: Qualitative point-to-point, qualitative point-to-interval (both formalised by Van Beek [13]), Allen qualitative interval-to-interval [14] and quantitative point-to-point [3]. The temporal relations allowed in the temporal reasoner are only convex disjunction, thus obtaining a trade off between expressive power and efficiency. In this level, convexity is checked at the same time as a translation from the high level relations of the language to metric point-to-point relations is produced.

The third layer, which contains the low level representation of the temporal entities and relations, is based on the FTCN (Fuzzy Temporal Constraint Network) [3] formalism. The representation is a graph composed of nodes (temporal variables representing time points) and fuzzy metric constraints between nodes (fuzzy numbers representing the temporal distance between two points). A minimal network that represents the minimal domains for temporal variables is calculated here. This network and the use of a local propagation mechanism (as in LATER [5]) allows us to achieve efficient query answering. The use of fuzzy numbers as constraints allows us to make use of the Possibility Theory to solve queries about necessity and possibility, by means of a fuzzy extension of classic modal operators MAY (Π) and MUST (N) thus obtaining a real value between zero and one as a result of a query.

To illustrate the syntax of the expressions and the translation process we provide a simple example. Both the assertions and the queries follow the same base format, (TemporalEntity TemporalConstraint TemporalEntity). For example, let us suppose we write the following expression: (IntervalA BEFORE EQUALS PointB); this relation can be translated into a pair of constraints: (PointBeginA BEFORE EQUALS PointB) and (PointEndA BEFORE EQUALS PointB) where PointBeginA and PointBeginB are the beginning and the end of IntervalA. As a second step, QUAN operator [15] is used to translate the qualitative relation BEFORE EQUALS to a fuzzy number represented by means of a trapezoidal possibility distribution (Figure 1). In this case, the BEFORE constraint is represented as $(1, 1, +\infty, +\infty, 1)$ and the EQUALS constraint is $(0, 0, 0, 0, 1)$, thus the union of both constraints is $(0, 0, +\infty, +\infty, 1)$.

3   Database Structure

Without losing generality, we can say that data may be temporal or atemporal, depending on whether they are associated to time entities or not. In the domain of our application (ICU), the system's structure must be adapted to the different sources of information, mainly those provided by monitored signals and patients' clinical data. Atemporal data are used to represent information about the patients' history, without any specific relation to time, for example, age or sex.

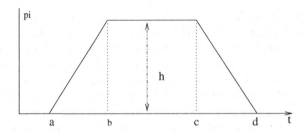

Fig. 1. Possibility distribution associated to the fuzzy number (a,b,c,d,h).

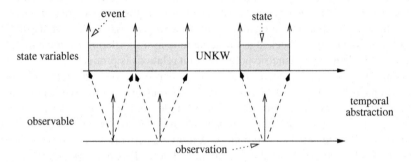

Fig. 2. Elements of the temporal abstraction process.

Temporal data include a time specification which can be specified by an absolute date or a temporal relation (by means of any expression allowed in the temporal language). As regards its temporal nature, information to be stored must belong to one of the following three main categories: observations -concrete measurements taken on any observable patient feature-, states -produced by the temporal abstraction process over the set of observations and which represent a time interval in which the value of a feature does not change-, and events -representing the begining and the end of a state- (for the relation of the structures see Figure 2). A conventional approach [10] is followed for clinical history data abstraction and the technique described in [16] is applied for signal abstraction.

The different tables in the database have been designed according to the previous categories of temporal concepts. Thus, three tables are considered: observations, states and events. The basic structure of tuples is comprised of three components: concept, attribute, and value. These elements correspond to the concept being dealt with, the name of one attribute belonging to the concept, and the value of that attribute. Observation tuples include an absolute date, indicating the time at which the observation was taken, whereas a temporal reference (a reference to an entity already present in the reasoner) is associated to the tuples in the state and events tables. This database structure constitutes a general structure that can be extended with any attributes imposed by the application domain. FuzzyTIME is perfectly adapted to these structures since it allows the application to deal with different temporal entities -points and intervals- and with both qualitative and quantitative information, including absolute dates and temporal constraints.

A graphical representation of the interrelation between the database and the internal representation of relations, points and intervals is shown in Figure 3. The temporal world layer is represented in the middle of the figure; a high level representation of entities (intervals like S and points like E1 or E2 in the figure) and relations (point-to-point either metric or qualitative, point-to-interval, interval-to-point and interval-to-interval) is maintained in that layer. This temporal world has a low level representation in the FTCN layer, where intervals are decomposed into an ordered pair of points and where qualitative relations are translated into metric ones. All the data relating to observations, states and events are stored in the database and can be retrieved with a reference that has a counterpart in the entities of the temporal world.

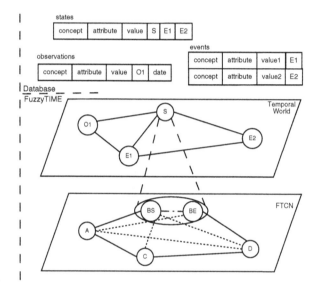

Fig. 3. Integration of FuzzyTIME with the database.

3.1 Data Updates

There are two kinds of updating operations: temporal and atemporal. First of all, semantic consistency must be checked against the domain ontology for both kinds of update. In our concrete case, the architecture includes an ontology server that offers the ICU ontology to the rest of modules. Once the semantic consistency is checked, the updates can be raalised. In the case of atemporal updates, the elements can be introduced into the database with a simple SQL sentence.

Additionally, temporal consistency with the data already stored must be checked for new temporal updates; this operation is done automatically by FuzzyTIME. Depending on the kind of temporal information, two different cases can be found: updating an absolute date or updating information on temporal variables. In the former case, for example in the case of observations, consistency checking is not necessary. The temporal information is asserted in FuzzyTIME and the temporal variable created by that insertion can be used as identifier for the temporal variable associated to the tuple in the database. For example, the expression OBSERVATION (pain, localisation, precordial) BEFORE 8:00 AM is asserted as such. In the case of having references to already defined temporal variables, the first step consist of retrieving these variables, the consistency checking must be performed and, finally, the tuple has to be inserted into the database if the temporal information to be asserted is consistent with that previously stored in the database.

3.2 Concept History Functions

Once the structure of the database has been designed, original language provided in FuzzyTIME, which is strictly temporal, must be extended in order to access the data stored in the database. To begin with, the definition of basic operations -like LAST, FIRST, NEXT, PREVIOUS, and NTH- is needed to browse data in a single concept history. Note that a topological order is established on data belonging to the same history, but this is not the case for data corresponding to different concept histories.

The argument for the FIRST and LAST functions is a tuple. This tuple can take several forms, e.g. wildcards: the tuple (concept, attribute, *) returns the first/last event (observation, or state) of the history associated with attribute with any value; or a list of values: the tuple (concept, attribute, NOT $\{v_1, ..., v_n\}$) returns the first/last event (observation, or state) of the history whose values do not match with any of the specified ones. With these functions, values matching expressions like LAST OBSERVATION (pain, intensity, NOT {high}) will retrieve the last observation of pain whose intensity is not high, i.e., either moderate or low.

The remaining functions, NEXT, PREVIOUS and NTH, allow the user to go through a history of events, states or observations, and can also be used in several ways:

- [NEXT | PREVIOUS] (concept, attribute, value, reference) returns following/ previous event (observation, or state) of (concept, attribute, value, reference) in the history.
- NEXT and PREVIOUS can also be applied to the result of FIRST and LAST functions.
- NTH (concept, attribute, value) returns the event, state, or observation in the nth position at the history list.

All the previously described functions return a database tuple that can be used in the query already defined in the temporal reasoning module. These functions can return a UNKW (unknown) value in the case of the concept being queried is undefined. With these simple functions, the user can go through a history in a simple loop with three steps: (1) retrieve the first tuple of the set, (2) establish the condition of the loop "until UNKW is returned", (3) retrieve the next tuple by means of the NEXT function.

3.3 Temporal Queries

In the first instance, the temporal reasoner only accepts temporal queries [2], so we have extended the language to cope with the operations imposed by its integration in the database. As well as the modal operators, i.e. necessity and possibility, universal and existential quantifiers have been introduced. These quantifiers allow us to deal with multiple appearances produced as result of a query to the database.

Queries, in their most basic form, are comprised of two operands and a temporal relation, -one of those defined in FuzzyTIME-, and can be classified according to the type of the operands. In the so-called level 0 queries, only the temporal entities (points and intervals) that have already been defined in the module for temporal reasoning can be included. The schema of this kind of query is:

– [MAY | MUST] (concept, attribute, value, reference) constraint [entity | date | (concept, attribute, value, reference)])

Thus, the first operand is any of the tuples mentioned (observations, states or events) plus a temporal reference; whereas the second operand can be either a tuple, with the same structure as the first operand, or the identifier of an entity or an absolute date. Both qualitative and qualitative relations are allowed, depending of the type of the operand.

This kind of query is directly translated into FuzzyTIME queries by means of the temporal references included in the database tuples, and the result of the queries will be a degree of possibility or necessity of the query. It has to be taken into account that any element with an associated temporal reference can be substituted by any function of those specified in the previous section.

For example, an expression like *"has the patient suffered the last strong pain within the last days before admission?"* can be written as MUST (LAST OBSERVATION (pain, intensity, high) LESS_THAN 3 DAYS BEFORE ADMISSION)). The next step is to retrieve the tuples that are compliant with the given values in the tuple (c, a, v) from the database; the second operand is the entity called ADMISSION, which corresponds with a time point already defined. These values are retrieved via a simple SQL query, such us, SELECT (concept, attribute, value, reference) FROM observation WHERE concept='pain' and attribute='intensity' and value='high', which returns a result set from the database. Having this result set, it is easy to find the entity that matches the temporal reference for each one of the valid tuples.

In the second type of queries, called level 1 queries, the first operand may be any tuple (observations, states or events) without a temporal relation; as second operand, any of the already defined temporal entities, or an absolute date, or tuple with a temporal reference can be used. In this case, since the query is extended over a subset of the temporal elements that comprises the history of the event, observation, or state on which the query is performed on, the universal and existential quantifiers can be used in conjunction with the modal operators MAY and MUST. This kind of queries can be formalized as follow:

– [MAY | MUST] ([FORALL | EXISTS] (concept, attribute, value) constraint [entity | date | (concept, attribute, value, reference)])

As in the previous case, elements associated with a temporal reference (states, events, or observations) can be replaced by any of the functions described in section 3.2. Solving these queries involves an intermediate step in the translation of the query into the FuzzyTIME language since special attention must be given to quantifiers. The universal quantifier is translated into a conjunction of queries. For example, to solve the following query "has the patient suffered all strong pains a few days before admission?", rewritten as MUST (FORALL OBSERVATION(pain, intensity, high) LESS_THAN 3 DAYS BEFORE ADMISSION)), the temporal references of all the tuples matching the OBSER-VATION predicate are retrieved. Let $\{t^1, \cdots, t^n\}$ be these variables, the previous query can be translated into $N(\bigwedge_{i=1}^{n}(t_i \ (LESS\_THAN \ 3 \ DAYS) \ t_{admission})$ which can be directly solved by FuzzyTIME. Queries involving existential quantifiers are translated into a disjunction of basic queries instead of a conjunction.

4   Conclusions

In this paper we have dealt with the integration of a general purpose module for temporal reasoning, FuzzyTIME, with a database where the domain information is stored. The extensible architecture of FuzzyTIME allows a seamless integration with any other module, in this case a database. The combined work of these components is necessary because both form part of a whole architecture, ACUDES [11], which benefit from (1) the major features of the temporal reasoner, such as the ability to deal with qualitative and quantitative temporal constraints and the efficient query answering process, and (2) the ability of the database manager for managing large amounts of data.

In the context of a decision support system in ICUs, more concretely in diagnosis, which is the domain where this system is applied, it is necessary to deal with temporal constraints. Therefore, a simple temporal extension of SQL like TSQL2 [6], which uses a timestamp column that represents a valid time for a tuple, is neither expressive not powerful enough to cope with the problem.

In the solution proposed in [9], the authors extend the relational model by redefining algebraic operators to deal with time and with (non fuzzy) qualitative temporal constraints between tuples. On the other hand, in [8] there is a theoretical approach to deal with indefinite temporal information on databases, but, again, only qualitative constraints are considered.

In our proposal, a specialised temporal manager is integrated on top of the database, and the original language has been extended to interact with a general structure for database tables. The result is a system able to perform operations over qualitative or quantitative constraints, such as asserting new temporal constrains, checking the consistency of constraints, and inferring new temporal constraints. Another contribution of our work is the ability to use the possibility theory modal operators for querying the database.

As regards the query language and the interaction with database, Section 3.2 provides basic functions for browsing concept histories and for retrieving specific occurrence. Furthermore, the kind of queries formerly allowed by FuzzyTIME has also been extended to take advantage of these new functions, making it possible to include existential and universal quantifiers in queries involving both temporal and atemporal information.

References

1. Horn, W.: AI in Medicine on its ways from Knowledge-Intensive Systems to Data-Intensive Systems. In: Artificial Intelligence in Medicine. Volume 23. (2001) 5–12

2. Campos, M., Cárceles, A., Palma, J., Marín, R.: A general purporse fuzzy temporal information management. In: EurAsia-ICT 2002. Advances in information and communication technology. ISBN: 3-85403-161-3., Teherán, Irán (2002) 93–97
3. Marín, R., Barro, S., Palacios, F., Ruiz, R., Martín, F.: An approach to fuzzy temporal reasoninng in medicine. Mathware & soft Computing **3** (1994) 265–276
4. Koubarakis, M., Skiadopoulos, S.: Querying temporal constraint networks in PTIME. In: Proceedings of the 6th National Conference on Artificial Intelligence (AAAI-99), Menlo Park, Cal., AAAI/MIT Press (1999) 745–750
5. Brusoni, V., Console, L., Terenziani, P.: Efficient query answering in LaTeR. In: TIME-95 International Workshop on Temporal Representation and Reasoning. (1995) 121–128
6. Snodgrass, R.T., ed.: The TSQL2 Temporal Query Language. Kluwer (1995)
7. Bertino, E., , Ferrari, E., Guerrini, G.: An approach to model and query event-based temporal data. In Morris, R., Khatib, L., eds.: 5th International Workshop on Temporal Representation and Reasoning — TIME'98, IEEE Computer Society Press (1998) 122–131
8. Koubarakis, M.: Databases and temporal constraints: Semantics and complexity. In Clifford, J., Tuzhilin, A., eds.: Recent Advances in Temporal Databases (Proceedings of the International Workshop on Temporal Databases), Springer-Verlag (1995) 93–109
9. Brusoni, V., Console, L., Terenziani, P., Pernici, B.: Qualitative and Quantitative Temporal Constraints and Relational Ratabases: Theory, Architecture, and Applications. IEEE Transactions on Knowledge and Data Engineering **11** (1999) 948–968
10. Shahar, Y.: Efficient algorithms for qualitative reasoning about time. Artificial Intelligence **90** (1997) 79–133
11. Palma, J., Marín, R., Campos, M., Cárceles, A.: ACUDES: Architecture for Intensive Care Units DEcision Support. In: Conference Procceedings of the second joint EMBS-BMES conference. 1938-1939.ISBN: 0-7803-7613-. (2002) 1938–1039
12. Barro, S., Marín, R., Mira, R., Patón, J.: A model and a language for the fuzzy representation and handling of time. Fuzzy Sets and Systems **61** (1994) 153–175
13. van Beek, P., Cohen, R.: Exact and approximate reasoning about temporal relations. Computational Intelligence **6** (1990) 132–144
14. Allen, J.F.: Maintaining knowledge about temporal intervals. In Brachman, R.J., Levesque, H.J., eds.: Readings in Knowledge Representation. Kaufmann, Los Altos, CA (1985) 509–521
15. Meiri, I.: Combining qualitative and quantitative constraints in temporal reasoning. Artificial Intelligence **87** (1996) 343–385
16. Felix, P., Barro, S., Marín, R.: Fuzzy constraint networks for signal pattern recognition. Artificial Intelligence. Special Issue:Fuzzy set and possibility theory-based methods in artificial intelligence (2003 (In Press).)

A Multimodal Logic Approach
to Order of Magnitude Qualitative Reasoning

Alfredo Burrieza[1] and Manuel Ojeda-Aciego[2]

[1] Dept. Filosofía, Universidad de Málaga, Spain
[2] Dept. Matemática Aplicada, Universidad de Málaga, Spain[*]

Abstract. In this work we develop a logic for formalizing qualitative reasoning. This type of reasoning is generally used, for instance, when one has a lot of data from a real world example but the complexity of the numerical model suggests a qualitative (instead of quantitative) approach.

1 Introduction

When working with a real world problem one often encounters a lack of quantitative (numerical) information among the observed facts. A possible solution to this absence of information is simply to develop methods for reasoning under an incompletely specified environment, and logic methods have been applied to give rise to reasoning schemes for fuzzy, imprecise and missing information.

A different approach is to apply ideas from qualitative reasoning and, specifically, order of magnitude reasoning (OMR) introduced in [7] and later extended in [2–4, 9, 11]. The underlying idea is that by reasoning in terms of qualitative ranges of variables, as opposed to precise numerical values, it is possible to compute information about the behavior of a system with very little information about the system and without doing expensive numerical simulation.

Qualitative reasoning works with continuous magnitudes by means of a discretization so that it is possible to distinguish all the relevant aspects required by the context/specification (and only these aspects).

The basis of OMR systems is computing with a set of coarse values, usually generated as abstract representations of precise values. This is of course the same approach taken by any qualitative reasoning system. The distinctive feature of OMR is that the coarse values are generally of different order of magnitude.

Depending on the way the coarse values are defined, different OMR calculi can be generated: It is usual to distinguish between Absolute Order of Magnitude (AOM) and Relative Order of Magnitude (ROM) models. The former is represented by a partition of the real line, in which each element of $\mathbb{R}$ belongs to a qualitative class. The latter type introduces a family of binary order-of-magnitude relations which establish different comparison relations between numbers. This can be illustrated by means of several important examples.

In [7] and extensions such as [2–4], coarse values are defined by means of ordering relations that express the distance between coarse values on a totally ordered domain

---

[*] Partially supported by projects BFM2000-1054-C02-02, TIC2003-09001-C02-01.

R. Conejo et al. (Eds.): CAEPIA-TTIA 2003, LNAI 3040, pp. 66–75, 2004.

in relation to the range they cover on that domain. Specifically, the seminal paper [7], distinguishes three types of qualitative relations, such as x *is close to* y, or x *is negligible w.r.t.* y or x *is comparable to* y; later on, some extensions were proposed in order to improve the original one with the inclusion of quantitative information, and allow for the control of the inference process [2–4].

There exist attempts to integrate both approaches as well, so that an absolute partition is combined with a set of comparison relations between real numbers [9, 11]. For instance, it is customary to divide the real line in seven equivalence classes and use the following labels to denote these equivalence classes of $\mathbb{R}$:

NL	NM	NS	PS	PM	PL
$-\beta$	$-\alpha$	0	α	β	

The labels correspond to "negative large", "negative medium", "negative small", "zero", "positive small", "positive medium" and "positive large", respectively. The real numbers α and β are the landmarks used to delimit the equivalence classes (the particular criteria to choose these numbers would depend on the application in mind). In [9] three binary relations (*close to, comparable, negligible*) were defined in the spirit of [7], but using the labels corresponding to quantitative values, and preserving coherence between the relative model they define and the absolute model in which they are defined.

Our aim in this paper is to develop a non-classical logic for handling qualitative reasoning with orders of magnitude. To the best of our knowledge, no formal logic has been developed to deal with order-of-magnitude reasoning. However, non-classical logics have been used as a support of qualitative reasoning in several ways: For instance, in [12, 10] is remarkable the role of multimodal logics to deal with qualitative spatio-temporal representations, and in [8] branching temporal logics have been used to describe the possible solutions of ordinary differential equations when we have limited information about a system.

In this paper, as a starting point of our proposal, we will use an arbitrary set of real numbers, not necessarily all the real line, partitioned in equivalence classes: three classes formed by so-called *observable numbers* (positive or negative) and *non-observable numbers* or *infinitesimals*[1] (including 0). In the class of infinitesimals we will not distinguish between positive or negative. The landmarks are defined by a pair of numbers α^+ and α^-, and the equivalence classes are denoted as follows:

- OBS^+ (positive observable include α^+)
- OBS^- (negative observable include α^-)
- INF (infinitesimals)

Once we have the equivalence classes in the real line, we can make comparisons between numbers by using binary relations such as

---

[1] This means elements too small to be observed. Not to be confused with the formal meaning in a hyper-real framework.

– *x is less than y*, in symbols $x < y$
– *x is less than and comparable to y*, in symbols $x \sqsubset y$.

where $\sqsubset$ is a restriction of the usual order of the real numbers ($<$) to numbers belonging to the same equivalence class.

We will introduce a minimal system to handle orders of magnitude based on the proposed approach, whose linear ordering will then be extended to $\mathbb{Q}$ and, finally, to $\mathbb{R}$.

In our syntax we will consider the operators $\overrightarrow{\Box}$ and $\overleftarrow{\Box}$ to deal with the usual ordering $<$, and the operators $\overrightarrow{\blacksquare}$ and $\overleftarrow{\blacksquare}$ to deal with $\sqsubset$. The intuitive meanings of each modal operator is as follows:

$\overrightarrow{\Box}A$ means *A is true for all number greater than the current one.*

$\overrightarrow{\blacksquare}A$ means *A is true for all number greater than and comparable to the current one.*

$\overleftarrow{\Box}A$ means *A is true for all number less than the current one.*

$\overleftarrow{\blacksquare}A$ means *A is true for all number less than and comparable to the current one.*

Although the treatment presented in this work is considerably simpler than those stated at the beginning of this section, still it is useful as a stepping stone for considering more complex systems, for which the logic has to be enriched by adding new modal operators capable to treat a bigger number of milestones, equivalence classes and/or qualitative relations.

This paper is organized as follows: In Section 2 the syntax and the semantics of the proposed logic is introduced; in Section 3 then a minimal axiom system is presented, whic axiomatizes validity in frames with an arbitrary set of real numbers is defined, then some extensions dealing with $\mathbb{Q}$ or $\mathbb{R}$ are given. In Section 4 the completeness proof is given, following a Henkin-style. Finally, in Section 5 some conclusions are drawn and prospects for future work are presented.

2   Syntax and Semantics of the Language $\mathcal{L}(MQ)$

The syntax of our initial language for qualitative reasoning is introduced below:
The alphabet of the language $\mathcal{L}(MQ)$ is defined by using:

– A stock of atoms or propositional variables, $\mathcal{V}$.
– The classical connectives $\neg, \wedge, \vee$ and $\rightarrow$ and the constants $\top$ and $\bot$.
– The unary modal connectives and $\overrightarrow{\Box}, \overleftarrow{\Box}, \overrightarrow{\blacksquare}$ and $\overleftarrow{\blacksquare}$.
– The constants α^+ and α^-
– The auxiliary symbols: (,).

Formulas are generated from $\mathcal{V} \cup \{\alpha^+, \alpha^-, \top, \bot\}$ by the construction rules of classical propositional logic adding the following rule: If A is a formula, then so are $\overrightarrow{\Box}A$, $\overleftarrow{\Box}A$, $\overrightarrow{\blacksquare}A$ and $\overleftarrow{\blacksquare}A$. The *mirror image* of A is the result of replacing in A each occurrence of $\overrightarrow{\Box}, \overleftarrow{\Box}, \overrightarrow{\blacksquare}, \overleftarrow{\blacksquare}, \alpha^+, \alpha^-$ by $\overleftarrow{\Box}, \overrightarrow{\Box}, \overleftarrow{\blacksquare}, \overrightarrow{\blacksquare}, \alpha^-, \alpha^+$, respectively. We shall use the symbols $\overrightarrow{\Diamond}, \overleftarrow{\Diamond}, \overrightarrow{\blacklozenge}$ and $\overleftarrow{\blacklozenge}$ as abbreviations respectively of $\neg\overrightarrow{\Box}\neg, \neg\overleftarrow{\Box}\neg, \neg\overrightarrow{\blacksquare}\neg$ and $\neg\overleftarrow{\blacksquare}\neg$.

Definition 1. *A* multimodal qualitative frame *for* $\mathcal{L}(MQ)$ *(or, simply, a* frame*) is a tuple* $\Sigma = (\mathbb{S}, +\alpha, -\alpha, <)$, *where*

1. $\mathbb{S}$ *is a nonempty set of real numbers.*
2. $<$ *is a strict linear order on* $\mathbb{S}$.
3. $+\alpha$ *and* $-\alpha$ *are designated points in* $\mathbb{S}$ *(called* frame constants*), and allow to form the sets* OBS^+, INF, *and* OBS^- *defined below:*

$$OBS^- = \{x \in \mathbb{S} \mid x \leq -\alpha\} \qquad INF = \{x \in \mathbb{S} \mid -\alpha < x < +\alpha\}$$
$$OBS^+ = \{x \in \mathbb{S} \mid +\alpha \leq x\}$$

We will use $x \sqsubset y$ as an abbreviation of "$x < y$ and $x, y \in EQ$, where $EQ \in \{OBS^+, INF, OBS^-\}$".

Definition 2. *Let* Σ *be a multimodal qualitative frame, a* multimodal qualitative model *on* Σ *(or* Σ-model*, for short) is an ordered pair* $\mathcal{M} = (\Sigma, h)$, *where* h *is a* meaning function *(or,* interpretation*)* $h: \mathcal{V} \longrightarrow 2^{\mathbb{S}}$. *Any interpretation can be uniquely extended to the set of all formulas in* $\mathcal{L}(MQ)$ *(also denoted by* h*) by using the usual conditions for the classical boolean connectives and the constants* $\top$ *and* $\bot$*, and the following conditions for the modal operators and frame constants:*

$$h(\overrightarrow{\Box}A) = \{x \in \mathbb{S} \mid y \in h(A) \text{ for all } y \text{ such that } x < y\}$$
$$h(\overrightarrow{\blacksquare}A) = \{x \in \mathbb{S} \mid y \in h(A) \text{ for all } y \text{ such that } x \sqsubset y\}$$
$$h(\overleftarrow{\Box}A) = \{x \in \mathbb{S} \mid y \in h(A) \text{ for all } y \text{ such that } y < x\}$$
$$h(\overleftarrow{\blacksquare}A) = \{x \in \mathbb{S} \mid y \in h(A) \text{ for all } y \text{ such that } y \sqsubset x\}$$
$$h(\alpha^+) = \{+\alpha\} \qquad h(\alpha^-) = \{-\alpha\}$$

The concepts of truth and validity are defined in a straightforward manner.

3   Axiomatic Systems for $\mathcal{L}(MQ)$

In this section we define several axiomatic systems for multimodal qualitative logic. A list of axiom schemes and inference rules are presented in order to build the different systems. We also consider all the tautologies of classical propositional logic.

Axiom schemata for $\overrightarrow{\Box}, \overrightarrow{\Diamond}$:

K1 $\overrightarrow{\Box}(A \to B) \to (\overrightarrow{\Box}A \to \overrightarrow{\Box}B)$

K2 $A \to \overrightarrow{\Box}\overleftarrow{\Diamond}A$

K3 $\overrightarrow{\Box}A \to \overrightarrow{\Box}\overrightarrow{\Box}A$

K4 $(\overrightarrow{\Diamond}A \wedge \overrightarrow{\Diamond}B) \to (\overrightarrow{\Diamond}(A \wedge B) \vee \overrightarrow{\Diamond}(\overrightarrow{\Diamond}A \wedge B) \vee \overrightarrow{\Diamond}(A \wedge \overrightarrow{\Diamond}B))$

K5 $\overrightarrow{\Box}\overrightarrow{\Box}A \to \overrightarrow{\Box}A$

K6 $\overrightarrow{\Box}A \to \overrightarrow{\Diamond}A$

K7 $(\overrightarrow{\Diamond}A \wedge \overrightarrow{\Diamond}\overrightarrow{\Box}\neg A) \to \overrightarrow{\Diamond}(\overrightarrow{\Box}\overrightarrow{\Diamond}A \wedge \overrightarrow{\Box}\neg A))$

Axiom schema for $\overrightarrow{\blacksquare}$:

C1 $\overrightarrow{\blacksquare}(A \to B) \to (\overrightarrow{\blacksquare}A \to \overrightarrow{\blacksquare}B)$

Mixed axiom:

M1 $\overrightarrow{\Box}A \to \overrightarrow{\blacksquare}A$

Axiom schemata for constants, where ξ denotes an element of the set $\{\alpha^+, \alpha^-\}$

c1 $\overleftarrow{\Diamond}\xi \vee \xi \vee \overrightarrow{\Diamond}\xi$

c2 $\xi \to (\overleftarrow{\Box}\neg\xi \wedge \overrightarrow{\Box}\neg\xi)$

c3 $\alpha^- \to \overrightarrow{\Diamond}\alpha^+$

c4 $\alpha^- \to \overrightarrow{\blacksquare}A$

c5 $(\overleftarrow{\Diamond}\alpha^- \wedge \overrightarrow{\Diamond}\alpha^+) \to \overrightarrow{\blacksquare}(\overleftarrow{\Diamond}\alpha^- \wedge \overrightarrow{\Diamond}\alpha^+)$

c6 $\overrightarrow{\Diamond}\alpha^- \to \overrightarrow{\blacksquare}(\alpha^- \vee \overrightarrow{\Diamond}\alpha^-)$

c7 $(\alpha^+ \wedge \overrightarrow{\blacksquare}A) \to \overrightarrow{\Box}A$

c8 $\overrightarrow{\blacksquare}A \to \overrightarrow{\Box}((\alpha^- \vee \overrightarrow{\Diamond}\alpha^-) \to A)$

c9 $(\overleftarrow{\Diamond}\alpha^+ \wedge \overrightarrow{\blacksquare}A) \to \overrightarrow{\Box}A$

c10 $(\overleftarrow{\Diamond}\alpha^- \wedge \overrightarrow{\Diamond}\alpha^+ \wedge \overrightarrow{\blacksquare}A) \to \overrightarrow{\Box}((\overleftarrow{\Diamond}\alpha^- \wedge \overrightarrow{\Diamond}\alpha^+) \to A)$

We also consider as axioms the corresponding mirror images.

Rules of inference:

    (MP)   Modus Ponens for $\to$

    (N$\overrightarrow{\Box}$)   If $\vdash A$ then $\vdash \overrightarrow{\Box}A$

    (N$\overleftarrow{\Box}$)   If $\vdash A$ then $\vdash \overleftarrow{\Box}A$

Definition 3. *The minimal system for $\mathcal{L}(MQ)$ is denoted MQ. It consists of the axioms given by K1–K4 plus M1, C1, c1–c10 and the corresponding mirror images. $MQ_{\mathbb{Q}}$ is the extension of MQ by adding K5, K6 and their mirror images. Finally, $MQ_{\mathbb{R}}$ is the extension of $MQ_{\mathbb{Q}}$ by adding K7 and its mirror image.*

The concepts of *proof* and *theorem* are defined in a standard way.

4   Soundness and Completeness

The proof of soundness is straightforward, since validity of the axioms and preservation of validity by inference rules is simply a standard calculation. Thus, we need only to focus on completeness, for which a Henkin-style proof can be constructed.

    The proof of completeness follows the step-by-step method as in [1]; therefore, some results about *consistent* (*maximal consistent*) sets of formulas are needed. Some familiarity with the basic properties of maximal consistent sets is assumed, we shall use $\mathcal{MC}$ to denote the set of all maximal consistent sets of formulas (*mc-sets*) of any of the systems introduced in the previous section. We denote by $\mathcal{AS}$ any such axiomatic system.

Definition 4. *Let* $\Gamma_1, \Gamma_2 \in \mathcal{MC}$. *Then:*

1. $\Gamma_1 \rhd \Gamma_2$ *if and only if* $\{A \mid \overrightarrow{\Box} A \in \Gamma_1\} \subseteq \Gamma_2$
2. $\Gamma_1 \blacktriangleright \Gamma_2$ *if and only if* $\{A \mid \overrightarrow{\blacksquare} A \in \Gamma_1\} \subseteq \Gamma_2$

The three lemmas below state some modal properties of the operators $\rhd$ and $\blacktriangleright$: the behaviour with respect to the relations just introduced, the transitivity and linearity of those orderings, and the existence of mc-sets with suitable properties. The statements only contain the behaviour of the specific (black) modal connectives, the usual (white) modalities have the same properties:

Lemma 1. *Let* $\Gamma_1, \Gamma_2 \in \mathcal{MC}$, *then:*

1. $\Gamma_1 \blacktriangleright \Gamma_2$ *if and only if* $\{A \mid \overleftarrow{\blacksquare} A \in \Gamma_2\} \subseteq \Gamma_1$
2. $\Gamma_1 \blacktriangleright \Gamma_2$ *if and only if* $\{\overrightarrow{\blacklozenge} A \mid A \in \Gamma_2\} \subseteq \Gamma_1$
3. $\Gamma_1 \blacktriangleright \Gamma_2$ *if and only if* $\{\overleftarrow{\blacklozenge} A \mid A \in \Gamma_1\} \subseteq \Gamma_2$
4. *(Lindenbaum's Lemma) Any consistent set of formulas in* $\mathcal{AS}$ *can be extended to an mc-set in* $\mathcal{AS}$.

Lemma 2. *Consider* $\Gamma_1, \Gamma_2, \Gamma_3 \in \mathcal{MC}$, *then*

1. *If* $\Gamma_1 \blacktriangleright \Gamma_2$ *and* $\Gamma_2 \blacktriangleright \Gamma_3$, *then* $\Gamma_1 \blacktriangleright \Gamma_3$.
2. *If* $\Gamma_1 \blacktriangleright \Gamma_2$ *and* $\Gamma_1 \blacktriangleright \Gamma_3$, *then either* $\Gamma_2 \blacktriangleright \Gamma_3$, *or* $\Gamma_3 \blacktriangleright \Gamma_2$, *or* $\Gamma_2 = \Gamma_3$.
3. *If* $\Gamma_2 \blacktriangleright \Gamma_1$ *and* $\Gamma_3 \blacktriangleright \Gamma_1$, *then either* $\Gamma_2 \blacktriangleright \Gamma_3$, *or* $\Gamma_3 \blacktriangleright \Gamma_2$, *or* $\Gamma_2 = \Gamma_3$.

Lemma 3. *Assume* $\Gamma_1 \in \mathcal{MC}$:

1. *If* $\overrightarrow{\blacklozenge} A \in \Gamma_1$, *then there exists* $\Gamma_2 \in \mathcal{MC}$ *such that* $\Gamma_1 \blacktriangleright \Gamma_2$ *and* $A \in \Gamma_2$.
2. *If* $\overleftarrow{\blacklozenge} A \in \Gamma_1$, *then there exists* $\Gamma_2 \in \mathcal{MC}$ *such that* $\Gamma_2 \blacktriangleright \Gamma_1$ *and* $A \in \Gamma_2$.

The following two lemmas are specific of our logic, since the behaviour of specific and general connectives is studied.

Lemma 4. *Consider* $\Gamma_1, \Gamma_2 \in \mathcal{MC}$ *such that* $\Gamma_1 \rhd \Gamma_2$, *then* $\Gamma_1 \blacktriangleright \Gamma_2$ *holds if and only if one of the following conditions below is fulfilled:*

1. $\{\overleftarrow{\lozenge}\alpha^- \wedge \overrightarrow{\lozenge}\alpha^+, \overleftarrow{\lozenge}\alpha^+, \overrightarrow{\lozenge}\alpha^-\} \cap \Gamma_1 \cap \Gamma_2 \neq \varnothing$
2. $\alpha^+ \in \Gamma_1$
3. $\alpha^- \in \Gamma_2$

Lemma 5. *Given* $\Gamma_1, \Gamma_2, \Gamma_3 \in \mathcal{MC}$ *we have:*

1. *If* $\Gamma_1 \blacktriangleright \Gamma_2$, *then* $\Gamma_1 \rhd \Gamma_2$
2. *If* $\Gamma_1 \blacktriangleright \Gamma_2$, $\Gamma_1 \rhd \Gamma_3$ *and it is not the case that* $\Gamma_1 \blacktriangleright \Gamma_3$, *then* $\Gamma_2 \rhd \Gamma_3$
3. *If* $\Gamma_2 \blacktriangleright \Gamma_1$, $\Gamma_3 \rhd \Gamma_1$ *and it is not the case that* $\Gamma_3 \blacktriangleright \Gamma_1$, *then* $\Gamma_3 \rhd \Gamma_2$
4. *If* $\Gamma_1 \rhd \Gamma_2 \rhd \Gamma_3$ *and* $\Gamma_1 \blacktriangleright \Gamma_3$, *then* $\Gamma_1 \blacktriangleright \Gamma_2 \blacktriangleright \Gamma_3$

We will sketch the proof of completeness by using the step-by-step method. The following definitions are needed in order to describe the construction method of each step in the proof.

The construction is built upon the concept of *pre-frame*.

Definition 5.

1. *A* pre-frame *is a tuple obtained by eliminating either one or both frame constants from a frame, that is, a pre-frame can be of the following forms: either* $\Upsilon = (\mathbb{S}, <)$ *or* $\Upsilon = (\mathbb{S}, +\alpha, <)$ *or* $\Upsilon = (\mathbb{S}, -\alpha, <)$.
2. *Given a pre-frame* Υ, *a* trace *of* Υ *is a function* $f_\Upsilon : \mathbb{S} \longrightarrow 2^{\mathcal{L}(MQ)}$ *such that, for all* $x \in \mathbb{S}$, *the set* $f_\Upsilon(x)$ *is a maximal consistent set.*

Definition 6.

1. *Given a frame* Σ, *a* trace *of* Σ *is a function* $f_\Sigma : \mathbb{S} \longrightarrow 2^{\mathcal{L}(MQ)}$ *such that, for all* $x \in \mathbb{S}$, *the set* $f_\Sigma(x)$ *is a maximal consistent set.*
2. *Let* f_Σ *be a trace of* $\Sigma = (\mathbb{S}, +\alpha, -\alpha, <)$. *Then* f_Σ *is called:*
   - Coherent *if it satisfies:*
     (i) $\alpha^+ \in f_\Sigma(+\alpha)$ *and* $\alpha^- \in f_\Sigma(-\alpha)$
     (ii) for all $x, y \in \mathbb{S}$:
       (a) If $x < y$ *then* $f_\Sigma(x) \rhd f_\Sigma(y)$
       (b) If $x \sqsubset y$, *then* $f_\Sigma(x) \blacktriangleright f_\Sigma(y)$
   - $\overrightarrow{\Diamond}$-prophetic *if it is coherent and for all formula A and all* $x \in \mathbb{S}$:

   $$\text{if } \overrightarrow{\Diamond} A \in f_\Sigma(x), \text{ there exists } y \text{ such that } x < y \text{ and } A \in f_\Sigma(y) \qquad (1)$$

   - $\overrightarrow{\blacklozenge}$-prophetic *if it is coherent and for all formula A and all* $x \in \mathbb{S}$:

   $$\text{if } \overrightarrow{\blacklozenge} A \in f_\Sigma(x), \text{ there exists } y \text{ such that } x \sqsubset y \text{ and } A \in f_\Sigma(y) \qquad (2)$$

   - $\overleftarrow{\Diamond}$-historic *if it is coherent and for all formula A and all* $x \in \mathbb{S}$:

   $$\text{if } \overleftarrow{\Diamond} A \in f_\Sigma(x), \text{ there exists } y \text{ such that } y < x \text{ and } A \in f_\Sigma(y) \qquad (3)$$

   - $\overleftarrow{\blacklozenge}$-historic *if it is coherent and for all formula A and all* $x \in \mathbb{S}$:

   $$\text{if } \overleftarrow{\blacklozenge} A \in f_\Sigma(x), \text{ there exists } y \text{ such that } y \sqsubset x \text{ and } A \in f_\Sigma(y) \qquad (4)$$

   - *The conditional expression (1) (resp. (2), (3), (4)) is called a* $\overrightarrow{\Diamond}$-prophetic *(resp.* $\overrightarrow{\blacklozenge}$-prophetic, $\overleftarrow{\Diamond}$-historic, $\overleftarrow{\blacklozenge}$-historic*) conditional for* f_Σ *wrt* $\overrightarrow{\Diamond} A$ *(resp.* $\overrightarrow{\blacklozenge} A$, $\overleftarrow{\Diamond} A$ *or* $\overleftarrow{\blacklozenge} A$*) and* x. *We also say in this case that such a conditional is simply a conditional for* f_Σ.
     f_Σ *is called* prophetic *if it is* $\overrightarrow{\Diamond}$-prophetic *(or* $\overrightarrow{\blacklozenge}$-prophetic*) and it is called* historic *if it is* $\overleftarrow{\Diamond}$-historic *(or* $\overleftarrow{\blacklozenge}$-historic*).*
3. *Let* f_Σ *be a trace of* $\Sigma = (\mathbb{S}, +\alpha, -\alpha, <)$. f_Σ *is called* full *if it is prophetic and historic.*

Definition 7.

1. *Let S be a denumerable infinite set. We consider the class, $\Xi_{\mathbb{S}}$, of finite frames, $(\mathbb{S}, +\alpha, -\alpha, <)$, where $\mathbb{S}$ is a nonempty finite subset of S. If $\Sigma_1 = (\mathbb{S}_1, +\alpha_1, -\alpha_1, <_1), \Sigma_2 = (\mathbb{S}_2, +\alpha_2, -\alpha_2, <_2) \in \Xi_{\mathbb{S}}$, we say that Σ_2 is an extension of Σ_1 if the following conditions are satisfied: $\mathbb{S}_1 \subseteq \mathbb{S}_2$, $<_1 \subseteq <_2$, $+\alpha_1 = +\alpha_2, -\alpha_1 = -\alpha_2$. In a similar way we define that a pre-frame Υ_1 is an extension of the pre-frame Υ_2.*
2. *Let f_Σ be a trace of a frame $\Sigma = (\mathbb{S}, +\alpha, -\alpha, <) \in \Xi_{\mathbb{S}}$.*
   - *Consider a $\overrightarrow{\Diamond}$-prophetic conditional for f_Σ (with respect to $\overrightarrow{\Diamond} A$ and x):*

     if $\overrightarrow{\Diamond} A \in f_\Sigma(x)$, there exists $y \in \mathbb{S}$ such that $x < y$ and $A \in f_\Sigma(y)$

     This conditional is said to be active, *if $\overrightarrow{\Diamond} A \in f_\Sigma(x)$ but there is no y such that $x < y$ and $A \in f_\Sigma(y)$; otherwise, if there exists y such that $x < y$ and $A \in f_\Sigma(y)$ the conditional is said to be* exhausted[2].
   - *The definition of* active *and* exhausted *$\overrightarrow{\blacklozenge}$-prophetic conditional are given in a similar manner.*
   - *For conditionals of type* historic *the definitions are similar.*

Theorem 1 (Completeness Theorem). *If A is a valid formula of $\mathcal{L}(MQ)$, then A is a theorem of MQ.*

Proof. The idea is to show that for any consistent formula A, it is possible to build a multimodal qualitative frame $\Sigma = (\mathbb{S}, +\alpha, -\alpha, <)$ and a full trace f_Σ, such that $A \in f_\Sigma(x)$ for some $x \in \mathbb{S}$. The frame Σ will be the countable union of a sequence of finite frames, $\Sigma_0, \Sigma_1, \ldots, \Sigma_n, \ldots$, taken from the class $\Xi_{\mathbb{S}}$ in Def 7. However, a preprocessing step is needed at the beginning of the construction; obviously, this preprocessing is of length at most two, since we have to guarantee the introduction of the frame constants $+\alpha$ and $-\alpha$.

Obtaining an Initial Frame. We define $\Upsilon_0 = (\mathbb{S}', <')$ where $\mathbb{S}' = \{x_0\}, <' = \varnothing$ and the trace f_{Υ_0} is defined as $f_{\Upsilon_0}(x_0) = \Gamma_0$ where Γ_0 is a maximal consistent set containing A, which exists by Lindenbaum's lemma. The next step depends on whether x_0 is a frame constant (we take $x_0 = -\alpha$ if $\alpha^- \in \Gamma_0$ or $x_0 = +\alpha$ if $\alpha^+ \in \Gamma_0$) or not.

On the one hand, assume that $x_0 = -\alpha$ (the case $x_0 = +\alpha$ is similar), then we have $\overrightarrow{\Diamond} \alpha^+ \in f_{\Sigma_0}(x_0)$. By Lemma 3(1) (with respect to white connectives) there exists Γ_1 such that $\alpha^+ \in \Gamma_1$. Now, we select the frame $\Sigma_0 = (\mathbb{S}_0, <_0)$ as follows:

   - $\mathbb{S}_0 = \{-\alpha, +\alpha\}$
   - $<_0 = \{(-\alpha, +\alpha)\}$

and the corresponding trace is defined as $f_{\Sigma_0} = f_{\Upsilon_0} \cup \{(\alpha^+, \Gamma_1)\}$, which is clearly coherent.

On the other hand, if we have $\alpha^- \neq x_0 \neq \alpha^+$, then we need to apply two steps as the previously described, one for introducing each frame constant.

---

[2] In other words, a conditional is said to be active if the conditional expression is not satisfied, whereas is said to be exhausted if the consequent is satisfied.

From the Initial Frame Onwards. Once we have an initial frame to work with, for the construction of Σ, we define an enumeration of elements in $S = \{x_i \mid i \in \mathbb{N}\}$ and an enumeration of formulas $A_0, A_1, \ldots, A_n, \ldots$ of the language $\mathcal{L}(MQ)$. Therefore, a code number can be assigned to each prophetic (historic) conditional in the usual way.

Assume that $\Sigma_n = (\mathbb{S}_n, <_n)$ and f_{Σ_n} are defined. Then, if no conditional is active, then $\Sigma_{n+1} = \Sigma_n$, $f_{\Sigma_{n+1}} = f_{\Sigma_n}$ and the construction is finished. Otherwise, i.e., if there are prophetic (or historic) conditionals for f_{Σ_n} with respect to $\overrightarrow{\Diamond} A$ (respectively, $\overleftarrow{\Diamond} A$, $\overrightarrow{\blacklozenge} A$, $\overleftarrow{\blacklozenge} A$) and x, which are active, then we choose the conditional C with the lowest code number. By the *exhausting lemma* to be introduced later, there exists an extension $\Sigma_{n+1} = (\mathbb{S}_{n+1}, <_{n+1}) \in \Xi_S$ of Σ_n together with an extension $f_{\Sigma_{n+1}}$ of f_{Σ_n} such that the conditional C for $f_{\Sigma_{n+1}}$ is exhausted. The trace of each finite frame is coherent, although in general, it fails to be either prophetic or historic. It can be proved that the final frame Σ, as defined, is such that f_Σ is full. Thus, A is verified by the *trace lemma* below.   q.e.d.

The lemmas used in the sketch of the proof of completeness are stated below.

Lemma 6 (Trace Lemma). *Let f_Σ be a full trace of a multimodal qualitative frame Σ. Let h be an interpretation assigning each propositional variable, p, the set $h(p) = \{x \in \mathbb{S} \mid p \in f_\Sigma(x)\}$. Then, for any formula, A, we have $h(A) = \{x \in \mathbb{S} \mid A \in f_\Sigma(x)\}$.*

Lemma 7 (Exhausting Lemma). *Let Ξ_S be as in Definition 7, f_{Σ_n} a coherent trace of a frame $\Sigma_n \in \Xi_S$, and suppose that there is a prophetic (historic) conditional, C, for f_{Σ_n} which is active. Then there is a frame $\Sigma_{n+1} \in \Xi_S$ and a coherent trace $f_{\Sigma_{n+1}}$, an extension of f_{Σ_n}, such that C is a conditional for $f_{\Sigma_{n+1}}$ which is exhausted.*

The completeness of systems $MQ_\mathbb{Q}$ and $MQ_\mathbb{R}$ are straightforward following [1].

5   Conclusions and Future Work

A minimal multimodal language for the handling of qualitative reasoning has been introduced, a sound and complete system for multimodal qualitative reasoning has been presented, and its completeness theorem has been sketched. The importance of using a logical apparatus in the treatment of qualitative reasoning is the possibility of mechanization of its reasoning system.

Obviously, this minimal language is still very poor in order to represent real-world interesting problems, for usually a greater number of landmarks are considered in AI applications of qualitative reasoning. As future work it is expected to extend the language, and automatize its proof procedure, namely:

1. Integrate further modalities expressed in terms of the Absolute and/or Relative Orders of Magnitude, such as closeness or negligibility, and considering a finer partition of the real line.
2. Develop a tableau calculus as proof procedure.

References

1. J. P. Burgess. Basic tense logic. In D. Gabbay and F. Guenthner, editors, *Handbook of Philosophical Logic: Volume II: Extensions of Classical Logic*, pages 89–133. Reidel, Dordrecht, 1984.

2. P. Dague. Numeric reasoning with relative orders of magnitude. In *Proc. 11th National Conference on Artificial Intelligence*, pages 541–547. The AAAI Press/The MIT Press, 1993.

3. P. Dague. Symbolic reasoning with relative orders of magnitude. In *Proc. 13th Intl. Joint Conference on Artificial Intelligence*, pages 1509–1515. Morgan Kaufmann, 1993.

4. M.L. Mavrovouniotis and G. Stephanopoulos. Reasoning with orders of magnitude and approximate relations. In *Proc. 6th National Conference on Artificial Intelligence*. The AAAI Press/The MIT Press, 1987.

5. M.L. Mavrovouniotis and G. Stephanopoulos. Formal order of magnitude reasoning in process engineering. *Computer Chem. Eng.*, 12(9/10):867–880, 1988.

6. N. Piera, M. Sánchez, and L.. Travé-Massuyès. Qualitative operators for order of magnitude calculus: robustness and precision. In *Proc. of 13th IMACS World Congress on Computation and Applied Mathematics*, pages 1–6. IMACS, 1991.

7. O. Raiman. Order of magnitude reasoning. *Artificial Intelligence*, 51:11–38, 1991.

8. B. Shults and B.J. Kuipers. Proving properties of continuous systems: qualitative simulation and temporal logic. *Artificial Intelligence*, 92:91–129, 1997.

9. M. Sánchez, F. Prats, and N. Piera. Una formalización de relaciones de comparabilidad en modelos cualitativos. *Boletín de la AEPIA (Bulletin of the Spanish Association for AI)*, 6:15–22, 1996.

10. H. Sturm, N. Suzuki, F. Wolter, and M. Zakharyaschev. Semi-qualitative reasoning about distances: A preliminary report. In *Logics in Artificial Intelligence*, volume 1919 of *Lecture Notes in Artificial Intelligence*, pages 37–56. Springer, 2000.

11. L. Travé-Massuyès, F. Prats, M. Sánchez, and N. Agell. Consistent relative and absolute order-of-magnitude models. In *Proc. Qualitative Reasoning 2002 Conference*, 2002.

12. F. Wolter and M. Zakharyaschev. Qualitative spatio-temporal representation and reasoning: a computational perspective. In G. Lakemeyer and B. Nebel, editors, *Exploring Artificial Intelligence in the New Millenium*. Morgan Kaufmann, 2002.

A New Genetic Approach for the Partitioning Problem in Distributed Virtual Environment Systems*

Pedro Morillo[1], Pedro López[2], Juan Manuel Orduña[2], and Marcos Fernández[1]

[1] Instituto de Robótica, Universidad de Valencia, Spain
Pedro.Morillo@uv.es
[2] Departamento de Informática, Universidad de Valencia, Spain
Juan.Orduna@uv.es

Abstract. The *Partitioning problem* is a key issue in the design of Distributed Virtual Environment (DVE) systems based on a server-network architecture. This problem consist of efficiently assigning the clients of the simulation (avatars) to the system servers. Despite the existing literature proposes different evolutive approaches for solving this NP-hard problem, an approach based on genetic algorithms is considered as the current best partitioning mechanism.

In this paper, we analyze the impact of the low diversity of the initial population in this algorithm, and we propose a new mechanism for generating initial populations of higher quality. We also propose a new set of crossover methods oriented to problem specifications. Both improvements define a new genetic algorithm that provides better solutions than any other existing approach, in terms of both quality function and execution time.

1   Introduction

Distributed Virtual Environment (DVE) systems have experienced a spectacular growth last years. These systems allow multiple users, working on different computers that are interconnected through different networks (and even through Internet) to interact in a shared virtual world. This is achieved by rendering images of the environment as a user located at that point in the virtual environment would perceived them. Each user is represented in the shared virtual environment by an entity called *avatar*, whose state is controlled by the user input. Since DVE systems support visual interactions between multiple avatars, every change in each avatar must be propagated to some avatars in the shared virtual environment. DVE systems are currently used in many different applications [20], such as collaborative design [18], civil and military distributed training [12], e-learning [17] or multi-player games [1, 7].

One of the key issues in the design of a scalable DVE system is the *partitioning problem*. It consists of efficiently assigning the workload (avatars) among different servers in the system [8]. The partitioning problem determines the overall performance of the DVE systems, since it has an effect not only on the workload that each server in the system supports, but also on the inter-server communications (and therefore on

---

* Supported by the Spanish MCYT under Grants DPI-2002-04438-C02-02 and TIC-2003-08154-C06-04.

R. Conejo et al. (Eds.): CAEPIA-TTIA 2003, LNAI 3040, pp. 76–85, 2004.

the network traffic). Despite the partitioning problem in DVE systems has been usually addressed with ad-hoc procedures [20, 9], recent works propose partitioning schemes following evolutive approaches [14–16]. One of these approaches, based on a genetic algorithm, offers good performances in terms of execution time and low values of quality function.

In this paper, we propose a set of improvements for this genetic approach in order to develop more scalable and cost-effective DVE systems. These improvements consists of maximizing the structural diversity of initial population and also of incorporating a new crossover mechanism. In this mechanism, each chromosome of the current population randomly chooses a crossover operation from a small set of oriented crossovers. Performance evaluation results show that, due to its ability of avoiding premature convergence of solutions, the proposed method can provide better solutions while requiring shorter execution time than other methods proposed in the literature.

The rest of the paper is organized as follows: Section 2 describes the partitioning problem and the proposed techniques for solving it. Section 3 shows the implementation of the proposed genetic approach for solving the partitioning problem. Next, Section 4 presents the performance evaluation of the proposed search method. Finally, Section 5 presents some concluding remarks and future work to be done.

2   The Partitioning Problem in DVE Systems

Architectures based on networked servers are becoming a de-facto standard for DVE systems [20, 9, 15]. In these architectures, the control of the simulation relies on several interconnected servers. Multi-platform client computers are connected to one of these servers. When a client modifies an avatar, it also sends an updating message to its server, that in turn must propagate this message to other servers and clients. Servers must render different 3D models, perform positional updates of avatars and transfer control information among different clients. Thus, each new avatar represents an increasing in both the computational requirements of the application and also in the amount of network traffic. When the number of connected clients increases, the number of updating messages must be limited in order to avoid a message outburst. In this sense, concepts like areas of influence (AOI) [20] or locales [2] have been proposed for limiting the number of neighboring avatars that a given avatar must communicate with. All these concepts define a neighborhood area for avatars, in such a way that a given avatar must notify his movements (by sending an updating message) only to those avatars located in that neighborhood. These avatars are denoted as neighbor avatars.

Depending on their origin and destination avatars, messages in a DVE system can be intra-server or inter-server messages. Figure 1 shows an example of a DVE system consisting of several servers interconnected through a network. This figure also shows an example of both intra-server and inter-server avatar updating messages.In this figure, avatars are uniformly distributed and they are represented as dots. Each server manages a given number of clients (avatars) and decides which avatars are the destinations for the messages received from other avatars. This figure also shows an example of both intra-server and inter-server avatar updating messages. Inter-server messages are those messages whose origin and destination avatars are assigned to different servers. Otherwise, the message is an intra-server message. In order to design scalable DVE systems, the number of inter-server messages must be minimized. Effectively, when clients send intra-server messages they only concern a single server. Therefore, they are minimizing the computing, storage and communication requirements for maintaining a consistent view of the virtual world to all avatars in a DVE system.

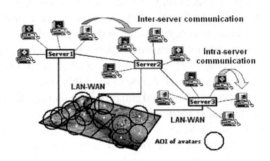

Fig. 1. Example of Multi-server DVE system

Lui and Chan propose in [8] propose a quality function, denoted as C_p, for evaluating each assignment of clients to servers. This quality function takes into account two parameters. One of them consists of the computing workload generated by clients in the DVE system, denoted as C_p^W. In order to minimize this parameter, the computing workload should be proportionally distributed among all the servers in the DVE system, according to the computing resources of each server. The other parameter of the quality function consists of the overall inter-server communication cost for sending the messages generated by all avatars, denoted as C_p^L. In order to minimize this parameter, avatars sharing the same AOI should be assigned to the same server. Quality function C_p is defined as

$$C_p = W_1 \, C_p^W + W_2 \, C_p^L \tag{1}$$

where W_1 and W_2 are two coefficients that weight the relative importance of the computational and communication workload, respectively ($W_1 + W_2 = 1$). These coefficients should be tuned according to the specific features of each DVE system. Using this quality function (and assuming $W_1 = W_2 = 0.5$) Lui and Chan propose an ad-hoc approach, called LOT, that re-assigns clients to servers [9]. The partitioning algorithm should be periodically executed for adapting the partition to the current state of the DVE system as it evolves (avatars can join or leave the DVE system at any time, and they can also move everywhere within the simulated virtual world). Lui and Chan also have proposed a testing platform for the performance evaluation of DVE systems, as well as a parallelization of the partitioning algorithm [9].

Since the partitioning problem in DVE systems can be considered as a a combinatorial optimization problem, different solutions based on metaheuristic techniques has been proposed [13–16]. Despite [13] describes a constructive strategy based on GRASP, the best partitioning results has been obtaining using evolutive techniques [15]. Among these evolutive techniques a genetic methods offer especially excellent results in terms of execution time and quality of the provided solutions.

Although the genetic approach proposed in [15] performs reasonably well, it is based on the generation of an initial population obtained by deriving a unique solution provided by a k-means clustering algorithm [16]. Despite this feature offers an improved initial population of feasible solutions it, does not focus on maximizing the structural diversity of chromosomes. As described in [11] and [4], this low level of structural diversity can lead the algorithm to reach a local minimum or even a poorer approximation to this value. Additionally, the crossover mechanism used by this algorithm is based on an auto-fertilization technique, where chromosomes are derived following a single-point crossover [5]. This crossover mechanism is excessively generalist, and it is possible to offer new crossover strategies more oriented to problem specifications.

3   A New Genetic Technique for Solving the Partitioning Problem

In order to improve the performance of our current approach for solving the partitioning problem in DVE systems, we propose a new version of the genetic algorithm. This new version focuses on maximizing the structural diversity of initial population and improving the crossover operator. The new algorithm replaces the current generation of the initial population with a new method based on random projections. Additionally, the crossover is performed by randomly choosing a mechanism from a list composed of five different crossover operators. All these five operators are very oriented to the specifications of partitioning problem in DVE systems.

3.1   Generation of a Heuristic Initial Population

Most of metaheuristic are based on the fast generation of an initial population of elements [15, 11]. This initial population usually represents a set of poor solutions to the problem, and it is evolved through a crossover operator until a stopping criterion (for example, a given number of iterations) is reached.

If the initial population has been correctly defined, then the metaheuristic algorithm easily obtains a good approximation to the global optimum. Moreover, as it is described in [11], if the initial population is not randomly selected then the algorithm should maintain a certain level of structural diversity among all the chromosomes, in order to properly represent the whole set of feasible solutions and to avoid the premature convergence of the search.

Taking into account these considerations, we propose a new mechanism, called *Projections algorithm (PA)*, in order to generate the new population of initial solutions. This fast algorithm provides a set of independent and well-diversified initial solutions to the problem.

PA consists of a given number of iterations n_c that defines the number of chromosomes in the population (population size). Each one of the n_c chromosomes represents a complete partitioning solution to the problem where all the N avatars $(A_0, .., A_{N-1})$ in the DVE are assigned to the M servers $(S_0, .., S_{M-1})$ in the system. An iteration consist of four steps (for the sake of clearness, we will consider in the following description that avatars move across a 2-D virtual world. The extrapolation to 3-D worlds is reasonably trivial), illustrated in Figure 2:

First, each avatar in the system is assigned to server S_0 (Fig.2a). Next, a random value θ between 0 and $\pi/2$ is generated. Since all avatars are located on a Cartesian plane, PA draws a straight line which passes through the zero coordinates (0,0) with a slope of θ radians (fig.2b). This line and its perpendicular define a new coordinate axis that is rotated θ radians with respect to the original position. Using a simple affine transformation (fig.2c), the old coordinates (X_i, Y_i) of each avatar can now be expressed with respect to the rotated axis by the new coordinates (X'_i, Y'_i). At this point, PA generates two different *binary search trees* with X'_i and Y'_i search keys of each avatar. Once both trees are created, the N/M different avatars in both trees with the highest and the lowest keys are put into four different sets [19]. In order to assign a set of avatars to a server, the third step of PA evaluates separately the different sets of avatars using the C_p function. Since both sets have the same cardinality N/M, PA algorithm only computes the C_p^L term. The term C_p^W is not computed, since it evaluates the standard deviation of the assigned avatars with respect to the the perfect balancing. The last step is to select the set with the lowest C_p^L value, and all avatars contained in this set are assigned to server S_1 (fig.2d). At this point, $N(M-1)/M$ avatars are still assigned to server S_0, and N/M avatars are assigned to server S_1. Next iteration allows server S_0 to lose another N/M avatars, which are assigned to S_2. PA algorithm finishes when the last group of avatars (with a size less or equal to N/M avatars) is assigned to server S_{M-1}. At this point, a number of avatars very close to N/M are assigned to each server server in the DVE system.

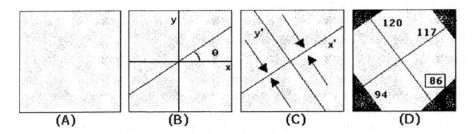

Fig. 2. Generation of the initial population based on *Projection Algorithm*

It is important to mention that the use of 4 binary search trees allows to improve diversity when selecting the sets of avatars to be assigned to the target server for each iteration. The random generation of rotation angles guarantees inherently independent solutions in the generation of individuals of the initial population. Moreover, this population allows the genetic approach to evolve solutions with good values of quality function C_p. These good C_p values are achieved by balancing the number of avatars among the servers and assigning to the same server the avatars that are closely located in the virtual scene.

3.2   Providing Randomness to Chromosome Crossover

In order to evolve chromosomes, the first approach for solving the partitioning problem in DVE systems, based on a genetic algorithm uses an auto-fertilization technique [16].

In this technique, each chromosome generates a new chromosome following a single-point crossover with a probability equal to one [5]. When the crossover operator is applied to all individuals of the population (the child population has been completely created) a elitist selection guarantees the survival of the best individuals. This crossover operator is excessively generalist and has been used often for solving different combinatorial problems.

The proposed technique is based on the random selection of crossover operators from a list. This list, which is accessed for each derivation, consists of five operators very oriented to problem specifications. The operator list consists of the following elements:

Operator 1. Random exchange of the current assignment for two *border* avatars. A given avatar A_i is a border avatar if it is assigned to a certain server S_r in the initial partition and any of the avatars in its AOI is assigned to a server different from S_r [14].

Operator 2. Once a border avatar A_i has been randomly selected, it is randomly assigned to one of the servers S_f hosting the border avatars of A_i.

Operator 3. Besides the step described in the previous operator, if it exists an avatar A_j such that A_j is assigned to S_f and it is a neighbor avatar of A_i, then A_j is assigned to S_r.

Operator 4. Since each avatar generates a certain level of workload in the server where it is assigned to [8], then it is possible to sort the servers of a DVE system according to the level of workload they support. If S_m and S_n are the servers with the highest and the lowest level of workload in the system, respectively, then a random avatar A_k assigned to S_m is assigned to S_n.

Operator 5. Besides the step described in the previous operator, a random avatar A_l, initially assigned to S_n, is now assigned to S_m.

4   Performance Evaluation

This section presents the performance evaluation results obtained with the proposed new genetic algorithm described in the previous section when it is used for solving the partitioning problem in DVE systems. Following the standard evaluation methodology described in [8] and used in [9, 13–16], we have empirically tested the new approach in two examples of a DVE system: a SMALL world, composed by 13 avatars and 3 servers, and a LARGE world, composed by 2500 avatars and 8 servers. We have considered two parameters: the value of the quality function C_p for the partition provided by the proposed search method and also the computational cost, in terms of execution time, required by the search method in order to provide that partition.

Our evaluation tool models the behavior of a generic DVE system with a server-network architecture on a real network of heterogeneous computers. Each server is implemented in a single PC, while up to 50 clients is allocated in the same PC. Following this configuration, a battery of DVE systems was tested. This battery was composed by 400 SMALL worlds and 300 LARGE worlds. We have used a 10 Mbps Ethernet as the interconnection network. The hardware platform used for the evaluation has been a Pentium IV at 1.7 GHz 256 Mbytes of RAM. The operating system was Windows 2000 Professional operating system.

4.1 Tuning of Genetic Algorithm

As described in [14, 16], the parameters of the genetic algorithm that should be tuned in order to achieve optimal performance are the population size, the number of generations, and the mutation rate.

Figure 3 shows the convergence of the proposed approach as the number of generations and mutation rate vary in a LARGE DVE configuration. This convergence is expressed in terms of fitness function C_p. Due to space limitations, the variation of the population size is not shown in this figure. The incidence of this parameter in the behavior of the algorithm is very similar to the incidence of the number of generations in the same DVE system.

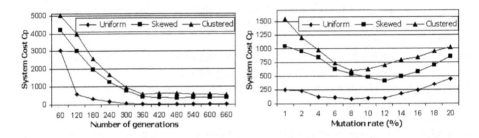

Fig. 3. C_p values obtained for different amounts of generations and mutation rates in a LARGE DVE system

Figure 3 shows (the graphic on the left) that for all the considered distributions, the C_p value provided by the proposed algorithm decreases as the number of iterations increases, until a value of 400 iterations is reached. From that point, quality function C_p slightly decreases or remain constant, depending on the considered distribution of avatars. The same behavior is shown for the population size when it reaches values close to 20 chromosomes. Although it is not shown here, values bigger than this number of iterations require too much execution time and do not reach significantly better solutions in terms of C_p. On other hand, a different behavior is observed when the mutation rate is varied (graphic on de right in figure 3). The values of quality function C_p provided by the proposed algorithm decrease as this parameter grows, until the system explore values close to 8-9%. From these points, genetic algorithm starts to obtain worse solutions in term of C_p. The reason for this behavior is that if an excessive number of mutations is performed for a given generation of individuals, then the evolving process of maintaining a set of high quality solutions is excessively degraded.

Therefore, tuning of the selected parameters for the proposed genetic method and for the LARGE DVE systems has been 400 iterations, 20 chromosomes and a mutation rate of 9%.

4.2 Evaluation Results

For comparison purposes, we have evaluated the performance of the proposed approach, as well as the *linear optimization technique* (LOT) described in [9] and also the basic genetic approach (BGA) presented in [16]. The latter method currently provides the best results for the partitioning problem in DVE systems. In the case of SMALL worlds we have also performed an exhaustive search through the solution space, obtaining the best partition as possible. Since this exhaustive method requires the exploration of a domain composed by 3^{13} (1.594.323) different solutions in SMALL worlds, this problem becomes unaffordable when LARGE worlds are considered (8^{2500} different solutions). On other hand, since the performance of the heuristic search methods may heavily depend on the location of the avatars, we have considered three different distributions of avatars: uniform, skewed, and clustered distribution.

Table 1 and table 2 show the evaluation results for a SMALL and LARGE virtual worlds, respectively. These tables show the C_p values corresponding to the final partitions provided by two versions of proposed genetic approach for a SMALL and LARGE virtual worlds, and also the execution times required in order to obtain these final partitions. Additionally, they also show the same results obtained for BGA and LOT methods.

Table 1. Results for a battery of SMALL DVE systems

	Uniform distribution		Skewed distribution		Clustered distribution	
	$T_{exe}(sec.)$	C_p	$T_{exe}(sec.)$	C_p	$T_{exe}(sec.)$	C_p
Exhaustive	3.411	6.54	3.843	7.04	4.783	7.91
LOT	0.0009	6.56	0.001	8.41	0.0011	8.89
BGA	0.002	6.54	0.003	7.04	0.005	7.91
V1	0.002	6.54	0.003	7.041	0.006	7.91
V2	0.003	6.54	0.003	7.04	0.006	7.91

Table 2. Results for a battery of LARGE DVE systems

	Uniform distribution		Skewed distribution		Clustered distribution	
	$T_{exe}(sec.)$	C_p	$T_{exe}(sec.)$	C_p	$T_{exe}(sec.)$	C_p
LOT	30.94	1637.04	32.18	3460.52	43.31	5903.80
BGA	6.65	1832.2	13.79	2825.6	29.22	4905.93
V1	6.24	547.2	14.05	612.9	28,74	1002.51
V2	6.41	321.3	14.59	450.8	28.65	791.94

In order to evaluate the improvements introduced by the methods proposed in this paper, *V1* version implements the BGA approach where the initial population has been created following the projection algorithm presented in section 3.2. In addition to this improvement, V2 version not only starts with this new initial population but also it implements the crossover mechanism described in section 3.1.

These tables show that both V1 and V2 approaches obtain similar results than LOT and BGA methods for all considered distribution of avatars in SMALL worlds. However, as it is described in [9] and [15], the main purpose of a partitioning method is to improve the scalability of DVE systems. Therefore, it must provide a significant performance improvement when it is used in LARGE DVE systems. The results obtained for the LARGE world show that the quality of the provided partitions are increased in terms of C_p values. Both V1 and V2 approaches require similar execution times than BGA method. However, V2 method is able to decrease C_p function from 1832.2s. to 321.3s when uniform distributions of avatars are considered. In the case of skewed and clustered distributions, C_p values are decreased in a similar proportion by both methods V1 and V2. These results show that by simply improving the structural diversity of the initial population (V1 version) it is possible to evolve the population of chromosomes until more efficient solutions.

5   Conclusions and Future Work

Current Distributed Virtual Environments (DVE) are usually designed following server-network architectures. In these architectures, a NP-hard problem called the partitioning problem has become a critical issue in order to design efficient and scalable DVE systems.

In this paper, we have analyzed and improved a recent method based on a genetic algorithm designed for solving this problem. This method currently provides the best results for the partitioning problem in DVE systems. One of the proposed improvements for this genetic method consists of using a new stochastic algorithm for the generation of the initial population that maximizes the structural diversity of chromosomes. On other hand, we have proposed the replacement of the traditional single-point crossover operator by a pool of five different crossover mechanisms oriented to problem specification.

Performance evaluation results show that the proposed implementation of the genetic method provides better solutions to the partitioning problem than the current approaches to the problem. Therefore, the proposed approach can improve the efficiency and scalability of DVE systems.

As future work to be done, we plan to design a parallel implementation of GRASP approach. This new design will be based on a master-slave configuration and will be implemented in conjunction with a post-optimization procedure.

References

1. M. Abrash, "Quake's game engine: The big picture", *Dr. Dobb's. Journal*.Spring, 1997.
2. D.B.Anderson, J.W.Barrus, J.H.Howard, Building multi-user interactive multimedia environments at MERL, in *IEEE Multimedia*, 2(4), pp.77-82, Winter 1995.
3. T.A. Funkhouser, "Network Topologies for Scalable Multi-User Virtual Environments", in *Proceedings IEEE VRAIS '96*, San Jose, CA. April, 1996.
4. J.H. Holland and D.E. Goldberg, "Genetic algorithms and machine learning: Introduction to the special issue on genetic algorithms", *Machine Learning*, 3, 1998.
5. K.E. Kinnear, "Alternatives to Automatically Function Definition", in Advances in Genetic Programming 1994, *MIT Press*, pp. 119-141.
6. E. Kirshenbaum, "Genetic Programming With Statically Scoped Local Variables", in *Proceedings of the Genetic and Evolutionary Computation Conference (GECCO) 2000*, July, 2000, pp. 459-468

7. M. Lewis and J. Jacboson, "Game Engines in Scientific Research", in *Communications of the ACM*, Vol 45. No.1, January 2002.
8. J.C.S. Lui, M.F. Chan and K. Oldfield, "Dynamic Partitioning for a Distributed Virtual Environment", *Dpt. of Computer Science*, The Chinese University of Hong Kong, 1998.
9. J.C.S. Lui and M.F. Chan, "An Efficient Partitioning Algorithm for Distributed Virtual Environment Systems", *IEEE Trans. Parallel and Distributed Systems*, Vol. 13, No.3, pp. 193-211. March 2002.
10. M.R. Macedonia, "A Taxonomy for Networked Virtual Environments", *IEEE Multimedia*, 4(1) 48-56, January-March 1997.
11. Z. Michalewicz, "Genetic Algorithms + Data Structures = Evolution Programs", *Springer-Verlag*, Second Edition, 1992.
12. D.C.Miller and J.A. Thorpe, "SIMNET: The advent of simulator networking", in *Proceedings of the IEEE*, Vol. 83, No.8, pp. 1114-1123. August, 1995.
13. P. Morillo and M. Fernández, "A GRASP-based algorithm for solving DVE partitioning problem", *in Proceedings of 2003 IEEE International Parallel and Distributed Processing Symposium Workshops (IPDPS-03)*, Nice, France, April, 2003.
14. P. Morillo, M.Fernández and J.M.Orduña, "An ACS-Based Partitioning Method for Distributed Virtual Environment Systems", *in Proceedings of 2003 IEEE International Parallel and Distributed Processing Symposium Workshops (IPDPS-03)*, Nice, France, April, 2003.
15. P. Morillo, M.Fernández and J. M. Orduña, "A Comparison Study of Modern Heuristics for Solving the Partitioning Problem in Distributed Virtual Environment Systems", in *International Conference in Computational Science and Its Applications (ICCSA' 2003)*, volume 2669 of Springer LNCS, pp. 458-467, Montreal, Canada. May 2003.
16. P. Morillo, M.Fernández and N.Pelechano, "A grid representation for Distributed Virtual Environments", *in Proceedings of 2003 1st European Across Grids Conference*, Santiago de Compostela, Spain, February, 2003.
17. T. Nitta, K. Fujita and S. Cono, "An Application Of Distributed Virtual Environment To Foreign Language", in *Proceedings of FIE'2000. IEEE Education Society.* Kansas City, Missouri, October 2000.
18. J.M. Salles, Ricardo Galli, A. C. Almeida et al, "mWorld: A Multiuser 3D Virtual Environment", in *IEEE Computer Graphics*, Vol. 17, No. 2. March-April 1997.
19. R. Sedgewick, "Algorithms in C", 3rd ed., Addison-Wesley, 1998.
20. S.Singhal and M.Zyda, "Networked Virtual Environments", *ACM Press*, New York, 1999.

A Proposal of Diagnosis for an ITS for Computational Logic[*]

Jose A. Maestro[1], Mª Aránzazu Simón[1], Mario López[2],
Alejandra Martínez[1], and Carlos J. Alonso[1]

[1] Grupo de Sistemas Inteligentes (GSI)
Dept. de Informática, Universidad de Valladolid, Spain
{jose,arancha,amartine,calonso}@infor.uva.es
[2] Telefónica I+D, Parque Tecnológico de Boecillo, Valladolid, Spain
mariolg@tid.es

Abstract. We describe in this paper an ITS called SIAL that supports the learning of problem solving skills in computational logic from obtaining the clause form of simple well formed formulae to hyperresolution. The core function in SIAL is the error diagnosis module, that has the role of detecting and interpreting the mistakes of the learner while he/she is solving the exercises. It combines both model-based and knowledge-based (expertise) diagnosis in order to achieve more accurate results. SIAL complements this core function with a flexible user interface and a pedagogical module that offers three modes of interaction adapted to the learner's level of expertise. SIAL is currently being tested by a group of volunteers in order to measure and tune its accuracy, as a preliminary step before performing tests in real conditions.

Keywords: Model-based Diagnosis, Intelligent Tutoring Systems, Computational Logic, Knowledge-based Systems

1 Introduction

New techniques for improving teaching quality, promoting students' motivation and more individualized learning are being demanded by modern universities. Using educational software may be seen as a valuable tool for fulfilling these demands. Intelligent Tutoring Systems (ITS) are computer programs that can be used in order to achieve that goal, thus we have been working on developing an ITS for reinforcing some topics in Artificial Intelligence (AI) subjects, specifically, automatic theorem proving (automated reasoning) related topics, as one of the most important milestones in AI (even in Computer Science) development and hence a main topic in basic AI courses and literature.

Although we devote great care and attention to explaining automated theorem proving basis to students, it was detected as a difficult topic for them to master. We observed the usefulness of computer aided instruction when teaching this AI topic in undergraduate courses. Standard programs as SWI-Prolog

[*] This work has been funded by the "Junta de Castilla y León" project VA04/99.

R. Conejo et al. (Eds.): CAEPIA-TTIA 2003, LNAI 3040, pp. 86–95, 2004.
© Springer-Verlag Berlin Heidelberg 2004

and others developed for the purpose such as SLI (Logic Inferential System), a theorem prover previously developed by our research group, were integrated in practical sessions, and a significant improvement in student performance was attained [1]. Despite that the SLI main feature is displaying a graphical representation of the refutation process, the main benefits observed with this experience were a higher student participation in the learning process, which increased their motivation and interest in the subject, and a better understanding of the concepts displayed. This experience led us to develop a new program: SIAL (Intelligent System for the Learning of Logic), more focused on pedagogical issues [1, 2].

Computational logic (first order logic), not only encompasses student's exercises covering the production of the clause form, predicate unification, application of resolution rule, etc., but also those problems related to the semi-decidability nature of this kind of logic [3]. The last area implies computational indecidability, that borders the limit of known mathematics, which makes the problem a very interesting challenge for developing an intelligent tutor.

The next sections are organized as follows: the SIAL environment is presented, then the system architecture is sketched, focusing on the diagnosis subsystem. Section 4 shows an example of the use of SIAL, and the paper finishes by presenting the main conclusions.

2   A Tutoring System for Computational Logic: SIAL

SIAL is an ITS designed to perform as a practical tool that automatically checks the user's solution to a proposed exercise. SIAL behaves like a *assistant* to diagnosis rather than an expert instructor, providing computational support in order to help the user to fix some concepts and problem solving procedures. It operates by proposing a set of exercises to the user (learner) which have to be solved using well known techniques and methods in computational logic.

The main objectives pursued with SIAL are:

- Improvement of learning by means of a software application that facilitates the assimilation of abstract concepts and problem solving skills.
- Availability of a laboratory application to monitor the student learning.

In the next subsections we describe SIAL, including the topics of computational logic covered by the system, the modes of interaction, the system architecture and the user interface.

2.1   SIAL Pedagogical Capabilities

The tutor is organized in thematic levels (Table 1), ranging from the simplest problem solving skills to the most complex ones [4]. Levels 1–6 include converting well-formed formulae (wff) to clause form, predicate unification, binary resolution, resolution refutation and factoring rule. These first six levels constitute the basic skills to be acquired, thus forming the basis for the following levels.

Levels 7 to 12 deal with methods for selecting clauses to yield a new resolvent and reducing the number of generated clauses. Pure literals, tautologies and

Table 1. Description of each level defined in SIAL, guiding and topic classification.

Level	Guiding	Topic	Description
1	Strong	Single	wff to clause form (without Skolemization process).
2	Strong	Single	wff to clause form (with Skolemization process).
3	Strong	Single	Unification procedure.
4	Strong	Compound	Resolution rule.
5	Strong	Compound	Strongly guided refutation resolution.
6	Strong	Compound	Factoring rule.
7	Weak	Compound	Weakly guided refutation resolution.
8	Weak	Compound	Pure literal removing.
9	Weak	Compound	Tautology removing.
10	Weak	Compound	Support set strategy.
11	Weak	Compound	Subsumption.
12	Weak	Compound	Hyperresolution (positive/negative hyperresolution).

subsumed clauses should be detected and removed. Also, set support strategy is included as a way to control the progressive increasing in the number of clauses. Level 12 introduces the hyperresolution rule.

SIAL levels can be grouped depending on the type of interaction the user is allowed to carry out. As the type of interaction influences the learning process, three kinds of interaction are considered: the most basic levels (1-6) perform *strongly guided* interaction, that encourages the user towards stepwise interaction. It is thought for low level learners that are expected to need a strong support from the system. The next levels (7-12) implement *weakly guided* interaction, where some intermediate steps can be avoided, going straight to the refutation stage. This is thought to be appropriate for middle-level users. Finally, the system implements an *automatic model* that performs as a usual theorem prover, on which the user can propose his own problem and ask the system to solve it.

Other grouping is possible. Levels 1–3 are devoted to only one topic at a time (producing the clause form/unification), so that the user can concentrate on an isolated topic. Levels 4–12 are defined to gather several topics. Each level above 4 can assume the functionality of each level below it, so that the user must integrate the knowledge already practiced jointly with a new technique, in the current problem solving process.

The idea of knowledge scaffolding [5] underlies this approach: the system selects lower level exercises for non-expert users and encourages the user to solve them in a stepwise fashion, whereas a higher level user must relate several different concepts and methods previously shown in order to obtain the solution, and is allowed a more flexible interaction with the system.

2.2   The System Architecture

SIAL is composed by the following four main modules (Figure 1):

1 Interface Module. This interacts with the user. Besides the *user interface*, it also contains the *user manager* and the *problem selector* modules, which

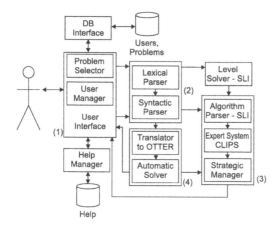

Fig. 1. SIAL system architecture.

manage the access to the user accounts and retrieve the following exercise to be solved. This module is also tightly related to the *help manager* and the *DB interface*.

2 Lexical-Syntactic Module. This is designated to control the user input.

3 Diagnostic Module. It is based on the tool called SLI (see Section 1) as the domain model. The system compares the SLI output with the user's answer. This approach is taken in each stepwise level and also in most of the non-stepwise levels. This module includes a *step-by-step theorem prover* (SLI), an *expert system engine* (CLIPS) and a *Strategic manager*. Also, this module can make use of the next one, in order to verify some of the user's answers.

4 Automatic Resolution Module. It makes use of OTTER, a first order logic theorem prover. This module is used in automatic resolution and whenever an internal complete refutation has to be obtained.

As the user progresses, the system selects exercises increasing slightly the level of complexity. The set of exercises and its associated level can be modified by the instructor, since this information is included in the database.

2.3   User Interface

The SIAL interface is designed to allow the user to interact in two ways: *graphical interaction* using the mouse and some dialogs, and *free interaction* through textual input. The graphical interaction is mainly used in putting wff into clause form (strongly guided mode), whereas dialogs are used in specific steps (unification, resolution, factorization, clause selection, ...). Advanced users are allowed a textual (free) interaction. Other interface features are:

Direct Manipulation. In order to avoid the unintentional introduction of new symbols, and to detect in each step the part of the expression being manipulated, the interaction allowed in the strongly guided mode relies on a direct

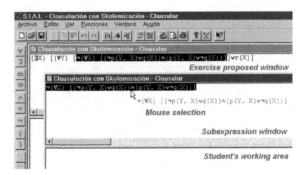

Fig. 2. A window of SIAL: converting to clause form window (strongly guided mode).

manipulation basis. A specific button bar has been developed for the process of putting the expressions into clause form. It has a button for each logical operator $(\wedge, \neg, \leftrightarrow, \ldots)$. The user introduces one of them in an expression by selecting it in the button bar and dragging it into the part of the expression where he wants the connector to be placed. The button bar has additional buttons for variable renaming, skolemization, expression removal and introduction/removal of carriage return.

Intelligent Interface. To facilitate the selection of (sub)expressions, an intelligent interface has been developed, which selects the whole subexpression affected by any symbol as the mouse passes over it. This feature is not only good for the ease of use, but also it fulfills a pedagogical goal: it helps the user to think always in the subexpression level, never on single characters.

Usability. One important objective in SIAL is to offer a functional and flexible interface. This led us to include several alternatives for manipulating expressions. A color code was established in order to improve the understanding of the operations being made. For instance, Figure 2 shows the dragging of a subexpression, which is displayed beside the cursor in red, indicating that the subexpression cannot be dropped in this part of the window to be manipulated. Also, unbalanced brackets are shown in red whereas balanced ones are in blue. Output is also graphical whenever it is possible. Within Levels 5–12 a refutation is the goal pursued so a graphical refutation tree is constructed. This output has also a color code: the last generated clause is displayed in red, unifiers in blue and duplicated clauses in green.

3   The Error Diagnosis Subsystem

Error diagnosis is the task of inferring the learner's knowledge by analyzing the user's behavior. It is a necessary task to support individual-adapted instruction. Many techniques have been proposed to develop a student model [6]. Model tracing is perhaps one of the most successful and some approaches using this technique have been proposed. A severe drawback of model-tracing tutors is the high cost of the development of an expert domain model.

In our case, error diagnosis is strongly influenced by the level of interaction allowed between the system and the student. Within the strongly guided levels, the student is encouraged to perform every step necessary to yield a solution. The input is usually entered by direct manipulation using the graphical interface. This interface is designed to act as a user input supervisor, restricting the number of possible errors. When an error is detected, the system interprets it using direct inference, matching the error with the student's mistake.

As the student gains familiarity with the basic skills, a more flexible interface is provided. Within the weakly guided levels, the general strategy changes and processing is divided into two main steps: (*i*) exercise statement and (*ii*) some new technique to solve the stated exercise. In the exercise statement step, the user is presented a set of first order logic sentences so that the corresponding set of final clauses must be provided. Due to the fact that the user only provides the final statement, the direct inference diagnosis method is almost impossible or unreliable at this step. In order to overcome this problem, the system follows a different method. It yields the set of clauses that cannot be matched to any one obtained internally as a diagnosis. This kind of weak diagnosis still provides the user with useful information about the quality of the answer, and lets the user focus the search of his/her mistake(s).

One of the main goals of the design of SIAL was to achieve a flexible interaction with the user, but the more freedom the user is allowed the more difficult to yield a diagnosis is, so up to two paradigms can be applied to obtain the diagnosis [7]: model-based diagnosis to ensure the user's answer validity and, sometimes whenever it is not possible to get an accurate diagnosis, an expertise-based diagnosis is tried. The next two subsections explain these two approaches.

3.1   Model-Based Diagnosis

Model-based diagnosis is a powerful diagnosing tool whenever a model is available. The model-based diagnosis uses the model to generate the correct output, the discrepancies between the model and the user's answer, and to decide what might be causing the errors [8].

In the development of SIAL a practical approach has been taken. A theorem prover (SLI), capable of producing the clause form from first order logic expressions and performing resolution refutation (for non-Horn clauses), is used as the domain model and supports the intelligent tutor. This also let us allow the user a very free interaction with the program as it can obtain the next correct solution from the last user's right answer. So there is no solution coded within the exercise statement since SIAL can obtain the correct solution on its own. Furthermore, the user can present his/her answer in a slightly different format from the one obtained internally, and the system is able to match both answers in order to compare them [9].

SIAL will accept (and assume) the user's answer if both expressions, the user's answer and SIAL internal solution, are equal except for alphabetic variations and for Skolem function and constant names in which also an alphabetic variation is allowed (*comparison criterion*). This approach is taken through al-

Original expression	Internal solution	User's answer	Result
$(\forall X)(p(X) \rightarrow q(X))$	$\neg p(X) \vee q(X)$	$\neg p(Y) \vee q(W)$	Rejected
$(\forall X)(\exists Y)(p(X) \rightarrow q(X,Y))$	$\neg p(X) \vee q(X, f\_sko3(X)))$	$\neg p(Z) \vee q(Z, g(Z))$	Accepted

Fig. 3. Two examples of answers to be compared and the comparison result.

most every check the system carries out, which means a more flexible interaction between the user and the tutor. The user will be able to choose the variable names, the skolem-function names, the skolem-function arguments, the predicates order, etc. Thus, SIAL is able to accept small solution variations generated by the user. Figure 3 shows two examples of use of the comparison criterion.

Now, the diagnosis approach is easy. If the user's answer cannot be accepted an error is detected. Almost every error detected in unification and resolution processes will rely on a subset of substitutions that does not comply with the comparison criterion established, so this subset can be used to explain why the user's answer is rejected. This approach can also be taken in every other process based on those mentioned. For instance, factoring and subsumption greatly rely on unification, in addition to the checking on the suitability of the literals chosen, so that an error detected at the unification process will be an error at the corresponding factoring/subsumption process. Also, the hyperresolution is based on resolution and unification processes; the detection carried out on those processes will be the most important part of the diagnosis process, jointly with the checking on the adequacy of the clauses selected.

Obtaining the clause form requires a special treatment. Even the strongly guided mode requires an additional processing as the most of the time it deals with logical expressions without any restriction. In this case, the comparison criterion only lets SIAL accept/reject the user's answer but it does not provide information enough in order to obtain an accurate diagnosis. It is even worst if the user carries out several simultaneous steps. To deal with this eventuality, both answers are converted into clause form and a one-to-one clause matching (using the comparison criterion) is tried. If such a match can be obtained then the user's answer is accepted or otherwise rejected. As a diagnosis is very difficult to obtain in this case, the method exposed in the next section is performed in order to provide the user with useful information about the error found.

3.2 Knowledge-Based (Expertise) Diagnosis

This kind of diagnosis is invoked only when a user's error is detected while clause form is being produced. To be able to yield a diagnosis, three basic suppositions have been adopted: (i) a single connector has been modified, (ii) the user has only made one mistake (the usual single-fault assumption), and (iii) the user is in strongly guided mode. Then, an error catalog is checked in order to locate the mistake made. This error catalog is implemented as an expert system, and the CLIPS engine is invoked to match the error. Some mistakes and their associated explanations are shown in Table 2. Each mistake is converted into a rule. The

Table 2. Pieces of the expert system. Some mistakes and the associate explanation.

Original expression	User expression	Explanation provided
$expr_l \leftrightarrow expr_r$	$(expr_l \rightarrow expr_r)$ $\vee (expr_r \rightarrow expr_l)$	"$\wedge/\vee$ mistake at connector substitution"
$expr_l \rightarrow expr_r$	$expr_l \vee \neg expr_r$	"$\rightarrow / \vee \neg$. Incorrect substitution. Negation has been placed on the wrong side"
$\neg(expr_l \wedge expr_r)$	$\neg(expr_l \vee expr_r)$	"$\neg \wedge /\neg \vee$. Incorrect substitution. The change of connector cannot be made"
$\neg(expr_l \wedge expr_r)$	$\neg expr_l \wedge \neg expr_r$	"$\neg \wedge /\neg \wedge \neg$. Incorrect substitution. The main connector has not been changed"

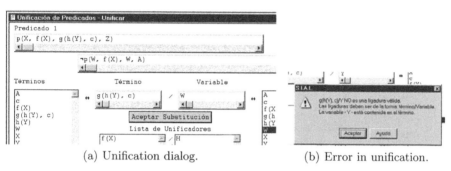

(a) Unification dialog.   (b) Error in unification.

Fig. 4. Strongly guided unification dialog.

set of rules can be viewed as a cause-effect network where the expert system performs a simple set covering strategy very close to the one proposed in [10]. Whenever it is not possible to yield a diagnosis, a default message is sent to the user asking him to carry out only one modification in the expression at a time.

4   A Running Example

SIAL has been implemented as a Master Thesis in the Comp. Sci. Dept. at the University of Valladolid (Spain). Nowadays the software application is being tested by a group of volunteers in order to check the accuracy of the diagnosis provided by the system, as a previous step to its testing in a real classroom situation. This section is mainly devoted to show some examples of the usual interaction between the student and SIAL using some input and output screens.

Figure 4(a) shows the strongly guided unification dialog. This dialog allows the user to unify two literals making up the sequence of bindings from the set of terms just below its corresponding literal. Each proposed binding is checked and applied to both literals if it is valid. Figure 4(b) shows an unification error. The user is informed that the proposed substitution $g(h(Y), c)/Y$ is not valid because $Y \in g(h(Y), c)$. The Help button shown in Figure 4(b) leads to a textual explanation of the corresponding misunderstanding topic.

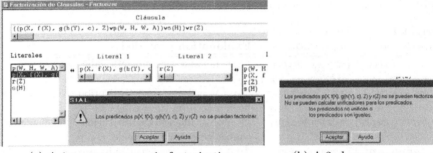

(a) A 1st error message in factorization.   (b) A 2nd error message.

Fig. 5. Strongly guided factorization dialog.

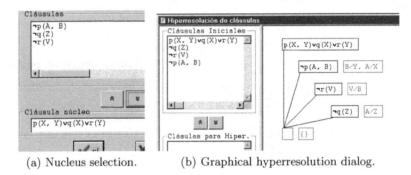

(a) Nucleus selection.   (b) Graphical hyperresolution dialog.

Fig. 6. Hyperresolution process.

Figure 5(a) shows the factorization dialog. An error message has been generated. It informs the user that the selected literals $p(X, f(X), g(h(Y), c), Z)$ and $r(Z)$ cannot be factorized together. A second mistake selecting the literals will produce a different message, the one shown in Figure 5(b), where the user is provided with a more detailed message: Unifiers cannot be obtained because of literals cannot be unified or are already equals.

Figure 6 shows part of the hyperresolution process implemented in SIAL. The dialog shown in Figure 6(a) lets the user select the nucleus clause from a set of clauses previously chosen, every other clause in the set (the satellites) must clash with the nucleus. Figure 6(b) shows the graphical hyperresolution yielded.

5 Conclusions

In this work, SIAL, an ITS for learning computational logic, has been presented, paying special attention to the error diagnosis subsystem, as it is one of the most important modules. This module makes use of an automatic theorem prover and an expert system for yielding a diagnosis. The combination of the model-based and expertise approaches allows us to provide the student with an accurate assistant. SIAL is able to interact with the user in different ways, depending on the skills already acquired. This feature influences the diagnosis provided by SIAL, since beginners will obtain a more precise error message than advanced users. The model-based approach chosen lets SIAL detect most of the user's errors accurately, inform the user about the error, and provide some hint to localize and fix the mistake.

References

1. Simón, A., Martínez, A., López, M., Maestro, J., Marqués, J., Alonso, C.: Learning Computational Logic with an Intelligent Tutoring System: SIAL. In: First International Congress on Tools for Teaching Logic, U. of Salamanca (2000) 161–168
2. Martínez, A., Simón, M., Maestro, J., López, M., Alonso, C.: Student Modelling and Interface Design in SIAL. In Intelligent Tutoring Systems. 5th International Conference, ITS 2000, Volume 1839 of LNCS., Springer (2000) 659
3. Chang, C.L., Lee, R.C.T.: Symbolic logic and mechanical theorem proving. Academic Press (1987)
4. Aranda, L., Torres, S., Trella, M., Conejo, R.: BabelWin: An environment for learning and monitoring reading and writing skills. In: Computers and Education in the 21st Century. Kluwer Academic Pub., The Netherlands (2000) 79–92
5. Vygotsky, L.: Mind in society: The development of higher psychological processes. Harvard University Press, Cambridge, MA (1978)
6. Dillenbourg, P., Self, J.: A framework for learner modelling. Interactive Learning Environments **2** (1992) 111–137
7. Ferrero, B., Fernandez-Castro, I., Urretavizcaya, M.: Multiple Paradigms for a Generic Diagnostic Proposal. In Intelligent Tutoring Systems. 5th International Conference, ITS 2000, Volume 1839 of LNCS., Springer (2000) 653
8. Price, C.: Computer-based diagnostic systems. Springer (1999)
9. Martin, B., Mitrovic, A.: Tailong Feedback by Correcting Students Answers. In Intelligent Tutoring Systems. 5th International Conference, ITS 2000, Volume 1839 of LNCS., Springer (2000) 383–392
10. Schreiber, G., Akkermans, H., Anjewierden, A., de Hoog, R., Shadbolt, N., Van de Velde, W., Wielinga, B.: Knowledge Engineering and Management, The CommonKADS Methodology. The MIT Press (1999)

A Reasoning Model for CBR_BDI Agents
Using an Adaptable Fuzzy Inference System

Rosalía Laza[1], Reyes Pavón[1], and Juan M. Corchado[2]

[1] Departamento de Informática
Universidad de Vigo
Campus As Lagoas, s/n, 32004, Ourense, Spain
{rlaza,pavon}@uvigo.es
[2] Departamento de Informática y Automática
Universidad de Salamanca
Plaza de la Merced s/n, 37008, Salamanca, Spain
corchado@usal.es

Abstract. This paper proposes to automate the generation of shellfish exploitation plans, which are elaborated by Galician extracting entities. For achieving this objective a CBR-BDI agent will be used. This agent will adapt the exploitation plans to the environmental characteristics of each school of shellfish. This kind of agents develops its activity into changing and dynamic environments, so the reasoning model that they include must be emphasised. The agent reasoning model is guided by the phases of the CBR life cycle, using different technologies for each phase. The use of an adaptative neuro-fuzzy inference system in the reuse phase must be highlighted.

1 Introduction

There are different types of agents and they can be classified in different ways [20]. One of these types are the so-called deliberative agents with a BDI architecture, which are characterized for having mental attitudes of Beliefs, Desires and Intentions; besides they have capacity to decide what to do and how to get their objectives according to their attitudes [20] [9] [14] [2].

Formalisation and implementation of BDI agents constitutes the field of research of many scientists [9] [14] [8] [16]. Some of them criticise the necessity of studying multi-modal logic for the formalisation and construction of such agents, because they have not been completely axiomatised and they are not computationally efficient. Rao and Georgeff [13] state that the problem lies in the wide distance between the powerful logic for BDI systems and practical systems. Another problem is that this type of agents is not able to learn, a necessary attitude for them since they must be constantly adding, modifying or eliminating beliefs, desires and intentions. Therefore it would be convenient to include a reasoning mechanism which involves a final apprenticeship.

The developed job shows how to build deliberative agents, using a case-based reasoning system (CBR), that solves the problems quoted previously. In the reasoning process of these agents, a GCS network (*Growing Cell Structures*) and an ANFIS model (*Adaptative Neuro-Fuzzy Inference Systems*) are utilized. The GCS network is used in the retrieve phase whereas the ANFIS model implements the phase of adaptation.

R. Conejo et al. (Eds.): CAEPIA-TTIA 2003, LNAI 3040, pp. 96–106, 2004.
© Springer-Verlag Berlin Heidelberg 2004

This paper is structured as follows. In section 2 the reasoning model of CBR-BDI agents is detailed. Section 3 proposes to automate the generation of shellfish exploitation plans, that are elaborated by Galician extracting entities; the results are also analysed in this section. Finally, in section 4 some conclusions are exposed.

2   Reasoning Model of CBR-BDI Agents

The relationship between CBR systems and BDI agents can be established implementing a case as a set of beliefs, together with an intention and a desire which caused the resolution of the problem. Using this relationship agents can be implemented (conceptual level) using CBR systems (implementation level). Then we are mapping agents into CBR systems. The advantage of this approach is that a problem can be easily conceptualised in terms of agents and then implemented in the form of a CBR system [3] [4] [5] [6]. Once the beliefs, desires and intentions of an agent are identified, the reasoning model can be established, in the way presented in this section.

The reasoning cycle of a typical CBR system includes four steps that are cyclically carried out in a sequenced way: retrieve, reuse, revise, and retain [1]. In the cases base, all experiences which can be used by a CBR-BDI agent are stored. Therefore, the first action which must be done is to find groups of similar cases, considering the values taken for the different variables.

In order to obtain such groups a GCS net is used. This kind of net is also used by other authors in the CBR retrieve phase[7]. The information provided by the net includes: a) how many groups are created, b) which cases take part in each group, c) which is the prototype case representing all the cases in the group and d) what is the distance between each case within the group and the prototype case.

For each identified set, a TSK rule is obtained [17]. These rules all together constitute the initial fuzzy inference system. The antecedent of each rule is a combination of variables which describe each case initial belief. They can be represented by a gauss function. In order to obtain the rule consequents, the least square method is used [11].

This initial fuzzy inference system will be used as previous knowledge in the ANFIS model, which will adjust the parameters of both antecedents and consequents, using the hybrid learning method explained in section 2.2. The refinement of these parameters is done using as input patterns the most similar cases retrieved in the previous phase. The result is a new fuzzy inference system, which will estimate the resolution of a new problem.

2.1 Retrieve Phase: GCS Network

The type of GCS used in this work is characterized by a two-dimensional space, where the units (cells) are connected and organised in triangles. Each cell in the network is associated with a weight vector, w, which has the same dimension as the input data. At the beginning of the learning process, the weight vector of each cell is initialised with random values. The basic learning process in a GCS network consists of topology modification and weight vector adaptations [10]. This vector is the prototype case of each cell of the network.

For each training case, the network performs a so-called *learning cycle*, which may result in topology modification and weight vector adaptation. In the first step of each learning cycle, the cell c, with the smallest distance between its weight vector, w_c, and the actual input vector, x, is chosen as the winner cell or best-match cell (see equation (1)).

$$c : \|x - w_c\| \leq \|x - w_i\| ; \forall i \in O \tag{1}$$

The second step consists of the adaptation of the weight vectors of the winning cell and their neighbouring cells; see equations (2) and (3). The terms ε_c and ε_n represent the learning rates for the winner and its neighbours respectively. Both learning rates are constant during learning, and $\varepsilon_c, \varepsilon_n \in [0, 1]$.

$$w_c(t+1) = w_c(t) + \varepsilon_c(x - w_c) \tag{2}$$

$$w_n(t+1) = w_n(t) + \varepsilon_n(x - w_n) ; \forall n \in N_c \tag{3}$$

In the third step of a learning cycle, each cell is assigned a *signal counter*, τ, that reflects how often a cell has been chosen as winner (see equations (4) and (5)).

$$\tau_c(t+1) = \tau_c(t) + 1 \tag{4}$$

$$\tau_i(t+1) = \tau_i(t) - \alpha\tau_i(t) ; i \neq c \tag{5}$$

The parameter α reflects a constant *rate of counter reduction* for the rest of the cells at the current learning cycle. Growing cell structures also modify the overall network structure by inserting new cells into those regions that represent large portions of the input data. The frequency of insertion update is controlled by the parameter λ, which is associated with the number of learning cycles between two cell insertions (see equations (6), (7) and (8)).

$$h_i = \tau_i \Big/ \sum_j \tau_j \quad ; \forall i, j \notin O \tag{6}$$

$$q : h_q \geq h_i ; \forall i \in O \tag{7}$$

$$r : \|w_r - w_q\| \geq \|w_p - w_q\| ; \forall p \in N_q \tag{8}$$

The GCS network indicates the prototype case of each node, its topology and calculates the scale parameters σ_j of each node [7]. This parameter measures the width in the gauss membership function. It can be seen in the Figure 1. Higher values of σ provide an area more extended of the node dominates in the environment of the centroide.

To calculate the node j, the prototype cases of its neighbour nodes are selected; then the average of the square-distance between them is calculated [18][19], that is:

$$\sigma_{jk}^2 = \frac{1}{N} \sum_{l=1}^{N} \|c_l - c_j\|^2 = \frac{1}{N} \sum_{l=1}^{N} (c_{lk} - c_{jk})^2 \tag{9}$$

where K is particular variable in cases.

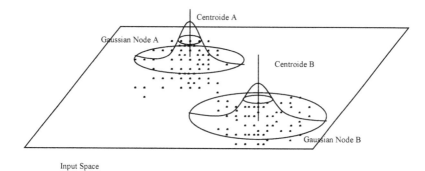

Input Space

Fig. 1. The point mean cases in the input environment.

This information is utilized for making the initial fuzzy inference system, which is utilized by the ANFIS model. This fuzzy inference system has a set of TSK rules; each node provides a fuzzy rule. The rules have the form:

$$R_j : if \ x_1 \ is \ A_{1j} \ and \ x_2 \ is \ A_{2j} \ and ... and \ x_M \ is \ A_{Mj}, then \ y \ = g_j(x_1, x_2, ..., x_M) \quad (10)$$

where $g_j(\cdot)$ is a polynomic function in x_j.

Each attribute is represented by a gauss function (equation (11)), which takes part of the antecedent of the rule.

$$A_{ij}(x_i) = \exp\left(-\frac{(c_k - x_i)^2}{2\sigma_k^2}\right) \quad (11)$$

where c is a prototype case and σ the distance.

The next step consists of obtaining the consequents of each TSK rule. The method utilized is least-square [11]. This initial fuzzy inference system is adapted with the ANFIS model.

In this phase the most similar cases to the new problem are retrieved. The problem is determined by a set of variables with particular values, which are used as inputs of the GCS net. Next, the searching for the node to which the new problem belongs is started, that is, the winner node must be found. This node is obtained by calculating the Euclidean distance between the new problem and every prototype case of each case. The node with the fewer distance will be the winner. All the cases associated to the winner node will be considered the most similar ones, and will be utilised in the following phase.

2.2 Reuse Phase: ANFIS Model

One of the first hybrid neuro-fuzzy systems for function approximation was Jang's ANFIS model [11]. ANFIS adjusts only the membership functions of the antecedent and the consequent parameters.

Because ANFIS uses only differentiable functions, it is easy to apply standard learning procedures from neural network theory. For ANFIS a mixture of backpropagation (gradient descent) and least squares estimation (LSE) is used. Backpropagation is used to learn the antecedent parameters, i.e. the membership functions, and LSE is used to determine the coefficients of the linear combinations in the rule's consequents.

A step in the learning procedure has two parts, which are shown in Table 1. In the first part the input patterns are propagated, and the optimal consequent parameters are estimated by an iterative least mean squares procedure, while the antecedent parameters are assumed to be fixed for the current cycle through the training set. In the second part the patterns are propagated again, and in this, epoch backpropagation is used to modify the antecedent parameters, while the consequent parameters remain fixed.

Table 1. Two passes in the hybrid learning procedure for ANFIS.

	Forward pass	**Backward pass**
Antecedent parameters	Fixed	Gradient descent
Consequent parameters	Least-square estimator	Fixed
Signals	Node outputs	Error signals

In this phase, the cases retrieved in the previous one are used, that is, the inference system provided by the GCS net. While the result is a fuzzy inference system adapted for solving a particular problem. With this system a result, which will be converted in the desire the CBR-BDI must achieve, is obtained.

Therefore, the next step the CBR-BDI agent must accomplish will be the planing of what actions to do to achieve this desire. The actions carried out for in the retrieved cases are obtained and the following process is done. An acyclical and directed structure whose first vertex is the new problem and the last one is the desire to achieve is created. The construction of this structure is done taking each one of the actions made in the retrieved cases and adapting their parameter values. Once the structure is built, Dijkstra algorithm [15] is used to determine the shortest path, taking as origin the new problem. The path determines the actions which must be done and a new intention is built. This intention reflects the solution to the posed problem.

Summarising, in this phase a sequence of actions starting from a new problem and the result which must be achieved, is proposed; that is, a new case.

2.3 Revision and Retain Phases

In this phase the solution obtained in the previous phase is evaluated. The revision can be carried out using Expert's Knowledge (rules) or simulation techniques [5], fuzzy inference system [7] or Belief-Revision techniques [12].

The new case (a problem, a solution and a result) is stored in the cases base. In this phase the produced error between estimated and real result is calculated. If the error is higher than a limit β the GCS network is rebuilt, because this means that a new input space which has not been considered before is being visited. Therefore the network must modify its topology and adapt the weights vector, even using the new stored cases.

3 Study Case: Shellfish Exploitation Plans Automation

In Galicia, there are a deep interest in ordering the fishing sector. Due to that, a set of rules for organising the marine resources exploitation were developed. According to those rules, the galician government is in charge of controlling and regulating both the extracting activity of marine resources in Galicia seashore and their commercial transactions which take place in the specific locations devoted to that aim.

In order to practice the extraction of marine resources it is necessary to present to the administration some documents named *shellfish exploitation plans*, which are elaborated for entities interested in exploiting Galician marine resources. Each extracting entity must prepare an exploitation plan for every resource it wants to obtain. The aim of these plans is to achieve the greatest continuous economical profit from marine resources by means of an appropriate planning for the extracting activity.

In Table 2, sections and topics included in an exploitation plan are shown.

Table 2. Exploitation plan summary.

General data	Goals	Evaluation	Pursuit
Shellfish men´s number	Production	Methods	Daily effort
Boats number	Economical	Conclusions	Daily production
Exploitation areas			

Extraction plan	Improvement actions	Financial plan
Probable schedule	Description	Incomes
Dates	Costs	Expenses
Limit (Kg/day)		Investment
Fishing traps		Capitalization
Points of control		
Selling ways		
Surveillance		

The shellfish exploitation plan presented by a extracting entity has values for a complete year and must be approved by the Fishing Authority. Since the moment of its approbation, the shellfish exploitation plan will regulate along the year the capture of the resources that it contains.

Notice that plans elaborated by the extracting entities incorporate general data, like shellfish men's number, selling ways, etc, but they also must include forecast about productive and economical goals, which have to be based on characteristics of extracting entities, environment and conditions of shellfish ecosystems.

Since the information managed by these plans is extensive enough, an automated system that gets, stores and analyses data about marine resources becomes essential. Appropriate tools for collecting data allow the acquisition of useful knowledge for managing marine resources by means of rational criteria. These tools provide help not only to entities in charge of exploitation, assisting them in the process of elaborating new plans, but also to administration, designing better fisheries policies that prevent overexploitation generated by an excessive fishing effort.

Nevertheless, the interest of the current shellfish management system goes beyond a simple statistical study, and pretends to adapt the exploitation plans to the characteristics of each school of shellfish and the necessities of Shellfish men. In this way, each year different management models can be applied and different technical solutions can be proposed in order to help in decisions making.

To obtain this objective, a CBR-BDI agent, like the one described in this work will be used. This agent will generate automatically the shellfish exploitation plan, allowing a reasonable and sustainable exploitation which is a desirable objective in all shellfish sector.

Next, an example of the application of a CBR-BDI agent for automatically generate shellfish exploitation plans for all Galician extracting entities devoted to clam is presented. All the information available in the shellfish exploitation plans belonging this resource and pertaining to previous years is used. This will allow to adjust the productive and economical goals. All the same, as a way of simplifying the example, only an estimation of productive goals (resource kilograms) will be done. If the rest of data were to be obtained, the same process must be followed.

In first place, it is necessary to define the CBR-BDI agent in the terms of the 4-tupla {E,CB,GAL,EK}, where E are the variables which describe the environment, CB is the case base (in terms of beliefs, desires and intentions), GAL is the general actions library and EK identifies the expert's knowledge [4].

The variables which describe the example environment are the typical ones for extracting entities (number of working days, number of shellfish men x number of days), for schools of shellfish like: environmental data (temperature, salty degree in water, PH, oxygen rate, transmittance and fluorescence), the size of the different school of shellfish (area and perimeter) and limits of allowed captures, besides the variable that must be forecast in the exploitation plan. This study is centred in the estimation of the number of marine resource kilograms that are to be recollected.

For building up the CBR-BDI system, a tool, called GABDI (abbreviation in Spanish of *BDI agents Generator*), is available. This tool facilitates the addition of information to the cases base.

In order to define the variables which define the environment, GABDI tool provides a form where the name and the rank of values the variable may take, can be introduced. Next step is to describe the actions which can be made over environment. Table 3 shows the actions which can be done to improve the recollection of a particular marine resource.

Table 3. Actions which can be done to improve the production of a marine resource.

Action nave	Input parameters	Output parameters
Transport	Oxygen	Oxygen, Kilograms
Move	Kilograms	Kilograms
Plantation	Kilograms	Kilograms
Seaweed removal	Oxygen	Oxygen, Kilograms
Plough	Area, Perimeter	Area, Perimeter, Kilograms

Next, the fulfilled intentions must be defined; that is, the actions done previously to solve old problems. Once identified the environmental variables, the actions which can be done and the actions done in the past, it is necessary to create the cases base. In order to achieve this objective, the states (beliefs) and the plan of done actions (intentions) must be indicated.

Now, in the cases base is stored all information available for the agent, so it can apply its reasoning model using the techniques described in section 2. The information managed by the CBR-BDI agent is saved in *csv* format.

3.1 Results Obtained

The correct functioning of the model has been proved experimentally, by means of a set of proofs. First proofs were made over 6554 stored cases, particularly, the ones representing the captures of the years 2000 and 2001 of clam. The forecasting was done over 192 situations belonging to year 2002.

The results corresponding to two systems were compared. One system is the initial fuzzy inference system obtained by GCS network (from here on GCS) and the other, the system proposed by the present work (from here on CBR-BDI agent). It must be highlighted that 82,8% of the times, the forecast of the CBR-BDI agent is better than the one provided by GCS system.

In first place, it has been proved if the samples that must be analysed follow a normal distribution. The proofs of normality applied were Z skewness and Z kurtosis. Since the result from these tests was negative, that is, they do not obey the normality hypothesis, a set of non parametrical proofs were applied. These proofs try to determine if a system is better than other analysing the data globally. The statistical techniques used in this latest case were the Sign Test and the rank sum of Wilcoxon for coincident pairs.

The Sign Test is designed specifically for proving hypothesis referents to median of a continuous population. Like the mean, the median is a measure of the centre or distribution position, because of that the Sign Test is also known as proof of position.

Since in the retrieve phase the GCS system provide a initial fuzzy inference system, it can be used to make the forecasting without the necessity of adapting its parameters by means of the ANFIS model. In order to prove that better results are obtained if the parameters are adapted, the two systems were compared: the provided by GCS and the CBR-BDI agent.

Table 4 shows the results after the application of The Sign Test over the two systems previously introduced. Results indicate that the error using the GCS system is bigger than the produced by CBR-BDI agent, with a confidence level of about 95%. Since p value is very small, it can be assured that in the case of the two extremes proof the null hypothesis is also rejected.

Table 4. The Sign Test between the initial fuzzy inference system and the CBR-BDI agent.

Test	Sign Test		
Alternative Hypothesis	GCS Error >= Agent Error		
Difference between pairs	N		
Positive	183		
Negative	9		
Zero	0		
Median difference	3088,466		
95.8% CI	2387,762	to +∞	(exact)
Sign Statistics	183		
1-extremo p	<0.0001	(exact)	

From the results obtained with the statistical sign test, it can be concluded that the CBR-BDI agent provides better results than the other two systems.

A powerful non parameter technique must compare the whole probability distributions not only the median. This test, which is called the rank sum of Wilcoxon, proofs the null hypothesis, that is, the probability distributions associated to the two populations are equivalent against the alternative hypothesis the probability distribution of a population is moved right (or left) with respect to the other.

In Table 5, the results of the rank sum of Wilcoxon test for two populations, as well as the error produced by GCS system and for the CBR-BDI system, are shown.

Table 5. Rank sum of Wilcoxon among GCS system and CBR-BDI agent.

Test Alternative Hypothesis	Rank sum of Wilcoxon test for coincident pairs GCS Error >= Agent Error		
Pairs difference	n	Rank sum	Rank median
Positive	183	18377,0	100,42
Negative	9	151,0	16,78
Zero	0		
Median difference	7285,193		
95.0% CI	5267,973	to +∞	(normal aproximation)
Wilcoxon's statistic	18377		
1-extreme p	<0.0001	(normal aproximation)	

Before doing the tests showed in Table 5, it was made the rank sum of Wilcoxon test for coincident pairs in the two extremes, in which the null hypothesis was rejected. In order to further refine this proof, it was analysed as alternative hypothesis, that the GCS system error were bigger or equal to CBR-BDI agent error, rejecting also the null hypothesis. The final conclusion was that population number 1 is moved to right of population number 2.

The rank sum of Wilcoxon test for coincident pairs reinforces the results obtained, in the sense that the CBR-BDI system provides better results than the other system. So that, it can be concluded that it is necessary to adapt the initial fuzzy inference system obtained by GCS network and that the ANFIS model is the best one to be utilised for that objective.

4   Conclusions

This job is part of the objectives of the action of research "Ampliación de sistemas de información geográfica orientado a la gestión de los recursos específicos a los demás recursos marisqueros de Galicia" approved by Xunta of Galicia with code: PGIDTCIMA 02/3. This research is carried out between CIMA (*Centro de Investigacións Mariñas*), University of Coruña and University of Vigo.

In this paper, it is showed how a CBR-BDI agent is able to learn and to give solutions to a particular problem. It utilizes a fuzzy inference system, which is adapted to the problem to solve.

The acceptance of this CBR-BDI agent, by the extracting entities, has been excellent. At this moment, it is being tested in different extracting entities. The satisfaction exhibited by the entities devoted to extract marine resources allows to foresee that the system will be completely implanted next year.

At present the elaboration of the shellfish exploitation plans is manual, slow and little reliable. In this action of research it is proposed a simple input data, besides the automatic preparation of the plans with that data.

As a final conclusion, it can be said that the model described in this research paper is capable of adding the partial knowledge provided by each incorporated technology, creating a global knowledge system, based on the case base reasoning method.

Acknowledgements

This research is supported by the Spanish national project TIC2002-04516-C03-01.

References

1. Aamodt A. y Plaza E.: Case-Based Reasoning: foundational Issues, Methodological Variations, and System Approaches, AICOM. Vol. 7. No 1, March. (1994)
2. Bratman M.E., Israel D., y Pollack M.E.: Plans and resource-bounded practical reasoning. Computational Intelligence 1988, 4. pages 349-355. (1988)
3. Corchado J. M., Laza R., Borrajo L., Yañez J. C. y Valiño M.: Increasing the Autonomy of Deliberative Agents with a Case-Based Reasoning System. International Journal of Computational Intelligence and Applications. ISSN: 1469-0268. (2003)
4. Corchado J.M. y Laza R.: Construction of BDI Agents from CBR systems. 1st German Workshop on Experience Management. Lecture Notes in Informatics Berlin, 7-8 Marzo. (2002)
5. Corchado J.M., Aiken J. y Rees N.: Artificial Intelligence Models for Oceanographic Forecasting. Plymouth Marine Laboratory. ISBN-0-9519618-4-5. (2000)
6. Corchado J.M., Laza R., Borrajo L., Yánez J.C., de Luis A. y Glez-Bedia M.: Agent-based Web Engineering. ICWE 2003, Third International Conference on Web Engineering, Oviedo, Asturias, Spain. July 14 -18, (2003)
7. Fdez-Riverola F, Corchado J. M. y Torres J.: An Automated Hybrid CBR System for Forecasting. Advances in Case-Based Reasoning. Craw S. and Preece A. (eds.), Springer. ISBN: 3-540-44109-3. (2002)
8. Georgeff M.P. y Lansky A.L.: Procedural knowledge. In Proceedings of the IEEE Special Issue on Knowledge 1986. Representation, volume 74. pages 1383-1398. (1986)
9. Jennings N.R.: On Being Responsible. In Y. Demazeau and E. Werner, editors, Decentralized A.I. 3. North Holland, Amsterdam, The Netherlands (1992)
10. Köhle, M., y Merkl, D.: Visualizing similarities in high dimensional input spaces with a growing and splitting neural network. En Proceedings of International Conference of Artificial Neural Networks, ICANN-96, (pp. 581-586), Bochum, Germany. (1996)
11. Nauck D., Klawonn F. y Kruse R.: Foundations of neuro-fuzzy systems. Publicación Chichester: John Wiley & sons, cop. 1997
12. Pavón R., Laza R., Gómez A. y Corchado J.M.: Automating the Revision phase of a Case-Based Reasoning system using Belief Revision. Soft Computing and Intelligent Systems for Industry. ICSC-NAISO Academic Press. Paisley, Scotland, United Kingdom. (2001)
13. Rao A.S. y Georgeff M.P.: BDI Agents: From Theory to Practice. First International Conference on Multi-Agent Systems (ICMAS-95). San Franciso, USA, June (1995)
14. Rao A.S. y Georgeff M.P.: Modeling rational agents within a BDI-architecture. In J. Allen, R. Fikes, and E. Sandewall, editors, Proceedings of the Second International Conference on Principles of Knowledge Representation and Reasoning. Morgan Kaufmann Publishers, San Mateo, CA. (1991)

15. Schulz F., Wagner D. y Weihe K.: Dijkstra´s Algorithm On-line: An Empirical Case Study from Public Railroad Transport. Algorithm Engineering. pages 110-123. (1999)
16. Shoham Y.: Agent-Oriented programming. Artificial Intelligence. 1993, 60(1): pages 51-92. (1993)
17. Takagi, T., y Sugeno, M.: Fuzzy identification of systems and its applications to modeling and control. IEEE Transactions on Systems, Man and Cybernetics, 15:116-132. (1985)
18. Warwick, K.: An overview of neural networks in control applications. Neural Networks for Robotic Control, M. Zalzala, Prentice-Hall. (1995)
19. Wasserman, P. D.: Advanced Methods in Neural Computing. Van Nostrand Reinhold. (1993)
20. Wooldridge M.: Intelligent Agents. Multiagent Systems. A modern approach to Distributed Artificial Inteligence. Edited by Gerhard Weiss, 1999. Pages 27-77. (1999)s

A Recurrent Neural Network for Airport Scales Location

Enrique Domínguez Merino and José Muñoz Pérez

Department of Computer Science, University of Malaga
Campus Teatinos s/n, 29071, Málaga
{enriqued,munozp}@lcc.uma.es

Abstract. The p-hub problem is a facility location problem that can be viewed as a type of airline network design problem. Given a finite set of nodes, each node (city) sends and receives some type of traffic (airline passengers) to and from other nodes (cities). The hub (airport) locations must be chosen from among these nodes to act as switching points. In this paper we consider the uncapacitated p-hub median problem with single allocation, where each non-hub node (origin and destination) must be allocated to exactly one of the p hubs. We provide a reduced size formulation and a competitive recurrent neural model for this problem. The architecture of the proposed neural network consists of two layers (allocation layer and location layer) of np binary neurons, where n is the number of nodes and p is the number of hubs. The effectiveness and efficiency of the proposed recurrent neural network under varying problem sizes are analyzed. Computational experience with another neural networks and heuristics is provided using data given in the literature.

1 Introduction

Hub location research has become an important area of location theory over the last two decades. This is due in part to the use of hub networks in modern transportation systems as network airlines design. These systems attend demand for travels between many origins and many destinations, where economies of scale exist in the cost for such travels. Rather than serving every origin-destination demand with a direct link, a hub network provides service via smaller set of links between origins/destinations and hubs, and between pairs of hubs. Such a network allows a large set of origins and destinations to be connected with relatively few links, via central hub facilities. The use of few links in the network concentrates flows and allows economies of scale to be exploited. Hub location problems involve locating hub facilities and designing hub network.

The location of hub facilities is an important issue arising in the design of airline passenger flow. Passengers generally have to travel longer distance and a longer time because non-stop services is reduced. However, the airline companies usually offer more frequent flight services because of fewer operating routes. A good airline network design is beneficial not only for the airline companies but also for many passengers; consequently, many airline companies are interested in locating their own hub airports.

Hub location problems may be classified by the way in which the demand points are assigned, or allocated, to hubs. One possibility is single allocation, in which each demand point is allocated to a single hub, i.e. each demand point can send and receive

R. Conejo et al. (Eds.): CAEPIA-TTIA 2003, LNAI 3040, pp. 107–115, 2004.

via only a single hub. A second possibility is multiple allocation, in which a demand point may send and receive via more than one hub.

The problem addressed in this paper models the situation where there are n cities (nodes), and p of these cities will be designed as hub airports. Each node in the network can interact with each other only via the hubs to which they have been allocated, and has to be connected to exactly one of the p hubs. More specifically, the problem studied in this paper is the uncapacitated, single allocation, p-hub median problem (which will be referred to as USAPHMP).

A quadratic integer programming formulation for this problem was proposed by O'Kelly [7]. Since O'Kelly original formulation, several researchers have used various heuristics to solve this problem. O'Kelly considered the use of two heuristics for solving an uncapacitated p-hub median problem which models flights paths of an airline company, and attempts to assign each airport to a fixed hub. Thus, the problem was reduced from location-allocation problem to an allocation problem alone. Klincewicz [6] examined ways of avoiding convergence of such heuristics to sub-optimal local minima by using tabu search and GRASP strategies, although the problem being considered was still the simplified problem of allocating nodes to a fixed hubs using a minimum distance rule. Skorin-Kapov and Skorin-Kapov [9] considered the use of tabu search for solving the complete location-allocation problem. Aykin [1] devised various others heuristics, Ernst and Krishnamoorthy [5] applied a simulated annealing heuristic and Smith, Krishnamoorthy and Palaniswami [8] considered a modified Hopfield network to solve the uncapacitated, single allocation, p-hub problem.

In this paper we proposed a recurrent neural model for solving this problem that we applied usefully to related problem like the p-median problem [3] . We provide a reduced size formulation and a competitive recurrent neural model for this problem. The architecture of the proposed neural network consists of two layers (allocation layer and location layer) of np binary neurons, where n is the number of nodes and p is the number of hubs. The process units (neurons) are grouped in assembles, where one neuron per assembly is active at the same time and neurons of same assembly are updated in parallel. The computational dynamics for the network has been defined and its convergence has been proved. Moreover, the energy function (objective function) always decreases as the system evolves according to the dynamical rule proposed. The advantage of the recurrent neural networks over more traditional techniques lies in their potential for rapid computational power when implemented in electronic hardware, and the inherent parallelism of the neural network. Of course, the proposed recurrent neural network has been simulated on a digital computer, and is therefore subjected to some limitations. Certainly, satisfactory hardware implementation is still subject of much research, and many design challenges lie ahead in this field. Yet there is little doubt that it is only a matter of time before VLSI implementations of large scale neural networks are possible. The effectiveness and efficiency of the proposed recurrent neural network under varying problem sizes are analyzed. Computational experience with another neural networks and heuristics is provided using data given in the literature.

The paper is organized as follows. In section 2 we review the problem formulations and we propose a new reduced size formulation. Section 3 presents the proposed competitive recurrent neural model. Section 4 describes the proposed neural network algorithm. Illustrative simulations and computational results using the well known 1970 Civil Aeronautics Board (CAB) data set are compared with others heuristics and reported in section 5. Finally, section 6 provides a summary and conclusions.

2 Problem Formulation

The hub location problem can be described as follows: given the location of a set of n nodes or cities, the volume of flow (w_{ij}) that must be shipped between each origin-destination pair and the cost per unit flow (c_{ij}) between each origin-destination pair. Then, we have to select p nodes from the set of them to be hubs. Hubs are airports or switching points for flow and they are fully connected. All flow travels via hubs and each non-hub node must be allocated to a unique hub node. The location of the hubs or airports and the allocation of the nodes or cities are chosen so that the total cost of the system is minimized. It should be noted that all flow that must be shipped between cities, have three separate components: collection (origin city to hub airport), transfer (hub airport to hub airport) and distribution (hub airport to destination city).

O'Kelly [7] gave the first formulation of USApHMP as a quadratic integer program. This formulation has n^2 variables, even so this problem is difficult to solve due to the non-convexity of the objective function. Subsequently a mixed integer linear program with $n^4 + n^2$ variables was developed by Campbell [2] to obviate the non-convexity of the objective function. Ernst and Krishamoorthy [5] developed a reduced mixed integer linear program using $n^3 + n^2$, and recently, Ebery [4] presented a formulation with $2n^2$ variables. In this paper, we proposed a new reduced formulation for the USApHMP using $2np$ variables. The proposed formulation is defined as follow

Minimize

$$\sum_{i=1}^{n}\sum_{j=1}^{n}\sum_{q=1}^{p}\sum_{k=1}^{n}\left[\beta w_{ik}c_{ij} + \gamma w_{ki}c_{ji} + \alpha \sum_{m=1}^{n}\sum_{r=1}^{p}w_{ik}c_{jm}x_{kr}y_{mr}\right]x_{iq}y_{jq} \tag{1}$$

Subject to

$$\sum_{q=1}^{p}x_{iq} = 1 \quad i = 1,2,...n \tag{2}$$

$$\sum_{j=1}^{n}y_{jq} = 1 \quad q = 1,2,...p \tag{3}$$

where

$$x_{iq} = \begin{cases} 1 & \text{if the node } i \text{ is allocated to cluster } q \\ 0 & \text{otherwise} \end{cases}$$

$$y_{jq} = \begin{cases} 1 & \text{if the node } j \text{ is the hub of cluster } q \\ 0 & \text{otherwise} \end{cases}$$

w_{ij} is the amount of flow from the node i to the node j

c_{ij} is the transportation cost associated between the nodes i and j

$\alpha \in [0,1]$ is the transfer coefficient

$\beta \in [0,1]$ is the collection coefficient

$\gamma \in [0,1]$ is the distribution coefficient

In the objective function (1), first and second terms are the cost of assigning a node to its hub for outgoing and incoming flows respectively. These terms are multiplied by two coefficients respectively: β (collection coefficient) and γ (distribution coefficient). The third component counts the costs of those interactions, which must flow between hubs. These inter-hub costs are multiplied by a parameter α to reflect the scale effects in interfacility flows. Constraint (2) ensures that each node is allocated to a unique cluster and restriction (3) ensures that one and only one hub is opened in each cluster. Note that this formulation is very simple.

3 Competitive Recurrent Neural Network Model

The proposed neural network consists of two layers (allocation layer and location layer) of interconnected binary neurons or processing elements. Each neuron i has an activation potential h_i and an output $S_i \in \{0,1\}$. In order to design a suitable neural network for this problem, the key step is to construct an appropriate energy function E for which the global minimum is simultaneously a solution of the above formulation. The simplest approach to constructing a desired energy function is the penalty function method. The basic idea in this approach is to transform the constrained problem into an unconstrained one by adding penalty function terms to the objective function (1). These terms cause a high cost if any constraint is violated. More precisely, increasing the objective function by a quantity, which depends on the amount by which the constraints are violated, eliminates some or all constraints. That is, the energy function of the neural network is given by the Liapunov energy function defined as

$$E = \sum_{i=1}^{n}\sum_{j=1}^{n}\sum_{q=1}^{p}\sum_{k=1}^{n}\left[\beta w_{ik}c_{ij} + \gamma w_{ki}c_{ji} + \alpha\sum_{m=1}^{n}\sum_{r=1}^{p}w_{ik}c_{jm}x_{kr}y_{mr}\right]x_{iq}y_{jq} +$$

$$+ \lambda_1\sum_{i=1}^{n}\left(1 - \sum_{q=1}^{p}x_{iq}\right)^2 + \lambda_2\sum_{q=1}^{p}\left(1 - \sum_{j=1}^{n}y_{jq}\right)^2 \tag{4}$$

where $\lambda_i > 0$ are penalty parameters that they determine the relative weight of the constraints. The penalty parameters tuning is an important problem associated with this approach.

In order to guarantee a valid solution and avoid the parameter tuning problem, we split our neural network in disjoint groups or assemblies according to the two restrictions, that is, for the p-median problem with n points, we will have n groups or assemblies, according to restriction (2), plus p groups or assemblies, according to restriction (3). Then, we will reorganize our neurons in two matrices (one matrix per neuron type) where a group is represented by a row or column of the matrix according to neuron type.

$$
\begin{array}{cccccc}
x_{11} & x_{12} & \cdots & x_{1p} & \rightarrow & \text{group 1} \\
x_{21} & x_{22} & \cdots & x_{2p} & \rightarrow & \text{group 2} \\
\vdots & \vdots & \ddots & \vdots & & \vdots \\
x_{n1} & x_{n2} & \cdots & x_{np} & \rightarrow & \text{group n}
\end{array}
$$

$$
\begin{array}{cccc}
y_{11} & y_{12} & \cdots & y_{1p} \\
y_{21} & y_{22} & \cdots & y_{2p} \\
\vdots & \vdots & \ddots & \vdots \\
y_{n1} & y_{n2} & \cdots & y_{np} \\
\downarrow & \downarrow & & \downarrow
\end{array}
$$

group n +1   group n + 2   group n + p

Fig. 1. Neuron organization for the USApHMP.

Fig. 1 shows two matrices, the first matrix contains the allocation neurons and the second contains the location neurons. The allocation neurons inside same group are in the same row of the matrix, and the location neurons inside same group are in the same column.

In this model one and only one neuron per group must have one as its outputs, so the penalty terms are eliminated from the objective function. The neurons inside same group are updated in parallel. Then we should ought introduce the notion of group update. Observe that the groups are updated sequentially. Then, the energy function of the neural network is reduced to

$$
E = \sum_{i=1}^{n}\sum_{j=1}^{n}\sum_{q=1}^{p}\sum_{k=1}^{n}\left[\beta w_{ik}c_{ij} + \gamma w_{ki}c_{ji} + \alpha\sum_{m=1}^{n}\sum_{r=1}^{p} w_{ik}c_{jm}x_{kr}y_{mr} \right] x_{iq}y_{jq} \tag{5}
$$

We avoid the parameter tuning problem for λ_1 and λ_2 in the eq. (4) with the new model due to the energy function of the new model (5) do not have penalty terms.

The activation potential of each neuron of the network are

$$
h_{x_{iq}} = -\sum_{j=1}^{n}\sum_{k=1}^{n}\left[\beta w_{ik}c_{ij} + \gamma w_{ki}c_{ji} + \alpha\sum_{m=1}^{n}\sum_{r=1}^{p} w_{ik}c_{jm}x_{kr}y_{mr} \right] y_{jq} \tag{6}
$$

$$
h_{y_{jq}} = -\sum_{i=1}^{n}\sum_{k=1}^{n}\left[\beta w_{ik}c_{ij} + \gamma w_{ki}c_{ji} + \alpha\sum_{m=1}^{n}\sum_{r=1}^{p} w_{ik}c_{jm}x_{kr}y_{mr} \right] x_{iq} \tag{7}
$$

where $h_{x_{iq}}$ is the activation potential of allocation neuron iq and $h_{y_{jq}}$ is the activation potential of the location neuron jq.

The central property of the proposed network is that the computational energy function always decrease (or remains constant) as the system evolve according to its dynamical rule

$$x_{iq}(k+1) = \begin{cases} 1 & \text{if } h_{x_{iq}}(k) = \max_{1 \le r \le P}\{h_{x_{ir}}(k)\} \\ 0 & \text{otherwise} \end{cases} \tag{8}$$

$$y_{jq}(k+1) = \begin{cases} 1 & \text{if } h_{y_{jq}}(k) = \max_{1 \le i \le N}\{h_{y_{iq}}(k)\} \\ 0 & \text{otherwise} \end{cases} \tag{9}$$

Note that we introduce the group-update concept or assembly-update concept, that is, all neurons of the same group or assembly are updated at the same time.

4 Neural Network Algorithm

The following procedure describes the proposed neural network algorithm (NNA):

1. Set the initial state by randomly setting the output of one neuron in each of $n+p$ groups to be one and all the others neurons in the group to be zero.
2. Select a group g where $1 \le g \le n+p$
3. Compute the inputs of the neurons in the group g by expression (6) when $1 \le g \le n$ or by expression (7) otherwise.
4. Update neurons by expression (8) when $1 \le g \le n$ or update neurons by expression (9) if $n+1 \le g \le n+p$
5. Repeat from step 2 until no more changes.

Clearly, this procedure is very similar to the dynamics of a recurrent neural network. The network updates itself in a systematic way while neurons are forced to assume a feasible solution. The feasibility is guaranteed, since every network configuration is forced to be a feasible solution. Thus, the algorithm can be seen as an efficient and convenient simulation approach to solve the proposed problem. Furthermore, the network is still implemented able in hardware, making the potential for rapid execution speed a further advantage.

5 Simulation Results

The data for this study are based on the well known CAB (Civil Aeronautics Board) data sets from the literature. Problems of size $n=10$ and 15 are extracted from this data set, while further problems are generated by varying the number of hubs $p \in \{2,3,4\}$ and the transfer cost $\alpha \in \{0.2,0.4,0.6,0.8,1\}$. The values of the collection and distribution coefficients are fixed at $\beta = \gamma = 1$. Exact results are again provided using the linear programming approach of Ernst and Krishnamoorthy [5]. The results are compared to the Hopfield network (HN) and the modified hill-climbing Hopfield network (HCHN) provided by Smith et al. [8]. All algorithms run on an Origin 2000 (Silicon Graphics Inc.) multiprocessor operated under IRIX 6.5 with 16 CPUs MIPS R1000.

Table 1. List airport names of CAB database.

Atlanta	Miami
Baltimore	Minneapolis
Boston	New Orleans
Chicago	New York
Cincinnati	Philadelphia
Cleveland	Phoenix
Dallas-Fort Worth	Pittsburgh
Denver	St. Louis
Detroit	San Francisco
Houston	Seattle
Kansas City	Tampa
Los Angeles	Washington DC
Memphis	

The results presented in Table 2 demonstrate quite clearly that the proposed NNA is able to compete effectively with the Hopfield neural networks approaches proposed by Smith et al. [8] in finding optimal or near-optimal solutions to the CAB data sets. The HN often converges to a poor quality solution, since it becomes caught in the first local minima it encounters. The HCHN considerably improves the quality of solutions with optimal solutions being located in 73% of the CAB problem instances. It is important to remember that the neural network results presented in Table 2 are simulations only, and are used to provide an indication of the quality of solutions, which could be expected from a hardware implementation of the networks. However, the amount of CPU time required to simulate the proposed NNA is the main advantage with respect the Hopfield network approaches. Thus, the CPU time for the HN and HCHN simulations are several orders of magnitude greater than those for the NNA. Moreover, the memory requirements for these simulations (HN and HCHN) also make it difficult to obtain solutions for problems greater than n=20. Although, this problem is not encountered in a hardware implementation, where an increase in problem size translates only to an increase in the number of amplifiers and resistors.

6   Conclusions

In this paper we have proposed a competitive recurrent neural network for airlines network design. We have considered the uncapacitated single allocation p-hub problem. It is important to consider the model because it is the most appropriate model in certain situations. We have proposed a new formulation that reduce the number of variables and constraints of the formulations provided by several authors [2,5,7]. As another neural solution approach, we proposed a competitive recurrent neural model. Although the networks results have been simulated on a digital computer, the proposed competitive neural network require a less amount of computational resource than the Hopfield networks approaches proposed by Smith et al. Moreover, the CPU time for the Hopfield networks simulations are several orders of magnitude greater than those for the proposed NNA.

Table 2. Results of CAB data sets for NNA, HN and HCHN.

n	p	α	Average Error (%)		
			NNA	HN	HCHN
		0.2	0.08	0.00	0.00
		0.4	0.05	0.00	0.00
	2	0.6	0.03	0.00	0.00
		0.8	0.02	0.00	0.00
		1	0.02	6.60	1.60
		0.2	0.13	18.80	0.00
		0.4	0.08	15.90	0.00
10	3	0.6	0.08	1.70	0.00
		0.8	0.07	0.00	0.00
		1	0.05	1.00	0.40
		0.2	0.24	0.00	0.00
		0.4	0.10	1.10	0.00
	4	0.6	0.10	4.80	0.00
		0.8	0.09	6.90	0.40
		1	0.08	0.70	0.40
		0.2	0.16	0.00	0.00
		0.4	0.14	0.00	0.00
	2	0.6	0.09	0.00	0.00
		0.8	0.08	3.00	0.20
		1	0.07	7.20	0.50
		0.2	0.09	0.20	0.00
		0.4	0.08	2.10	0.00
15	3	0.6	0.16	0.60	0.00
		0.8	0.12	3.50	0.00
		1	0.13	1.40	1.00
		0.2	0.11	0.00	0.00
		0.4	0.11	4.60	0.00
	4	0.6	0.14	2.80	0.00
		0.8	0.15	1.90	0.00
		1	0.18	3.70	1.20

In the computational experience, we have shown that the proposed neural model worked well, only 0.1% average error for the CAB data sets, and found optimal or near-optimal solutions quickly. Therefore, the proposed recurrent neural network might be used for large problems. While other heuristics are quite fast, neural networks have the potential to solve large size problems even faster by employing the parallel and hardware implementation for which they were design.

References

1. T. Aykin (1995), "The hub location and routing problem", *European Journal of Operational Research* (83), 200-219
2. J.F. Campbell (1994). "Integer programming formulations of discrete hub location problems", *European Journal of Operational Research* (72), 387-405
3. E. Domínguez and J. Muñoz (2002), "An efficient neural network for the p-median problem", *Lectures Notes on Artificial Intelligence* (2527), 460-469

4. J. Ebery (2001), "Solving large single allocation p-hub problems with two or three hubs", *European Journal of Operational Research* (128), 447-458
5. Ernst and M. Krishnamoorthy (1996), "Efficient algorithms for the uncapacitated single allocation p-hub median problem", *Location Science* (4), 139-154
6. J. G. Klincewicz (1992), "Avoiding local minima in the p-hub location problem using tabu search and grasp", *Annals of Operational Research* (40), 283-302
7. M. E. O'Kelly (1987), "A quadratic integer program for the location of interacting hub facilities", *European Journal of Operational Research* (32), 393-404
8. K. Smith, M. Krishnamoorthy and M. Palaniswani (1996), "Neural versus traditional approaches to the location of interacting hub facilities", *Location Science* 4(3), 155-171
9. D. Skorin-Kapov and J. Skorin-Kapov (1994), "On tabu search for the location of interacting hub facilities", *European Journal of Operational Research* (73), 502-509

Adaptive P2P Multimedia Communication Using Hybrid Learning*

Juan A. Botía, Pedro Ruiz**,
Juan A. Sánchez, and Antonio F. Gómez Skarmeta

Departamento de Ingeniería de la Información y las Comunicaciones
Universidad de Murcia

Abstract. Multimedia communication in mobile and ad hoc networks used by real time applications can be improved by adding intelligent and adaptive cababilities. This new functionality will allow them to adapt to contantly and unpredictably changing network conditions. Derived from this adaptivity, the user will perceive a more or less constant quality instead of the high variable quality perceived in nowadays applications. In this work, we maintain the following thesis: both machine learning and intelligent agents will play an important role in the improvement of the aplications we mentioned above. Machine learning, by means of reinforcement learning will provide adaptivity. Intelligent agents will ease P2P computation. This paper focuses on approaches for both topics.

1 Introduction

A mobile ad hoc network (MANET) is a spontaneous association of terminals equipped with wireless interfaces, which form a network. These networks do not require any infrastructure and all the network-layer functions need to be distributed among each of the different nodes. For example, when two distant nodes need to communicate, intermediate nodes act as relays so that multi-hop paths can be created. So, ad hoc nodes perform the functions both of host and routers. These networks are characterized by continuously and unpredictably changing network conditions, mainly due to the movement of the nodes (which provokes topology changes), and other issues at the lower layers like fading, collisions, etc. Traditional real-time multimedia applications are unable to perform well over these networks, and some adaptive functionalities are required at the application layer, to deal with such problems. These new applications called "adaptive applications" are challenged with new components to detect the current network conditions and adapt their internal settings (e.g. audio codecs, video rates, etc.) accordingly.

The main focus of traditional multimedia applications is the reduction of the data rate when the network bandwidth becomes scarce, and the increase of the

---

* Work supported by the FIT-070000-2003-662, FIT-1603002003-41 and TIC2002-04021-C02-01 projects).
** This work has been partially funded by Spanish Ministry of Science and Technology (MCYT) under the Ramón y Cajal Programme.

R. Conejo et al. (Eds.): CAEPIA-TTIA 2003, LNAI 3040, pp. 116–125, 2004.

data rate whenever more resources become available. Of course, this behaviour improves the QoS perceived by the user. However, the relation between user-perceived QoS and the data-rate required to achieve that QoS is not linear. So, when the network conditions become very bad, a correct change in the internal application settings, could greatly reduce the data rate, while keeping the QoS to an acceptable level. The main problem, is that for these applications to do that, they have to be aware of the user-perception of QoS. This modeling is very complex because it usually has subjective components which cannot be modeled analytically.

In this work we propose an hybrid approach for the design of a mechanism in charge of managing the configuration of a multimeda peer-to-peer application. This configuration mechanism seeks for the best user satisfaction. The hybridization must be understood in terms of the different machine learning techniques [10] we use. We will first obtain an inductive model, using supervised learning, to predict the user perceived quality given concrete network conditions and multimedia application settings. Following, once we are able to score a concrete situation, we will apply reinforcement learning [12] to learn a strategy to decide when and how to change application settings, taking into account the score of the inductive model.

Intelligent agents [14] will be used to ease the control of the P2P multimedia applications. We also propose in this work the use of FIPA (*Foundation for Intelligent Physical Agents*) agents to wrap the elements afore mentioned and to seamesly integrate them in previously existing multimedia applications.

The rest of the paper is structured as follows: section 2 explains the problem we are faced to. Section 3 introduced the hybrid approach we have used to obtain the adaptive mechanism. Following, section 4 briefly presents the agents architecture we use to integrate the adaptivity in multimedia applications. Finally, section 5 expose lessons learned in this work and pending tasks.

2   Adaptive Multimedia Applications

Quality of Service (QoS) as defined in ITU-T recommendation E.800, ITU-E.800 [2] is "the collective effect of service performance, which determines the degree of satisfaction of a user of a service". It is characterized by a combination of service performance factors such as operability, accessibility, retainability and integrity. Thus, it is clear that the user plays an important role in QoS evaluations.

We will start by introducing the application architecture [4]. Main building blocks of it appear at figure 1. The main items in this architecture are the following: (a) multimedia application components like audio, video, slides for a remote presentation, etc., (b) the QoS signaling mechanism and (c) the adaptation logic. The QoS signaling mechanism is the protocol in charge of sending and receiving reports describing the network conditions from the other end. When such a report is received it is passed to the Adaptation Logic as an additional input. Additionally, the Adaptation Logic is in charge of deciding which set of parameters is best suited to the current network conditions.

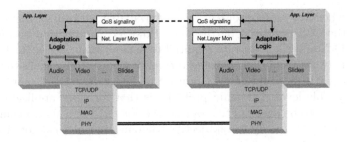

Fig. 1. General adaptive architecture

The most difficult part for the Application Logic is the decision on what components to adapt, and which setting to change, when the application is exceeding the available bandwidth. Many adaptive applications to date, just reduce data rates to use less than the available bandwidth. However, they do not deal with the main difficulty, which is taking the correct decision while taking into consideration the subjective user-perception implications about it.

3   Hybrid Learning for P2P Control

In this section we will introduce the scheme we have designed to perform hybrid learning. Section 3.1 will introduce the supervised learning part and section 3.2 will present the learning by reinforcement part.

3.1   Supervised Learning for User Modeling

In order to inductively model the QoS perception of an user, we have to produce a learning data set. And this has to be compound by examples of situations referring to a particular network condition and a particular multimedia application sending to and receiving data from the network. Network conditions have been reproduced by using a reflector. This is a software tool collocated in the middle of a dedicated link between two communicating nodes. It will be in charge of simulating different levels of available bandwidth and estimating packet losses. The multimedia application used, ISABEL-Lite, is a reduced version of ISABEL [1] which allows both manual and automatic change of its settings. This settings must be understood in terms of audio and video codecs. Audio and video codecs are in charge of capturing, coding, sending, decoding and presenting audio and video data respectively. More especifically, for the video we can also specify the size, the number of frames per second sent and a quality factor.

Table 1 summarizes all attributes and the corresponding range of values, which compound the data set used to model the user. Notice that the last row refers to the score given by the user.

The data set consists of 864 instances, each one scored by an user. The data set can be considered to be balanced with the following distribution of examples

Table 1. Parameters appearing at the example set used for rule induction by SLIPPER

Parameter	Values	Explanation
BW	{33, . . . , 384}	Limit of network bandwidth
LOSS	0..100	% loss packets
AUDCOD	PCM, G711-u, G722, GSM	Audio codec
VIDCOD	MJPEG, H.263	Video codec
FSIZE	CIF, QCIF, 160x128	Size of video frames
QFVIDEO	5, 10, 15, 30, 60	Quantify factor of video codec
FPS	{0, . . . , 12}	Frames by second sent
QoS	1, 2, 3, 4, 5	User perceived quality

by score: 241 (27.8%) examples with score 1, 83 (10.4%) for score 2, 181 (20.9%) examples with score 3, 233 (26.9%) with 5 and finally, 125 (14.46%) for the highest score.

Learning experiments have been performed using SLIPPER [6]. This algorithm does not directly use the classic search bias of divide an conquer for rule induction. Instead, it bases its strategy on boosting [7]. It uses a weak learner (i.e. a very simple rule induction algorithm) which boost by modifying learning instances probability each iteration to focus on instances not correctly classified yet. In fact, we also tested IREP, IREP* [8] and RIPPER [5]. Former algorithms which do not use boosting and all of them under-performed SLIPPER. We will consider the possibility of using other kinds of algorithms like, for example, ordinal regreesion ones. This algorithms predict discrete outputs taking into account a given order between values.

Best classification capacity model we have obtained with SLIPPER appears at figure 2. Ten fold crossvalidation gave a missclassification error of 10%. It is compound by 12 rules and an example is classified as pertaining to the first class (from the upper to the lower class) in which the sum of the confidence values of matching rules in the class is higher than the corresponding negative value. Using that model we can approximate user perceived QoS. However, what we really need is a mechanism to decide, when thing go wrong in the session, what changes have to be applied to the application settings. For that, we will use reinforcement learning.

3.2   Reinforcement Learning for Adaptivity

In this section we will introduce our approach to obtain the adaptivity scheme. This will be in charge of deciding when and how to change the configuration of our multimedia application to obtain, in the long term, an optimun user satisfaction. The decision model we will obtain will be a multi-layer perceptron [3]. Learning the parameters (i.e. the weights of the arcs in the network) is done by reinforcement learning [13].

In learning by reinforcement, we make use of an entity called agent [12] which is situated in the environment. Its situation comes depicted by the environment particular state at time t, let it be denoted with s_t. The learner agent can perform a set of actions in the environment. Each time the agent executes an action a, it receives a reward from the environment, r. The agent then has to appropiately

```
if matchConfidence {
        [QFVIDEO >= 60, VIDCOD = MJPEG, FSIZE = QCIF, LOSS <= 10, FPS >= 6] -> 2.8792
        [AUDCOD = GSM, BW >= 80, QFVIDEO >= 30, FSIZE = QCIF, FPS <= 6] -> 1.4357
        [AUDCOD = GSM, BW >= 128, LOSS = 0, QFVIDEO >= 30, FPS >= 3, VIDCOD = MJPEG]
            -> 1.7013
        [] -> -2.4188
} > 0 then 5 else if matchConfidence {
        [BW >= 384, QFVIDEO >= 40, FSIZE <= 2] -> 2.7121
        [QFVIDEO >= 30, VIDCOD = MJPEG, LOSS <= 3, AUDCOD = G722] -> 1.1756
        [FSIZE = CIF, QFVIDEO >= 30, LOSS <= 3, AUDCOD = G722, BW >= 80] -> 1.4437
        [] -> -1.5044
} > 0 then 4 else if matchConfidence {
        [LOSS >= 30] -> 2.1188
        [QFVIDEO <= 5] -> 1.4142
        [LOSS >= 16, FPS <= 3] -> 1.5438
        [] -> -1.0984207275826066
} > 0 then 1 else if matchConfidence {
        [LOSS >= 16] -> 1.9109
        [QFVIDEO <= 10, FSIZE = QCIF] -> 1.5861
        [FSIZE = 160X128, QFVIDEO <= 40,
         VIDCOD = H.263] -> 1.2546
        [] -> -0.3953
} > 0 then 2 else 3
```

Fig. 2. Rule model to estimate user perceived QoS

choose each action it executes in order to maximice the reward obtained at the long term. In the context of this particular application, the agent will learn a state-value function, let it be denoted with $V^\pi(s_t)$. This function will be used to predict the long term reward the agent would obtain if, being at time t, it selects the action given by the policy π (i.e. the criteria used to select an action among all the possible ones). This approach is typically used for prediction but we will use it for control. In typical control problems, not only the state is taken into account in the value function but also the actions. This time, the agent has to learn a good aproximation of a function, let it be denoted with $Q^\pi(s, a)$ for the current policy π and for all states s and actions a.

Learning is done by iteratively updating the Q function by means of the following expression:

$$Q(s, a) \leftarrow Q(s, a) + \alpha[r + \gamma Q(s', a') - Q(s, a)],$$

where the pair (s', a') refers to the state s' to which the environment goes to, from s when action a is executed and a' is the action executed at state s'. Constants α and γ are the learning rate and the discount factor, respectively.

In this particular domain, we directly act on the problem. For example, a possible action could be to set the video codec to MJPEG or either to change video size to QCIF or even do nothing at all. Inmediate rewards, obtained from executed actions, will be approximated by using the rules model of figure 2.

The estimator will be learnt by using SARSA, without using the elegibilities mechanism (i.e. $\lambda = 0$, see [12], pag. 163). Elegibilities speed up convergence to a good aproximation of the Q function, however, in previous simulations we did not perceive any improvement in using that technique.

A world state will be given by concrete network conditions as simulated by the reflector (i.e. packet losses), and settings of the multimedia application. Con-

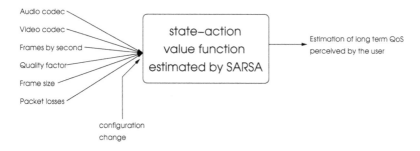

Fig. 3. Functional diagram for the adaptive strategy to be learnt by SARSA

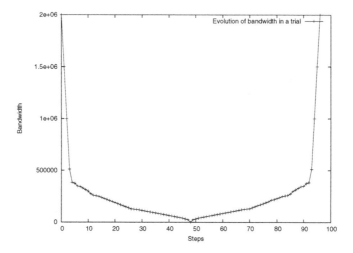

Fig. 4. Bandwidth evolution used in SARSA trials

sequently, an action will be a change in the state (except by packet losses, which would be given by the reflector). It must be noticed that available bandwidth can not be considered as another dimension of the environment features vector as this parameter can not be obtained from the real application. It can only be simulated with the reflector. A functional scheme, in terms of modules inputs and outputs appears depicted at figure 3.

Again, we have used the ISABEL Light Videophone along with the reflector to reproduce a real application and network conditions the agent will use to learn from. The videophone simulates both communication end points. It reproduces, with no end, a musical clip with a total of 400 video frames which sends to itself through the reflector. This, in turn, is in charge of simulating the network link between the end points. Each one of the learning trials or episodes uses the same bandwidth values changing through time. Bandwidth follows the curve appearing at figure 4. Notice that the density of different bandwidth values grows while approximating to values between 256 and 0KB. That is because this range of values are more sensitive to changes. Depending on the amount of data injected to the network by the videophone and on the reflector simulated bandwidth, the reflector will generate a concrete packet losses percentage. Both the videophone and the reflector accept commands from outside through a socket. By openning telnet connections to the videophone we can configurate application settings. For example, with the string `set(AUDIO::PCM,VIDEO::MJPEG,QCIF,8,5.0)` we tell the videophone to set the audio codec to PCM, the video codec to MJPEG, the video size to QCIF, the frame rate to 8 and the quality factor to 5. Bandwidth can be set at the reflector in the same way. We can also read packet losses from the reflector by using a *read* command with the same socket. Communication through sockets is important here because the learning scheme has been developed by using Java and the reflector and videophone are developed in C++. The learning global scheme appears at figure 5.

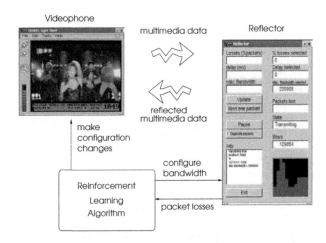

Fig. 5. Arquitectura de aprendizaje global con videófono, reflector y algoritmo SARSA

We have obtained the best results with a multilayer perceptron of 30 hidden nodes, a reinforcement learning rate of 0.05 and a discount factor of 0.9, being the learning rate for the neural network of 0.01. Each one of the episodes was compound by 970 movements (10 actions for each different bandwidth value appearing at figure 4).

Effective learning progress will be demonstrated by using a number of different curves. The first one corresponds to the accumulated r values obtained in each episode, for all s_{t+1} visited states. It is labeled with (a) at figure 6. Notice that, from the very begining, it grows until it becomes stable. Another interesting point is shown by (b) curve. It refers to packet losses. In the begining, it shows a minimun level of packet being lost in the network. This is because the learner stands at very conservative states (i.e. states using a low bandwidth and, subsequently, low user scores are obtained). As long as the learning process evolves, packet losses ratio becomes stable between a 3 and a 5% (an acceptable value). RMSE decreases, as expected. Regarding the five curves appearing at

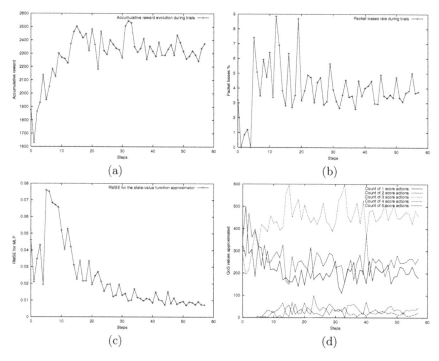

Fig. 6. Curve labeled with (a) shows the evolution of accumulated rewards through episodes. The one labeled with (b) represents the packet losses percentage. The (c) curve is the evolution of the Rooted Mean Squared Error (RMSE) for the multilayer perceptron which approximates the estate-valor function. At (d) we have the number of each different scores obtained during learning

graph (d), we can se how that curves which represent low scores (1 and 2 scores) decrease. Also, the number of actions with good quality increase (i.e. 3 scores) and the amount of good and very good quality actions increase.

4   P2P Control Implementation with FIPA Agents

In this section we will explain an initial implementation we have developed for the adaptive control of the videophone. Our long term goal is to built a complete ambient intelligence [9] system. This concept emphasize the context in which the user is situated. This context depends on the device through which he is connected to the system, the physical network, his personal interests (i.e. his user profile) and available services at the current context. Now, we are working on the first and second mentioned factors.

If we want to provide an implementation of the adaptive level of the architecture (see figure 1) based on intelligent agents, we have to revise the QoS basic signalling mechanism along with the adaption logic (a detailed analysis of the issue can be found at [11]).

The QoS signalling mechanism provides with information of the network state to the other end point at the communication channel. A point to point transport mechanism can be defined in charge of informing the transmitter about the quality the receiver is obtaining. This QoS can be compound by the packet losses ratio and the mean jitter. Each one of the QoS signalling packets can be added a sequence number and the estimated bandwidth. We can express this kind of packets with XML, like in the following example:

```
<?xml version="1.0" encoding="UTF-8"?>
<qosreport>
  <sequence>34</sequence>
  <lostpackets>9.3465</lostpackets>
  <delay>0.093</delay>
  <preferences></preferences>
  <estimatedbw>128000</estimatedbw>
</qosreport>
```

in which we have included an empty preferences part. Agents simply have to exchange messages like that, by using a performative to convey them.

To this moment, implementation is being carried out on laptops, by using videophones coded in C++ and intelligent agents with the JADE platform.

Adaption logic is in charge of deciding when and how to act on application settings. This functionality is given by the multilayer perceptron that, for each action, produces an estimate of how good it will be in the long term. The decision mechanism consists on choosing the action with highest return value. When an **inform** message is received with a **<qosreport>** content, we use the neural network and apply changes.

5   Conclusions

In this work, we have presented an hybrid approach based on both supervised and reinforcement learning. This has been used to obtain and adaptation mechanism to maintain an acceptable QoS in the context of multimedia applications like a videophone. We also outlined initial details of the FIPA agents based architecture to provide a complete ambient intelligence application. Results still can be improved. A possible improvement is that of using ordinal regression models instead of classification ones to approximate the quality perceived by the user. In this way, error estimations would be more precisse as score labels are ordered. However, and with no doubt, this work suposses a very promising start point with respect to the role that artificial intelligence will play in the improvement of ad hoc networks communication. Moreover, another posibility is using simple regression for the same problem.

References

1. *The ISABEL CSCW application.*
   [On line] http://www.agora2000.com/productos/isabel.html.
2. Recommendation E.800 (08/94). *Terms and Definitions Related to Quality of Service for Adaptable Multimedia Communication.* ITU-T, 1994.

3. Christopher M. Bishop. *Neural Networks for Pattern Recognition*. Clarendon Press, Oxford, 1995.
4. Juan A. Botía, Pedro Ruiz, Jose Salort, and Antonio Skarmeta. Improving user-perceived qos in mobile ad hoc networks using decision rules induction. In *Proceedings of the Canadian Conference of Artificial Intelligence*, Ontario, Canada, June 2003.
5. W. Cohen. Fast effective rule induction. In *Proceedings of the Twelfth International Conference on Machine Learning*, pages 115–123, Lake Tahoe, CA, 1995.
6. W. Cohen and Y. Singer. A simple, fast, and effective rule learner. In *Proceedings of the Conference of American Asociation for Artificial Ingelligence*, 1999.
7. Yoav Freund and Robert E. Schapire. A short introduction to boosting. *Journal of Japanese Society for Artificial Intelligence*, 14(5):771–780, September 1999.
8. Johannes Fürnkranz. Separate-and-conquer rule learning. *Artificial Intelligence Review*, 13(1):3–54, February 1999.
9. W.A IJsselsteijn G. Riva, F. Davide, editor. *Being There: Concepts, effects and measurement of user presence in synthetic environments*. IOS Press, Amsterdam, The Netherlands, 2003.
10. Tom M. Mitchell. *Machine Learning*. McGraw-Hill, 1997.
11. Pedro M. Ruiz. *Multicast Architecture for MANET Extensions to Fixed IP Networks Supporting Real-Time Adaptive Applications*. PhD thesis, University of Murcia, 2002.
12. R. Sutton and A. Barto. *Reinforcement Learning. An Introduction*. MIT Press, 1998.
13. Richard S. Sutton. Learning to predict by the methods of temporal differences. *Machine Learning*, 3:9–44, 1988.
14. Michael Wooldridge. *An Introduction to MultiAgent Systems*. Willey, 2002.

An Approach for Ontology Building
from Text Supported by NLP Techniques

Rafael Valencia-García[1], Dagoberto Castellanos Nieves[2],
Pedro José Vivancos Vicente[1], Jesualdo Tomás Fernández Breis[3],
Rodrigo Martínez-Béjar[1], and Francisco García Sánchez[1]

[1] Departamento de Ingeniería de la Información y las Comunicaciones, Campus de Espinardo,
Universidad de Murcia, CP 30071, Murcia, Spain
{valencia,pedroviv}@um.es, rodrigo@dif.um.es
[2] Facultad de Informática y Matemática, Universidad de Holguín
Av. XX Aniversario s/n, CP 80100, Holguín, Cuba
dago@facinf.uho.edu.cu
[3] Departamento de Informática y Sistemas, Facultad de Informática,Campus de Espinardo,
Universidad de Murcia, CP 30071, Murcia, Spain
jfernand@dif.um.es

Abstract. In this work, we present an approach to simplify Knowledge Acquisition Processes (KAPs) by means of extracting knowledge directly from natural language texts. The ultimate goal is to acquire knowledge straight from experts' language. This approach uses a morphologic analyzer to improve the setting-in-a-context between knowledge elements (e.g., concepts and attributes). Another objective is achieving language independency. Here, the knowledge acquired from texts is represented by means of ontologies.

1 Introduction

Extracting knowledge directly from natural language text is a challenging task. It would allow extracting knowledge easily and, what is more significant, without the intervention of knowledge engineers. Our ultimate goal is the development of tools capable of extracting knowledge from text, on the one hand, and interacting directly with experts of any application domain, on the other. To do this, we agree with [3] in the sense that people who know a language should in part know the rules of such language. In particular, we account for this assumption in designing and implementing a morphologic analyzer. This paper presents a technique for generating knowledge from text through the combination of knowledge modelling techniques and natural language processing, two disciplines that have been following different roads. The main idea behind the approach presented here is simple: the system stores the knowledge found by the expert to automatically identify this knowledge whenever it reappears. Knowledge has been represented in this work by means of ontologies. In literature, ontologies are commonly defined as specifications of domain knowledge conceptualisations [15]. Due to the nature of an ontology, there is not a unique (valid) manner for defining ontologies [8]. Moreover, several definitions have historically been given to the term ontology, although an ontology is commonly considered to be an enumeration of the relevant concepts in an application area, as well as a definition

R. Conejo et al. (Eds.): CAEPIA-TTIA 2003, LNAI 3040, pp. 126–135, 2004.
© Springer-Verlag Berlin Heidelberg 2004

of classes of concepts and relationships among these classes [4]. A series of functions to capture knowledge has been implemented to represent the knowledge acquired through ontologies.

The structure of the paper can be described as follows. Section 2 presents an overview of the approach presented in this work. Section 3 and 4 account for the algorithms used for parsing natural language texts, indicating also how to set words into their corresponding context. In Section 5, an example of the application of the framework is described. Section 6 explains the system implementation and its application to a real domain. Related work is discussed in Section 7. Finally, in Section 8 some final conclusions are remarked.

2   Overview of the Approach

The aim of this work was to implement a system able to extract knowledge from natural language texts. More precisely, we have focused on building an ontology from a text. Ontologies permit to divide knowledge into categories such as concepts, attributes, relationships, rules, axioms, etc. These knowledge entities can appear explicitly in the text, although sometimes knowledge is only referred to implicitly. Thus, the approach attempts to find explicit knowledge entities from the text. The starting point is an empty knowledge base. In this phase, the system is unable to find knowledge in the text and the expert has to introduce knowledge manually. However, experts do not just find knowledge in a single fragment, but they also identify expressions which that knowledge can be derived from. The expert identifies all the knowledge entities of the fragment and (s)he also tells the system the expressions in which they appear. These expression-knowledge associations are stored by the system in order to be reused for new knowledge findings thereafter. The expert has only to identify these associations once, and from that moment onwards, the system will perform automatically, and the expert's task will just consist of confirming the results output by the system. In principle, we might think that in a system with a huge knowledge base, the expert has just to take a seat, divide the text into minor fragments and confirm the system's proposals. Unfortunately, the process is not that simple. The system checks the fragments for expressions with already associated knowledge. A word with associated knowledge may appear in plural or singular, replaced by a pronoun, etc and verbs may appear in different inflected forms (number, tenses, etc.).

In a huge knowledge base, it is likely to find expressions with multiple knowledge associations, as words can have various meanings. These meanings refer to other knowledge pieces in the knowledge base. For instance, an attribute does not exist on its own, it refers to a conceptual entity. A relationship implies the existence of at least two knowledge entities. Thus, the system has to identify knowledge in fragments as well as knowledge referenced by it. The process reveals some problems: (1) searching for meaningful expressions in a text; (2) deciding what to do when an expression has more than one knowledge association in the knowledge base; and (3) identifying knowledge referred to by "non-concepts". The first two problems are faced here in the search phase whereas the third one is dealt with in the setting-in-a-context phase, for which the system uses a morphologic analyser. The morphological analyzer uses the learning algorithm C4.5 [10] to classify each word of a sentence. For each word, the instance related to it will be obtained, and this word will be classified by C4.5. Further details about this analyzer may be found in [12].

3 Parsing Text and Looking for Knowledge

The starting point for using the approach is a set of expressions in the current fragment with no associated knowledge. The system completes a full cycle once all words of the current fragment have been analyzed. Next, it takes the remaining non-analyzed words of the text fragment (current words) and looks for similar words in the already existing expressions in the knowledge base. Then, for each expression of the knowledge base similar to the current word, if it is considered to be an acceptable expression, these actions are performed: (1) obtain and sort the knowledge associated to the expression present in the knowledge base; (2) create a new expression that matches the knowledge base expression and associates previously sorted associated knowledge to than expression; and (3) add the new expression to the list of fragment expressions with its associated knowledge.

When no good options are found, the user has to be provided with the possibility of defining new knowledge associated to the expression. Alternatively, these expressions might also be straightforwardly ignored (e.g., preposition, particle, conjunction, interjection, pronoun, and determiner). The similar function is in charge of identifying which expressions of the knowledge base are similar to the current word of the fragment. In its simplest case, it would be an "equal" function. Nevertheless, this function cannot deal with compound expressions as such; therefore a new function is needed, namely "isPrefix", which function checks whether the current word is a substring of another word or not. It would also be desirable that the function could deal with word families (types associated to a single lemma/lexeme) and other language peculiarities. For instance, if the expression "causes" already exists in the knowledge base and the current fragment contains the word "caused", it would be desirable that the system realized that both words actually allude to the same verb (lemma). This issue might be partially implemented using parts-of-speech taggers and lemmatisers. Here, a word in the current fragment is "similar" to an expression in the knowledge base if the expression starts with the current word.

The acceptable function is an extension to the "similar" one. It is introduced to determining whether the current word and a similar expression are not just "similar by chance". The "isPrefix" function has an important drawback: if the current word is the article "a", any expression starting with "a", as "assurance", "added value", "a hundred" or "advert" will be (candidates to be) considered as similar. Therefore, this function limits the number of acceptable options amongst the similar ones. This function has been designed with strong requirements: an existing expression in the database is acceptable if it appears as such in the current fragment.

Current words in a text fragment are always single constituents. However, database expressions can contain more than one word (multiple-word expressions). If a word is acceptable, then the current fragment will contain all the words of the database expression. Thus, the current word needs to be enlarged to cover all the words of the database expression, creating a new object that contains all the words.

The correctly recognized relationships between expressions and their associated knowledge are stored in the database. Once an expression is obtained holding certain properties (through the functions similar and acceptable), knowledge associated with that expression is searched for in the database. Whenever different association possibilities in the database exist, the system sorts them out and displays them.

Whenever different possibilities are considered as inferred knowledge from an expression, the system rearranges and sorts them according to the following criteria: (1) person-dependency, who recognized the knowledge, (2) domain dependency, the type of domain and (3) spatial location, whether the expression belongs to the same fragment and/or text. In particular, there are currently 11 different possible sorting criteria. Once knowledge sorting has concluded, the search phase ends. At this point, the system is likely to have processed both the current fragment and the set of expressions present in its database. Additionally, inferred knowledge would have been sorted out according to the above criteria in an attempt to overcome ambiguity.

4 The Setting-in-a-Context Phase

Once the search phase has been performed, the system is fitted with a list of associated knowledge expressions. However, the system's task does not finish then, unless the inferred knowledge is a concept; if the inferred knowledge is a different knowledge entity (i.e., attribute, value, relation) some operations need to be performed. In what follows, we shall explain the operations that need to be performed for different knowledge entities. In other works, the conceptualisation was very limited and was dependent on a concrete language, namely, English, where attributes usually follow concepts (see for instance [13]). This property was used by a system to look for concepts which attributes belong to. So, when the system finds an attribute in the search phase, the system searches for the most left-nearby concept in the current fragment. However, that is not always correct. For example, in the following fragment: "... due to the weight of the table", the concept table is on the right of its attribute weight. Therefore, with the previous process, the conceptualisation would be incorrect. In order to solve conceptualisation problems, we use grammar patterns, which are own by each language and that indicate a relation between words by knowing only their grammar category. Thus, by using these patterns we can approach this process to be language independent. The grammar patterns used for English in this work, which are shown in Table 1, are based in the ones presented in [14].

We say "property" because the existing relation between two words is a priori unknown (e.g A word is an attribute of a concept, or a value of an attribute). Once the search phase has finished, the system will perhaps have several attributes, concepts, and values. When the system has to find the relations between those knowledge entities, it use of such patterns. For example, in the following fragment: "… the red car …", if the system has tagged red as value and car as concept in the search phase, by using the pattern 'Adj + Noun' the system will find a relation between the concept car and the value red. All relations are assumed to be binary. That is, two elements need to be found. Let us consider this fragment now: "...antioxidants inhibit the activation of the NF-kB transcription factor... ". This type of structure is quite frequent when identifying participants in relations: one of the candidates is on the left hand-side of the expression, inferring the relation, and the other one on the right hand-side. The system searches for expressions with inferred knowledge on the left and right hand-side, and candidates are selected according to various criteria:

- If the current expression is associated to a relation of the type "is-a" or "part-of", any ontological category can be chosen as a candidate as these relations can only exist between concepts. Therefore, the system searches for two concepts, one on the left and another on the right hand-side of the current expression. It is very rare that any of the candidates of a relation is a value (the system is designed to ignore values).
- If an attribute is found, the process of searching for a related concept is the same as the one described above to provide a context for attributes.

The search process is similar to the one described in previous sections. Candidates are searched (1) in a pre-determined number of expressions for which the user has associated knowledge, (2) in the expressions obtained in the search phase and, finally (3) in the user expressions.

Table 1. Grammar patterns.

Previous word(s)	Current word	Relation	Example
Adjective	Adjective	The previous word is a property of the current one	Sweetie lovely Diffusible binding
Adverb	Adverb	The previous word is a property of the current one	Very popular
	Adverb	The previous word is a property of the current one	Very strongly
Adjective		The previous word is a property of the current one	Tall boy Individual gene
Noun	**Noun**	The previous word is a property of the current one	Telephone directory Gen activity
Noun+prep+ (det)		The current Noun is a property of the first one	The table of wood Model of the molecule

5   Example of Knowledge Acquisition Process

In this section, we introduce an example to describe the operation of the knowledge acquisition process. Hence, we will suppose that we have the knowledge base shown in Table 2. and that we are processing the following text fragment: "*A tight mutant is a mutant which displays its non-wild type phenotype distinctly and clearly while a leaky mutant displays a much less distinct phenotype compare to wild type*". First, we will show the results of the morphological analysis, and then, we will illustrate how knowledge is found in this fragment.

Table 2. Knowledge Base.

Is	**Taxonomic Relation**	phenotype	**Concept**
is a	**Taxonomic Relation**	...	
is a class of	**Taxonomic Relation**	tight	**Value**
is a part of	**Mereological Relation**	tight Mutant	**Concept**
...		type	**Attribute**
leaky Mutant	**Concept**	...	
Non-wild	**Value**		
...			

Morphological Analysis
A (Determiner) tight (Adjective) mutant (Noun) is (Verb) a (Determiner) mutant (Noun) which (Pronoun) displays (Verb) its (Determiner) non-wild (Adjective) type (Noun) phenotype (Noun) distinctly (Adverb) and (Conjunction) clearly (Adverb) while (Conjunction) a (Determiner) leaky (Adjective) mutant (Noun) displays (Verb) a (Preposition) much (Adverb) less (Adverb) distinct (Adjective) phenotype (Noun) compared (Verb) to (Preposition) wild (Adjective) type (Noun).

Parsing Text and Looking for Knowledge
As it was previously stated, the words classified as preposition, particle, conjunction, interjection, pronoun, and determiner are considered to be semantically meaningless. So, the system does not search any knowledge associated to them. The system searches first knowledge associated to *tight*. Thus, the system searches in the knowledge base for similar expressions. In this case, the *similar* expressions to *tight* are {tight, tight mutant}, since they contain "tight" as a prefix. Then, the system searches for the most *acceptable* expression. In this case it finds the expression "tight mutant" in the text, so it infers that "tight mutant" is a concept. The next word to be analyzed is "is". The *similar* words in the knowledge base are {is, is a, is a class of, is a part of}. However, the system realizes that "is a" is acceptable. Thus, the system infers a taxonomic relation associated to the expression "is a". The process continues and the system will finally obtain the following knowledge from the text:

> {tight mutant (Concept), is a (Taxonomic relation), mutant (Concept), non-wild (Value), type (Attribute), phenotype (Concept), leaky mutant (Concept) }

Setting-in-a-Context Phase
At this point, the system does not need to perform any more operations with the expressions whose associated knowledge entity is a concept. Otherwise, the corresponding knowledge entity needs to be conceptualised. In this example, the expressions "non-wild", "type" and "is a" have to be set into the correct context. Now, the system makes use of the grammar patterns to relate the knowledge. For instance, the expression "non-wild" was labeled as a Value in the previous phase. Following with the example, the system will need to find its related attribute. The expression "non-wild" is an adjective and the expression "type" is a Noun. According to the fourth grammar pattern, "non-wild" is a property of "type". Hence, the system infers that "non-wild" is a value of the attribute "type". Next, the system has to associate the attribute "type" to a concept. Since "type" is a noun and "phenotype" is a noun, a grammar pattern is found. The system knows that "type" is a property of "phenotype". By looking at the previous phase, "phenotype" is a concept and "type" is an attribute, so the system infers that "type" is an attribute of the concept "phenotype". The last expression to be conceptualized is "is a", which represents a taxonomic relation. The system has to find the participants of the relationship. For this purpose, the system searches on the left and the right side of the linguistic expression "is a" to find the participants of the relationship. Here, the participants have to be concepts. In this example, the system infers a taxonomic relation between the expressions "tigh mutant" and "mutant".

6 Implementing a Software Tool

A software tool based on the approach described above has been designed and implemented for acquiring knowledge from texts (text needs to be specified in a text file; i.e., in ASCII format). The tool is fitted with two distinct working modes: (1) the query mode and (2) the maintenance mode. In the maintenance mode, users are provided with the full functionality of the tool (adding new experts and tasks, associating experts to tasks; saving the work/session(s) in the database, loading previously saved work, etc). The query mode has a reduced functionality. The user can neither perform management activities nor save work/sessions in the database. Other differences between both modes are: (a) in the maintenance mode, the user inserts knowledge with the help of the tool; the system proposes knowledge to the user by making use of natural language recognition techniques; and (b) in the query mode, the user cannot insert new knowledge as ontologies are built automatically. Non-expert users cannot carry out the following actions: input knowledge into the system, select the expert, select the task, select a text for recognition. In our tool, five ontological knowledge categories are used, namely:

- Concepts: these represent a class of objects in the domain.
- Attributes: these represent the properties of a given concept.
- Values: attributes belong to a domain; attributes such as length are numeric whereas attributes like colour are enumerated. The elements of those domains are the possible values attributes can take.
- Relations: relations in a domain ontology play the same role as in a relation/entity model, although some constraints have been imposed. In this tool, relations are binary and pre-defined: IS-A, PART-OF, ASSOCIATION, INFLUENCE.
- Axioms: an axiom is a domain rule. For instance, Force = mass * acceleration.

The taxonomic and mereological relations do only exist between two concepts. The remaining relations can exist between whatever two ontological categories, although a relation cannot be part of another relation.

The system may recognize entities from such categories except for axioms. The structure of the ontologies resulting of our system performance can be seen in Figure 1. The tree on the left hand-side of Figure 1 is the ontology, having three main branches: concepts, relations, and rules (i.e., axioms). Axioms appear as branches of the "rules" node. Each concept has branches for allocating its attributes and each of these has for its values. The relations are represented as branches of the "relationships" node, and the instances of the relations can be viewed on the right side of the screen (i.e., the IS-A relation in Figure 1).

In order to evaluate the usefulness of the approach in real settings, a case study (experiment) was performed. It consisted in applying it to several sub-domains of Computer Science with 'simulated experts', namely, 5th year students instructed for the experiment (one expert per sub-domain). The instruction was done through the provision of abundant information concerning the sub-domain they were encouraged to work in. Concerning motivation, a list containing descriptions of each sub-domain (already well-known by them through the corresponding subjects studied in the career) utilised in the case study was first shown to them. Then, they selected those found to be most 'attractive' to them. With this, we tried to ensure each 'expert' was motivated enough to do his/her job in the experiment. With all, each expert was given

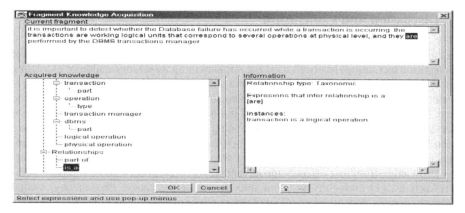

Fig. 1. Analysis of a text fragment.

a text from the domain which (s)he had been instructed on. Then, we checked whether the assumptions pointed out before were too strong or not. The results of the knowledge acquisition process from text in this experiment show that, at least, the simulated experts used in this case study overcame the technical, implicit restrictions of our approach and extracted and represented explicit knowledge from text, as it was our goal. The data of the experiment and the resulting ontologies can be accessed at our web page.

7 Related Work

The way we approach knowledge structuring differs from the one presented in [5,11]: in that our knowledge entities are concepts, attributes, values, relations, and rules whereas in the quoted work, the discussion is about concepts, roles, individuals and axioms. Another difference with [5,11] is that the concept acquisition process is performed differently, too: our system's suggestions are hypotheses the user accepts or rejects, whereas in [8], the process is structured into three phases: (1) generating quality labels for hypotheses; (2) estimating the credibility of the hypotheses; and (3) computing the order of preference of the hypotheses.

The expression-oriented analysis to capture knowledge from text in the system presented here is somewhat more general than the classic word-based approach described in [3], for whom words can be derived from other words by means of transformation rules. Semantics associated to terms has been dealt with also elsewhere. In particular, in [6] the author recognises that semantic variations permit to recognise, for example, verbal and adjectival phrases as conceptually equivalent to nominal terms. Concerning tools for terms acquisition from text, there are others well-known in literature, for instance LEXTER [2], which was built for term acquisition from French corpora. In our work we go beyond the term extraction to distinguish several kinds of semantic terms through several ontological knowledge categories. The use of ontologies for knowledge acquisition from text is discouraged in [7,9] for domains in which changes in expert knowledge is rapid and substantial. However, we believe to have shown that our approach can easily be adapted to new requirements.

8   Discussion and Conclusion

In this paper, an approach that combines knowledge acquisition and natural language recognition techniques has been used for implementing a system capable of extracting knowledge from natural language texts in a supervised mode. The methodology presented in this work offers a new and promising method for knowledge acquisition from text. The system has been evaluated in one case study (i.e., a Computer Science domain) and several ontologies corresponding each to a different sub-domain have been built by applying the framework described in this paper to a set of natural language texts on the referenced domain. We are confident that this approach of acquiring knowledge from text offers some advantages with respect to pure linguistic methods such as: (1) ambiguity is taken into account (i.e., person dependency, spatial location, domain dependency); (2) rhetoric is not considered; (3) implicit knowledge can be identified and added by the user; (4) the system is incremental and automatic; and (5) the system's performance and transparency are acceptable.

The way in which the acquisition process has been divided into (i.e., 'search' and 'setting-in-a-context' phases) allows, in principle, the system to be used for any language. However, some considerations need to be made regarding these two phases. We propose some improvements concerning the context-in-a-setting phase regarding different knowledge entities: (a) relations (i.e., solving situations such as those in which no participants appear on either side of the relation; a possible solution might be checking whether the concept is directly followed by an attribute; here, we might think that it is more likely that the attribute is the second participant and not the concept); (b) pronouns (these are not dealt with in this work and would be another interesting issue to be treated). Regarding future work, we plan to perform a statistical evaluation of the system in some other domains such as medicine, where we have already performed some promising experiments.

Acknowledgements

We thank the Spanish Ministry for Science and Technology for its support for the development of the system through projects TIC2002-03879, FIT-110100-2002-78, FIT-150500-2002-376, FIT-150500-2003-499, FIT-150500-2003-503, FIT-110100-2003-73, FIT-150500-2003-505, and Murcian Regional Government through project 2I03SIU0039. We also thank the European Commission for its support under project ALFA II0092FA.

References

1. M. Aronoff, Word Formation in Generative Grammar, MIT Press, 1976.
2. D. Bourigault, LEXTER, a Natural Language tool for terminology extraction, In Proceedings, 7th EURALEX International Congress, 771-779, Goteborg, Sweden, 1996.
3. N. Chomsky, Knowledge of Language: Its Nature, Origin, and Use, Praeger, 1986.
4. J.T. Fernández-Breis, D. Castellanos-Nieves, R. Valencia-Garcia, P.J. Vivancos-Vicente, R. Martínez-Béjar, and M. De las Heras-González, Towards Scott domains-based topological ontology models. An application to a cancer domain, in Proceedings of International Conference on Formal Ontology in Information Systems. Maine, EEUU, 2001.

5. U. Hahn, & K. Schnattinger, An Empirical Evaluation of a System for Text Knowledge Acquisition. In Proceedings of the European Knowledge Acquisition Workshop, 129-144, Sant Feliu de Guixols, Spain, 1997.
6. C. Jacquemin, Spotting and Discovering Terms through Natural Language Processing, MIT Press, 2001.
7. D.M. Jones & R.C. Paton, Acquisition of Conceptual Structure in Scientific Theory. In E.Plaza & R. Benjamins (Eds), Proceedings of the European Knowledge Acquisition Workshop, 145-158, Sant Feliu de Guixols, Spain, 1997.
8. M. A. Musen, 'Domain Ontologies in Software Engineering: Use of Protegé with the EON Architecture', Methods of Information in Medicine, 37, 540-550, (1998).
9. D.E. O'Leary, 'Impediments in the use of explicit ontologies for KBs development.', International Journal of Human-Computer Studies,46, 327-338, (1997).
10. J.R. Quinlan, C4.5: programs for Machine Learning, San Mateo : Morgan Kaufmann, 1993.
11. M. Romacker, and U. Hahn, Context-based Ambiguity Management for Natural Language Processing, Lecture Notes in Artificial Intelligence 2116, 184-197, (2001).
12. J.M. Ruiz-Sánchez, R. Valencia-García, J.T. Fernández-Breis, R. Martínez-Béjar, R. and P. Compton, An approach for incremental knowledge acquisition from text. Expert Systems with Applications, 25(2):77-86, (2003).
13. R.I., Sánchez-Carreño, J.T. Fernández-Breis, R. Martínez-Béjar & P. Cantos-Gómez, 'An ontology-based approach to knowledge acquisition from text', Cuadernos de Filología Inglesa ,9(1) ,191-212, (2000).
14. L. Thomas, Beginning Syntax, Oxford Blackwell, 1993.
15. G. Van Heijst, A. T. Schreiber, & B. J. Wielinga, 'Using explicit ontologies in KBS development'. International Journal of Human-Computer Studies, 45, 183-292, (1997).

An Efficient Preprocessing Transformation
for Functional Dependencies Sets
Based on the Substitution Paradigm*

Ángel Mora, Manuel Enciso,
Pablo Cordero, and Inmaculada Pérez de Guzmán

E.T.S.I. Informática, Universidad de Málaga, 29071, Málaga, Spain
{pcordero,enciso}@uma.es, {amora,guzman}@ctima.uma.es

Abstract. Functional Dependency is a fundamental notion of the Relational Model. Since the introduction of this successful theoretical framework in the 70's, there have been several works focussed on their automated treatment. The pioneer line of this area was the use of Functional Dependencies Logics. Unfortunately, this line has presented several limitations, most of them caused by the crucial role of the transitivity paradigm in the axiomatic system. In [11] we introduce a new Functional Dependencies Logic which does not use the transitivity rule. This logic uses a new *substitution* rule and the design of its axiomatic system has been guided by the notion of *optimality*.
In this paper we show the advantages of such a logic. We introduce a pre-processing transformation which removes redundancy of a given set of Functional Dependencies and allows a more efficient further treatment by other well known indirect algorithms. Besides that, we carry out an empirical study to prove the practical benefits of our approach.

1   Introduction

Functional Dependencies (FD) are an important element of the Relational Model [10]. They establish a relation among the attributes (fields) of the system and allow the development of a method to eliminate data redundancy. This method, named *FD normalization* [25], depurates relational databases to get a more efficient information management.

Up to now, normalization was considered a secondary task in software development and the proof is that no many CASE tool have skill to store and manipulate Functional Dependencies. The automated manipulation of FD to get normalized databases has not a high priority in Software Engineering. This lack of interest relies on two problems: first, to discover all the FDs in a database requires a high degree of expertise and system knowledge and secondly, the management of FD is not a trivial task[1].

Recently, Functional Dependencies are playing a more important role in Computer Science. This growing interest is due to a collection of works which use Artificial Intelligence techniques to find functional dependencies and other types of data associations

---

* This work has been partially supported by the Cycit project 1109-2000.
[1] Some well known problems related with FD are NP-hard problems.

R. Conejo et al. (Eds.): CAEPIA-TTIA 2003, LNAI 3040, pp. 136–146, 2004.
© Springer-Verlag Berlin Heidelberg 2004

which were *hidden* to database designers. These works have open the door to discover knowledge in databases and give a solution to the first problem cited above. The Rough Set Theory introduced by Pawlack [24] and some Data Mining techniques [7, 16] have been used to discover knowledge in database: in [6] to find keys, in [17] to discover FD in large databases and in [15] to deduce FD and Multivalued Dependencies in a given relation. Neural networks have been used in [22] to examine the database and find significant dependencies. In [19] the authors study functional dependencies in q-Horn Theories, and discusses their use in knowledge condensation. More recently, some authors have related FD with emergent technologies. Thus, the extension of FDs to XML has been studied in [2, 8].

The second problem, that is, the automated manipulation of FD has been also tackled with Artificial Intelligence. There exists in the bibliography a collection of equivalent functional dependencies logics which allow a formal specification of FDs and provide axiomatic systems as a formal basis to design automated deduction methods. These FD logics are introduced by well-known database authors: P. Atzeni [4], R. Fagin [14], A. Kogan [18], J. Paredaens [23], J. Ullman [25], etc.

Nevertheless, none of these logics are used to design an automated method to depurate sets of functional dependencies. In fact, there is a set of works which use indirect methods to manage FDs [9, 18, 20, 21]. The neglect of all these FD logics is due to a common characteristic: all of their axiomatic systems rely on the transitivity rule. The important role of transitivity avoids the design of efficient transformations and obscures the use of other rules which may be useful to reduce the original problem.

By the other hand, the management of sets of functional dependencies has focussed in the problem of *minimality*: the notion of redundant FD set is centered solely in the number of FD. As P. Atzeni says in [4], there is an strong problem based in the notion of *optimality*. Optimality looks for a set of FD with less size, i.e., when the total number of attributes in the FDs can be reduced.

In [11] we introduce a substitution operator which is the basis of a new rule for FD inference systems. This new rule is directly based on the notion of optimality and, as we shall see in this work, can be used to reduce efficiently the size of the FD sets. In fact the substitution operator may be considered as a primitive rule, rendering a new kind of FD logic, the $\mathbf{SL}_{FD}$ logic [11]. The main novelty of our logic is that it does not use transitivity rule as the basis of the inference system.

In this work we have design a preprocessing transformation which uses the substitution operator of $\mathbf{SL}_{FD}$ logic to prune the original FD set, rendering in polynomial time an equivalent FD set with less size. We show how substitution paradigm may be used to reduce the original problem (so, it can be treated in less time by other well-known algorithms). Furthermore, we have tested empirically the substitution transformation which allows us to reveal the importance of optimality and minimality.

The work is organized as follows: section 2 presents some well-known definitions and results concerning the relational model. We will use Paredaens logic in section 3 and will present the substitution operator in section 4. In section 5 we will introduce the pre-processing transformation based on substitution and we will test its efficiency. Conclusions will be presented in the last section of this paper.

2   Relational Model Preliminaries

E.F. Codd[2] is considered the father of the Relational Model [10], the first conceptual data model with a formal basis which have survive with minor changes since the 70's decade.

Codd stores data in **tables** and labels each column of the table with an identifier named *attribute*. For each a attribute, the data of the corresponding column are referred to be values of a set named $dom(a)$. Thus, if $\mathcal{A}$ is a finite set of attributes, we are interested in $R \subseteq \Pi_{a \in \mathcal{A}} dom(a)$ relations.

Each row of the table is denominated *tuple of the relation*. If t is a tuple of the relation and a is an attribute, then $t(a)$ is the a-component of t.

Definition 1. *Let R be a relation over $\mathcal{A}$, $t \in R$ and $X = \{a_1, \ldots, a_n\} \subseteq \mathcal{A}$. The* **projection** *of t over X, $t_{/X}$, is the restriction of t to X. That is, $t_{/X}(a_i) = t(a_i)$, for all $a_i \in X$.*

Definition 2 (Functional Dependence). *Let R be a relation over $\mathcal{A}$. Any affirmation of the type $X \mapsto Y$, where $X, Y \subseteq \mathcal{A}$, is named* **functional dependence** *over R. We say that R* **satisfies** *$X \mapsto Y$ if, for all $t_1, t_2 \in R$ we have that: $t_{1/X} = t_{2/X}$ implies that $t_{1/Y} = t_{2/Y}$. We denote by FD_R the following set:*

$$FD_R = \{X \mapsto Y \mid X, Y \subseteq \mathcal{A}, R \text{ satisfies } X \mapsto Y\}$$

W. W. Armstrong shows the semantics of the FD in the following proposition which characterizes the properties that satisfies the set FD_R (the proof was presented in [3]):

Proposition 1 (Armstrong Axioms). *Let R be a relation over $\mathcal{A}$, then[3]:*

1. *If $Y \subseteq X \subseteq \mathcal{A}$ then $X \mapsto Y \in FD_R$.*
2. *If $X \mapsto Y \in FD_R$ then $X \mapsto XY \in FD_R$.*
3. *If $X \mapsto Y, Y \mapsto Z \in FD_R$ then $X \mapsto Z \in FD_R$.*
4. *If $X \mapsto Y, X \mapsto Z \in FD_R$ then $X \mapsto YZ \in FD_R$.*
5. *If $X \mapsto Y \in FD_R$ then $X \mapsto Y - X \in FD_R$.*
6. *If $X \mapsto Y \in FD_R$, $X \subseteq U \subseteq \mathcal{A}$ and $V \subseteq XY$ then $U \mapsto V \in FD_R$.*
7. *If $X \mapsto Y, X' \mapsto Z \in FD_R$, $X' \subseteq XY$, $X \subseteq U \subseteq \mathcal{A}$ and $V \subseteq ZU$ then $U \mapsto V \in FD_R$.*

3   The Paredaens Logic

In the above section we present the notion of functional dependence (definition 2) and show some properties which allow the management of all the FDs that are satisfied in a given relation (proposition 1). In this section we introduce Paredaens Logic [23] named $\mathbf{L}_{Par}$, which allows the formal specification and manipulation of FDs. As we mention in

---

[2] E.F. Codd died on April the 18th. We are in doubt with him for their revolutionary idea about data storage and management and we particularly appreciate his tireless fight at the beginning of the 70's, when academic and business organizations had no faith in his Relational Model.

[3] If X and Y are sets of attributes, XY denotes the set $X \cup Y$.

the introduction, there exists other well-known logics [4, 14, 18, 25] that are equivalent[4] to $\mathbf{L}_{Par}$. Moreover, all of them are correct and complete, i.e. their axiomatic systems are congruent with the notion of satisfiability introduced in definition 2 and they cover proposition 1.

Definition 3 (The $\mathbf{L}_{Par}$ Language). *Let Ω be an infinite numerable set of atoms and let $\mapsto$ be a binary connective, we define the language*

$$\mathcal{L}_{Par} = \{X \mapsto Y \mid X, Y \in 2^{\Omega} \text{ and } X \neq \varnothing\}$$

In the literature, attributes must be non-empty. Nevertheless we may consider the empty attribute, denoted $\top$, and extend the original language of $\mathbf{L}_{Par}$.

Now, we introduce the axiomatic system $\mathcal{S}_{Par}$:

Definition 4. $\mathbf{L}_{Par}$ *is the logic given by the pair ($\mathcal{L}_{Par}, \mathcal{S}_{Par}$) where $\mathcal{S}_{Par}$, has as axiom scheme $\lfloor Ax_{Par} \rfloor$: $\vdash_{\mathcal{S}_{Par}} X \mapsto Y$, if $Y \subseteq X$ and the following inference rules:*

$\lfloor Trans \rfloor$	$X \mapsto Y, Y \mapsto Z \vdash_{\mathcal{S}_{Par}} X \mapsto Z$	**Transitivity Rule**
$\lfloor Augm \rfloor$	$X \mapsto Y, \vdash_{\mathcal{S}_{Par}} X \mapsto XY$	**Augmentation rule**

In $\mathcal{S}_{Par}$ we have the following derived rules (these rules appear in [23]):

$\lfloor Union \rfloor$	$X \mapsto Y, X \mapsto Z \vdash_{\mathcal{S}_{Par}} X \mapsto YZ$	**Union Rule**
$\lfloor Comp \rfloor$	$X \mapsto Y, W \mapsto Z \vdash_{\mathcal{S}_{Par}} XW \mapsto YZ$	**Composition Rule**
$\lfloor Inters \rfloor$	$X \mapsto Y, X \mapsto Z \vdash_{\mathcal{S}_{Par}} X \mapsto Y \cap Z$, where $Y \cap Z \neq \varnothing$	**Intersection Rule**
$\lfloor Reduc \rfloor$	$X \mapsto Y \vdash_{\mathcal{S}_{Par}} X \mapsto Y\text{-}X$, where $Y\text{-}X \neq \varnothing$	**Reduction Rule**
$\lfloor Frag \rfloor$	$X \mapsto YZ \vdash_{\mathcal{S}_{Par}} X \mapsto Y$	**Fragmentation Rule**
$\lfloor gAugm \rfloor$	$X \mapsto Y \vdash_{\mathcal{S}_{Par}} U \mapsto V$, where $X \subseteq U$ and $V \subseteq XY$	**Generalized Augmentation Rule**
$\lfloor gTrans \rfloor$	$X \mapsto Y, Z \mapsto U \vdash_{\mathcal{S}_{Par}} V \mapsto W$, where $Z \subseteq XY, X \subseteq V$ and $W \subseteq UV$	**Generalized Transitivity Rule**

The concepts of deducted *wffs*, denoted $\Gamma \vdash_{\mathcal{S}_{Par}} \varphi$ and FD equivalent sets, denoted $\Gamma \vdash_{\mathcal{S}_{Par}} \Gamma'$ are introduced as usual.

4   A New Tool for Removing Redundancy

In [11] we propose the introduction of two substitution rules that allow to remove redundancy in a efficient way. Moreover, these rules have a strong formal base, the lattice theory and concretely the concept of ideal-ond for formalizing the redundancy notion. We summarize these concepts:

---

[4] We selected Paredaens Logics with no loss of generality, because all the other FD logics have the same structure in their syntax, semantics and axiomatic system.

Definition 5. *Let $\Gamma \subseteq \mathcal{L}_{Par}$, and $\varphi = X \mapsto Y \in \Gamma$. We say that φ is* **superfluous in** *Γ if $\Gamma \backslash \{\varphi\} \vdash_{S_{Par}} \varphi$. We say that φ is* **l-redundant in** *Γ if exists $\varnothing \neq Z \subseteq X$ such that $(\Gamma \backslash \varphi) \cup \{(X - Z) \mapsto Y\} \vdash_{S_{Par}} \varphi$. We say that φ is* **r-redundant in** *Γ if exists $\varnothing \neq U \subseteq Y$ such that $(\Gamma \backslash \varphi) \cup \{X \mapsto (Y - U)\} \vdash_{S_{Par}} \varphi$. We say that Γ* **have redundancy** *if it have an element φ that it is superfluous or it is l-redundant or it is r-redundant in Γ.*

The rules that we will introduce are transformations of $\mathcal{S}_{Par}$-*equivalence*. This way, the application of these rules does not imply the incorporation of new *wff*, but the substitution of *wffs* by simpler ones, with an efficiency improvement.

The following theorem allow us to introduce the substitution rules, see the proof in [11].

Theorem 1. *Let $X \mapsto Y, U \mapsto V \in \mathcal{L}_{Par}$ with $X \cap Y = \varnothing$.*

(a) *If $X \subseteq U$ then $\{X \mapsto Y, U \mapsto V\} \equiv_{\mathcal{S}_{Par}} \{X \mapsto Y, (U - Y) \mapsto (V - Y)\}$. Therefore, if $U \cap Y \neq \varnothing$ or $V \cap Y \neq \varnothing$ then $U \mapsto V$ is l-redundant or r-redundant in $\{X \mapsto Y, U \mapsto V\}$ respectively.*

(b) *If $X \nsubseteq U$ and $X \subseteq UV$ then $\{X \mapsto Y, U \mapsto V\} \equiv_{\mathcal{S}_{Par}} \{X \mapsto Y, U \mapsto (V - Y)\}$. Therefore, if $V \cap Y \neq \varnothing$ then $U \mapsto V$ is r-redundant in $\{X \mapsto Y, U \mapsto V\}$.*

The above theorem allows us to define the substitution and r-substitution rules as follows:

$\lfloor Sust \rfloor$ $X \mapsto Y, U \mapsto V \vdash_{\mathcal{S}_{Par}} (U\text{-}Y) \mapsto (V\text{-}Y)$ if $X \subseteq U$, , $X \cap Y = \varnothing$

$\lfloor rSust \rfloor$ $X \mapsto Y, U \mapsto V \vdash_{\mathcal{S}_{Par}} U \mapsto (V\text{-}Y)$, where $X \subseteq UV$, , $X \cap Y = \varnothing$

The following example shows the advantages of the substitution rules.

Example 1. Given $\Gamma = \{a \mapsto bc, ab \mapsto ce, bd \mapsto ac, af \mapsto b, cd \mapsto ba\} \subseteq \mathcal{L}_{Par}$, we can apply the substitution rules to obtain FDs sets with less redundancy.

Rule	Γ
$\lfloor Sust \rfloor$: $a \mapsto bc, ab \mapsto ce \vdash_{\mathcal{S}_{Par}} a \mapsto e$	$a \mapsto bc, a \mapsto e, bd \mapsto ac, af \mapsto b, cd \mapsto ba$
$\lfloor Union \rfloor$: $a \mapsto bc, a \mapsto e \vdash_{\mathcal{S}_{Par}} a \mapsto bce$	$a \mapsto bce, bd \mapsto ac, af \mapsto b, cd \mapsto ba$
$\lfloor Sust \rfloor$: $a \mapsto bce, af \mapsto b \vdash_{\mathcal{S}_{Par}} af \mapsto \top$	$a \mapsto bce, bd \mapsto ac, af \mapsto \top, cd \mapsto ba$
$\lfloor Ax_{Par} \rfloor$: $\vdash_{\mathcal{S}_{Par}} af \mapsto \top$	$a \mapsto bce, bd \mapsto ac, cd \mapsto ba$
$\lfloor Sust \rfloor$: $a \mapsto bce, bd \mapsto ac \vdash_{\mathcal{S}_{Par}} bd \mapsto a$	$a \mapsto bce, bd \mapsto a, cd \mapsto ba$
$\lfloor rSust \rfloor$: $bd \mapsto a, cd \mapsto ba \vdash_{\mathcal{S}_{Par}} cd \mapsto b$	$a \mapsto bce, bd \mapsto a, cd \mapsto b$

We would like to remark the importance of the substitution rules. No FD axiomatic system has such a rule that is able to detect and eliminate redundancy in an efficient way from a set of FDs. Integrating substitution rules to an axiomatic system has the following advantages:

– Systematic application of the rules of the axiomatic system.
– Elimination of redundant attributes from the determinant and determinate of FDs.

We show now an interested FD normal form.

Definition 6 (Reduced Functional Dependency Set). *[5, 1]*
   A set Γ of FDs is in reduced form if for all $X \mapsto Y$ then $X \cap Y = \varnothing$.

The following theorem ensures a good properties concerning the FDs in reduced form.

Theorem 2. *Given $X, Y, Z \in 2^{\Omega}$, then we have that $\{X \mapsto Y\} \equiv_{S_{Par}} \{X \mapsto (Y - X)\}$*

In databases it is usual to work with reduced FDs. The following example illustrates the importance of this definition and shows what happens if $\Gamma \subseteq \mathbf{L}_{Par}$ contains non reduced FDs

Example 2.
Let $\mathcal{A} = \{a, b, c, d\} \subseteq \Omega$ and $\Gamma = \{ab \mapsto bd, abc \mapsto de\} \subseteq \mathbf{L}_{Par}$.
In this DFs set, substitution rules cannot be applied to eliminate redundancy in Γ as there is no fulfillment of hypothesis $X \cap Y \neq \varnothing$ that appears in Theorem 1.
Nevertheless, Theorem 2 proves that Γ is equivalent to the set of reduced FDs $\Gamma' = \{ab \mapsto d, abc \mapsto de\} \subseteq \mathbf{L}_{Par}$. To that end, we will simply apply the rule $\lfloor Reduc \rfloor$ to Γ with linear cost.
The rule $\lfloor Sust \rfloor$ can be applied to obtain $ab \mapsto d, abc \mapsto de \vdash_{S_{Par}} abc \mapsto e$ and eliminate the r-redundant attribute d from $abc \mapsto de$.
We thus obtain $\Gamma' = \{ab \mapsto d, abc \mapsto e\}$, which is S_{Par}-equivalent to Γ.

From now on we consider *wffs reduced* of $\mathbf{L}_{Par}$. In the following section, we will introduce a preprocessing transformation and we will carry out an empirical test of its efficiency.

5 A Pre-processing Transformation Based on the Substitution Paradigm

In this section we will present the design and implementation[5] of a pre-processing transformation that will allow us to transform any given set of FDs into another equivalent one with less redundancy. This transformation is directly based on the substitution rules we just introduced.

Besides that, we present an empirical study of this preprocessing transformation which allows us to analyze the benefits of the new substitution rules.

First we will show the design in pseudo-code that describes how we will use the rules that take part in the transformation that we propose to eliminate redundancy in FDs sets. Such transformation does not completely eliminate all the redundancy. The pre-processing transformation establishes an efficient preprocessing pruning based mainly on the substitution rules, and allows for the application of any other depuration method over the new FD set, which is shorter than the original one. In some cases, our preprocessing transformation captures the redundancy of the original FD set entirely, with the corresponding benefits for the efficiency.

The transformation depicted in figure 1 applies the following steps[6]:

---

[5] We use Prolog to implement the preprocessing transformation. We have used SWI-Prolog version 5.1.8.

[6] The transformation has quadratic complexity.

removeRedundancy

Input: Γ (a set of FDs)

Output: Γ' (a FDs set with less redundancy)

<u>*BEGIN*</u>

      1. $\lfloor\ Reduc\ \rfloor$

      2. $\lfloor\ Union\ \rfloor$

     <u>*Repeat*</u>

          3. Substitution $\lfloor\ Sust\ \rfloor$ + $\lfloor\ rSust\ \rfloor$

     <u>*until*</u> more substitution cannot be applied

      4. Check if it is possible to apply

          Generalized Transitivity

  <u>*END*</u>

Fig. 1. A Pre-processing transformation

- In step 1, the rule $\lfloor Reduc \rfloor$ transforms FDs into reduced FDs.
- In step 2, the rule $\lfloor Union \rfloor$ renders FDs with disjoint determinants.
- In step 3, we exhaustively apply the substitution rules. After each application of substitution if the result requires it, the union rule or the $\top$ elimination will be applied before the following substitution.
- In step 4, we will check if it is necessary to apply transitivity. This way, we will check if the original set has been thoroughly treated.

It is convenient to remark that before starting step 3 the size of the FDs set has been reduced with limited linear cost. We will achieve an important improvement with respect the rest of the FDs algorithms as all of them apply the rule $\lfloor Frag \rfloor$ as their first transformation, which causes an increase in the number of FDs.

The following example (introduced in [13]) shows the application of this preprocessing transformation to a set of FDs.

Example 3. We apply **removeRedundancy** to :
$\Gamma = \{b \mapsto a, b \mapsto g, b \mapsto h, d \mapsto a, bn \mapsto h, ab \mapsto d, ab \mapsto e, ab \mapsto f, ab \mapsto g, abc \mapsto d, abc \mapsto j, abc \mapsto k\}$

Step 1 $\lfloor Reduc \rfloor$

Step 2

    $\lfloor Union \rfloor$ $b \mapsto a, b \mapsto g, b \mapsto h \vdash_{S_{Par}} b \mapsto agh$ [7]

    $\lfloor Union \rfloor$ $ab \mapsto d, ab \mapsto e, ab \mapsto f, ab \mapsto g \vdash_{S_{Par}} ab \mapsto defg.$

    $\lfloor Union \rfloor$ $abc \mapsto d, abc \mapsto j, abc \mapsto k \vdash_{S_{Par}} abc \mapsto djk.$

Step 3

    $\lfloor Sust \rfloor$ $b \mapsto agh, bn \mapsto h \vdash_{S_{Par}} bn \mapsto \top$ [8]

    $\lfloor Ax_{Par} \rfloor$ $\vdash_{S_{Par}} bn \mapsto \top$ [9]

    $\lfloor Sust \rfloor$ $b \mapsto agh, ab \mapsto defg \vdash_{S_{Par}} b \mapsto def$

    $\lfloor Union \rfloor$ $b \mapsto agh, b \mapsto def \vdash_{S_{Par}} b \mapsto adefgh$

    $\lfloor Sust \rfloor$ $b \mapsto adefgh, abc \mapsto djk \vdash_{S_{Par}} bc \mapsto jk$

    $\lfloor rSust \rfloor$ $d \mapsto a, b \mapsto adefgh \vdash_{S_{Par}} b \mapsto defgh$

Step 4 It is not necessary to apply GTransitivity.

---

[7] We remove $b \mapsto a, b \mapsto g, b \mapsto h$ and we add $b \mapsto agh$.

[8] We substitute $bn \mapsto h$ by $bn \mapsto \top$.

[9] We remove $bn \mapsto \top$.

We obtain the following depurated FD set : $\Gamma' = \{b{\rightarrow}defgh, d{\rightarrow}a, bc{\rightarrow}jk\}$. This same example is depurated in [13] using 16 $^+$-closures and in [12] applying 5 $^+$-closures and and 6 r-closures[10]. Our **removeRedundancy** transformation obtains the same result without using a closure operator.

5.1 Statistics of the Application of the Substitution Rules

We have not found Benchmarks that allow us to carry out comparisons with other author's results, nor utilize `fdsAleatory` that allows us to randomly generate a set Γ of FDs over a set of attributes $\mathcal{A}$.

We must emphasize that the results of the application of the algorithm are similar starting from `NumSet`= 50. As a matter of fact, as can be seen in the following table, application percentages of each rule suffer no significant variation in 50, 100, 150 and 200 tested FDs sets.

$NumSets$	Step 1 $Reduc$	Step 2 $Union$	Step 3 $Subst$
50	12.06	7.45	80.49
100	11.73	7.67	80.60
150	11.84	6.01	82.15
200	11.79	6.88	81.33

Therefore, we consider in our experiment 50 random sets of FDs. In all the experiments the percentage of times that each one of the rules that take place in the transformation (Step 1, Step 2, Step 3) is measured. Likewise, we check if it is also necessary to apply the transitivity rule because there is still redundancy and, finally, we provide the percentage in which the size of the problem has been reduced with the preprocessing transformation. The have carried out tree experiments:

Experiment 1. In this experiment we will vary the `NumFDs` parameter, that determines the maximum size of Γ. The random generator receives this argument and produces a set of FDs with $1 \leq |\Gamma| \leq$ `NumFDs`. In the following table we see the results of applying the transformation for `NumFDs`= $10, 20, 30, 40, 50, 60$.

$NumFDs$	Step 1 $Reduc$	Step 2 $Union$	Step3 $Subst$
10	27	13.2	59.80
20	10.59	7.48	81.93
30	7.41	5.05	87.54
40	4.89	4.68	90.43
50	4.12	4.16	91.72
60	3.29	4.55	92.16

---

[10] A closure operation defined by those authors.

We also remark, as an important result, that in a $38,33\%$ of the FDs sets it is not necessary to apply the transitivity rule and also that the substitution has been able to reduce the scheme to a $56,24\%$ of its initial size.

Experiment 2. In this experiment, we generate 50 random sets of FDs (NumSet= 50) with a maximum of 50 (NumFDs= 50) and we will take as a parameter the number of attributes, that is, $1 \leq |\mathcal{A}| \leq$NumAtr. We can see in the following table the results of applying the preprocessing transformation for NumAtr= $10, 20, 30, 40, 50, 60$.

	Step 1	Step 2	Step 3
NumAtr	*Reduc*	*Union*	*Subst*
10	14.33	17.63	68.04
20	8.61	8.52	82.87
30	5.69	6.75	87.57
40	5.03	5.11	89.86
50	4.22	4.57	91.21
60	3.75	3.77	92.47

In this experiment, in a $19,33\%$ of the cases it is not necessary to apply the transitivity rule and the scheme has been reduced in a $47,09\%$.

Experiment 3. In real world databases, the number of attributes that appear in an FD is not very large, that is why we consider this study case. In the follwoing experiment, we generate 50 random sets of FDs (NumSet= 50), a maximum of 50 FDs (NumFDs= 50),we take as a parameter the number of attributes ($1 \leq |\mathcal{A}| \leq$NumAtr) and we restrict the length of the determinant and determinate of the FDs to a third, and to a fifth of NumAtr. We see in the following table the results of applying the rules.

	1/3			1/5		
NumAtr	*Reduc*	*Union*	*Subst*	*Reduc*	*Union*	*Subst*
10	23.8	23.53	52.67	41.89	29.82	28.34
20	12.95	13.31	73.74	22.97	18.26	58.77
30	8.15	7.59	84.26	12.77	9.43	77.79
40	7.24	5.21	87.55	13.16	7.94	78.9
50	6.20	3.55	90.24	11	4.59	84.4
60	5.93	2.49	91.59	8.33	2.56	89.11

For the first case, (LengthMaxLeft=LengthMaxRight=$\frac{NumAtr}{3}$), in a $25,33\%$ of the cases, it is not necessary to apply transitivity and the scheme has been reduced to a $56,86\%$ of its size. For the second case (LengthMaxLeft= LengthMaxRight= $\frac{NumAtr}{5}$) these values are $30,00\%$ and $51,38\%$ respectively.

5.2   Conclusions

As we show in [11], substitution rules make possible the design of a new kind of FDs logics that are not centered in the transitivity paradigm. In this work, we have demonstrated how a preprocessing transformation enables us to prune effectively the problem of eliminating redundancy in FDs sets. As a main advantage with respect to indirect algorithms proposed in the literature, our transformation uses directly an axiomatic systems to eliminate redundancy and it is possible to give explanations.

As can be seen in all the experiments carried out, the percentages of application of the substitution rules are very high and are increased substantially with the complexity of the FDs set. Specifically, the experiments enable us to draw the following general conclusions:

- In a $28, 25\%$ of FDs sets it is not necessary to apply transitivity and the preprocessing transformation eliminates redundancy efficiently.
- The size of FDs sets has been reduced in a $52, 89\%$.
- When the number of attributes is increased, the number of cases in which it is not necessary to apply transitivity is also increased. This demonstrates that the substitution rule is specially adequate for dealing with large databases schemes.
- The percentages of application of the substitution rules are independent from the number of attributes and from the length of the FD[11].

References

1. S. TORGERSEN, *Automatic design of relational databases*, Ph. D. Thesis. TR 89-1038, 1989
2. M. L. LEE, T. W. LING, AND W. L. LOW, *Designing functional dependencies for XML*, Lecture Notes in Computer Science. EDTB 2002 Proceedings 2287, pp. 124–141
3. W. W. ARMSTRONG, *Dependency structures of data base relationships* , Proc. IFIP Congress. North Holland, Amsterdam, 1974, pp. 580–583
4. P. ATZENI AND V. D. ANTONELLIS, *Relational Database Theory*, The Benjamin/ Cummings Publishing Company Inc., 1993
5. G. AUSIELLO, A. D'ATRI, AND G. SACCA, *Graph Algorithms for Functional Dependenciy Manipulation*, J. ACM 30 (4), 1983
6. D. A. BELL, *From data properties to evidence*, IEEE Transactions on Knowledge and Data Engireering 5 (6), 1993 pp. 965–968
7. D. A. BELL AND J. W. GUAN, *Computational methods for rought classifications and discovery*, J. American Society for Information Sciences. Special issue on Data Minig, 2004
8. P. BUNEMAN, W. FAN, J. '. R. O. M. SIMÉÉ, AND S. WEINSTEIN, *Constraints for semistructured data and XML*, SIGMOD Record (ACM Special Interest Group on Management of Data) 30 (1), 2001, pp. 47–54
9. J. CHOOBINEH AND S. S. VENKATRAMAN, *A methodology and tool for derivation of functional dependencies from business forms*, Information Systems 17 (3), 1992, pp. 269-282
10. E. F. CODD, *The Relational Model for Database Management: Version 2. Reading, Mass.* , Addison Wesley, 1990
11. P. CORDERO, M. ENCISO, I. P. D. GUZMÁN, AND A. MORA, *SLFD Logic: Elimination of data redundancy in Knowledge Representation*, Lecture Notes - LNAI 2527, Advances in AI, pp. 141-150, Springer-Verlag
12. A. DE MIGUEL, M. PIATTINI, AND E. MARCOS, *Diseño de Bases de Datos Relacionales*, Ed. Ra-ma, 1999
13. J. DIEDERICH AND J. MILTON, *New Methods and Fast Algorithms for Database Normalization*, ACM Transactions on Database Systems 13 (3), 1988, pp. 339–365

---

[11] As an unusual case, in experiment 3, when the FDs are small and also the size of the determinate, many *collapsed* FDs are generated to which *Reduc* is applied.

14. R. FAGIN, *Functional Dependencies in a Relational Database and Propositional Logic*, IBM. Journal of research and development 21 (6), 1977, pp. 534–544
15. P. A. FLACH AND I. SAVNIK, *Database dependency discovery: A machine learning approach*, AI communications 12 1999, pp. 139–160
16. J. W. GUAN AND D. A. BELL, *Rough computational methods for information systems*, Artificial Intelligence 105, 1998, pp. 77-103
17. Y. HUHTALA, J. KÄRKÄINEN, P. PORKKA, AND H. TOIVONEN, *TANE: An efficient algorithm for discovering functional and approximate dependencies*, The computer Journal, 42 (2), 1999
18. T. IBARAKI, A. KOGAN, AND K. MAKINO, *Functional dependencies in Horn theories*, Artificial Intelligence 108 (1-2), 1999, pp. 1-30
19. T. IBARAKI, A. KOGAN, AND K. MAKINO, *On functional dependencies in q-Horn theories*, Artificial Intelligence 131, 2001, pp. 171-187
20. S. LOPES, J.-M. PETIT, AND F. TOUMANI, *Discovering interesting inclusion dependencies: application to logical database tuning*, Information Systems 27 (1), 2002, pp. 1-19
21. H. MANNILA AND K.-J. RAIHA, *Algorithms for Inferring Functional Dependencies from Relations*, Data and Knowledge Engineering 12, 1994, pp. 83–99
22. R. ORRE, A. LANSNER, A. BATE, AND M. LINDQUIST, *Bayesian neural networks with confidence estimations applied to data mining*, Computational Statistics & Data Analysis 34, 2000, pp. 473-493
23. J. PAREDAENS, P. DE BRA, M. GYSSENS, AND D. V. VAN GUCHT, *The Structure of the Relational Database Model*, EATCS Monographs on Theoretical Computer Science, 1989
24. Z. PAWLAK, *Rough Set: theoretical aspects of reasoning about data*, Kluwer. Dordercht, Netherlands, 1991
25. J. D. ULLMAN, *Database and Knowledge-Base Systems*, Computer Science Press, 1988

An Evolutionary Algorithm
for Solving Word Equation Systems

César L. Alonso[1], Fátima Drubi[2], and José Luis Montaña[3],[*]

[1] Centro de Inteligencia Artificial, Universidad de Oviedo
Campus de Viesques, 33271 Gijón, Spain
calonso@aic.uniovi.es
[2] Departamento de Informática, Universidad de Oviedo
Campus de Viesques, 33271 Gijón, Spain
[3] Departamento de Matemáticas, Estadística y Computación
Universidad de Cantabria
montana@matesco.unican.es

Abstract. In 1977 Makanin stated that the solvability problem for word equation systems is decidable ([10]). Makanin's algorithm is very complicated and the solvability problem for word equations remains NP-hard ([1]). We show that testing solvability of word equation systems is a NP-complete problem if we look for solutions of length bounded by some given constant greater than or equal to two over some single letter alphabet. Up to this moment several evolutionary strategies have been proposed for other NP-complete problems, like 3-SAT, with a remarkable success. Following this direction we introduce here an evolutionary local search algorithm for solving word equation systems provided that some upper bound for the length of the solutions is given. We present some empirical results derived from our algorithm which indicate that our approach to this problem becomes a promising strategy. Our experimental results also certify that our local optimization technique clearly outperforms a simple genetic approach.

1 Introduction

Given a word equation like, for instance:

$$x01x1y = 1y0xy \ . \tag{1}$$

where x, y are variables, trying to find a solution giving values to the variables over $\{0,1\}^*$ (strings over the alphabet $\{0,1\}$) or show it has none, is a surprisingly difficult problem. As appears in [5], the problem of solving equations in algebras is a well-established area in Computer Science called Unification. Solving equations in strings has applications in many areas such as string unification in PROLOG-3 or unification in theories with associative non-commutative operators, which, due to the current state of the art of the problem, are still of

---

[*] Partially supported by the Spanish grant BFM2000-0349.

R. Conejo et al. (Eds.): CAEPIA-TTIA 2003, LNAI 3040, pp. 147–156, 2004.

no practical use. Other applications such as pattern-matching with variables, imprimitiveness, periodicity or conjugation can be seen in ([7]).

Due to their theoretical an practical relevance, word equation systems (WES) have been extensively studied. Partial solutions to WES were known long ago: in [9], [12] or [14] we can find semi-decision procedures which give a solution if the system has one but they could run forever otherwise. Other partial results can be found in Hmelevskiĭ where the problem is solved for equations in three variables (see also [6]). In 1977, Makanin solved the problem in its complete generality giving the first algorithm to find solutions for arbitrary string equations if there exist and determining the no existence of solutions otherwise (see [10]). The time complexity of this algorithm is $2^{2^{P(n)}}$ nondeterministic time, where $P(n)$ is a single exponential function of the size of the equation n ([8]). In recent years a lot of work related to the word equation systems problem has been done, giving better complexity upper bounds ([5], [11]), or solving particular instances of the problem as the case where each variable appears at most twice in the equation ([13]).

From the structural point of view it is known that the solvability problem for word equations is NP-hard, even if one considers solutions with the length bounded by a linear function and the right side of equations contains no variables (see ([1]). In this context the main open problem is to close the gap between NP and $2^{2^{P(n)}}$, and show that the length of a minimal solution is at most singly exponential w.r.t. the size of the equation (see [11] for a detailed discussion of this question). In this situation, handling NP-hard problems with genetic algorithms (G.A.) is a great challenge; and G.A. have demonstrated to be useful on problems with a combinatorial explosion of possible solutions.

In the present paper we introduce an evolutionary algorithm, which incorporates some kind of local optimization for the problem of solving systems of word equations as that in (1), assuming that an upper bound for the length of the solutions is given. So far we have not found in the literature any references for solving this problem in the framework of evolutionary strategies involving local search. The paper is organized as follows: in section 2 we explicitly state the WES problem with bounds and the 3-SAT reduction to it, showing the NP-completeness. Section 3 describes the evolutionary algorithm with the local search procedure. In section 4, we present the experimental results, solving some word equation systems randomly generated forcing solvability. Finally, section 5 contains some conclusive remarks on this contribution and addresses future research directions.

2   The Word Equation Systems Problem

Let A be an alphabet of constants and let Ω be an alphabet of variables. We assume that these alphabets are disjoint. As usual we denote by A^* the set of words on A, and given a word $w \in A^*$, $|w|$ stands for the length of w; ε denotes the empty word.

Definition 1. *A word equation over the alphabet A and variables set Ω is a pair $(L, R) \in (A \cup \Omega)^* \times (A \cup \Omega)^*$, usually denoted by $L = R$. A word equation system (WES) over the alphabet A and variables set Ω is a finite set of word equations $S = \{L_1 = R_1, \ldots, L_n = R_n\}$, where, for $i \in \{1, \ldots, n\}$, each pair $(L_i, R_i) \in (A \cup \Omega)^* \times (A \cup \Omega)^*$.*

Definition 2. *Given a WES over the alphabet A and variables set Ω, $S = \{L_1 = R_1, \ldots, L_n = R_n\}$, a solution of S is a morphism $\sigma : (A \cup \Omega)^* \to A^*$ such that $\sigma(a) = a$, for $a \in A$, and $\sigma(L_i) = \sigma(R_i)$, for $i \in \{1, \ldots, n\}$.*

The WES problem, in its general form, is stated as follows: given a WES over the alphabet A and with variables set Ω, $S = \{L_1 = R_1, \ldots, L_n = R_n\}$, find a solution if there exists anyone or determine the no existence of solutions otherwise. The problem we are going to study in this contribution is not as general as stated above, but it is also a NP-complete problem, as we show in Theorem 5 below. In our formulation of the problem also an upper bound d for the length of the variable values in a solution is given. We name this variation the d-WES problem.

d-WES Problem: Given a WES over the alphabet A with variables set Ω, $S = \{L_1 = R_1, \ldots, L_n = R_n\}$, find a solution $\sigma : (A \cup \Omega)^* \to A^*$ such that $|\sigma(x)| \leq d$, for each $x \in \Omega$, or determine the no existence otherwise.

Example 3. For each $d \geq 1$, let F_d and $WordFib_d$ be the d-th Fibonacci number and the d-th Fibonacci word over the alphabet $A = \{0, 1\}$, respectively. For any $d \geq 2$ let S_d be the word equation system over the alphabet $A = \{0, 1\}$ and variables set $\Omega = \{x_1, \ldots, x_{d+1}\}$ defined as:

$$x_1 = 0$$
$$x_2 = 1$$
$$01x_1x_2 = x_1x_2x_3$$
$$\cdots$$
$$01x_1x_2x_2x_3 \ldots x_{d-1}x_d = x_1x_2x_3 \ldots x_{d+1}.$$

Then, for any $d \geq 2$, the morphism $\sigma_d : (A \cup \Omega)^* \to A^*$, defined by

$$\sigma_d(x_i) = FibWord_i,$$

for $i \in \{1, \ldots, d+1\}$, is the only solution of the system S_d. This solution satisfies $|\sigma(x_i)| = F_i \leq F_{d+1}$, for each $i \in \{1, \ldots, d + 1\}$. Recall that $FibWord_1 = 0$, $FibWord_2 = 1$ and $FibWord_i = FibWord_{i-2}FibWord_{i-1}$ if $i > 2$.

Remark 4. Example 3 is quite meaningful itself. It shows that any exact deterministic algorithm which solves the WES problem in its general form (or any heuristic algorithm solving all instances S_d) must have, at least, exponential worst-case complexity. This is due to the fact that the system S_d has polynomial size in d and the only solution of S_d, namely σ_d, has exponential length w.r.t d.

A problem which does not allow to exhibit the exponential length argument for lower complexity bounds is the d-WES problem stated above. Up to this moment, we are not able to prove an exponential worst-case complexity lower bound for it, but the corresponding solvability problem, let us name it the d-SWES problem, becomes NP-complete. The d-SWES problem is stated as follows:

d-*SWES Problem:* Given a WES over the alphabet A with variables set Ω, $S = \{L_1 = R_1, \ldots, L_n = R_n\}$, determine if there exists a solution $\sigma : (A \cup \Omega)^* \to A^*$ satisfying $|\sigma(x)| \leq d$, for each $x \in \Omega$.

Next, we show the reduction from 3-SAT to the 2-SWES problem. It is easy to see that this reduction holds for any $d \geq 2$.

Theorem 5. *For any $d \geq 2$ the d-SWES problem is NP-complete.*

Proof. Clearly the d-SWES problem belongs to the class NP. For the completeness, let us suppose that $S = \{C_0, \ldots, C_m\}$ is an instance for the 3-SAT problem, where

$$C_i = \{\widetilde{x}_{3i}, \widetilde{x}_{3i+1}, \widetilde{x}_{3i+2}\}; \ \widetilde{x}_j \in \{v, \overline{v}\}, \ v \in Variables(S)$$

Then, we build from S, in polynomial time, the following d-SWES instance over the single letter alphabet $A = \{1\}$:
for each $v \in Variables(S)$ we introduce the new variables y_v, z_v and the equation

$$y_v z_v = 1 \ . \tag{2}$$

Now, for each clause $C_i = \{\widetilde{x}_{3i}, \widetilde{x}_{3i+1}, \widetilde{x}_{3i+2}\}$ we introduce the new variables c_i and the equation

$$c_i \widetilde{v}_{3i}, \widetilde{v}_{3i+1}, \widetilde{v}_{3i+2} = 111 \ . \tag{3}$$

where $\widetilde{v}_j = y_v$ if $\widetilde{x}_j = v$ and $\widetilde{v}_j = z_v$ if $\widetilde{x}_j = \overline{v}$, $v \in Variables(S)$

Under these conditions, it is straightforward to see that, the 3-SAT instance S is satisfiable if and only if the WES defined by the sets of equations (2) and (3) with 2 as length bound for the variables, has a solution in A^*.

□

3   The Evolutionary Algorithm

In this section, we present an evolutionary algorithm for solving the d-WES problem. Before describing in detail the genetic operators acting on the chromosomes of our algorithm we introduce the following notation: given an alphabet A and some string over A, $\alpha \in A^*$, for any pair of positions i, j, $1 \leq i \leq j \leq |\alpha|$, in the string α, $\alpha[i, j] \in A^*$ denotes the substring of α given by the extraction of $j - i + 1$ consecutive many letters i through j from string α. In the case $i = j$, we denote by $\alpha[i]$ the single letter substring $\alpha[i, i]$, which represents the i-th symbol of the string α.

3.1 Individual Representation

Given an instance for the d-WES problem, that is, a word equation system $S = \{L_1 = R_1, \ldots, L_n = R_n\}$ with n equations and m variables, over the alphabet $A = \{0, 1\}$ and variables set $\Omega = \{x_1, \ldots, x_m\}$, if a morphism σ is candidate solution for S, then for each $i \in \{1, \ldots, m\}$, the size of the value of any variable x_i, $|\sigma(x_i)|$, must be less than or equal to d. This motivates the following definition.

Definition 6. *With the above assumptions, given an instance S for the d-WES problem, a chromosome $\bar{\alpha}$ (representing a candidate solution for S) is a list of m strings $\{\alpha_1, \ldots, \alpha_m\}$ where, for each $i \in \{1, \ldots, m\}$, $\alpha_i = \alpha_i' \alpha_i''$ is a word over the alphabet $\bar{A} = \{0, 1, B\}$ of size $|\alpha_i| = d$, such that the value of the variable x_i, is represented in the chromosome by the substring $\alpha_i' \in A^*$. The string α_i'' is a word over the single letter alphabet $\{B\}$. The symbol B, in the extended alphabet $\bar{A}$, stands for the blank symbol.*

3.2 Choosing a Suitable Fitness Function

Given a word equation system $S = \{L_1 = R_1, \ldots, L_n = R_n\}$ over the alphabet $A = \{0, 1\}$ with set variables $\Omega = \{x_1, \ldots, x_m\}$ and a chromosome $\bar{\alpha} = \{\alpha_1, \ldots, \alpha_m\}$, representing a candidate solution for S, the fitness of $\bar{\alpha}$ is computed as follows:

First, in each equation, we substitute, for $j \in \{1, \ldots, m\}$, every variable x_j for the corresponding string $\alpha_j' \in A$, and, after this replacement, we get the expressions $\{L_1(\bar{\alpha}) = R_1(\bar{\alpha}), \ldots, L_n(\bar{\alpha}) = R_n(\bar{\alpha})\}$ where $\{L_i(\bar{\alpha}), R_i(\bar{\alpha})\} \subset A^*$ for all $i \in \{1, \ldots, n\}$.

For each $i \in \{1, \ldots, n\}$, let $l_i = |L_i(\bar{\alpha})|$ and $r_i = |R_i(\bar{\alpha})|$ be the size of the left and right side in the expression $L_i(\bar{\alpha}) = R_i(\bar{\alpha})$, respectively, and let

$$s_i = \#\{k \in \{1, \ldots, min\{l_i, r_i\}\} : L_i(\bar{\alpha})[k] = R_i(\bar{\alpha})[k]\},$$

this is, the number of matching symbols in the expression $L_i(\bar{\alpha}) = R_i(\bar{\alpha})$. Then, the fitness of the chromosome $\bar{\alpha}$, $f(\bar{\alpha})$, is defined as:

$$f(\bar{\alpha}) = \sum_{i=1}^{n} (Max\{l_i, r_i\} - s_i).$$

According to the previous definition of the fitness of a chromosome and due to Definition 6 one can easily prove the following fact.

Proposition 7. *Let $S = \{L_1 = R_1, \ldots, L_n = R_n\}$ be a word equation system over the alphabet $A = \{0, 1\}$ with set variables $\Omega = \{x_1, \ldots, x_m\}$ and let $\bar{\alpha} = \{\alpha_1, \ldots, \alpha_m\}$ be a chromosome representing a candidate solution for S. Define the morphism $\sigma : (A \cup \Omega)^* \to A^*$ as $\sigma(x_i) = \alpha_i'$, for each $i \in \{1, \ldots, m\}$. Then the morphism σ is a solution of system S if and only if the fitness of the chromosome $\bar{\alpha}$ is equal to zero, that is $f(\bar{\alpha}) = 0$.*

3.3   Genetic Operators

Selection: We make use of the roulette wheel selection procedure (see [3]).

Crossover: Given two chromosomes $\bar{\alpha} = \{\alpha_1, \ldots, \alpha_m\}$ and $\bar{\beta} = \{\beta_1, \ldots, \beta_m\}$, the result of a crossover is a chromosome constructed applying a local crossover to every of the corresponding strings α_i, β_i. According to Definition 6 suppose that, for each $i \in \{1, \ldots m\}$, $\alpha_i = \alpha_i' \alpha_i''$ and $\beta_i = \beta_i' \beta_i''$, where $\alpha_i', \beta_i' \in A^*$ and α_i'', β_i'' are words over the single letter alphabet $\{B\}$. Fixed $i \in \{1, \ldots m\}$, the crossover of the strings α_i, β_i, denoted as cr_i, is given as follows. Assume $a_i = |\alpha_i'| \leq |\beta_i'|$ then, the substring $cr_i[1, a_i]$ is the result of applying uniform crossover ([3]) to the strings $\alpha_i' \in A^*$ and $\beta_i'[1, a_i]$. Next, we randomly select a position $k_i \in \{a_i + 1, \ldots, d\}$ and define $cr_i[a_i + 1, k_i] = \beta_i'[a_i + 1, min\{k_i, |\beta_i'|\}]$ and $cr_i[k_i + 1, d] = B^{d-k_i} \in \{B\}^*$. We clarify this local crossover by means of the following example:

Example 8. Let $\alpha_i = 01BBBBB$ and $\beta_i = 100011B$ be the variable strings. In this case, we apply uniform crossover to the first two symbols. Let us suppose that 11 is the resulting substring. This substring is the first part of the resulting child. Then, for the corresponding parents substrings, $BBBBB$ and $0011B$, if the selected position were, for instance, position 4, the second part of the child would be $00BBB$, and the complete child would be $1100BBB$.

Mutation: We apply mutation with a given probability p. The concrete value of p in our algorithms is given in Section 4 below. Given a chromosome $\bar{\alpha} = \{\alpha_1, \ldots, \alpha_m\}$, the mutation operator applied to $\bar{\alpha}$ consists in replacing each gene of each word α_i with probability $\frac{1}{d}$, where d is the given upper bound. Remember that the possible values of the genes are $\{0, 1, B\}$, so after mutation, we need to move, for each variable, the blank symbols to the tail of the string.

3.4   Local Search Procedure

We present here the local search procedure which is sketched below. The local search procedure takes as input a chromosome $\bar{\alpha} = (\alpha_1, \ldots, \alpha_m)$, and yields a chromosome $\bar{\beta} = (\beta_1, \ldots, \beta_m)$, which satisfies the following properties. First, if f is the fitness function, it holds $f(\bar{\beta}) \leq f(\bar{\alpha})$. Second, the output chromosome $\bar{\beta}$ cannot be improved either by flipping any single entry of any α_i' or by modifying (by one unit) the length of any single string α_i'. At this point recall that for any $i \in \{1, \ldots, n\}$, the word $\alpha_i = \alpha_i' \alpha_i''$, where $\alpha_i' \in \{0, 1\}^*$ stands for the value of the variable x_i and α_i'', is a word over the single letter alphabet $\{B\}$ of size $d - |\alpha_i'|$. In this context, modifying by one unit the length of α_i' means either to add a bit $0 - 1$ at the end of the string α_i' or to replace the last bit of α_i' by a blank symbol B.

The computational local search process produces a sequence of chromosomes

$$\bar{\alpha} = \bar{\gamma}_0, \ \bar{\gamma}_1, \ \ldots, \ \bar{\gamma}_s = \bar{\beta}$$

satisfying the following properties:

1. $f(\bar{\gamma}_{j+1}) < f(\bar{\gamma}_j)$, $j \in \{0, \ldots, s-2\}$;
2. for each $i \in \{1, \ldots, m\}$ and for each $j \in \{0, \ldots, s-1\}$, $\gamma_{j+1_i}{}'$ is the result of flipping the bits from $\gamma_{j_i}{}'$, and $|\, |\gamma_{j+1_i}{}'| - |\gamma_{j_i}{}'|\, | \leq 1$;
3. $\bar{\gamma}_s = \bar{\gamma}_{s-1}$

Below, we display the pseudo-code of the local search procedure taking as input a chromosome with m string variables of size d (one for each variable).

```
Repeat
     for i=1 to m do
          String_i:=String_i_of_Chromosome;
          New_string_i:=flip_and_modify_length(String_i)
     Chromosome:=(New_string_1,...,New_string_m)
     until New_string_i=String_i for each i in {1,...,m}
```

Notice that, according to the individual representation (see Definition 6), a string $\alpha_i = \alpha_i'\alpha_i''$, turns out to be $\alpha_i' B^{d-a_i}$ (where $a_i = |\alpha_i'|$). The procedure flip_and_modify_length, having this string α_i as input, runs first over each bit of α_i', and then flips the corresponding bit if it produces a gain in the fitness function. Hence α_i' moves to $\alpha_{i\,flip}'$ keeping the length, i. e. $a_i = |\alpha_i'| = |\alpha_{i\,flip}'|$. Next, α_i is modified, and consequently a_i, if there is an improvement in the fitness, producing as final output the best from the following four strings:

$$\alpha_{i\,flip}' B^{d-a_i}, \quad \alpha_{i\,flip}' 0 B^{d-(a_i+1)}, \quad \alpha_{i\,flip}' 1 B^{d-(a_i+1)}, \quad \alpha_{i\,flip}'[1, a_i - 1] B^{d-(a_i-1)}$$

Summarizing, the pseudo-code of our evolutionary algorithm is the following:

```
Generation := 0;
Population := initial_population;
evaluate(Population);
while (not_termination_condition) do
     Best := best_individual(Population);
     New_population := {Best};
     while (|New_population| < |Population|) do
          Pair := select_parents(Population);
          Child := crossover(Pair);
          Child := mutation(Child, probability);
          Child := local_search(Child);
          New_population := insert(Child, New_population);
     Population := New_population;
     Generation := Generation + 1
```

Remark 9. Note that, with respect to the evolutionary algorithm, the initial population is randomly generated. The procedure evaluate(population) computes the fitness of all individuals in the population. Finally, the termination condition is true when a solution is found (the fitness at some individual equals zero) or the number of generations attains a given value.

4   Experimental Results

We have performed our experiments over problem instances having n equations, m variables and a solution of maximum variable length q, denoted as pn-m-q. We run our program for various upper bounds of variable length $d \geq q$. Let us note that, m variables and d as upper bound for the length of a variable, determine a search space of size $(\sum_{i=0}^{d} 2^i)^m = (2^{d+1} - 1)^m$.

Since we have not found in the literature any benchmark instance for this problem, we have implemented a program for random generate word equation systems with solutions, and we have applied our algorithm to these systems[1].

All runs where performed over a processor AMD Athlom XP 1900+; 1,6 GHz and 512 Mb RAM. For a single run the execution time ranges from two seconds, for the simplest problems, to five minutes, for the most complex ones. The complexity of a problem is measured through the average number of evaluations to solution.

4.1   Probability of Mutation and Size of the Initial Population

After some previous experiments, we conclude that the best parameters for our program are **population size** equals 2 and **probability of mutation** equals 0.9. It may seem something singular such a small population size and such a large probability of mutation but, analyzing many of the evolutive algorithms for solving 3-SAT problem, ([2] or [4]), we see that all of them have the property of very small size of population (frequently size one) and very large probability of mutation (sometimes 1). Motivated by this situation, we have run our algorithm without crossover and only applying mutation, and the obtained results, rather successful, were not as good as using the above mentioned parameters allowing crossover.

4.2   Local Search vs. Simple Genetic Algorithm

We show the local search efficiency executing some experiments without local search. Also we execute the experiments only applying local search to individuals randomly generated, i.e. without crossover and mutation. In all the executions, the algorithm stops if a solution is found or the limit of 1500000 evaluations is reached. The results of our experiments are displayed in the following table based on 50 independent runs for each instance. As usually in this type of problems, the performance of the algorithm is measured first of all by the *Success Rate (SR)*, which represents the portion of runs where a solution has been found. Moreover, as a measure of the time complexity, we use the *Average number of Evaluations to Solution (AES)* index, which counts the average number of fitness evaluations performed to find a solution in successful runs.

4.3   Conclusions

The results of the experiments reported in Table 1, indicate that the use of evolutive algorithms is a promising strategy for solving the d-WES problem, and

---

[1] Available on line in http://www.aic.uniovi.es/Tc/spanish/repository.htm

Table 1. Experimental results for various sizes of search space (S.S.). We have also run the simple genetic algorithm without local search (SR0 & AES0) and a purely local search algorithm (SR1 & AES1). The elements of column U.B. are the different upper bounds.

P. instance	U.B.	S.S.	SR	SR0	SR1	AES	AES0	AES1
p10-8-3	3	2^{32}	100%	98%	100%	3593.14	243568	1725.22
p25-8-3	3	2^{32}	100%	100%	100%	771.66	86942	446.48
p10-8-3	4	2^{40}	100%	72%	100%	7094	464914	4250.42
p25-8-3	5	2^{48}	100%	74%	100%	1405.06	393360	1171.22
p25-8-3	6	2^{56}	100%	42%	100%	2502.06	644780	1846.3
p5-15-3	3	2^{60}	100%	50%	100%	19332.8	290949	85397.9
p10-15-3	3	2^{60}	100%	62%	100%	9788.18	458878	209762
p15-12-4	4	2^{60}	100%	100%	100%	644.94	193523	789.6
p10-8-3	7	2^{64}	100%	4%	100%	221302	60725	18062.5
p25-8-3	8	2^{72}	100%	16%	100%	4946.56	389959	4934.46
p10-8-3	10	2^{88}	76%	0%	100%	577926	–	86715.5
p5-15-3	5	2^{90}	100%	6%	40%	192842	366681	770198
p10-15-3	5	2^{90}	98%	10%	12%	362663	712000	801046
p10-15-5	5	2^{90}	100%	2%	0%	104509	801145	–
p25-23-4	4	2^{115}	96%	0%	28%	493575	–	870265
p25-23-4	5	2^{138}	78%	0%	2%	593530	–	220356
p15-25-5	5	2^{150}	96%	0%	0%	359897	–	–
p5-15-3	10	2^{165}	4%	0%	0%	464710	–	–
p25-8-3	20	2^{168}	100%	0%	100%	31189.3	–	157516

that our algorithm has a good behavior also dealing with large search space sizes. Note, as well, that the local search in combination with our crossover and mutation is much better than the simple genetic approach and also better than a purely local search procedure. Nevertheless, these promising results, there are some hard problems, as p10-8-3 or particulary p5-15-3, over which our algorithm has some difficulties trying to find a solution and in other ones, as for example p25-8-3, the program always finds just the same. In both cases, the found solution is always the same and agrees with that proposed by the random problem generator. In this sense, we have not a conclusion about the influence either of the number of equations or of the ratio size of the system/number of variables, on the difficulty of the problem.

5   Summary and Future Work

In this paper we have introduced an effective evolutive algorithm for solving the d-WES problem. The main novelty with respect to previous work on this subject is the use of heuristics. Unfortunately the performance of our heuristic method cannot be compared, at least on the set of instances we have randomly generated, with any exact algorithm, because, due to its very high complexity, no implementation of deterministic algorithms for the d-WES problem is available.

In a work in progress, we plan to design an evolutionary algorithm for the general problem of solving systems of word equations (WES) that profits a logarithmic compression of the size of a minimal solution of a word equation via Lempel–Ziv encodings of words. Such encoding dramatically reduces the size of the search space. We hope that this reduction may allow to avoid the restriction of looking for short solutions (bounded length solutions) and treat the WES problem in its complete generality.

References

1. Angluin D.: Finding patterns common to a set of strings, J. C. S. S. 21(1) (1980) 46-62
2. Eiben, A., van der Hauw, J.: Solving 3-SAT with adaptive Genetic Algorithms. 4th IEEE Conference on Evolutionary Computation, IEEE Press (1997) 81-86
3. Goldbert, D. E.: Genetic Algorithms in Search Optimization & Machine Learning. Addison Wesley Longmann, Inn. (1989)
4. Gottlieb, J.,Marchiori, E., Rossi, C.: Evolutionary Algorithms for the Satisfiability Problem. Evolutionary Computation 10 (1) (2002)
5. Gutiérrez, C.: Solving Equations in Strings: On Makanin's Algorithm. Lucchesi, C.L., Moura, A.V. (eds.) L.N.C.S. 1380 (1998) 358-373
6. Hmlevskiĭ, J.L.: Equations in Free Semigroups. Trudy Mat. Inst. Stelov 107 (1971)
7. Karhumaki, J., Mignosi, F, Plandowski W.,: The expressibility of languages and relations by word equations in ICALP'97, LNCS 1256 (1997) 98-109
8. Koscielski, A., Pacholski, L.: Complexity of Makanin's algorithm, J. ACM 43(4) (1996) 670-684
9. Lentin, A.: Equations in Free Monoids. Automata Languages and Programming (M. Nivat ed.) North Holland (1972) 67-85
10. Makanin, G.S.: The Problem of Solvability of Equations in a Free Semigroup. Math. USSR Sbornik 32 (1977) 2 129-198
11. Plandowski, W., Rytter, W.: Application of Lempel-Ziv encodings to the Solution of Words Equations. Larsen, K.G. et al. (Eds.) L.N.C.S. 1443 (1998) 731-742
12. Plotkin G.D.: Building-in Equational Theories. Mach. Int. 7 (1972) 73-90
13. Robson, J.M., Diekert, V.: On quadratic Word Equations. Meinel, C. et al. (Eds.) L.N.C.S. 1563 (1999) 217-226
14. Siekmann J.: A Modification of Robinson's Unification Procedure. M. Sc. Thesis (1972)

Analysis of the Functional Block and Operator Involved in Fuzzy System Design

O. Valenzuela[1], Lozano Marquez[1], Miguel Pasadas[1], Ignacio Rojas[2],
Manuel Rodríguez[2], and Fernando Rojas[2]

[1] Department of Mathematics, University of Granada, Granada 18071, Spain
[2] Dept. of Computer Architecture and Computer Technology, University of Granada, Spain

Abstract. A great deal of research has been carried out into the main architectures, learning abilities and applications of fuzzy systems. Studies have addressed the problem of selecting different T-norm, T-conorm, types of membership function, different defuzzifier operator and fuzzy implication operator; these constitute the essential functional components of fuzzy inference process. In this paper, and statistical analyses have been carried out into the influence on the behaviour of the fuzzy system arising from the use of different alternatives of the main functional block. Thus, as a complement to the existing intuitive knowledge, it is necessary to have a more precise understanding of the significance of the different alternatives. In the present contribution, the relevance and relative importance of the parameters involved in such a design are investigated by using a statistical tool, the ANalysis Of the VAriance (ANOVA).

1 Introduction

Fuzzy logic and particularly fuzzy controllers have been widely applied to both many consumer products and many industrial process controls. A typical configuration of fuzzy system consists of four principal units: (1) fuzzifier which converts a crisp input to a fuzzy term set; (2) fuzzy rule base which stores fuzzy rules describing how the fuzzy system performs; (3) fuzzy inference engine which performs an approximate reasoning by associating input variables with fuzzy rules; and (4) defuzzifier which converts the fuzzy output to a crisp value for the actual system. The performance of the fuzzy system is influenced by the selection of the fuzzy sets of the linguistic variables, the shapes of membership functions, the fuzzy rule base, the inference mechanism (T-norm, T-conorm and fuzzy implication operator),and the defuzzification method. There exist many possibilities to select the set of basic operations in the fuzzy inference process. As there are many possibilities to select the set of basic operators used in the fuzzy inference process, the search for the fuzzy operators that are most suitable for the different steps of a fuzzy system, their characterization and evaluation, can be included among the most important topics in the field of fuzzy logic. A better insight into the performances of the alternative operators would make it easier to develop a fuzzy application. Examining the specialized literature, it is clear that the selection of the best fuzzy implication operator has become one of the main question in the design of a fuzzy system, being occasionally contradictory (at presently there are more than 72 fuzzy implication proposed and investigated). An ap-

R. Conejo et al. (Eds.): CAEPIA-TTIA 2003, LNAI 3040, pp. 157–166, 2004.

proach to the problem from a different perspective is given. The question is to determine whether the selection of the fuzzy implication operator is more important with respect to the behaviour of the fuzzy system than the operators (mainly T-norm) involved in the definition of the implication function and in the rest of the inference process. Also, which implication operators have similar behaviour?

The structure of a fuzzy system comprises a set of IF-THEN fuzzy rules,Ψ, composed of r rules, R_p (p=1,...,r): $\Psi=\{R_p ; p=1, ..., r\}$. Each rule has the form: *IF X is A THEN Y is B* where A and B are fuzzy variables (linguistic variables such as old, small, high, etc.) described by membership functions in universes of discourse U and V, respectively, where the variables X and Y take their values. To interpret the fuzzy relationship that defines the fuzzy rules, a fuzzy implication operator, I, is used to produce the conclusion of the rule using the compositional rule of inference:

$$\mu_B(y) = \underset{x \in U}{Sup}\{T'(\mu_{A'}(x), I(\mu_A(x), \mu_B(y)))\} \tag{1}$$

where μ_A and μ_B are the membership functions of A and B, and I is the implication operator which is defined in terms of the so called T-norm and T-conorm operators. When the fuzzy rules have more than one input variable in the antecedent part (rules in the form IF X_1 is A_1 AND ... X_m is A_m THEN Y is B_1), the membership value $\mu_A(X^t)$ is calculated by:

$$\mu_A(X^t) = T\left(\mu_{A1}(X_1), ... \mu_{Am}(X_m)\right) \tag{2}$$

where $X^t = (X_1(t), ..., X_m(t))$ is the vector of the input crisp signals fed to the fuzzy system in the time t, and T represents a T-norm operator. In this way, the most important elements in the fuzzy inference process are the fuzzy implication operator, I, the T-norm and T-conorm operators. Triangular norms and conorms are widely used in many contexts. In particular,

- Triangular norms have been used in statistical metric spaces [10] in order to construct the laws which determine the joint distribution of two random metric variables.
- In fuzzy set theory the two laws define intersection and union of fuzzy sets ([16])and
- characterize the decomposable fuzzy measures.
- In the fuzzy logic framework they determine the different types of inference rules.
- In the axiomatic theory by Forte–Kampé de Fèriet the norm is related with the independence notion and the conorm with the incompatible events [1].

In the literature there are many possibilities for the selection of the fuzzy operators that determine how each individual rule is evaluated and how to obtain a final conclusion of all the rules in conjunction. The proper definition of connectives (conjunction, disjunction, negation, implication, etc) constitutes a central issue in the theoretical and applied studies of the area [2]. This paper analyzes the performance of some fuzzy implications proposed in the bibliography together with the operators needed for their definition and for the fuzzy inference process. To do this, an appropriate statistical tool has been used: the multifactorial analysis of the variance ANOVA [3][4], which consists of a set of statistical techniques that allow the analysis and comparison of experiments, by describing the interactions and interrelations between either the quantitative or qualitative variables (called factors in this context) of the system.

2 Application of ANOVA in the Design of a Fuzzy System

The ANalysis Of the VAriance (commonly referred to as ANOVA) is one of the most widely used statistical techniques. The theory and methodology of ANOVA was developed mainly by R.A. Fisher during the 1920s [3]. ANOVA belies its name in that it is not concerned with analyzing variances but rather with analyzing the variation in means. ANOVA examines the effects of one, two or more quantitative or qualitative variables (termed factors) on one quantitative response. ANOVA is useful in a range of disciplines when it is suspected that one or more factors affect a response. ANOVA is essentially a method of analyzing the variance to which a response is subject into its various components, corresponding to the sources of variation which can be identified.

Suppose the easy case that the number of factors affecting the outcome of the experiment is two. We denote by $X_{i,j}$ (i=1, ... n1; j=1,..., n2) the value observed when the first factor is at the i-th level and the second at the j-th level. It is assumed that the two factors do not act independently and therefore that there exists an interaction between them. In this case, the observations fit the following equation:

$$X_{i,j,k} = \mu + \alpha_i + \beta_j + (\alpha\beta)_{i,j} + \varepsilon_{i,j,k} \tag{3}$$

where μ is the fixed effect that is common to all the populations, α_i is the effect associated with the i-th level of the first factor and β_j is the effect associated with the j-th level of the second factor. The term $(\alpha\beta)_{i,j}$ denotes the joint effect of the presence of level i of the first factor and level j of the second one; this, therefore, is denominated the interaction term. The term $\varepsilon_{i,j,k}$ is the influence on the result of everything that could not be assigned or of random factors. The null hypothesis is proposed that each term of the above equation is independent of the levels involved; in other words, on the one hand we have the two equality hypotheses for the levels of each factor:

$$H_{01} : \alpha_1 = ... = \alpha_i = ... = \alpha_{n1}$$
$$H_{02} : \beta_1 = ... = \beta_j = ... = \beta_{n2} \tag{4}$$

and on the other, the hypothesis associated with interaction, which can be expressed in an abbreviated way as:

$$H_{03} : (\alpha\beta)_{ij} = 0, \quad \forall i, j \tag{5}$$

The hypothesis of the equality of several means arises when a number of different treatments or levels of the main factors are to be compared. Frequently one is interested in studying the effects of more than one factor, or the effects of one factor when certain other conditions of the experiment vary, which then play the role of additional factors. With ANOVA, we test a null hypothesis that all of the population means are equal against an alternative hypothesis that there is at least one mean that is not equal to the others. We find the sample mean and variance for each level of the main factor. Using these values, we obtain two different estimates of the population variance. The first one is obtained by finding the sample variance of the n_k sample means from the overall mean. This variance is referred to as the *variance between the means*. The second estimate of the population variance is found by using a weighted average of the sample variances. This variance is called the *variance within the means*. Therefore, ANOVA allows us to determine whether a change in the measure of a given variable is caused by a change in the level of a factor or is just originated by a random effect. In this way, it allows us to distinguish between the components which cause the variations appearing in a set of statistical data and to determine whether the discrepancies *between* the means of the factors are greater than would reasonably be expected according to the variations *within* these factors.

The two estimates of the population variance are then compared using the **F-ratio** test statistic. Calculating the sum of the squares of the observations extended to the levels of all the factors (S_T) and the sum of squares within each level (S_R), and dividing S_T and S_R by the appropriate number of degrees of freedom (**D.F**), obtaining s_T and s_R respectively, the F-ratio is computed as s_T/s_R. This calculated value of the F-ratio for each factor is then compared to a critical value of F of Snedecor with the appropriate degrees of freedom to determine whether we should reject the null hypothesis. When there is no treatment effect, the ratio should be close to 1. If a level of a main effect has a significant influence on the output variable (observed variable, in our case the Error Index), the observed value of F will be greater than the F-Snedecor distribution, with a sufficiently high confidence level (usually 95%). In this case the null hypothesis is rejected and it is argued that at least one of the levels of the analyzed factor must affect the response of the system in a different way. The F-ratio test assumes normal populations with equal variance and independent samples. The analysis is sensitive to inequality of variance (heteroscedasticity) when the sample sizes are small and unequal and care should be taken in interpreting the results.

The comparison between the F-ratio and the F-Snedecor distribution is expressed through the significance level (**Sig. Level**). If this significance level is lower than 0.05 then the corresponding levels of the factor are statistically significant with a confidence level of 95%. Thus, this is the main statistical parameter that will be considered in next Sections in order to derive conclusions about the different factors influencing the design of a fuzzy system.

As a first step, ANOVA determines whether or not the null hypothesis is true, indicating whether all the effects of the different levels of each factor are mutually equivalent and whether the interactions of a certain order are null. From this point, the goal is to verify which factors produce meaningful alterations in the output when their levels change. In the case of the null hypothesis being rejected, a more profound study must be carried out to classify the levels of the most significant factors, taking into account the size of their effects and seeking differences in the output response produced when using a given level of those factors [3]. The levels of a factor that are not statistically different form a homogeneous group and therefore the choice between the various levels belonging to a given homogeneous group has no significant repercussion on the response. Thus, once we discover that some of the factors involved in the design of an fuzzy system do not fulfil the null hypothesis, a study is carried out of the levels of this factor that may be considered statistically non-significant, using Multiple Range Test tables for this purpose; these tables describe the homogeneous groups possible for each of the levels of the factor being analyzed.

In the statistical study performed in next sections, the factors considered are the implication operators, T-norm and T-conorm, the type of defuzzifier and the shape of the membership function. Table 1 gives the different levels considered in each factor when carrying out multifactorial ANOVA (this is not a one-way ANOVA, because we considered all the factors simultaneously). Each of these factors has different levels. For example minimum, product, Einstein, Giles, Dombi, Hamacher and Yager are the levels considered for the type of T-norm. The response variable used to perform the statistical analysis is the mean square error in the output transfer function of a fuzzy system, when some of the levels of the factor considered vary with respect to a reference design. The changes in the response variable are produced when a new combination of T-norm, T-conorm, fuzzy implication function, defuzzification method or membership function is considered, thus changing the structure of the fuzzy system.

3 Selection the Main Parameter in the Design of a Fuzzy System

In the specialized literature, it is proposed that a huge amount of operators can be used as implication operators in the fuzzy control inference process. The fuzzy implication functions can be classified as follows: 1) Strong Implications (S-Implications). This family corresponds to the definition of implications in fuzzy logic based on classical Boolean logic. Examples belonging to this family are the Diene, Dubois-Prade and Mizumoto implications. 2) Quantum Logic Implications (QL-Implications). These type of implications have the form $I(a,b)=S(N(a), T(a,b))$, where T is a T-norm. An example of this type of operator is the Zadeh implication. 3) Residual Implications (R-Implications). The functions belonging to this family reflect a partial ordering on propositions, and are obtained by residuation of a T-norm in the form $I(a,b)=$ $\sup\{\beta\in[0,1] / T(a,\beta) \leq b\}$. Examples of this class of functions are the Gödel, Lukasiewicz and Sharp fuzzy implications. 4) Interpretation of the implication as a conjunction. The form of this function is $I(a,b)=T(a,b)$, which is clearly not an operator that fulfils the condition to be considered as a fuzzy implication. However, in the fuzzy control field, implications which are represented by a T-norm, such as the minimum (Mamdani) or product (Larsen), are usually used for the design of the inference process [8].

With respect to the T-norm and T-conorm operators, many studies on the mathematical properties of these functions and their influence on the fuzzy inference process have been made [11]. Dozens of mathematical functions, each more complex and difficult to implement than the last, have been proposed [5],[11],[12][15]. Moreover, parametrical operators [5] [15] have been frequently used. Because of the great variety of proposed T-norms, it might be thought that some of them should be able to combine fuzzy sets as human beings aggregate information. In practice the minimum and product operators are used for the conjunction of fuzzy sets because of their simplicity of implementation. However, there are empirical studies [5] that have pointed out that these classical operators do not represent the way human beings aggregate information.

Concerning the shape of the membership function considered, we have selected the most used in the bibliography: triangular, trapezoidal and gaussian. Also, we have include an splined-based curve, denominated as Π-shape membership function. This function is defined by Matlab™ software as:

$$\mu_{\Pi-shape} = pimf(x,[a,b,c,d]) \tag{6}$$

where a and d specify the "feet" of the curve, while b and c specify its "shoulders". The generalized bell-shaped membership functions is defined by:

$$\mu_{gbellmf(a,b,c)} = \frac{1}{1 + \left|\dfrac{x-c}{a}\right|^{2b}} , \mu_{sigmoidal} = \frac{1}{1 + e^{-a1(x-c1)}} * \frac{1}{1 + e^{-a2(x-c2)}}$$

(7)

where the parameter b is positive, c is the center and a is a dilation factor. Finally the *Product of two Sigmoidal functions* is the previous equation, where $a1$ and $a2$ have different sign, and $c1$ and $c2$ are the centers.

Table 1. Levels of each factor considered in the statistical analysis.

	Membership Function	Fuzzy implication operator	T-norm	T-conorm	Defuzzifier
Level 1	**Triangular**	**Mamdani (R_m)**	**Minimum**	**Maximum**	**Middle of Maxima**
Level 2	Trapezoidal	Stochastic (R_{st})	Product	Goguen	First of Maxima
Level 3	Gaussian	Kleene-Dienes (R_b)	Einstein	Einstein	Last of Maxima
Level 4	Product of two Sigmoidal	Lukasiewicz (R_a)	Giles	Giles	Height Defuz.
Level 5	Generalized bell curve	Cao (R_{Cao})	Dombi ($\gamma=0.5$)	Dombi ($\gamma=0.5$)	Centre of Area
Level 6	Π-shape memb. functions	Early-Zadeh (R_z)	Dombi ($\gamma=1$)	Dombi ($\gamma=3$)	ξ-Quality ($\xi=1$)
Level 7		Gödel (R_g)	Hamacher ($\lambda=0.5$)	Hamacher	ξ-Quality ($\xi=2$)
Level 8		Gaines (R_{gaines})	Yager ($\beta=2$)	Yager ($\beta=2$)	Slide Defuz ($\delta=0.1$)
Level 9		Wu (R_W)	Yager ($\beta=4$)	Yager ($\beta=4$)	Slide Defuz ($\delta=0.9$)

During the last few years a great deal of research work has focused on the use of different types of defuzzifier and on the analysis of the properties of new defuzzification methods [5]. For example [14] introduces a parameterized family of defuzzification operators, called Semi LInear DEfuzzification (SLIDE). To carry out the statistical study, a selection is made of a set of alternatives representative of each of the factors to be considered. As previously remarked, the response variable used to perform the statistical analysis is the mean square error in the output transfer function of a fuzzy controller, when the factors considered change with respect to a reference. This reference is the combination of implication function, T-norm, T-conorm and defuzzifier shown in bold print in Table 1, that give the different levels considered in each factor to carry out the multifactorial ANOVA.

4   Results of the ANOVA Statistical Study

For the statistical study, a total of 40 fuzzy controllers were examined using systems found in the bibliography, with different numbers and types of membership functions and rules, in order to obtain wide-ranging results. Therefore, all the possible configurations of factors used (T-norm, T-conorm, fuzzy implication, defuzzification method and membership functions) are evaluated for each of the 40 different knowledge bases. The statistical study was carried out using fuzzy system with two input variables and one output, being the number of rules defining each system in the interval [16,49]. For each fuzzy system different simulations have been carried out corresponding to the number of combination of the levels presented in Table 1 (6*9*9*9). The objective of the statistical analysis is to determine the influence in the behaviour of the system (the output surface) when the different alternative to define the levels of the main factor considered in the fuzzy inference process are modified. All the fuzzy systems have a complete set of rules.

Table 2 gives the four-way variance analysis for whole set of examples of fuzzy systems studied. The analysis of variance table containing the sum of squares, degrees of freedom, mean square, test statistics, etc, represents the initial analysis in a compact form. This kind of tabular representation is customarily used to set out the results of ANOVA calculations. As can be seen from Table 2, the defuzzification method and the type of T-norm present the greatest statistical relevance because the higher the F-Ratio or the smaller the Significance level, the greater the relevance of the corresponding factor. The fuzzy implication operator and the T-conorm selected are not so significant. These conclusions are also confirmed by the multiple range tables for the different factors (Table 3). Analyzing the different levels of each of these main factors, it is possible to understand their influence on the characteristics of the inference process and on the fuzzy implication, enabling levels with the same response repercussion to be grouped homogeneously. From Table 3, it is clear that there are two homogeneous groups of implication operators that are not disjoint, thus there exists fuzzy implication which can be classified within the two groups. One group includes the R_m, R_g, R_a, R_{st}, R_{Gaines}, R_W and R_{Cao} implication operators and the other contains R_g, R_a, R_{st}, R_{Gaines}, R_W, R_{Cao}, R_b and R_z. The biggest difference in the mean appears between the Mamdani operator (which, indeed, should be considered as a T-norm operator and not an implication one) and the Zadeh operator. Table 3 shows the results for the T-norm operators, giving three homogeneous groups. The analysis for the T-conorm factor, there are two not disjoint homogeneous groups, with similar behaviour on the design of a fuzzy system. It is important to point out that the ANOVA analysis is capable of ordering the T-norms and T-conorms from more to less restrictive.

Table 2. ANOVA table for the analysis of the main variables in fuzzy inference process.

Main Factors	Sum of Squares	D.F	F-Ratio	Sig.level
Fuzzy implication operator	3.4	8	1.12	0.312
Membership functions	2.1	5	1.53	0.213
T-norm	6.1	8	2.25	0.031
T-conorm	3.1	8	1.13	0.412
Defuzzifier	12.2	8	5.35	0.000

Table 3. Multiple Range test for the variables analized.

Levels of variable Fuzzy Implication operator	Mean	Homogeneous Groups	
1: Mamdani (R_m)	.41	X	
4: Lukasiewicz (R_a)	.65	X	X
7: Gödel (R_g)	0.95	X	X
2: Stochastic (R_{st})	1.11	X	X
8: Gaines (R_{Gaines})	1.24	X	X
5: Cao (R_{Cao})	1.51	X	X
9: Wu (R_W)	1.85		X
3: Kleene-Dienes (R_b)	2.12		X
6: Early-Zadeh (R_z)	2.46		X
Limit to establish significant differences: ± 1.41			
Levels of variable T-norm operator	Mean	Homogeneous Groups	
1: Minimum	0.13	X	
9: Yager (β=4)	0.68	X	X
6: Dombi (γ=1)	1.19	X	X
2: Product	1.66		X
8: Yager (β=2)	1.74		X
7: Hamacher (λ=0.5)	1.87		X	X
3: Einstein	1.98		X	X
5: Dombi (γ=0.5)	3.23		X
4: Giles	3.29		X
Limit to establish significant differences: ± 1.41			
Levels of variable T-conorm operator	Mean	Homogeneous Groups	
1: Maximum	0.11	X	
6: Dombi (γ=3)	0.24	X	
9: Yager (β=4)	0.33	X	X
7: Hamacher	0.52	X	X
8: Yager (β=2)	0.71	X	X
2: Goguen	0.85	X	X
3: Einstein	1.12	X	X
5: Dombi (γ=0.5)	1.16	X	X
4: Giles	1.73		X
Limit to establish significant differences: ± 1.41			
Levels of variable Defuzzifier method	Mean	Homogeneous Groups	
1: Middle of Maxima	0.11	X	
9: Slide Defuzzification (δ=0.9)	0.53	X	X
7: ξ-Quality Defuzzification (ξ=2)	0.84	X	X
2: First of Maxima	1.59		X
3: Last of Maxima	1.74		X
4: Height Defuzzification	2.82		X
8: Slide Defuzzification (δ=0.1)	3.24		X
6: ξ-Quality Defuzzification (ξ=1)	3.35		X
5: Centre of Area	3.55		X
Limit to establish significant differences: ± 1.41			

Table 3. (Cont.)

Levels of variable Membership functions method	Mean	Homogeneous Groups	
1: **Triangular**	0.35	X	
2: Gaussian	0.69	X	X
6: Π-shape membership functions	0.95	X	X
2: Trapezoidal	1.39	X	X
5: Generalized bell curve	1.84	X	X
4: Product of two Sigmoidal functions	2.39		X
		Limit to establish significant differences: ± 1.41	

In Table 3 the levels of the defuzzifier have been grouped into three groups (the last ones with empty intersections, which means that there are no similarities between them). The first group is composed by the Middle of Maxima, Slide and ξ-Quality Defuzzification with δ=0.9 and ξ=2, respectively. The second group is composed by the Slide (δ=0.9), ξ-Quality (ξ=2) First Maximum and the Last Maximum. Finally, the third group includes the Height defuzzification, Slide (δ=0.1), ξ-Quality (ξ=1) and the Centre of Area.

Although indeed, it cannot make sure that the conclusions can be extrapolate to all the application fields in fuzzy logic, it is possible to establish similarities among different levels of the main factor considered in the statistical analysis, so that the fuzzy system designer doesn't have to worry in excess in the selection of different alternatives for the realization of the fuzzy inference process. For example, although an abundant bibliography exists on the different alternatives for the implementation of a T-conorm, the designer of fuzzy system, should be worry more about other parameters that define the fuzzy system than if an operator T-conorm of the Dombi family with γ = 3 or of Yager with β = 4has been used.

5   Conclusion

The goal of this paper is to get a better insight into determining the factor that have the most relevant influence on the design and performance of a fuzzy system, in order to establish the main factor to be carefully studied when a real application is developed. To do this, an appropriate statistical tool has been used: multifactorial analysis of the variance, that allow the analysis and comparison of experiments, by describing the interactions and interrelations between either the quantitative or qualitative variables (called factors in this context) of the system. The selection of an appropriate implication operator is unfortunately one of the most confusing tasks a designer must face. Choosing an implication operator from the many viable options is a hard task, not just because there is a chance of selecting the wrong one, but because it is difficult to justify the choice. Furthermore, we have to consider that the final output is not only determined by the implication operator but also by the accompanying aggregation operator (mainly T-norm and T-conorm), the defuzzification method and the shape of the membership functions. These different alternativves yields more than a hundred combinations to be examined when considering the different methods found in the literature. The present statistical study was motivated by the great variety of alternatives that a designer has to take into account when developing a fuzzy system. Thus, instead of the existing intuitive knowledge, it is necessary to have a more precise understanding of the significance of the different alternatives.

Acknowledgements

This work has been partially supported by the Spanish CICYT Project DPI2001-3219.

References

1. Carlo Bertoluzza,Viviana Doldi, "On the distributivity between t-norms and t-conorms" Accepted in Fuzzy Sets and Systems, 2003
2. C.Fodor, T.Keresztfalvi, Nonstandard conjunctions and implications in fuzzy logic, *International Journal of Approximate Reasoning* 12, 69-84, 1995
3. R.A.Fisher, The Comparison of Samples with Possibly Unequal Variances", Annals of Eugenics 9 (1936) 174-180 (Also in R.A.Fisher, *Contribution to Mathematical Statistics*, New York: Wiley, 1950).
4. G.Casella, R.L.Berger, "Statistical Inference", *Duxbury Press*, 1990.
5. D.Driankov, H.Hellendoorn, M.Reinfrank, *An introduction to fuzzy control*, Springer-Verlag. 1993.
6. J.Harmse, Continuous fuzzy conjunctions and disjunctions, *IEEE Trans. of Fuzzy Systems* 4 (3), 295-314, 1996.
7. Erich Peter Klement, Radko Mesiar and Endre Pap Problems on triangular norms and related operators, Fuzzy Sets and Systems, Accepted, 2003
8. Erich Peter Klement, Radko Mesiar, Endre Pap, "Triangular Norms", Kluwer Academic Pub, 2000
9. J.B.Kiska, M.E.Kochanska, D.S.Sliwinska, The influence of some fuzzy implication operators on the accuracy of a fuzzy model - Part I, II *Fuzzy Sets and Systems*,15, 111-128, 223-240, 1985.
10. B.Schweizer,A.Sklar,Statistical metric spaces,Paci c J.Math.10 (1960)313 –334.
11. I.B.Turksen, Interval-valued fuzzy sets and 'compensatory AND', *Fuzzy Sets and Systems* 51, 295-307, 1992.
12. E.Trillas, S.Cubillo, C.Campo, A few remarks on some T-conditional functions, *IEEE International Conference on Fuzzy Systems* (1997), 153-156
13. R.R. Yager, Fuzzy sets and approximate reasoning in decision and control, *IEEE International Conference on Fuzzy Systems* (1992) 418-428.
14. R.R.Yager, D.P. Filev, SLIDE: A Simple adaptive defuzzification method, *IEEE Transactions on fuzzy systems*,1, 69-78, 1993.
15. R.R.Yager, Criteria importances in OWA aggregation: an application of fuzzy modelling, *IEEE International Conference on Fuzzy Systems* (1997), 1677-1682
16. Z.Wang,G.J.Klir,Fuzzy Measure Theory,Plenum Press,New York,1992.

Analysis of the Topology Preservation of Accelerated Growing Neural Gas in the Representation of Bidimensional Objects

Francisco Flórez Revuelta, Juan Manuel García Chamizo,
José García Rodríguez, and Antonio Hernández Sáez

Departamento de Tecnología Informática y Computación, Universidad de Alicante,
Apdo. 99, 03080 Alicante, Spain
{florez,juanma,jgarcia,ahernandez}@dtic.ua.es

Abstract. Self-organizing neural networks endeavour to preserve the topology of an input space by means of competitive learning. This capacity is used for the representation of objects and their motion. In addition, these applications usually have real-time constraints imposed on them. This paper describes several variants of a Growing Neural Gas self-organizing network that accelerate the learning process. However, in some cases this acceleration causes a loss in topology preservation and, therefore, in the quality of the representation. Our study quantifies topology preservation using different measures to establish the most suitable learning parameters, depending on the size of the network and on the time available for adaptation.

1 Introduction

Through competitive learning, self-organizing neural models adapt the reference vectors of neurons and the network that interconnects them, thereby obtaining a network that tries to preserve the topology of a high-dimensional input space [1], that is, similar patterns are mapped onto adjacent neurons and, vice versa, neighbouring neurons activate or code similar patterns. This capability is usually employed to extract the most important features of an input space in order to improve or to facilitate a later classification. In our laboratory we use these neural models in a different way, approximating a self-organizing network, Growing Neural Gas (GNG) [2], to an input space of the same dimensionality and thereby obtaining a reduced representation of the data manifold. Our interest lies in the final structure of the network that interconnects the neurons and that allows the representation of objects [3] (figure1). These models are also capable of continuously readapting to new input patterns, it not being necessary to recommence the learning process. This latter capacity has particular applications in motion analysis [4].

These two applications – representation of objects and of their motion – are in many cases subject to high temporal constraints, which is why the complete adaptation of the network within the available time must be assured. This is made possible by modifying the learning parameters of the GNG so as to terminate within the time available. Nevertheless, this modification can affect the quality of the adaptation, measured in terms of the topology preservation of the input space.

R. Conejo et al. (Eds.): CAEPIA-TTIA 2003, LNAI 3040, pp. 167–176, 2004.

In other applications with no time limit the process of adaptation to the network can be interrupted. What this means is that a good preservation of the topology should be maintained throughout the learning process in order to ensure a correct representation of the input space.

Several modifications to accelerate learning are considered in this paper and applied to the representation of two-dimensional objects. We also consider the degree of topology preservation depending on the learning parameters and on the time available for their adaptation.

Fig. 1. Representation of two-dimensional objects using a self-organizing network.

2   Growing Neural Gas

Growing Neural Gas is an incremental neural model that does not require a prior specification of network size (as happens with other methods). From a minimal network, a growth process takes place that is continued until a termination condition is fulfilled. In contrast with other methods - where learning falls basically in decaying parameters - the learning parameters are constant in time.

The GNG learning algorithm for approximating the network to the input manifold is as follows:

1. Start with two neurons a and b at random positions w_a and w_b in $\mathcal{R}^d$.
2. Generate an input signal ξ according to a density function $P(\xi)$.
3. Find the nearest neuron (winner neuron) s_1 and the second nearest neuron s_2.
4. Increase the age of all the edges emanating from s_1.
5. Add the square of the distance between the input signal and the winner neuron to an error counter for s_1:

$$\Delta error(s_1) = \left\| w_{s_1} - \xi \right\|^2 \tag{1}$$

6. Move the winner neuron s_1 and its topological neighbours (neurons connected to s_1) towards ξ according to learning steps ε_w and ε_n, respectively:

$$\Delta w_{s_1} = \varepsilon_w (\xi - w_{s_1}) \tag{2}$$

$$\Delta w_{s_n} = \varepsilon_n (\xi - w_{s_n}) \tag{3}$$

7. If s_1 and s_2 are already connected by an edge, set the age of this edge to 0. If no connection exists, create one.

8. Remove any edges older than a_{max}. If this results in isolated neurons (those without emanating edges), remove these as well.
9. For each number λ of input signals generated, insert a new neuron as follows:
   - Determine the neuron q with the maximum accumulated error.
   - Insert a new neuron r between q and its most distant neighbour f :

$$w_r = 0.5 \left(w_q + w_f \right) \tag{4}$$

   - Insert new edges connecting the neuron r with neurons q and f , removing the old edge between q and f .
   - Decrease the error variables for neurons q and f , multiplying them by a constant α. Start the error variable of r with the new value for the error variable for q and f .
10. Decrease all error variables by multiplying them by a constant β.
11. If the stopping criterion is not yet achieved, return to step 2.

To sum up, the adaptation of the network to the input space takes place in step 6. The insertion of connections (step 7) between the two neurons nearest to each input pattern eventually establishes a Delaunay triangulation induced by the input space [1]. Elimination of connections (step 8) removes the edges that should no longer form part of this triangulation. This is done by eliminating the connections between neurons that are no longer close by or that have nearer neurons. Finally, the accumulated error (step 5) allows the identification of those zones of the input space where it is necessary to increase the number of neurons to improve mapping.

3   Modifying Growing Neural Gas Parameters to Accelerate Learning

Termination of GNG competitive learning is usually determined by the insertion of all the neurons until a predetermined size is obtained. Nevertheless, if a temporal factor is included as a condition for termination, in some cases it will not be possible to complete the adaptive process, with the consequent loss of topology preservation from the creation of connections between neurons that should not be joined or the absence of others that should be created (figure 2). This will create differences between the final configuration of the network and the Delaunay triangulation that should have been established.

If a complete network is required, with all its neurons and within a predetermined time, the learning algorithm needs to be modified to accelerate termination. The main factor affecting learning time is the number of input signals generated per iteration, since new neurons are inserted (step 9 above) at smaller intervals, with less time required to complete the network.

Another alternative is to insert more than one neuron per iteration, with step 9 of the learning algorithm (above) repeated as often as necessary. (See [6] for a description of the insertion of two neurons per iteration, depending on circumstances). In our case, several neurons are inserted in those zones where the greatest accumulated error exists.

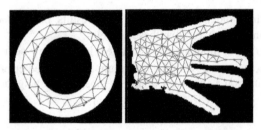

Fig. 2. Incomplete (incorrect) adaptations due to early termination of the learning process.

Nevertheless, these alternatives affect the preservation of the topology of the input space, i.e. the quality of the representation (figure 3). For this reason, different measures of topology preservation will be used here in order to evaluate the correction of the different adaptations over time.

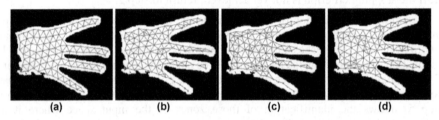

Fig. 3. Final adaptations according to the number of neurons inserted per iteration: (a) 1, (b) 2, (c) 5 and (d) 10.

4 Measures of Topology Preservation

The quality of the adaptation of self-organizing neural networks is mainly measured in two aspects: resolution and preservation of the topology of the input space.

The resolution measure usually employed is the quantization error [5], expressed as:

$$\mathcal{E} = \sum_{\forall \xi \in \mathbb{R}^d} \left\| w_{s_\xi} - \xi \right\| p(\xi) \tag{5}$$

where s_ξ is the nearest neuron to each input pattern ξ.

The first measure developed to evaluate topology preservation was the topographic product [7], which compares the neighbourhood relationship between each pair of neurons in the network with respect to both their position on the map and their reference vectors:

$$P = \frac{1}{\mathcal{N}(\mathcal{N}-1)} \sum_{j=1}^{\mathcal{N}} \sum_{k=1}^{\mathcal{N}-1} \log \left(\left(\prod_{l=1}^{k} \frac{d^V\left(w_j, w_{n_l^A(j)}\right)}{d^V\left(w_j, w_{n_l^V(j)}\right)} \cdot \frac{d^A\left(j, n_l^A(j)\right)}{d^A\left(j, n_l^V(j)\right)} \right)^{1/2k} \right) \tag{6}$$

where j is a neuron, w_j is its reference vector, n_l^V is the l-th closest neighbour to j in the input manifold V according to a distance d^V, and n_l^A is the l-th nearest neuron to j in the network A according to a distance d^A. In order to use this measure for non-linear input spaces the geodesic distance [8] is employed as d^V.

Another measure is the topographic function [9], which compares the resulting neural network with the Delaunay triangulation induced by the input space, measuring the number of neurons with adjacent receptive fields but which are not connected and vice versa.

It would be desirable for all measures to take into account both aspects of resolution and topology preservation. This is not the case for the above measures, however, even though both the topographic product and the topographic function assume resolution as implicit in the competitive learning of self-organizing models.

Kaski and Lagus [10] proposed a goodness measure C that combined both aspects. First obtained is the closest reference vector for each input pattern, and then the path from that neuron to the second-closest reference vector in the map. The result is the sum of these distances.

Deviations from zero in these three measures indicate a loss in topology preservation, with the sign indicating, in the case of the product and the topographic function, whether the dimensionality of the network is larger or smaller than that of the input space to be represented.

5 Comparative Study of the Different Alternatives

In this section we will compare the quality of the representation of different networks in which some learning parameters have been modified to accelerate adaptation. Some others of the learning parameters are fixed ($\varepsilon_1 = 0.1$, $\varepsilon_2 = 0.01$, $\alpha = 0.5$, $\beta = 0.0005$, $a_{max} = 250$). The different alternatives will be denoted as GNG_x^λ where λ indicates the number of input signals and x represents the number of neurons per iteration.

Our study included all the input spaces depicted in Figure 1. Since results are very similar, in the interest of brevity we will only discuss the results obtained for the most complex input space (the hand).

Table 1(a) gives the learning times for the different options when the pre-established termination condition is a network size of 100 neurons. Table 1(b) shows the number of neurons in each network by the time the fastest variant (GNG_{10}^{10000}) terminates. Obviously, inserting several neurons or reducing the signals per iteration means that networks of greater size are obtained in less time.

Figures 4 and 5 depict topology preservation for the studied alternatives, not only of the final networks, but of the intermediate networks generated during the adaptive process. In this way it is possible to consider the degree of topology preservation of the network should learning be interrupted by an external event.

Table 1. (a) Learning time for networks with 100 neurons and (b) number of neurons in the networks at 0.12 seconds.

Variant	Time (sec.)
GNG_1^{10000}	1
GNG_1^{5000}	0.57
GNG_1^{2500}	0.30
GNG_1^{1000}	0.13
GNG_2^{10000}	0.56
GNG_5^{10000}	0.24
GNG_7^{10000}	0.17
GNG_{10}^{10000}	0.12

(a)

Variant	Neurons
GNG_1^{10000}	18
GNG_1^{5000}	30
GNG_1^{2500}	51
GNG_1^{1000}	93
GNG_2^{10000}	30
GNG_5^{10000}	62
GNG_7^{10000}	79
GNG_{10}^{10000}	100

(b)

5.1 Topology Preservation Depending on the Number of Neurons

Figure 4 shows topology preservation of the GNG variants depending on the number of neurons in the network and as the learning process advances. This is of interest in cases where, although there are no temporal constraints to limit the adaptive process, a possible maximum size of the network is established, e.g. 100 neurons.

Quantization error is similar for all the alternatives since the resolution depends mainly on the number of neurons in the network. The slower alternatives, which better situate each neuron, naturally present a lower quantization error.

In the initial adaptation stages the networks attempt to make a rapid representation of the input space, and for this reason the preservation of the topology fluctuates considerably. When a small number of neurons are inserted, this is stabilized. Nevertheless, if the faster options are employed, topology preservation is poorer throughout the adaptive process, since there are edges between neurons that should not be connected and vice versa. Similar results are obtained for combined resolution and topology preservation measures. Included also as a combined measure is the product of the quantization error and the topographic product.

One particular observation is that, above a certain number of neurons, the different measures stabilize; in Figure 4, for example, stabilization occurs when the networks reach a size of around 40 neurons.

5.2 Topology Preservation Depending on the Time Available

Figure 5 shows topology preservation throughout the adaptation process of the network, with no restrictions in the number of neurons but with a time limit. In this case, the time limit set is that necessary to complete the variant GNG_1^{10000} with 100 neurons.

It can be observed that the faster variants, by creating a greater number of neurons (table 2), produce a better resolution and, therefore, a smaller quantization error.

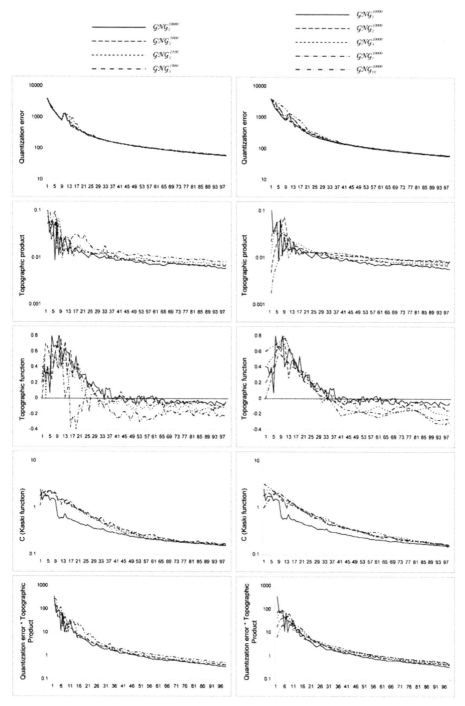

Fig. 4. Topology preservation according to different numbers of neurons.

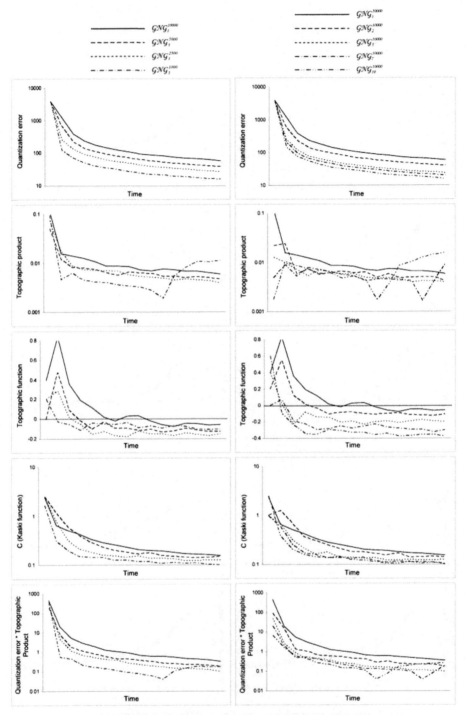

Fig. 5. Topology preservation according to the time available.

Table 2. Number of neurons created in a preestablished time.

Variant	Neurons	Variant	Neurona
$\mathcal{GNG}_1^{10000}$	100	$\mathcal{GNG}_2^{10000}$	146
$\mathcal{GNG}_1^{5000}$	149	$\mathcal{GNG}_5^{10000}$	247
$\mathcal{GNG}_1^{2500}$	221	$\mathcal{GNG}_7^{10000}$	294
$\mathcal{GNG}_1^{1000}$	350	$\mathcal{GNG}_{10}^{10000}$	372

Differences in topology preservation of the different options are not significant when measured using the topographic product. Nevertheless, because the number of input signals per iteration is insufficient to adapt all the neurons, topology preservation is lost when the number of neurons is high.

The topographic function, on the other hand, shows differences in topology preservation, indicating that the faster networks have incorrect connections.

Finally, the combined measures are highly dependent on the quantization error and are, therefore, more suitable for larger networks.

6 Discussion

Growing Neural Gas topology preservation is affected by both learning parameters and the time available. Faster methods improve resolution but in many cases cause topology preservation to deteriorate. This is because the relationship between the number of neurons and the input signals per iteration decreases, which would indicate that there is an upper limit to the network size for each learning acceleration alternative. It can, however, also be observed that there is no improvement in the quantization error or in topology preservation above a certain number of neurons. This would indicate that a minimum network size is necessary to obtain an acceptable representation of objects. Likewise, topology preservation should be kept between acceptable limits during the longest possible learning time, in case some external event should interrupt the adaptation.

Related research is presently underway in which we are studying the degree of topology preservation for other self-organizing models (Neural Gas [11], GWR [12]). Our intention is to identify the characteristics of these networks that will allow a suitable and rapid representation of an input space, with a view to developing new combined self-organizing neural networks.

The application of these models to the representation of objects and their motion will be made possible by adapting the different learning parameters so that a good quality representative network is obtained within the time available.

Acknowledgements

This work has been partially funded by the Science and Technology Agency of the Valencian Autonomous Government (Spain) under project CTIDIA/2002/109.

References

1. Martinetz, T., Schulten, K.: Topology Representing Networks. Neural Networks, 7(3) (1994) 507-522
2. Fritzke, B.: A Growing Neural Gas Network Learns Topologies. In Advances in Neural Information Processing Systems 7, G. Tesauro, D.S. Touretzky y T.K. Leen (eds.), MIT Press (1995) 625-632
3. Flórez, F., García, J.M., García, J., Hernández, A.: Representation of 2D Objects with a Topology Preserving Network. In Proceedings of the 2nd International Workshop on Pattern Recognition in Information Systems (PRIS'02), Alicante. ICEIS Press (2001) 267-276
4. Flórez, F., García, J.M., García, J., Hernández, A.: Hand Gesture Recognition Following the Dynamics of a Topology-Preserving Network. In Proc. of the 5th IEEE Intern. Conference on Automatic Face and Gesture Recognition, Washington, D.C. IEEE, Inc. (2001) 318-323
5. Kohonen, T.: Self-Organizing Maps. Springer-Verlag, Berlin Heidelberg (1995)
6. Cheng, G., Zell, A.: Double Growing Neural Gas for Disease Diagnosis. In Proceedings of Artificial Neural Networks in Medicine and Biology Conference (ANNIMAB-1), Goteborg, Vol. 5. Springer (2000) 309-314
7. Bauer, H.-U., Pawelzik, K.R.: Quantifying the Neighborhood Preservation of Self-Organizing Feature Maps. IEEE Transactions on Neural Networks, 3(4) (1992) 570-578
8. Flórez, F., García, J.M., García, J., Hernández, A.: Producto Topográfico Geodésico: Mejora para medir la preservación de la topología de redes neuronales auto-organizativas. In Proceedings of the X Conferencia de la Asociación Española de Inteligencia Artificial (CAEPIA'2003), San Sebastián, Vol. II. Servicio Editorial de la Universidad del País Vasco (2003) 87-90
9. Villmann, T., Der, R., Herrmann, M., Martinetz, T.M.: Topology Preservation in Self-Organizing Feature Maps: Exact Definition and Measurement. IEEE Transactions on Neural Networks, 8(2) (1997) 256-266
10. Kaski, S., Lagus, K.: Comparing Self-Organizing Maps. Lecture Notes in Computer Sciences, 1112. Springer, Berlin (1996) 809-814
11. Martinetz, T, Schulten, K.: A "Neural-Gas" Network Learns Topologies. In Artificial Neural Networks, T. Kohonen, K. Mäkisara, O. Simula y J. Kangas (eds.) (1991) 1:397-402
12. Marsland, S., Shapiro, J.; Nehmzow, U.: A self-organising network that grows when required. Neural Networks, 15 (2002) 1041-1058

Application of Crossover Operators
Based on Confidence Interval in Modeling Problems
Using Real-Coding Genetic Algorithms[*]

Rafael del Castillo Gomariz, César Hervás Martínez, Sebastián Ventura Soto,
and Domingo Ortiz Boyer

Department of Computing and Numerical Analysis, University of Córdoba
14071 Córdoba, Spain
grupo@ayrna.org

Abstract. In this work we develop and compare multi-parent crossover operators based on the extraction of characteristics from the best individuals in the population (average, median, standard deviation and quantiles). These statistics evolve in parallel with the algorithm. The proposed operators are used in combination with a real-coded genetic algorithm for the evolution of polynomial functions to solve microbial growth problems. Their performance is compared to other crossover operators for real-coded genetic algorithms. Both the prediction errors made in the modelling of systems and the objectivity and speed in the identification of models show the viability of this type of models that mix base functions with evolutionary computation.

1 Introduction

Nowadays, the modelling of systems is one of the most interesting problems in many scientific branches. The resolution of this problem has been classically approached by using regression techniques in order to minimize an error function, over a model type previously established by the researcher. Most often the functional model to apply is non-linear and it usually presents a high dimensionality, making the process considerably more complicate, as there is scarce additional information, or none at all.

The most common approximation functions are linear and generalized linear models, flattened hyperplanes, response surfaces, artificial neural networks, Fourier series, wave functions, decision trees and flattened kernel functions. All of them provide explicit models for the relationship between the predictive variables x and the response variable y [2] (only one in our case).

In this work we present an methodology for the estimation of Response Surface (RS) polynomial models through Real-Coded Genetic Algorithms (RCGA) using specific real-coded crossover operators: BLX-α [3], an adaptation of BLX-α, and the recently developed multi-parent crossovers CIXL and CIXL2 [4].

In Section 2 we introduce multiparent crossover operators. Section 3 presents a general approach to the evolution of RS models with RCGAs and a crossover operator

---

[*] This work has been funded by the spanish Ministry of Science and Technology, MCyT, through Project TIC 2002-04026-C02, and by FEDER funds.

R. Conejo et al. (Eds.): CAEPIA-TTIA 2003, LNAI 3040, pp. 177–186, 2004.

adapted from BLX-α. Section 4 shows the results of a equality of means test over two factors: grade of the initial RS and type of crossover used. Conclusions are drawn and presented in Section 5.

2   Crossover Algorithms Based on Confidence Intervals

In the resolution of RS polynomial models, the multi-parent crossover operators give to the RCGA the additional value of being able to use information from several individuals to create a new one, with a better fitness if possible. We present in this section a type of multi-parent crossover algorithm based on the location and dispersion characteristics of the genes from the best individuals in the population. These characteristics will be used to build virtual parents that inherit the traits associated to the previous estimators.

The aforementioned idea leads to the definition of two crossover operators based on Confidence Intervals using the norms L_2 (CIXL2) and L_1 (CIXL1), whose equilibrium between exploration and exploitation seems to be very suitable for this type of problems. Their performance in model identification problems has been made clear in [6], where they have been applied to non-linear regression problems taken from "the Statistical Reference Datasets Projects (STRDP)" which can be consulted in http://www.nist.gov/itl/div898/strn/nls.

2.1   Intervals Associated to Median and Mean
as Location Parameters of the Genes

Let β be the set of the n individuals in the population and let $\beta^* \subset \beta$ be the set formed by the best n individuals (the ones with highest fitness). If we consider that the genes β_i of the chromosomes β^* are independent random variables following a continuous distribution function H (β_i), with a location parameter μ_{β_i}, then we have the model β_i $= \mu_{\beta_i} + e_i$, being e_i a random variable, for each $i=1,...$ p.

If we suppose, for each i, that the best n individuals actually form a simple random sample $(\beta_{i1}, \beta_{i2, \dots} \beta_{in})$ of the β_i distribution then the model takes the form

$$\beta_{ij} = \mu_{\beta_i} + e_{ij}, \text{ for } j=1,..., n \tag{1}$$

Now, from the model proposed in (1), if we consider the norm L_1, given by $\|\beta_i\|_1 = \sum_{j=1}^{n} |\beta_{ij}|$, and we look for an estimator of μ_{β_i} associated with the negative gradient method, that is, S1 (μ_{β_i}) = -dD$_1$ (μ_{β_i})/dμ_{β_i}, where the dispersion function induced by the norm L_1 is D$_1$ $(\mu_{\beta_i}) = \sum_{j=1}^{n} |\beta_{ij} - \mu_{\beta_i}|$, and we define H as the distribution function of the β_i, then we have that the negative gradient estimator of the location parameter through the norm L_1 is the median of the β_i distribution. That is, $\mu_{\beta_i} = M_{\beta_i}$ being its distribution binomial with parameters n and ½. From this distribution we can already build confidence intervals for the location parameter, populational median, whose estimator is the sample median M_{β_i} of the genes of the n better individuals, for a generic sample of size n, with a confidence coefficient $1-\alpha$. In this case we apply the Neyman method for calculating confidence intervals and we have that

$$I_{1-\alpha}(\mu_{\beta_i}) = [\beta_{i(k+1)}, \beta_{i\,(n-k)}], \tag{2}$$

being $\beta_i(k+1)$ and $\beta_i(n-k)$ the values of the genes associated to the position $k+1$ and $n-k$ when the sample has been sorted, and where the k value is determined from the underlying binomial distribution.

If we take into consideration the norm L_2, defined as $\|\beta_i\|_2 = \sum_{j=1}^{n} \beta_{ij}^2$, it can be proved that the negative gradient estimator of the location parameter through the norm L_2 is the average of the distribution β_i. Assuming that the distribution of the genes $H(\beta_i)$ is normal, the confidence interval is calculated as:

$$I_{1-\alpha}(\mu_{\beta_i}) = [\bar{\beta_i} - t_{n-1,\alpha/2} \times \bar{S}_{\beta_i}/\sqrt{n} ; \bar{\beta_i} + t_{n-1,\alpha/2} \times \bar{S}_{\beta_i}/\sqrt{n}] \tag{3}$$

where t_n-1 is a Student t distribution with $n-1$ degrees of freedom.

From the previous confidence intervals we build 3 virtual parents: one formed by all the lower limits (*CILL*), other formed by all the upper limits (*CIUL*) and a third one (*CIM*) formed by the average (if using CIXL2) or median (if using CIXL1) values of the confidence intervals of each gene. The *CILL* and *CIUL* individuals divide the domain of each gene, D_i, into 3 subintervals I_i^L, I_i^{IC} and I_i^R, such that $D_i \equiv I_i^L \cup I_i^{IC} \cup I_i^R$, $I_i^L \equiv [a_i, CILL_i]$, $I_i^{IC} \equiv (CILL_i, CIUL_i)$ and $I_i^R \equiv [CIUL_i, b_i]$, being a_i and b_i the lower and upper limits of the domain D_i.

The crossover operators will create a single offspring β^s from the individual $\beta^f \in \beta$, the individuals *CILL, CIUL* and *CIM*, and their fitnesses, in the following way:

- If $\beta_i^f \in I_i^L$ then, if the fitness of β^f is bigger than that of *CILL*, then $\beta_i^s = r(\beta_i^f - CILL_i) + \beta_i^f$, else $\beta_i^s = r(CILL_i - \beta_i^f) + CILL_i$;
- If $\beta_i^f \in I_i^{IC}$ then, if the fitness of β^f is bigger than that of *CIM*, then $\beta_i^s = r(\beta_i^f - CIM_i) + \beta_i^f$, else $\beta_i^s = r(CIM_i - \beta_i^f) + CIM_i$;
- If $\beta_i^f \in I_i^R$ then, if the fitness of β^f is bigger than that of *CIUL*, then $\beta_i^s = r(\beta_i^f - CIUL_i) + \beta_i^f$, else $\beta_i^s = r(CIUL_i - \beta_i^f) + CIUL_i$,

where r is a random number in the interval $[0,1]$.

3   Estimation and Design of Polynomial Base Functions with RCGA

In general, the modelling of a system whose equation is known is a problem of conventional regression. In this type of problems there is a functional relationship between a series of independent variables x_i and a dependent variable y, in the form:

$$y = f(\beta_0, \beta_1, ..., \beta_m, x_1, ..., x_n) \tag{4}$$

where β_i are the coefficients to be adjusted in order to minimize the sum of squared residuals. This optimization problem can be solved with a classical algorithm, or with a genetic algorithm. If we opt for the second option we would codify the individual as a set of genes, each one representing a coefficient.

3.1   Response Surface Models and Genetic Algorithms

Response surface models explain a large variety of phenomena. The expression that defines them is a grade G polynomial in each variable [5][8]. Therefore they are functions following the form

$$f(x_1, x_2, ..., x_n) = c_0 + \sum_{i=1}^{n} c_i x_i + ... + \sum_{\substack{i_1, i_2 ... i_G = 1 \\ i_k \le i_{k+1}}}^{n} c_{i_1 i_2 ... i_G} x_{i_1} x_{i_2} ... x_{i_G} \tag{5}$$

where G is the grade of the model, x_i are the independent variables, n is the number of independent variables and β_i are the coefficients.

If we want to model the structure of a phenomenon by using the aforementioned model, we will codify individuals with as many genes as the coefficients in the model that we pretend to develop. This number of coefficients depends on the number of variables and the grade of the model in question but, as we already mentioned, the interpretability of the models is a very desirable characteristic in every type of modeling, and that leads us to seek simple models. The codification of an individual uses one gene for each coefficient of the model. However, this gene has two well-differentiated parts. On one hand, there is an allele which indicates the presence or absence of the corresponding term (monomial) in the model; and on the other hand there is another allele to codify the value of the coefficient in question.

Figure 1 shows an individual that represents a grade 2 RS with 3 variables, adapted to this method. To obtain expressions with the minimum number of terms, we include one term in the fitness function that rewards the smaller (i.e. simpler) models. In this way, our problem turns into a problem with two objectives: on one hand, it is convenient that the error is minimum, but, on the other hand, it is also interesting to obtain models with a small number of coefficients.

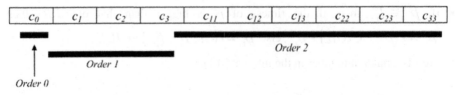

Fig. 1. Individual that represents a response surface of order 2 with 3 independent variables.

Since the number of objectives is very reduced, we did not consider a multi-objective algorithm and to simplify we chose a fitness function that calculates a linear combination of them, weighing up their importance with a coefficient.

3.2 Microbian Growth Models

In this work we develop a model for the growth prediction of the altering microorganism *Leuconostoc mesenteroides ssp. mesenteroides* [9], which has been frequently isolated as a responsible for the alteration of different types of meat products. The available data have been 210 signal-time curves of Leuconostoc Mesenteroides growth under different conditions of temperature T (10.5, 14, 17.5, 21 and 24° C), pH (5.5, 6, 6.5, 7 and 7.5), sodium chloride concentration NaCl (0.25, 1.75, 3.25, 4.75 and 6.25%) and sodium nitrite concentration NaNO2 (0, 50, 100, 150 and 200 ppm). These 210 curves correspond to 30 different experimental conditions chosen according to a Composite Central Design[1] of experiments. From each one of these 30 conditions, 7 experiment replicas were conducted. Five of the experimental results sets were chosen at random to form the training set, and the remaining two formed the generalization set. Thus the training set is composed of 150 curves and the generalization (or test) one by 60.

Next, these resultant values of absorbancy, considered throughout the time, were adjusted by means of an exponential Baranyi and Roberts-type model [1] with the help of the DMFit 1.0 program (József Baranyi, Institute of Food Research, Norwich Research Park, Norwich NR4 7UA, UK). The results were the training and generalization values of the kinetic growth parameters lnlag, grate and yend (the logarithm of the adaptation phase, the growth rate and the maximum density) of the microorganism for each experimental condition.

3.3 Genetic Algorithm

Table 1 summarizes the parameters used for the genetic algorithm. The fitness function presents two terms; the first one represents the error term (according to the minimization of the squared residuals sum) and the second one represents the complexity term of the model (according to the minimization of the number of coefficients).

The first term is a transformation of the standard error of prediction (%SEP), an adimensional coefficient of the form:

$$SEP = \frac{100}{\bar{y}} \sqrt{\frac{\sum_{i=1}^{n}(y_i - \hat{y}_i)^2}{n}}, \tag{6}$$

where y_i represents the value of the function in this point, $\hat{y}_i$ is the estimated value and, $\bar{y}$ the mean value of all the y_i. The second term modulates linearly the number of terms in the expression, growing as the number n_T of terms decreases. In this way, the fitness expression would be:

---

[1] This type of experiments design focuses the sampling on the central values of the experimental variables.

$$A = (1-\alpha)(1-\frac{SEP}{K}) + \alpha\left(1 - \frac{n_T - n_{Tm}}{n_{TM} - n_{Tm}}\right) \quad (7)$$

where the coefficients n_{Tm} and n_{TM} represent respectively the minimum and maximum number of coefficients that the model can represent, and the constant K, whose values ($1 \leq K < \infty$) are obtained heuristically, modulates the SEP value to weight the differences among patterns in order to get equilibrium between the two objectives.

Table 1. Parameters used in the genetic algorithms for the modelling of the response surfaces.

GENERAL ASPECTS OF THE ALGORITHM			
Population size		500 individuals	
	Duplication	$p_d=0.2$	Tournament selection
	Crossover	$p_c=0.6$	Tournament selection
			BLX-α ($\alpha=0.5$)
			CIXL1 and CIXL2 (*1-α= 0.7, n=5*)
	Mutation	$p_m=0.2$	Random selection
			Non uniform mutation (parameter *b*= 5)
Stop criterium		500 generations	

This nondecreasing fitness function takes a maximum value of 1, which could be possible only if the standard error of prediction was null and the model had t_m terms.

The number of genes forming each individual of the population will depend on the grade of the chosen RS for the model. The crossover operators used in the genetic algorithm have been the BLX-α crossover [3], three adaptations of this crossover to this problem, and the multi-parent crossovers CIXL1 and CIXL2 [4]. The mutation operator has been the Non Uniform. These operators, specific for the real coding, have been adapted to be able to work with the double codification previously explained.

All the algorithms have been implemented in Java using Sun Microsystems Java Development Kit version 1.3.1, and the JCLEC class library for evolutionary computation [10]. The analysis of variance for the comparison of means has been performed using the statistics software SPSS version 11.0.

3.4   Adaptation of the BLXα Crossover

We have designed an adaptation of the BLX-α operator (even though it could have been any other arity-2 crossover designed for RCGA). Let $\beta^1 = \{(s_1^1, c_1^1), ..., (s_i^1, c_i^1), ..., (s_p^1, c_p^1)\}$ and $\beta^2 = \{(s_1^2, c_1^2), ..., (s_i^2, c_i^2), ..., (s_p^2, c_p^2)\}$ be two parents chosen for crossover, with p genes each one and representing two RS models with p coefficients. Each gene corresponds to a monomial in the corresponding RS, and each allele represents, respectively a selector that indicates the presence or absence of the monomial in the model and the value of the coefficient associated to the term. These two

parents will generate two offsprings $\beta^{h1} = \left\{(s_1^{h1}, c_1^{h1}), ..., (s_i^{h1}, c_i^{h1}), ..., (s_p^{h1}, c_p^{h1})\right\}$ and
$\beta^{h2} = \left\{(s_1^{h2}, c_1^{h2}), ..., (s_i^{h2}, c_i^{h2}), ..., (s_p^{h2}, c_p^{h2})\right\}$. The genes of the best parent will be inherited more likely than those of the other, so that each gene $\left(s_i^{h1}, c_i^{h1}\right)$ and $\left(s_i^{h2}, c_i^{h2}\right)$ will have the following values:

If round $\left(s_i^1\right) =$ round $\left(s_i^2\right)$

$then$ $s_i^{h1} \leftarrow s_i^{h2} \leftarrow$ round $\left(s_i^1\right)$

$(c_i^{h1}, c_i^{h2}) \leftarrow$ application of BLXα over the alleles (c_i^1 and c_i^2)

$else$ $apt1 \leftarrow$ fitness of parent β^1 ; $apt2 \leftarrow$ fitness of parent β^2
n_1 and $n_2 \leftarrow$ two random integers with a probability $apt1/(apt1+apt2)$ of taking value 1 and probability $apt2/(apt1+apt2)$ of taking value 2

$(s_i^{h1}, c_i^{h1}) \leftarrow (s_i^{n_1}, c_i^{n_1})$; $(s_i^{h1}, c_i^{h1}) \leftarrow (s_i^{n_2}, c_i^{n_2})$

$EndIf$

That is, the generated offspring will inherit the terms existing in both parents and the BLXα crossover will be applied to the coefficients of these terms. When the terms exist only in one of the parents, the more fit this parent is compared to the other, the more possibilities of passing to the offspring they will have.

4   Results

We have searched for an optimal topology as well as the coefficients of the model using RS of grades 2 to 5, so as to check if our methodology is able to find models for different topologies previously used. It means that the size of the weight space to estimate increases exponentially with the grade of the starting polynomial. For each one of the 3 growth parameters we have analyzed if there are significative differences in the mean values of the generalization SEP according to the grade of the polynomial (RS2 to RS5) and according to the four types of crossover operators used (BLXα, BLXαAD1, CIXL1 and CIXL2). An test for equality of means has been performed, taking into account both intrapopulation variances and interpopulation variances. For each cell of the ANOVAII model, 30 runs were performed[2], using the parameters discussed in the previous section, and we can affirm with a significance level of 99% that for the three performed analysis, one for each parameter of the growth curves:

1. There are significative differences in the variances associated to each cell (Sig=0.000). There are significative differences in the averages: according to the interaction between the grade of the starting polynomial and the type of crossover used (Sig=0.000), according to the polynomial grade (Sig=0.000) and according to the crossover type (Sig=0.000). There are not significant differences when starting with RS2 or RS3, but they appear when starting with RS4 or RS5.

---

[2] Currently, more tests are being executed to confirm the results.

Table 2. Statistic results summary (Mean, Standard Deviation) in the three experiments.

Parameter/SR Crossover	lnlag / SR3		grate / SR2		yend / SR2	
	Mean	StdDev	Mean	StdDev	Mean	StdDev
BLX-alfa	7.92	0.52	15.51	4.01	15.71	0.51
BLXAD1	8.15	1.51	15.62	2.19	15.87	0.69
CIXL1	7.25	0.55	11.79	2.11	15.58	0.39
CIXL2	12.55	2.59	21.17	6.67	21.32	8.88

$$\text{lnlag} = 1.8585 - 0.2366(T) - 0.0938(pH) + 0.273(NaCl) + 0.1029(NaNO_2) + 0.0374(pH)^2$$
$$-0.1294(pH)(NaCl) - 0.0569(pH)(NaNO_2) - 0.0923(pH)(NaCl)(NaNO_2) \tag{8}$$

$$\text{Grate} = 0.1802 + 0.0718(T) + 0.0250(T)^2 + 0.0206(NaCl)^2 - 1.9315(T)^2(NaNO_2)$$
$$-10.4226(pH)^2(NaNO_2) + 0.0071(pH)(NaCl)^2 - 0.0102(NaCl)^3 \tag{9}$$
$$+12.3471(NaCl)^2(NaNO_2)$$

$$\text{yend} = -0.6844 + 0.1522(T) - 0.2222(NaCl) - 0.2437(NaNO_2) + 0.0591(pH)(NaCl)$$
$$-0.0427(NaCl)^2 + 0.1510(T)^2(pH) + 4.3559(T)^2(NaCl) + 0.0301(pH)(NaNO_2)$$
$$+0.0186(pH)^3 + 5.2791(pH)^2(NaCl) - 0.017(pH)(NaCl)(NaNO_2) \tag{10}$$
$$-9.6772(NaCl)(NaNO_2)^2$$

2. In the models where the dependent variable is *lnlag*:
- The RS of grade 3 produces the best total results (for the six crossovers) in mean (8.97). The means and variances are shown in Table3.
- There are no significative differences in mean between the crossovers BLX and CIXL1. But there are between them and the crossover CIXL2. The CIXL1 crossover is the one that produces the best results in mean starting with a grade 2 polynomial and especially grade 3. These differences are significant if we eliminate the results of the crossovers CIXL2.
- We concluded using polynomials of grade 3 and the CIXL1 crossover. In this way the statistic results of the 30 proofs are shown in Table 3. The best model chosen according to %SEP and smaller number of parameters is shown in equation 8.
3. In the models where the dependent variable is *grate*:
- The RS of grade 2 produces the best total results (for the six crossovers) in mean (16.02). The means and variances are shown in Table 3.
- There are no differences in mean between the crossovers BLX and CIXL1. But there are between them and the crossover CIXL2. The CIXL1 crossover is the one that produces the best results in mean starting with a grade 2 polynomial, being these differences significant if we eliminate the results of the crossover CIXL2
- We concluded using polynomials of grade 2 and CIXL1 crossover. In this way, the statistic results of the 30 proofs are shown in Table 3. The best model chosen according to %SEP and smaller number of parameters is shown in equation 9.

Table 3. Data of the best models obtained in the three experiments with CIXL1.

	Lnlag	grate	yend
%SEP Training	7.17	8.51	-11.88
%SEP Test	7.05	9.22	-13.49
Num. coefficients	9	9	13
Fitness	0.69	0.65	0.48

4. In the models where the dependent variable is *yend*:
- The RS of grade 2 produces the best total results (for the six crossovers) in mean (17.12). The means and variances of the %SEP for RS2 and the 6 crossovers are shown in Table 3.
- There are no differences in mean between the crossovers BLX and CIXL1. But there are between them and the crossover CIXL2. The crossover CIXL1 is the one that produces the best results in mean starting with a grade 2, but these differences are not significant even though we eliminate the results of the crossover CIXL2.
- We concluded using polynomials of grade 2 and CIXL1 crossover. In this way, the statistic results of the 30 proofs are shown in Table 3. The best model chosen according to %SEP and smaller number of parameters is shown in equation 30.

5   Conclusions

We have experimentally demonstrated how, starting from overdimensionated response surface models, our methodology finds the model fitting the phenomenon's response. A fitness function has been proposed that considers the quadratic relative errors and weights up the simplicity of the model as well. This makes the expressions evolve until they present a minimum size, improving their interpretability through the decrease of the number of terms in the polynomial function and their capacity of generalization. A specialized genetic algorithm has been implemented, using a double codification and specifically adapted operators. These operators, CIXL1 and CIXL2, make possible to extract the adaptive statistic characteristics of the best individuals and to use them to lead the search in the most effective way. In particular we checked that with the CIXL1 crossover operator we obtained better results, proposing its use in this type of algorithm. This procedure represents an advantage over the use of statistic tests to eliminate coefficients and identify the model exactly, much more tedious and, in some cases, biased by the subjective appreciations of the investigator. We also checked that with this algorithm it is possible to reach better results than the ones obtained with non-linear regression.

References

1. Baranyi, J., Roberts, T. A.: 1994. A dynamic approach to predicting bacterial growth in food. Int. J. Food Microbiol., Vol. 23 (1994) 277-294
2. Denison, D., Holmes, C., Mallick, B., Smith, A.: Bayesian Methods for Non-linear Classification and Regression. John Wiley & Sons, Chichester (2002)
3. Eshelman, L.J., Schaffer, J.D.: Real-coded genetic algorithms and interval-schemata. Foundations of Genetic Algorithms, Vol. 21, Morgan Kaufmann (1993) 187-202
4. Hervás, C., Ortiz, B., García, N.: Theoretical Análisis of the Confidence Interval Based Crossover for Real-Coded Genetic Algorithms. Parallel Problem Solving from Nature PPSN VII, 2439, Springer-Verlag, Granada (2002) 153-161
5. Myers Raymond, H.M., Montgomery, D. C.: Response Surface Methodology: Process and Product Optimisation Using Designed Experiments. Second Edition, John Wiley & Sons, New York (2002)

6. Ortiz, D., Hervás, C., Muñoz, J.: Genetic algorithm with crossover based on confidence intervals as an alternative to least squares estimation for non-linear models. Metheuristic International Congress, Porto (2001)
7. Ortiz, D.: Operadores de cruce basado en intervalos de confianza en algoritmos genéticos con codificación real, Tesis Doctoral, Málaga (2001)
8. Rawlings, J.O., Pantula, S.G., Dickey, D.: Applied regression analysis: A research tool. Springer-Verlag, New York (1998)
9. Rodríguez Pérez, R.: Elaboración de modelos predictivos de crecimiento microbiano de lactobacilus plantarum.Tesis Doctoral. Departamento de Bromatología y Tecnología de los alimentos. Universidad de Córdoba (2003)
10. Ventura, S., Ortíz, D., Hervás, C. JCLEC. Una librería de clases Java para Computación Evolutiva. Congreso Español de Algoritmos Evolutivos y Bioinspirados (2002)

ASPerson : Agent System for Personalizing Web Contents over Wireless Connection*

Woncheol Kim[1], Eenjun Hwang[1], and Wonil Kim[2,**]

[1] Graduate School of Information and Communication
Ajou University, Suwon 442-749, Korea
{wc323,ehwang}@ajou.ac.kr
[2] College of Electronics Information Engineering
Sejong University, Seoul, 143-747, Korea
wikim@sejong.ac.kr

Abstract. Recent popularity of hand-held devices and pervasiveness of e-commerce have increased web accesses through mobile devices. However, due to the limited screen size, users have to scroll a lot to locate what they want. Even worse, network connections are usually too slow to support most of the data-intensive applications. Therefore, an efficient scheme for navigating web contents through these devices should be addressed in this arena. In this paper, we propose a web agent system, *ASPerson* that enables users to browse ordinary web pages efficiently even on the small screen mobile devices. It extracts any specific sections of interest from web pages and reorganizes them based on user preference for convenient browsing.

1 Introduction

Recently, due to the rapid progress of web and mobile technology; web pages have been accessed more frequently than ever using mobile devices. However, most existing web pages are written in HTML and optimized for desktop computers. Even though the screen resolution and computing power of mobile devices have been improved, they are still not as capable as desktop computers. They inherently have small screen, low network bandwidth, low battery capacity and weak computing power. These limitations impose serious problems when mobile users navigate web pages. Browsing web pages using a small screen device is inconvenient and inefficient. For example, it needs multiple scrolling and takes much longer time to access any desired contents. Nevertheless, more people want to access web pages through mobile devices. Many works have been done to relieve this problem and can be divided into two categories: 1) personalizing or recommending for each user and 2) trimming unimportant contents. Personalized service is based on the prediction of user's action

---

* This research was supported by University IT Research Center Project.
** Author for correspondent, +82-2-3408-3782

R. Conejo et al. (Eds.): CAEPIA-TTIA 2003, LNAI 3040, pp. 187–196, 2004.

from the past usage pattern. However, it is not easy to acquire information that reflects each user's interest. Trimming service may suffer from missing some valuable information, unless each user's preference is identified accurately during the trimming process. In this paper, we propose an agent system, *ASPerson* to provide a personalized news service automatically to mobile users based on their preference. The system utilizes a unit called *newslet* that expresses a topic in a typical web page. In fact, a *newslet* can be defined as a meaningful area to a particular user. *ASPerson* makes it feasible to navigate web pages on a small screen even over low bandwidth connection.

The rest of this paper is organized as follows. Section 2 discusses related works and our approach. Section 3describes the process of extracting user preference from web log. Section 4 shows overall system architecture. Section 5 describes the system performance through several simulations, and finally Section 6 concludes the paper.

2 Related Works

There have been many researches on navigating web pages efficiently through small display devices. Pda++ [1] was proposed to zoom on the display. CZ [2] web and Widgets [3] have been suggested for summarizing web pages. In WEST [4], a scheme called "focus + context" was proposed to provide an overview of a web page. Power Browser [5] divides web pages into semantic textual units and composes summary based on the unit. Bickmore et al. [6] suggested an accordion style summarization using structural page transformation and sentence elision in Digestor. Trevor et al. [7] used a new user interface that splits current mode of integrating "link following" and "reading" into separate mode, namely, navigating and acting.

One of the current trends on the web related applications is how to display as much information as possible in a page. However, with this, it is getting more difficult to find information on a mobile device. On the other hand, previous researches did not consider personalized service, although every visitor has different interest and behavior. For personalized service, many researches have used web mining [8, 9, 10] methods. Web mining can help discover knowledge information and improve web site design. Usually, preprocessing is used before web mining due to the incompleteness of available data. In order to discover any usage pattern or user interest, pattern discovery methods such as statistical analysis, clustering, classification, sequential pattern and dependency modeling are used. The goal of pattern analysis is to filter out uninteresting rules or patterns from the set found in the pattern discovery phase.

In this paper, we also adopt web usage mining to support personalized services to mobile users. More specifically, in order to provide personalized news services, we propose a segmentation unit called *newslet*. For the segmentation, we first identify various topics of a news web page, and then consider each news section as a *newslet*. This means that a web page is divided into several topics. Detailed steps are as follows:

- **User preference analysis:** In this step, various browsing behaviors of mobile web visitors are gathered. Previous browsing behaviors with the web site are analyzed for web browsing patterns. Those browsing patterns are used to provide personalized news contents. Here, we will use the link information to find user's traversal patterns of web page.
- **Extracting newslets:** In this step, we analyze web pages and extract a collection of *newslets*. During the web page analysis, we extract topic areas from each page using weights of keywords and the number of links in the HTML elements.
- **Reorganizing newslet sequence:** In this step, we reorder *newslets* appropriately for the mobile devices. Those *newslets* in which users have more interest should be displayed before the one that users have less interest on the screen. Consequently, mobile user with small display and low bandwidth can receive convenient news services without multiple scrolling.

Our *newslet* scheme can automatically personalize the contents of a web page according to individual user's preference, and reduce low network bandwidth. Moreover, it can present the whole contents of a web page on a small screen. This will increase the readability and understandability of mobile web page users.

3 Finding User Preference

Finding user preference page sequence involves three steps. First, representative keywords are extracted from news pages. And then page sequences are extracted from user behavior pattern. Finally, news pages are divided into *newslets* by the topic or function.

3.1 Extracting Keywords from News Web Pages

A news page contains many topics that can be divided into categories such as politics, economics and sports. In order to decide the category to which a given *newslet* belongs, we check the weights of selected keywords in the *newslet*. To do that, we first describe how to extract related keywords from the news page. During this step, extracting too many keywords might cause an ambiguity in the decision of the news section boundary. Therefore, we assign higher weight to important sentences. The sentence rank itself is decided by the sum of weights and scores of related keywords. In addition, in order to choose important sentences from the web page, we use the Luhn's keyword cluster technique [11], the frequencies of the keywords in the <Title> tag and the modified keyword weight.

First of all, we decide whether a sentence is important or not, For example, if the sum of keyword weights in the sentence becomes higher than a predefined weight threshold, we consider it as a significant sentence. Then we assign the rank of each sentence using the keywords in the <Title> tag and extract keywords from the high-ranked sentences. Finally, we consider different font size, color and thickness. Since web page authors are generally decorating keywords to emphasize the sentences, the sentence with the decorated keywords is more important than the other sentences.

3.2 Browsing Sequence Extraction from User Patterns

We use traversal pattern algorithm to extract meaningful user access patterns from the browsing behavior history for news pages. In the web environment where pages are linked together, users tend to traverse pages back and forth by following the link. As a result, some pages will be revisited because of its location rather than its content. For example, in a web page of structure shown in Fig. 1, to reach a sibling web page, users will use the backward icon and then go to a sibling page instead of typing its URL. Consequently, while extracting user access patterns from the log file, such backward references should be taken into consideration.

In this paper, assuming that the backward reference is used for ease of traveling, we concentrate on the discovery of forward reference patterns. During navigation, as soon as a backward reference occurs, its forward reference path is considered to terminate. This forward reference path is called as maximal forward reference.

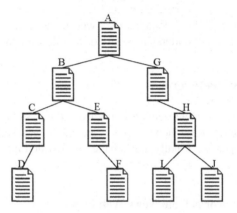

Fig. 1. Traversal pattern example.

Suppose the log file contains the following traversal path (A, B, C, D, C, B, E, F, E, B, A, G, H, I, H, J) for web pages of structure shown in Fig 1. Then, maximal forward references are ABCD, ABEF, AGHI, and AGHJ, when using algorithm in [12]. Here, we use link anchor text, the text that appears between the <a> tags in a link. For example <a href="http://www.ajou.ac.kr">ajou university, welcome to ajou </a>, "ajou university, welcome to ajou" is the link text. We call the keywords of link anchor as Link Anchor Keywords (LAKs). Since link anchors contain significant information about the link, we use the LAKs to classify each news sections.

After extracting maximal forward references, LAKs are created in the order of visited links. For example, assume that the user visited links in the order of A, B, C, D, and that extracted LAKs were Computer, IT, mobile devices, Microsoft. Then we can guess that those LAKs are relevant to the IT news section. After all, we will decide its news category using keyword matching with LAKs. This step will repeat iteratively until exhausting maximal forward references.

3.3 Newslet Extraction from News Pages

Extracting a table block from a web page has several problems. First, since an HTML document has a tree structure internally and permits a table within a table recursively, it is difficult to see a table as one unit of topic. Even though a news page is divided by topic or function, since the HTML tag is restricted, we cannot give appropriate meaning to each topic area. In this paper, we extract topic areas of each news page using weights of keywords and the number of the links in the HTML element.

Whenever the user navigates a specific page, the proposed system analyzes the HTML document, extracts the HTML element and then constructs its parse tree. After that, the first node of the parse tree is stored in the queue.

Next, it removes a node element from the queue. When the number of the child node's links is larger than or equal to a threshold, then it is considered to represent some different topic. We define such node as a *newslet* and store it into a *newslet* queue; otherwise, it is more likely to be integrated to its parent. This process is repeated until there are no more elements in the queue. The keywords in the selected *newslet* area are extracted to identify its meaning.

4   System Overview of News Contents Reorganization

Navigation of web pages on the mobile devices can be limited by many factors such as battery capacity, network bandwidth, and small display. In this paper, we implemented our prototype system in the proxy server that is an extension to the HTTP proxy server. That is, all the relevant functions for reconstructing web pages are running on the proxy server. Fig 2 shows the overall system architecture. When a mobile user requests a news page, the target web page will be displayed by the following steps.

1. When the user accesses the web page using a mobile device, the Extracting Engine module analyzes user patterns. In addition, the extracting engine module stores analyzed user interests into the database.
2. When the User Analyzer module of the proxy server receives a request from the WWW server, it identifies the user and acquires user information through the user interest database. Then it transmits user information and the web page to the HTML parser module.
3. When the HTML parser module receives the web page, it constructs a parse tree for the web page. After that, Link Analyzer module extracts link information in order to make a *newslet*. The *Newslet* Divider module analyzes the number of linked HTML nodes in order to identify facility areas and construct a *newslets* for the web page.
4. Page Reconstruct and Rearrangement module rearrange the *newslets'* sequences in order to find news sections of user interest. The sections that the user has more interest in should be displayed on the top part of the screen.

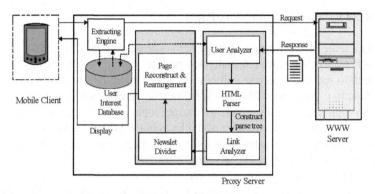

Fig. 2. System Overview.

5   Experiments

While most web pages are designed with at least 800 x 600 or 1024 x 768 resolution, small devices usually have 320 x 240 resolution. We construct *newslet* that can fit into 320 x 240 resolution device. We have simulated a prototype system that supports browsing of HTML web pages using embedded Visual Basic 3.0 with a mobile emulator. It equipped with small display with web ability.

5.1   Scenario

We use log file in order to discover user access pattern. Typical log file contains a lot of information such as IP address of visitors, user identifier, access time, methods of request, the URL of the requested page, used protocol, and the number of transmitted bytes etc. Preprocessing is performed to filter out irrelevant data such as image file information, error code and protocol.

After that, we extract maximal forward references and LAKs in the order of visited links. The news section is determined by the maximal forward reference using LAKs. Fig 3 shows how to extract user's preferred news sections using the link information. LAKs are obtained from the link information and then user's preferred news sections are identified from the LAKs. Assuming that a user accesses pages in the order of P, B, E, T, M, S as shown in Fig 3, our proposed system would reorganize the web pages and send them in the following order: P→B→E→T→M→S.

5.2   Evaluation

To evaluate the efficiency of our system, we have performed several experiments for various types of news pages. We evaluate its performance by measuring (i) the number of scrolls involved and (ii) the page size.

Link information	LAKs (Link anchor keywords)	News section
~/ newsArticle.jhtml?type=politicsNews&storyID=2844205	Congress, Try, Solve ,Medicare Problems	Politics (P)
~/ newsArticle.jhtml?type=politicsNews&storyID=2844971	Israel, Palestinians, Peace, Steps	
.....	.....	
~/_tsclsii/markets/marketstory/10090182.html	Stocks, Turn, Mixed,	Business (B)
~/financeNewsArticle.jhtml?type=businessNews&storyID=2845238	Jobless, Claims, Fall, Continued, Claims, Up	
.....	.....	
~/ newsArticle.jhtml?type=entertainmentNews&storyID=2844570	Thanks, Memory, Americans, Rock	Entertain-ment (E)
~/ newsArticle.jhtml?type=entertainmentNews&storyID=2842373	Idol, Fox, Pop, Albums, Charts	
.....	.....	
~/ newsArticle.jhtml?type=technologyNews&storyID=2843665	Computer, European Broadband, mobile	Technology (T)
~/ newsArticle.jhtml?type=technologyNews&storyID=2837894	Microsoft, Windows, Linux	
.....	.....	
~/ newsArticle.jhtml?type=internetNews&storyID=2842114	Matrix, Reloaded, radio, television,	Movie (M)
~/ newsArticle.jhtml?type=internetNews&storyID=2839697	X-Men, United, Hulk, Movie	
.....	.....	
~/newsArticle.jhtml?type=politicsNews&storyID=2840773	Bush, G8, Iraq, Debate	Politics (P)
~/ newsArticle.jhtml?type=politicsNews&storyID=2843578	Anti-War, Polish, Mayor, Bush Visit	
.....	.....	
~/newsArticle.jhtml?type=golfNews&storyID=2820132	Leading, prize-money, winners, U.S., PGA, tour,	Sports (S)
~/newsArticle.jhtml?type=baseballNews&storyID=2820183	Language, Police, baseball, homerun	
.....	.....	

Fig. 3. Finding news sequence.

Table 1 shows the number of scrolling without reorganization. Typical news sections for Politics, Technology, Business, Sports, Entertainment, and Movies are indicated as P, T, B, S, E, and M respectively. We assume a typical news page is viewed in the order of P, B, T, S, E, M, and mobile screen can show three news sections at a time.

First of all, we calculate the number of up/down scrolls to check whether the reorganized pattern is adequate or not. In order to evaluate the efficiency of our reorganizing scheme, we calculate the total number of user scrolls to read the given sequence of article.

Table 1. The number of scrolls without reorganization.

User	Display sequence without reorganization	User sequence	The number of scrolls for each sequence	Total number of scrolls
A		P,B,E,T,M,P,E	0,0,2,0,1,3,2	8
B		M,B,E,P,B,M,B	3,2,1,2,0,3,2	13
C	P,B,T,S,E,M	M,E,B,P,S,T,S	3,0,2,1,1,0,0	7
D		M,T,S,M,E,T,M	3,1,0,1,0,1,1	7
E		E,M,S,T,P,B,P	2,1,0,1,2,0,0	6
F		P,B,S,E,T,M,T	0,0,0,1,1,0,1	3

The fixed display sequence of news sections is P, B, T, S, E and M, in case reorganization is not involved. User A access news pages in the order of P, B, E, T, M, P and E. Since the simulated device can show three sections at a time, the user A can only see (P, B, T). First when the user A access news section P, he/she does not need to scroll to see P. He/she does not need scrolls to access B either. Next, user A accesses news sections E, and in this case he/she needs to scroll up two times to access E showing (T, S, E) at the screen. Next, the user A does see T without any scroll. In order to see news section M, user A should perform one scroll only; therefore mobile screen shows (S, E, M). Finally user A performs five scroll-downs to see news section P and E. The total number of scrolls for user A is therefore 8 (2+1+3+2).

Table 2. The number of scrolling with reorganization.

User	Display sequence with Reorganization	User sequence	The number of scrolling for each sequence	Total number of scrolling
A	P,B,E,T,M,S	P,B,E,T,M,P,E	0,0,0,1,1,2,0	4
B	M,B,E,P,S,T	M,B,E,P,B,M,B	0,0,0,1,0,1,0	2
C	M,E,B,P,S,T	M,E,B,P,S,T,S	0,0,0,1,1,1,0	3
D	M,T,S,E,P,B	M,T,S,M,E,T,M	0,0,0,0,1,0,0	1
E	E,M,S,T,P,B	E,M,S,T,P,B,P	0,0,0,1,1,1,0	3
F	P,B,S,E,T,M	P,B,S,E,T,M,T	0,0,0,0,1,1,0	2

The case where reorganization is involved is shown in Table 2. Now, the personalized display sequence is P, B, E, T, M and S. The user A can only see P, B, E, because the simulated device can show three sections on the screen as in the earlier case. User A accesses news pages in the order of P, B, E, T, M, P, E. First when the user A accesses news section P, he/she does not need to scroll to see P. He/she does not need scrolls to access B and E either. Next, user A accesses news sections T, and in this case user A need one scroll-up, watching (B, E, T) at the screen. In order to see news section M, user A should perform just one scroll-up, leaving E, T and M on the screen. Finally user A scrolls down two times to see news section P. User A does not need scrolling because mobile screen already has P, B and E. Therefore, the user A needs only 4 scrolls in total. Consequently, reorganization scheme of user preference is more convenient to mobile users.

Table 3 compares the file size and display size before and after the page reconstruction. From the table, we see that with the proposed scheme, the file size and display size were reduced a lot. The average file size and display size were decreased by 72% and 74%, respectively.

Table 3. Page file of web pages after rebuilding.

Page	Original page size	Newslet size
CNN	122.4 Kb	25.5 Kb
BBC	110.6 Kb	23.2 Kb
MSNBC	123.4 Kb	25.6 Kb
ABCNews.com	115.8 Kb	22.5 Kb
Google news	118.2 Kb	30.7 Kb
USATODAY	128.1 Kb	28.1 Kb
CBS SportsLine	117.4 Kb	27.2 Kb
CNET news.com	114.3 Kb	29.7 Kb
TechWeb	126.6 Kb	27.0 Kb

From the experiment result, we see that the decreased file size relieves the low bandwidth limitation of mobile display devices and the deduction of display size relieves the small display limitation.

Different page sequences due to user interest are shown in Fig 4, where display screen shows user interests in the order of Politics, Business, Entertainment, etc and Business, Entertainment, Technology, etc, for user A and B, respectively. Consequently, contents on the small screen are personalized according to the user interest.

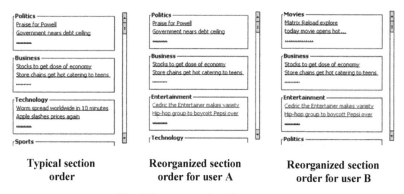

Typical section	Reorganized section	Reorganized section
order	order for user A	order for user B

Fig. 4. Reconstruction of news page.

6   Conclusions

In this paper, we proposed a web agent system for personalizing web pages to mobile users. Basic approach is to divide a typical web page into several regions called *newslet* depending on the topic or function. We extract preference sections from news web pages and automatically reorganize them. We have developed a simulated prototype system and performed several experiments to show its effectiveness. Especially, we focused on two factors: the number of scrolls involved and the resulting file size. A *newslet* is much smaller in file size compared to the original page, which helps relieve network bandwidth limitation of wireless connection. Consequently, it enables mobile users to browse ordinary news web pages on small screen.

References

1. B. B. Bederson, J. D. Hollan, "Pda++: A Zooming Graphical Interface for Exploring Alternate Interface Physics,"ACM Symposium on user Interface Software and Technology, 1994.
2. B.Fisher, M. Agelidis, J. Dill, P. Tan, G. Collaud, and C. Jones, "CZWeb: Fish-eye Views for Visualizing the World-Wide Web", Proceedings of the 6th International World Wide Web Conference, 1997.
3. T. Kamba, S. A. Elson, T. Harpold, T. Stamper, and P. Sukaviriya, "Using small screen space more efficiently," Proceedings of CHI'96, ACM Press, 1996.
4. S. Bjrk, L.E. Holmquist, J. Redstrm, I. Bretan, R. Danielsson, J. Karlgren, and K. Franzn, "WEST: A Web Browser for small Terminals,"ACM Sysmposium on User Interface Software and Technology, 1999.
5. Buyukkokten, H. Garcia-Molina, and A. Paepcke, T. Winograd, "Power Browser: Efficient Web Browsing for PDAs,"Proceedings of CHI'2000, ACM Press, Amsterdam, 2000.
6. T. W. Bickmore, B. N. Schilit, "Digestor: Device-independent Access to the World Wide Web,"Proceedings of the 6th international World Wide Web Conference, Santa Clara, CA, 1997.
7. J. Trevor, D. M. Hilbert, B. N. Schilit and T. K. Koh, "From Desktop to Phonetop: A UI For Web Interaction On Very Small Devices", ACM Symposium on User Interface Software and Technology, 2001.
8. Baldonado Lizhen Liu; Junjie Chen; Hantao Song "The research of Web mining," Intelligent Control and Automation, Proceedings of the 4th World Congress on, Volume: 3, 2002 Page(s): 2333 -2337 vol.3.
9. Jaideep Srivastava, Robert Cooley, Mukund Deshpande, Pang-Ning Tan, "Web Usage Mining: Discovery and Applications of Usage Patterns from Web Data" SIGKDD Explorations 2000.
10. Osmar R. Zaiane, Man Xin, Jiawei Han Advances in Digital Libraries "Discovering Web Access Patterns and Trends by Applying OLAP and Data Mining Technology on Web Logs" (1998).
11. De Bra and R.D.J. Post. "Information retrieval in the World-Wide Web: making client-based searching feasible." Proceedings of the First International World-Wide Web Conference. 1994.
12. Ming-Syan Chen, Jong Soo Park, Philip S. Yu "Efficient Data Mining for Path Traversal Patterns", IEEE Transactions on Knowledge and Data Engineering, Vol 10, No, 2, pp. 209-221.

Automatic Computation
of the Fundamental Matrix from Matched Lines*

Oscar A. Pellejero, Carlos Sagüés, and J. Jesús Guerrero

Dpto. de Informática e Ingeniería de Sistemas (U.Z.)
María de Luna 3, E-50018 Zaragoza, Spain
{oscarph,csagues,jguerrer}@posta.unizar.es
Phone 34-976-761940, Fax 34-976-761914

Abstract. This paper addresses the recovery of epipolar geometry using homographies computed automatically from matched lines between two views. We use lines because they have some advantages with respect to points, particularly in man made environments. Although the fundamental matrix cannot be directly computed from lines, it can be deduced from homographies obtained from them. We match lines lying on a plane, estimating simultaneously a planar projective transformation with a robust method. A homography allows us to select and to grow previous matches that have been obtained combining geometric and brightness image parameters. Successive homographies can be computed depending on the number of planes in the scene. From two or more, the fundamental matrix can be obtained.

1 Introduction

The recovery of epipolar geometry has been more broadly treated using points [1]. The use of lines as image features has some advantages, mainly in man made environments. Straight lines can be accurately extracted in noisy images, they capture more information than points, and they may be used where partial occlusions occur. The epipolar geometry cannot be computed directly from lines, but it can be made through homographies [2].

Line matching, which has also been previously treated [3], is more difficult than point matching [4] because the end points of the extracted lines are not reliable. Besides that, there is no geometrical constraint, like the epipolar, for lines in two images. The putative matching of features based on image parameters has many drawbacks, resulting in non matched or wrong matched features.

Perspective images of planar scenes are usual in the perception of man made environments, and how to work with them is well known. Points or lines on the world plane in one image are mapped to points or lines in the other image by a plane to plane homography, also known as a plane projective transformation [5]. This is an exact transformation for planar scenes or for small baseline image pairs. We match lines between two images computing simultaneously a planar projective transformation.

---

* This work was supported by projects DPI2000-1265, DPI2000-1272.

R. Conejo et al. (Eds.): CAEPIA-TTIA 2003, LNAI 3040, pp. 197–206, 2004.
© Springer-Verlag Berlin Heidelberg 2004

So, the first homography allows us to select and to grow previous matches which have been obtained combining geometric and brightness image parameters [6]. After that, successive homographies can be computed until no more of them could be obtained. As we use least median of squares to compute the homography and several homographies are supposed, we play with some percentile to select the inliers and outliers. From at least two homographies the fundamental matrix can be directly obtained.

After this introduction, we will present the process to obtain the initial matches which will be used to compute the homography (§2). The robust estimation of homographies from lines, and the process to obtain the final matches using geometrical constraints given by the homographies, is explained in §3. After that, we present in §4 how to compute fundamental matrix once we have information about two homographies of the scene. Experimental results with real images are presented in §5. Finally, §6 is devoted to exposing the conclusions.

2   Initial Matches

Lines are extracted using our implementation of the method proposed by Burns [7]. This method computes spatial brightness gradients to detect the lines in the image. Pixels having the gradient magnitude larger than a threshold are grouped into regions of similar direction of brightness gradient. These groups are named line-support regions (LSR). A least-squares fitting into the LSR is used to obtain the line. For each one, we store four geometric parameters: midpoint coordinates (x_m, y_m), the line orientation (θ) and the length of the extracted line (l). We also use two brightness attributes: agl and c (average grey level and contrast).

We determine correspondences between lines in two images without knowledge about motion or scene structure. The initial matching is made using the weighted nearest neighbor. Naming $\mathbf{r_g}$ the difference of geometric parameters between both images $(1, 2)$, $\mathbf{r_g} = [x_{m1} - x_{m2}, y_{m1} - y_{m2}, \theta_1 - \theta_2, l_1 - l_2]^T$, and $\mathbf{r_b}$ the variation of the brightness parameters between both images, $\mathbf{r_b} = [agl_1 - agl_2, c_1 - c_2]^T$, we can compute two Mahalanobis distances, one for geometric parameters, $\mathbf{d_g} = \mathbf{r_g}^T \mathbf{S}^{-1} \mathbf{r_g}$, and the other for brightness parameters, $\mathbf{d_b} = \mathbf{r_b}^T \mathbf{B}^{-1} \mathbf{r_b}$. To establish the matches, we test the geometric and the brightness compatibility. A line in the first image can have more than one compatible line in the second image. From the compatible lines, the line having the smallest $\mathbf{d_g}$ is selected as putative match. Details are in [6].

3   From Lines to Homographies

The representation of a line in the projective plane is obtained from the analytic representation of a plane through the origin: $n_1 x_1 + n_2 x_2 + n_3 x_3 = 0$. The equation coefficients $\mathbf{n} = (n_1, n_2, n_3)^T$ correspond to the homogeneous coordinates of the projective line. All the lines written as $\lambda \mathbf{n}$ are the same as $\mathbf{n}$. As cameras have a limited field of view, observed lines have usually n_3 close to 0. Similarly, an image point $\mathbf{p} = (x_1, x_2, 1)^T$ is also an element of the projective plane. A projective transformation between two projective planes (1 and 2) can be represented by a linear transformation $\mathbf{H}_{21}$, in such a way that $\mathbf{p}_2 = \mathbf{H}_{21}\mathbf{p}_1$. Considering the above equations for lines in both images, we have $\mathbf{n}_2 = \left[\mathbf{H}_{21}^{-1}\right]^T \mathbf{n}_1$. A homography requires eight parameters to be completely defined, because there is an overall scale factor. A corresponding point or line gives two linear equations in terms of the elements of the homography. Thus, four corresponding lines assure a unique solution for $\mathbf{H}_{21}$, unless three of them are parallel or intersect in the same point. To have an accurate solution it is interesting to have the lines as separate as possible in the image.

3.1   Computing Homographies from Corresponding Lines

Here, we will obtain the projective transformation of points ($\mathbf{p}_2 = \mathbf{H}_{21}\mathbf{p}_1$), but using matched lines. To deduce it, we suppose the start (s) and end (e) tips of a matched line segment to be $\mathbf{p}_{s1}, \mathbf{p}_{e1}, \mathbf{p}_{s2}, \mathbf{p}_{e2}$, which will not usually be corresponding points. The line in the second image can be computed as the cross product of two of its points (in particular the observed tips) as

$$\mathbf{n}_2 = \mathbf{p}_{s2} \times \mathbf{p}_{e2} = [\mathbf{p}_{s2}]_\times \mathbf{p}_{e2}, \tag{1}$$

where $[\mathbf{p}_{s2}]_\times$ is the skew-symmetric matrix obtained from vector $\mathbf{p}_{s2}$.

As the tips belong to the line we have, $\mathbf{p}_{s2}^T \mathbf{n}_2 = 0$; $\mathbf{p}_{e2}^T \mathbf{n}_2 = 0$. As the tips of the line in the first image once transformed also belong to the corresponding line in the second image, we can write, $\mathbf{p}_{s1}^T \mathbf{H}_{21}^T \mathbf{n}_2 = 0$; $\mathbf{p}_{e1}^T \mathbf{H}_{21}^T \mathbf{n}_2 = 0$. Combining with equation (1) we have,

$$\mathbf{p}_{s1}^T \mathbf{H}_{21}^T [\mathbf{p}_{s2}]_\times \mathbf{p}_{e2} = 0 \; ; \; \mathbf{p}_{e1}^T \mathbf{H}_{21}^T [\mathbf{p}_{s2}]_\times \mathbf{p}_{e2} = 0. \tag{2}$$

Therefore each couple of corresponding lines gives two homogeneous equations to compute the projective transformation, which can be determined up to a non-zero scale factor. Developing them according to the elements of the projective transformation, we have

$$\begin{pmatrix} Ax_{s1} \; Ay_{s1} \; A \; Bx_{s1} \; By_{s1} \; B \; Cx_{s1} \; Cy_{s1} \; C \\ Ax_{e1} \; Ay_{e1} \; A \; Bx_{e1} \; By_{e1} \; B \; Cx_{e1} \; Cy_{e1} \; C \end{pmatrix} \mathbf{h} = \begin{pmatrix} 0 \\ 0 \end{pmatrix},$$

where $\mathbf{h} = (h_{11} \, h_{12} \, h_{13} \, h_{21} \, h_{22} \, h_{23} \, h_{31} \, h_{32} \, h_{33})^T$ is a vector with the elements of $\mathbf{H}_{21}$, and $A = y_{s2} - y_{e2}$, $B = x_{e2} - x_{s2}$ and $C = x_{s2}y_{e2} - x_{e2}y_{s2}$, being (x_{s1}, y_{s1}) the coordinates of the start tip $\mathbf{p}_{s1}$.

Using four corresponding lines, we can construct a 8×9 matrix $\mathbf{M}$. In order to have a reliable transformation, more than the minimum number of matches and an estimation method may be considered. Thus from n matches a $2n \times 9$ matrix $\mathbf{M}$ can be built, and the solution $\mathbf{h}$ can be obtained from SVD decomposition of this matrix [5]. In this case the relevance of each line depends on its observed length, because the cross product of the segment tips is related to the segment length.

It is known that a previous normalization of data avoids problems of numerical computation. As our formulation only uses image coordinates of observed tips, data normalization proposed for points [8] has been used.

3.2   Robust Estimation

The least squares method assumes that all the measures can be interpreted with the same model, which makes it very sensitive to out of norm data. Robust estimation tries to avoid the outliers in the computation of the estimate. From the existing robust estimation methods [9], we have chosen the least median of squares method. This method makes a search in the space of solutions obtained from subsets of minimum number of matches. The algorithm to obtain an estimate with this method can be summarized as follows:

1. A Monte-Carlo technique is used to randomly select m subsets of 4 features.
2. For each subset S, we compute a solution in closed form $\mathbf{H}_S$.
3. For each solution $\mathbf{H}_S$, the median or other percentile M_S of the squares of the residue with respect to all the matches is computed.
4. We store the solution $\mathbf{H}_S$ which gives the minimum percentile M_S.

A selection of m subsets is good if at least in one subset the 4 matches are good. Assuming a ratio ϵ of outliers, the probability of one of them being good can be obtained [10] as, $P = 1 - \left[1 - (1 - \epsilon)^4\right]^m$.

Once the solution has been obtained, the outliers can be selected from those of maximum residue. As in [9] the threshold is fitted proportionally to the standard deviation of the residue, estimated as [10], $\hat{\sigma} = 1.4826 \left[1 + 5/(n - 4)\right] \sqrt{M_S}$. Assuming that the measurement error is Gaussian with zero mean and standard deviation σ, then the square of the residues follows a χ_2^2 distribution with 2 degrees of freedom. Taking, for example, that a 95% probability is established for the line to fit in the homography (inlier) then the threshold will be fixed to $5.99 \, \hat{\sigma}^2$.

3.3   Growing Matches from Homography

From here on, we introduce the geometrical constraint introduced by the estimated homography to get a bigger set of matches. Thus final matches consist of two sets. The first one is obtained from the initial set of matches selected after the robust computation of the homography that passes an overlapping test compatible with the transformation of the segment tips additionally. The second set of matches is obtained using all the segments not matched initially and those previously rejected. With this set of lines a matching process similar to the basic matching is carried out. However, now the matching is made with the nearest neighbor segment transformed with the homography. The transformation is applied to the end tips of the image segments using the homography $\mathbf{H}_{21}$ to find, not only compatible lines but also compatible segments in the same line. In the first stage of the matching process, there was no previous knowing of camera motion. However, in this second step the computed homography provides information about an expected disparity and therefore the uncertainty of geometric variations can be reduced.

3.4 Several Homographies

Previously, we have explained how to determine a homography from lines, assuming some of the lines used are outliers. The first homography can be computed in this way, assuming that a certain percentage of matched lines between images are good matches of lines in the plane to be extracted, and the others are outliers. We have not got a priori knowledge about which plane of the scene is going to be extracted first, but the probability of being chosen increases with the number of lines on it. If we execute the process two times, the same plane will be extracted with high probability, unless the number of lines in two main planes of the scene are similar. So, the only reasonable way to extract a second plane of the scene consists of eliminating lines used to determine first homography, expecting the second plane to have the largest number of lines then. Here we are assuming that lines belonging to the first plane do not belong to the second plane. That is true except for the intersection line between both planes.

So, once we have computed a first homography we should eliminate all lines belonging to that plane, that is to say, the lines which verify the homography. Probably it is better to eliminate all lines belonging to the region where the plane has been extracted, but at the moment it is not easy to determine the limits of the region, and other planes could exist inside.

4 Fundamental Matrix from Homographies

Fundamental matrix is a 3×3 matrix of rank 2 which encapsulates the epipolar geometry. It only depends on cameras' internal parameters and on relative motion.

As the images are obtained with the same camera whose projection matrix in a common reference system are $\mathbf{P}_1 = \mathbf{K}[\mathbf{I}|\mathbf{0}]$, $\mathbf{P}_2 = \mathbf{K}[\mathbf{R}|\mathbf{t}]$ (being $\mathbf{R}$ the camera rotation, $\mathbf{t}$ the translation and $\mathbf{K}$ the internal calibration matrix), then, the fundamental matrix can be expressed as $\mathbf{F}_{21} = \mathbf{K}^{-T} \left([\mathbf{t}]_\times \mathbf{R}\right) \mathbf{K}^{-1}$. It can be computed from corresponding points [1], in such a way that epipolar constraint for points in both images can be expressed as $\mathbf{p}_2^T \mathbf{F}_{21} \mathbf{p}_1 = 0$.

It can also be computed from homographies obtained through two or more planes. In this way when there are planar structure, corresponding lines in two images can be used. If at least two homographies $(\mathbf{H}_{21}^{\pi_1}, \mathbf{H}_{21}^{\pi_2})$ can be computed between both images corresponding to two planes (π_1, π_2), a homology $\mathbf{H} = \mathbf{H}_{21}^{\pi_1} \cdot (\mathbf{H}_{21}^{\pi_2})^{-1}$, that is a mapping from the second image into itself, exists. Under this mapping the epipole in second image $(\mathbf{e}_2)$ is a fixed point and therefore $\mathbf{e}_2 = \mathbf{H} \, \mathbf{e}_2$. So $(\mathbf{e}_2)$ may be determined by the eigenvector of $\mathbf{H}$ corresponding to unary eigenvalue [5]. From two planes, the fundamental matrix can be either computed as $\mathbf{F}_{21} = [\mathbf{e}_2]_\times \mathbf{H}_{21}^{\pi_1}$ or $\mathbf{F}_{21} = [\mathbf{e}_2]_\times \mathbf{H}_{21}^{\pi_2}$.

Our algorithm consists of an iteration of robust estimation of a homography and elimination of lines verifying it. We can iterate while planes are extracted. Then, if we have extracted two or more, we can compute the fundamental matrix as we have described previously. If we have estimated a first homography, any new homography will not be good for fundamental matrix estimation. A fundamental matrix computed from two close planes is inaccurate. This can be avoided checking the condition number of the homology $\mathbf{H} = \mathbf{H}_{21}^{\pi_1} \cdot (\mathbf{H}_{21}^{\pi_2})^{-1}$. If $\mathbf{H}_{21}^{\pi_1}$ and $\mathbf{H}_{21}^{\pi_2}$ are two homographies of the same plane, the condition number of the homology $\mathbf{H}$ would be close to 1. We demand a greater value than a threshold. However, a large value is not suitable, because large condition numbers indicate a nearly singular matrix. So the condition number should fit into a fixed range. In this way, if second homography leads us to a homology with a condition number out of the fixed range, it is discarded and lines belonging to that plane are also eliminated, in order to let us get a new homography with the rest.

Moreover, knowledge of one homography of the scene restricts others. Linear subspace constraints on homographies have been previously derived in [11]. They showed that the collection of homographies of multiple planes between a pair of views span a 4-dimensional linear subspace. This constraint, however, requires the number of planes in the scene to be greater than 4. Zelnik-Manor and Irani apply it [12], replacing the need for multiple planes with the need for multiple views. They only need two planes, and often a single one (under restricted assumptions on camera motion). We work only with two images, and more than four planes in a scene are not always available, but easier constraints are possible. In fact, the knowledge of first homography allows us to compute the second only from three matched lines, and knowledge of first and second let us compute the third from two.

This method may fail if only one plane in the scene exists, or in case of pure rotation, because epipolar geometry is not defined and only one homography can be computed, but an automatic detection of this situation is made through condition number of the homology.

5   Experimental Results

The proposed method works properly with indoor images and outdoor images provided that at least two planes, containing enough lines, exist in the scene.

To measure the goodness of the computed fundamental matrix we use the first order geometric error computed as the Sampson distance [5] for points extracted and matched manually,

$$\sum_i \frac{(\mathbf{p}_2^T \mathbf{F}_{21} \mathbf{p}_1)^2}{(\mathbf{F}_{21} \mathbf{p}_1)_f^2 + (\mathbf{F}_{21} \mathbf{p}_1)_s^2 + (\mathbf{F}_{21}^T \mathbf{p}_2)_f^2 + (\mathbf{F}_{21}^T \mathbf{p}_2)_s^2} \tag{3}$$

here $()_f$ and $()_s$ indicate the first and second components of the corresponding vectors.

The square root resulting on dividing such value between the number of points used, gives us a measure in pixels comparable with other pairs of images. One pixel of error could have been introduced in the manual selection of point matches. Since point matches are different for every image pair, measure noise is also different, and comparisons should be done with care.

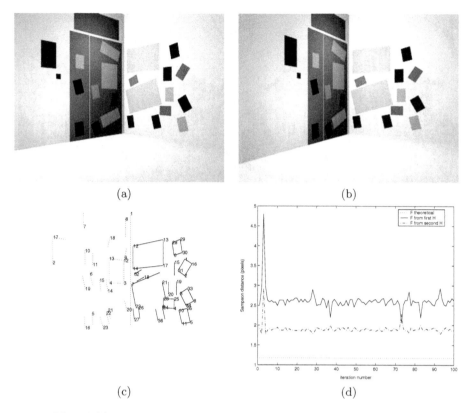

(a)   (b)

(c)   (d)

Fig. 1. (a) and (b) Synthetic images to compute the fundamental matrix. (c) Matches belonging to each plane in one execution. We show only one image because all matches are correct. (d) Sampson distance, with the two fundamental matrices computed from homology for 100 iterations and theoretical fundamental matrix. Sampson distance for theoretical matrix gives us a measure of quality of manually selected points. Notice that the average distance for fundamental matrices computed is only about a pixel over theoretical matrix.

The first experiment is made with synthetic images (Fig. 1). The motion of the camera includes translation and rotation. The first image camera centre is on an equidistant line to the planes showed, four meters from each one. The motion is a rotation of 15 degrees using as axis the intersection line of both planes. We can compute theoretically the epipole and the fundamental matrix knowing the camera motion. The theoretical epipole can be compared with the obtained epipole, computing the angle of both epipoles in relation to the camera center. We have done 100 executions forcing the condition number over 1.4. The mean value of this error is 1.7628 degrees with a standard deviation of 0.6037. We want to emphasize that, in this case and for a standard execution, all final matches of lines between images are correct and are considered as belonging to the correct plane.

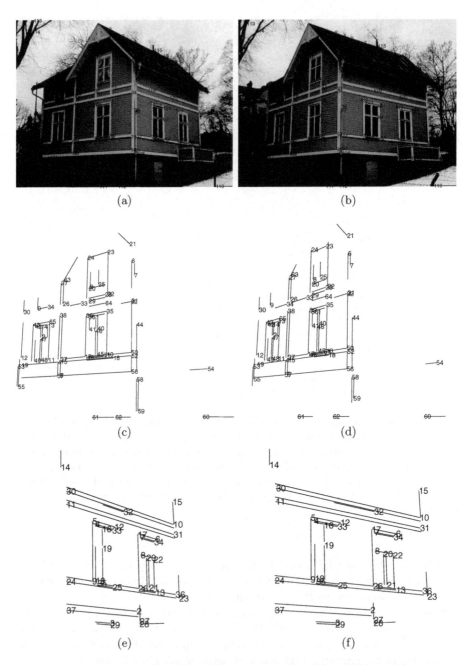

Fig. 2. Real images to compute the fundamental matrix. (a) and (b) Initial matching of straight lines. (c) and (d) Matches in the first homography. (e) and (f) Matches in the second homography. In both extracted planes we obtain new matches, whereas outliers are reduced significantly. (Images supplied by D. Tell, KTH Stockholm).

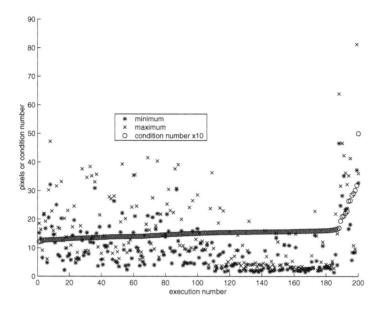

Fig. 3. Sampson distance per point for 200 executions. In each one two fundamental matrices are obtained. We show the minimum and the maximum of both Sampson distance, and the condition number of the homology obtained in the execution multiplied by 10. Executions are ordered by condition number. We can notice that it exists an interval of values from 1.53 to 1.64 (executions 125 to 185 approximately) where Sampson distance takes smaller values. These values can be used to decide the goodness of an execution.

We also show an experiment carried out with real outdoor images. Initial matches of lines and final matches obtained computing two homographies in one execution can be seen in Fig. 2. Outliers are common in initial matching, whereas in final matching they are rare. Moreover, lines not considered initial matches, appear after estimating the homography. However, lines not belonging to the region of the plane in the image also appear in this phase, because they are close to satisfying the constraint imposed by it, because they are nearly collinear with corresponding epipolar line. We think they do not spoil neither the computed homography, nor therefore the fundamental matrix estimation. We have executed the algorithm 200 times, ordering executions by condition number. In this experiment the condition number has not been limited in any way, in order to analyze its influence on the quality of fundamental matrix. In Fig. 3, we show the Sampson distance and the condition number obtained in each execution. We can notice that it exists an interval (from execution 125 to 185 approximately), where Sampson distance takes low values. That is to say, we can use condition number to determine when an execution is good. In this experiment, an execution with condition number between 1.53 and 1.64 can be considered good. Out of this range, fundamental matrix should be discarded, and a new execution done.

6   Conclusions and Future Work

We have presented a method to compute automatically the fundamental matrix between two images using lines.

The proposed method works properly with indoor images and outdoor images provided that at least two planes, containing enough lines, exist in the scene. The condition number of the obtained homology can be used to decide the goodness of the fundamental matrix.

However, matches obtained not always belong to the corresponding region of the plane extracted. Lines used for the computation of one homography are discarded for the following homographies, but we should check that regions containing such lines are not overlapping. Another improvement consists of constraints between homographies. Knowledge of one homography of the scene restricts others. The use of regions associated to planes and constraints between homographies will lead us to a faster and more accurate algorithm.

References

1. Zhang, Z.: Determining the epipolar geometry and its uncertainty: A review. International Journal of Computer Vision **27** (1998) 161–198
2. Rother, C., Carlsson, S.: Linear multi view reconstruction and camera recovery using a reference plane. International Journal of Computer Vision **49** (2002) 214–223
3. Schmid, C., Zisserman, A.: Automatic line maching across views. In: IEEE Conference on CVPR. (1997) 666–671
4. Zhang, Z., Deriche, R., Faugeras, O., Luong, Q.: A robust technique for matching two uncalibrated images through the recovery of the unknown epipolar geometry. Artificial Intelligence (1995) 87–119
5. Hartley, R., Zisserman, A.: Multiple View Geometry in Computer Vision. Cambridge University Press, Cambridge (2000)
6. Guerrero, J., Sagüés, C.: Robust line matching and estimate of homographies simultaneously. IbPRIA. Pattern Recognition and Image Analysis, LNCS 2652. (2003) 297–307
7. Burns, J., Hanson, A., Riseman, E.: Extracting straight lines. IEEE Trans. on Pattern Analysis and Machine Intelligence **8** (1986) 425–455
8. Hartley, R.: In defense of the eight-point algorithm. IEEE Trans. on Pattern Analysis and Machine Intelligence **19** (1997) 580–593
9. Zhang, Z.: Parameter estimation techniques: A tutorial with application to conic fitting. Rapport de recherche RR-2676, I.N.R.I.A., Sophia-Antipolis, France (1995)
10. Rousseeuw, P., Leroy, A.: Robust Regression and Outlier Detection. John Wiley, New York (1987)
11. Shashua, A., Avidan, S.: The rank 4 constraint in multiple ($\geq$ 3) view geometry. In: Proc. European Conf. Computer Vision, St. Louis, Missouri (1996) 196–206
12. Zelnik-Manor, L., Irani, M.: Multiview constraints on homographies. IEEE Transactions on Pattern Analysis and Machine Intelligence **24** (2002) 214–223

BOGAR_LN: An Agent Based Component Framework for Developing Multi-modal Services Using Natural Language

Francisco J. Garijo[1], Sonia Bravo[2], Jorge Gonzalez[2], and Emilio Bobadilla[2]

[1] Telefónica I+D
Emilio Vargas 6
28043 Madrid
fgarijo@tid.es
[2] INAD
C/Albacete 5, Edificio AGF, 3ª Planta
28027 Madrid
{jorm,sbravos,eba}@inad.es

Abstract. This paper describes BOGAR_LN an agent-based component-ware framework which consist of a multi-layered library and support tools for component creation, retrieval, management, and reuse. BOGAR_LN library provides application developers with four categories of reusable component models: Agent Organization models , Agent models, Resource models, and Basic computing entities. For each category, there are generic components which represents abstract reusable patterns and application oriented components. Component instances are made up of three blocks of information: design description in UML, code implementation in Java, and an extensible collection of attribute-value descriptors. The initial repertoire of repository components, comes from previous experiences in developing Agent based telecom services. The paper also presents the metrics and the evaluation approach to assess the benefits of the framework. Evaluation data have been gathered by using the framework to develop a mixed-initiative spoken dialog system for appointment management over the telephone. Results showed significant reductions on both project duration and cost. Compared to previous developments the time and the engineering effort required to build the service, was on average 65% less when using BOGART_LN.

1 Introduction

Agent technology has the maturity demanded for successful inclusion in large scale industrial applications, however its utilization into commercial systems is merely testimonial. Demonstrating the advantages of agent technology face to conventional software technologies still a challenging issue.

In the telecom area there has been several research initiatives to asses and evaluate the benefits of agent technology [5] [7] [8] [23]. Experimental results confirm the advantages of agent technology when it is used in harmony with the concepts, the methodologies and the development environments for distributed software systems. Professional development of agent based systems requires the extension of method-

R. Conejo et al. (Eds.): CAEPIA-TTIA 2003, LNAI 3040, pp. 207–220, 2004.

ologies for object-oriented software development to agent-oriented applications as well as the identification of tools to support this methodology. This issue was addressed by EURESCOM project P907 [1999-2001]. The project defined the MESSAGE methodology (Methodology for Engineering systems of software agents) [2][7], which consists of applicability guidelines, a modelling notation, and a process for analysis and design of agent systems. MESSAGE extends the basic UML concepts of Class and Association with knowledge level agent centric concepts, and adopts the Rational Unified Process [18] as the software development process. It also proposes a set of meta-models defined in OMG's Meta-model Facility [17], that capture different views of multi-agent systems: Organization Model, to describe the overall structure of the system; Goal/Task Model, to determine what the MAS and constituent agents do in terms of the goals they work to attain, and the tasks they must accomplish in order to achieve goals; Agent Model, that contains a detailed and comprehensive description of each individual Agent and Role within the MAS; Domain (Information) Model, that acts as a repository of information (both entities and relations) concerning the problem domain, and Interaction Model, which is concerned with agent interactions with human users and other agents. Similar divisions can be found in other agent oriented methodologies such as MAS-CommonKADS [13], Vowel Engineering [4], and GAIA [25]. The MESSAGE contribution is that each meta-models provides the concepts, the underlying structure, and the rules for producing UML application models. Using MOF allows flexible notation and facilitates building design and implementation tools [5][11]. Extensions to MESSAGE modelling notations can be found in INGENIAS [14] and RT MESSAGE [16].

Although Agent centred concepts and notations proved to be suitable for analysis and preliminary design, developers need also guideline and support for other stages of the life cycle such as requirements, detailed design, implementation, testing and deployment. The transition from general design to detail design, and from detail design to implementation set up two complementary problems: Firstly how to identify computational models for implementing the functionality of the agents, and second how to translate those models into efficient implementations running in the target platform.

One solution experimented in MESSAGE consisted on defining a family of design patterns in UML, which are instances of the meta-models and incorporate computing models derived from previous engineering experiences [6] [23]. Design models for gents are component-based [22], and cover the more popular styles of agent architecture such as reactive and cognitive architecture. Agent based components provide standard external interfaces, and uniform internal structure, which in turn is made up of generic components, to achieve specific functionality, such as agent control, agent management, agent perception and communication, and agent internal state. Interaction among internal components is through their standard interfaces. This enables that each component might be implemented with different paradigms and technologies. For example a control mechanism might be implemented through a rule based processor, or a frame based processor; communication might be message oriented through FIPA protocols, operational oriented using RMI or CORBA, or other.

Experience in Telefonica I+D developing conversational services with spoken natural language interfaces, confirm the advantages of this approach. Viewing agents as reusable software component provides several advantages:1) Applications are developed by selecting and assembling the appropriate components. 2) Integration and inter-operability among agents, and standard component-ware technology and supporting tools is assured. 3) Developers unfamiliar with agent concepts and notations may choose agent based components to fulfil specific functionality of their application. This enables agent technology to be easily assimilated into current engineering practice.

In addition to agents, three categories of patterns were identified: 1) Organisations patterns modelling agent based applications; 2) Resource patterns encapsulating computing entities providing services to agents. These services include message oriented middleware, transaction monitors, security and authentication services, information services, databases, visualization, speech recognition and generation, etc.; 3) Basic components which models components for building new agent and resource models. These category includes abstract data types, specialized libraries, domain ontologies, rule processors, buffers, etc.

Working with such variety of heterogeneous components set up the need for developing tools that support specification and management of application components, and reuse. The BOGAR system was designed to achieve this goal by providing the following functionality.

- Creating and managing agent-oriented application components. Each component is characterised by three blocs of information: an extensible collection of attribute-value descriptors which defines semantic information attached to the component; component design in UML and component code in Java. BOGAR provides a component repository service to catalogue, store and retrieve components from partial descriptions.
- Facilitating the reuse process. BOGAR provides functions for component search, selection, analysis, and assembly. It also provides advice and guidance for adaptation and modification.

BOGAR's implementation allowed to carry out one of the pioneering experiences to evaluate the benefits using agent based components for developing conversational services with natural language interfaces.

The following sections describe the principal features of the BOGAR framework, the component model, and the evaluation results. Final considerations, open issues and future work are addressed in the conclusion section.

2 BOGAR_LN Overview

BOGAR_LN (Biblioteca de OrGanizaciones, Agentes, Recursos y componentes básicos) is an agent-based component management system for component creation, retrieval, management, and reuse. BOGAR_LN has been conceived to attain a double objective:

- Providing organisations and software engineering teams with a component library and services to capture, store, manage, and disseminate their engineering knowledge.
- Supporting designers and developers for finding, analyzing, and integrating repository components into their application.

BOGAR_LN library contains an agent-centred collection of software components, which have been synthesized through practical experience in developing conversational services with natural language interfaces. In addition to searching and browsing facilities, the system provides advice and guidance to developers for adapting components to their application requirements. For complex components like agents, the system shows the steps needed for adaptation, indicating those internal components which might be changed, and giving examples of modification.

2.1 Component Characteristics

The concept of component used in BOGAR is aligned with standard definitions in software engineering [22] [23]: "self-contained piece of software, with contractually specified interfaces and context dependencies. It Encapsulates some coherent functionality. and supports independent deployment and composition by third party".

BOGAR components are characterised by three types of information:

- Component descriptors. This is an extensible collection of attribute-value pairs which allows: a) cataloguing the component according to different criteria such as identity, category, genericity, type, domain, and others; b) defining the component features and execution constraints such as functionality, dependency relationships with other components, hardware and software requirements, and other restrictions.
- Component design defined in UML using standard UML based tools.
- Component code conformant to design descriptions. This code is written in JAVA. There are also components written in C and C++ which have been wrapped with Java interfaces.

Component descriptors, design, and code constitute the component material substrate, with which developers might handle the software component like an entity similar to the components known in different engineering disciplines.

2.2 Component Types. Agents as Basic Components in the Engineering Process

BOGART allows cataloguing, storing and managing all kinds of software components. What differentiates BOGAR from other components repositories is that its component model and supporting functionality is specifically suited for agent based development. Therefore the fundamental entity which articulate the repository taxonomy, is the agent.

Agent components provides an external view which is made up of their external interfaces, and an uniform internal structure – Fig. 1 –.There are two type of interfaces: a) Agent management interfaces providing methods to activate, stop, delete, and monitor the agent; b) Agent communication interface to allow agent interaction with different entities that can be either agents – using agent communication languages (ACL) –, or computing entities in the environment such as web servers, data bases, call managers, messaging servers, mail servers, directory services, etc.

Agent's internal structure is formed by the necessary subsystems to perform the perception-assimilation-control –act cycle. These subsystems are defined as internal components encapsulating its specific functionality, and communicating through

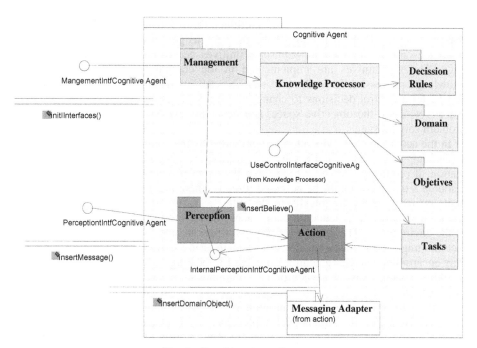

Fig. 1. Cognitive Agent Pattern.

standard interfaces. A great variety of agent models can be obtained, depending on the characteristics of their perception mechanism, their control process, or their actuation model.

In the applications developed at Telefónica I+D in the period 1997-2003,two categories of agent components have been used.

Cognitive Agents. Their architectural pattern – Fig.1 – is based on a BDI cognitive processor.

The design model provides computational components to define different kinds of knowledge:

- Ontologies to model the application domain.
- Intentions. Agent intentions are defined through the collection of objectives that the agent should achieve.
- Tasks and actions. They represent methods or procedures to obtain the information required to achieve the objectives. Actions are computing primitives that allow the agent to get new beliefs by different mechanisms such as inference processes, acting over the environment assimilating incoming information, and communicating with other agents.
- Strategy and decision making. The decision model is declarative. Strategy and tactic rules might be defined for controlling objective generation, choosing the most suitable tasks to achieve a particular objective, and changing the focus of the resolution process by suspending the resolution of an objective and selecting a new one.

The processing loop is based on a multithread implementation of the perception-reason-act-cycle. In the reasoning phase, the knowledge processor select and execute inference and problem-solving-control primitives according to the agent's knowledge. These primitives are implemented in the computing infrastructure of the knowledge processor. They allow to start internal inference process, execute tasks, and perform control decisions to change the focus of resolution, refine the existing objectives, clean the objective space, and generate new objectives according to the problem solving state.

In the actuation phase, the interfaces provided by the computing entities in the environment – e.g. agents, and resources – are used to obtain information. This information, if produced, will be sent through the agent perception interfaces. Although resource's interfaces might be accessed directly, there is a need for adaptor components, which hide the complexity for locating, accessing and extracting information from the resource. The actuation component provides to the agent a high level view of the environment. The knowledge processor uses its interfaces to carry out actions. Actions might be implemented as simple method invocations of internal classes, or may encapsulate launching complex process for locating and accessing the resources, including synchronous or asynchronous communication, exception handling, retries, time-outs, etc.

In the perception phase, asynchronous events and communication messages are received. The perception component implements the agent communication interfaces. Its processing model include extraction, filtering, storing, and assimilation mechanisms to transform incoming information into cognitive entities, which will be stored into the cognitive memory by the knowledge processor.

Reasoning cycles may conflict with information assimilation cycles. By default the reasoning has priority over information assimilation, however this priority might be modified dynamically. Typically, the knowledge processor starts with a reasoning phase where a set of objectives are generated. Strategy knowledge is used to select the most appropriate objective, and to start the resolution process by interpreting its specific resolution knowledge. This knowledge is defined by situation-action rules, where the situation part specify a partial state of the cognitive memory including the objective and its internal state, and the action part contains statements for launching inference process or executing tasks. Inference process may generate new believes which in turn might activate new resolution rules. When this rule chaining process stops, the knowledge processor adds to the cognitive memory the entities elaborated by the perception. This will create new conditions where strategic rules and objective resolution rules may be applied to continue solving the pending objectives.

In addition to the packages show in figure 1, the design pattern also includes the classes and diagrams for defining all the computing entities mentioned above, such as events, believes, messages, tasks, objectives, etc.

Reactive Agents. They differs from cognitive agents in its perception and control model. The perception works as an event handling mechanism. The control is modelled as an Extended Finite State Machine (EFSM) which consumes events stored in the perception, and perform transitions by changing its internal state, and invoking actions in the actuation model. Reactive agents behaves like event-consuming process which change its internal state and execute operations according to their state transition table. Agent behaviour is defined be specifying the events, the transition table in XML, and the actuation model.

2.3   Agent's Organizations, Resources and Basic Components

To achieve their goals, agents need to interact with the computing entities in their environment. Agents view this entities as "resources". More formally, in agent based applications we have called resources those computing entities that are not agents, and are used by the agents to obtain information for achieving their objectives. Examples of resources are: Data bases, protocol stacks, text to speech translators, speech processors, visualization systems, syntactic analysers, etc. As Agents do, resources should offer standard interfaces. This facilitates the management, use, and deployment in different processors.

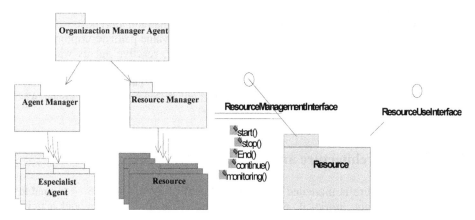

Fig. 2. Organization pattern and Resource pattern.

Although there might be applications with only one agent, complex applications usually involve several agents communicating among them and accessing different kinds of resources. This model, in which a group of agents collaborate to achieve the system functionality corresponds to an agent organization – Fig 2 –. The architectural pattern for the agent organization has been defined through meta-modelling [5] [9]. This pattern is made up of agents playing specific roles such as agent managers, agent specialist, and resources.

2.4   Conceptual Model of the Component Library

The library structure has been defined to accommodate components according to different criteria – component category, role in the application, genericity, application domain, and component functionality. BOGAR conceptual model contemplates four categories of components: Organization, Agent, Resource and Basic component. This characterization, is inspired on methodological proposals such as Vowels[4], MESSAGE [7] and INGENIAS [14] Each category is divided into two subcategories:

Generic Components. They are component patterns that are used to generate particular engineering components. Its structure and its behaviour are parameterized. The parameters values may be class, methods, interfaces or components. By giving appropriate values to the component's parameters specific components are obtained that then can be used in applications.

Specific Components. They can be downloaded from the library and assembled for building conversational services, if their installation and deployment requirements are met.

Generic and specific components can be further classified according to predefined attributes, such as the subcategory and the domain, and specific component descriptors that can be defined by the library administrator. For example the agent component in figure – is catalogued as follows: Entity type: Agent; Genericity: generic; Subtype: Cognitive; Domain: undefined; Component-Specific Descriptors: undefined. New sub-categories of generic cognitive agents for specific domains may be created by specifying domain values. The system administrator may also refine the classification model by defining an open list of attribute-value pairs descriptors in the Component-Specific Descriptors attribute. For example, reactive agents which appears in the organization pattern as agent managers, have been classified as follows: Entity type: Agent; Genericity: specific; Subtype: Reactive; Domain: generic; Component-Specific Descriptors: [Control Model: Extended Finite State Automata; Action model: parameterless].

3 BOGAR Architecture and Functionality

BOGAR architecture is modelled as an organization of agents – Fig.3. – to enable component catalogue, retrieval, management, and reuse. Its design model and its implementation was done by reusing the existing collection of agent-based components. These components, and the new components developed for building BOGAR – e.g. BOGAR organization, BOGAR agents, resources, and basic components –, were also catalogued and stored in the repository.

The agent organisation that implements the component framework is made up of the following agents:

Management Agents. Their role is to create, supervise and control other computing entities. They are also responsible for creating and activating all the computing infrastructure – objects and threads – necessary for the managed entities to achieve their function. Once the managed entities are created, the agent manager start checking that their functioning is correct. In cases where there are errors fault diagnostic and control actions are performed, to inform, restore, abort, or delete the affected entities. The organization has a hierarchical control model. The organization manager agent creates and controls the agent manager and the resource manager agent. These, in turn, have the responsibility of creating and supervising the specialist agents and the resources respectively. The managements agents are reactive agents whose code is 95% re-used from one application to another.

Specialist Agents. These implement the library management functions. The following agents exist:

   Access Agent. This agent is responsible for user's authentication giving access to personalized functionality according to user's profile. The system supports two types of users: library administrators and developers. The supporting func-

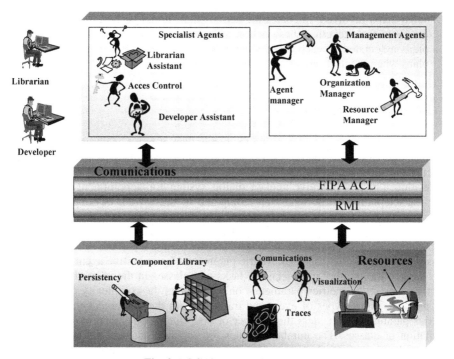

Fig. 3. BOGAR_LN Architecture.

tionality for each user role, is provided by cognitive agent assistants, which are activated when the access agent informs them of successful completion of the authentication process.

Librarian Assistant Agent. The mission of the library administrator is to catalogue new components and to guarantee the consistency, integrity, and correct functioning of all components stored in the library. The administrator assistant agent provides the administrator with graphical interfaces and tools for the cataloguing, searching, modifying, storage and removal of library components.

Developer Assistant Agent. It provides developers with the means for searching, browsing, and downloading components. It also provides advice and guidance for reusing the components. The search functions for component location allow visual navigation through the library conceptual model. The user may get the list of components associated to an abstract concept and progressively refine the search by specifying additional criteria such as component type, genericity, sub-type, etc. When the developer ask for detailed examination of component design and/or component code, the agent activates the pre-defined tools for design – Rational Rose – and encoding – J. Builder –. In the case of not having compatible commercial tools, HTML descriptions of the components are also available which might be viewed with standard HTML browsers. The Developer Agent provides advice and guidance for transforming the generic components into application components. It shows the user the sequence of step necessary to carry out the transformation process, and if required, for each step, it displays the subsystems involved, indicates the actions that should be performed, and opens the tools for executing these actions. Transformation process are modelled as plans associated to each component type. The agent select and interpret these plans when the user requests help for reusing the components.

4 BOGAR_LN Evaluation

Metrics were established to determine the percentage of reuse of library components, and the time and effort required for design and implementation of application components and subsystems. Evaluation data have been gathered by using the framework to develop a mixed-initiative spoken dialog system for appointment management over the telephone. These data were compared to those from developing previous conversation services without the framework.

Different metrics parameters were defined for each development phase and for each component type. In the design phase, metrics parameters focus on the number of classes and diagrams carried out. Metric parameters for cognitive agent components, also include the number of objectives, tasks and classes in the re-used domain. For reactive agents, the metrics parameters only considers the complexity of the control automaton – status, types of event and transitions. In the implementation phase, the metrics parameters considers the number of code lines corresponding to the implementation of classes. The number of rules for cognitive agents, and the number of states of the Finite State Automata of reactive agents, are also considered.

The new service developed using the framework – "The CITA2 service" is a natural language telephony-based appointment management service that allows the employees of a company to schedule, reschedule, consult and **cancel** appointments, with members of their managing staff. The system answer telephone calls, dialogue with users to achieve their requests, and manage meeting scheduling for each manager. The system implementation is also based on an organization of cooperating agents and organization resources. The interaction with the user is controlled by the cognitive agents which perform a goal driven behaviour, and mixed-initiative dialogue model. Speech understanding model, agents reasoning capabilities, and dialogue strategies are domain oriented. The system listen to users identify them, ask questions to get missing information or to confirm data, and use the data for achieving its pending goals. There is not restriction for users on the way to talk to the system. For new scheduling appointments, the system checks for availability in the manager's agenda, giving alternative appointments, and inviting the user to chose one of them. The user is not constraint to follow the system indications, it may enter new data for one operation, select new operations or abandon the service. Semantic verification of the recognized information allows the system to point out erroneous or misunderstood information, and starting dialogues for flexible correction of the data, taking into account the dialogue context.

4.1 Evaluation Results in the Design Phase

Results in table 1 show reusability rates of over 60%, which approach 100% in the case of reactive agents.

Internal infrastructure components of the cognitive agent such as the agent's management, the perception, and the cognitive control, are 100% reused during design. Designer activities should only focus on defining the domain dependent components of the service to develop: objectives, tasks and domain classes.

Table 1. Results in the Design Phase.

Component Type	Number of Components	Classes and diagrams	Reusability	Time reduction
Cognitive Agent	2	201	56,5%	45%
Reactive Agent	3	155	97,6%	95%
Resource	5	112	66,3%	55%
Totals	**10**	**468**	**72,4%**	**65%**

The library provides completely designed resources that can be used 'as is', for example the syntactic analyzer, the call manager and the voice recognition / generation resources. However substantial design effort might be devoted to design service specific resources such as the meeting agenda for the managing staff.

The design phase usually suffers the pressures to shorten the development times. Having pre-designed elements simplifies the activities on this phase and helps the designer to be centred in the most complex elements, which must be detailed and documented before the implementation phase.

4.2   Evaluation Results in the Implementation Phase

Reusability percentages for the reactive agents overcome 95%. The development time decreases in a similar way, because the biggest effort consists on the implementation of the automaton actions that has been specified in the design phase.

Table 2. Results in the implementation phase.

Component Type	Number of Components	Code Reusability	Lines of code	Time reduction
Cognitive Agent	3	69,3%	8766	65%
Reactive Agent	2	97,8%	9743	95%
Resource	5	37,6%	8422	30%
Totals	**10**	**70%**	**36.931**	**65%**

Reusability percentages of the cognitive agents are bigger than those of design phase, near 65%. The agent's infrastructure is totally reused, but the cognitive domain dependent components of the application must be implemented. Their cost depends on the complexity of the dialogue processes – objectives and tasks –, and the entities forming the domain ontology. When a similar service exists into the library, the reusability percentage increases because part of the domain dependent work can be reused – objectives, tasks and the ontology classes –. Many objectives from the CITA2 project where reused from another services, for example: the system activation, the service terminating, the data confirmation, and the help support. In some cases it has been necessary to modify them partially, but these modifications have been made without hardly effort, simply following the design diagrams most of the time.

The reusability of the resources decrease from 55% in design to 30% in implementation. This is due to the variations in the reusability of application resources. Whilst there are resources completely reused from one application to another, – for example speech recognition and generation –, the reusability percentage of service specific resources like the meeting agenda management, is insignificant – less than 3% –.

Overall, the average reusability score is remarkable, it comes closer to 65% .

5   Conclusions and Further Work

BOGAR_LN library contains the components obtained and used to develop agent based applications in the last five years. Overall, there are 69 Mb of documentation, design and code corresponding to 32 components, indexed and catalogued into different categories – organizations, agents, resources and basic components –The two systems developed with the component framework – BOGAR and CITA2 –, are fully operative, running on low cost machines, under Linux or Windows OS. Flexible deployment of agents and resources might be done by deploying them on a single processing node, or separated over different nodes. This facilitates application performance and scalability.

Using the components allows substantial reduction in development time and effort – 65% less –. Cost reduction is achieved without minimising or skipping activities like design, documentation and testing. The number of errors in the testing phase, and error detection/correction cycle duration, also decrease. The testing period for CITA2, was one third of those spent for previous services, and the amount of errors was 60% smaller.

The BOGAR_LN framework has revealed as a valuable instrument for an engineering team. Its component management features allow to catalogue the project results according to corporate methodology standards and team development tools. Thus the results of the development processes are centralized and they become easily accessible to developers. BOGAR_LN multi-layered library and supporting tools offers developers the following features:

- An open collection of reliable and proven components that can be adapted and assembled for building new services.
- Architecture patterns and instances of these patterns, including both design descriptions and implementation code. Application examples enable developers easy assimilation of the agent based components, their utilisation and reuse. Applications are modelled according to the Organisation patterns, which are made up of instances of agent based patterns and resources. These in turn are made up of more fine grained components.
- Advice and guidance plans for adapting each type of generic component to specific domains. These plans might updated, and new plans might be attached to the components.

Although the evaluation has focus on the design and implementation phases, significant reductions have been observed in the analysis and testing phases too. In the testing phase it would be convenient to store in the library the testing models by associating to each component its corresponding testing specifications scenarios and results. This would contribute to increase the reliability of the components, reducing costs for integration testing, and system testing.

In the near future work should continue to enrich the library with new components, specially generic components, and adding new features that allow to:

- Specify and validate the properties of the components.
- Define new relationships among components, incorporating dependency checking and constraint verification mechanisms for component adaptation and composition.
- Enhance user support for component reuse facilitating the validation of component properties and composition constraints. Translation assistance from design models to efficient implementation code, rules, and XML descriptions, is also required.

References

1. B. Bauer, F. Bergenti, P. Massonet, J. Odell: Agents and the UML: A Unified Notation for Agents and Multi-agent Systems AOSE 2001 Springer Verlag LNAI 2222 pp 148-150.
2. G. Caire, F Leal., R Evans, F Garijo, J Gomez P Kearney, J Stark, Philippe Massonet Agent Oriented Analysis using MESSAGE/UML. In Agent Oriented Software Engineering, July 2001 LNAI 2222 Springer 2002 pp119,135.
3. FIPA Foundation for Intelligent Physical Agents www.fipa.org/
4. Y. Demazeau "La méthode VOYELLES", dans Systèmes Multi-Agents : Des Théories Organisationnelles aux Applications Industrielles, Mandiau et al, eds, Hermès, hiver 2001.
5. F. J. Garijo J. J. Gómez-Sanz, J. Pavón. Multi Agent System Organisation : an engineering view. MAAMAW 2001 Annecy, Francia Mayo 2001.
   http://grasia.fdi.ucm.es/publications.html.
6. F. J. Garijo, J. Tous, S. Corley, M. Tesselaar Development of a Multi-Agent System for cooperative work with network negotiation capabilities. Lecture Notes in Computer Science, Vol 1437. pp 222-232. Albayrak & Garijo Eds. Springer-Verlag. 1998.
7. P907 MESSAGE: Methodology for Engineering Systems of Software Agents D2.
   http:// www.eurescom.de/public/projectresults/ P900-series/907d2.asp -
8. S. Corley , J. Hickie, J. Kennedy , M. Dennis F. Garijo Agent-Oriented Workflow Management for Telecommunications Business Processes Proc of 6ᵗʰ International Conference on Intelligent Networks, Bordeaux, Januray 2000.
9. J. J. Gómez-Sanz, J Pavón, F. J. Garijo: Meta-models for building multi-agent systems. Proceedings of the 2002 ACM Symposium on Applied Computing SAC 2002: March 10-14, 2002, Madrid, Spain, pp 37-41.
10. J. J. Gómez-Sanz, J. Pavón, F. J. Garijo: Intelligent Interface Agents Behavior Modeling. MICAI 2000 Acapulco Mexico, LNAI 1793 Springer Verlag 598-609.
11. J. J. Gómez-Sanz, J. Pavón,: Meta-modelling in Agent Oriented Software Engineering Advances in Artificial Intelligence IBERAMIA 2002 Sevilla, Spain LNAI 2527 Springer Verlag pp 606-615.
12. Huhns, M. S., "Multiagent Systems and Societies of Agents," MIT Press, 2000.

13. Iglesias, C., Garijo, M., Gonzalez, J. C., and Velasco, J. R., "Analysis and design of multi-agent systems using MAS-CommonKADS," in Singh, M. P., Rao, A., and Wooldridge, M. J. (eds.) *Intelligent Agents IV* LNAI Volume 1365 ed. SpringerVerlag: Berlin, 1998.
14. **INGENIAS**. grasia.fdi.ucm.es/ingenias/index_marco_esp.htm
15. JIAC - Java-based Intelligent Agent Componentware http://www.dai-labor.de/en/main/jiac_iv/general
16. V. Julian and V. Botti Developing Real-Time Multi-Agent Systems IberAgents 2002 Malaga http://sirius.lcc.uma.es/iberagents/julian.pdf
17. Kruchten, P. (1999) *The Rational Unified Process*. Addison-Wesley.
18. OMG. *Meta Object Facility (specification) V.1.3.* formal/2000-04-03. http://www.omg.org
19. P. Ricordel & Y. Demazeau, "From Analysis to Deployment : a Multi-Agent Platform Survey", Engineering Societies in the Agents' World (ESAW'00), ECAI 00, Springer Verlag, pp. 93-105, Berlin, August 2000.
20. J. Treur, Y. Demazeau & P.-Michel Ricordel, "Situation and Prospective of Agent-Based Engineering", in Knowledge Engineering and Agent Technology, Cuena et al, eds, IOS Series on Frontiers in AI and Applications , Summer 2001.
21. Odell, J., Parunak, H. V. D. & Bauer, B. Extending UML for Agents. In Proceedings of the Agent-Oriented Information Systems Workshop at the 17th National conference on Artificial Intelligence (2000).
22. OMG CORBA Component Model RFP http://www.omg.org/library/schedule/CORBA_Component_Model_RFP.htm
23. C Szyperski, Component Software - Beyond Object-Oriented Programming, Addison-Wesley, 432 pages, hardcover, 1997, ISBN 0-201-17888-5.
24. D. Walshe, J. Kennedy, S. Corley, G. Koudouridis, F. Van Laenen, V. Ouzounis, F. J. Garijo, and J. Gomez Sanz. An Interoperable Architecture for Agent-Oriented Workflow Management . Proc of IC-AI'2000: The 2000 International Conference on Artificial Intelligence. Monte Carlo Resort, Las Vegas, Nevada, USA June 26-29, 2000 IC. CSREA-Press. ISBN 1-892512-59-9.
25. Wooldridge, M., Jennings, N. R., and Kinny, D., "The Gaia Methodology for Agent-Oriented Analysis and Design," *Journal of Autonomous Agents and Multi-Agent Systems*, vol. 15 2000.

Building Software Agents from Software Components[*]

Mercedes Amor, Lidia Fuentes Fernández,
Lawrence Mandow, and José María Troya

Dept. Lenguajes y Ciencias de la Computación
Universidad de Málaga
Málaga, Spain
{pinilla,lff,lawrence,troya}@lcc.uma.es

Abstract. The widespread use of the Internet has favored the development of distributed multi-agent systems. The development of agent-based applications is carried out with Agent-Oriented Software Engineering methods, techniques and tools. Although there are several different platforms and methodologies for software agents design, the lack of flexible agent architectures makes the development of multi-agent systems a tiresome and hard task. Current agent architectures provided by these platforms and methodologies do not offer enough flexibility for the development of flexible software agents, placing little emphasis on reuse. This paper presents a software agent development approach using a component-based architecture that promotes building agents from reusable software components. The basis of our approach is the use of component-based software development concepts and the separation of concerns principle to separate agent functionality into independent entities increasing the maintainability and adaptability of the agent to new environments and demands. This architecture simplifies the software agent development process, reducing it to the description of the agents' software components and interaction protocols using XML documents. The power of Java and Jess technologies has been exploited in the implementation of our compositional model of software agents.

1 Introduction

The ever increasing use of the Internet in everyday tasks makes necessary the development of capable software for dynamic, open, and distributed environments. Unlike other technologies used in the development of distributed Web applications, software agents seem to present the necessary features, like autonomy or self adaptation, to support the development of flexible and open systems.

Agent-oriented Software Engineering (AOSE) is a new discipline devoted to the development of Multi-Agent Systems (MAS). The goal of AOSE is to provide methods, techniques, and tools for the development and maintenance of agent-based software [1]. The design of MAS is focused in the modeling of internal components for the different agents, using the agent architecture provided by a particular agent platform like Jade [2], Zeus [3] or FIPA-OS [4].

---

[*] This research was funded in part by the Spanish MCYT under grant TIC: 2002-04309-C02-02.

R. Conejo et al. (Eds.): CAEPIA-TTIA 2003, LNAI 3040, pp. 221–230, 2004.

In the case of Zeus, the agent architecture is made up of a set of subsystems that allow task planning and execution, data storage, and exchange of messages between other components. The agent's internal architecture connects these subsystems through hard coded explicit references. Unlike Zeus, FIPA-OS and Jade try to decouple the agents' internal elements through the definition and use of interfaces. Although the latter agent platforms present more flexible architectures, they do not encourage the reuse of tasks and components across different platforms beyond well known object oriented mechanisms. Therefore, the developer has to program from scratch the complete functionality of the agent for each individual application. Most of the ongoing work aims at providing more flexible agents offering new architectures [5][6], or modifying existing ones [7].

We propose a compositional architecture for agent development that makes easier the task of building new agents from reusable software components. This architecture breaks down the agent's functionality into completely independent components, facilitating component addition or substitution, providing a greater degree of adaptation of the resulting agent. Furthermore, to achieve a better functional decomposition of the software agent, those properties that appear (cut-across) in several components are modeled as *aspects* according to current AOSD practice [8].

As a result, different abstractions that are part of the agent, like behavior, interaction protocols, or message distribution through a transport service, are internally separated in different entities within the architecture. This separation allows the modification of these components at run-time without affecting the others. For example, an agent will be able to adapt to its environment, training in a new interaction protocol or turning into a new agent, after acquiring new functionalities that were not included beforehand as part of the agent.

The implementation of software agents in one of the existing agent platforms is a tiresome and error-prone task that forces the developer to learn some high level programming language as well as the architecture and API of the chosen agent platform. On the other hand, in our architecture the development of new agents is accomplished by simply providing deployment files with the necessary information mainly about functionality, interaction protocols, and message distribution that initially structure the agent. This proposal offers clear advantages on the developers' side. Fewer errors are generated during development due to the reuse of reliable and error-free components purchased in the component market (Commercial Off-the-Shelf components, or Web services). Agent development mainly implies component assembly, minimizing programming errors and shortening development time in agent-based applications. Developers can be supported with tools that check the correctness of component combination.

In the next section we present our compositional architecture for software agent design, including the Java/Jess implementation of the *connector* component, responsible for the agent's coordination. Then, we present an example of the application development process with this approach. Finally, some conclusions are drawn.

2   A Compositional Architecture for Software Agents

Figure 1 shows an UML class diagram of the proposed architecture. UML stereotypes are used in the modeling of the <<Connector>>, <<Component>>, <<Mediator>>, <<Distribution>>, and <<Interface>> entities.

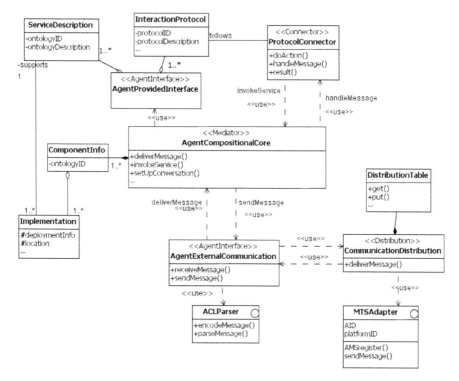

Fig. 1. UML class diagram of the Compositional Architecture for Software Agents.

In this architecture, the agent's functionality is provided by software components. In other agent architectures it is usual to find code related to agent actions or tasks together with code related to agent coordination. Therefore, it is difficult to reuse agent functionalities when the coordination changes. Applying the *separation of concerns* principle, we model component coordination with a new entity, called *connector* (a more detailed description can be found in section 2.1). Connectors (represented in this diagram by the *Connector* entity) coordinate the different interactions or conversations of the agent according to a communication protocol. A single agent may take part in several conversations simultaneously, each one controlled by a different connector. All instantiated connectors differ only in the coordinated protocol, whose description is passed upon instantiation.

In our architecture, agent behavior is provided by reusable software components, which offer the set of core services, as well as the application-dependent functionality. Actually, any software component can be incorporated as part of the agent's functionality, from COTS (*Commercial Off-The-Shelf*) components to Web services [9]. The syntax and semantics of the software components interfaces are described in the DAML-S service description ontology [10]. Since we use DAML-S as an interface description language, components' services are identified and invoked inside our architecture in an implementation independent way. Interaction protocols include calls to components' services also in DAML-S.

Coordination and functionality are composed dynamically at runtime by means of the Mediator entity. During protocol execution, the *AgentCompositionalCore (ACC)* component maps actions requested by connectors to services offered by registered components in DAML-S. Once determined which component offers the service, ACC locates the component and invokes the service according to its DAML-S description. In addition, when an agent starts a new conversation, the Mediator is the component that creates a new connector to control the interaction according to some protocol.

Our architecture separates other agent abstractions in independent entities. The *AgentInterface* components are in charge of agent external characterization, like the format used to represent exchanged ACL messages, a description of its functionality, and a list of the supported conversation protocols. The encoding format of messages exchanged within an interaction is also bundled in a separated entity. Thus, the codification of ACL messages in a concrete FIPA format is not merged with the agent platform access, nor with the behavior of the agent. Each parser has to realize a common interface to code and decode output and input messages. In the model, for each different ACL format supported, we provide an *ACLParser* plug-in (*ACLparser* interface in Figure 1) that parses ACL messages formatted according to a concrete FIPA ACL representation. Each parser processes input messages and discards those with syntactic errors according to a concrete ACL representation.

Other *AgentInterface* component, the *AgentProvidedInterface*, contains the agent's public interface, which is an extension of the traditional software component's public interface adapted to a software agent. In our case, the agent offers a public interface that includes a description of the agent's functionality (provided by the plug-ins, i.e. software components), and a list of the communication protocols supported by the agent, among other elements. Thus, this component keeps the description of the supported protocols, used by the ACC component at runtime to create connectors when the agent starts or takes part in a new protocol-driven interaction.

In order to produce agents able to be executed in any FIPA-compliant agent platform, we have separated everything related with the use of Message Transport Service (MTS), bundling it into a distribution *aspect*. This distribution aspect will be later bound to the particular adaptors (*plug-ins*) of the corresponding agent platforms on which the agent instance run. Then, the actual distribution of messages using a particular message transport service offered by a FIPA-compliant agent platform is performed by an independent entity, the *CommunicationDistribution* component in Figure 1. This component will forward output and input messages through an agent platform adaptor. Such adaptor defines a common interface that must be realized by each concrete adaptor instance of the target agent platform(s). Each adaptor will deal with the delivering and reception of messages using the specific services of such platform(s) (*MTSAdapter* interface in Figure 1). Since agent platform dependencies are encapsulated as external plug-ins, our agents can be adapted to engage in any FIPA-compliant agent platform, and even be used in more than one agent platform simultaneously making it more versatile and adaptable.

In the next section we will briefly explain how to describe a communication protocol, and give details about the implementation of the connector that uses this description to coordinate the execution of the protocol.

2.1 Connector Implementation

In the proposed architecture, connectors coordinate protocol execution. Connectors accept and interpret protocol descriptions at run-time. Therefore interaction protocols do not need to be pre-coded in the connectors. Protocol descriptions include the definition of the messages exchanged, as well as the internal actions carried out by the agent during protocol execution. The interaction protocol is linked or connected this way with the agent's functionality.

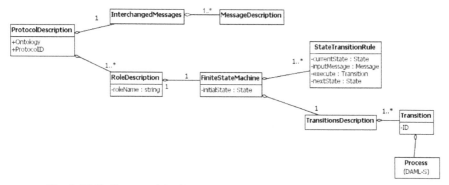

Fig. 2. UML diagram of the XML schema describing an interaction protocol.

The UML class diagram in Figure 2 depicts the structure of a protocol description. Agent interaction protocols are defined by finite state machines, whose states represent the current status of the conversation, and whose edges represent the messages being sent between agents. The protocol is described by means of the set of exchanged messages and a separate finite state machine modeling the behavior of each side of a conversation (the initiator and the responder). Each finite state machine is represented by a set of state transition rules .The transition from one state to another carries out the execution of the agent's functionality. The *TransitionDescription* element encloses the set of agent actions that are invoked during protocol execution. Instead of a simple sequence of invocations to the agent internal functionality, it is possible to use more complex control structures to coordinate the execution of the agent functionality. Since DAML-S provides the basis for the definition of agent's functionality as services, we use again the control structures defined in the *Process Model* of DAML-S to encompass a set of agent actions in a transition description. A more complete description of this protocol specification scheme appears in [11].

The connector interprets these descriptions and uses them to coordinate protocol execution at run-time. A single generic connector has been implemented in JESS [12], a rule-based language written entirely in Java. This generic connector can interpret and coordinate the execution of any protocol described with the XML schema shown in Figure 2.

The UML class diagram of our Connector component is shown in Figure 3. Different coordination functions have been separated into different classes. The *Message-Matcher* class matches received messages to those included in the protocol description. The *FSM* class encapsulates a coordination engine that controls the protocol's behavior according to a state machine. The *ExecutionContext* class plans and monitors each transition execution.

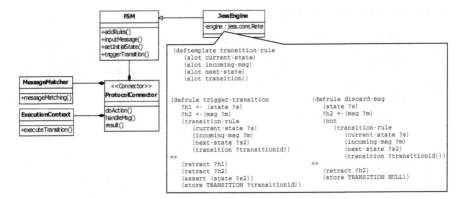

Fig. 3. Connector component implementation.

Each time a connector is created to coordinate some protocol, these three objects are instantiatied. Each one is instantiated for a particular protocol described in XML. The *MessageMatcher* object will use message descriptions to match (*messageMatcher* method) incoming messages to valid protocol messages, and returns message identifiers. The *FSM* element controls execution according to the transition diagram included in the description. Finally, the *ExecutionContext* object will use the description of protocol transitions to invoke agent actions and monitor their execution.

The *JessEngine* subclass offers the implementation of a coordination engine in Jess. This implementation uses rule-based programming to coordinate the execution of a communication protocol. This class uses the rules describing the protocol's transition diagram to infer the particular transition for each incoming message, and updates the protocol's state. The rule base includes two inference rules that model any transition diagram. A set of facts represents the transition diagram according to the template shown in Figure 3. And finally, two facts represent the protocol's state describing the current state and the last message, e.g. *(state idle)* and *(msg cfp)*. These last facts are the only ones that change during protocol execution.

The *trigger-transition* rule, shown in Figure 3, activates when a fact representing an incoming message is asserted and another fact describes a transition rule for the current state and the incoming message. When the rule fires, the state changes and the identifier of the transition to be executed is signaled using the *TRANSITION* variable. The *discard-msg*, also shown in Figure 3, activates to discard a protocol's message that does not produce a transition.

It is worth noting that these two inference rules model the behavior of any protocol defined as a state machine. Therefore it is not necessary to implement different connectors for each possible protocol.

Most agent architectures decompose the agent's internal functionality into different tasks, which are carried out during an interaction. The definition and implementation of these tasks must adhere to a set of inheritance and interface realizations. In addition, these tasks include hard code related to their coordination with other tasks. Each task is dependent on the agent platform since it is implemented in a particular API. This dependency makes difficult the reuse of the functionality in other applications and platforms. In our architecture, each agent action is associated to a service provided by a component. There are no dependencies though, since the connectors plan and invoke actions in a conversation, they do not execute them directly. Component services are invoked by the mediator entity, which performs the dynamic composition of components and connectors when a connector requests a service invocation.

3 Software Agent Design

This section shows the proposed agent development approach. The process will be illustrated through the development of a software agent for an Internet-based auction system. In our example the agent should be capable of exchanging messages with a FIPA-OS auctioneer agent according to the English auction protocol. The agent should be able to bid during the auction, and must buy if it finally wins. Our goal is to reuse the already-developed FIPA-OS auctioneer agent and develop a new agent capable of interacting with it. According to the specified protocol and functionality of the proposed sample agent we should follow these steps,

1. Locate software components with the needed bidding and buying functionalities. The agent architecture and composition mechanism do not impose constraints over these software components. It is only required to describe the provided interface with DAML-S. In this example we can use a third vendor Java component that offers the desired functionality through two methods: *bid* and *buy*. The public interface of this component is described in the *file:///c:/onto/e-market.daml* DAML-S document and implemented in the *ca3.behaviour.emarket.class* Java file.
2. Describe the negotiation protocol using the XML schema detailed in the previous section. Our agent will interact with the auctioneer agent during the auction following this protocol. If we use other agent platforms we have to code the interaction protocol and the agent's behavior invoked during protocol execution. This is not the case in the proposed architecture. Figure 4 shows part of the protocol description in XML, which corresponds to the accompanying state diagram, modeling the participant's behavior during the auction. When the conversation starts a connector

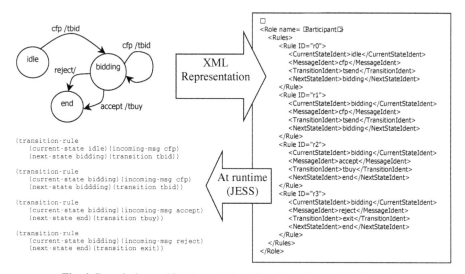

Fig. 4. Description and Implementation of an Agent Interaction Protocol.

will use this XML code to add the facts shown in the lower left corner of Figure 4 to the initial fact list of the *JessEngine* object. These facts will be used in Jess to infer the protocol's behavior. The description of the negotiation protocol needs to be made only once, and can be reused in other applications. The set of agent actions enclosed in the description of the transitions *tbid* and *tbuy* (omitted in the XML code in Figure 4) will refer to DAML-S descriptions of the services *bid* and *buy* provided by the component *emarket*. The protocol's XML description will be made accessible to the agent through a URI *(file:///C:/xml/EnglishAuction.xml)*.

3. Adaptors need to be plugged into the agent for the different transport services used for the exchange of messages. Adaptors should implement the Java interface *MTSAdapter* to be included in the architecture. The architecture currently provides adaptors for the message transport services of the FIPA-OS, JADE, and Zeus agent platforms.

4. Finally, create a deployment file including the agent configuration, specifying the components and descriptions located in the previous steps that will provide the desired agent behavior and capabilities in the auction.

The XML schema of the deployment document for our auction agent is shown in Figure 5. The file must contain information regarding possible codification formats for the messages the agent will use. In this example we know a priory that ACL messages will be coded using the String representation. Also, We also need to provide information about the software components (*emarket* component) that will be registered in the agent as part of its functionality, including their location and deployment information. The *protocol* element in the document includes a reference to the document that describes the *EnglishAuction* protocol, used by the agent to take part in the auction (the *EnglishAuction.xml* file), and the protocol identifier (*EnglishAuction*). Finally, a reference to the implementation of the FIPA-OS adaptor that will be used to send and receive messages to and from the auctioneer agent is included as deployment information.

```xml
<?xml version="1.0" encoding="UTF-8"?>
...
<!-- Fichero de despliegue de un agente de subasta-->
    <aclRepresentation><format>
          <ID>String</ID>
          <URI>file:///c:/code/ca3.acladapter.StringEncoding.class</URI>
    </format></aclRepresentation>
    <behaviour><component>
          <ontology>file:///c:/onto/e-market.daml</ontology>
          <URI>file:///c:/code/ca3.behaviour.emarket.class</URI>
    </component></behaviour>
    <coordination><protocol>
          <ID>EnglishAuction</ID>
          <URI>file:///C:/xml/EnglishAuction.xml</URI>
    </protocol></coordination>
    <distribution><platform>
          <adapterTo>FIPAOS</adapterTo>
          <URI>file:///c:/code/ca3.distribution.FIPAOSAdapter.class</URI>
    </platform></distribution>
</deployment>
```

Fig. 5. Deployment file for an agent taking part in an auction.

Hopefully, we will not need to program new functionality, since components with bidding and buying functionality can be reused from other agent applications of e-commerce just including the description in DAML-S of its provided interface in the deployment file.

In our approach the development of a new agent is, in the best-case scenario, reduced to the description in XML documents of the supported interaction protocols and the components that will be assembled in the agent architecture. Otherwise, if no COTS component is found, a software component providing the desired services needs to be developed. However, to develop agent functionality it is not necessary to inherit from any class or implement any interfaces, increasing its reusability in other application domains, and especially in agents from other platforms. In addition, the flexibility provided by the component-based architecture allows updating the agent configuration given in the initial deployment file. At runtime the agent can add functionality by plugging into software components. Also, the agent can be trained in new interaction protocols just incorporating the corresponding protocol description, or the agent is able to format exchanged messages in a different ACL format or engage in a different agent platform once the appropriate adaptor is plugged into the agent.

4 Conclusions

This paper presents a compositional architecture for software agents, which provides the infrastructure for the development of agents from reusable software components. The architecture combines *components* and *aspect* technologies, and separates functionality, agent coordination, and message distribution, in different entities. The separation of coordination in an independent component, and the use of JESS, allows the reuse of a single connector to coordinate any communication protocol. This connector needs only an XML description of the protocol's behavior (modeled with a state machine), valid messages, and the actions carried out as part of the interaction.

Our agents can be designed regardless of deployment and runtime features like the agent platform or the message encoding. However, though these details are particularized by the deployment information, new components can be included at runtime to address new requirements, and already registered components can be updated with new releases. We do not suggest just another agent platform. Instead, we propose a model to design component-based agents that can be reused on top of the existing platforms and can be easily adapted to new requirements that affect agent coordination, functionality and/or deployment even at runtime.

This proposal offers some benefits derived from the compositional approach: The (re)use of third-vendor components reduces programming errors during implementation, since they are supposed to be tested and error-free; we can provide development tools to support and guide the assembling of the software components, reducing the time and the effort required to develop agent-based applications. We enforce developing an agent from reusable components allowing application developers to choose the best components from industry. Moreover, our agents benefit from a platform independency derived from the application of the separation of concerns principle, which lets them to live in most of the agent platforms.

We are currently working in the development of a graphic environment to ease the development of software agents and to guide the developer in the specification of new protocols and the development of the software agents through the automatic generation of the agent's deployment and protocol description documents.

References

1. Iglesias, C.A., Garijo, M., Gonzalez, J.C., *A Survey of Agent-Oriented Methodologies*, in Intelligent Agents V – Proceedings of the Fifth International Workshop ATAL 98, Springer-Verlag, 1998.
2. TILAB, *JADE: Java Agent Development Framework*. http://jade.cselt.it
3. BtexaCT, *The Zeus Agent Building Toolkit*. http://193.113.209.147/projects/agents/zeus
4. Emorphia, *FIPA-OS*. http://fipa-os.sourceforge.net
5. Brazier, F.M.T et al., *Compositional Design and Reuse of a Generic Agent Model*. Applied Artificial Intelligence Journal vol 14, no. 5, 2000.
6. García, A.F., Lucena, C., *An Aspect-Based Object-Oriented Model for Multi-Agent Systems*. Advanced Separation of Concerns Workshop, 2001.
7. Griss M.L. et al., *Using UML State Machine Models for More Precise and Flexible JADE Agent Behaviours*. Agent Oriented Software Engineering, LNCS 2585, pp. 113-125, Springer-Verlag, 2003.
8. Aspect-Oriented Software Development: http://www.aosd.net
9. Amor, M., Fuentes, L. and Troya, J.M., *Putting Together Web Services and Compositional Software Agents*. Web Engineering, LNCS 2722, pp. 44-53, Springer-Verlag, 2003.
10. DARPA: DAML-S. http://www.daml.org
11. Amor, M., Fuentes, L. y Troya, J.M., *Training Compositional Agents in Negotiation Protocols*. Next publication in Integrated Computer-Aided Engineering International Journal (2003).
12. Distributed Computing Systems at Sandia National Laboratories, *Jess, The Java Expert System Shell*. http://herzberg.ca.sandia.gov/jess/

Clustering Main Concepts from e-Mails

Jesús S. Aguilar-Ruiz[1], Domingo S. Rodriguez-Baena[1],
Paul R. Cohen[2], and Jose Cristóbal Riquelme[1]

[1] Department of Computer Science, University of Seville, Spain
{aguilar,dsavio,riquelme}@lsi.us.es
[2] Intelligent Systems Division, ISI, University of South California, USA
cohen@isi.edu

Abstract. E–mail is one of the most common ways to communicate, assuming, in some cases, up to 75% of a company's communication, in which every employee spends about 90 minutes a day in e–mail tasks such as filing and deleting. This paper deals with the generation of clusters of relevant words from E–mail texts. Our approach consists of the application of text mining techniques and, later, data mining techniques, to obtain related concepts extracted from sent and received messages. We have developed a new clustering algorithm based on neighborhood, which takes into account similarity values among words obtained in the text mining phase. The potential of these applications is enormous and only a few companies, mainly large organizations, have invested in this project so far, taking advantage of employees's knowledge in future decisions.

1 Introduction

Ontologies have shown their usefulness in application areas such as intelligent information integration, information brokering and natural–language processing [15]. We can represent the knowledge existing in a domain using a conceptual diagram composed by a group of objects and the relations among them [4]. This sample of knowledge, created from a set of relational terms, from a specific vocabulary, is the aspect of ontology on which our research is focused.

Information Extraction systems were designed to filter, to select and to classify the increasing amount of information available nowadays, mainly on the Web. Most of them were based on shallow natural language processing techniques, but semantics was not really used, due to the unavailability of generic ontologies. Important efforts concentrate on developing tools for semi–automatic building of domain–specific ontologies, mainly based on text mining techniques.

Nowadays, a number of studies and techniques focus on textual information contained in electronic documents (e–mails, presentations, technical reports, etc.) [13]. Text can be a rich source of information, but this information is coded in such a way that decoding it becomes quite difficult. Learning, natural language processing, information extraction and mathematical approaches have been combined to decode and extract the content of texts [8].

The objective of this research is to extract ontological information from email using text and data mining techniques. In this paper, our goal is not to construct

R. Conejo et al. (Eds.): CAEPIA-TTIA 2003, LNAI 3040, pp. 231–240, 2004.
© Springer-Verlag Berlin Heidelberg 2004

ontologies, but rather, to find groups of concepts that are commonly discussed in email. Email with family members involves a different set of concepts than email with colleagues in computer science, or with administrative assistants, or automobile mechanics. One way to extract concepts is to look for words that "go together" in text. If words co–occur more often than one would expect by chance, it may be because these words refer to one or more related concepts. These groups of concepts can provide us with an idea about what topics are in texts, making possible to organize the knowledge of users in order to take advantage of it for future decisions.

The document is organized as follows: in Section 2 we will briefly justify and show the current interest in this research; in Section 3 the entire system is described, using a simple example throughout every step; the experiments will be presented and discussed in Section 4; finally, the most important conclusions will be summarize in Section 5.

2   Motivation

E–mail has turned into one of the most common ways of communication in the last few years. Recent studies show that e–mail can make up to 75% of the company's communication, in which every employee spends about 90 minutes a day in organizing e–mail–tasks such as filing and deleting. The number of sent and received messages increase between 35% and 50% every year [10]. For comparison, US corporations spend roughly $1.5 trillion per year, only counting averaged salaries for the time workers spend reading, replying to, and organizing their e–mail. However, the entire US military budget in 2002 was $ 360 billion [6]. The knowledge extracted from e–mails can help us to organize, by subject or importance, the information handled by a group, or to categorize the employees of a company according to the content of their e–mails, allowing us, for instance, to locate a person specialized in data mining because the words data mart or clustering are common in his e–mails [2].

Researchers at Hewlett Packard have been experimenting with analyzing the flow of 185.773 e–mails among 485 users in an organization over a two–month period, concluding that it is possible to identify the power structure of an organization, communities (both known and unknown), and the leadership within these groups [1]. On a practical level, managers, for example, might use information gleaned from email studies to help businesses run more smoothly by making sure teams are communicating effectively and determining who is collaborating on certain projects. That study only examined the headers of emails, as already did Schwartz and Wood in 1993 [14], by mining 1.2M email headers to detect interests between people using graph theory.

The potential of the applications derived from obtaining useful knowledge from the textual information contained in e–mails is enormous [9]. For instance, KnowledgeMail [7], is able to create a user profile that can locate an expert on a specific topic when his/her knowledge is needed by other member of a company. Logically, these types of applications start to make sense in large companies, in which the use of the knowledge generated can result in an important time and capital saving for the company. That is the case of the Central Intelligence Agency, that invested $1 million in knowledge–management software developer Tacit Knowledge Systems, and between $1 and $5 millions in Stratify's software to mine unstructured data from e–mail systems, web pages, etc., at the end of 2001 [3].

Not only private companies, but also some universities are becoming interested in this field; for example, Carnegie Mellon University is currently involved in a research project dealing with the intelligent treatment of e–mail.

3   Description

We process the information in email messages in a sequence of steps, beginning with text mining and then data mining. The steps of the system are the following:

1. Preprocessing: our knowledge base will be composed of words in messages so we will have to filter the least relevant elements from texts: punctuation marks, language elements such as articles, pronouns, conjunctions, etc.
2. Text Mining: we will apply a method designed to obtain relations among words to the data set we have obtained from the previous filtering. To do this, it is necessary that we observe the similarity between words. The calculation of similarity is based on proximity frequency of words in text. That is, two words are similar if they appear one next to each other more than it is statistically expected.
3. Data Mining: given a set of lists, obtained in the previous step and formed by pairs of words and their similarities, we will apply data mining techniques to generate conceptual groups. In particular, we will use a clustering technique, specifically developed for this project, based on the neighbourhood concept.

In Figure 1 we show the process described previously, which has a set of e–mails as input and ontologies as output.

3.1   Preprocessing

The goal of this step is to remove irrelevant information, so a simple filter algorithm is applied. A set of strings with little semantic information is deleted from the text. Among them, are punctuation marks, articles, pronouns and some high-frequency, low content words. Afterwards, the text is semantically denser, as very related words will be closer to each other due to the deletion of other irrelevant words in between.

3.2   Text Mining

There are many ways to associate words within a text [8]. We will use a sliding window of size K throughout the text. The content of each window will inform about the statistical relationship among its words.

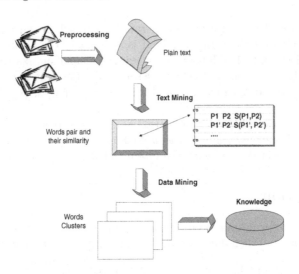

Fig. 1. Providing knowledge from e–mails.

Let P_1 and P_2 be two words. If they appear near each other more than one would expect by chance, we say that P1 and P2 are similar. To measure this similarity Ψ, let us suppose that P_1 and P_2 are separated by K words in a text sequence. Suppose also that there are $f_1 = 1$ appearances of P_1 in a sequence of length N. Then we can model the probability that P_2 falls within K words of P_1 as follows: the probability that a random location in the sequence falls within K words of P_1 is $p = \frac{2K}{N}$. Suppose there are $f_2 = 5$ occurrences of P_2. The probability that exactly δ of them will fall within K words of P_1 is just a binomial probability where the number of events is $f_2 = 5$, the number of successes is δ, and p is as described earlier. That is $P(X = \delta) \sim Binomial\left(N, \frac{2K}{N}\right)$. This is easily generalized to $f_1 > 1$ because $p = \frac{2Kf_1}{N}$, and then $P(X = \delta) \sim Binomial\left(N, \frac{2Kf_1}{N}\right)$.

We take $K = 10$ and then use a window with $2K+1$ positions (K on both the left and the right hand of the word being analyzed). This method will generate the similarity values for each pair of words. At the end, a file composed by a set of (P_1, P_2, Ψ), in which P_1 and P_2 are the two words and Ψ is the similarity value calculated as described earlier.

3.3   Data Mining

The final goal of this process is to obtain sets or clusters of words, so the existing relationship among members of the same cluster is based on the similarity. This phase can be divided in two steps:

1. Preprocessing: in which the similarity file generated in the previous step is processed to create a data structure that contains the information organized in such a way that the data mining technique can deal with it properly.

2. Clustering: we have developed a new neighborhood–based clustering technique adapted to the features of these data. This technique will provide a set of related words clusters from which we will study their inter–relationships to provide ontologies.

Preprocessing. The similarity value Ψ provides us an idea about the relationship between two words in the text. Because Ψ is usually very small we will use logarithms, so the numbers will be negatives. That is, larger negative value means greater similarity. After a preliminary study, we observe that there are pairs of words with very high similarity. This words used to appear at the bottom of messages as the signature (sender name, address, organization, etc.). We set a threshold, obtained from the normal distribution, based on the mean and the deviation, and eliminate a number of pairs composed by frequents words in texts, mainly associated with the sender.

In the next step, we generate a data structure in which every word is added to a word list, ordered by similarity. These lists have a variable length and give us an idea about the context of each word in the text. This data structure will serve as input for the clustering algorithm, called SNN (Similar Nearest Neighbour), which is based on the word neighbourhood and is described next.

Clustering. Our approach to clustering, the SNN (Similar Nearest Neighbour) algorithm has three main features:

- SNN is deterministic and its results do not depend on the order in which it is presented items. Many clustering algorithms do not have this property.
- SNN starts taking as initial set of representative patterns all of them at once. Next, it will join related patterns until the algorithm ends, following an incremental and hierarchical criterion. Other algorithms take a subset of representative patterns, so results might vary depending on the quality of the initial selection.
- SNN has no input user–defined parameters. The vast majority of clustering algorithms need user parameters. The number of clusters required by the user is the most common, as in K–means clustering algorithm [12] (this non–hierarchial method initially takes the number of components of the population equal to the final required number of clusters). In fact, some works have tried to find good methods to initialize the K–means algorithm [11]. Nevertheless, there are some others like the number of representative examples, as in CURE [5]. Our algorithms SNN provides automatically the most suitable number of clusters.

To describe the clustering algorithm, we will first provide some definitions.

Let e be a word, we say that the enemy of e is the first word in the list of associated words ordered by similarity that surpasses the threshold λ, previously set. The neighbourhood N_s of a word e is the set of words which are nearer e than the enemy of e, that is, their similarities are lower than enemy's similarity. The neighbourhood N_C of a cluster C is the set composed by all the neighbourhoods of each word belonging to the cluster C. $N_C(C) = \bigcup_{e \in C} N_s(e)$. Two clusters,

```
 1. Procedure S-NN(in: E, λ; out: RSC)
 2.    SC := ∅
 3.    for each e_i ∈ E, 1 ≤ i ≤ |E|
 4.       RSC[i] := {e_i}
 5.       NSC[i] := N_s {e_i, λ}
 6.    end for
 7.    SC := RSC
 8.    RSC := Reduction(SC, NSC)
 9.    while SC ≠ RSC do
10.       for each C_k ∈ RSC, 1 ≤ k ≤ |RSC|
11.          NSC[k] := N_c(C_k)
12.       end for
13.       SC := RSC
14.       RSC :=Reduction(SC, NSC)
15.    end while
16. end S-NN

17. Function Reduction(in: C, S; out: R)
18.    R := C
19.    for each pair (i,j), with 1 ≤ i ≤ j ≤ |C|
20.       if S[i] = S[j]
21.          R[i] := R[i] ∪ C[j]
22.          remove R[j]
23.       end if
24.    end for
25. end Reduction
```

Fig. 2. S–NN algorithm.

C_1 and C_2, will be cluster–neighbours if $N_C(C_1) = N_C(C_2)$. A reduced set of clusters RSC is a subset of clusters from the original set of clusters in which any two clusters are not neighbours, i.e, any two cluster–neigbours have been joined. We will identify each cluster in the reduced set of clusters RSC as the patterns that belong to the cluster, i.e., the patterns that were obtained by means of unions of neighbour–clusters.

Once the necessary definitions to support the algorithm have been presented, we will describe the algorithm depicted in Figure 2.

The input parameter E represents the structure obtained by the similarity search algorithm applied to the initial plain text, that is, pairs of words with their similarity value, and the output parameter is RSC, the reduced set of clusters, where each one comprises a group of instances.

$$P_1, P_2, \Psi_{1,2} = Similarity(P_1, P_2)$$

$$P_1, P_3, \Psi_{1,3} = Similarity(P_1, P_3)$$

$$\dots\dots\dots\dots\dots\dots\dots\dots\dots\dots\dots\dots\dots$$

$$P_{n-1}, P_n, \Psi_{n-1,n} = Similarity(P_{n-1}, P_n)$$

The input parameter is E, containing the instances, SC is an auxiliary set of clusters and RSC is initially set with clusters containing only one instance (lines 2–6). After initializing RSC and obtaining every word's neighbourhood, we apply a first reduction of this set of clusters. This is done because we need to take into account the value of λ in the first reduction. As we can see, the first time NSC is calculated (line 5), λ is present. However, next calculations do not take into account this value. This is not a parameter of the clustering algorithm per se, but a threshold to filter some words in the initial lists. When K is large, it is recommended to reduce the value of λ.

The process is repeated until RSC has no change at an iteration (line 9). The neighbourhood of every cluster is calculated (lines 10–12) in order to analyze the possible reduction of the set of cluster, task done by the Reduction function (line 14). The reduction of a set of clusters follows the next criterion: one cluster will be removed (line 22) if there exists another cluster which has exactly the same neighbourhood (line 20). In this case, the members of both clusters are joined (line 21).

The idea behind the algorithm is very simple: two clusters are neighbours if they have exactly the same neighbours. Obviously, the concept of neighbourhood is limited by the participation of the enemy, which indicates what neighbours each cluster has. The criterion used in this paper could be relaxed in two ways: considering the reduction when the neighbours of a cluster are a subset of the neighbours of the other or when the intersection among the neighbours of the two clusters is non–empty. As for the first as the second variation, the number of clusters is even smaller. The experiments shown in this paper were carried out by using the original criterion: the equality. However, we are going to study these other two criteria in further research.

4   Experiment

To illustrate the method, we have designed a simple practical example based on two emails. They represent the conversation between a professor of a university department and his secretary about making a reservation to a flight. The aim is to obtain relevant words within clusters generated with the proposal technique. The e–mails are the following:

> *Good Morning Maggie,*
> *I'd like to book a flight from London to NYC for Thursday evening, about seven. I must be at the University to give a talk related to the Argos project the following morning. I'd really prefer a nonstop flight, because the last time I took a connecting flight, it left late and I missed the connection.*
> *Don't worry about the hotel reservation. I'm going to spend the weekend in a friend's house. Thank you. –P*

> *Good Morning professor,*
> *I have been talking to the travel agency and there is a nonstop flight at 9:31 from Heathrow. Is that too late? One more question, will you be flying coach or you prefer business class? Well, I'll try to find a seat available in business class, ok? And finally, I charge it to the Argos Project, I suppose. Well, let's see what I can come up with. Maggie.*

Firstly, the textual information of both emails is filtered, eliminating elements not interesting such us commas, points, articles, pronouns, conjunctions, etc. The result of this operation is a plain text in which all the relevant words are put together, keeping the same order than in the original emails.

GOOD MORNING MAGGIE LIKE BOOK FLIGHT LONDON NYC THURSDAY EVENING SEVEN MUST BE UNIVERSITY GIVE TALK FOLLOWING MORNING RELATED ARGOS PROJECT PRE-FER NONSTOP FLIGHT LAST TIME TOOK CONNECTING FLIGHT LEFT LATE MISSED CONNEC-TION WORRY HOTEL RESERVATION GOING SPEND WEEKEND FRIEND HOUSE THANK GOOD MORNING PROFESSOR ....

In the next step, we calculate the similarity by passing a window of length $2K+1$ (with $K = 10$) through the plain text. For each pair of words we provide a value of similarity. The final result is other file with the structure shown in Table 1: two words and the similarity between them.

Table 1. Table with pairs or words and their similarity.

word	word	similarity
GOOD	MORNING	-18.086
GOOD	FLIGHT	-4.873
PROJECT	TALK	-3.023
CLASS	BUSINESS	-9.620
FLIGHT	PROFESSOR	-6.413
TRAVEL	UNIVERSITY	-3.880
FLIGHT	NONSTOP	-3.560
GOOD	BOOK	-3.009
COACH	SEAT	-5.324
PROFESSOR	MORNING	-6.837
...	...	...

Now, we apply the first part of the algorithm, as a previous step for the clusters generation by SNN. We calculate the initial neighbourhoods, which is shown in Table 2.

Table 2. Words and associated neighborhood.

[GOOD]	[MORNING, FLIGHT,BOOK]
[FLIGHT]	[GOOD, FLIGHT, NONSTOP,...]
[PROFESSOR]	[FLIGHT, MORNING, BOOK, ...]
...	...

Next, clusters with similar neighbourhood are joined and the new neighbourhood of each cluster is calculated. For example, [GOOD] and [PROFESSOR] have the same neighbourhood, so they will pass joined to the next iteration. In addition , the neighbourhood of [GOOD, PROFESSOR] will contain the instance NONSTOP (because it is neighbour of FLIGHT at iteration 1). For this reason we will find that [GOOD, PROFESSOR]=[MORNING, FLIGHT,BOOK]+[NONSTOP]. Iteration 3 does the same: firstly it searches for possible joining and afterwards calculates the new neighbourhood for each cluster. In this way the iterations are repeated: calculating similarity between clusters, reducing the number of clusters and increasing the neighbourhood of the new clusters generated. The process ends when there is no modification of clusters at one iteration, so the termination criterion is natural and totally independent of the user, removing this parameter, very common in the great majority of clustering algorithms.

Table 3. Clusters from 57.817 words collected from e–mails.

C1: [ARRIVE BALTIMORE DEPART ECONOMY COACH **FLIGHT** HARTFORD
      TERMINAL WASHINGTON]
C2: [ABILITY FIELD **INVESTIGATION** LANGUAGES MAINTAINING PROFESSIONAL
      PROGRAMMING PUBLICATIONS SPECIFIC THEORETICAL]
C3: [ACCOUNT **FUNDING** GOVERNOR GRANT INVESTIGATOR REQUIRED]
C4: [ACQUIRING BEHAVIOR DIRECTLY **MILITARY** TACTICS]
C5: [ASSISTANTS ASSOCIATION CONDUCT DESIGNS **FACULTY**
      IMPLEMENTS MEMBER]
C6: [ASSISTS COORDINATION EQUIPMENT **LAB** RESPONSIBLE]
C7: [**CARD** CREDIT DEBIT REMEMBER]

Finally, we have a reduced set of clusters as a result, each cluster containing the words that have certain degree of similarity. For instance, in our example there would be the following final clusters:

[GOOD PROFESSOR FLIGHT BOOK HOUSE...]
[TALK ARGOS UNIVERSITY PROJECT...]
[HOTEL FRIEND WORRY ...]
...

Once the clusters have been obtained, we can analyze the relevant concepts based on words within them. In each cluster we detect the most relevant elements as the one that has the biggest value of similarity with respect to the rest of words in the cluster. In Figure 3, the two main concepts and their relations are shown: project and flight. The elements associated with them are in the cluster, not being the most relevant ones.

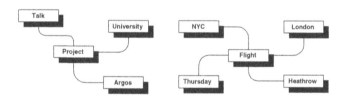

Fig. 3. Main concepts.

The example designed to explain the process has very few words. However, the system has been proven in a real organization and with real e–mail messages. The text obtained, after applying the first filter over punctuation marks, articles, etc, contained more than 10.000 different words, that generated a file with 57.817 pairs of related words, with their respective similarity values. A summary of the results is shown in Table 3, in which appear the most significant clusters. The words in bold represent the main elements of every cluster.

5   Conclusions

In this paper we addresses a problem that is becoming considered relevant in large organizations: the generation of clusters from E–mail texts. The objective of this research consists of extracting useful knowledge represented by clusters from textual information contained in a large number of emails using text and data mining techniques. Our approach consists of the application of text mining techniques to filter spurious words and find similarities among words and, later, data mining techniques, to obtain relational concepts, grouped in clusters, and extracted from the sent and received messages electronically. A new neighborhood–based clustering algorithm, SNN, is also introduced in this paper. Experiments generated from 57.817 pairs of related words show the quality of our approach.

References

1. L.M. Bowman. Email flow can show company power structure. *ZD Net UK News*, March 2003.
2. P. W. Eklund and R. Cole. Structured ontology and information retrieval for email search and discovery. *ISMIS*, pages 75–84, 2002.
3. E. Goodridge Intelligence Agency Bets On Knowledge Management. *Information-Week*, Dec. 3, 2001.
4. T. Gruber. Towards principles for the design of ontologies used for knowledge sharing. *Intl. J. of Human and Computer Stud-ies*, 2/3(46):293–310, 1997.
5. S. Guha, R. Rastogi and K. Shim. CURE: an efficient clustering algorithm for large databases. *ACM SIGMOD International Conference on Management of Data*, pages 73–84, 1998.
6. J. Dao. Pentagon Seeking A Large Increase In Its Next Budget. *New York Times*, January 7, 2002.
7. KnowledgeMail. *http://www.tacit.com*, 2003.
8. C. D. Mannig and H. Schutze. *Foundations of Statistical Natural Language Processing*. MIT Press, 1999.
9. E. Moreale and S. Watt. Organisational information management and knowledge discovery in email within mailing lists. *IDEAL*, pages 87–92, 2002.
10. V. Murphy. You've Got Expertise. *Forbes Magazine*, February, 2001.
11. J. M. Pena, J. A. Lozano and P. Larranaga. An empirical comparison of four initialization methods for the k-means algorithm. *Pattern Recognition Letters*, 20, 1027–1040, 1999.
12. D. Pollard. Quantization and the method of k-means. *IEEE Transactions on Information Theory*, 2/3(46):293–310,28(2):199–205, 1982.
13. F. Sebastiani. Machine learning in automated text categorization. *ACM Computing Surveys*, 1(34):1–47, 2002.
14. M. Schwartz and D. Wood. Discovering shared interests among people using graph analysis of global electronic mail traffic. *Communication of the ACM*, 36(8):1–47, 1993.
15. G. Wiederhold and M. Genesereth. The conceptual basis for mediation services. *IEEE Expert / Intelligent Systems*, 12(5):38–47, September/October 1997.

Definition of Postural Schemes
for Humanoid Robots

Telmo Zarraonandia, Javier de Lope, and Darío Maravall

Department of Artificial Intelligence
Faculty of Computer Science
Universidad Politécnica de Madrid
Campus de Montegancedo, 28660 Madrid
{telmoz,jdlope,dmaravall}@dia.fi.upm.es

Abstract. Each of the positions to be adopted by a humanoid robot
to make a particular movement can be considered as a postural scheme
associated with that particular movement. For example, if we want the
robot to complete a given step sequence, the robot should increase or
decrease the positions of its links to arrive at the desired position, whilst
maintaining its stability. Other possible examples of movement execution
are sideways movement, walking upstairs, etc. In this paper, we propose
a method for defining postural schemes that guarantee stability in all
the intermediate positions of the movements. This method is based on
the direct kinematics of the robot.

1 Introduction

Many different solutions have been proposed for solving the problem of robot
mobility, and many different configurations have been developed enabling robots
to move in a range of different environmental conditions. One of the solutions
on which more interest has focused recently is the one based on biped robots.
Although the stability and velocity of this kind of robots is not as good as for
other models, they responsed to the human aim to develop models similar to
their creators.

Recent advances in mechanical and electronic robot components and the
research drive in this area derived from events like the RoboCup [1] have led to
the development of successful models, such as the Honda humanoids, the Waseda
humanoid robot and the MIT Leg Lab robots.

However, the design of biped robots able to walk like humans do is still an
extremely difficult task to achieve, mainly because of stability problems derived
from the use of only two support links.

Two methods are usually used to guarantee robot stability in its movements.
The first one is formally known as *static balance*, and it aims to achieve stability
by maintaining the projection of the center of masses (COM) of the robot inside
the area inscribed by the feet that are in contact with the ground. The second
one, usually know as *dynamic balance*, uses the zero moment point (ZMP), which
is defined as the point on the ground around which the sum of all the moments

R. Conejo et al. (Eds.): CAEPIA-TTIA 2003, LNAI 3040, pp. 241–250, 2004.
© Springer-Verlag Berlin Heidelberg 2004

of the active forces equals zero [2]. If the ZMP is within the convex hull of all contact points between the feet and the ground, the biped robot is stable and will not fall over [3, 4].

Nevertheless, linear walking is not the only type of movement we may want to achieve for a biped robot. If we aim to create a prototype able to play football and compete in events like the RoboCup, it will need to be able to move sideways to cover the goal, step backwards to receive a pass or move one leg to kick the ball. In other words, it must be able to accomplish a wide range of postures, which, if adopted consecutively, allow the robot to perform these actions.

The paper is organized as follows. Section 2 introduces the basis of the proposed method and comments some advantages of its implementation. Sections 3 and 4 describe the humanoid robot and its direct kinematics, respectively. Some general concepts on stability criteria on the robot postures are commented in the section 5. Section 6 reviews two different postural schemes, the first one is composed of positions with both feet on the ground and straight legs, the second includes the positions involved in the robot taking a single step. Finally, the conclusions and future work are presented.

2   Proposed Method

In this paper, we propose a method for ascertaining the values that we should assign to the joints of a humanoid robot to achieve the desired postures. This is basically an inverse kinematics problem. As is known, the analytical resolution of the inverse kinematics of a robot with a high degree of joint configuration redundancy is practically unapproachable. Besides, the solutions produced by this method are specific for a particular robot configuration.

The proposed method considers the use of an artificial network for solving the inverse kinematics. Different neural networks are employed for each posture or set of postures. The input is the desired position and orientation of the free foot and the output is the set of joint values that not only satisfy the input conditions but also conform the most stable posture.

After testing different kinds of artificial neural networks architectures, the one we considered best suited is a two-layer backpropagation network. The input layer has a maximum of 6 neurons (three for the position in Cartesian coordinates and three for the orientation expressed as a combination of the RPY equivalent angles). The output layer has 12 neurons, one for each angle or degree of freedom of the humanoid robot. The hidden layer contains a different number of neurons depending on the posture and the training set. Usually it is composed by 4 to 12 neurons.

The use of neural networks has several advantages. One is that it is an adaptive solution that can be implemented in hardware using the appropriate electronic device [5]. For our case, we are using a field programmable gate array (FPGA) that is programmed with a specific neural network. For example, for the linear walking gait, alternative swings of both legs must be done, so two neural networks are needed, for the inverse kinematics of the right and left legs. The appropriate neural network to solve that particular movement is alternatively loaded in the FPGA.

Before this can be done, the direct kinematics of the robot will need to be studied. This will tell us which configuration will be adopted by the robot for a particular set of joint values. We will also need to establish a method to obtain the training cases for the net. This will be crucial for the process, as if the best cases are not selected, the solutions proposed by the net may result in inadequate postures that may cause robot instability. Finally, we will need to examine which net configuration is the best for solving the problem.

This paper covers the first two points. It examines the direct kinematics of the robot and a method for obtaining the training cases for the neural network. Details on the artificial neural network architecture and the employed training algorithms can be found in [6].

3   Robot Model

The model of the robot we are going to consider for the study is a humanoid robot made up of two legs and hips. Each leg is composed of six degrees of freedom, which are distributed as follows: two for the ankle – one rotational on the pitch axis and the other rotational on the roll axis –, one for the knee – rotational on the pitch – and three for the hip – each of them rotational on each of the axes. The prototype is now under development. Fig. 1 shows the physical model of the robot. A more detailed description of the robot dimensions and movement range is given in [7].

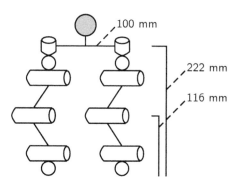

Fig. 1. Physical model of the robot

4   Direct Kinematics of the Robot

Generally, we can define the direct kinematics problem as follows: to determine the position and orientation of the end-effector of a robotic arm as a function of its joint variables and referred to a coordinate system fixed to its base.

We can consider our biped robot as a robotic arm or a chain of rigid links, which are pairwise connected to each other by joints. One of the robot feet will always be in contact with the ground, and it will be considered as the robotic arm base or first link. The other foot will be free to move around the space, and it will be considered as the end-effector or last link. Hence, we can restate the problem as: given a set of values for the robot joints and considering one foot as fixed to the ground, find the position and orientation of the other one.

To solve the problem, we have assigned a coordinate frame to each of the joints of the robot. We have also calculated the Denavit and Hartenberg parameters – θ_i, a_i, d_i, α_i – of each of the links. Now, it will be possible to map one coordinate frame to its precedent link frame by means of the four well-known geometrical transformations, as its expressed in the following equations:

$$
{}^{i-1}A_i = R(z, \theta_i)\, T(0, 0, d_i)\, T(a_i, 0, 0)\, R(x, \alpha_i) =
$$
$$
= \begin{bmatrix}
\cos\theta_i & -\cos\alpha_i \sin\theta_i & \sin\alpha_i \sin\theta_i & a_i \cos\theta_i \\
\sin\theta_i & \cos\alpha_i \cos\theta_i & -\sin\alpha_i \cos\theta_i & a_i \sin\theta_i \\
0 & \sin\alpha_i & \cos\alpha_i & d_i \\
0 & 0 & 0 & 1
\end{bmatrix}
\tag{1}
$$

where ${}^{i-1}A_i$ is the matrix expression of the homogeneous transformation to map the frame associated with the link $i-1$ and the frame associated with the link i.

For our particular case and considering the right foot as fixed to the ground, the assignment of the coordinate frames to the robot joints is illustrated in Fig. 2. Table 1 shows the D-H parameter definition of each of the links.

The position and orientation of the left with respect to the right foot will be denoted by the homogeneous transformation matrix:

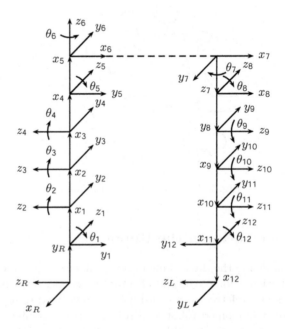

Fig. 2. Coordinate system associated with the robot joints

Table 1. D-H parameters for the robot links

Right Leg				Left Leg				
Frame	θ_i	d_i	a_i	α_i	Frame	θ_i	d_i	a_i	α_i
R	$\pi/2$	0	L_1	$-\pi/2$	7	θ_7	0	0	$\pi/2$
1	θ_1	0	0	$\pi/2$	8	$\theta_8 + \pi/2$	0	L_9	$\pi/2$
2	θ_2	0	L_3	0	9	θ_9	0	L_{10}	0
3	θ_3	0	L_4	0	10	θ_{10}	0	L_{11}	0
4	θ_4	0	L_5	$-\pi/2$	11	θ_{11}	0	0	$-\pi/2$
5	$\theta_5 + \pi/2$	0	0	$\pi/2$	12	θ_{12}	0	L_{13}	$-\pi/2$
6	θ_6	0	L_7	π	L	0	0	L_{14}	0

$$^{R}T_L = \begin{bmatrix} ^{R}R_L & ^{R}\boldsymbol{p}_L \\ 0 & 1 \end{bmatrix} = {}^{R}T_0 \times {}^{0}T_1(\theta_1) \times \ldots \times {}^{5}T_6(\theta_6) \times$$
$$^{6}T_7(\theta_7) \times \ldots \times {}^{11}T_{12}(\theta_{12}) \times {}^{12}T_L \qquad (2)$$

where $^{R}R_L$ denotes the rotation matrix of the left foot with respect to the right foot coordinate frame, $^{R}\boldsymbol{p}_L$ is known as *position vector* and denotes the position of the left foot with respect to the right foot coordinate frame and each $^{i}T_j$ denotes the homogeneous coordinate transformation matrix from link i to link j.

As described above, the nine values that conform the *rotation matrix* need to be calculated to determine the free foot orientation. Nevertheless, we can specify the orientation by means of a fewer number of values using the *RPY* equivalent angles, that is, the values of the rotations around the *roll*, *pitch* and *yaw* axes, which are necessary for mapping one coordinate frame to other one. Using this notation, we will reduce the neural network inputs to six: three for the desired coordinate position – *position vector* – and three for the desired orientation – *RPY* equivalent angles –.

$$^{R}R_L = \begin{bmatrix} a_{11} & a_{12} & a_{13} \\ a_{21} & a_{22} & a_{23} \\ a_{31} & a_{32} & a_{33} \end{bmatrix} \quad \begin{array}{l} a_{11} = \cos\theta_P \cos\theta_R \\ a_{12} = \sin\theta_Y \sin\theta_P \cos\theta_R - \cos\theta_Y \sin\theta_R \\ a_{13} = \cos\theta_Y \sin\theta_P \cos\theta_R + \sin\theta_Y \sin\theta_R \end{array}$$

$$\qquad (3)$$

$$\begin{array}{ll} a_{31} = -\sin\theta_P & a_{21} = \cos\theta_P \sin\theta_R \\ a_{32} = \sin\theta_Y \cos\theta_P & a_{22} = \sin\theta_Y \sin\theta_P \sin\theta_R + \cos\theta_Y \sin\theta_R \\ a_{33} = \cos\theta_Y \cos\theta_P & a_{23} = \cos\theta_Y \sin\theta_P \sin\theta_R - \sin\theta_Y \cos\theta_R \end{array}$$

The study of the positions and movements in the inverse case, that is, when the left foot is fixed to the ground and the right foot is able to move, would result in a coordinate frame assignment similar to the one described above. Nevertheless, and as a consequence of the symmetry in the robotic configuration, it will not lead to any important conclusions concerning the proposed method and will not be developed here.

5   Stability Criteria and Constraints

Once the kinematic model of our robot has been defined, it will be used to solve the inverse kinematic problem, that is, to find the values for the joints of the robot that will result in a specific position and orientation of the free foot.

Many different solutions could be proposed to solve the problem. However, they would all have to cope with several difficulties. The first is that, for a specific set of joint values, it is obvious that we can always obtain a given position and orientation of the free foot. Nevertheless this does not necessarily hold for the inverse problem, that is, we may not find a set of joint values that match the desired position and orientation. Furthermore, different joint configurations can produce the same foot position and orientation.

Therefore, we need to define a set of criteria to determine which one of the range of possible configurations should be selected to map a specific position and orientation. In our case, these criteria would be the stability criteria and *posture naturalness*, that is, that the posture of the robot must be as close as possible to the one a human would adopt to achieve that particular position and orientation.

To decide which is the most stable of a set of possible configurations, the static balance criteria will be applied. We consider that a configuration will be more stable closer the projection of the center of mass is to the center of the support polygon formed by the feet. If the projection is outside the polygon, the configuration will not be taken into account. The height of the COM will also affect system stability, as the system will be more stable, the lower the COM is. However, we are not interested in postures that place the hip too low down, as we want the postures of the robot to be as natural as possible.

At this stage of our work, we are considering the distribution of the mass to be uniform for every link. We also consider that every link has a symmetrical shape. The COM of each link will then be placed at the geometric center of the link. As this applies to each of the robot links, we can determine the global COM of the model using:

$$x_{com} = \frac{1}{M} \sum_{i=1}^{N} m_i x_i \quad ; \quad y_{com} = \frac{1}{M} \sum_{i=1}^{N} m_i y_i \quad ; \quad z_{com} = \frac{1}{M} \sum_{i=1}^{N} m_i z_i \quad (4)$$

where (x_i, y_i, z_i) is the geometric center of the link i, m_i is the mass of the link i, M is the mass of the robot, and N the number of links.

Once the physical model of the robot is completely developed, these formulas will be replaced by other ones taking into account the physical characteristics of each of the links.

6   Postural Schemes

As we mentioned at the beginning of the paper, neural networks will be employed to solve the robot inverse kinematics. The idea is that if the desired position and orientation of the free foot are the network inputs, the output will be the required values for the 12 joints that not only satisfy the inputs but also generate the most stable and natural posture according to the criteria and constraints described in the previous section. Obviously, for this to be achieved, the key to the process is network training, that is, the selection of the training cases.

Based on the model of the robot and the direct kinematics described above, a set of joint and Cartesian coordinates pairs has been generated to be used as training data for the neural network. At this stage of the research two sets of postural schemes have been considered. The first one will be composed of positions with both feet on the ground and straight legs, which are uniformly distributed across a given coordinate range. The second scheme includes the positions involved in the robot taking a single step.

By distinguishing between these two sets, we will be able to perform two separate investigations to find out which neural network produces better results for each of the schemes.

6.1   Standing Postural Scheme

The aim of this first scheme is to learn robot postures along the roll and pitch axes. These postures are restricted to both feet being in full contact with the ground, the knees not being bent and there being no rotation around the hip roll axes. Fig. 3 shows the final positions of the free foot. We only have to generate values for the ankle joints and hip joints that rotate around the *pitch* and *roll* axes to output cases of this type. As the two feet are in full contact with the

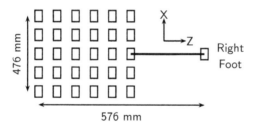

Fig. 3. Free feet positions on the final postures set of training cases

ground, the support polygon is formed by their corners. As we want to get the most stable posture, the projection of the COM should obviously be in the center of the polygon. Therefore, the angles formed by the legs and the ground must be the same. To obtain the movement of the foot along the *pitch* axis, we only have to assign α values to the joints that rotate around the *roll* axis so that:

$$\theta_1 = -\alpha \ ; \quad \theta_8 = -\alpha \ ; \quad \theta_5 = -\alpha \ ; \quad \theta_{12} = -\alpha \tag{5}$$

Similarly, to obtain the movement of the foot along the *roll* axis, we will assign β values to the joints that rotate around the *pitch* axis. We find two different cases depending on which foot we want to place ahead. For the left one:

$$\theta_2 = \beta \ ; \quad \theta_4 = -\beta \ ; \quad \theta_9 = \beta \ ; \quad \theta_{11} = -\beta \qquad (6)$$

And, for the right foot:

$$\theta_2 = -\beta \ ; \quad \theta_4 = \beta \ ; \quad \theta_9 = -\beta \ ; \quad \theta_{11} = -\beta \qquad (7)$$

To output the training cases for this first postural scheme, we have to generate two sets of values α and β that uniformly cover all the angle ranges of the roll and pitch axes. The final set of cases will be formed by all the possible combinations of the two sets. Table 2 shows the range of values we have considered for each joints type.

Table 2. Joint value ranges for the final postural scheme

Right Leg			Left Leg		
θ_i	Min	Max	θ_i	Min	Max
θ_1	$-30°$	$30°$	θ_7	$0°$	$0°$
θ_2	$-30°$	$0°$	θ_8	$-30°$	$0°$
θ_3	$0°$	$0°$	θ_9	$-30°$	$30°$
θ_4	$-30°$	$30°$	θ_{10}	$0°$	$0°$
θ_5	$-30°$	$0°$	θ_{11}	$-30°$	$0°$
θ_6	$0°$	$0°$	θ_{12}	$-30°$	$0°$

6.2 Walking Postural Scheme

The aim of the second scheme is to learn all the robot postures required to take a step on the roll axis. For this to be achieved, we have to generate a set of joint and Cartesian coordinates pairs, which describes possible postures to be adopted by the robot throughout the step gait (Fig. 4).

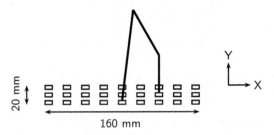

Fig. 4. Free feet positions for the walking postural scheme

To output the training cases, we will take the final postures from the first scheme and will move the free foot along the *yaw* axis by increasing the angle of the hip joint rotational around the *pitch* axis. For each of these values and to guarantee that the *roll* foot position does not change and the sole of the foot remains parallel to the ground, knee and ankle joint values will be recalculated according to the following expressions:

$$\theta_{10} = \theta_9 - \arcsin\left[(L_1 + L_2)\sin\alpha - \left(\frac{L_1\sin\theta_9}{L_2}\right)\right] \tag{8}$$

$$\theta_{11} = \theta_9 - \theta_{10} \tag{9}$$

where α denotes the initial value for the hip joint, θ_9 its new value, θ_{10} and θ_{12} denote the angles for the knee and ankle joints, L_1 is the distance from knee to hip and L_2 the distance from knee to ankle.

As in the configurations of this scheme, the robot has only one foot in contact with the ground, the polygon of support is formed only by the right foot, and the projection of the COM must remain as close as possible to the center of this rectangle. For this to be achieved, some sort of a swinging movement of the hip towards the support foot will be required. Therefore, a set of angles for the hip and ankle joints that produce this movement will need to generated, assuming that the hip remains parallel to the ground:

$$\theta_1 = \alpha \ ; \quad \theta_5 = \alpha \ ; \quad \theta_8 = -\alpha \ ; \quad \theta_{12} = -\alpha \tag{10}$$

The next step will be to make all the possible combinations of the set of values for the swinging movement and the set obtained initially to produce the movement along the *yaw* and *roll* axis to get a new set of candidate cases to train the net. The position of the COM is calculated for each of these cases. If its projection is not inside the borders of the polygon of support, the configuration is removed from the set.

Finally, two or more joint configurations may result in the same or a very similar position of the free foot. As we want the net to learn the best of the range of all the configurations, a filter has to be applied to detect and select the best configuration according to the criteria described in the previous sections. Table 3 shows the ranges of the joint angles for this scheme.

Table 3. Range of angle positions for the walking postural scheme

	Right Leg			Left Leg	
θ_i	Min	Max	θ_i	Min	Max
θ_1	0°	9°	θ_7	—	—
θ_2	−15°	0°	θ_8	−9°	0°
θ_3	0°	0°	θ_9	−15°	0°
θ_4	0°	15°	θ_{10}	0°	90°
θ_5	0°	9°	θ_{11}	−30°	30°
θ_6	—	—	θ_{12}	−9°	0°

7   Conclusions and Further Work

A method for outputting the training set for a neural network that solves the inverse kinematics of a humanoid robot with 12 degrees of freedom has been presented. The training cases cover different kinds of postures that the robot migth need to adopt to perform a single step.

Our current work is related to the selection of an appropriate learning set for the artificial neural network. We have observed that the nets require fewer neurons in the hidden layer if the training sets are composed by a minor number of cases. Also, we obtain a best generalization of the learned function and the typical problem of overfitting is reduced. Therefore, it is very important to define a set of stability criteria for creating each postural scheme.

The next stage of our work will be to define a mechanism for selecting the most appropriate postural scheme from a predefined library that matches with a particular desired movement. New postural schemes definitions for other common robot movements will also be developed.

The other side of our work will be related to the implementation of our simulation work in the physical robot prototype. Specifically we are working on the final mechanical aspects of the humanoid robot, designing the hardware interface with sensors and motors, and implementing the artificial neural networks on a FPGA.

References

1. Kaminka, G., Lima, P., Rojas, R. (eds.) (2003) RoboCup 2002: Robot Soccer World Cup IV, LNAI 2752. Springer-Verlag, Berlin
2. Vukobratovic M., Brovac, B., Surla, D., Sotkic, D. (1990) Biped Locomotion. Springer-Verlag, Berlin
3. Huang, Q., Yokoi, K., Kajita, S., Kaneko, K., Arai, H., Koyachi, N., Tanie, K. (2001) Planning walking patterns for a biped robot. IEEE Trans. on Robotics and Automation, **17**(3), 280–289
4. Furuta, T., Tawara, T., Okumura, Y., Shimizu M., Tomiyama, K. (2001) Design and construction of a series of compact humanoid robots and development of biped walk control strategies. Robotics and Autonomous Systems, **37**(2–3), 81–100
5. Linares-Barranco, B., Andreou, A.G., Indiveri, G., Shibata, T. (2003) Special issue on neural networks hardware implementations, IEEE Trans. on Neural Networks, **14**(5), 976–979
6. De Lope, J., Zarraonandia, T., González-Careaga, R., Maravall, D. (2003) Solving the inverse kinematics in humanoid robots: A neural approach. In J. Mira, J.R. Álvarez (eds.) Artificial Neural Nets Problem Solving Methods, LNCS 2687. Springer-Verlag, Berlin, 177–184
7. De Lope, J., González-Careaga, R., Zarraonandia, T., Maravall, D. (2003) Inverse kinematics for humanoid robots using artificial neural networks. In R. Moreno-Díaz, F.R. Pichler (eds.) Computer Aided Systems Theory – EUROCAST-2003, LNCS 2809. Springer-Verlag, Berlin, 448–459

Designing a Semantic Portal
for Collaborative Learning Communities

M. Felisa Verdejo, Beatriz Barros, J. Ignacio Mayorga, and Tim Read

Lenguajes y Sistemas Informáticos, UNED, Madrid, Spain
{felisa,bbarros,nmayorga,tread}@lsi.uned.es

Abstract. This paper presents the design of a semantic portal for collaborative learning communities and describes a persistence mechanism that stores objects enriched with a contextual description. The latter enables the knowledge reutilization in many learning activities and scenarios constituting, as such, a collective memory of the community. The current work is based on two theoretical foundations: the expressive capacity of ontologies, which offers a computer system new possibilities for using the knowledge it contains and the Activity Theory (AT) framework, which permits describing and structuring collaborative learning scenarios.

1 Introduction

In constructivist theories, human learning is postulated as a process of knowledge *construction* by the learner, based upon previous knowledge and interaction with the environment. The importance of the interaction has already been noted by Sociocultural Theory [8], which claimed that individual cognition is the result of interiorization by the subject, of interpersonal interactions in a shared culture and social context. Thus, there is a shift on the object of study from individual cognition to persons-acting-with-mediational-means, one of them, language. So called "situated" conceptions [2] of human learning go further, emphasizing the interdependence of cognition and context, and present learning as a social process of participation and belonging to a community of practice. In this approach knowledge is a socially mediated product, built through communication, discussion , clarification and negotiation.

Collaborative learning supported by computers, known as CSCL, is a relatively recent multidisciplinary research area [3]. From a pedagogical perspective, it has its roots in social constructivism and situated learning, pivoting around the ideas of action, interaction, and participation. From a computer science perspective, the idea is to model and design the software that supports these ideas, i.e., to create systems that facilitate action and human interaction in a social context of practice with a shared learning goal.

One of the first systems inspired by these principles was CSILE, which provided mechanisms to represent the argumentation and the knowledge shared in a learning community [6]. The underlying architecture of this system was a hypermedia database that stored the contributions of the participants, together with categorization facilities and connections between them.

R. Conejo et al. (Eds.): CAEPIA-TTIA 2003, LNAI 3040, pp. 251–259, 2004.

Artificial Intelligence techniques suggest many interesting opportunities for improving the design of CSCL systems. One of the first aspects is to explicitly model the community of learning, its organization, structure and the processes that are carried out, including the description of the possible software tools that are used for human action and interaction within the community. The use of ontologies is an adequate approach to explain, share and re-use knowledge. The mechanisms of representation and re-use allow the existence of distributed knowledge communities which provides multiple opportunities to enrich knowledge associated with working in groups, re-using information from one activity to another, offering different points of view depending on the objectives or interacting with information from various sources among other possibilities.

This conceptualisation of collaboration must be explicit. We need to represent the distinct aspects of the description of collaboration in order to use it as a base to describe the objects/artefacts that the community produces. Through the use of the proposed knowledge-based representation, an ontology, the new artefacts are created in a semantic context, so that reasoning techniques can be applied to generate the metadata to annotate automatically these new instances. In addition, the location in the ontology will allow better searches than those permitted by a mere syntactical annotation. As well it is possible to extend/refine the ontology to adapt the search mechanisms to each community necessities.

In section 2 of this paper, the ontology that has been created and will serve as a baseline to generate a semantic portal for collaborative learning communities[1] will be presented, using the technology of Protégé[2]. The portal provides access to a series of services to knowledge communities, including the possibility to define and carry out projects inspired from a repertoire of scenes called DexT (*digital experimentation tools*), which include access to possible experiments with real or virtual instruments available in various scientific areas such as: Astronomy, with the use of a telescope, Seismology, with access to on line measuring equipment, Organic Chemistry, with basic laboratory equipment, Biodiversity, with the use and control of a greenhouse, etc... At the same time, the portal provides tools that help define the structure and the development of the project, one of them being the **Active Document** (AD). In this case, the view of the ontology presented covers the theoretical frame of reference where the AD is based, the **Activity Theory (AT)** [5], which identifies the human and mediational units that define a group activity and captures aspects of its sociocultural relationships in terms of object, rules and division of labour.

A basic feature to carry out the activities is having a common repository, a group memory which can inter-operate with the modelling, collaboration and communication tools, and which also provides mechanisms to allow the community to easily inspect/search the artefacts they have generated and stored. Therefore, we have defined a Repository accessible through the portal that sustains the work processes in the knowledge communities and that serves as a collective memory for the co-

---

[1] Portal for the project COLDEX: *Collaborative Learning and Distributed Experimentation*, IST-2001-32327.

[2] http://protege.stanford.edu/

constructed knowledge and the activities carried out. This repository supports a contextual search adapted to the necessities of each community. The portal then sustains a distributed knowledge-based repository we call **Learning Object Repository** (LOR), which we describe in section 3. This approach will allow us to offer a package with richer functionalities for the use of the system. Starting from basic functionalities, so described in the ontology, it will be possible to combine and obtain new ones that were not anticipated and which adapt to the necessities of each user and learning scenario. Finally, in the conclusions section, we offer a summary of the work carried out and an outline of future action.

2   Description of the Ontology to Structure the Knowledge Communities Portal

The conceptual model for the knowledge communities portal has been expressed through an ontology (shown, in part, in figure 1) and it contemplates a variety of possibilities to define the organization of learning groups, the structure of the activities and the collaboration when developing a project. Specifically, there is a complete collaborative knowledge design model included in the ontology, based on the AT, materialized in the Active Document, further described in section 2.1.

Protégé (protege.stanford.edu) is a well-known environment, which allows creating and maintaining ontologies. It has a number of advantages, which make it appro-

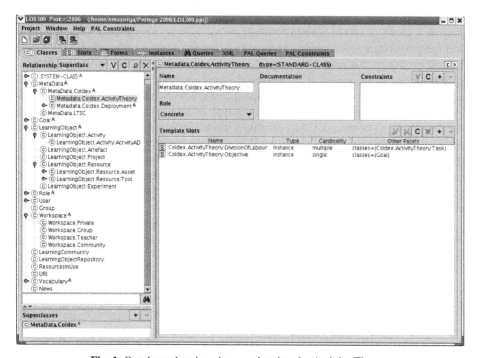

Fig. 1. Ontology showing classes related to the Activity Theory.

priate for our modelling task. It is "open-source" and it is contributed by a large and growing community, which is actively involved in its evolution by providing modules (plug-ins) for a number of useful new features. Thus, for instance, it supports a wide variety of formats, such as OWL or RDF(S). Furthermore, it offers first-order logic languages, which permit, both through a GUI and programmatically, making semantic queries for retrieving information stored in or inferable from the ontology. We have used PROTEGE to build the ontology underlying the current portal prototype.

From a conceptual point of view, we can define the portal as a service and activity centre for knowledge communities. A *knowledge community* is made up of members, which are people who are registered in the system (they have access to the system). A community can carry out projects. The participants in a *project* are members of the community with the password that allows them wider access.

A project is set up in the framework of one of the DeXTs that the portal offers. A *DeXT,* as previously mentioned, has a *thematic* field and it suggests a group of ideas/*challenges* to explore experimentally. A DEXT can also include ideas for projects based on a diversity of collaboration models, scripts for accessing remote data gathering instruments, descriptions of various modelling or simulation tools that are useful for the development of the project, designs for experiments with a specific instrument, etc. and kits to physically build artefacts (for instance Lego Mindstorms to build robots). A knowledge community can select or raise a challenge and tackle it through a *project*.

A project will be organized with a "model of organization" where phases will be defined, and in each "phase" a series of collaborative activities will be carried out: observation, modelling, analysis, phenomenon interpretation, among others. In the project, a series of *resources* can be used: *assets* such as experimental data, tutorials, and *tools* (software *tools*, remote or local instruments..) and a series of results/objects will be produced. An *activity* can be characterized by a group of attributes: type of collaboration, place where it is produced (local or remote), structure (open, predefined, ...), as well as possible participant roles. The portal offers *workspaces* for every project, workareas characterized by a type of accessibility, and an organization for the objects to be stored. Conceptually, a work area is a repository resource with a catalogue, which allows the system itself to annotate some of the metadata describing the results that the users store there, keeping in mind the context of the project where they are produced. Also, by defining the area of storage, conceptually, as an element of the ontology, each project can re-use, extend, or create a conceptual scheme that reflects its annotation, indexing, and search needs.

On the other hand, a knowledge community can publish (part of) its results to share with other communities through the portal's Learning Object Repository (LOR), which is, again, conceptualised as an ontology.

2.1 The Theory of the Activity
as a Base for the Design of Collaborative Activities

The AT serves as a framework to represent the activities of groups of people where the technology plays a mediating role. Within this theory, an analysis model has been developed to identify and represent the human and artificial elements related to a group activity, capturing socio-cultural relations in the environment that are relevant to the situation in which they are produced. In the AT, the basic unit is the "activity" for which the following are defined: the involved "community" and the "social norms" which control their function, "the division of labour" that is followed to perform an activity, the mediation tools (physical and mental) which are provided for the action and interaction, "the subject" that carries out the activity, and the object of the activity.

The AT has been used, mostly in the Nordic countries, for the manual analysis and evaluation of the educational practice; however, using it to generate CSCL systems has not been widely explored. We know two proposals, which came about at the same time, where the AT inspires the conception of a CSCL system, as described in [1], from a CSCW perspective, and the AD, whose architecture is detailed in [7]. The AD defines (1) a formal notation based in the AT to produce design specifications of collaborative activities and (2) a system to process the specification of an activity and automatically generate a computer system in order to be able to carry it out.

A *learning community* can define a project through the authoring tools of the AD, which processes the specification and configures a client that includes complete functionality for the development of the defined project. If the AD is chosen, the project can also be organized in phases, each of which represents a certain quantity of activities that involve one community. In this case, each *activity* is defined in the terms of the AT, so an activity can be divided into tasks, as shown in the right part of the window in figure 1, and participation norms can be defined. Some of these norms are formally expressed through the explicit definition of *roles*. The community participants carry out a task in which they can play various roles, such as *student*, *teacher*, or *expert*, among others. The community can be organized into small *groups* and each group can carry out different tasks in one project. In the case of the AD system for the definition of each task, different roles as well as the assigned mediation tools can be specified. **These tools are expressed in the specification of the activity as resource references** of the LOR that are applied for that specific problem which is being solved. In the case of using the AD, the project workspace is not only a storage area but it also includes a toolbar. Figure 2 shows a snapshot of the portal interface for a registered user of a community; on the left part the menu and on the central part the personalized view of the available workspaces for that user. The open folder shows the tools available and the objects already created.

3 The LOR as a Subsystem

The characterization of learning objects, as well as the metadata to describe them is a topic of growing interest in the different international forum of standardization. In our proposal, we have kept in mind the given aspects necessary in order to import/export objects with other systems. However, the content of our repertoire is much richer, so the notion of "learning object" is extended to include other elements, in particular

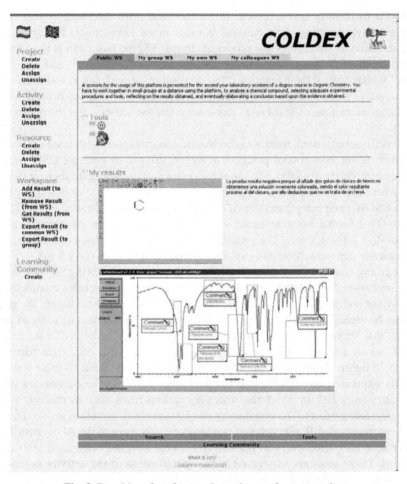

Fig. 2. Portal interface for a registered user of a community.

specifications of collaborative activities. For example, IMS[3] is starting to consider them within the "learning design" interest group [4]. For us, the idea of learning objects repository includes all available resources for the communities: (1) data in different formats (images captured by a telescope, laboratory photos, spectrums, series of measurements, and also hypotheses presented in an experiment, elaborated data such as annotated model results, questionnaires, reports from projects already carried out, etc.), which would enter in the type of "asset", or "aggregate" when it has a structure, (2) tools and (3) design specifications of learning activities ("template"). The definition of the objects/resources, and the resources themselves are, thus, stored in a complex external independent structure, the LOR. The use of this type of storage pattern allows the distributed re-utilization of the resources and their explicit definition.

---

[3] IMS *Global Learning Consortium* http://www.imsglobal.org/

Therefore, from an operative point of view, the LOR can be seen from three perspectives: (i) as a resource provider, (ii) as a means of active storage for a community in the carrying out of a project, and (iii) as a library of collaborative learning scenario patterns to generate a CSCL environment.

i. The LOR as a resource provider.

An approximation of the LOR is to see it as a library capable to manage resources, the learning objects; here, we are interested in the possibilities of reference, access, or distribution of the objects. The LOR bases its function on ontologies, which allows it to amplify the possibilities and to improve the search, the retrieval, and the possibility of querying with respect to using an unstructured vocabulary and a group of metadata to describe the objects. The LOR facilitates the use of the semantic value added by these ontologies. In particular, these resources in the AD are the ones that can be referred and instantiated to solve tasks associated to the activities.

ii. The LOR as a dynamic storage system for the learning process.

The LOR is also a dynamic means persistence mechanism where the results generated as part of the activities that are being carried out are saved and can be used as new resources for the following activities. This perspective amplifies the degree of collaboration since it provides a common mechanism to share previously generated data in a flexible and re-usable manner. In figure 3, it can be seen an aspect of the interface where the operation to add an object to the LOR has been selected and, in this case, all the values of the descriptors have been chosen automatically by the system either taken or inferred from the context of the creation of an object, an "asset", which is stored along with the standard metadata for this type of object, as well as those belonging to the definition and context of the creation relative to the theme, learning objective, project, phase, activity, task, tool, etc.

iii. The LOR as a means of storage for specifications of general collaborative activities.

The functionality of the LOR allows the use of collaborative activity models that can be instanced with the adequate content to automatically obtain the learning scenarios adapted to a concrete domain. The ontologies and the possibility to annotate objects simplify the job of the author to define the learning environment for a specific context. This is the vision of the LOR obtained when working from the authoring tools of the AD system.

The LOR has a person/computer interface, which can be used from the portal. The basic group of LOR functions (such as adding, comparing, searching, exporting, exploring, or refining, among others) is represented in a **taxonomy of functions.** This offers new and improved possibilities of choice through an interface that applies the stored knowledge in this structure to adapt the response to the concrete needs of a specific community at any given time. In this way, the interface can adapt dynamically to the changing circumstances of the use of the system by different communities and in different learning activities. The LOR is especially inter-operational with other tools/devices, not only with the AD or the authoring tools of the AD, but also as we

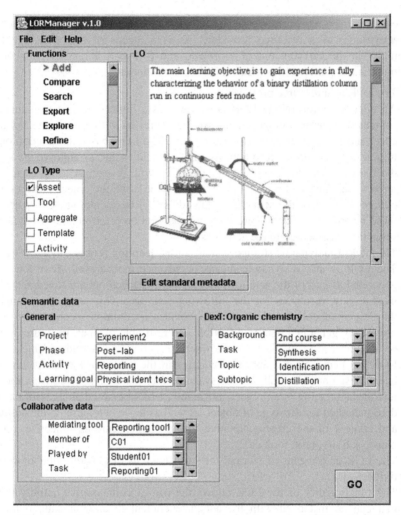

Fig. 3. Interface where the operation to add an object to the LOR is selected.

have explained with the workspace (importing and exporting is possible), and other collaborative tools.

4 Conclusions

In this article we have presented the design of an ontology to generate a first proto-type for a semantic portal that will serve collaborative learning communities. This portal interacts with a repository of learning objects, which, in addition to being a resource provider for other systems, is also a means of storage for virtual communi-ties and a library to generate collaborative learning environments. Concretely, in relation to this last point, the Active Document system has been embedded as a component. The AD is a system that processes the specification of a complex learning activity and it automatically generates a computer system that allows a group to carry it out.

The portal is in an initial design phase and is currently still in the process of formative evaluation with communities that will interact at a distance with the portal and the different systems/tools. This will allow us to refine the ontologies that are presented and consider more functions for the learning objects repository. These participatory design cycles will allow us to contrast the validity of the proposals that sustain this study as well as the establishment of the approximation followed.

Finally, with respect to the ontologies' development, it is worth to mention that we started using KAON (8) in a first step. At this point, we are using Protégé for this task mainly for such features, as robustness, scalability and the possibility of first-order and access logic querying, which makes it easier to concentrate on the conceptual aspects of the ontology creation and maintaining.

Acknowledgements

This report has been funded partially by the projects of COLDEX (IST-2001-32327) and EA_2C_2 (CICYT TIC2001-007).

References

1. Bourguin, G. & Derycke, A. (2001). "Integrating the CSCL Activities into Virtual Campuses: Foundations of a new infrastructure for distributed collective activities". In P. Dillenbourg, A. Eurelings, K. Hakkarainen (eds.) *European Perspectives on Computer-supported Collaborative learning*, pp. 123-130.
2. Brown, J.S., Collis, A. & Duguid, P. (1989) "Situated cognition and the culture of learning" *Educational Researcher,* Vol. 18, No. 1, pp. 32-42.
3. Koschmann, T. (1996) *CSCL: Theory and Practice of an emerging paradigm.* Lawrence Erlbaum Associates.
4. IMS-LD http://www.imsglobal.org/learningdesign/ ldv1p0/imsld_infov1p0.html
5. Nardi, B.A. (1996) *Context and Consciousness. Activity Theory and Human-Computer Interaction*, MIT Press.
6. Scardamalia, M. & Bereiter, C. (1991) "Higher Levels of Agency for Children in Knowledge Building: A Challenge for the Design of New Knowledge Media", *The Journal of the Learning Sciences*, Vol. 1, No. 1, pp. 37-68.
7. Verdejo, M.F. Barros, B. Read, T. & Rodriguez-Artacho, M. (2002). "A system for the specification and development of an environment for distributed CSCL scenarios". In *ITS'2002: Advances in Artificial Intelligence.* Springer-Verlag (Lecture Notes in Computer Science). Vol. 2363.
8. Verdejo, M.F. Barros, B. Mayorga J.I., Read, T. (2003) Diseño de un portal semántico para comunidades de aprendizaje colaborativ CAEPIA'2003, pp. 329-338.

Dialogue Act Classification in a Spoken Dialogue System[*]

María José Castro[1], David Vilar[1], Pablo Aibar[2], and Emilio Sanchis[1]

[1] Departament de Sistemes Informàtics i Computació
Universitat Politècnica de València, E-46022 València, Spain
{mcastro,dvilar,esanchis}@dsic.upv.es
[2] Departament de Llenguatges i Sistemes Informàtics
Universitat Jaume I de Castelló, E-12071 Castelló, Spain
aibar@lsi.uji.es

Abstract. A contribution to the understanding module in a spoken dialogue system is presented in this work. The task consists of answering telephone queries about timetables, prices and services for long distance trains in Spanish. In this system the representation of the meaning of an utterance is accomplished by means of *frames*, which represent the type of information of the user turn, and *cases*, which provide the information given in the sentence. The input of the understanding module is the output of the speech recognizer and its output is used by the dialogue manager.

We focus on the classification process of the dialogue user turn with respect to the second level, i.e., the identification of the type or types of *frames* given in the utterance and on the effect of the spontaneous speech recognition errors in the classification accuracy. As classifiers for the user turns we employ multilayer perceptrons, in order to use specific understanding models for each type of *frame*.

1 Introduction

Dialogue systems are one of the outstanding goals of language technology. In this kind of systems, one of the main concerns is the *understanding* of the user turns, in contrast to speech recognition systems, where the goal is the correct *transcription* of the user utterances. This allows us to ignore some words, focusing our attention on those which provide us with useful information for extracting the meaning of the utterance.

In this paper we present a contribution to the understanding module of the BASURDE [1] dialogue system. The task consists of answering telephone queries about timetables, prices and services for long distance trains in Spanish. In this system the representation of the meaning of an utterance is accomplished by means of *frames*, which represent the type of information of the user turn, and *cases*, which provide the information given in the sentence. The input of the

---

[*] Thanks to the Spanish CICYT agency under contracts TIC2003-07158-C04-03 and TIC2002-04103-C03-03 for funding.

R. Conejo et al. (Eds.): CAEPIA-TTIA 2003, LNAI 3040, pp. 260–270, 2004.

understanding module is the output of the speech recognizer and its output is then used by the dialogue manager. We have tried several stochastic based approaches to the understanding module [2–5]. Recently, other approaches to specific understanding modules have been presented [6].

In this work we focus on the classification process of the dialogue user turn with respect to the second level, i.e., the identification of the type or types of frames given in the utterance and on the effect of the spontaneous speech recognition errors in the classification accuracy. Due to the multiple error sources in a dialogue system (recognition errors, unexpected answers, etc.) it is convenient to have a reliable method for detecting which type of frame has been uttered. Once the dialogue act has been determined, the posterior extraction of the attributes and values of the utterance is simplified, as we work in a restricted analysis domain. A connectionist approach to the classification problem is studied in this paper. Our previous work on this topic can be found in [7–9].

2   The Dialogue Structure

One of the most frequent ways to represent the dialogue structure is by using dialogue acts [10, 11], which represent the successive states of the dialogue. The labels must be specific enough to account for the different intentions of each of the turns, but general enough in order to easily adapt them to different tasks. In this work we begin with a corpus of 215 dialogues acquired using the Wizard of Oz technique, with 1 440 user turns. The reduced size of this corpus poses a problem for the correct estimation of the model parameters. With this set of dialogues we defined three levels for labeling [12]:

Dialogue Acts: This first level is task-independent and represents the general intention of the user turn. It comprises the following labels: Opening, Closing, Undefined, Not_Understood, Waiting, Consult, Acceptance, Rejection, Question, Confirmation, Answer.

Frames: The second level is task-specific and represents the kind of message provided by the user, the so called *frame*. In our case we defined 15 labels which, together with their relative frequencies, are shown in Table 1.

Cases: The third level takes into account the values given in the utterances, like city names, dates, etc.

The labeling of the corpus was carried out using a semiautomatic process: some dialogues were manually labeled and used to train some preliminary models, which in turn were used to label the rest of the corpus. The final result was manually reviewed. An example of the three level labeling is shown in Figure 1. One important feature of this labeling scheme is that one dialogue turn can have more than one label associated with it (see the second example of Figure 1), which allows a better specification of the meaning, but it also makes the posterior classification and segmentation tasks harder.

Table 1. The 15 frame classes and their relative frequencies

Frame Class	%
Affirmation	26.75
Departure_time	18.27
New_data	13.16
Price	12.29
Closing	10.07
Return_departure_time	5.30
Rejection	4.34
Arrival_time	3.57
Train_type	3.37
Confirmation	1.73
Not_understood	0.63
Trip_length	0.24
Return_price	0.19
Return_train_type	0.05
Return_departure_time	0.05

3 Lexicon and Codification of the User Turns

In the problem we are dealing with, the morphological variance of the words is not important because it does not give any additional information for the classification task. This allows us to define a set of categories and lemmas, in order to reduce the size of the vocabulary. We have defined the following categories:

1. *General categories*, like city names, week days, ordinal and cardinal numbers...
2. *Task-specific categories*, like train type or ticket type.
3. *Lemmas*: verbs in infinitive form, singular nouns and without article.

It is worth noting that some words that normally are considered "stopwords" and can be deleted in a great number of tasks, in our case they play a very important role. One clear example of this kind of words are the prepositions, that are the key to distinguish between the origin and the destination of a train. Using these prepositions we performed an additional step, splitting the general category "city_name" into the two categories "from_city_name" and "to_city_name".

After this preprocessing we reduced the size of the vocabulary from 616 to 265 words. Lastly we deleted those words with a frequency below a fixed threshold f_p (but without deleting the user turns they appear in) given that, due to their low frequency, they do not provide significant information for the discrimination of the classes. In the same way, we only considered those turns labeled with frame classes whose frequency is above the value f_c, because we do not have enough training samples available for a correct estimation of the parameters of these less frequent classes. In our case we fixed f_p and f_c both to a value of 5 (absolute frequency), which reduces the size of the corpus to 1 339 user turns, comprising a final vocabulary of 120 words and the first 10 classes of Table 1.

Original sentence:	Quería saber los horarios del Euromed Barcelona–Valencia.
	I would like to know the timetables of the Euromed train
	from Barcelona to Valencia.
1st level (speech act):	Question
2nd level (frames):	Departure_time
3rd level (cases):	Departure_time (Origin: barcelona, Destination: valencia,
	Train_type: euromed)
Original sentence:	Hola, buenos días. Me gustaría saber el precio y los
	horarios que hay para un billete de tren de Barcelona a La
	Coruña el 22 de diciembre, por favor.
	Hello, good morning. I would like to know the price and
	timetables of a train from Barcelona to La Coruña for the
	22nd of December, please.
1st level (speech act):	Question
2nd level (frames):	Price, Departure_time
3rd level (cases):	Price (Origin: barcelona, Destination: la_coruña,
	Departure_time: 12/22/2002)
	Departure_time (Origin: barcelona, Destination: la_coruña,
	Departure_time: 12/22/2002)

Fig. 1. Example of the three-level labeling for two user turns. The Spanish original sentence and its English translation are given

Once the vocabulary has been fixed, the codification of each input utterance is a 120 bit vector, each bit indicating the presence or absence of a word of the vocabulary in the utterance. This coding scheme neglects the information that can be obtained taking the sequentiality of the utterance into account, but we consider that this information is not fundamental in our classification problem. This codification is a natural approach to the input format of the connectionist classifier. An example of the result of the preprocess and codification of the user turn is shown in Figure 2.

4   Multiclass Classification Using Neural Networks

We have used multilayer perceptrons (MLPs) to classify the user turns, for being one of the most widely used artificial neural networks for classification tasks. In our case the input layer gets the user turn coded as a bit vector, as explained above, and the number of output units is defined as the number of class labels of the classification task. Each unit in the (first) hidden layer defines an hyperplane in the representation space. Those hyperplanes will form the decision boundaries of the different classes. Using sigmoid activation functions, the MLPs can smooth these boundaries, adapting them to classification tasks [13]. The activation level of an output unit can be interpreted as an approximation of the a posteriori probability of the input sample belonging to the corresponding class [14].

In this way, if we face an uniclass classification problem, i.e. if the input set is formed by samples of the form

$$\{(\mathbf{x}_n, c_n)\}_{n=1}^{N}, \quad c_n \in \mathcal{C}, \tag{1}$$

Original sentence	Quería saber los horarios del Euromed Barcelona-Valencia.
	I would like to know the timetables of the Euromed train
	from Barcelona to Valencia.
Preprocessed sentence	de, horario, nom_ciudad_destino, nom_ciudad_origen,
("Bag of words")	querer, saber, tipo_tren
	of, timetable, to_city_name, from_city_name, want, know,
	train_type
▷Input local coding	0 0 0 0 0 0 0 0 0 0 0 0 0 0 0 0 0 0 0 1 0 0 0 0 0 0 0 0 0 0 0
	0 0 0 0 0 0 0 0 0 0 0 0 0 0 1 0 0 0 0 0 0 0 0 0 0 0 0 0 0 0 0
	0 0 0 0 0 1 1 0 0 0 0 0 0 0 0 0 0 0 0 0 0 0 0 0 0 0 0 1 0 0
	0 0 1 0 0 0 0 0 0 0 0 0 0 0 1 0 0 0 0 0 0 0 0 0 0 0
	(7 active input units)

Original sentence	Hola, buenos días. Me gustaría saber el precio y los
	horarios que hay para un billete de tren de Barcelona a La
	Coruña el 22 de diciembre, por favor.
	Hello, good morning. I would like to know the price and
	timetables of a train from Barcelona to La Coruña for the
	22nd of December, please.
Preprocessed sentence	buen, de, día, hola, horario, nom_ciudad_destino,
("Bag of words")	nom_ciudad_origen, nom_mes, num_cardinal, querer, para,
	saber, tren
	good, of, morning, hello, timetable, to_city_name,
	from_city_name, month_name, cardinal_number, want, for,
	know, train
▷Input local coding	0 0 0 0 0 0 0 0 0 1 0 0 0 0 0 0 0 0 1 0 0 0 1 0 0 0 0 0 0 0
	0 0 0 0 0 0 0 0 0 0 1 0 0 1 0 0 0 0 0 0 0 0 0 0 0 0 0 0 0 0
	0 0 0 0 0 1 1 1 0 1 0 0 0 0 1 0 0 0 0 0 0 0 0 0 0 0 0 1 0 0
	0 0 1 0 0 0 0 0 0 0 0 0 0 0 0 0 1 0 0 0 0 0 0 0 0 0
	(13 active input units)

Fig. 2. Example of the local coding for two user turns

where $\mathcal{C} = \{c^1, c^2, \ldots, c^{|\mathcal{C}|}\}$ is the set of $|\mathcal{C}|$ class labels, the classification rule will assign the sample $\mathbf{x}$ to the class $k^\star(\mathbf{x})$ with the biggest a posteriori probability, which can be estimated using an MLP:

$$k^\star(\mathbf{x}) = \operatorname*{argmax}_{k \in \mathcal{C}} \Pr(k|\mathbf{x}) \approx \operatorname*{argmax}_{k \in \mathcal{C}} g_k(\mathbf{x}, \omega), \qquad (2)$$

where $g_k(\mathbf{x}, \omega)$ is the value of the kth output of the MLP given the input sample $\mathbf{x}$ and the set ω of parameters of the MLP.

In our task, however, we face a multiclass classification problem, where an utterance can have more than one dialogue act associated with it[1]. That is, the training set is constituted by samples which are pairs of the form

$$\{(\mathbf{x}_n, C_n)\}_{n=1}^N, \quad C_n \subseteq \mathcal{C}. \qquad (3)$$

---

[1] In related dialogue act classification works [11] a hand segmentation of the user turns was needed in order to obtain units corresponding to one unique frame class. With this previous segmentation a n-gram based classifier was used.

Original sentence	Quería saber los horarios del Euromed Barcelona–Valencia.
	I would like to know the timetables of the Euromed train from Barcelona to Valencia.
2nd level	Departure_time
▷**Output coding**	0 1 0 0 0 0 0 0 0 0 (1 out of 10 classes)
Original sentence	Hola, buenos días. Me gustaría saber el precio y los horarios que hay para un billete de tren de Barcelona a La Coruña el 22 de diciembre, por favor.
	Hello, good morning. I would like to know the price and timetables of a train from Barcelona to La Coruña for the 22nd of December, please.
2nd level	Price, Departure_time
▷**Output coding**	0 1 0 1 0 0 0 0 0 0 (2 out of 10 classes)

Fig. 3. Example of the coding of the frame type or types

Table 2. Partition of the dataset (80% for training and 20% for test) and type of the user turns (uniclass–UC and multiclass–MC)

Data	Total	UC	MC
Training	1 071	692 (65%)	379 (35%)
Test	268	175 (65%)	93 (35%)

In our classification task, the class set $\mathcal{C}$ contains the 10 most frequent frame classes defined in Table 1. Our goal is to classify a user turn into one or more frame classes $K^\star(\mathbf{x})$ whose posterior probabilities, estimated using multilayer perceptrons, are above a threshold:

$$K^\star(\mathbf{x}) = \{k \in \mathcal{C} \mid \Pr(k|\mathbf{x}) \geq \mathcal{T}\} \approx \{k \in \mathcal{C} \mid g_k(\mathbf{x}, \omega) \geq \mathcal{T}\} \qquad (4)$$

where the threshold $\mathcal{T}$ must also be estimated during the training process.

Under this approach, the classes are coded with a $|\mathcal{C}|$-dimensional bit vector, where the desired output units for each training sample are fixed to 1 for the correct frame class or classes and to 0 for the rest. Figure 3 shows an example of the coding of the desired output.

5 Experiments

For the experimentation a random splitting of the 1 339 user turns was carried out. A training set comprising about 80% of the data was formed, and the remaining 20% was used for testing. Table 2 shows the distribution of the data, along with the uniclass and multiclass frequency in each partition.

5.1 Training the MLPs

The training of the MLPs was carried out using the neural network simulation software kit "SNNS: Stuttgart Neural Network Simulator" [15]. In order to successfully use neural networks as classifiers several aspects have to be considered,

Table 3. MLP topologies and parameters

Topology:	One hidden layer: 2, 4, 8, 16, 32, 64
	Two hidden layers: 2–2, 4–2, 4–4, 8–2, ..., 64–64
Learning algorithm:	Backpropagation (with and without momentum term), Quickpropagation
Learning rate:	0.05, 0.1, 0.2, 0.3, 0.4, 0.5
Momentum:	0.1, 0.2, 0.3, 0.4, 0.5
Maximum increment:	1.75, 2

Table 4. Error rate of the speech recognition system

	Without processing		*Processed*	
Data	WER	Sentence	WER	Sentence
Training	18.71	55.56	17.53	52.90
Test	20.65	58.96	19.15	55.06

such as the network topology, the training algorithm and the selection of its parameters [13–15]. We carried out experiments with different network topologies, with an increasing number of units: one hidden layer with 2 units, two hidden layers with 2 units each, two hidden layers of 4 and 2 units, one hidden layer of 4 units, etc. Different learning algorithms were also used: the incremental version of the backpropagation algorithm, with and without momentum term, and the quickpropagation algorithm, studying at the same time the influence of their parameters like learning rate and momentum term. In the training process a random presentation of the samples was used. In each case a stop criterion based on a validation set was used, where a randomly chosen subset of approximately 20% of the training samples was used in order to stop the learning process and select the best configuration.

In the training phase we first tested the influence of the MLP topology. Different MLPs were trained with an increasing number of units, using the standard backpropagation algorithm, with a sigmoid activation function and learning rate equal to 0.2, selecting the best topology based on the mean squared error on the validation set.

Once the topology was fixed, we continued our experimentation training MLPs of this topology with the above mentioned algorithms, with different combinations of learning rate and momentum, and with different values of maximum increment for the quickpropagation algorithm (see Table 3).

5.2 Performance of the Speech Recognizer

Table 4 shows the results obtained using our speech recognizer based on semicontinous Hidden Markov Models. First, the correct transcription and the output of the recognizer are compared using the word error rate (WER) measure, and the percentage of bad recognized sentences is also given.

Table 5. Classification error rate of the user turns

		Test				
		Text			Voice	
Training	Total	a UC	MC	Total	UC	MC
Text	11.19	7.43	18.28	48.13	50.86	43.01
Text+Voice	27.24	17.71	34.70	46.64	38.29	62.37
Voice	25.00	16.57	40.86	44.40	40.57	51.61

Secondly, the results of the same measures is given after the categorization and lemmatization explained in Section 3. The results are shown for both the training and the test partitions.

5.3 Text and Voice Experiments

A common practice in understanding and voice recognition systems is to train the models with correct data (i.e., the correct transcription of the user utterances) and to test with the transcription of a speech recognizer. Connectionist classifiers, as most classifiers do, try to minimize the error of the training data and therefore a tacit assumption is made, namely that both training and test data are generated using the same model. This is not consistent with the above described approach. Therefore we have carried out a series of experiments in order to study the influence of training with text or voice data.

Learning with Text Data. In a first phase and in order to test if the classifier can be successfully used in this task we trained an MLP (with the above described methodology) with text data. The best result on the validation set was obtained with an MLP of two hidden layers of 32 units each and training with the backpropagation algorithm with momentum term, using a learning rate equal to 0.3 and a momentum term of 0.5. In order to determine the classification threshold, the validation data was classified using values of the threshold between 0.1 and 0.9. The best classification rate was obtained using a threshold value of 0.5 (see Figure 4).

Using this MLP and the threshold equal to 0.5 we achieved an error rate[2] of 11.19% on the correctly transcribed test set. If we test this MLP (trained with text data) on the output of the speech recognizer the error rate grows up to 48.13%. All the results are shown in Table 5.

Learning with Text and Voice Data. In a second phase, starting with the above trained MLP, we retrained the classifier on the same training set, but using the data of the speech recognizer both as the training data and as the

---

[2] In all the experiments, we considered a missclasification of the sample as an error. That is, in the case of the multiclass user turns we require that all the corresponding class labels are detected.

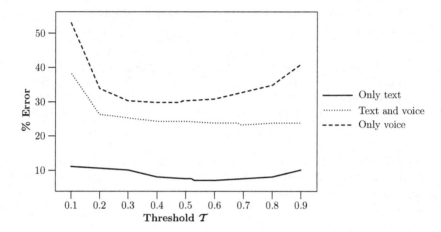

Fig. 4. Sweep on the threshold values for classification using the validation data on the three experiments

validation data for the stop criterion. With this retrained MLP an analogous process as before was carried out in order to estimate the threshold, which was fixed to a value of 0.7. The classification results, both for text and voice data, are shown in Table 5. These results show a degradation of the performance on the text data (as expected) and only a non-significant improvement on the voice data.

Learning with Voice Data. Lastly, the MLPs were trained using the "real" data, i.e. directly using the data recognized by the speech recognizer system. The best topology was an MLP with two hidden layers of 16 units each. The best results were obtained using a learning rate equal to 0.2, and the best threshold value was 0.4. The results are shown in Table 5. A small improvement on the voice data is achieved, but not quite significant, perhaps due to a excessively high error rate of the speech recognizer (nearly 20% word error rate after processing the output).

6   Conclusions

The classification error rates of the user turns (Table 5) show a great degradation of performance when voice data is used. This is mostly due to the poor results of the speech recognition system (see error rate in Table 4). Nevertheless, we have empirically shown that it is convenient to use the "real" data in the training phase in order for the classifier (a MLP in our case) to be able to generalize the typical errors of the recognizer.

On the other hand, it is shown that the classification task is more difficult for multiclass user turns than for the uniclass ones. We have also tried to train and test only with the uniclass data and the results were significantly better.

Another evident conclusion of these results is that we need a two-level classification: when the confidence of the classification is high, the classification is taken as correct and the user turn will be precessed with one or more specific understanding models. If this is not the case, i.e. if the confidence of the classification is low, the turn will be rejected and a general understanding module will be used. Therefore, the estimation of the classification threshold should minimize the number of classifications errors (as we have done now) and also minimize the number of false classifications.

Lastly, we are working on the improvement of the automatic speech recognizer and the acquisition of new samples, that is, the dialogue corpus will be extended, so we will be able to repeat the experiments with a higher amount of data.

References

1. Bonafonte, A., Aibar, P., Castell, N., Lleida, E., Mariño, J.B., Sanchis, E., Torres, M.I.: Desarrollo de un sistema de diálogo oral en dominios restringidos. In: Primeras Jornadas de Tecnología del Habla, Sevilla (Spain) (2000)
2. Pla, F., Molina, A., Sanchis, E., García, F.: Language Understanding Using Two-Level Stochastic Models with POS and Semantic Units. In: Proc. of 4th International Conference on Text, Speech and Dialogue (TSD'01). (2001)
3. Segarra, E., Sanchis, E., García, F., Hurtado, L.F.: Extracting semantic information through automatic learning. In: Pattern Recognition and Image Analysis. Proc. of IX SNRFAI'01, Benicàssim (Spain) (2001)
4. Sanchis, E., García, F., Galiano, I., Segarra, E.: Applying dialogue constraints to the understanding process in a Dialogue System. In: Proc. of 5th International Conference on Text, Speech and Dialogue (TSD'02), Brno (Czech Republic) (2002)
5. Vilar, D., Castro, M.J., Sanchis, E.: Connectionist classification and specific stochastic models in the understanding process of a dialogue system. In: Proc. Eurospeech'03, Geneva (Switzerland) (2003)
6. Hacioglu, K., Ward, W.: Dialog-Context Dependent Language Modeling Combining N-grams and Stochastic Context-Free Grammars. In: Proc. International Conference on Acoustics, Speech and Signal Processing (ICASSP'01). (2001)
7. Castro, M.J., Sanchis, E.: A Simple Connectionist Approach to Language Understanding in a Dialogue System. In: Advances in Artificial Intelligence – Iberamia 2002. Volume 2527 of LNAI. Springer-Verlag (2002)
8. Sanchis, E., Castro, M.J.: Dialogue Act Connectionist Detection in a Spoken Dialogue System. In: Soft Computing Systems. Design, Management and Applications. Volume 87 of Frontiers in Artificial Intelligence and Applications. IOS Press (2002)
9. Vilar, D., Castro, M.J., Sanchis, E.: Comparación de métodos de detección de actos de diálogo. In: Actas de las II Jornadas en Tecnologías del Habla, Granada (España) (2002)
10. Nagata, M., Morimoto, T.: First steps toward statistical modeling of dialogue to predict the speech act type of the next utterance. Speech Communication **15** (1994)
11. Stolcke, A., Ries., K., Coccaro, N., Shriberg, E., Bates, R., Jurafsky, D., Taylor, P., Martin, R., Van Ess-Dykema, C., Meteer, M.: Dialogue Act Modeling for Automatic Tagging and Recognition of Conversational Speech. Computational Linguistics **26** (2000)

12. Martínez, C., Sanchis, E., García, F., Aibar, P.: A Labelling Proposal to Annotate Dialogues. In: Proc. LREC'02., Las Palmas de Gran Canaria (Spain) (2002)
13. Rumelhart, D.E., Hinton, G.E., Williams, R.J.: Learning internal representations by error propagation. In Rumelhart, D.E., McClelland, J.L., eds.: PDP: Computational models of cognition and perception, I. MIT Press (1986)
14. Bishop, C.M.: Neural networks for pattern recognition. Oxford University Press (1995)
15. Zell, A., Mamier, G., Vogt, M., Mache, N., Hübner, R., Döring, S., Herrmann, K., Soyez, T., Schmalzl, M., Sommer, T., Hatzigeorgiou, A., Posselt, D. Schreiner, T., Kett, B., Clemente, G., Wieland, J.: SNNS: Stuttgart Neural Network Simulator. User Manual, Version 4.2. Institute for Parallel and Distributed High Performance Systems, University of Stuttgart, Germany. (1998)

Distributed Non-binary Constraints*

Miguel A. Salido[1] and Federico Barber[2]

[1] Dpto. Ciencias de la Computación e Inteligencia Artificial, Universidad de Alicante
Campus de San Vicente, Ap. de Correos: 99, E-03080, Alicante, Spain
msalido@dsic.upv.es
[2] Dpto. Sistemas Informáticos y Computación, Universidad Politécnica de Valencia
Camino de Vera s/n, 46071, Valencia, Spain
fbarber@dsic.upv.es

Abstract. Nowadays many real problems can be modeled as Constraint Satisfaction Problems (CSPs). In many situations, it is desirable to be able to state both *hard* constraints and *soft* constraints. Hard constraints must hold while soft constraints may be violated but as many as possible should be satisfied. Although the problem constraints can be divided into two groups, the order in which these constraints are studied can improve efficiency, particulary in problems with non-binary constraints. In this paper, we carry out a classification of hard and soft constraints in order to study the tightest hard constraints first and to obtain ever better solutions. In this way, inconsistencies can be found earlier and the number of constraint checks can be significantly reduced.

1   Introduction

Many problems arising in a variety of domains such as planning, scheduling, diagnosis, decision support, scheduling and design can be efficiently modeled as Constraint Satisfaction Problems (CSPs) and solved using constraint programming techniques. Some of these problems can be modeled naturally using non-binary (or n-ary) constraints. Although, researchers have traditionally focused on binary constraints [9], the need to address issues regarding non-binary constraints has recently started to be widely recognized in the constraint satisfaction literature.

One approach to solving CSPs is to use a depth-first backtrack search algorithm [3]. General methods for solving CSPs include *Generate and test* [7] and *Backtracking* [6] algorithms. Many works have been carried out to improve the *Backtracking* method. One way of increasing the efficiency of *Backtracking* includes the use of *search order* for variables and values. Some heuristics based on *variable ordering* and *value ordering* [5] have been developed, because of the additivity of the variables and values. Constraints are also considered to be *additive*, that is, the order of imposition of constraints does not matter; all that matters is that the conjunction of constraints be satisfied [1].

---

* This work has been supported by the grant DPI2001-2094-C03-03 from the Spanish Government.

R. Conejo et al. (Eds.): CAEPIA-TTIA 2003, LNAI 3040, pp. 271–280, 2004.

In spite of the additivity of constraints, only a few works have be done on binary constraint ordering mainly for arc-consistency algorithms [10], [4], but little work has be done on non-binary constraint ordering (for instance in disjunctive constraints [8]), and only some heuristic techniques classify the non-binary constraints by means of the arity. However, less arity does not imply a tighter constraint. Moreover, when all non-binary constraints have the same arity, or these constraints are classified as hard and soft constraints, these techniques are not useful.

In this paper, we propose a heuristic technique called *Hard and Soft Constraint Ordering Heuristic* (HASCOH) that classifies the non-binary constraints, independently of the arity so that hard constraints are studied before soft constraints and then the tightest constraints are studied before the loosest constraints. This is based on the *first-fail* principle, which can be explained as

"To succeed, try first where you are more likely to fail"

HSACOH manages CSPs in a distributed way so that each agent is committed to a set of constraints. The hard constraints that are more likely to fail are studied first using a search algorithm. In this way, inconsistent tuples can be found earlier so that backtrackings are avoided. Without loss of generality, we do not consider preferences in soft constraints, that is, all soft constraints are equally important. Thus, soft constraints are studied after the hard constraints in order to satisfy as many soft constraints as possible. This model allows agents to run concurrently to achieve partial solutions for any-time complete solutions.

2   Preliminaries

CSP: A constraint satisfaction problem (CSP) consists of a set of variables $X = \{x_1, x_2, ..., x_n\}$; a set of finite domains $D = \{D_1, D_2, ..., D_n\}$, where each variable $x_i \in X$ has a set D_i of possible values; and a finite collection of constraints restricting the values that the variables can simultaneously take. We will classify these constraints as hard and soft constraints: hard constraints must hold while soft constraints may be violated, but should be satisfied as much as possible.

State: one possible assignment of all variables; the number of states is equal to the Cartesian product of the domain size.

Partition: A partition of a set C is a set of disjoint subsets of C whose union is C. The subsets are called partition blocks.

Distributed CSP: A distributed CSP is a CSP in which the variables and constraints are distributed among automated agents [11]. Each agent has several variables and attempts to determine their values. However, there are interagent constraints and the value assignment must satisfy these interagent constraints.

Objective in a CSP: A *solution* to a CSP is an assignment of values to all the variables so that at least all the hard constraints are satisfied. Typical tasks of interest are to determine whether a solution exists, to find one or all solutions and to find an optimal or a good solution relative to a preference criterion.

3   Constraint Ordering: An Any-Time Proposal

Our main objective is to classify the problem constraints in an appropriate order depending on the desired goals. One way to manage the problem constraints is by means of the natural order in which they are inserted into the problem. However, when managing hard and soft constraints there is a natural and reasonable order where the hard constraints are managed first and the soft constraints are managed later. This natural constraint ordering is presented in Figure 1. Each hard and soft constraint satisfies a portion of the search space, but no ordering is carried out to avoid constraint checking.

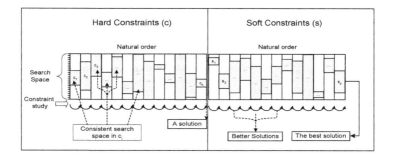

Fig. 1. Natural ordering of hard and soft constraints

In many real problems, the main objective is to obtain a solution that satisfies hard constraints, as soon as possible, and as many soft constraints as possible. In this case, an any-time proposal may be appropriate. A feasible solution may be improved at any time by another solution that satisfies more soft constraints. Thus, both hard and soft constraints are classified from the tightest ones to the loosest ones. This constraint ordering is presented in Figure 2.

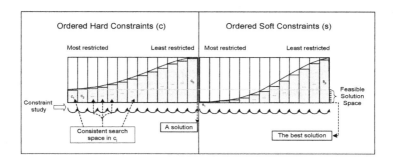

Fig. 2. Constraint ordering in the any-time proposal

The search space of the correctly ordered hard and soft constraints has a behavior which is similar to the behavior of the left tails of normal curves, in which the height of each curve is bounded by the entire search space. The height of the tail of the hard constraints represents the valid search space for the problem. This restricted search space is the only valid search space for finding problem solutions and the rest of the search space can be removed.

Furthermore, the height of the tail of the soft constraints may be zero, because soft constraints are generally over-constrained. However, these constraints are dispensable and the objective is to satisfy as many soft constraints as possible. These soft constraints are classified from the tightest one to the loosest one. Thus, the first solution generated by the study of hard constraints is checked with all soft constraints and this solution is labeled with the number of satisfied soft constraints. Due to the any-time behavior, the following solution satisfying all hard constraints is checked with the soft constraints from the tightest one to the loosest one, and this constraint checking is aborted when its label can not be greater than the label of the first solution. Thus, at any time, the best solution is maintained with its label, and a future solution is checked with soft constraints while its label may reach the label of the current best solution.

Here, we will focus on this any-time behavior in which, depending on the user requirements, the solutions can be improved in order to satisfy more soft constraints. Thus our main objective is to classify both hard and soft non-binary constraints in the appropriate order to be solved by some of the current techniques that manage non-binary constraints in a natural way [2].

4   Our Distributed Model: HASCOH

Agent-based computation has been studied for several years in the field of artificial intelligence and has been widely used in other branches of computer science. HASCOH is meant to be a framework for interacting agents to achieve a consistent state. The main idea of our multi-agent model is based on carrying out a partition of the hard constraints, in k groups called *blocks* of constraints, so that the tightest constraints are grouped and studied first by autonomous agents.

To this end, a preprocessing agent carries out a partition of the hard constraints, similar to a sample in finite population, in order to classify both hard and soft constraints from the tightest *hard* constraints to the loosest soft constraints. Then, a group of agents called *hard block agents* concurrently manages each block of hard constraints, generated by the preprocessing agent. Also, an agent called *soft agent* manages all soft constraints. Each *hard block agent* is in charge of solving its partial problem by means of a search algorithm. Thus, a problem solution is incrementally generated from the first *hard block agent* to the last *hard block agent*. Without loss of generality we consider all variables are involved in the hard constraints. Afterwards, the *soft agent* is committed to checking the solutions obtained by the *hard block agents*. Therefore, as an any-time proposal, and depending on the time available, these solutions may be improved by means of the concurrent search in order to find a solution that satisfies as many constraints as possible.

Figure 3 shows the multi-agent model, in which consistent partial states (s_{ij}) are concurrently generated by each *hard block agent* and sent to the following

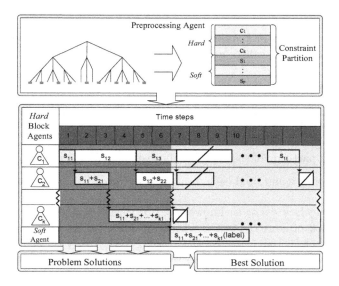

Fig. 3. Multi-agent model

hard block agent until a consistent state is found (by the last *hard block agent*). For example, state: $s_{11} + s_{21} + \ldots + s_{k1}$ is a problem solution. Then, the *soft agent* checks this solution, and it is labeled with the number of satisfied soft constraints. We must take into account that a solution is incrementally generated, however partial solutions are concurrently generated due to many partial solutions will not take part in a solution.

4.1   Preprocessing Agent

The preprocessing agent classifies the constraints in the appropriate order by means of a sample from a finite population in statistics where there is a population, and a sample is chosen to represent this population. In our context, the population is composed by the states generated by means of the Cartesian Product of variable domain bounds and the sample is composed by $s(n)$ random and well distributed states (s is a polynomial function) in order to represent the entire population. As in statistic, the user selects the size of the sample ($s(n)$). The preprocessing agent studies how many states $st_i : st_i \leq s(n)$ satisfy each constraint c_i. Thus, each constraint c_i is labeled with p_i: $c_i(p_i)$, where $p_i = st_i/s(n)$ represents the probability that c_i satisfies the whole problem. Therefore, the computational complexity is $|c|s(n)$. Thus, the preprocessing agent classifies the *hard* constraints in ascending order of the labels p_i and the soft constraints in descending order of the labels p_i. The behavior of a preprocessing agent is shown in Figure 4. It can be observed that a sample of states is selected from the spanning tree. Each state is checked with the constraints and the evaluation value T_{si} may be stored to be used by local search algorithms. Furthermore, each constraint c_i is labeled in order to be classified. Thus, as we pointed in Figure 3, these ordered constraints are partitioned in k blocks (geometrically distributed) to divide the problem in k interdependent subproblems. Each subproblem will be solved by an agent, called *block agent*.

4.2   Hard Block Agent

A *block agent* is a cooperating agent with a set of properties. We make the following assumptions (Figure 4(right)):

- There is a partition of the set of hard constraints $C \equiv \bigcup_{i=1}^{k} C_i$ generated by the preprocessing agent, and each *hard block agent* a_j has a block of constraints C_j.
- Each *hard block agent* a_j knows a set of variables, V_j, which are involved in its block of constraints C_j. These variables fall into different sets: *used variables* set $(\overline{v}_j)$ and *new variables* set (v_j), that is: $V_j = \overline{v}_j \cup v_j$.
- The domain D_i corresponding to variable x_i is maintained in the first *hard block agent* a_t in which x_i is involved, (i.e.), $x_i \in v_t$.
- Each *hard block agent* a_j assigns values (by a search algorithm) to variables that have not yet been assigned, that is, a_j assigns values to variables $x_i \in v_j$, because variables $x_k \in \overline{v}_j$ have already been assigned by previous agents $a_1, a_2, ..., a_{j-1}$.
- Each *hard block agent* a_j knows the consistent partial states generated by the previous agents $a_1, a_2, ..., a_{j-1}$. Thus, agent a_j knows assignments of variables included in sets: $\overline{v}_1, \overline{v}_2, ..., \overline{v}_{j-1}$.

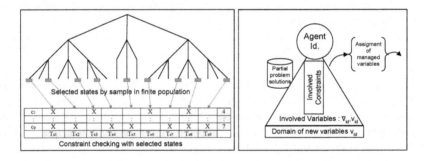

Fig. 4. Behavior of preprocessing agent and hard block agent

Hard block agents cooperate to achieve a consistent state. *Hard block agent* 1 tries to find a consistent state for its partial problem. When it has a consistent partial state, it communicates this partial state to *hard block agent* 2. *Hard block agent* 2 studies the second set of tightest *hard* constraints using the variable assignments generated by *hard block agent* 1. Meanwhile, agent 1 tries to find any other consistent partial state. So, each *hard block agent* j $(j \leq k)$, using the variable assignment of the previous hard block agents $1, 2, .., j - 1$, tries to concurrently find a more complete assignment. A problem solution is obtained when the last *hard block agent* k finds a consistent state.

4.3 Soft Agent

Once *hard block agents* find a consistent state, this solution is sent to the *soft agent*. This agent is committed to checking solutions with soft constraints in order to return the best solution at any-time.

The first solution generated by the hard block agents is sent to the *soft agent*. The *soft agent* checks this solution with all soft constraints to evaluate the goodness of this solution. Thus, this solution is labeled with the number of satisfied soft constraints. The second solution generated by the *hard block agents* is also sent to the *soft agent*, and this solution is checked with soft constraints starting from the tightest ones. The constraint checking continues as long as the label of this solution may be greater than the label of the first solution. For instance, if there are ten soft constraints and the first solution satisfies seven soft constraints (its label is 7), the second solution will be checked with the soft constraints (from the tightest to the loosest). When this solution is not consistent with two soft constraints, the soft constraint checking is aborted, because this solution will not satisfy more constraints than the first solution. Thus, any other solution will be checked with soft constraints as long as its label may reach the label of the current best solution.

Example: The 4-queens problem is a classical search problem in the artificial intelligence area. We have extended this problem to include soft constraints. The problem is to place four queens z_1, z_2, z_3, z_4 on a 4×4 chessboard so that no two queens can capture each other. Thus, hard constraints impose the condition that no two queens are allowed to be placed on the same row, the same column, or the same diagonal. We also add two soft constraints: queen 1 value must be less or equal than queen 2 value: $z_1 \leq z_3$ and the sum of queen 1 and queen 2 values must be less or equal than queen 3 value: $z_1 + z_2 \leq z_3$. This modified 4-queens problem is internally managed in Figure 5.

Figure 5 shows the behavior HASCOH. The preprocessing step checks how many partial states (from a given sample: 16 tuples $\{(1,1), (1,2), \cdots, (4,3), (4,4)\}$) satisfy each constraint and classifies them afterwards. It can be observed that some hard constraints are tightest than others. Constraints c_1, c_4, c_6 only satisfy 6 partial states, while constraints c_2 and c_5 satisfy 8 partial states and constraint c_3 satisfies 10 partial states. Furthermore, soft constraint 2 is tightest than soft constraint 1.

5 Evaluation of HASCOH

In this section, we compare the performance of our model HASCOH with two well-known and complete CSP solvers: *Generate and Test* (GT) and *Backtracking* (BT), because they are the most appropriate techniques for observing the number of constraint checks. This empirical evaluation was carried out with two different types of problems: benchmark problems and random problems.

Benchmark Problems: The n-queens problem is a classical search problem in the artificial intelligence area. The 4-queens problem was studied in the previous section.

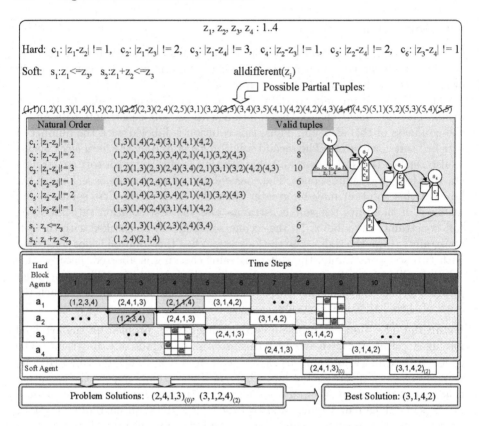

Fig. 5. The 4-queens problem in our distributed model

Table 1. Number of constraint check saving using our model with GT and BT in the n-queens problem

	HASCOH+GT	HASCOH+BT
queens	*Constraint Check Saving*	*Constraint Check Saving*
5	2.1×10^4	2.4×10^2
10	4.1×10^{11}	3.9×10^7
20	1.9×10^{26}	3.6×10^{18}
50	2.4×10^{70}	3.6×10^{52}
100	2.1×10^{143}	2.1×10^{106}
150	5.2×10^{219}	3.7×10^{161}
200	9.4×10^{295}	8.7×10^{219}

In Table 1, we present the amount of constraint check saving in the n-queens problem using GT with our model (HASCOH+GT) and BT with our model (HASCOH+BT). Here, our objective is to find all solutions. The results show that the amount of constraint check saving was significant in HASCOH+GT and Mod+BT due to the fact that our model classifies the constraints in the appropriate order, so that the tightest constraints were checked first, and inconsistent tuples were discarded earlier.

Random Problems: Benchmark sets are used to test algorithms for specific problems. However, in recent years, there has been a growing interest in the study of the relation among the parameters that define an instance of CSP in general (i.e., the number of variables,number of constraints, domain size, arity of constraints, etc). Therefore, the notion of randomly generated CSPs has been introduced to describe the classes of CSPs. These classes are then studied using empirical methods.

In our empirical evaluation, each set of random constraint satisfaction problems was defined by the 4-tuple $< n, c, s, d >$, where n was the number of variables, c the number of hard constraints, s the number of soft constraints and d the domain size. The problems were randomly generated by modifying these parameters. We considered all constraints as global constraints, that is, all constraints had maximum arity. Thus, Table 2 sets three of the parameters and varies the other one in order to evaluate the algorithm performance when this parameter increases. We evaluated 100 test cases for each type of problem and each value of the variable parameter.

Table 2. Number of constraint checks using Backtracking filtered with Arc-Consistency

problems	BT-AC constraint checks	HASCOH +BT-AC constraint checks	problems	BT-AC constraint checks	HASCOH +BT-AC constraint checks
$< 5, 5, 5, 10 >$	14226.5	2975.5	$< 3, 5, 5, 10 >$	150.3	33.06
$< 5, 10, 5, 10 >$	60250.3	5714.2	$< 3, 5, 5, 20 >$	260.4	55.2
$< 5, 20, 5, 10 >$	203542.2	12548.5	$< 3, 5, 5, 30 >$	424.3	85.26
$< 5, 30, 5, 10 >$	325487.4	17845.7	$< 3, 5, 5, 50 >$	970.5	180.1
$< 5, 50, 5, 10 >$	513256.7	24875.5	$< 3, 5, 5, 70 >$	2104.8	380.9
$< 5, 75, 5, 10 >$	704335.1	34135.3	$< 3, 5, 5, 90 >$	4007.4	701.7
$< 5, 100, 5, 10 >$	895415.3	43396.6	$< 3, 5, 5, 110 >$	7851.4	1205.1

The number of constraint checks using BT filtered by *arc-consistency* (as a preprocessing) (BT-AC) and BT-AC using our model (HASCOH+BT-AC) is presented in Table 2. On the left side of the table, we present the number of constraint checks in problems where the number of hard constraints was increased from 5 to 100 and the number of variables, soft constraints and the domain size were set at 5,5 and 10, respectively: $< 5, c, 5, 10 >$. The results show that the number of constraint checks was reduced in all cases. On the right side of the table, we present the number of constraint checks in problems where the domain size was increased from 10 to 110 and the number of variables, the number of hard constraints and the number of soft constraints were set at 3,5 and 5, respectively: $< 3, 5, 5, d >$. The results were similar and the number of constraint checks was also reduced in all cases.

6   Conclusions and Future Work

In this paper, we propose a distributed model for solving Constraint Satisfaction Problems (CSPs) in which agents are committed to solving their partial problems by means of search algorithms. The solutions are incrementally created by each hard block agent in order to satisfied the hard constraints and as many soft constraints as possible. Hard and soft constraints are ordered to reduce the number of constraint checks.

As future work, we are working on a distributed model in which *block agents* can dynamically interchange constraints, depending on the evaluation values, so that the preprocessing agent can be removed and block agents can carry out this constraint partition.

References

1. R. Barták, 'Constraint programming: In pursuit of the holy grail', *in Proceedings of WDS99 (invited lecture), Prague, June*, (1999).
2. C. Bessière, P. Meseguer, E.C. Freuder, and J. Larrosa, 'On forward checking for non-binary constraint satisfaction', *Artifical Intelligence*, 205–224, (2002).
3. J.R. Bitner and Reingold E.M., 'Backtracking programming techniques', *Communications of the ACM 18*, 651–655, (1975).
4. I.P. Gent, E. MacIntyre, P. Prosser, and T Walsh, 'The constrainedness of arc consistency', *Principles and Practice of Constraint Programming*, 327–340, (1997).
5. R.M. Haralick and Elliot G.L., 'Increasing tree search efficiency for constraint satisfaction problems', *Artificial Intelligence*, **14**, 263–313, (1980).
6. V. Kumar, 'Depth first search', *In Encyclopedia of Artificial Intelligence*, **2**, 1004–1005, (1987).
7. V. Kumar, 'Algorithms for constraint satisfaction problems: a survey', *Artificial Intelligence Magazine*, **1**, 32–44, (1992).
8. M.A. Salido and F. Barber, 'A polynomial algorithm for continuous non-binary disjunctive CSPs: extended DLRs', *Knowledge-Based Systems, In press*, **16**, (2003).
9. E. Tsang, *Foundation of Constraint Satisfaction*, Academic Press, 1993.
10. R. Wallace and E. Freuder, 'Ordering heuristics for arc consistency algorithms', *In Proc. of Ninth Canad. Conf. on A.I.*, 163–169, (1992).
11. M. Yokoo, E.H. Durfee, T. Ishida, and K. Kuwabara, 'The distributed constraint satisfaction problem: Formalization and algorithms', *Knowledge and Data Engineering*, 673–685, (1998).

Dynamic User Modeling
in a System for Personalization of Web Contents*

Alberto Díaz[1] and Pablo Gervás[2]

[1] CES Felipe II – Universidad Complutense de Madrid
C/ Capitán 39, 28300 Aranjuez, Madrid
adiaz@cesfelipesegundo.com
[2] Departamento de Sistemas Informáticos y Programación
Facultad de Informática, Universidad Complutense de Madrid
c/ Juan del Rosal, 8, Madrid 28040
pgervas@sip.ucm.es

Abstract. This paper presents a system for personalization of web contents based on a user model that stores long term and short term interests. Long term interests are modeled through the selection of categories and keywords for which the user need information. However, user needs change over time as a result of his interaction with received information. For this reason, the user model must be capable of adapting to those shifts in interest. In our case, this adaptation or dynamic modeling is performed by a short term model obtained from user provided feedback. The experiments that have been carried out determine that the combined use of long and short term models performs best when both categories and keywords are used for the long term model.

1 Introduction

Web content appears in many forms over different domains of application, but in most cases the form of presentation is the same for all users. The contents are static in the sense that they are not adapted to each user. Content personalization is a technique that tries to avoid information overload through the adaptation of web contents to each type of user.

A personalization system is based on 3 main functionalities: content selection, user model adaptation, and content generation. For these functionalities to be carried out in a personalized manner, they must be based on information related to the user that must be reflected in his user profile or user model (Mizarro&Tasso, 2002).

Content selection refers to the choice of the particular subset of all available documents that will be more relevant for a given user, as represented in his user profile or model. In order to effect this choice one must have a representation of the documents, a representation of the user profile, and a similarity function that computes the level of adequacy of one to the other.

---

* This research has been partially funded by the Ministerio de Ciencia y Tecnología (TIC2002-01961).

R. Conejo et al. (Eds.): CAEPIA-TTIA 2003, LNAI 3040, pp. 281–290, 2004.

User model adaptation is necessary because user needs change over time as a result of his interaction with information (Billsus&Pazzani, 2000). For this reason the user model must be capable of adapting to those interest changes, it must be dynamic. This adaptation is built upon the interaction of the user with the system, which provides the feedback information used to evolve the profile.

In our case, content generation involves generating a new result web document that contains, for each selected document, its title, its relevance as computed by the system, a summary, and a link to the full document.

In this paper we focus on user model adaptation and the various possible combinations of modeling alternatives for this process. The aim is to identify which is the best way of carrying out the user model adaptation process to improve content selection.

2 Available Methods and Techniques

Existing literature provides different techniques for defining user interests: keywords, stereotypes, semantic networks, neural networks, etc. A particular set of proposals (Chiu&Webb, 1998; Billsus&Pazzani, 2000) model users by combining long term and short term interests: the short term model represents the most recent user preferences and the long term model represents those expressed over a longer period of time. To determine whether a document is relevant for a given user the short term user model is used wherever it can provide a satisfactory answer. The long term model is used only as a backup solution for cases in which the short term model fails to provide an answer.

The representation of the text content of the documents is usually achieved by means of techniques based on term weight vectors (Salton, 1989). The vector associated with a document can be obtained by eliminating the words contained in a stop list and extracting the stems of the remaining words by means of a stemmer. Weights are usually calculated by means of the tf · idf formula, based on frequency of occurrence of terms (Salton, 1989).

Various classification algorithms are available for carrying out content selection depending on the particular representation chosen for user models and documents: cosine formula, rules associated to stereotypes, neural networks, nearest neighbour, naive Bayes classifier, etc.

The feedback techniques needed to achieve a dynamic modeling of the user are based on feedback given by the user with respect to the information elements selected according to his profile. The information obtained in this way can be used to update accordingly the user models in representation had been chosen: term weights, semantic networks, rules associated to stereotypes, etc.

In particular, a system based on intelligent agents is applied in (Nakashima &Nakamura97) to a digital newspaper. The user model stores "conscious" information about the user as terms with an associated weight and "unconscious" information as terms associated with aspects such as age, sex, occupation, marital status, city, etc. A selection is computed using a combination of both types of information. For the first one, relevance is based on "conscious" user terms appearing in the document, with additional relevance accorded to terms appearing in the title. For the second, a similar computation is applied over the terms associated with each aspect of the "unconscious" part of the model.

The next process must be carried out each day for each user u to obtain / update the user terms associated to the "conscious" part of the model:

Two set of documents are distinguished according to the feedback provided by the user: $R_u(+)$, is the set of documents for which the user has provided positive feedback, $R_u(-)$, is the set of documents for which no feedback has been provided. The set of all documents is R_u.

The access value for term t in document d for user u is defined as:

$$a_{tdu} = \begin{cases} P \cdot (T \cdot title_{td} + body_{td}) & si \, d \in R_u(+) \\ -N \cdot (T \cdot title_{td} + body_{td}) & si \, d \in R_u(-) \end{cases}$$ (1)

where $title_{td}$ is the frequency of appearance of term t in the title of document d, $body_{td}$ is the frequency of appearance of term t in the body of document d, P is the weight applied to positive feedback, N is the weight for no-feedback and T is the weight applied to the title. The particular values chosen are: $P = 0.9$, $N = 0.9$ and $T = 2$.

In this way, a term will have a high access value if it appears frequently in titles and bodies of documents with positive feedback, and it will have a low access value if it appears in documents for which no feedback is provided. This value computes the representativity of terms as a function of user feedback.

The update rate of a term t for a user u is computed as:

$$p_{tu} = \frac{\sum_{d \in R_u} a_{tdu}}{max(\left| \sum_{d \in R_u} a_{tdu} \right|)}$$ (2)

In this way, the access values for all the terms are added together and normalised to ensure that the term with highest update rate has value 1, and the rest take values between 0 and 1.

The new interest value for term t for user u is obtained with the following formula:

$$N_{tu} = \begin{cases} O_{tu} + ((1 - O_{tu}) \cdot S \cdot p_{tu}) & si \, p_{tu} \geq 0 \\ O_{tu} - (O_{tu} \cdot S \cdot |p_{tu}|) & si \, p_{tu} < 0 \end{cases}$$ (3)

where O_{tu} indicates the old interest value for term t for user u and S indicates the speed of change of the degree of interest of a term. The higher the value of S, the faster the degree of interest will change, in the sense that there will be more difference between its initial value and the new value. The value chosen for S is 0.8.

3 Our Proposal

We propose a browsable user model or user profile that represents user interests from three different points of view (Amato&Straccia, 1999). The user model stores three types of information: personal information, information concerning the format in which information is to be received, and specific information about user interests according to various reference systems that will be used to carry out the personalization.

When a user accesses an information filtering system, he defines a more or less static set of interests that are stored in his user profile. For Web personalization we can have a similar situation in which the user has a set of fixed reference interests about which he wants to receive information on a regular basis. These interests will make up the long term model. However, user needs change over time as a result of the interaction with information (Bilssus&Pazzani, 2000). For this reason, it is probable that the interests of a user will not remain static but will in the short term suffer temporary oscillations around this initial reference. The interests associated with these oscillations will constitute the short term model. Our proposal is based on the combination of both models to represent user's information needs.

Long term user interests are modelled with respect to two reference frameworks: one based on a domain specific system of classification, and another based on the content of the documents.

A basic reference system is the classification system specific to the particular domain under consideration - for instance, in a digital newspaper, this system will be based on the set of sections used by the newspaper -. This system is composed of a set of first level categories that represent different types of information - for instance, examples of sections of digital newspapers would be: national, international, sport, etc. Each web document belongs to a category of that classification system. Information concerning these categories is stored as a matrix where rows correspond to categories and columns correspond to users. Users may assign a weight to each category to indicate their interest in them (C_{cu}).

The other system of reference is based on the content of documents. The user can enter a number of keywords to characterise his interests. The appearance of these keywords in the documents will be taken to indicate that the document may be interesting to the user. For each keyword the user introduces a weight that indicates its importance to him. These keywords are stored, for each user u, as a term weight vector (k_u).

Short term interests are represented by means of feedback terms. These terms are obtained from user provided feedback over the documents he receives. That is, the user provides positive or negative feedback over the documents he receives, and a set of representative terms is extracted from them. This information is handled by the user model adaptation process, which returns a term weight vector (t_u) for each user.

This term weight vector is taken to represent the current short term interests of that user. Short terms interests tend to correspond to temporary information needs whose interest to the user wanes after a short period of time. Therefore their weight must be progressively decreased over time.

Documents are downloaded from the web as HTML documents. For each document, title, category, URL and text are extracted and stored for ulterior processing. Term weight vector representations are obtained by application of stop lists, stemmer, and the tf · idf formula for computing actual weights.

The only restrictions that must be fulfilled by a domain for the proposed model to be applicable are that there exist textual information associated with web documents and that a domain specific classification exist to classify the documents.

4 Content Selection

Content selection refers to the choice of those among the available documents that are particularly relevant for a user, according to his profile. Once particular representations have been fixed for documents and user model, it becomes feasible to establish which documents are more adequate for each user.

Since we have different reference frameworks in the user model we will indicate how content selection is performed with respect to each one of them, and later we will explore different possible combinations of the resulting selections. Combinations will be based on the relevance obtained for each document within each particular reference framework, and the relative weight used for each reference framework in a particular combination. For all combinations, the final result is a ranking of the set of documents according to the computed overall relevance.

4.1 Selection with Respect to the Long Term Model

As each web document has a preassigned category, selection with respect to this reference framework is immediate. Each document is assigned the weight associated with the corresponding category in the particular user model. The relevance between a document d, belonging to a category c, and a user model u is directly the value assigned to category c by user u:

$$r_{du}^c = C_{cu} \tag{4}$$

The relevance between a document d and the keywords of a user model is computed using the cosine formula for similarity within the vector space model (Salton, 1989):

$$r_{du}^k = sim(d_d, k_u) \tag{5}$$

When all documents have been ordered with respect to the various reference frameworks, the results are integrated using a particular combination of reference frameworks. Therefore, the total relevance between a document d and a user model u is computed with the following foyrmula:

$$r_{du}^l = \frac{\alpha r_{du}^c + \beta r_{du}^k}{\alpha + \beta} \tag{6}$$

where Greek letters α and β represent the importance assigned to each reference framework (α, for categories and β, for keywords). For this combination to be significant, relevance obtained for each framework must be normalised with respect to the best results for the document collection under consideration.

5   User Model Adaptation

Adaptation of the user model involves obtaining / updating a short term model of the user from the feedback information provided by the user. This model can be used to improve the process of selection in the personalization system.

5.1   Obtaining the Short Term Model

The short term model is obtained as a result of the process of adaptation of the user model. The user receives a web document that contains an automatically generated summary (Acero et al. 2001) for each of the 10 web documents that the system has found more relevant according to his user profile. With respect to this information the user may interact with the system by giving positive or negative feedback - refraining from providing feedback is interpreted as a contribution as well, taken to imply indifference - for each of the information elements that he has received. The feedback terms of the short term model are obtained from the news items for which either positive or negative feedback has been provided.

Because these terms represent an interest of the user over a short period of time, an algorithm is used to decrement their value over time: each day the starting value of the new weights is obtained by subtracting 0.1 from the previous day's value. Terms that reach a weight less or equal to 0 are eliminated from the model.

To select / update the new feedback terms all documents are preprocessed in the same way as was done for the selection process: stop lists and stemmer are applied. The starting point for the adaptation process are the terms of the representation of the documents, with their associated frequency (tf).

The algorithm in (Nakashima&Nakamura, 1997) is then applied to obtain the feedback terms. The feedback process for the "conscious" part of their model is used to obtain the short term model of our proposal. As an innovation, the set $R_u(-)$ is taken to be the set of documents for which the user has provided negative feedback. Also the set R_u is now the set of all documents for which feedback of some kind has been provided.

The final result of this process is a set of terms ordered according to their new interest value. A subset of them is selected - the 10 most relevant ones - to obtain / update the feedback terms of the short term model.

5.2   Selection with Respect to the Short Term Model

Relevance between a document d and a short term user model u is computed in the same way used for the keywords of the long term model, but using the term weight vector obtained in the process of adaptation of the user model:

$$r_{du}^{s} = r_{du}^{t} = sim(d_d, t_u)$$

(7)

5.3 Selection with Respect to the Combined Long Term - Short Term Model

When all documents have been ordered with respect to the different sources of relevance, the results are integrated using a particular combination of reference frameworks. Therefore, the total relevance between a document d and a user model u is computed with the following formula:

$$r_{du} = \frac{\chi r_{du}^c + \delta r_{du}^k + \varepsilon r_{du}^t}{\chi + \delta + \varepsilon} \tag{8}$$

where Greek letters χ, δ, and ε represent the importance assigned to each of the reference frameworks -χ, for categories, δ, for keywords, ε, for feedback terms. For this combination to be significant, the relevance obtained from each reference framework must be normalised with respect to the best results over the document collection being used.

6 Evaluation

As an example of web documents for experimentation we have chosen the web pages of the digital edition of a Spanish newspaper[1]. Experiments are evaluated over data collected for 11 users and the news items corresponding to 5 consecutive days - Monday to Friday - of the digital edition of the ABC Spanish newspaper. These days correspond to the period 6th -10th May 2002. The number of news items per day is respectively 128, 104, 87, 98 and 102.

To carry out the evaluation, judgements from the user are required as to which news items are relevant or not for each of the days of the experiment. To obtain these judgements users were requested to check the complete set of news items for each day, stating for each one whether it was considered interesting or not. Users were explicitly asked not to confine their judgements on interest to relevance with respect to the initial user profiles they had constructed on first accessing the system, but rather to include any news items that they found interesting on discovery, regardless of their similarity with respect to their initial description of their interest. It is hoped that enough information to cover these rogue items will be captured automatically and progressively by the system through the feedback adaptation process.

6.1 Metrics

Since our experimental set up combines a binary relevance judgement from the users and a ranking of news items provided by the system, it was decided to use normalised precision (Salton, 1989; Mizarro, 2001) as our evaluation metric. In addition, with respect to equal relevance values for consecutive positions of the ranking, the average ranking of the whole set of conflicting positions has been taken as ranking for each

---

[1] This provides a consistent format, which simplifies systematic processing.

and all of them. This adjustment avoids the problem of ordering items at random within the ranking when they have equal relevance.

Normalised precision is computed using the following formula:

$$Pr = 1 - \frac{\sum_{i=1}^{REL} \log RANK_i - \sum_{i=1}^{REL} \log i}{\log N! / ((N - REL)! REL!)} \qquad (9)$$

where REL is the number of relevant documents, $RANK_i$ is the ranking of document i, and N is the total number of documents.

6.2 Statistical Significance

Data are considered statistically significant if they pass the *sign-test*, with paired samples, at a level of significance of 5% ($p \leq 0.05$). This decision is based on the fact that no specific assumption is made concerning the distribution of data, and that due to the different normalisation processes carried out, it is more convenient to consider relative values instead of absolute values (Salton, 1989).

6.3 Experiments

The following experiments have been carried out to check the validity of the proposed model. Each experiment combines different possibilities for long term modeling - only categories, only keywords, and categories and keywords together - either acting on their own or in combination with the short term model. This implies giving different values to the parameters χ, δ and ε of formula (8).

6.3.1 Experiment 1

This experiment compares the long term model using only keywords L(Ke) (χ=0, δ=1, ε=0), with the short term model S (χ=0, δ=0, ε=1) and with a combination of both models L(Ke)S (χ=0, δ=1, ε=1).

Table 1. Relative increments in normalised precision between different combinations of L(Ke) and S, L(Ca) and S, and L(Ca,Ke) and S.

Experiment 1	Pr	Experiment 2	Pr	Experiment 3	Pr
L(Ke)S > L(Ke)	26.9	L(Ca)S > L(Ca)	26.9	L(Ca,Ke)S > L(Ca,Ke)	8.5
L(Ke)S > S	16.1	L(Ca)S > S	29.0	L(Ca,Ke)S > S	32.9
S > L(Ke)	8.5	L(Ca) > S	10.9	L(Ca,Ke) > S	22.4

The only statistically significant result (Table 1) is that L(Ke)S > L(Ke). This means that combining the long and short term models, is better than using only the long term model. There is also a relative improvement of the combination with respect to the short term model, but it is not statistically significant. The short term model performs better than the long term model, but again not significantly.

6.3.2 Experiment 2

This experiment compares the long term model using only categories L(Ca) (χ=1, δ=0, ε=0), with the short term model S (χ=0, δ=0, ε=1) and with the combination of both models L(Ca)S (χ=1, δ=0, ε=1).

The statistically significant results (Table 1) are that L(Ca)S > S and L(Ca)S > L(Ca). This means that the combination is always better than using each model separately. The long term model performs better than the short term, but without significance.

6.3.3 Experiment 3

This experiment compares the long term model using both categories and keywords L(Ca,Ke) (χ=1, δ=1, ε=0), with the short term model S (χ=0, δ=0, ε=1) and with the combination of both models L(Ca,Ke)S (χ=1, δ=1, ε=1).

All results are statistically significant (Table 1). This means that the combination performs better than either model on its own, and the long term model is better than the short term model.

6.3.4 Experiment 4

This experiment compares the best performing combinations of previous experiments - long and short term models used together - when the long term model is built using only keywords L(Ke)S (χ=0, δ=1, ε=1), only categories L(Ca)S (χ=1, δ=0, ε=1) and a combination of both L(Ca,Ke)S (χ=1, δ=1, ε=1).

Table 2. Relative increments in normalised precision between different combinations of L and S together.

	Pr
L(Ca,Ke)S > L(Ca)S	2.9
L(Ca,Ke)S > L(Ke)S	12.6
L(Ca)S > L(Ke)S	11.2

All results are statistically significant (Table 2). This means that the long term / short term combination that uses categories and keywords in the long term model is better than the combinations that use either only categories or only keywords for the long term model. Using categories only for the long term model is better than using keywords only.

7 Conclusions

This paper presents the improvement in personalisation achieved by the inclusion of a process of user model adaptation, due to the fact that the selection that is obtained by combining the long term and short term profiles performs better than the one obtained by using the long term model on its own.

The results show that using a combination of a long term model based on categories and keywords, together with a short term model, improves the adaptation to the user because values of normalised precision increase.

The only restrictions for this model to be applicable to a particular domain are that there exist textual information associated to each web document, and that a domain dependent classification be available to classify the documents to be considered.

References

1. Amato, G. & Straccia, U., 1999. "User Profile Modeling and Applications to Digital Libraries". Third European Conference on Research and Advanced Technology for Digital Libraries (ECDL'99), Springer-Verlab LNCS 1696, pp. 184-197.
2. Acero, I., Alcojor, M., Díaz, A., Gómez, J.M., Maña, M., 2001. "Generación automática de resúmenes personalizados". Procesamiento del Lenguaje Natural, 27 (2001), pp. 281-290.
3. Billsus, D. & Pazzani. M.J., 2000. "User Modeling for Adaptive News Access", User Modeling and User-Adapted Interaction Journal 10(2-3), pp. 147-180.
4. Chiu, B. & Webb, G., 1998. "Using decision trees for agent modeling: improving prediction performance", User Modeling and User-Adapted Interaction (8), pp. 131-152.
5. Mizzaro, S., 2001. "A New Measure Of Retrieval Effectiveness (or: What's Wrong With Precision And Recall)". International Workshop on Information Retrieval (IR'2001), Infotech Oulu, pp. 43-52.
6. Mizarro, S. & Tasso, C., 2002. "Ephemeral and Persistent Personalization in Adaptive Information Access to Scholarly Publications on the Web". 2nd International Conference on Adaptive Hypermedia and Adaptive Web Based Systems, Málaga, España, Mayo 2002.
7. Nakashima, T. & Nakamura, R., 1997. "Information Filtering for the Newspaper". IEEE Pacific Rim Conference on Communications, Computers and Signal Processing, August 1997. Victoria, B.C., Canada.
8. Salton, G., 1989. Automatic Text Processing: The Transformation, Analysis and Retrieval of Information by Computer, Addison-Wesley Publishing, Reading, Massachusets, 1989.

Embracing Causality
in Inducing the Effects of Actions

Ramon P. Otero

Department of Computer Science
University of Corunna
Corunna 15071, Galicia, Spain
otero@udc.es

Abstract. The following problem will be considered: from scattered examples on the behavior of a dynamic system induce a description of the system. For the induced description to be concise and modular, we use a generic action formalism based on causality, that is representable in logic programming. It is relatively simple to induce a description of a dynamic system that suffers from the frame problem. The known solutions to the frame problem require a non-monotonic formalism. Unfortunately induction under non-monotonic formalisms, e.g. normal logic programs, is not well understood yet. We present a method for induction under the non-monotonic behavior needed to solve the frame problem. Technically we introduce a causality predicate for the target fluent and induce a description of the causality of the fluent instead of the fluent itself. The description of causality together with the appropriate inertia axiom models the behavior of the original target fluent. The main advantage of this method is that the induction of the effects of actions can be made with well known induction methods on monotonic formalisms, such as Horn programs.

1   Introduction

Over the years, the problem of learning a description of a dynamic system was extensively considered, e.g., in the area of learning automata. Automata-based descriptions are clearly understood and have efficient algorithms for inference. But it is not easy to extend a description to cope with additional behaviors and the size of the description becomes very large for actual domains.

In this work we will consider action formalisms, an alternative approach for describing dynamic systems. From a point of view of automata, action formalisms provide a concise and highly modular description of the transition relation of the domain. Action formalims are logic-based, but unfortunately rely on non-monotonic logics.

The method of addressing this learning problem, started from Inductive Logic Programming (ILP). In this area of machine learning, a logic program is induced from examples of its conclusions. Some action formalisms can be represented in logic programs. Then induction of action descriptions can be solved with ILP.

R. Conejo et al. (Eds.): CAEPIA-TTIA 2003, LNAI 3040, pp. 291–301, 2004.
© Springer-Verlag Berlin Heidelberg 2004

Other authors already followed this method [Moyle 2002, Lorenzo and Otero 2000] with restricted success. The reason is that ILP methods are only defined for definite logic programs, while action formalisms need normal programs to represent the nonmonotonic behavior using negation as failure (NAF). In definite logic programs, action descriptions have the frame problem (section 3).

The method followed in this work appeals to causality. Causality in action has provided solutions to the frame and ramification problems still to be solved in other formalisms. In induction, causality will provide a method to translate the nonmonotonic induction problem of the effects of actions to a form in which monotonic methods of ILP can be used, nevertheless providing a complete method for induction of action descriptions, and solving the frame problem in induction.

In the next section induction of the effects of actions is defined after a short introduction of action formalisms and ILP. Section 3 shows the presence of the frame problem in monotonic induction. The method of induction is presented in section 4 with some examples and characterization results. Then the method is extended (section 5) for its applicability to realistic domains. We conclude discussing the results and commenting on related work.

2   Induction of Action Descriptions

Every action description of a dynamic system distinguish between the evolving properties of the domain that are represented by *fluents*, and the *actions* that cause change in these properties. In logic programing, actions and fluents are represented as predicates. The steps through which the domain evolves are represented by a situation term, that is given as argument to every fluent $f(S)$, and action $a(S)$.

Then an action description, in logic programming, is a set of program rules with the following general form,

$$f(S) \leftarrow a(S), \ prev(S, PS), \ f'(PS), \ldots \tag{1}$$

Where f stands for a fluent and a for an action. The fluent atoms $f'(PS)$ are optional and always refer to the previous situation PS (assume the appropriate definition for predicate $prev(S, PS)$, e.g. $prev(2, 1)$). These rules are called *action laws* and describe the effects of performing action a at situation S as some fluent f being true at the same situation, under the *precondition* that other fluents $f'(PS)$ are true at the previous situation. Note that no reference far from the previous situation is allowed and that the rules cannot use constants in situation arguments, i.e. action laws hold for every situation.

Descriptions like this can be used to infer the effects of performing a sequence of actions from an initial state of the domain (*temporal prediction*). To this end a set of facts on the fluents at the initial situation, e.g. $f(0) \leftarrow$, $f'(0) \leftarrow$, and a corresponding set for the sequence of actions, e.g. $a(1) \leftarrow$, $a'(2) \leftarrow$, $a(3) \leftarrow$, is added to the program. The effects correspond to the consequences of the program on fluents at the different situations.

When inducing the effect of actions, the problem is somehow the opposite. From a set of ground instances of fluents and actions at the situations inside a sequence infer the corresponding set of rules. Following usual methods, we will define induction for one fluent at a time.

Note that the representation we introduced so far, does not allow for ground descriptions starting at different initial states (with different sets of ground fluent facts at situation 0) to be present simultaneously inside the program. Then we introduce another reference for the initial state that is also given as argument to every fluent and action. An action law will have the general form[1] $f(S, N) \leftarrow a(S, N),\ prev(S, PS),\ f'(PS, N), \ldots$ while a ground fact like $f(2, n1)$ will represent fluent f is true at situation 2 when starting from initial state $n1$.

Even in the case of fixed initial state, we cannot represent different sequences of actions in the program. Lets call *narrative* a particular sequence of actions starting from a particular initial state. The term we added before will be used to allow the representation of different narratives in the program.

Definition 1 (Induction of Effects of Actions) *Let*

i) A_i be a set of ground facts on the actions at the situations in a narrative i,
ii) F_i' a corresponding set of ground facts on the fluents at the same narrative,
iii) F_i^+ (positive examples) a set of ground facts on some selected target fluent f, and
iv) F_i^- (negative examples) another set of ground facts on it.

Given several collections of these four sets for different narratives, a set of rules P in the form of action laws is a solution to induction of target fluent f if and only if, for every narrative i,

$$(P \cup F_i' \cup A_i) \models F_i^+ \quad and \tag{2}$$
$$(P \cup F_i' \cup A_i) \not\models F_i^- \tag{3}$$

The definition follows those of a general induction problem in ILP. From a set of positive examples E^+ and negative examples E^- on some predicate, and under some background Horn program B, a set of definite rules H is solution iff $B \cup H \models E^+$, $B \cup H \not\models E^-$, being also $B \cup H \not\models \bot$. The correspondence with induction in actions is $E^+ = \bigcup_i F_i^+$, $E^- = \bigcup_i F_i^-$, $B = \bigcup_i (A_i \cup F_i')$, and $H = P$.

In particular we will use the method of Inverse Entailment (IE) [Muggleton 1995], for which an efficient implementation, called Progol, is available. IE and its implementation Progol, allows the specification of the intended form of the induced rules through the use of *mode declarations*. Search is then restricted to this bias. This is important for induction in actions, because any solution not in the form of an action law will not actually constitute a solution. Under some conditions, IE is a complete induction method [Muggleton 1998] for Horn programs providing every solution in the form of definite rules, this will be enough for the induction of the effect of actions.

---

[1] When it is clear from the context, we usually omit this additional reference to N to improve readability.

3   The Frame Problem in Induction

To show the existence of the frame problem in induction consider the simple
well-known example of the Yale Shoting Scenario (YSS). There is a turkey and
a gun, the gun can be loaded or not, and the turkey will be dead when shooting
with the gun loaded. There are actions shoot s, load l, and wait w; and fluents
loaded ld, and dead d. An example of a learning problem in this scenario is the
induction of a description of fluent d from sets of examples on narratives like the
following.

situation	0	1	2	3	4	5
dead		nd	nd	nd	nd	d	d
loaded		nld	nld	ld	ld	ld	ld
actions			s	l	w	s	w

Where nd (not dead) is the complementary fluent to d and nld the complementary of ld; recall that actions are represented at the same situation of their
effects, instead of the previous one. A direct coding of this problem in the ILP
system Progol can be as follows.

$$
\begin{aligned}
B \quad & nld(0).\ nld(1).\ ld(2).\ ld(3).\ ld(4).\ ld(5).\ \ldots \\
& s(1).\ l(2).\ w(3).\ s(4).\ w(5).\ \ldots \\
E^+ \quad & d(4).\ d(5).\ \ldots \\
& nd(0).\ nd(1).\ nd(2).\ nd(3).\ \ldots \\
E^- \quad & :-d(0).\ :-d(1).\ :-d(2).\ :-d(3).\ \ldots \\
& :-nd(4).\ :-nd(5).\ \ldots \\
\hline
H \quad & d(S):-\ s(S),\ prev(S,PS),\ ld(PS). \\
& d(S):-\ w(S),\ prev(S,PS),\ d(PS). \\
& d(S):-\ l(S),\ prev(S,PS),\ d(PS). \\
& nd(S):-\ w(S),\ prev(S,PS),\ nd(PS). \\
& nd(S):-\ l(S),\ prev(S,PS),\ nd(PS). \\
& nd(S):-\ s(S),\ prev(S,PS),\ nld(PS),\ nd(PS).
\end{aligned}
$$

The facts and constraints grouped under B, E^+ and E^- are the input to the
system. The negative examples on E^- are represented as constraints. The rules
grouped under H are the induced output by the Progol system. (Not shown is a
ground description of predicate $prev(S,PS)$ also in B.)Looking at H, two kinds
of rules have been induced, with the general forms:

$$f(S) \leftarrow a(S),\ prev(S,PS),\ f'(PS) \tag{4}$$

$$f(S) \leftarrow a(S),\ prev(S,PS),\ f(PS),\ f'(PS) \tag{5}$$

Where f stands for a fluent (d and nd) and a for an action, being f' a fluent
different from f. Rules in the form (4) are (genuine) action laws, while those in
the form (5) are called *frame axioms*. Note the number of frame axioms (five)
compared with action laws (one).

Action laws explain the example instances when there is a change in truth,
e.g. $d(4)$ true after $d(3)$ false. Frame axioms explain the example instances when

they persisted from the previous situation, note the head fluent $f(S)$ is also a condition of the rule at the previous situation $f(PS)$. Indeed all the rules are needed because all of the examples provided must be covered by H solution.

Every representation of actions must contain rules that describe persistent fluents after an action. It is the form of these rules – and the number of them – that states whether a representation has or not the frame problem. In the solution induced we have one frame axiom for each combination of fluent and action in the domain. Precisely because H contains so many frame axioms, the description induced has the frame problem. The frame problem is solved when the description of persistent fluents is made in a compact form, typically with a single rule for each fluent without referencing any action, or with a single rule for the domain, lets call these rules *inertia axioms*. For example, the rules $d(S) := prev(S, PS), d(PS), not\ nd(S)$ and $nd(S) := prev(S, PS), nd(PS), not\ d(S)$ would replace the five frame axioms.

Most of the methods of induction are defined on monotonic formalisms, then it can be said that every solution on them will have the frame problem. There are also some restricted nonmonotonic induction methods, but as far as our knowledge, their applicability on the frame problem has not been shown. Methods of nonmonotonic induction are still under study. It must be also said that as far as the induced model of the domain, solutions with the frame problem contain all the possible solutions. Solving the frame problem in induction will not provide additional models for the domain.

4   The Method

The method is based on the following. Frame axioms are induced because there are examples on fluents that persist. But we actually know the compact form for these rules, the inertia axioms, given the set of fluents. If the induction method were able to work under nonmonotonic normal programs, just making the inertia axioms present during induction in the background B, would provide solutions free from the frame problem.

Nevertheless there is a simple alternative, if frame axioms cover persistent examples, we can avoid their induction by not providing the persistent examples. In order to carefully make the selection of examples, we appeal to causality. A generic causal formalism of action will be used, that can be consider a summary of different causal approaches [Lin 1995,Gustafsson and Doherty 1996].

Step 1. For every fluent in the domain, define two predicates $f(S)$ and $nf(S)$, to represent when the fluent is true and when it is false. Add also the constraint

$$:- f(S), nf(S). \tag{6}$$

This representation avoids the CWA of LP for fluents and allows the reference to the negative fluent without using NAF, thus inside definite LP. The CWA for fluents is not interesting, because when some fluent instance cannot be proved it is better to assume it persisted than to assume it is false.

Step 2. For the target fluent $f(S)$ define an additional fluent $pf(S)$ (also $pnf(S)$ for $nf(S)$) as follows,

$$pf(S) :- f(S),\ prev(S, PS),\ nf(PS). \tag{7}$$

$$pnf(S) :- nf(S),\ prev(S, PS),\ f(PS). \tag{8}$$

Fluent $pf(S)$ is the causality predicate representing when the target fluent $f(S)$ is caused (and true). (Respectively $pnf(S)$ represents the target is caused and false.) From the set of examples on the target fluent f, these two rules will extract the corresponding set of examples on its causality. These two rules represent the initial idea of causality, namely, when there is a change in a fluent, the fluent must be caused.

Step 3. For the target fluent $f(S)$ define the fluent $npf(S)$ (also $npnf(S)$ for $nf(S)$) as follows,

$$npf(S) :- nf(S). \tag{9}$$

$$npnf(S) :- f(S). \tag{10}$$

Fluent $npf(S)$ is the complementary of $pf(S)$, i.e. represents the target fluent $f(S)$ is not caused. As in the previous step, from the set of examples, these two rules will extract the corresponding set on its non-causality. Note that non-causality is not defined from a persistent example, but instead from the complementary fluent being true. The fluent cannot be caused and true if it is false. Instead, if non-caused is defined from persistent, some solutions will be forbiden.

Step 4. Apply a complete monotonic induction method of ILP, e.g. IE, as in Definition 1 but with target fluent $pf(S)$ (then also for $pnf(S)$) instead of the original target $f(S)$. The instances of $pf(S)$ being the positive examples and those of $npf(S)$ the negative ones for the induction of $pf(S)$. (Respectively the instances on $pnf(S)$ and $npnf(S)$, are the positive and negative examples for $pnf(S)$.) The causality of the target fluent will be induced in the form of action laws:

$$pf(S) :- a(S),\ prev(S, PS),\ f'(PS), \ldots \tag{11}$$

Note that the induced rules cannot correspond to frame axioms, simply because we did not provide positive examples on persistent fluents.

Step 5. To complete the solution add to the induced causal action laws (11) the inertia axiom for the original target $f(S)$, and a rule transfering causality to truth. (Also for the complementary $nf(S)$, not shown.)

$$f(S) :- prev(S, PS),\ f(PS),\ not\ pnf(S). \tag{12}$$

$$f(S) :- pf(S) \tag{13}$$

Recall the example on the YSS. We already used step 1 defining f and nf for each fluent. After steps 2 and 3 are applied we got the following extended description of the example narrative.

situation	0	1	2	3	4	5
dead	nd	nd	nd	nd	d	d
loaded	nld	nld	ld	ld	ld	ld
actions		s	l	w	s	w
caused E$^+$					pd	
caused E$^-$	npd	npd	npd	npd		

At step 4 the following is provided to the ILP system Progol.

B $nld(0).\ nld(1).\ ld(2).\ ld(3).\ ld(4).\ ld(5).\ \dots$
$s(1).\ l(2).\ w(3).\ s(4).\ w(5).\ \dots$
$d(4).\ d(5).\ \dots$
$nd(0).\ nd(1).\ nd(2).\ nd(3).\ \dots$
E^+ $pd(4).\ \dots$
E^- $:- pd(0).\ :- pd(1).\ :- pd(2).\ :- pd(3).\ \dots$
H $pd(S) :- s(S),\ prev(S, PS),\ ld(PS).$

A single rule in H is enough to cover all the causality of dead. The solution to induction is H and the rules (step 5):

$$d(S) :- prev(S, PS),\ d(PS),\ not\ pnd(S).$$
$$d(S) :- pd(S)$$

Unfortunately the method is only applicable (see step 2) to narratives verifying a condition on the target fluent instances. In the next section the method will be extended to cope with this restriction.

Definition 2 (complete narrative) *A narrative is* target-complete *if there is a ground fact on the target fluent at every situation in the narrative.*

Theorem 1. *For narratives* target-complete *solutions by the method correspond one-to-one to solutions of induction of the effects of actions without the frame problem (Definition 1).*   ■

Completeness and soundness of the method rely on the completeness (and soundness) of the monotonic ILP method used (It must be complete at least for solutions in the form of action laws and the additional restrictions required must also hold). The induction of the causality of the target fluent pf is induction in Horn LP, thus every solution is provided. On the other hand, the completeness and soundness also rely on the solution to the frame problem used being an actual solution to it, e.g., every solution with the frame problem has a corresponding representation with inertia axioms and vice versa. To complete the proof note that the examples on the causality of the target are selected to allow every possible causality: when there is a change in the fluent, it must be caused thus an action law is needed to cover these examples; but for negative examples only those on which the complementary fluent holds are provided, in these examples the fluent cannot be caused and true. For any other case, there can be solutions with or without the fluent caused. Finally, every solution by the method does not have the frame problem because no induction on persistent fluent instances is done.

5   Dealing with Missing Examples

Consider the following motivating example on a narrative in the YSS. There is a missing example on the target fluent at situation 3 (the narrative is not target-complete).

situation	0	1	2	3	4
dead		nd	nd	nd	?	d
loaded		nld	nld	nld	ld	ld
actions			s	w	l		s
caused E^+					$pd?$	$pd?$
caused E^-	npd	npd	npd	$npd?$	

By step 2 of the method causality is defined from two consecutive example instances. Then because of missing example at situation 3, no $pf(3)$ nor $pf(4)$ is obtained (nor $npd(3)$). Nevertheless it is clear that there is a change between situations 2 and 4. If a causality example is not provided here, target instance $d(4)$ will not be covered by some solutions, what makes the method unsound.

Missing example instances in the target predicate are common in learning. It is precisely because of these missing instances that alternative solutions to induction provide different generalizations; in this sense, more missing instances allow more generalization in the solution. Induction in action seems to behave the other way around, missing examples instead of facilitating induction turn it more complex. Note also that there is no problem with missing examples when induction is directly applied as showed before. But recall also that all these solutions have the frame problem. This points out the close relationship between dealing with missing examples and solving the frame problem in induction. In the discussion section, we comment on this.

The extension of the method is based on the following. Consider a narrative with a *missing segment*, i.e., several consecutive situations without example on the target fluent. Consider also that the examples just before and after the missing segment are complementary, e.g. nf and f; it is clear that there is a change in a situation in the missing segment or in the situation just after the segment, but the narrative does not tell where it is. Thus a missing segment like this represents the following input for induction: there is a positive example on causality among the situation instances inside the segment and the inmediate next situation.

Learning problems from examples provided as before have been already considered in machine learning under Multiple Instance (MI) learning. MI methods are able to deal with induction problems where each positive example is specified by a set of instances, instead of just one, meaning that at least one of the instances in the set is a positive example, but it is not known which one. MI methods can be represented in general ILP systems (see for instance [Finn et al.1998]) and we will follow this approach to extend the method for missing segments while still relying on regular ILP. The extension is presented by describing the additional tasks at the steps of the restricted method.

Step 1. (cont.) Define an extra argument for every action, e.g. $a(ES, S)$. For every missing segment in every narrative define a new constant to name it, e.g. $m34$, and give this constant as argument ES to every ground action inside the segment and to the action at the immediate situation after the missing segment, e.g. $l(m34, 3)$. For the rest of the action instances the ES argument is that of the situation, e.g. $w(2, 2)$. The extra argument on actions is used to denote the missing segment the action belongs to, in case there is one.

Step 2. (cont.) For every missing segment with complementary target instances at the situations immediately before and after the segment, a caused instance is defined as follows: If the situation inmediately after the segment has an f (resp. nf) instance define $pf(es)$ (resp. $pnf(es)$), where es is the constant name of the missing segment. Note that a single instance of causality is extracted from a missing segment, and that the instance is at the segment (es) as a whole.

Step 3. (no extension needed)

Step 4. (cont.) Now the induced action laws will have one of the forms:

$$pf(S) :\!- \ a(S, S), \ prev(S, PS), \ f'(PS), \ldots \tag{14}$$

$$pf(ES) :\!- \ a(ES, S), \ prev(S, PS), \ f'(PS), \ldots \tag{15}$$

Modify rules (15) by making the situation variable of pf that of S, the (regular) situation of the action in the rule. Then discard in every rule the extra situation argument of the action, so the rules become the usual action laws.

Step 5. (no extension needed)

For the previous example on the YSS with a missing segment, after the extensions at step 1 and 2 are applied we have,

situation	0	1	2	3	4
dead		nd	nd	nd	$?$	d
loaded		nld	nld	nld	ld	ld
actions			$s(1,1)$	$w(2,2)$	$l(m34,3)$	$s(m34,4)$
caused E^+						$pd(m34)$
caused E^-	npd	npd	npd		

After steps 3 and 4, the single rule induced H is

$$pd(ES) :\!- \ s(ES, S), \ prev(S, PS), \ ld(PS).$$

that is transformed in the familiar rule $pd(S) :\!- \ s(S), \ prev(S, PS), \ ld(PS)$. And step 5 (as before) completes the solution.

Theorem 2. *Solutions by the extended method correspond one-to-one to solutions of induction of the effects of actions without the frame problem (Definition 1).* ∎

Intuitively, the method works as follows. When induction has to cover one caused example at a missing segment $pf(es)$, any of the actions at the segment can be choosen by using the reference es on them. Once a particular action is selected $a(es, s)$ the exact situation of change in the segment is also fixed, s, then any other reference for preconditions on other fluents is restricted to that situation s.

6 Discussion and Related Work

The method is applicable to induction under other causal formalisms of action [Lin 1995,Gustafsson and Doherty 1996] as the differences with the causality used here are not important for action laws.

Furthermore though causality is used during induction, it can be discarded in the final solutions making the method valid for action formalisms without causality. As an example the following transformation provides descriptions of actions in Answer Set Programming (ASP) [Lifschitz 1999].

Step 5. (alt.) (adapted for ASP) For every induced causal action laws (11) put the head directly on the original target $f(S)$, instead of the causal fluent pf.

Complete the solution adding the following inertia axiom for the original target $f(S)$, (Also for the complementary $nf(S)$, not shown.)

$$f(S) :- prev(S, PS), \ f(PS), \ not \ nf(S). \tag{16}$$

This example points out that the descriptions induced are valid also for temporal explanation problems and for planning, besides temporal prediction. For instance, in ASP these problems can be solved after the addition of general rules for the fluents at the initial situation (temporal explanation), and general rules providing every possible sequence of actions (planning). These 'generation' rules do not depend on the behavior of the domain but on its signature (like inertia axioms).

One important area of application of the method is planning. The domain description in planning is usually based on STRIPS. The main difference with our causal formalism is the existence in STRIPS of a global unique precondition for every effect of an action. The method can be easily adapted to induce for these languages. On the other hand note that the solution to the frame problem in STRIPS-like representations is implicit, i.e. there is no explicit inertia axiom rule in the descriptions. Our method solves the frame problem in a general form that is also valid for STRIPS-like representations.

Two other approaches followed the same initial idea, namely induce action descriptions with ILP. In [Moyle and Muggleton 1997] the approach was introduced for Event Calculus descriptions, being [Moyle 2002] the most recent work. The methods proposed there are different and rely on working with NAF rules (for inertia) during induction, but it has been shown [Sakama 2000] [Otero 2001] that monotonic induction does not extend well to normal programs. The approach in [Lorenzo and Otero 2000] also uses some causality, in the sense that the examples on causality must be directly provided, and must be complete, i.e. a CWA on them is assumed, thus the so called nonmonotonic setting in induction is used. This restricts the range of applicability of the method, as causality is usually not directly observable in the domains. In our approach causality is extracted from observations in the truth of fluents, and no CWA is assumed on it. Furthermore we allow also direct examples on the fluent pf. An important difference with these two approaches is that they are restricted to target-complete narratives. This can be understood as 'solving' the frame problem in induction by translating the frame problem to the evidence (set of examples) that must be complete, including every change and every non-change. As we mentioned before, non-monotonic ILP methods [Sakama 2000,Otero 2001] would provide alternatives to solve the frame problem. But currently they are defined under strong restrictions [Sakama 2000] and seem not enough to deal with the frame problem. Or they are not as efficient as monotonic ones [Otero 2001]. Note that even if a general nonmonotonic ILP method were available, methods using them would be less efficient than the one presented here.

References

[Finn *et al.*1998] P. Finn, S. Muggleton, D. Page, and A. Srinivasan. Pharmacophore discovery using the inductive logic programming system progol. *Machine Learning*, 30:241–271, 1998.

[Gustafsson and Doherty 1996] J. Gustafsson and P. Doherty. Embracing occlusion in specifying the indirect effects of actions. In *Proc. of the 5th Int. Conf. on Principles of Knowledge Representation and Reasoning*, 1996.

[Lifschitz 1999] V. Lifschitz. Action languages, answer sets and planning. In *The Logic Programming Paradigm: a 25-Year Perspective*, pages 357–373. Springer Verlag, 1999.

[Lin 1995] Fangzhen Lin. Embracing causality in specifying the indirect effects of actions. In *Proc. of the 14th International Joint Conference on Artificial Intelligence, IJCAI'95*, pages 1985–1991, 1995.

[Lorenzo and Otero 2000] D. Lorenzo and R. Otero. Learning to reason about actions. In *Proc. of the 14th European Conference on Artificial Intelligence, ECAI 00*, pages 316–320, 2000.

[Moyle and Muggleton 1997] S. Moyle and S. Muggleton. Learning programs in the event calculus. In *Proc. of the 7th Int. Workshop on Inductive Logic Programming, ILP 97, LNAI 1297*, pages 205–212, 1997.

[Moyle 2002] S. Moyle. Using theory completion to learn a robot navigation control program. In *Proc. of the 12th Int. Conf. on Inductive Logic Programming, ILP 02*, 2002.

[Muggleton 1995] S. Muggleton. Inverse entailment and Progol. *New Generation Computing*, 13:245–286, 1995.

[Muggleton 1998] S. Muggleton. Completing inverse entailment. In *Proc. of the 8th Int. Workshop on Inductive Logic Programming, ILP 98, LNAI 1446*, pages 245–249, 1998.

[Otero 2001] R. Otero. Induction of stable models. In *Proc. of the 11th Int. Conference on Inductive Logic Programming, ILP 01, LNAI 2157*, pages 193–205, 2001.

[Sakama 2000] C. Sakama. Inverse entailment in nonmonotonic logic programs. In *Proc. of the 10th Int. Conf. on Inductive Logic Programming, ILP 00, LNAI 1866*, pages 209–224, 2000.

Employing TSK Fuzzy Models
to Automate the Revision Stage of a CBR System

Florentino Fernández-Riverola[1] and Juan M. Corchado[2]

[1] Dept. Informática. University of Vigo, Campus As Lagoas s/n,
32004, Ourense, Spain
riverola@uvigo.es
[2] Dept. de Informática y Automática, University of Salamanca, Plaza de la Merced s/n,
37008, Salamanca, Spain
corchado@usal.es

Abstract. CBR systems are normally used to assist experts in the resolution of problems. During the last few years, researchers have been working in the development of techniques to automate the reasoning stages identified in this methodology. This paper presents a fuzzy logic based method that automates the review stage of case-based reasoning systems and aids in the process of obtaining an accurate solution. The proposed methodology has been derived as an extension of the Sugeno Fuzzy model, and evaluates different solutions by reviewing their score in an unsupervised mode. The method has been successfully used to completely automate the reasoning process of a biological forecasting system and to improve its performance.

1 Introduction

Case based reasoning (CBR) systems have been successfully used in several domains such as diagnosis, prediction, control and planning [1-3]. However, a major problem of these systems is their difficulty to evaluate the proposed solution and, if it is necessary, repairing it using domain-specific knowledge. This is usually done by means of interacting with a human expert and it is highly dependent of the problem domain. Also there are very few standard techniques to automate their construction, since each problem may be represented by a different data set and requires a customized solution. This is a current weakness of CBR systems and one of their major challenges. For several years we have been working in the identification of techniques to automate the reasoning cycle of CBR systems [3-5]. This paper presents a Takagi Sugeno Kang fuzzy (TSK) based model to automate the process of case revision, that may be used in problems in which the cases are characterized predominantly by numerical information.

Fuzzy modeling is one of the techniques currently being used for modeling of nonlinear, uncertain, and complex systems. An important characteristic of fuzzy models is the partitioning of the space of system variables into fuzzy regions using fuzzy sets [6]. In each region, the characteristics of the system can be simply de-

R. Conejo et al. (Eds.): CAEPIA-TTIA 2003, LNAI 3040, pp. 302–311, 2004.

scribed using a rule. A fuzzy model typically consists of a rule base with a rule for each particular region. Fuzzy transitions between these rules allow for the modeling of complex nonlinear systems with a good global accuracy.

During the last years, several researchers show how fuzzy models can be combined with CBR systems to implement some stages of their reasoning cycle. In this way, some works have focused on the handling of fuzzy descriptions in the retrieval step [7], on the learning of fuzzy concepts from fuzzy examples [8], on the integration with rule-based reasoning [9], and on the logical modeling of the inference mechanisms based on similarity measures [10]. In this paper, we explore the advantages of applying fuzzy logic to the revision stage of a CBR system, showing how this phase can be completely automated in most IBR systems.

An instance based reasoning system developed for predicting biological parameters, will be used to illustrate the efficiency of the solution here discussed. The forecasting of diatoms (a type of single-celled algae) is very important to obtain a valuable freshwater bioindicator, eliminating the need for a single group of organisms that can continually register the health of masses of water. This paper first explain in detail the TSK method and its theoretical background. The biological problem in which this technique has been used is presented, and finally we show how this approach has been implemented to forecast diatoms at different water masses.

2 TSK Fuzzy Revision Method

First we explore the possibility of obtaining an initial fuzzy model learning symbolic rules from artificial neural networks. Then, we show how the construction and training of the fuzzy revision subsystem can be done and finally, we present a suitable way of incorporating the proposed method to the CBR cycle.

2.1 Obtaining the Initial Fuzzy Model

In order to represent the domain knowledge, different types of fuzzy models can be used. The Mamdani model [11], which uses linguistic rules with a fuzzy premise part and a fuzzy consequent part, is often used in knowledge acquisition. Another structure that has been used extensively in literature is the Takagi-Sugeno [12] model. In this paper our fuzzy revision stage is based on the TSK fuzzy model, due to the form of its rules what makes them more appropriate for most problems that can be numerically represented.

The two common approaches for obtaining fuzzy models from data are parameter adaptation and fuzzy clustering. In the first case, one tunes an initial partition of the premise space, while in the second case a partition suitable for a given number of rules is sought automatically. Both techniques can be combined too [13].

A novelty method of fuzzy clustering able to extract interpretable fuzzy rules from a RBF neural network [14] is proposed in [15] and applied successfully in the work of [16].

```
      Function GENERATE_TSK_RULE_BASE (input: confRBF; output: confFS)
      {
00    begin.
01        confFS ← ∅ /* at the beginning the fuzzy rule base does not contain any rule */
02        for each center c ∈ confRBF do /* each center or cluster represents a rule */
03            RULE ← ∅ /* an empty rule is built */
              /* each attribute v represents a system measurement */
04            for each value of the attribute v do
05                assign_membership_function_to_antecedent_value: RULE ← (v, Gaussc)
06                add_consequent: RULE ← connector_weight_hidden_layer_output_layer
07            confFS ← RULE /* a new rule is added to the rule base */
08    end.
      }
```

Fig. 1. Generating the initial TSK rule base.

Figure 1 provides a concise description of the algorithm that generates the fuzzy rule base of the equivalent fuzzy system, where *confRBF* represents the configuration of the trained network and *confFS* stands for the set of fuzzy rules that describes the fuzzy system.

2.2 Constructing the Fuzzy Modeling Subsystem for Revision

Starting from the TSK fuzzy rule base obtained from the algorithm proposed in Figure 1, a measure of similarity is applied with the purpose of reducing the number of fuzzy sets describing each variable. We use a similarity measure for identifying similar fuzzy sets and replace these by a common fuzzy set representative for the original ones. If the redundancy in the model is high, merging similar fuzzy sets for each variable might result in equal rules that also can be merged, thereby reducing the number of rules as well. As a result, the new fuzzy rule base increments the capacity of generalization of the original TSK fuzzy system.

In order to generate several fuzzy rule bases with different degrees of generalization, it is necessary to establish a λ-limit from which two membership functions can be considered analogous and therefore can be joined [13]. In our revision method, the parameter λ goes from 0.9 to 0.6 with decrements of 0.1 [16], generating four fuzzy rule bases corresponding with four TSK fuzzy systems.

The algorithm starts in an iterative way grouping membership functions attribute by attribute. In each iteration, the similarity between all the membership functions for a given attribute is calculated, selecting the pair of functions that holds a higher degree of similarity providing that $S > \lambda$. The selected pair of functions are joined and the rule base is brought up to date with the new membership function. The algorithm continues until the maximum similarity between two memberships functions belonging to any attribute is less or equal to λ. Finally, the fuzzy rules with similar antecedent part are merged, and the consequent of the new rule is estimating by means of Equation (1).

$$C_r = \frac{1}{k} \sum_{i=1}^{k} C_i .$$ (1)

where C_r is the consequent of the new generated rule and k represents the number of rules with similar antecedent.

Function GENERATE_REVISION_SUBSYSTEM (input: λ, confFS; output: confRS-λ)

{
```
00    begin.
01      for each variable a ∈ confFS do /* for all the premise variables of the system */
02          obtain_membership_functions: MF ← confFS(a) /* membership functions for a */
03          select_the_most_similar_pair_of_fuzzy_sets: pairMF ← MaxSimilarity(MF)
04          while similarity(pairMF) > λ do /* while functions overcome the threshold */
05              merge_selected_pair_of_fuzzy_sets: MF ← Merge(pairMF)
06              update(confFS) /* update the rule-base */
07              select_the_most_similar_pair_of_fuzzy_sets: pairMF ← MaxSimilarity(MF)
08      merge_rules_with_equal_premise_parts: confSR-λ ← Merge(confFS)
09    end.
```
}

Fig. 2. Generating the fuzzy revision subsystem.

Figure 2 provides a concise description of the algorithm that generates each one of the TSK fuzzy systems, starting from the initial fuzzy system and applying to it a different λ value. In the algorithm, λ holds the degree of similarity between membership functions, *confFS* stands for the initial fuzzy rule base and *confFS-λ* represents the fuzzy inference system generated starting from the original one with a λ generalization degree.

2.3   Training the Fuzzy Revision Subsystem

The process of training the fuzzy revision subsystem can be viewed as a wrapper algorithm that envelops the whole CBR cycle. We propose the use of a clustering retrieve method, in order to maintain a local adaptation (importance vector) of each fuzzy system for each class of identified problems [16].

   In this model, the fuzzy systems are associated with each class identified by the retrieval stage, mapping each one with its corresponding importance vector as said before. There is one importance vector for each class or "prototype". These fuzzy systems are used to validate and refine the proposed solution. Given a new problem and a proposed solution for it, each of the fuzzy systems that compose the revision subsystem generates a solution that is pondered according to the importance vector associated to the class to which the problem belongs. The importance value of the fuzzy set that best suits a particular class is increased, whilst the others are proportionally decreased.

The importance vector associated with the retrieved class is modified when the error percentage with respect to the real value is calculated. The fuzzy system that has produced the most accurate prediction is identified and the error percentage value previously calculated is added to the degree of importance associated with it.

This process in the adaptation of the importance vector (initially, all the fuzzy systems hold the same weight value), is carried out because it is difficult to ascertain in advance the optimum level of generalization for a given data set.

2.4 Reviewing the Initial Solution

When a new problem arise and the reuse stage of the CBR proposes a solution for it, the parallel solution carried out by the TSK fuzzy revision method is compared and its difference (in percentage) is calculated. The proposed revision schema is based on the definition of two revision limits: *acceptance_limit* and *reject_limit*. Although the precise values of these parameters depend on the problem domain, we have identified after carrying out several experiments that a correct initial approximation is to assign values of 10% and 30% respectively [16].

These limits refer to the variation rate between the initial proposed solution and the solution obtained from the TSK fuzzy system. The adoption of this schema leads to the definition of three possible behaviors:

- If the variation rate is less or equal than the *acceptance_limit*, the initial solution is endorsed by the fuzzy revision subsystem and it is presented as the final solution for the new problem.
- If the variation rate is greater or equal than the *reject_limit*, it means that the fuzzy revision subsystem contradicts the initial solution, so the CBR system is unable to solve the problem.
- If the variation rate is in the open interval defined by the two limits, then the fuzzy revision subsystem adapts the initial solution pondering by 50% each possible solution. The output of the CBR system is the modified solution.

An important point in the previous explained operation, is that the fuzzy revision method is able to identify those situations in which the CBR system is unable to provide a correct solution for a given problem.

2.5 Integrating the TSK Fuzzy Revision Method in the CBR Cycle

As we said before, a notable point in the proposed method is the utilization of importance vectors in the retrieval stage. This is necessary in order to be able to track the learning capacity of the fuzzy systems in a local way. Given a new problem, the importance vector associated with the winner class is modified independently of the others, so that we can maintain the rest unchanged.

For problem domains in which it is not possible to apply a clustering schema as retrieval algorithm, our method could be used in a global fashion maintaining a common vector that holds the weights of each fuzzy system, but the accuracy of the solutions will diminish. To palliate this negative effect, a better adjustment of the acceptance and reject limits will be necessary [16].

Figure 3 shows how our revision method can be combined within the CBR cycle in order to form an automated CBR system. It is necessary to highlight the possibility of computing in parallel the solutions provided for stages ii and iii, as well as the presence of a knowledge base for keep the configuration of the whole system.

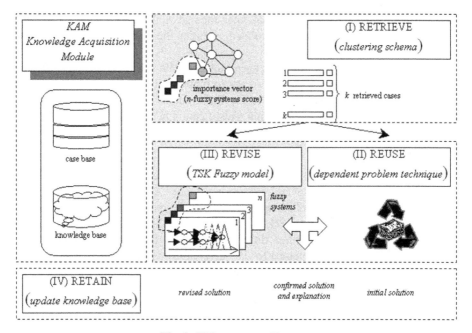

Fig. 3. CBR system architecture.

A crucial aspect in the proposed method is the generation of the initial TSK fuzzy system rule base. This can be done following the advice of human experts, learning symbolic rules from artificial neural networks, using evolutionary strategies, applying fuzzy clustering to the data or using a hybrid approach.

3   IBR for Biological Forecasting

A forecasting biological system capable of predicting the concentration of diatoms (a type of single-celled algae) in different water masses, has been developed applying the proposed revision method discussed in this paper. The possibility of forecasting the concentration of diatoms is very important to obtain a valuable freshwater bioindicator, eliminating the need for a single group of organisms that can continually register the health of water masses. Indices based on diatom composition give more accurate and valid predictions than benthic macroinvertebrates, as they react directly to pollutants.

The system has the architecture showed in Figure 3, where the retrieval stage is carried out using a GCS (Growing Cell Structures) network [17]. The GCS facilitates the indexation of cases and the selection of those that are most similar to the problem descriptor following a clustering schema. The reuse and adaptation of cases is carried out with a RBF (Radial Basis Function) network [14], which generates an initial solution creating a forecasting model with the retrieved cases. The revision stage is carried out using the proposed revision method based on a set of β-TSK Fuzzy models. Finally, the learning stage is carried out when the real value of the variable to predict is measured and the error value is calculated, updating the knowledge structure of the whole system.

The β-TSK revision subsystem has been included with the intention of developing a robust model, based on a technology easy to implement and that can automate the process of defining the revision step of the IBR system, identifying and cutting off incorrect predictions as well as providing a justification in the form of fuzzy rules.

3.1 The Instance

In the context of the previously presented domain, data are recorded at different sampling intervals belonging to several monitoring points. A KA (*Knowledge Acquisition*) module is in charge of collecting and handling the data to construct the instance base. The raw data (temperature, PH, oxygen and other physical characteristics of the water mass) are measured at three different depth and form a basic input profile. These data values are complemented by data derived from satellite images stored on a database. The satellite image data values are used to generate cloud and superficial temperature indexes which are then stored with the problem descriptor and subsequently updated during the IBR operation. Data from the previous 2 weeks (W_{n-1}, W_n) is used to forecast the concentration of diatoms one week ahead (W_{n+1}). This time-window has been found to give sufficient resolution to characterize the problem instance for the forecasting of such single-celled algae organisms [4]. The instance base generated by the KA module consists on approximately 6.300 instances similar to the previous one belonging to homogeneous water masses.

3.2 The β-TSK Fuzzy Revision Subsystem

To create the revision subsystem for the presented forecasting problem, we have generated four fuzzy systems (in this case β=4) using the algorithm showed in Figure 2. Equation (1) was applied to merge the consequents of similar rules. The number of final fuzzy rules for each fuzzy system is identified in Table 1.

The complexity reduction rate gives an idea of the generalization achieve by each fuzzy system compared with the original one. When similar fuzzy sets for each variable are collapsed, the fuzzy system gains in generalization ability but also diminishes its accuracy. It can be seen as a process that goes from specific knowledge to general one, and can be used to detect and correct the situations in which the IBR system performs an invalid prediction caused by the selection of similar instances that have different solutions. This is the main reason for which the continuous adaptation of the importance vector needs to be done in a local way.

Table 1. Number of rules in each TSK fuzzy system.

λ-Value	Number of Rules	Complexity Reduction Rate
original	50	-
0.9	42	16%
0.8	39	22%
0.7	28	44%
0.6	15	70%
0.5	-	-

An important point, is to know how many fuzzy systems need to be generated. From several experiments with different real and artificial data sets, we have found that a complexity reduction rate above 70% does not help in the revision of incorrect solutions, due to the presence of few rules that combine incorrect fuzzy sets.

3.3   Forecasting with the Instance-Base Reasoning System

Several experiments have been carried out to illustrate the effectiveness of the IBR system, which incorporates the β-TSK Fuzzy revision subsystem. Experiments have been carried out using the instance base provided by the KA module which contains data from several water masses. We show in Figure 4.a the errors on a data set of 448 instances randomly taken from the instance base (composed of more than 6.000 instances) using the IBR system developed without a revision subsystem.

Whilst the mean average error was found to be 512.164,3 cell/liter and the number of inadmissible predictions (those with an error ≥ 1.000.000 cell/liter) reached the 14,3%, the results obtained with the same IBR system but upgraded with the β-TSK Fuzzy revision subsystem far overcome these results. In the second case, the mean average error drop to 370.421,1 cell/liter and the rate for inadmissible predictions goes to 7,6%. Figure 4.b shows the results obtained with the new TSK Fuzzy revision algorithm improving the performance of the IBR system.

To better understand the gain after the successful implementation of the revision subsystem in the IBR system, Figure 4.c outlines the differences between the two error series showed before.

Further experiments have been carried out to compare the performance of the IBR augmented system with several other forecasting approaches. These include standard statistical forecasting algorithm and the application of several neural networks methods. In all the cases, the IBR with β-TSK Fuzzy revision subsystem outperforms the others techniques improving the final accuracy.

Starting from the error series generated by the different models, the Kruskall-Wallis test has been carried out. Since the P-value is less than 0,01, there is a statistically significant difference among the models at the 99,0% confidence level. Figure 4.d shows a multiple comparison procedure (Mann-Withney test) used to determine which models are significantly different from the others. It can be seen that the IBR with β-TSK Fuzzy revision subsystem presents statistically significant differences with the rest of the models.

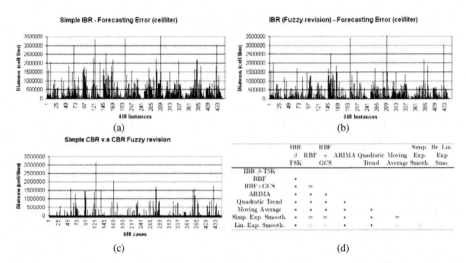

Fig. 4. Average error of the predictions carried out with the IBR system with and without the β-TSK Fuzzy revision subsystem in 448 forecasts.

The reason for this straightforward improvement is due to the ability of the set of TSK fuzzy systems to monitoring the results provided by the RBF network, cutting off inadmissible predictions and adapting those which are valid but not too accurate. All this work can be done in parallel with the initial prediction given by the RBF network, and the process of adapting the weights for each fuzzy system can be maintained by the adopted retrieval clustering schema.

4   Conclusion

We have demonstrated a new technique for case/instance revision, which could be used to automate the revision stage of instance based reasoning systems. The basis of the method is a set of TSK fuzzy models. The simplified rule bases allow us to obtain a more general knowledge of the system and gain a deeper insight into the logical structure of the system to be approximated. The proposed revision method then help us to ensure a more accurate result, to gain confidence in the system prediction and to learn about the problem and its solution.

It has been shown to provide accurate results on an exemplar-forecasting task: the prediction of diatoms as fresh water bioindicator. As diatoms occur in almost all aquatic environments in abundance, only small samples are required for reliable community assessment, diatoms have short cell cycles and they colonize new habitats rapidly.

The reviewing and adaptation of the initial solutions is a very simple operation using the proposed method and presents no major computational obstacles, moreover it can be done in parallel. The whole system may be used with any number-based data set; an area of ongoing research is the automatic determination of the optimal value for the β parameter and several experiments are in progress.

References

1. Watson, I.: Applying Case-Based Reasoning: Techniques for Enterprise Systems. Morgan Kaufmann (1997)
2. Pal, S.K., Dillon, T.S., Yeung, D.S.: Soft Computing in Case Based Reasoning. Springer Verlag, London, U.K. (2000)
3. Fyfe, C., Corchado, J.M.: Automating the construction of CBR Systems using Kernel Methods. International Journal of Intelligent Systems, (2001) Vol 16, No 4
4. Fdez-Riverola. F., Corchado, J.M.: FSfRT: Forecasting System for Red Tides. Applied Intelligence. Soft Computing in Case-Based Reasoning. *In press* (2003)
5. Corchado, J.M., Aiken, J.: Hybrid Artificial Intelligence Methods in Oceanographic Forecasting Models. IEEE SMC Transactions Part C. (2003)
6. Zadeh, L.A.: Fuzzy Sets. Inf. Contr., (1965) Vol 8, 338-353
7. Jaczynski, M., Trousse, B.: Fuzzy logic for the retrieval step of a case-based reasoner. Proc. of the EWCBR'94, (1994) 313-321
8. Plaza, E., López de Mántaras.: A case-based apprentice that learns from fuzzy examples. Methologies for Intelligent Systems, (1990) Vol 5, 420-427
9. Dutta, S., Bonissone, P.P.: Integrating case rule-based reasoning. Int. J. of Approximate Reasoning, (1993) Vol 8, 163-203
10. Plaza, E., López de Mántaras, Armengol, E.: On the importance of similitude: an entropy-based assessment. Report IIIA 96/14, IIIA-CSIC, University of Barcelona, Bellaterra, Spain (1996)
11. Mandani, E.H.: Applications of fuzzy algorithms for control of a simple dynamic plant. Proc. Inst. Electr. Eng., (1974) No 121, 1585-1588
12. Takagi, T., Sugeno, M.: Fuzzy identification of systems and its applications to modeling and control. IEEE Transactions on Systems, Man and Cybernetics, (1985) Vol 15, 116-132
13. Setnes, M., Babuška, R., Kaymak, U., Lemke, R.: Similarity measures in fuzzy rule base simplification. IEEE Transactions on Systems, Man and Cybernetics, (1998) Vol 28, 376-386
14. Fritzke, B.: Fast Learning with Incremental RBF Networks. Neural Processing Letters, (1994) Vol 1, No 1, 2-5
15. Jin, Y., Seelen, W. von., Sendhoff, B.: Extracting Interpretable Fuzzy Rules from RBF Neural Networks. Internal Report IRINI 00-02, Institut für Neuroinformatik, Ruhr-Universität Bochum, Germany (2000)
16. Fdez-Riverola, F.: Neuro-symbolic model for unsupervised forecasting of changing environments, Ph.D. Dissertation, Dept. Informática, University of Vigo (2002)
17. Fritzke, B.: Growing Self-Organizing Networks-Why?. Proc. European Symposium on Artificial Neural Networks, (1996) 61-72

Enhancing Consistency Based Diagnosis with Machine Learning Techniques[*]

Carlos J. Alonso[1], Juan José Rodríguez[2], and Belarmino Pulido[1]

[1] Grupo de Sistemas Inteligentes, Dpto. de Informática, Universidad de Valladolid
[2] Lenguajes y Sistemas Informáticos, Universidad de Burgos

Abstract. This paper proposes a diagnosis architecture that integrates consistency based diagnosis with induced time series classifiers, trying to combine the advantages of both methods. Consistency based diagnosis allows fault detection and localization without prior knowledge of the device fault modes. Machine learning techniques are able to induce time series classifiers that may be used to identify fault modes of a dynamic systems. The diagnostician performs fault detection and localization resorting to consistency based diagnosis through possible conflicts. Then, a time series classifier, induced from simulated examples, generates a sequence of faults modes, coherent with the result of the fault localization stage, and ordered by fault modes confidence. Finally, to simplify the diagnosis task, it is considered as a subtask of a supervisory system, who is in charge of identifying the working conditions for the physical system.

1 Introduction

There is a wealth of techniques and different approximations that have been used to attempt the automation of the diagnosis task. Not even categorizing the different proposal is an easy task, and it is not the objective of this work. Nonetheless, we dare to resume the main approaches according to [2], that identified four main families: Knowledge Based Systems – expert systems – , Case Based Reasoning, Machine Learning and Model Based Systems. Notwithstanding that there exist proposals which do not fit well into any of the previous categories, these diversity of approaches reflects the fact that the diagnosis of complex systems is still an open problem, and that no single technique may claim its pre-eminence on every kind of problem.

Nevertheless, researchers are attempting to design diagnosticians for real problems that may be considered as representatives of the highest complexity: dynamic systems, with a large number of components, a small set of observable variables, with models that are not well known and are difficult to estimate, with interactions not totally known among components, where the presence of control systems may mask faulty behaviors and where the changes of configuration of the system, logical and physical, is an added handicap. The domain of industrial continuous processes is a good representative of this difficult class of problems.

[*] This work has been supported by the Spanish MCyT project DPI2001-4404-E and the "Junta de Castilla y León" project VA101/01.

R. Conejo et al. (Eds.): CAEPIA-TTIA 2003, LNAI 3040, pp. 312–321, 2004.
© Springer-Verlag Berlin Heidelberg 2004

Focusing our discussion on the model based diagnosis community, the main research effort in order to tackle real world difficult problems has been directed toward modeling issues, recognizing that modeling is a key question in model based diagnosis. Other communities have emphasized the development of hybrid systems that integrates different diagnosis techniques. Although some efforts have been made in this direction, [12], we think that there is a lot of work to be done to define a common framework to smoothly integrate model based diagnosis with other diagnosis techniques. However, we feel that there is another step to be taken to improve a diagnostician performance, and this implies a small change on the current perception of how to tackle a diagnosis problem. Usually, diagnosis is considered as an isolated task, or closely related to Fault detection – which provides inputs for diagnosis – and Reconfiguration – which exploits diagnosis outputs. This introduces, in a natural way, the idea of supervision, as a set of tasks aimed to guarantee that the system under supervision satisfies some external criteria. Moreover, this basic architecture may be further extended to include others functionalities that may highly improve the performance of the diagnosis task, adjusting the diagnostic task settings to the current scenario.

Global supervision may identify the context where the diagnosis task takes place. Consequently, it allows to test on-line if the implicit diagnosis hypotheses hold. For instance, aspects like validity range of the models, proper range of the external settings or even identification of external disturbances may be considered by a supervisory system. The identification of these circumstances is essential to improve the robustness of any diagnosis algorithm.

This paper proposes an hybrid diagnosis system which uses consistency based diagnosis for fault detection and localization and machine learning to induce time series classifiers employed for fault identification. In this way we preserve one of the main advantages of consistency based diagnosis, that is, it only relays on models of correct behavior. Additionally, the knowledge related to faults modes is captured via machine learning techniques. Moreover, the information obtained in the localization step, i.e. diagnosis à la Reiter, is considered in a simple but effectively manner by the induced classifiers in charge of fault identification. The diagnostician is part of a global supervisory system, that identifies the operation protocol of the physical devices. Different operation protocols may require different models and/or different time series classifiers.

The rest of the paper is organized as follows. Next section introduces the basic tasks for global supervision system. Afterward, section 3, we describe a machine learning technique especially designed to induce time series classifiers that will be used for fault identification. Later on, section 4, we describe how to integrate these classifiers with the consistency based approach to diagnosis, which is supported by the possible conflict concept. The paper ends with a brief discussion.

2   Diagnosis as a Supervisory Task

Diagnosis of complex dynamic systems must not be conceived as an isolated task that may be invoked on any circumstance. Generally,any diagnosis system, whatever diagnosis technique it relies on, will resort to a set of simplifying hypotheses in order to facilitate fault diagnosis. Consequently, before invoking a diagnosis task, it would be advisable to characterize the condition of the system to be analyzed to know if the diagnosis hypotheses, generally implicit in the diagnostician, are satisfied.

This process of putting in context the diagnosis task may be tackled considering diagnosis as part of a global supervision task of a dynamic system. The concept of global supervision that we will employ to frame the diagnosis task was introduced in [1], where eight basic task were proposed to accomplish on line supervision of industrial continuous process. To identify the context where the diagnosis will be performed, only four task are needed. These tasks, that may be considered as the kernel of a supervisory system, are: State Assessment, Monitoring, Operation Mode and Fault Diagnosis.

This task taxonomy make use of the concept of state (of the system) and operation protocol. Thought these concepts were introduced in the domain of industrial processes, they may be extrapolated to other domains. Thus, the state of the system will be described by a vector that includes the inputs, the desired outputs and the medium and long term constraints. Then, a state is valid or feasible if and only if the physical system is able to obtain the desired outputs with current inputs and constraints. The interest of these concepts stems from the fact that many artificial systems are designed to work on a small set of feasible states. Moreover, every feasible state use to have a small set of operation protocols, that defines the physical and logical settings that constrain how the systems is governed. Examples of operation protocol settings are controllers configuration, set points, etc. Basically, once the operation protocol is fixed, we have delimited the relevant aspect of the situation where diagnosis is going to be made. Once introduced the concept of state and operation protocol, we may briefly describe the basic tasks of a supervisory system:

State Assessment: It is defined as the task that establishes the current state of the system and its operation protocol.

Monitoring: Given a set of variables, monitoring task identifies the subset of variables that departs from their desired trajectories according to some criteria.

Operation Mode: Operation mode is the task that supervises that the plant is commanded according to the selected operation protocol.

Fault Diagnosis: Fault diagnosis task has to localize faulty equipment. In addition, it may identify the causes of faults.

State assessment is the task in charge of determining the context of the supervisory systems. It may be considered as a special kind of condition monitoring. It is, probably, the most difficult task to automate. Nonetheless, it is possible to design decision support systems that, yielding the ultimate responsibility to the technical/managerial staff, assist on the performance of this task and make available this high level decisions to the rest of tasks. Monitoring has been decoupled from Fault Diagnosis because it may be invoked due to the requirement of a different task, like Operation Mode. Moreover, it allows to employ different techniques for fault detection and fault diagnosis, which may be of interest on complex dynamic problems. Operation Mode takes care of those problems related with an erroneous commanding of the systems. This concept is similar to the external fault concept used by [3].

The hybrid diagnosis system that we propose in section 4 assumes that we know the current operation protocol, Monitoring continuously watch the system – actually, in this system, a by-product of model based diagnosis – and the diagnosis task is invoked only if Operation Mode do not detect a violation of the operation protocol. A deviation of the operation protocol may invalidate the models of the plant, which is a handicap for consistency based diagnosis. Even more sensitive to such deviations are the machine learning techniques. Space limitations do not allow to present in depth this issue, but the ultimate cause is that example based induction basically identifies behavior patterns of variables related to faults and these patterns may vary significantly under different operation protocols.

3   Machine Learning Techniques for Fault Identification

Machine learning techniques has been successfully used to automate fault diagnosis, inducing trees or rules from examples, [8], or training artificial neural networks, [13]. These techniques try to identify behavioral patterns associated to the different faults, and allow to perform fault identification. However, the majority of the machine learning techniques do not take into account the dynamic aspects of a problem and, consequently, fail to exploit the temporal information that so meaningful seems to be to human trouble shooters – although see [4] for an exception. Considering that the main patterns, to identify faults in dynamic environments, consist on the evolution over time of variables related with the current fault, we decided to focus the problem as of classifying multivariate time series. The classifiers, introduced in section 3.1, are induced from examples. If enough faulty examples are available, the classifiers may be induced without further knowledge. Currently, we are working on an experimental test bed to induce the classifiers from simulation of faults models.

3.1   Time Series Classifiers

The considered classification system is based on the family of learning methods named "boosting", using very simple base classifiers: only one literal. At present, an active research topic is the use of *ensembles* of classifiers. One of the most popular methods for creating ensembles is boosting, [11]. It works assigning a weight to each example. Initially, all the examples have the same weight. In each iteration a *base* (also named *weak*) classifier is constructed, using any other classification method, according to the distribution of weights. Afterwards, the weight of each example is readjusted, based on the correctness of the class assigned to the example by the base classifier. The final result is obtained by weighted votes of the base classifiers.

The used base classifier are interval predicates. There are two kinds: relative and region based. Relative predicates consider the differences between the values

Table 1. Classifier example. For each literal, there are 3 numbers. They are the weights associated for each of the 3 classes of the data set.

Literal	1st class	2nd class	3rd class
true_percentage(E, x, 1_4, 4, 36, 95)	-0.552084	3.431576	-0.543762
not true_percentage(E, x, 1_4, 16, 80, 40)	1.336955	0.297363	-0.527967
true_percentage(E, x, 3, 49, 113, 25)	-0.783590	-0.624340	1.104166
decreases(E, x, 34, 50, 1.20)	-0.179658	0.180668	0.771224
not true_percentage(E, x, 4, 14, 78, 15)	0.899025	-0.234799	-0.534271

in the interval. Region based predicates are based on the presence of the values of a variable in a region during an interval. This section only introduces the predicates, [9] gives a more detailed description, including how to select them efficiently. The considered predicates are:

- increases(Example, Variable, Beginning, End, Value). It is true, for the Example, if the difference between the values of the Variable for End and Beginning is greater or equal than Value.
- decreases(Example, Variable, Beginning, End, Value). Idem when the difference is less or equal.
- stays(Example, Variable, Beginning, End, Value). It is true, for the Example, if the range of values of the Variable in the interval is less or equal than Value.
- always(Example, Variable, Region, Beginning, End). It is true, for the Example, if the Variable is always in this Region in the interval between Beginning and End.
- sometime(Example, Variable, Region, Beginning, End). Similarly, when the variable stays for sometime.
- true_percentage(Example, Variable, Region, Beginning, End, Percentage). It is true, for the Example, if the percentage of the time between Beginning and End where the variable is in Region is greater or equal to Percentage.

Table 1 shows a classifier. It was obtained from a three classes data set. This classifier is composed by 5 base classifiers. For each literal there are 3 numbers, the weights associated for each class. In order to classify a new example, a weight is calculated for each class, and then the example is assigned to the class with greater weight. In the classifier, there is a weight for each base classifier and literal. For each class, its weight is the sum of the weights of the true literals for the example minus the sum of the weights of the false literals.

3.2 Using the Classifiers for Fault Identification

Normally, when a classifier is used, the only expected result is the selected class. For fault identification, it would be desirable to obtain an ordering of the different fault modes. This ordering contains information that may be useful for the human responsible on the command of the process. On the other hand, some faults are discarded in the previous phase, so the desired output is an ordering of the remaining candidates. The ADABOOST [11] algorithm assigns for each class a determined value, the weighted vote of the individual classifiers for that class. These value can be used for considering the result of the classifier not as a unique class but as an ordering of the set of classes. If some classes have been discarded in a previous step, then it is only necessary to compute the weighted vote for the remaining classes.

An open question is how to measure the adequacy of a classification with these features, that is, the result is an ordering of the sets of labels. One possibility is to consider the average number of classes that appear before the correct class. In order to obtain a measure with a range independent of the number of classes, the value of the average number of classes that are before the correct one is divided by the number of classes minus one. In this way, that value will be between 0 and 1. This measure is called *position error*. The classical error, here will be called *classification error*, with the objective of avoiding confusions. A position error of 0% indicates that the correct class is always the first, a 100% indicates that the correct one is always the last. If the order of classes were assigned randomly, the average value of this error would be 50%.

The classifiers have been obtained using full series as training examples. They are trained with series that start and end at steady states, with the faults happening somewhere in between. Nevertheless, it is not an option to wait for a full series in order to use the classifiers, we want to apply the classifiers as soon as a fault is detected. Hence, the classifiers must deal with partial time series, and they must produce a classification, as good as possible, considering the available information. We call this feature *early classification*.

From all the literals in the classifier, some of them will have a defined result for the partial example, because their intervals refer to areas that are already available in the example. Nevertheless, for other literals their results will be unknown because their intervals still are not available for the example. The learning method produces as a result a linear combination of literals. The literals that still have an unknown result, will be simply omitted from the classifier. The classification given to a partial example will be the linear combination of those literals that have known results.

3.3   Experimental Validation

The considered dataset is introduced in [10]. It is proposed as a benchmark for classification systems of temporal patterns in the process industry. This data set was generated artificially. This is a 4 series, 16 classes problem. There are 1600 examples, 100 of each class. Half of the examples are for training and the other half for testing. The results shown are the average of 5 runnings, because the learning method has a stochastic component.

This section shows the obtained results using simultaneously relative and region-based predicates. The classification error as a function of the number of base classifiers is shown in table 2. For 100 literals, the error is 0.45%. The result reported in [10], using recurrent neural networks and wavelets is an error of 1.4%, but 4.5% of the examples are not assigned to any class. As expected, position error is much smaller than classification error. Using only 10 literals, its value is 2.21%. This is a 16 classes problem. Hence, the average of the number of classes that are selected before the correct class is $15 \times 0.0221 = 0.315$.

Table 2. Experimental results.

error / number of literals

Iterations	10	20	30	40	50	60	70	80	90	100
Classification error	20.60	7.23	4.05	1.60	1.35	1.23	0.90	0.78	0.68	0.45
Position error	2.21	0.74	0.39	0.16	0.13	0.11	0.08	0.06	0.05	0.03

Early classification: error / series length percentage

Percentage	10	20	30	40	50	60	70	80	90	100
Classification error	93.75	89.88	76.05	73.40	62.90	39.60	7.25	1.35	0.80	0.45
Position error	100.00	42.46	12.71	10.38	7.91	3.39	0.62	0.10	0.06	0.03

Early classification results are shown in table 2. For this case, the error is considered as a function of the observed percentage of the series length. The considered classifiers are composed by 100 literals. For the classification error it is necessary to have observed, at least, the 70% of the series in order to obtain useful classifications. The results for the position error are, logically, more optimistic. For the 30% of the series length the position error is 12.71%. This means that the average number of classes before the correct one, for a data set with 16 classes, is $15 \times 0.1271 = 1.91$.

4   Integration of Consistency Based Diagnosis with Possible Conflicts and Time Series Classifiers

It is well known that consistency based diagnosis supports fault detection and localization from models of correct behavior. In order to obtain a more detailed diagnosis, fault modes must be introduced, which allows fault identification. In a simulation based approach to consistency based diagnosis, this requires on-line simulation of fault modes. However, on-line simulation of faults modes is a problematic issue. Hence, a more qualitative description of faulty behavior is desirable. The time series classifiers introduced in the previous section employ a qualitative description of the system variables evolution to perform fault identification. Consequently, a natural integration of both approaches would consist on performing fault detection and localization based on consistency, and fault identification with the time series classifiers.

Somehow surprisingly, the integration of both techniques may be fulfilled in several ways. We have opted for giving higher priority to the consistency based diagnosis output, because we wanted to preserve its logical soundness property. To achieve this behavior, the induced time series classifiers are slightly modified. Let us denote by $CLASSIFIER(t)$ an invocation of the induced time series classifier with a fragment of series from time t to min(current time, t+maximum series length). Each call to $CLASSIFIER(t)$ will return a list of fault modes ranked by their voted weight. Let us denote by $CLASSIFIER(t, c)$ an invocation to the modified classifier, being c a set of consistency based diagnosis candidates. A call to $CLASSIFIER(t, c)$, will compute the list obtained firstly invoking $CLASSIFIER(t)$ and secondly removing those fault modes not associated to components of c. For efficiency reasons, this behavior is accomplished eliminating from the original classifier the outputs related to fault modes that do not correspond to components of c, but this is a minor issue. To further simplify the problem, singled fault hypothesis is assumed; otherwise, the induction of the time series classifiers becomes a combinatorial problem.

With these previous assumptions, the integration of both techniques is particularly simple if consistency based diagnosis relies on the concept of *possible conflict* because due to the capability of the induced classifiers to consider only a fragment of a time series – early classification – and to discard the fault modes not associated with the current candidates, the integration only requires to invoke the time series classifiers into the iterative and incremental cycle of diagnosis with *possible conflicts*. A detailed description of consistency based diagnosis with *possible conflicts* can be found in [7]. We include a brief summary for the sake of self-containment. The main idea behind the *possible conflict* concept, [5], is that the set of subsystems capable to generate a conflict can be identified off-line. This identification can be done in three steps. The first one generates an abstract representation of the system, as an hypergraph. In this representation there is only information about constraints in the models, and their relationship to knwown and unknown variables in such models. The second step looks for minimal overconstrained sets of relations, which are essential for model-based diagnosis. These subsystems, called *minimal evaluation chains*, represent a necessary condition for a conflict to exist. Each minimal evaluation chain, which is a partial sub-hypergraph of the original system description, need to be solved using local propagation criteria alone. To fulfill this last requirement we add extra knowledge, representing every possible way a constraint can be solved by means of local propagation. As a consequence, each minimal evaluation chain generates a directed and-or graph. In each and-or graph, we search for every possible way the system can be solved using local propagation, if any. Each possible way is called a *minimal evaluation model*, and it can predict the behavior of a part of the whole system. Moreover, since conflicts will arise only when models are evaluated with available observations, the set of constraints in a minimal evaluation model is called a *possible conflict*.

Those models can be used to perform fault detection. If there is a discrepancy between predictions from those models and current observations, the possible conflict would be responsible for such a discrepancy and should be confirmed as a real conflict. Afterwards, diagnosis candidates are obtained from conflicts following Reiter's theory. In previous works we have shown that possible conflicts is a compilation technique which, under certain assumptions, is equivalent to on-line conflict calculation in GDE, [6].

In a dynamic environment, diagnosis with possible conflicts is performed in an iterative and incremental way. To include fault identification, we only have to add a new step, 5.d, to the basic cycle[1]:

---

[1] Where OBS_{pc_i} denotes the set of input observations available in SD_{pc_i}, $PRED_{pc_i}$ represents the set of predictions obtained from SD_{pc_i}, OBS'_{pc_i} denotes the set of output observations in SD_{pc_i}, and δ_{pc_i} is the maximum value allowed as the dissimilarity value between OBS'_{pc_i} and $PRED_{pc_i}$. $CLASSIFIER(t, c)$ denotes and invocation to the time series classifier with a fragment of series from t to the min(current time, t+maximum series length) and with the set of candidates c. t_0 is the time of the last iteration prior to the first conflict confirmation.

1. the system must be analyzed looking for any minimal evaluation chain;
2. those minimal evaluation chains with no evaluation model must be rejected,
3. exactly one minimal evaluation model associated to a minimal evaluation chain must be selected,
4. build the executable model of the possible conflict pc_i, SD_{pc_i}, from the description of the minimal evaluation model,
5. *repeat*
   (a) simulate SD_{pc_i} using OBS_{pc_i} and producing $PRED_{pc_i}$,
   (b) *if* $| PRED_{pc_i} - OBS'_{pc_i} |> \delta_{pc_i}$ *then* confirm pc_i,
   (c) *if* a new pc_i is confirmed, *then* compute the new set of candidates
   (d) update fault modes ranking with $CLASSIFIER(t_0,$ set of candidates$)$
   until there is no pc_i to be simulated.

The proposed diagnosis process will incrementally generate the set of candidates consistent with observations. Simultaneously, it will order the available fault modes according to their confidence, in a process with an error rate that decreases as bigger fragments of the variables evolution is available.

5   Discussion

This work presents a different approach to diagnosis of dynamic systems. The proposal pretends to be effective in complex dynamic systems. Consequently, it is assumed that the diagnostician is an integral part of a supervision systems. On simpler settings, where system configuration and operation point are fixed, the diagnostician could work as an independent module.

Special effort has been done to keep the best properties of consistency based diagnosis, that is, it only needs models of correct behavior and diagnosis is sound an complete respect to the used models. At the same time, we try to alleviate its major drawback: diagnosis tends to be unfocused due to the absence of fault information. This fault information is introduced resorting to machine learning techniques. Although in the majority of the cases the generation of faulty examples will resort to simulation of faulty modes, simulations for training are made off-line. Another important advantage of the proposed method is that fault model for training do not require to know the precise value of the parameters that describe the fault. Moreover, some level of variations on these parameters may facilitate the induction process. Notice, also, that the proposed way to integrate both techniques do not lose the completeness of the system, guaranteed by the consistency based phase. If a non considered faulty model arises, the system is still able to do fault localization.

The induced models, time series classifiers, describe in a natural way some temporal properties of the faulty behavior. They are designed to work with time series and their symbolic nature allows to adapt them to accept series of different length. This property provides several opportunities for a natural integration on the iterative cycle of consistency based diagnosis. Actually, the integration proposed in this work is just one of the simpler possibilities available.

This work is part of an ongoing research activity, and further experimental effort has still to be done. Preliminary test with a small set of fault modes on a single operation mode seems to be promising, but the systematic induction of the classifiers has still to be solved.

References

1. G. Acosta Lazo, C. J. Alonso González, and B. Pulido Junquera. Basic tasks for knowledge based supervisin in process control. *Engineering Application of Artificial Intelligence*, 14:441–455, 2002.
2. K. Balakrishnan and V. Honavar. Intelligent diagnosis systems. *Journal of Intelligent Systems*, 8, 1998.
3. S. Cauvin, M.-O. Cordier, C. Dousson, P. Laboire, F. Levy, J. Montmain. M. Pocheron, I. Servet, and L. Travé-Massuyès. Monitoring and alarm interpretation in industrial environments. *AI Comunications*, 11(3–4):139–173, 1998.
4. C. Feng. Inducting temporal fault diagnostic rules from a qualitative model. In S. Muggleton, editor, *Inductive Logic Programming*. Academic Press, 1992.
5. B. Pulido and C. Alonso. An alternative approach to dependency-recording engines in consistency-based diagnosis. In *AIMSA-00*, volume 1904 of *LNAI*, pages 111–120. Springer Verlag, 2000.
6. B. Pulido and C. Alonso. Possible conflicts, ARRs, and conflicts. In *13th International Workshop on Principles of Diagnosis (DX-02)*, pages 122–128, Semmering, Austria, 2002.
7. B. Pulido, C. Alonso, and F. Acebes. Lessons learned from diagnosing dynamic systems using possible conflicts and quantitative models. In *IEA/AIE-2001*, volume 2070 of *LNAI*, pages 135–144, 2001.
8. J. R. Quinlan. *C4.5: programs for machine learning*. Morgan Kaufmann, 1993.
9. Juan J. Rodríguez, Carlos J. Alonso, and Henrik Boström. Boosting interval based literals. *Intelligent Data Analysis*, 5(3):245–262, 2001.
10. Davide Roverso. Multivariate temporal classification by windowed wavelet decomposition and recurrent neural networks. In 3rd *ANS International Topical Meeting on Nuclear Plant Instrumentation, Control and Human-Machine Interface*, 2000.
11. Robert E. Schapire. A brief introduction to boosting. In 16th *International Joint Conference on Artificial Intelligence*, 1999.
12. L. Travé-Massuyès and R. Milne. Gas turbine condition monitoring using qualitative model based diagnosis. *IEEE Expert*, pages 22–31, 1997.
13. V. Venkatusugramanian and K. Chan. A neural network methodology for process fault diagnosis. *AIChE J.*, 35:1993–2001, 1995.

Exploiting Disambiguated Thesauri
for Information Retrieval in Metadata Catalogs*

Javier Nogueras-Iso, Javier Lacasta, José Ángel Bañares,
Pedro R. Muro-Medrano, and F. Javier Zarazaga-Soria

Computer Science and Systems Engineering Department, University of Zaragoza
María de Luna, 1, 50018-Zaragoza, Spain
{jnog,jlacasta,banares,prmuro,javy}@unizar.es

Abstract. Information in Digital Libraries is explicitly organized, described, and managed. The content of their data resources is summarized
into small descriptions, usually called metadata, which can be either introduced manually or automatically generated. In this context, specialized thesauri are frequently used to provide accurate content for subject
or keyword metadata elements. However, if a Digital Library aims at
providing access for the general public, it is not reasonable to assume
that casual users will use the same terms as the keywords used in metadata records. As an initial step to fill the semantic gap between user
queries and metadata records, the authors of this paper already created
a method for the semantic disambiguation of thesauri with respect to
an upper-level ontology (WordNet). This paper presents now the integration of this disambiguation within an information retrieval system, in
this case adapting the vector-space retrieval model. Thanks to the disambiguation, both metadata records and queries can be homogenously
represented as a collection of WordNet synsets, thus enabling the computing of a similarity value, which ranks the results.

1 Introduction

As opposite to the largely unstructured information available on the Web, information in Digital Libraries (DLs) is explicitly organized, described, and managed. In order to facilitate discovery and access, DL systems summarize the
content of their data resources into small descriptions, usually called metadata, which can be either introduced manually or automatically generated (index
terms automatically extracted from a collection of documents). The focus of this
paper is DLs working with metadata records using an agreed metadata schema.
Indeed, most DLs use structured metadata in accordance with recognized standards such as MARC21 (http://lcweb.loc.gov/marc/marc.html) or Dublin Core

---

* The basic technology of this work has been partially supported by the Spanish
Ministry of Science and Technology through the projects TIC2000-1568-C03-01 from
the National Plan for Scientific Research, Development and Technology Innovation
and FIT-150500-2003-519 from the National Plan for Information Society. The work
of J. Lacasta has been partially supported by a grant from the Aragón Government
and the European Social Fund (ref. B139/2003).

R. Conejo et al. (Eds.): CAEPIA-TTIA 2003, LNAI 3040, pp. 322–333, 2004.

(http://www.dublincore.org). Moreover, in order to provide accurate metadata, metadata creators use specialized thesauri to fill the content of typical keyword sections. According to ISO-2788 (norm for monolingual thesauri), a thesaurus is a set of terms that describe the vocabulary of a controlled indexing language, formally organized so that the a priori relationships between concepts (e.g. synonyms, broader terms, narrower terms and related terms) are made explicit. Thesauri provide a specialized vocabulary for the homogeneous classification of resources and for supplying users with a suitable vocabulary for the retrieval.

There are numerous catalog systems that use thesauri as the basis for discovery services. For instance, the system presented in [1] aims at identifying human experts in different subjects of an application domain. There, a concept index was built manually and experts were associated with these concepts. After the user specifies a set of concepts, the system searches for experts who either know about one of those concepts or know about concepts "closely" related to "the user's concepts of interest". That is to say, the system evaluates the semantic relatedness using the network representation of the thesaurus. The hits returned are ranked according to the distance between query concepts and the concepts assigned to each expert.

However, if a DL aims at providing access to the general public (not only constrained to the community of experts that created the resources in the DL), it is not reasonable to assume that casual users will use the same query terms as the keywords used in metadata records. This discordance between query terms and metadata keywords is even worse in the case of DLs handling resources from different application domains, where metadata creators have probably used different thesauri (increasing the heterogeneity of keywords). This situation implies that discovery in DLs cannot be implemented as a simple word matching between the user queries and metadata records. On the contrary, a DL should be able to understand the sense of the user's vocabulary and to link these meanings to the underlying concepts expressed by metadata records.

In order to fill the semantic gap between user queries and metadata records, we proposed in [2] a method for the semantic disambiguation of thesauri with respect to an upper-level ontology, which is closer to the user expressions. Concepts contained in user queries are usually extracted by means of natural language processing techniques (beyond the scope of this paper) that also make use of similar upper-level ontologies. Therefore, it seems reasonable to use the semantic disambiguation of thesauri as a mechanism that harmonizes concepts in metadata records and user queries. In particular, our method provides the disambiguation against WordNet [3], a large-scale lexical database developed from a global point of view that can provide a good kernel to unify, at least, the broader concepts included in distinct thesauri. Our method can be classified as an unsupervised disambiguation method and applies a heuristic voting algorithm that makes profit of the hierarchical structure of both WordNet and the thesauri. Whereas thesaurus hierarchical structure provides the disambiguation context for terms, the hierarchical structure of WordNet enables the comparison of senses from two related thesaurus terms.

This disambiguation facilitates a unifying system to express user queries and metadata records but it does not constitute itself the final objective. The final purpose is to integrate this disambiguation within an Information Retrieval System (IRS). In fact, the indexing with WordNet synsets is not new in the context of general text retrieval, [4] shows some experiments and revises some related works. In general, the conclusion of these works is that WordNet indexing can improve performance whenever the disambiguation accuracy rate is high (in some cases not less than 90% [5]). These conclusions are probably not extensible to the IRS proposed in this paper because they were indexing free text and this IRS is constrained to the keywords section of metadata. However, it is expected that the disambiguation accuracy in our IRS will be very high. The first reason is that we are disambiguating the own keywords. As opposed to free text retrieval, we are not going to extract concepts from words that are not essential to the document meaning. Additionally the thesaurus hierarchy provides an accurate and limited context for disambiguation.

As a logical continuation of [2], this works aims at verifying the applicability of our disambiguation method within an information retrieval system. In particular, this paper presents the adaptation of the vector-space retrieval model [6] to the context of metadata catalogs. Other classical models, like the probabilistic or neural-net based models, would probably perform better in more heterogeneous contexts. However, the initial hypothesis was that in this context, where metadata records are the summary of the desired resource, a simple model may provide satisfactory results.

The rest of the paper is organized as follows. Section 2 presents the information retrieval system with the adaptation of the indexing technique to the specific features of metadata schemas. The indexing technique makes profit of the metadata keywords section, whose content has been strategically filled in by selecting terms from disambiguated thesauri. Thanks to the disambiguation, both metadata records and user queries can be homogenously represented as a collection of WordNet synsets (concepts in WordNet), thus enabling the computing of a similarity value, which ranks the results returned by the digital library. Section 3 presents some of the results from the initial experiments of the retrieval system. It has been tested against a geographic catalog, i.e. a catalog containing metadata records that describe data with some kind of location reference. And finally, this work ends with some conclusions and future lines.

2   The Retrieval Model

An information retrieval model can be defined as the specification for the representation of documents, queries, and the comparison algorithm to retrieve the relevant documents. The vector-space retrieval model [6] proposes a framework in which partial matching is possible and it is characterized by the use of a weight vector representing the importance of each index term with regard to a metadata record (document). Hence, the framework F, which represents the collection of records and the user queries, consists of a M-dimensional vector space, where each dimension corresponds with each distinct index term in the glossary (denoted as T and being M the size of the glossary). Following expressions show vector representations of a document $d_j \in D$ (documents in the collection) and a query $q \in Q$ (set of user queries):

$$d_j = ((t_1, w_{1,j}), (t_2, w_{2,j}), ..., (t_M, w_{M,j})); q = ((t_1, w_{1,q}), (t_2, w_{2,q}), ..., (t_M, w_{M,q})) \quad (1)$$

where $t_1, t_2, ... t_M \in T$ are the M synsets belonging to the glossary; $w_{i,j}$ represents the weight given to an index term with respect to d_j; and $w_{i,q}$ is the weight given to an index term with respect to q. Finally, this model provides a function to compute the degree of similarity between each metadata record and a user query q, enabling the ranking of records with respect to q. Following equation shows the exact formula to compute the similarity value (denoted as $Sim(d_j, q)$) which is based on the cosine of the angle formed by the vector representing the metadata record and the vector of the user query [7].

$$Sim(d_j, q) = \frac{\vec{d_j} \cdot \vec{q}}{|\vec{d_j}| \times |\vec{q}|} = \frac{\sum_{k=1}^{M} w_{k,j} \times w_{k,q}}{\sqrt{\sum_{k=1}^{M} w_{k,j}^2} \times \sqrt{\sum_{k=1}^{M} w_{k,q}^2}} \quad (2)$$

Next subsections explain the process to obtain the index terms of metadata records and queries and their weights.

2.1   The Indexing of Metadata Records

Before applying a retrieval algorithm, documents (metadata records) in the collection must be summarized into a set of representative keywords called index terms. In this context of metadata catalogs, metadata records are precisely a summary of media documents (image, text or whatever). Furthermore, the advantage in this context is that metadata creators introduce explicitly the concepts within the keywords section. Nevertheless, the retrieval model of a metadata catalog cannot be based uniquely on a simple matching between a query word and the words contained in keywords section. On one hand, different metadata creators may not share the same criteria to select a harmonized (homogenous) set of keywords. And on the other hand, this simple matching would be comparable with a classic Boolean information retrieval model, where query terms are compared with keywords contained in records to decide whether the record is relevant or not without providing any ranking.

As mentioned in the introduction, one way to increment the descriptive potential of the keywords section is to select terms belonging to formalized controlled lists of terms or thesauri. In this way, more sophisticated methods to resolve terminological queries could be applied. However, there is not a universal thesaurus to classify every type of resource and metadata creators make use of different thesauri or controlled lists depending on the application domain. Therefore, the set of keywords, although using thesauri and controlled lists, are still quite heterogeneous. For example, in the context of geographic information, catalogs may include geographic information about topography, cadaster or communications. Hence, we proposed in [2] the semantic disambiguation of

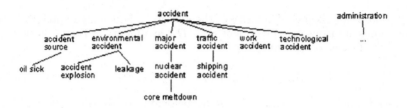

Fig. 1. Example of thesaurus branches

thesaurus terms to avoid this heterogeneity. The main objective of this semantic disambiguation method is to relate the different thesauri to an upper-level
ontology like WordNet [3].

WordNet is structured in a hierarchy of synsets which represent a set of synonyms or equivalent terms. The initial step of the disambiguation process is to
divide the thesaurus into branches (a branch corresponds to a tree whose root is
a term with no broader terms and that is constituted by all the descendants of
this term in the "broader term/narrower term" hierarchy). The branch provides
the disambiguation context for each term in the branch. Secondly, the disambiguation method finds all the possible synsets that may be associated with the
terms in a thesaurus branch. And finally, a voting algorithm is applied where
each synset related to a thesaurus term votes for the synsets related to the rest
of terms in the branch. The main factor of this score is the number of subsumers
in synset paths (the synset and its ancestors in WordNet). The synset with the
highest score for each term is elected as the disambiguated synset. Table 1 shows
the final score of synsets for the branch *accident* in Fig. 1. For the sake of clarity, some terms and their corresponding synsets have not been shown. A more
detailed explanation of the algorithm to obtain the score can be found in [2].

Table 1. Disambiguation of a thesaurus branch

Term	Subterm	Synset path	score	lia
accident				
		event→happening→trouble→misfortune→mishap→accident	3,143	0,551
		event→happening→accident	2,560	0,449
accident→accident source				
	accident			
		event→happening→trouble→misfortune→mishap→accident	2,304	0,552
		event→happening→accident	1,873	0,448
	source			
		entity→object→artifact→creation→product→work→publication →reference	0,713	0,231
		entity→object→location→point→beginning	0,705	0,228
		entity→object→artifact→facility→source	0,685	0,221
		entity→life_form→person→communicator→informant	0,397	0,128
		entity→life_form→person→creator→maker→generator	0,397	0,128
		psychological_feature→cognition→content→idea→inspiration →source	0,186	0,060
		abstraction→relation→social_relation→communication →written_communication→writing→document→source	0,009	0,003
accident→accident source→oil slick				
		entity→object→film→oil_slick	0,214	1,000

...

Therefore, once a new metadata record has been completed, it is possible to obtain the collection of synsets corresponding to the thesaurus terms. Besides, as the metadata creator probably selected terms from different thesauri, there may be repetition of synsets in the obtained collection. Hence, given the keywords section of a metadata record, it is possible to extract a collection of synsets, which are indeed the index terms and may be characterized by a weight proportional to the number of occurrences and the liability of the disambiguated synset.

As concerns the vector model, one of the best weighting schemes for index terms (the synsets) is the one proposed in [7], which tries to balance the effect of intra-clustering similarity (features that better describe a subset/cluster of documents in the collection) and inter-clustering dissimilarity (features which better distinguish a subset from the remaining documents in the collection) of documents (see equation 3). Assuming this weighting scheme, the first step to calculate the weight of a synset is to obtain the frequency of a synset t_i in a metadata record d_j. For a classical information retrieval system, this frequency (denoted as $freq_{i,j}$) would be simply the number of occurrences of an index term. But in this case, we cannot obviate that the disambiguation of thesaurus terms is heuristic and we wanted to consider the score obtained for each synset in the disambiguation process. Therefore, given a thesaurus term s, we have estimated the liability of the elected synset t_i with respect to the other non-elected synsets which were initially associated with the term s. This liability value, denoted as $lia_{s,i}$, is computed as the division between the score of the elected synset and the sum of the scores of all synsets related to a thesaurus term. Column lia in table 1 shows an example of such percentage. $freq_{i,j}$ is finally computed as the sum of the liability of each synset t_i that is indirectly referenced by the terms included in a metadata record d_j. Secondly, it is necessary to obtain the normalized frequency $f_{i,j}$, which is computed as the division between $freq_{i,j}$ and the maximum frequency (computed over all synsets t_l referenced by d_j). Next step is the calculation of the inverse frequency idf_i of a synset t_i, i.e. the logarithm of the division between the size of the collection (denoted as N) and the number of records referenced by this synset (denoted as n_i). The point here is that if a synset is referenced in many metadata records, it is not very useful to discriminate them. Finally, the total weight $w_{i,j}$ is computed as the product between $f_{i,j}$ and idf_i.

$$freq_{i,j} = \sum_{s \in d_j} lia_{s,i}; \; f_{i,j} = \frac{freq_{i,j}}{max_{t_l}(freq_{l,j})}; \; idf_i = \log N/n_i; \; w_{i,j} = f_{i,j} \times idf_i; \quad (3)$$

Additionally, subsection 3.2 proposes a variant of the indexing to augment the number of index terms for each metadata record.

2.2   The Indexing of Queries

Regarding the queries formulated by users, it is also necessary to find index terms characterizing these queries. Indeed, the query performed by the user specifies, although vaguely, the set of metadata records that he/she wants to discover. As well as metadata records have been summarized into a collection of synsets, queries must be also synthesized into a set of WordNet synsets. That is to say, in parallel to the indexing of metadata records, every word belonging to the query must be searched into WordNet and then, their possible senses, in the form of synsets, should be processed to obtain a representative collection of synsets. The first question here was whether we should also try the disambiguation of queries or not. By disambiguation of queries it is meant the election of the synset that better represents each query word among its possible synsets found in WordNet. In the context of our experiments it was assumed that the queries contained only a few words and not necessarily connected (i.e. with no synsets in common). Therefore the final decision was the non-disambiguation of queries. Besides, some works like [8] showed that trying to disambiguate the query in addition to the corpus made the results worse, especially in cases where the query was very short. Additionally, it must be mentioned that the use of synsets provides an implicit expansion of query words because each synset represents a set of synonyms (the word typed by the user and all its possible synonyms). In [9] Voorhees essayed different strategies for query expansion using the different types of associations between WordNet synsets and it was concluded that they provided little benefit, at least in the environment (general text retrieval for TREC conference, http://trec.nist.gov/) where the experiments were performed.

Finally, regarding query weights, a variant from the weighting scheme in [7] is applied to compute the weight of every synset with respect to the query q:

$$w_{i,q} = (0.5 + 0.5 \times (freq_{i,q}/max_{t_l}(freq_{l,q}))) \times idf_i \tag{4}$$

This variant, suggested in [10], gives a minimum weight of 0.5 to the normalized frequency. In this case, $freq_{i,q}$ is computed as the number of indirect references to the synset t_i.

3   Testing the Retrieval Model

3.1   Metadata Corpus

The formal precision (number of relevant hits divided by the number of hits) and recall (number of relevant hits divided by the number of relevant documents) measures used to quantify retrieval effectiveness of information retrieval systems are based on evaluation experiments conducted under controlled conditions. This requires a testbed comprising a fixed number of documents, a standard set of queries, and relevant and irrelevant documents in the testbed for each query. This is the case of TREC (http://trec.nist.gov/), an annual conference for academic and industrial text retrieval systems, which provides 2 GB document collection with about half a million documents. However, we could not find such a controlled testbed in the context of metadata catalogs and we had to construct our own testbed.

As an initial metadata corpus, the contents of the Geoscience Data Catalog (http://geo-nsdi.er.usgs.gov/) at U.S. Geological Survey (USGS) were downloaded. The USGS is the science agency for the U.S. Department of the Interior that provides information about Earth, its natural and living resources, natural hazards, and the environment. And despite being a national agency, it is also sought out by thousands of partners and customers around the world for its natural science expertise and its vast earth and biological data holdings. At the moment of download (March 2003), this catalog contained around 1,000 metadata records in XML format describing geographic data. The metadata records are compliant with the American standard CSDGM (Content Standard for Digital Geospatial Metadata, http://www.fgdc.gov), which includes a keywords section where the metadata creator can specify different values and the thesauri to which they belong. One of the reasons to select this catalog was our experience in Spatial Data Infrastructures [11]. However, the results of this work are extensible to any type of digital library using metadata schemas that contains a keyword section. Another important reason to select this catalog was that it provides a full text and field based search engine called ISearch [12], which enables at least the comparison of records retrieved.

Once the metadata records were imported in our metadata database, it was found that only 753 of the imported records contained thematic keywords. Furthermore, only 340 of these records contained keywords (an average of 3.673 keywords per record) belonging to formalized thesauri: NGMDB ("National Geologic Map Database Catalog themes, augmented", http://ngmdb.usgs.gov/) with 72 terms appearing 1105 times in the collection; and GTE ("Gateway to the Earth", http://alexandria.sdc.ucsb.edu/~lhill/usgs_terms/usgs/html9/) with 648 terms appearing only 144 times in the collection. Thus, given that uniquely these thesauri were suitable for the disambiguation, our information retrieval system could use only a small part of the downloaded collection. However, there were 656 records with an average of 7.87 terms belonging to unspecified thesauri, which were entitled in metadata records as "General" or "none". Therefore, we tried to transform these keywords from unspecified thesauri into terms belonging to GEMET, NGMDB and GTE. In particular, we selected GEMET ("General European Multilingual Environmental Thesaurus", http://www.mu.niedersachsen.de/cds/) because it is a quite comprehensive thesaurus for geographic information that consists of 5,542 terms organized in 109 branches and translated into 12 languages. In this transformation, we also solved some small morphological differences between the included terms and the terms of the disambiguated thesauri, e.g. difference between singular and plural versions. Thanks to this modification of metadata records, the final collection contained 711 records with an average of 5.594 theme keywords belonging to the three disambiguated thesauri.

In order to obtain performance measures, a series of topics(queries) and their relevance to metadata records were also necessary. For that purpose, the metadata corpus was enhanced by assigning manually the relevance with respect to a series of topics. This way, it would be possible to evaluate the precision and recall of different retrieval systems. The topics selected were based on the keywords with highest frequency in the collection. Fig. 2 displays the 10 topics selected, the thesauri to which they belong and their "narrower term/broader term" relations. Then, the metadata records were hand-tagged applying two basic rules: "if an specific term a is found in a record m, the record m will be relevant with respect to the broader terms of term a"; and "if a generic term a is found in a record m, the record m will not be relevant with respect to the narrower terms of term a".

Finally, we wanted to compare the effectiveness of our IRS with respect to a typical word-based retrieval system. But instead of using ISearch for this text retrieval system, the "Oracle Intermedia Text package" [13] was used. Oracle enables the creation of text indexes on text columns that may contain a wide range of Document Object Like data, including XML documents. And by means of the *CONTAINS* operator it is also possible to perform word queries on these columns (including tag based queries for XML documents) and obtain a relevance score. The cause for the replacement of ISearch by Oracle was the disparity in the remote and local data contents. On one hand, the online USGS Catalog updates its contents periodically. And on the other hand, we had modified locally the theme keywords to increment the use of disambiguated thesauri. Anyway, the ranking algorithms of ISearch and Oracle are very similar. To obtain the relevance score, both systems use an inverse frequency algorithm based on the vector-space model formulas. In fact, before the transformation of keywords, a series of tests were performed against online ISearch and Oracle (containing same records in XML) and equivalent results were obtained.

3.2   The Experiments

The first experiments of our IRS were devoted to observe the influence of inverse frequency and the number of keywords in each metadata record. For instance, let us observe the results obtained with the query *geology erosion* (associated with 5 synsets: 2 with *geology* and 3 with *erosion*) in table 2, which are ranked by similarity. Although the first two hits have only one match with the query synsets, they are ranked higher than the record in third position, which has three synset matches. On one hand, this is due to the fact that two of the synsets matches correspond to the synsets associated with *geology*, whose inverse frequency is very low. These synsets are very frequent in the collection and the vector-space model tries to balance this effect: "the fewer a term occurs in, the more important it must be". And on the other hand, third hit references a total number of 13 synsets, while the first two hits reference only 3. As the number of referenced synsets grows, the norm of the vector representing the record will increase, increasing as well the denominator in the similarity formula. This denominator favours metadata records with fewer keywords. Although some times this means that such metadata records are better focused on a subject, other times is simply due to a worse quality in metadata cataloguing. It was tested the possibility of obviating the denominator. But this variation was rejected because the results were not satisfactory: there was almost no graduation for the similarity in simple queries as the previous one. Besides, as the number of query terms and synset matches increases, the norm of the vectors representing the records is not so influent.

Then, we wanted to test one of the obvious advantages of our information retrieval system in comparison with other search engines based on word indexing.

Table 2. Returned results for the query *geology erosion*

Order	Title	Sim
1	Beach profile data for Maui, Hawaii	0.375
2	Beach profile data for Oahu, Hawaii	0.375
3	Possible Costs Associated with Investigating and Mitigating Some Geologic Hazards in Rural Parts of San Mateo County, California	0.318
. . .		

It is that the queries can contain words that have not been necessarily included in metadata keywords, e.g. synonyms of these keywords that match with the same WordNet synsets. For instance, we performed two queries with two synonyms, *fuel* and *combustible*, which correspond to the same WordNet synset. Our IRS always returned 138 hits but Oracle only returned records (138 hits with same score) for the query *fuel*, which was the word included in the keyword section.

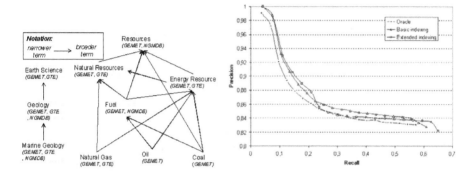

Fig. 2. Concept Map   **Fig. 3.** Average Precision-Recall curves

After these initial experiments, we decided to augment the number of synsets representing the metadata records. For this expansion, we included the disambiguated synsets that were associated to the broader terms of the terms included in keyword section. For instance, the broader term of *coal* in GEMET is *fossil fuel*, and thus metadata records with term *coal* were indexed with the disambiguated synset of *coal* as well as with the disambiguated synset of *fossil fuel*. The idea was that if a user asks for resources about *fossil fuel*, he might be interested in different types of fossil fuels (e.g. *coal*, *natural gas* or *petroleum*). Of course, the weight of the synset for the broader term must be lower than the weight for the real term included in the metadata record. In particular, the liability of the synsets which are associated with broader terms was divided by 2. Thanks to this modification, our IRS returned 121 hits for the query *fossil fuel*, one hit more than the query *coal*. Meanwhile, Oracle returned no hits for query *fossil fuel*. This is due to the fact that Oracle *CONTAINS* operator only performs simple word matching, and only the word *fuel* is included in metadata records.

Finally, we compared the performance of the basic indexing of our IRS, the extended indexing of our IRS and the Oracle text retrieval. Fig. 3 displays the average precision-recall curves obtained with the aforementioned topics and for the different types of retrieval systems. Basically, it can be concluded that the precision obtained is similar in the three cases. The main advantage of the IRS proposed in this paper is that the recall measures are improved: an increase of 6.60% in the case of basic indexing with respect to Oracle; and an increase of 13.94% in the case of extended indexing.

4   Conclusions and Future Lines

This paper has presented the adaptation of a vector-space information retrieval model to the context of metadata catalogs. The indexing of metadata records assumes that the metadata schema includes a keyword section or subject element, something quite usual in most metadata schemas. Besides, the indexing technique is based on the inclusion in this section of terms selected from disambiguated thesauri. The index terms are precisely the synsets associated with the selected thesaurus term during the disambiguation process of the thesaurus. Furthermore, this basic indexing of metadata records was modified to augment the number of index terms. Apart from collecting the synsets associated with a thesaurus term, the indexing method also included the synsets associated with the broader terms in the thesaurus hierarchy. These synsets coming from broader terms were assigned a lower weight. This modification was based on the assumption that metadata records represented by these synsets (from broader terms) are still semantically close to queries including the broader concept. This expansion could have been also continued with the synsets associated with other related terms. However, works like [1] suggest not considering concepts at distance two or more from an initial concept.

The viability of the retrieval model has been tested with a collection of metadata records describing geographic resources and the results have been compared with a typical text retrieval system (based on word matching). These first experiments have shown that the precision obtained is comparable with a typical text retrieval system. And as regards recall, it has been noticed an increase in the number of relevant documents returned with respect to the text retrieval system. Anyway, it is necessary to test the method with a bigger corpus of metadata records and better classified with additional disambiguated thesauri.

The main disadvantage of the IRS presented in this paper is that the thesauri disambiguation may not be adequate for very specialized thesauri. WordNet is an upper-level ontology that lacks for domain-specific terminology. Nevertheless, the intention of this work is to approximate as much as possible the terms used in metadata records and the concepts extracted from "general-purpose" queries. And WordNet is a public domain electronic lexical database which may be considered as one of the most important resource available to researchers in computational linguistics, text analysis and many related areas.

On the other hand, an improvement in the computation of the weight of each index term would be to consider the importance of the thesaurus, to which the terms in the keyword section belong. A term selected from a specific thesaurus like GEMET may be more relevant than a term belonging to a thesaurus that compiles only a hundred of categories. Finally, it must be mentioned that this retrieval method could be extended by indexing other metadata fields (or elements) like *title*, or *abstract*. Besides, the value of similarity could be integrated into more complex information retrieval systems as another factor to compute the final value for the degree of similarity.

References

1. Clark, P., Thompson, J., Holmback, H., Duncan, L.: Exploiting a thesaurus-based semantic net for knowledge-based search. In: Proc 12th Conf on Innovative Application of AI (AAAI/IAAI'00). (2000) 988–995
2. Mata, E.J., Ansó, J., Bañares, J.A., Muro-Medrano, P.R., Rubio, J.: Enriquecimiento de tesauros con wordnet: una aproximación heurística. In: Actas IX CAEPIA, Gijón (2001) 593–602
3. Miller, G.A.: Wordnet: An on-line lexical database. Int. J. Lexicography **3** (1990)
4. Gonzalo, J., Verdejo, F., Chugur, I., Cigarran, J.: Indexing with WordNet synsets can improve Text Retrieval. In: Proc. COLING/ACL'98 Workshop on Usage of WordNet for Natural Language Processing. (1998)
5. Sanderson, M.: Word sense disambiguation and information retrieval. In: Proceedings of the 17th International Conference on Research and Development in Information Retrieval. (1994)
6. Salton, G., ed.: The SMART retrieval system - Experiments in Automatic Document Processing. Prentice Hall, Inc., Englewood Cliffs, NJ (1971)
7. Salton, G., McGill, M.J.: Introduction to Modern Information Retrieval. McGraw-Hill (1983)
8. Voorhees, E.M.: Using WordNet to disambiguate Word Senses for Text Retrieval. In: SIGIR '93, Proc. 16th annual international ACM SIGIR conf. on Research and Development in Information Retrieval. (1993) 171–180
9. Voorhees, E.M.: On Expanding Query Vectors with Lexically Related Words. In: Text REtrieval Conference. (1993) 223–232
10. Salton, G., Buckley, C.: Term-weighting approaches in automatic text retrieval. Information Processing & Management **24** (1988) 513–523
11. Bernabé, M.A., Gould, M., Muro-Medrano, P.R., Nogueras, J., Zarazaga, F.J.: Effective steps toward the Spain National Geographic Information Infrastructure. In: Proc 4th AGILE Conference on Geographic Information Science, Brno, Czech Republic (2001) 236–243
12. Nassar, N.: Searching With Isearch, Moving beyond WAIS. Web Techniques magazine, www.webtechniques.com (1997)
13. Scherer, D., Brennan, C.: Exploring Oracle Text Basics. Oracle Magazine **March/April** (2001)
    http://www.oracle.com/oramag/index.html.

Face Detection with Active Contours
Using Color Information

Jae Sik Chang[1], Eun Yi Kim[2], and Hang Joon Kim[1]

[1] Dept. of Computer Engineering, Kyungpook National Univ., Daegu, South Korea
{jschang,kimhj}@ailab.knu.ac.kr
[2] Scool of Internet and Multimedia, Konkuk Univ., Seoul, South Korea
eykim@konkuk.ac.kr

Abstract. This paper proposes a method for detecting facial regions in complex environments. To obtain accurate facial boundaries, active contours are used. In the active contour model, a contour is presented by zero level set of level function ϕ, and evolved via level set partial differential equations. The advantages of the proposed method include 1) the robustness to noise, 2) accurate detection regions of multiple face with various viewpoints and sizes. To assess the effectiveness of the proposed method, it was tested with several natural scenes, and the results are compared with these of geometric active contours. Experimental results show the effectiveness of the proposed method.

1 Introduction

Human face detection has been considered as an interest research area, mainly due to developments of applications of multimedia and surveillance systems.

Accordingly, various techniques and algorithms have been proposed and they can be roughly classified into four categories [1]; knowledge-based approaches, feature invariant approaches, template matching approaches and appearance-based approaches. Among these approaches, template matching approaches have been widely used. This approach stores several templates describing the face, facial features, and their relations. And it computes the correlation values between a given image and the templates to detect facial regions [1]. Although it is simple, the use of this approach is restricted to the detection of the frontal facial images. This limitation is due to rigidity of templates, so deformable templates were proposed to model facial features. The method deforms the predefined templates, and matches deformed template and a given image. These operations are iteratively executed until the best fit of the template is founded [1].

Although these methods have good performance, some technical problems for face detection are remained as it used to be. For example, detecting accurate boundary of facial region is difficult task due to noise and degradation in image and various viewpoints of faces. And when tracking is needed, detection and detection type in first frame are more important. In order to overcome these problems, we use an active

R. Conejo et al. (Eds.): CAEPIA-TTIA 2003, LNAI 3040, pp. 334–343, 2004.
© Springer-Verlag Berlin Heidelberg 2004

contour model, a description of a object boundary which is iteratively adjusted until it best match the object of interest [2]. Because of their elasticity, Active contours are used frequently to detect and track boundaries of non-rigid objects [3,4,5]. Original Active contours act as an edge-detector, i.e. an initial contour around the object to be detected evolves to its normal direction and stop on the boundary that has large gradient values [4,5].

This paper investigates the application of the active contours to the face detection problems. The facial region detection is formulated as an energy minimization problem, leading to the solution via an active contour model, in the Bayesian framework. Instead of gradient information used in general active contour models, we use the color information of human faces that is represented by a skin color model. And for representation and evolving of contours, we use the level set method [4,5,6]. The experimental results show that our method is effective to detect faces that have various viewpoints and scales in noisy images.

2 Proposed Method

In this paper, the facial region detection is formulated as an energy minimization problem, leading to the solution via an active contour model, in the Bayesian framework. In proposed method, the label field has two kinds of label for facial region and background region, respectively. Our goal is to estimate a boundary, between the two regions, which minimize the energy functional, for this, we used an active contour model based on color information of human faces. In the active contour model used, closed curve as contour is presented by zero level set of level function ϕ, and evolved via level set partial equations.

2.1 Problem Formulation

The input image G is considered as formed by two regions: facial region(R) and background region (R^c). Let $S=\{(i,j): 1\le i \le M_1, 1\le j \le M_2\}$ denote the $M_1 \times M_2$ lattice, such that the elements in S index the image pixels. Let $\Lambda = \{\lambda, \lambda^c\}$ denote the label set, where λ and λ^c are labels for facial region and background region, respectively. Let $X =\{X_{ij} \mid X_{ij} \in \Lambda\}$ be the family of random variables defined on S. Let ω be a realization of X. The goal is to identify ω that maximizes the posterior distribution for a fixed input image g. That is,

$$X^* = \arg\max_{\omega} P(G = g \mid X = \omega)P(X = \omega) . \tag{1}$$

Eq. (1) can be represented as the following pixel-wise equation:

$$X^* = \arg\max_{\omega} \prod_{(i,j)\in R}\left[P(G_{ij} = g_{ij} \mid X_{ij} = \lambda)P(X_{ij} = \lambda)\right]$$
$$\times \prod_{(i,j)\in R^c}\left[P(G_{ij} = g_{ij} \mid X_{ij} = \lambda^c)P(X_{ij} = \lambda^c)\right]. \tag{2}$$

Then, Eq. (2) can be formulated as an energy minimization problem as follows:

$$\vec{\gamma}^* = \underset{\vec{\gamma}}{\arg\min} E(\vec{\gamma}), \text{ where } \begin{aligned} E(\vec{\gamma}) &= -\int_{R_{\vec{\gamma}}} \log\left[P(G_{ij} = g_{ij} \mid X_{ij} = \lambda)P(X_{ij} = \lambda)\right] dx \\ &\quad - \int_{R_{\vec{\gamma}}^c} \log\left[P(G_{ij} = g_{ij} \mid X_{ij} = \lambda^c)P(X_{ij} = \lambda^c)\right] dx \end{aligned} \tag{3}$$

In Eq. (3), $\vec{\gamma}(s):[0,1] \rightarrow \Re^2$ is a closed planar curve that we use as an estimator of ∂R, $R_{\vec{\gamma}}$ the region enclosed by $\vec{\gamma}$ is the estimator of the region R, while its complement $R_{\vec{\gamma}}^c$ is the estimator of the background R^c.

2.2 Minimization of Energy Functional

For minimization of energy, we do steepest descent with respect to $\vec{\gamma}$. For any point $\vec{\gamma}(s)$ on the curve $\vec{\gamma}$, as

$$\frac{d\vec{\gamma}(s)}{dt} = -\frac{\partial E(\vec{\gamma})}{\partial \vec{\gamma}(s)}, \tag{4}$$

where the right-hand side is (minus) the functional derivative of the energy [7,8].

Taking the functional derivative yields the motion equation for a point $\vec{\gamma}(s)$, for more detail refer [7].

$$\frac{d\vec{\gamma}(s)}{dt} = \begin{aligned} &\underbrace{[\log P(G_{\vec{\gamma}(s)} = g_{\vec{\gamma}(s)} \mid X_{\vec{\gamma}(s)} = \lambda) - \log P(G_{\vec{\gamma}(s)} = g_{\vec{\gamma}(s)} \mid X_{\vec{\gamma}(s)} = \lambda^c)]\vec{n}(\vec{\gamma}(s))}_{term1} \\ &\underbrace{+[\log P(X_{\vec{\gamma}(s)} = \lambda) - \log P(X_{\vec{\gamma}(s)} = \lambda^c)]\vec{n}(\vec{\gamma}(s))}_{term2} \end{aligned}, \tag{5}$$

where $\vec{n}(x)$ is the unit normal to $\vec{\gamma}$ at x pointing outward of $R_{\vec{\gamma}}$. This equation is identical to the motion equation for boundary of region competition proposed by *Zhu et al.* for image segmentation [7].

2.3 Level Set Formulation

We solve Eq. (5) numerically by discrediting the interval [0,1] on which $\vec{\gamma}$ is defined, thus leading to a representation of $\vec{\gamma}$ in terms of a finite number of points or nodes. This leads to an explicit representation of $\vec{\gamma}$. A better alternative is to represent the curve $\vec{\gamma}$ implicitly by the zero level set of a function $\phi: \Re^2 \rightarrow \Re$, with the region inside $\vec{\gamma}$ corresponding to $\phi > 0$ [4,5,6].

In the case of face detection based on color information, the evolution equation for ϕ corresponding to Eq. (5) becomes

$$\frac{d\phi_{ij}}{dt} = \underbrace{\left[\log P(G_{ij} = g_{ij} \mid X_{ij} = \lambda) - \log P(G_{ij} = g_{ij} \mid X_{ij} = \lambda^c)\right]}_{term1} \|\nabla\phi\| \\ + \underbrace{\left[\log P(X_{ij} = \lambda) - \log P(X_{ij} = \lambda^c)\right]}_{term2} \|\nabla\phi\|. \tag{6}$$

2.4 Estimation of the Probabilities

Let $\Omega = \{ \omega = (\omega_{11}, \omega_{12}, \ldots, \omega_{M1M2}) | \omega_{ij} \in \Lambda, (i,j) \in S \}$ denote the set of all possible realization of X, and let ω be a realization of Ω. X can be an MRF on S with respect to neighborhood system if the following condition holds [9]:

$$P(X_{ij} = \omega_{ij} | X_{kl} = \omega_{kl}, (i,j) \neq (k,l)) = P(X_{ij} = \omega_{ij} | X_{kl} = \omega_{kl}, (k,l) \in \eta_{ij}). \tag{7}$$

Then, $P(\omega)$ has Gibbs distribution as follows[9]:

$$P(\omega) = \exp(-U(\omega)) = \exp[-\sum_{c \in C} S_c(\omega)]. \tag{8}$$

In Eq.(8), C is a possible set of cliques, where a clique is defined as a set of pixels in which all the pairs are mutual neighbors. $U(\omega)$ imposes the spatial continuity of the labels where $S_c(\omega)$ is spatial potential. The proposed method assumes that the only nonzero potentials are those corresponding to two-pair cliques. Then $S_c(\omega) = -\alpha$ if all labels in c are equal, otherwise $S_c(\omega) = \alpha$.

We assume that the color values of the face region are homogeneous and consistent with having been generated by prespecified probability distribution called "skin color model", and the distribution of the background region is complicated, so it is difficult to be prespecified and is complicated.

We use the skin color model proposed by *Yang et al.* [10] for describing the color information of human faces. Therefore, the skin-color model is approximated by a 2D-Gaussian model $N(m, \Sigma^2)$.

The likelihood function of λ for g_{ij} is described as follows:

$$P(G_{ij} = g_{i,j} | X_{i,j} = \lambda)$$

$$\propto \frac{1}{2\pi\sigma_r\sigma_g\sqrt{1-\rho^2}} \times \tag{9}$$

$$\exp\left\{-\frac{1}{2(1-\rho^2)}\left[\frac{(r-\bar{r})^2}{\sigma_r^2} + \frac{(g-\bar{g})^2}{\sigma_g^2} - 2\rho\frac{(r-\bar{r})(g-\bar{g})}{\sigma_r\sigma_g}\right]\right\}.$$

We can obtain the equation followed,

$$\log P(g_{i,j} | \omega_{i,j} = \lambda) \approx -F(r,g), \tag{10}$$

where

$$F(r,g) = \left[\frac{(r-\bar{r})^2}{\sigma_r^2} + \frac{(g-\bar{g})^2}{\sigma_g^2} - 2\rho\frac{(r-\bar{r})(g-\bar{g})}{\sigma_r\sigma_g}\right]. \tag{11}$$

As mentioned above, we use the color information of human faces for the likelihood function of λ for g_{ij}. Since the distribution of the background region is complicated, it is difficult to be pre-specified in real images. We use a threshold θ for the likelihood function of λ^c for g_{ij}. θ can be obtained as follows.

$$\theta = \log P(G_{ij} = g_{ij} | X_{ij} = \lambda^c) = -F(\bar{r} + 3\sigma_r, \bar{r}) = -F(\bar{g} + 3\sigma_g, \bar{g}) = -9. \tag{12}$$

Accordingly, Eq. (6) can be represented by the following equation, which is defined as a level set evolution equation:

$$\frac{d\phi(x)}{dt} = \underbrace{\{(-F)-\theta\}\|\nabla\phi\|}_{term1} + \underbrace{[(-\sum_{o\in C}S_c(\lambda))+(-\sum_{o\in C}S_c(\lambda^c))]\|\nabla\phi\|}_{term2} \qquad (13)$$

2.5 Implementation

The initial level set function ϕ_o can be implemented using a distance mapping technique. In our experimentation, we have used Euclidian distance mapping to generate the level set function $\phi(X,t)$ that embeds the parametric closed initial curve $\bar{\gamma}(t=0)$, as the initial zero level set. The level set evolution equation given in Eq.(13) is iteratively implemented using simple forward difference with respect to neighbor pixels of zero level pixels. If n is the iterative contour parameter, then

$$\frac{\phi^{n+1}(x)-\phi^n(x)}{\Delta t} = \{(-F)-\theta\}\|\nabla\phi\|+[(-\sum_{o\in C}S_c(\lambda))+(-\sum_{o\in C}S_c(\lambda^c))]\|\nabla\phi\| . \qquad (14)$$

The norm of gradient term $\|\nabla\phi\|$ in Eq.(14) is implemented using Sobel operators.

After each iteration, The approximate final propagated contour i.e., the zero level set is constructed ($\phi = 0$) and label field is updated from $\phi^{n+1}(x)$. Contour reconstruction is obtained by determining the zero crossing grid location in the level set function [11]. If ϕ_{ij} is a positive value, the label of position (i,j) is set to λ, otherwise λ^c. The stopping criterion is satisfied, when the difference of the number of the pixel inside contour ($\bar{\gamma}$) is less than a threshold value. The threshold value is chosen by manually.

3   Experimental Results

This paper investigates the application of the active contours to the face detection problems. This chapter focuses on evaluating the proposed method. First section presents the facial region detection results for several images. Then, the comparison between the proposed method and another method was showed.

3.1   Facial Detection Results

In order to assess the effectiveness of the proposed method, experiments were performed on color images including facial regions that have various poses and viewpoints. The skin-color model is obtained from 200 sample images. Means and covariance matrix of the skin color model are as follows:

$$m=(\bar{r},\bar{g})=(117.588,79.064),$$

$$\Sigma=\begin{bmatrix} \sigma_r^2 & \rho_{X,Y}\sigma_g\sigma_r \\ \rho_{X,Y}\sigma_r\sigma_g & \sigma_g^2 \end{bmatrix}=\begin{bmatrix} 24.132 & -10.085 \\ -10.085 & 8.748 \end{bmatrix}.$$

An active contour model is a semi-automatic method that needs an initial contour and then the results are affected by the location of the initial contour. Original geometric active contours or balloon snakes move uni-directionally, i.e. contours only

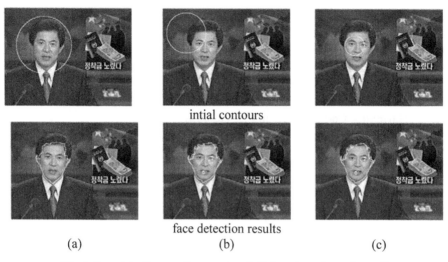

intial contours

face detection results

(a)   (b)   (c)

Fig. 1. Face detection results on various initial contours (experiment 1).

expand or shrink, therefore, some arbitrary initialized contour can miss the object. In proposed method, proposed active contour model moves bi-directionally because we used the color information of human faces. So, our method allows for arbitrary initialization of initial contour. Fig.1 shows the experimental results on various initial contours.

To fully demonstrate the effectiveness of the proposed method, it was performed on the images including multiple facial regions and noisy images. In order to represent and evolve the contour, the proposed method use level sets which allow automatic topological changes. It makes the proposed method detect multiple faces. An experiment result on the image which includes more than one face is shown in Fig.2

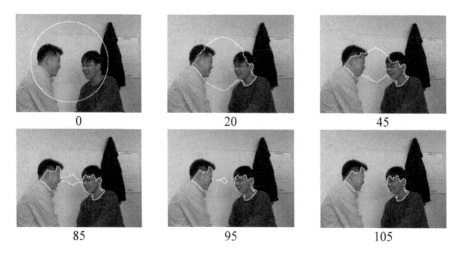

0   20   45

85   95   105

Fig. 2. Results of experiments on a image include multiple faces. The iteration number is indicated below the pictures (experiment 2).

The contour split up into several parts, and finally two of them are converged to boundaries of faces and others are disappeared. This result represents that the proposed method runs independently on the number of faces in the given image. This experiment was performed with $\Delta t=1$, $\alpha=0.2$, initial contour $((x - 128)^2 + (y - 109)^2 = 92^2)$ and the threshold value of stopping criteria is 5.

3.2 Performance Comparisons and Discussions

To assess the validity of the proposed method, it was compared with the geometric active contour model presented in [4]. The model represents and evolves the contour using level sets. In the method using the model, the contour shrinks iteratively and the contour stops on the boundary that has high gradient values. For each video frame, ground truth was created by manually constructing accurate boundaries of each facial region. This is used to calculate the accuracy and the miss detection rate so as to evaluate performance of the proposed method. The accuracy and the miss detection rate are defined by

$$A = \frac{num(D \cap G) + num(D^c \cap G^c)}{imageSize} \times 100 \ ,$$

$$M_i = \frac{num(D \cap G^c) + num(D^c \cap G)}{imageSize} \times 100 \ , \text{respectively,}$$

where
    $D = \{ \ d \mid d = $ pixels of facial regions detected by the proposed method$\}$
    $G = \{ \ g \mid g = $ pixels of facial regions detected manually$\}$: ground truth ;
    $num(\bullet)$: # of pixels in the region.

Fig.3 shows the result of face detection using the geometric active contour model. The experiment performed on the same initial condition that is used on experiment 1(a).

| 0 | 10 | 40 |
| 100 | 200 | 395 |

Fig. 3. Results of face detection using the geometric active contour model proposed by *Caselles et al.* [4] (experiment 3).

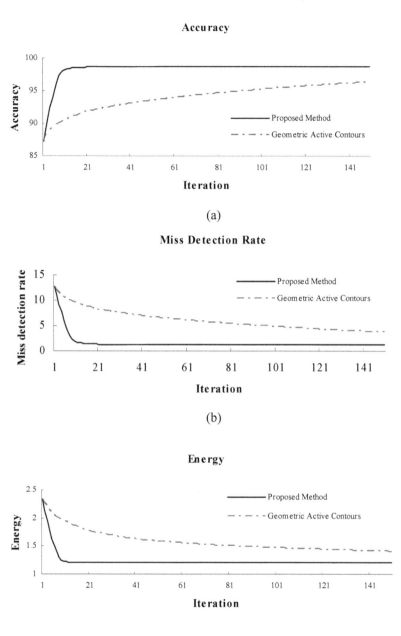

Fig. 4. The comparisons of the two methods in terms of accuracy, miss detection.

Fig. 4 shows the comparisons of the two methods in terms of accuracy, miss detection rate and energy. As you can see, accuracy (miss detection rate and energy) of the proposed method increases (decreases) dramatically and maintain stable phase.

4 Conclusions

In this paper, an active contour was used for detecting facial regions, regardless of pose, viewpoints, and noise. An input image is modeled using a Markov random field (MRF), which is effective in describing the spatial dependency of neighboring pixels and robust to degradation and noise. And MAP was used for optimality criterion, so that the face detection is formulated as an energy minimization. For minimizing the energy, we used a active contour model based on the color information of human faces. In the active contour model, a contour is presented by zero level set of level function ϕ, and evolved via level set partial differential equations.

Experimental results show the effectiveness of the proposed method. However, the proposed method is a semi-automatic method, where it need a initial contour inputted by manually. Future works include determining the initial contour efficiently and adaptation the proposed method to real applications such as video monitoring system, face recognition system, etc.

Acknowledgement

This work was partially supported by both Brain Korea 21 and grant NO. R04-2003-000-10187-0 from the Basic Research Program of the Korea Science & Engineering Foundation, respectively.

References

1. M. H. Yang. D. J. Kriegman and N. Ahuja, "Detecting Faces in Images: A Survey," *IEEE Transactions On PAMI*, Vol. 24, No. 1, pp. 34-58, 2002.
2. S. D. Fenster, J. R. Kender, "Sectored Snakes: Evaluating Learned Energy Segmentations," *IEEE Transaction On PAMI*, Vol. 23, No. 9, pp. 1028-1034, 2002.
3. M. Kass, A. Witkin and D. Terzopoulos, "Snakes: Active contour models," *Int. J. Comput. Vis.*, vol. 1, pp.321-331, 1988.
4. V. Caselles, F. Catte, T. Coll and F. Dibos, "A geometric model for active contours in image processes," *Numer. Math.*, vol. 66, pp.1-31, 1993.
5. T. F. Chan and A.Vese, "Active Contours Without Edges," *IEEE Transactions On Image Processing,* vol. 10, No. 2, pp.266-277, 2001.
6. S. Osher and J. A. Sethian, "Fronts propagating with curvature-dependent speed: Algorithms based on Hamilton-Jacobi Formulation," *J.Comput. Phys.*, vol. 79, pp.12-49, 1988.
7. S. C. Zhu and A. Yuille, "Region Competition: Unifying Snakes, Region Growing, and Bayes/MDL for Multiband Image Segmentation," *IEEE Transaction On PAMI*, Vol. 18, No. 9, pp. 884-900, 1996.
8. A. R. Mansouri, "Region Tracking via Level Set PDEs without Motion Computation," *IEEE Transactions On PAMI*, Vol. 24, No. 7, pp. 947-961, 2002.
9. E. Y. Kim, S. W. Hwang, S. H. Park, and H. J. Kim, "Spatiotemporal Segmentation Using Genetic Algorithms", *Pattern Recognition*, Vol. 34, No. 10, pp. 2063-2066,2001.

10. J. Yang and A. Waibel, " A real-time face tracker," Proceedings of the Third *IEEE Workshop on Applications of Computer Vision,* Sarasota, Florida, 1996, pp.142-147 ("Tracking Human Faces in Real-Time," Technical Report, CMU-CS-95-210, 1995).

11. S. Kulkarni and B. N. Chatterji, "Accurate shape modeling with front propagation using adaptive level sets," *Pattern Recognition Letters*, to be published.

Formal Verification of Molecular Computational Models in ACL2: A Case Study*

Francisco J. Martín-Mateos, José A. Alonso,
Maria José Hidalgo, and José Luis Ruiz-Reina

Computational Logic Group
Dept. of Computer Science and Artificial Intelligence, University of Seville
E.T.S.I. Informática, Avda. Reina Mercedes, s/n. 41012 Sevilla, Spain
http://www.cs.us.es/{~fmartin,~jalonso,~mjoseh,~jruiz}

Abstract. Theorem proving is a classical AI problem with a broad range of applications. Since its complexity is exponential in the size of the problem, many methods to parallelize the process has been proposed. One of these approaches is based on the massive parallelism of molecular reactions. ACL2 is an automated theorem prover especially adequate for algorithm verification. In this paper we present an ACL2 formalization of a molecular computational model: Adleman's restricted model. As an application of this model, an implementation of Lipton's experiment solving SAT is described. We use ACL2 to make a formal proof of the completeness and soundness properties of this implementation.

1 Introduction

In the last years the interest in developing new computational models based on biological models has increased [2, 13]. One of the main advantages of these models is the massive parallelism associated with some process. This reduces considerably the complexity of some problems (with respect to the elemental operations in the model). However, the biological implementation of these models is not often possible and, when it can be done, the cost of the experiments could force to increase our confidence in their correction.

ACL2 [7] is a programming language, a logic for reasoning about programs in the language, and a theorem prover supporting formal reasoning in the logic. Automated reasoning systems in general and ACL2 in particular, are usually used to build formal models of "digital systems", software and hardware [9, 15]. Using the proof techniques of these systems, we can prove properties of the formalized models. In this paper, we present an application of the ACL2 system to formalize and verify computational models based on biological models. In particular, we formalize a molecular computational model and one of the first biological experiment solving a NP-complete problem.

Adleman's first experiment [1] shows that NP-complete problems could be solved by means of manipulation of DNA molecules. Based on Adleman's ideas,

---

* This work has been supported by project TIC2000-1368-C03-02 (Ministry of Science and Technology, Spain), cofinanced by FEDER funds.

R. Conejo et al. (Eds.): CAEPIA-TTIA 2003, LNAI 3040, pp. 344–353, 2004.

R.J. Lipton [11] solved an instance of the satisfiability propositional problem. In this sense, new experiments has been done recently [3, 10]. In this paper we present our ACL2 formalization of Adleman's restricted model. This formalization is done in such a way that the subsequent development is generic: the specific operations are not important, but only their properties. In [14] a formalization of Lipton's experiment is given as an iterative algorithm based on the elemental operations of Adleman's restricted model. We define recursive functions implementing this formalization and we prove the completeness and soundness properties of these functions.

2   The ACL2 System

ACL2 [7] is a programming language, a logic for reasoning about programs in the language, and a theorem prover supporting formal reasoning in the logic. The ACL2 logic is a quantifier-free, first-order logic with equality, describing an extension of an applicative subset of Common Lisp. The syntax of terms is that of Common Lisp and the logic includes axioms for propositional logic and for a number of Lisp functions and data types. Rules of inference of the logic include those for propositional calculus, equality and instantiation. The ACL2 theorem prover mechanizes that logic, being particularly well suited for obtaining automatized proofs based on simplification and induction. For a detailed description of ACL2, we refer the reader to the book [6].

By the *principle of definition*, new function definitions are admitted as axioms only if there exists a measure in which the arguments of each recursive call decrease with respect to a well-founded relation, ensuring in this way that no inconsistencies are introduced by new definitions. Some higher order functionality is provided by means of the `encapsulate` mechanism [8] which allows the user to introduce new function symbols by axioms constraining them to have certain properties (to ensure consistency, a witness local function having the same properties has to be exhibited). Inside an `encapsulate`, the properties stated need to be proved for the local witnesses, and outside, they work as assumed axioms. This mechanism behaves like an universal quantifier over a set of functions abstractly defined with it. So, any theorem proved about these functions is true for any functions with the same properties as the assumed in the `encapsulate`.

The user can start a proof attempt invoking the `defthm` command establishing the property she wants to prove. The ACL2 theorem prover is automatic in the sense that once `defthm` is invoked, the user can no longer interact with the system. However, the user can (and usually must) guide the prover by adding lemmas and definitions that are used in subsequent proofs as rewriting rules. A typical ACL2 proof effort consists of formalizing the problem in the logic and helping the prover to find a preconceived proof by means of a suitable set of rewriting rules. These rules can be found by inspecting the failed proofs. That is the methodology we followed in this case study.

For the sake of readability, the ACL2 expressions in this paper are presented using a notation closer to the usual mathematical notation than its original

Common Lisp syntax. Some of the functions are also used in infix notation. The complete files with definitions and theorems are available on the Web in http://www.cs.us.es/~fmartin/acl2/molecular/.

3   Adleman's Restricted Model

In [2] some abstract models for molecular computing are described. The first model proposed works with test tubes with a set of DNA molecules, i.e. a multiset of finite sequences over the alphabet $\{A, C, G, T\}$. Nevertheless, it may be preferable to use molecules other than DNA, using an alphabet Σ which is not necessarily $\{A, C, G, T\}$. Further, though DNA has a natural structure which allows to order the occurrence of elements and hence deal with sequences, this may not be true for other types of molecules. Then, the members of a tube will be multisets of elements from Σ. In the sequel, we consider an alphabet Σ and we call *aggregate* a multiset of elements from this alphabet.

The above considerations are the basis of the restricted model of molecular computation. This model works on test tubes with a multiset of aggregates (i.e. a multiset of multisets of elements from Σ). On these tubes, the following operations can be performed:

- *Separate*(T, x): Given a tube T and an element $x \in \Sigma$, produces two new tubes, $+(T, x)$ and $-(T, x)$, where $+(T, x)$ is the tube consisting of every aggregate of T which contains the element x and $-(T, x)$ is the tube consisting of every aggregate of T which does not contain the element x:

$$+(T, x) = \{\gamma \in T : x \in \gamma\}$$

$$-(T, x) = \{\gamma \in T : x \notin \gamma\}$$

- *Merge*(T_1, T_2): Given tubes T_1 and T_2, produces the new tube $T_1 \cup T_2$, which is the multiset union of the multisets T_1 and T_2.
- *Detect*(T): Given a tube T, decides if T contains at least one aggregate; that is, returns "yes" if T contains at least one aggregate and returns "no" if it contains none.

These operations are performed in the laboratory in the following way. If a *Merge* of tubes is required, this is accomplished by pouring the contents of one of the tubes into the other. If a *Separate* or a *Detect* operation is required on a tube then some technical operations (magnetic bead system, polymerase chain reaction, get electrophoresis, ...) are performed on it. This model is called "restricted" in the sense that the molecules themselves do not change in the course of a computation.

To formalize the restricted model in ACL2, we use lists to represent multisets. Then, a test tube is represented as a list of aggregates and an aggregate is represented as a list of elements from Σ. So, the functions associated with the molecular operations work on lists.

We consider two functions, `separate+` and `separate-`, associated with the *Separate* operation. The first one returning the value $+(T, x)$ and the second one the value $-(T, x)$. The *Merge* operation is associated with the function `tube-merge`. Finally, we consider the function `detect` associated with the *Detect* operation.

The definition of these functions is not so interesting as their properties. The properties of any algorithm built on the restricted model must be independent of the implementation of the operations. This will ensure the properties of the algorithm even when it was evaluated in a molecular laboratory. Therefore, we define them by means of the `encapsulate` mechanism, constraining them to have certain properties. These properties are the following:

ASSUMPTION: `member-separate+`
$\quad \gamma \in \mathtt{separate+}(T, x) \leftrightarrow x \in \gamma \wedge \gamma \in T$

ASSUMPTION: `member-separate-`
$\quad \gamma \in \mathtt{separate-}(T, x) \leftrightarrow x \notin \gamma \wedge \gamma \in T$

ASSUMPTION: `member-tube-merge`
$\quad \gamma \in \mathtt{tube-merge}(T_1, T_2) \leftrightarrow \gamma \in T_1 \vee \gamma \in T_2$

ASSUMPTION: `member-detect`
$\quad \mathtt{detect}(T) = \mathbf{t} \leftrightarrow \exists e \in T$

If we want to test any algorithm built on the restricted model, we must provide concrete functions implementing the basic operations and prove the encapsulated properties for them. Anyway, introducing these properties by means of `encapsulate`, we ensure that the proof of subsequent properties are independent of these concrete implementations.

4   Lipton's Experiment

Adleman's experiment [1] solved an instance of the Hamiltonian path problem over a directed graph with two designated vertices, by implementing a brute force procedure in a laboratory of molecular biology. To solve the problem, an initial test tube with DNA molecules encoding all the paths in the graph was built. This tube was subjected to some operations based on DNA manipulation, and every aggregate encoding a path which was not a valid solution of the problem was removed.

Lipton shows in [11] how to solve an instance of the satisfiability problem for Propositional Logic, using the ideas of Adleman. To achieve this, he described every relevant assignment of a propositional formula by means of paths on a directed graph associated with the variable set of the formula. Specifically, given a propositional formula in conjunctive normal form, $F = c_1 \wedge \ldots \wedge c_p$, where the clauses $c_i = l_{i,1} \vee \ldots \vee l_{i,r_i}$, and the set of variables $Var(F) = \{x_1, \ldots, x_n\}$, the associated directed graph $G_n = (V_n, E_n)$ is defined as follows:

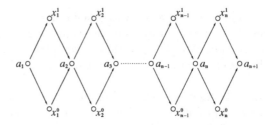

Fig. 1. Directed graph associated with a propositional formula with n variables

$$V_n = \{x_i^j : 1 \leq i \leq n, 0 \leq j \leq 1\} \cup \{a_i : 1 \leq i \leq n+1\}$$
$$E_n = \{(a_i, x_i^j), (x_i^j, a_{i+1}) : 1 \leq i \leq n, 0 \leq j \leq 1\}$$

This graph, shown in figure 1, verifies the following properties:

- There are 2^n paths from a_1 to a_{n+1}.
- There exists a natural bijection between the above set of paths and the relevant assignments of F, according to the following criteria: given a path from a_1 to a_{n+1}, $\gamma = a_1 x_1^{j_1} a_2 x_2^{j_2} \dots x_n^{j_n} a_{n+1}$, then the assignment $\hat{\gamma}$ is associated with it, such as $\hat{\gamma}(x_i) = j_i$, $1 \leq i \leq n$.

The initial test tube contains DNA molecules codifying the paths from a_1 to a_{n+1}, and so every relevant assignment of F. The alphabet and the initial test tube considered are the following:

$$\Sigma = \{a_i, x_i^j, a_{n+1} : 1 \leq i \leq n, 0 \leq j \leq 1\}$$

$$T_0 = \{\{a_1, x_1^{j_1}, a_2, x_2^{j_2}, \dots, x_n^{j_n}, a_{n+1}\} : 1 \leq i \leq n, j_i \in \{0, 1\}\}$$

Lipton's experiment can be described as follows: for each clause in the initial formula, every aggregate representing an assignment falsifying this clause is removed. The way to work with clauses is the following: for each literal in the clause, every aggregate representing an assignment in which this literal is true is preserved, and the remaining aggregates are removed. This experiment has been formalized in [14], where it has been expressed as an iterative algorithm based on the elemental operations of Adleman's restricted model:

Input: T_0 (as described above)
    For $i \leftarrow 1$ **to** p **do**
        $T_{i,0} \leftarrow \emptyset$
        $T_{i,0}'' \leftarrow T_{i-1}$
        For $j \leftarrow 1$ **to** r_i **do**
            $T_{i,j}' \leftarrow$ `separate+`$(T_{i,j-1}'', l_{i,j}^1)$
            $T_{i,j}'' \leftarrow$ `separate-`$(T_{i,j-1}'', l_{i,j}^1)$
            $T_{i,j} \leftarrow$ `tube-merge`$(T_{i,j-1}, T_{i,j}')$
        $T_i \leftarrow T_{i,r_i}$
    `detect`(T_p)

where, for each literal $l_{i,j}$ in the initial formula:

$$l_{i,j}^1 = \begin{cases} x_m^1 & \text{if } l_{i,j} = x_m \\ x_m^0 & \text{if } l_{i,j} = \neg x_m \end{cases}$$

In this formalization, the first loop deals with the clauses in the initial formula. The tube $T_{i,0}''$ is the set of aggregates before processing the clause c_i, and the tube $T_{i,0}$ acts as accumulator for the aggregates representing an assignment making c_i true. The second loop deals with the literals in a clause. The aggregates representing an assignment in which the literal is true (that is, the aggregates with the element $l_{i,j}^1$) are in the tube $T_{i,j}'$ which is merged with the accumulator, the remaining are in the tube $T_{i,j}''$ which is used with the next literal. When every literal in a clause has been processed, the tube T_{i,r_i} contains the aggregates from the tube $T_{i,0}''$ representing an assignment making true that clause.

It must be noticed that the complexity of this experiment, with respect to the basic molecular operations, is $O(k)$, where k is the number of literals. This low complexity is mainly due to the massive parallelism of molecular reactions. Of course, our simulation in ACL2 is sequential, and it loses this advantage. The basic molecular operations (with constant time cost) are performed in ACL2 by exhaustive analysis, and this dramatically increases the complexity.

Next, we present our implementation of Lipton's experiment in ACL2. First of all we must notice that the above algorithm depends on the initial test tube (T_0) and on the propositional formula (F), by means of the $l_{i,j}^1$. Then, we have defined a function with two arguments, the formula and the tube. On the other hand, the iterative formulation presented above is not adequate for its implementation in the functional language of ACL2. We have made a recursive formulation equivalent to the iterative version. In fact, we have defined two functions, one for each loop. The function dealing with the external loop works recursively on the number of clauses of F, and the other one works recursively on the number of literals of the selected clause.

Our implementation does not use the *Detect* operation, instead it returns the final tube in the external loop (T_p). This is useful to formulate the soundness and completeness properties of the functions implementing the experiment as we will show in the next section.

First of all we define the function 1-element, that builds the element $l_{i,j}^1$ from the literal $l_{i,j}$. Literals are represented using integers, thus, for all $i > 0$, literal x_i is represented with the integer i, and $\neg x_i$ with $-i$. To represent the elements $l_{i,j}^1$ we use pairs: the element x_i^0 is represented with the pair (i . 0) and the element x_i^1 with the pair (i . 1).

DEFINITION:
    1-element$(L) =$
        if $L < 0$ then $(-L$. 0$)$
        else $(L$. 1$)$

Next, we define a function implementing the internal loop. Its inputs are a main tube T (corresponding to $T_{i,j}''$ in the iterative version presented above), an accumulator tube acc (corresponding to $T_{i,j}$) and a clause C (corresponding to c_i). The aggregates in the main tube containing the element $l_{i,1}^1$ are merged with the accumulator tube in a new one. The aggregates in the main tube that do not contain the element $l_{i,1}^1$ are poured in a new main tube. The new main and accumulator tubes are used in the recursive call on the rest of the literals:

DEFINITION:
```
sat-lipton-clause(C,T,acc) =
    if endp(C) then acc
    else let* T⁺ = separate+(T,1-element(car(C)))
              T⁻ = separate-(T,1-element(car(C)))
              Nacc = tube-merge(acc,T⁺)
        in sat-lipton-clause(cdr(C),T⁻,Nacc)
```

The main function deals with the external loop. Its inputs are a tube T (corresponding to the initial tube T_0 in the iterative version presented above) and a formula F in conjunctive normal form. This function applies the internal loop on this tube, an initially empty accumulator tube and the first clause of the formula. The result of this process is used as initial tube in the recursive call on the rest of clauses:

DEFINITION:
```
sat-lipton-cnf-formula(F,T) =
    if endp(F) then T
    else let NT = sat-lipton-clause(car(F),T,nil)
        in sat-lipton-cnf-formula(cdr(F),NT)
```

5   Using ACL2 to Prove Correctness

Once formalized in ACL2 the abstract model with its assumed properties, and defined the functions implementing the experiment in this formalization, we can prove in the system the termination, soundness and completeness properties of these functions. The termination property is straightforward (in the recursive calls the length of F or C decreases) and it is proved without additional help from the user. The soundness and completeness properties are the following:

1. Soundness: $\forall \gamma \in T_p, (\hat{\gamma}(F) = 1)$
2. Completeness: $\forall \gamma \in T_0, (\hat{\gamma}(F) = 1 \Rightarrow \gamma \in T_p)$

where F is a propositional formula in conjunctive normal form and $\hat{\gamma}(F)$ is the truth value of F in the assignment $\hat{\gamma}$ (the truth value of a formula in conjunctive normal form is extended as usual).

These properties of the algorithm have two hidden assumptions:

1. F is a formula in conjunctive normal form (cnf-formula-p).
2. γ is an aggregate with the form: $\{a_1, x_1^{j_1}, a_2, x_2^{j_2}, \ldots, x_n^{j_n}, a_{n+1}\}$
   with $1 \le i \le n$ and $j \in \{0, 1\}$

To deal with the first of these assumptions, we have formalized some concepts related to propositional logic. The functions literal-p, clause-p and

cnf-formula-p characterize respectively literals (non-null integer numbers), clauses (lists of literals) and formulas in conjunctive normal form (lists of clauses).
To represent assignments, we use association lists. In these lists a propositional
variable can have associated any value; if this value is 1, the variable is interpreted as true, otherwise it is interpreted as false. The functions literal-value,
clause-value and cnf-formula-value compute respectively the truth value in
an assignment of a literal, clause or formula in conjunctive normal form.

We use lists to represent aggregates in the following way: the aggregate
$\{a_1, x_1^{j_1}, a_2, x_2^{j_2}, \ldots, x_n^{j_n}, a_{n+1}\}$ is represented by the list

$$((\text{A . 1}) \ (1 . j_1) \ (\text{A . 2}) \ \ldots \ (n . j_n) \ (\text{A . n}))$$

In this way, we use the same expression to represent an aggregate γ and the associated assignment $\hat{\gamma}$. The pairs (A . i) are ignored when we use this expression
to represent an assignment.

We have checked that the following property is enough to characterize the
aggregates: for each variable x_i in the original formula, there must exist one
and only one x_i^j in the aggregate[1]. We have defined three functions checking this
property. The first one (literal-aggregate-p) checks the property with respect
to the variable of a literal, the second one (clause-aggregate-p) with respect
to the variable set of a clause and the third one (cnf-formula-aggregate-p)
with respect to the variable set of a formula in conjunctive normal form. In the
sequel, when we say that γ is an aggregate w.r.t. a literal, a clause or a formula,
we mean that γ is an aggregate with respect to its variable or its variable set.

Now, we can formulate the completeness property:

THEOREM: completeness-sat-lipton-cnf-formula
   $(\gamma \in T \wedge$ cnf-formula-p$(F) \wedge$ cnf-formula-aggregate-p(γ, F)
       $\wedge$ cnf-formula-value$(F, \gamma) = 1)$
   $\rightarrow \gamma \in$ sat-lipton-cnf-formula(F, T)

Let us briefly describe the proof process of this theorem. The ACL2 prover
tries to prove it by induction. Based on its heuristics, the system uses the induction scheme suggested by the function sat-lipton-cnf-formula. This produces
the following subgoals:

1) endp$(F) \rightarrow P(\gamma, F, T)$
2) ¬endp$(F) \wedge P(\gamma,$cdr$(F),$sat-lipton-clause$($car$(F),T,$**nil**$)) \rightarrow P(\gamma, F, T)$

where $P(\gamma, F, T)$ denotes the property we want to prove.

As we can see, the first subgoal is straightforward (in this case the value of
sat-lipton-cnf-formula(F, T) is T) and the second one is not easy. Using the
simplification process, the system transforms the second subgoal obtaining the
following:

---

[1] Therefore, the elements a_i in the aggregates are not necessary. Nevertheless, we have
  to consider them to faithfully reflect the original experiment.

$(\gamma \in T \wedge \text{consp}(F) \wedge \text{clause-p}(C) \wedge \text{cnf-formula-p}(F')$
$\qquad \wedge \text{clause-aggregate-p}(\gamma,C) \wedge \text{cnf-formula-aggregate-p}(\gamma,F')$
$\qquad \wedge \text{clause-value}(C,\gamma) \neq 0 \wedge \text{cnf-formula-value}(F',\gamma) = 1$
$\qquad \wedge \gamma \notin \text{sat-lipton-clause}(C,T,\text{nil}))$
$\quad \rightarrow \gamma \in \text{sat-lipton-cnf-formula}(F,T)$

where C is $\text{car}(F)$ and F' is $\text{cdr}(F)$.

In a first attempt, the proof of this subgoal fails. Inspecting the failed proof, we found that a very similar property should be proved about the function sat-lipton-clause. One possibility is the following:

THEOREM: completeness-sat-lipton-clause
$\quad (\gamma \in T \wedge \text{clause-p}(C) \wedge \text{clause-aggregate-p}(\gamma,C) \wedge \text{clause-value}(C,\gamma) = 1)$
$\quad \rightarrow \gamma \in \text{sat-lipton-clause}(C,T,acc)$

Once again, the system tries to prove this theorem using the induction scheme suggested by the function sat-lipton-clause. Inspecting the proof attempt we can also conclude that some property about separate+ should be proved. This property is the following:

THEOREM: completeness-separate+
$\quad (\gamma \in T \wedge \text{literal-p}(L) \wedge \text{literal-aggregate-p}(\gamma,L) \wedge \text{literal-value}(L,\gamma) = 1)$
$\quad \rightarrow \gamma \in \text{separate+}(T,\text{1-element}(L))$

This theorem is proved using elemental properties about aggregates and their associated assignments. Using this theorem, the system can prove the completeness property of sat-lipton-clause and, finally, the completeness property of sat-lipton-cnf-formula.

The proof of the soundness property is obtained in a similar way. The associated ACL2 event is the following:

THEOREM: soundness-sat-lipton-cnf-formula
$\quad (\text{cnf-formula-p}(F) \wedge \text{cnf-formula-aggregate-p}(\gamma,F)$
$\qquad\qquad\qquad \wedge \gamma \in \text{sat-lipton-cnf-formula}(F,T))$
$\quad \rightarrow \text{cnf-formula-value}(F,\gamma) = 1$

6   Conclusions

In this work we have presented a formalization of Adleman's restricted model, one of the first molecular computational models. This formalization has been done in a generic framework in which the concrete implementation of its operations is not important, but only their properties. Using this formalization we have defined functions simulating Lipton's experiment solving SAT. Finally, the completeness and soundness properties of these functions have been proved.

The formalization of unconventional models of computation is a suitable way of working with them when we do not have real models (e.g. we do not have a laboratory implementing molecular computational models). This formalization brings us the possibility of simulate real experiments or develop new ones.

Furthermore, using an automated reasoning system allows to formally prove properties of the simulated experiments. The automatic system helps to develop these proofs avoiding a hand development.

We have presented a recursive formalization, in opposite to the iterative version presented in [14]. This fact is due to the applicative nature of ACL2. This approach suggests the application of proof techniques based on induction (as usual in ACL2), to prove the correctness properties of the functions simulating the experiment, as opposed to the needed with an iterative version, based on Hoare logic. In [5] we have reproduced the development presented here in the PVS system [12], as part of a project about formal specification of molecular computational models in this system.

References

1. Adleman, L.M.: Molecular computation of solutions to combinatorial problems. Science, 266:1021–1024, 1994.
2. Adleman, L.M.: On constructing a molecular computer. DNA Based Computers, DIMACS Series, 27, pp. 1–21. American Mathematical Society, 1996.
3. Braich, R.S., Chelyapov, N., Johnson, C., Rothemund, P.W.K. and Adleman, L.: Solution of a 20-Variable 3-SAT Problem on a DNA Computer. Science, 296:499–502, 2002.
4. Beaver, D.: A universal molecular computer. DNA Based Computers, DIMACS Series, 27, pp. 29–36. American Mathematical Society, 1996.
5. Graciani, C., Martín–Mateos, F.J. and Pérez–Jiménez, M.J.: Specification of Adleman's Restricted Model Using an Automated Reasoning System: Verification of Lipton's Experiment. LNCS vol. 2509 pp. 126–136, 2002.
6. Kaufmann, M., Manolios, P. and Moore, J S.: Computer-Aided Reasoning: An Approach. Kluwer Academic Publishers, 2000.
7. Kaufmann, M. and Moore, J S.: ACL2 Version 2.7, 2002.
   Homepage: http://www.cs.utexas.edu/users/moore/acl2/
8. Kaufmann, M. and Moore, J S.: Structured Theory Development for a Mechanized Logic. Journal of Automated Reasoning, 26(2): 161–203, 2001.
9. Moore, J S.: Piton: a mechanically verified assembly-level language. Kluwer Academic Publisher, 1996.
10. Lee, I.-H., Park, J.-Y., Jang, H.-M., Chai, Y.-G. and Zhang, B.-T.: DNA Implementation of Theorem Proving with Resolution Refutation in Propositional Logic. LNCS vol. 2568, pp. 156–167, 2003.
11. Lipton, R.J.: DNA solution of hard computational problems. Science, 268:542–545, 1995.
12. Owre, S., Rushby, J.M., Shankar, N. and Stringer–Calvert, D.W.J.: PVS System Guide. Homepage: http://pvs.csl.sri.com/
13. Paun, G.: Computing with membranes. Journal of Computer and System Sciences, 61(1):108–143, 2000.
14. Pérez–Jiménez, M.J., Sancho, F., Graciani, C. and Romero, A.: Soluciones moleculares del problema SAT (in spanish). Lógica, Lenguaje e Información, JOLL'2000, pp. 243–252. Ed. Kronos, 2000.
15. Russinoff, D.: A mechanically checked proof of IEEE compliance of the floating point multiplication, division and square root algorithms of the AMD-K7 processor. LMS J. of Comp. Math., vol. 1, pp. 148–200, 1998.

Fuzzy Logic Based Torque Ripple Minimization
in Switched Reluctance Motors

Mahdi Jalili-Kharaajoo

Young Researchers Club, Islamic Azad University, Iran
P.O. Box: 14395/1355, Tehran, Iran
mahdijalili@ece.ut.ac.ir

Abstract. In this paper a fundamental control issue in switched reluctance motor (SRM), the torque ripples, is addressed. Normally, torque ripple minimization is achieved by using a look-up tables, i.e., the look-up table uses stored magnetic characteristics to provide the reference current, on-angle, and off-angle for a given torque. Due to highly nonlinear characteristics of the SRM, all the techniques suggested in the past to minimize torque ripples are not fully successful. Moreover, their performance depends greatly on the accuracy of the magnetic characteristics measurements of the motor on which most of these algorithms work. In this work the reference phase current tern is modulated with the aid of fuzzy logic, which is well suited to compensate for the nonlinearities the system, so that the torque ripples are further suppressed. Performance of the proposed strategy is verified by computer simulation.

1 Introduction

The switched reluctance motor (SRM) has becoming an attractive alternative in variable speed drives, due to its advantages such as structural simplicity, high reliability and low cost [1,2]. Many papers have been written about SRM concerning design and control [3]. An important characteristic of the SRM is that the inductance of the magnetic circuit is a nonlinear function of the phase current and rotor position. So, for the control and optimization of this drive, a precise magnetic model is necessary. To obtain this model is not an easy task, because the magnetic circuit operates at varying levels of saturation under operating conditions [4]. Further, the nonlinear characteristic of this plant represents a challenge to classical control. To overcome this drawback, some alternatives have been suggested in [5], using fuzzy and neuronal systems. However, at present, it has found limited industrial applications because of its inherent torque ripples caused by the nonlinear mechanism of torque production in the motor.

Here a method is presented, based on fuzzy logic, for further modulation of the currents, obtained as in [6], to suppress the ripples. Fuzzy logic is well suited to the problems with a large degree of nonlinearity and uncertainty. There are several reports of successful applications of fuzzy logic for the control of electric motors and servos [7,8,9]. In this work, torque ripple minimization is carried out from a control point of view, i.e., generation of a current profile using modern control theory so as to suppress the torque ripples. Since the torque developed by the SRM is dependent on

R. Conejo et al. (Eds.): CAEPIA-TTIA 2003, LNAI 3040, pp. 354–363, 2004.

the current in each phase as a function of the rotor positions, the proposed Fuzzy-Logic-based-Current-Modulator (FLCM) adds a correction term, as a function of rotor position, to the reference current obtained by the procedure outlined in [6]. The FLCM takes rotor position and torque error as the inputs. The corrected current is then passed through another control block that regulates the rate of rise/fall of current. The output of this block is the final modulated current, which is fed to the stator winding. The on-line measurement of electromagnetic torque and rotor position is essential for the implementation of the algorithm.

The rest of the paper is organized as follows. Section 2 briefly describes the SRM used in this study along with an outline of the reference current generation scheme as per the algorithm reported in [6]. Section 3 presents the proposed current modulation algorithm. Section 4 evaluates the performance of the algorithm by computer simulation studies. Section 5 provides the conclusion.

2 Switched Reluctance Motor Torque Model

The SRM has a salient pole stator with concentrated coils and also a salient pole rotor which has no magnets or conductors. The basic principles of inductance variation and torque production are described in detail in [1]. A four-phase motor is used in the following analysis. All the four phases are assumed to be symmetrical. In the descriptions to follow, reference to a generic phase is reflected as a subscript in the variables with the knowledge that the analysis is applicable to the individual phases with appropriate relative phase differences between them. Because of double saliency of the motor and the operation of the motor under magnetic saturation, the inductance of phase j ($j=1, \ldots, 4$), L_j, is a function of both rotor position y and the current I_j. However, under the assumption of linear magnetics, inductance vs rotor position profile can be approximated over one rotor pole pitch as shown in Fig. 1 (solid line). The parameters in Fig. 1 are defined as: β_s is stator pole arc; β_r is rotor pole arc ($\beta_s < \beta_r$); α_r is rotor pole pitch ($\beta_s + \beta_r < \alpha_r$); L_a is aligned phase inductance and L_u is unaligned phase inductance. The inductance profile can be mathematically described by

$$L_1(\theta) = \begin{cases} L_u + K\theta, 0 \le \theta \le \beta_s \\ L_a, \beta_s \le \theta \le \beta_r \\ L_a - K(\theta - \beta_s - \beta_r), \beta_r \le \theta \le \beta_r + \beta_s \\ L_u, \beta_r + \beta_s \le \theta \le \alpha_r \end{cases} \tag{1}$$

where

$$K = \frac{L_a - L_u}{\beta_s} \tag{2}$$

for the phase j:

$$L_j(\theta) = L_1(\theta)[\theta - \frac{\alpha_r}{4}(j-1)] \tag{3}$$

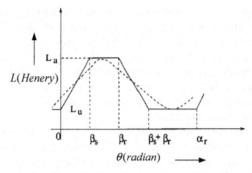

Fig. 1. Approximated inductance vs rotor position for phase # 1.

When a single phase of the SRM is energized, the torque developed, T_j, is

$$T_j(\theta_e, I_j) = N_r \frac{\partial}{\partial \theta_e} W_e(\theta_e, I_j) \tag{4}$$

where θ_e and N_r are the electrical angle and the number of rotor poles respectively, and $\theta_e = N_r \theta$. The co-energy, W_e, is defined as

$$W_e(\theta_e, I_j) = \int_0^{I_j} \phi_j(\theta_e, I_j) dI_j \tag{5}$$

where ϕ_j is the flux linkage and is expressed as

$$\phi_j(\theta_e, I_j) = L_j(\theta_e) I_j(\theta_e) \tag{6}$$

Hence, the final expression for the torque can be obtained as

$$T_j(\theta_e) = \frac{N_r}{2} \sum_{j=1}^{4} \frac{\partial L_j(\theta_e)}{\partial \theta_e} I_j^2(\theta_e) \tag{7}$$

For the design of the optimal current profile in [6], a 128-point fast Fourier transform (FFT) is performed on the positive part of the derivative function $\partial L_j(\theta_e)/\partial \theta_e$ with no restriction on the conduction period. The nonlinear torque model is transformed into a linear one with a simple change of variable

$$y_j(\theta_e) = I_j^2(\theta_e) \tag{8}$$

in this work we will use the result of [6].

3   Fuzzy Current Modulator Design

The complete algorithm consists of two steps. Step 1 describes a fuzzy logic based current compensation scheme while step 2 incorporates the $dI_j / d\theta$ control algorithm.

3.1 Step 1

In this step, an incremental current is added to the previously obtained reference current from the FFT calculations, i.e.

$$I_j = I_j^{ref} + K_t \alpha(\Delta I_j) \tag{9}$$

where I_j^{ref} is reference current for phase j, ΔI_j is current correction term, α is confidence factor; and $K_t = a$ is gain.

The current correction term ΔI_j is obtained by a fuzzy rule base. The rule base is constructed with two inputs. They are the rotor position and the normalized error between the desired and the actual torque. As the rotor rotates, various phases pass through positive torque-producing region (when the inductance of the phase is rising), zero torque-producing region (the inductance is almost constant), and negative torque-producing region (inductance is falling) in cyclic fashion. The normalized torque error is defined as

$$e = \frac{T_d - T_m}{T_d} \tag{10}$$

where T_d is desired torque, and T_m is actual motor torque.

The fuzzy rule base for each phase is constructed on the following observations/rules:

1. If e is positive and the phase is passing through a positive torque-producing region, then increase the phase current.
2. If e is negative and the phase is passing through a negative torque-producing region, then increase the phase current.
3. If e is almost zero, then no correction is required.
4. If the phase is passing through a zero torque-producing region, then essentially no correction term should be added to the reference current.

Fuzzy sets are designed for the angular position, θ, and the normalized error, e, as shown in Fig. 2. A typical set of output membership functions is shown in Fig. 3. However, it is stressed that because the crisp value of the output depends on the cen-

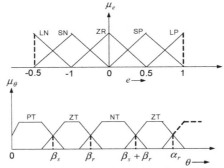

LP=Large Positive, LN=Large Negative, SP=Small Positive, SN=Small Negative
ZR=Near Zero, PT=Positive Torque, NT=Negative Torque, ZT=Zero Torque

Fig. 2. Membership function for e and θ foe phase #1.

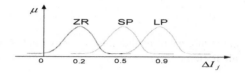

Fig. 3. Membership function for ΔI_j.

tral values of the output fuzzy sets, the exact shapes of the membership functions do not matter.

The ΔI_j, as obtained from Fig. 3, is principally based on torque error and the sign of torque generated in the region of interest. However, one important information that is not taken into account is the rate of change of torque with respect to θ_e, ($dT_m / d\theta_e$), which is also proportional to the square of the current. For example, say, it is desired to increase the current (inferred from the fuzzy reasoning process) to decrease some positive torque error. But, if in that region $dT_m / d\theta_e$ is negative, and then the compensations in the error will not be as per the expectations. In this case, a better compensation can be achieved if the correction term ΔI_j is slightly reduced. Hence, we prefer to multiply the ΔI_j by another factor called, here, as the confidence factor, a. This confidence factor is decided based on the following simple strategy.

$$D = \frac{dT_m}{d\theta_e} \tag{11}$$

1. If $D > 0$, and $e > 0$, then $\alpha = \alpha_1$.
2. If $D > 0$, and $e < 0$, then $\alpha = \alpha_2$.
3. If $D < 0$, and $e > 0$, then $\alpha = \alpha_2$.
4. If $D < 0$, and $e < 0$, then $\alpha = \alpha_1$.

Finally, before the reference current is added with the correction term, the term $\alpha(\Delta I_j)$ is multiplied by a gain depending upon the desired average torque level. This gain is required because the correction term is derived from the fuzzy rule base based on the normalized torque error. This gain is justifiably made proportional (in a fuzzy sense) to the desired torque level. Thus the gain, K_t, is decided from a very simple heuristic rule.

1. If T_d is small (S), K_t is small (S)
2. If T_d is medium (M), K_t is medium (M)
3. If T_d is large (L), K_t is large (L)

The membership function for T_d (for a specified operating range of torque; here it is chosen to be 15 N m.) is shown in Fig. 4. Here, also, a center-average defuzzifier is used for obtaining the crisp value of K_t as before and K_q ($q=1,...,3$) are the central values of the respective fuzzy sets for K_t (small, medium, and large). The membership functions, whose shapes are not important (as mentioned earlier), for the output fuzzy sets are shown in Fig. 5.

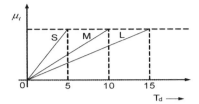

Fig. 4. Membership functions for *Td*.

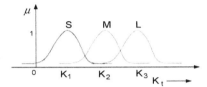

Fig. 5. Membership functions for K_t.

3.2 Step 2

In this step the rate of rise and fall of the currents is limited. It is essential to suppress the ripples caused during the phase commutation interval. A fuzzy logic system is used for this purpose. The final correction law is

$$
I_j^f =
\begin{cases}
I_j + \eta_1 \left| \dfrac{dI_j}{d\theta_e} \right|_{fuz} \Delta\theta_e, & if \ \dfrac{dI_j}{d\theta_e} > 0 \\[4mm]
I_j - \eta_2 \left| \dfrac{dI_j}{d\theta_e} \right|_{fuz} \Delta\theta_e, & if \ \dfrac{dI_j}{d\theta_e} < 0
\end{cases}
\tag{12}
$$

The $\left| dI_j / d\theta_e \right|_{fuz}$ is determined from fuzzy inference mechanism with a view to smoothing the fall and rise of phase currents. The gains η_1 and η_2 are such that $\eta_1 > \eta_2$. They are included in order to have unequal rate of rise and fall of currents in any two consecutive phases. This is essential to handle some typical situations, i.e., when one major current-sharing phase is switched on and another similar phase is to be switched off. Torque produced by the newly energized phase is very low. Also, because of sharp fall of current in the other phase, the total torque drops giving rise to ripples. By making $\eta_1 > \eta_2$, the current in the incoming phase is forced to rise more rapidly while, at the same time, the current in the outgoing phase falls slowly. An optimal adjustment of these two gains is expected to yield better results.

At each step, the crisp value of input $\left| dI_j / d\theta_e \right|$ is fuzzified by Gaussian member-ship functions, as shown in Fig. 6. Five fuzzy sets are chosen: VS_i=very small, S_i=small, M_i=medium, L_i=large, VL_i=very large. The subscripts *i* and o stand for the

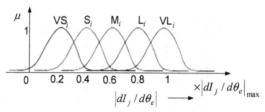

Fig. 6. Membership functions for input $\left|dI_j / d\theta_e\right|$.

input and output fuzzy sets respectively. The $\left|dI_j / d\theta_e\right|_{max}$ is to be decided based on system knowledge. For the worst case change of current, we set its value at $I_m / 0.05\beta_s N_r$, where the mechanical overlap between two consecutive torque-producing regions is chosen to be $0.05\beta_s$ in step 1. However, to allow for little over-head, we choose it as

$$\left|\frac{dI_j}{d\theta_e}\right| = \frac{1.1I_m}{0.05\beta_s N_r} = DI^{max} \tag{13}$$

All the fuzzy sets have equal standard deviation $(=0.2\ DI^{max})$. The rule base for the smoothening mechanism consists of following five general rules. The rule base is chosen based on the simplest reasoning that the rate of change of current are lessened (a necessity for high-speed applications) without great reductions in the magnitude of current.

$$DI^{th} = \left|\frac{dI_j}{d\theta_e}\right| \tag{14}$$

1. If DI^{th} th is VL_i, then make it L_o.
2. If DI^{th} th is L_i, then make it M_o.
3. If DI^{th} th is M_i, then make it S_o.
4. If DI^{th} th is S_i, then make it VS_o.
5. If DI^{th} th is VS_i, then make it ZR_o.

The crisp value of $\left|dI_j / d\theta_e\right|_{fuz}$ is again obtained by center-average defuzzifica-tion. The membership functions for the output fuzzy sets are shown in Fig. 7 where $DI_n\ (n=1,...,5)$s are the central values of the respective output fuzzy sets. Finally, I'_j is computed from (12). These are the currents that are directed to flow in the respective phase windings of the SRM.

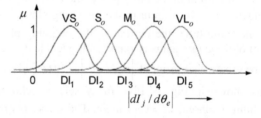

Fig. 7. Membership functions for output $\left|dI_j / d\theta_e\right|$.

4 Simulation Results

The switched reluctance motor parameters are chosen as

Output power=7.5 kW; number of phases=4; Number of stator poles (Ns)=8; number of rotor poles (Nr)=6;L_u=10mH;L_a=110mH; α_r =1.05rad; β_s = 0.35rad; β_r = 0.42 rad.

For the fuzzy membership functions the following values are chosen

$CV_1 = 0.2$ $CV_2 = 0.5$ $CV_3 = 0.9$

$K_1 = 1.0$ $K_2 = 3.0$ $K_3 = 5.0$

$DI_1 = 0.35\ DI^{max}$ $DI_2 = 0.26\ DI^{max}$ $DI_3 = 0.18\ DI^{max}$

$DI_4 = 0.09\ DI^{max}$ $DI_5 = 0.045\ DI^{max}$

$\alpha_1 = 1.5, \alpha_2 = .8,\ \ \eta_1 = 1.3, \eta_2 = 0.7$

Test simulations have been performed for the torque range of 0-15 Nm. A well-established model that incorporates magnetic saturation is considered for the motor [11].Fig. 8(a) and (b) shows the current profiles for two consecutive phases for a desired torque of 7 N-m, without modulation and with modulation respectively. The current clipper has been included for analysis in both the cases in order to emphasize the elegance of the modulation algorithm alone. The effects of the current modulation algorithm can be clearly observed. Fig 9 shows a comparison of the steady state torque profiles for a desired torque of 7 N m. As it is clearly observed, it achieves two objectives simultaneously, i.e., improvement in the average torque value and suppression of the peak-to-peak ripples in the steady state torque profile. Fig. 10 displays the simulation results for a torque of 10 Nm.

From the test results, it is clear that the proposed current modulation algorithm provides substantial improvement in the steady state torque profile of the SRM. It is also observed that the modulation provides significant boost to the average torque level. However, it is strongly felt that a variable torque-gain is required.

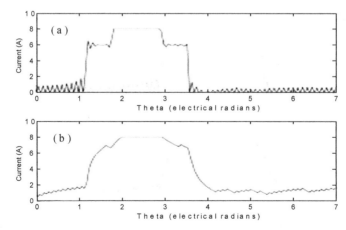

Fig. 8. (a) Current profiles for two phases (without modulation) for Td=7 Nm; (b) current profiles for two phases (with modulation) for Td=7 Nm.

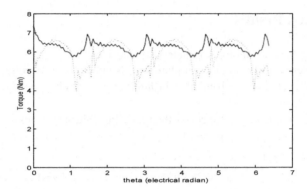

Fig. 9. Comparison of the steady state torque profiles for Td=7 Nm with modulation (solid line) and without modulation (dotted line).

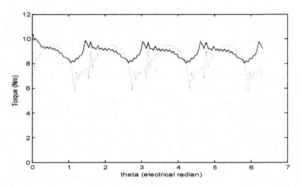

Fig. 10. Comparison of steady state torque profiles for Td=10 Nm with modulation (solid line) and without modulation (dotted line).

5   Conclusion

A sequence of systematic steps has been presented to modulate the current wave-forms, designed to be optimal under the assumption of linear magnetics, so as to compensate for the nonlinear magnetics of the SRM. Although the study, here, rests upon a previous work [6], it is an elegant algorithm to refurbish the current profile for obtaining high precision direct torque control. The two remarkable aspects of the proposed algorithm are:

1. There is a significant improvement in the elimination of the torque ripples. On an average, the % peak-to-peak torque ripple is reduced from 40 to 15%.
2. The steady state average torque also gets a boost. The absolute (percentage) average torque error has been improved from 20 to 5%, on an average.

The striking feature of this new scheme is that it is fairly simple to comprehend. All the steps of the algorithm have been derived from strong physical points of view.

References

1. Miller T.J.E., *Switched Reluctance Motors and their Control*, Magna Physics Publishing and Clarendon Press-Oxford, 1993.
2. Le-Huy, Switched Reluctance Motor Drive: A Survey, *II Seminário Internacional de Motores Elétricos e Acionamentos Reguláveis Proceeding*, São Paulo, Brazil, pp. 121 - 138, May, 1991.
3. Gribble J.J., P.C. Kjaer, C. Cossar, T.J.E.Miller, Optimal Commutation Angles for Current Controlled Switched Reluctance Motors, *Power Electronics and Variable Speed Drives, Conference Publication No. 429, IEE*, pp. 87 - 91, September, 1996.
4. Elmas Ç., S. Sagiroglu, I. Çolak, G. Bal, Modelling of a nonlinear Switched Reluctance Drive Based on artificial Neural Networks, *Power Eletronics and Variable Speed Drives-Conference Proceeding*, pp. 7-12, 1994.
5. Reay D.S., M.M. Moud, T.C. Green, B.W. Williams, Switched Reluctance Motor Control Via Fuzzy Adaptive Systems, *IEEE Control Systems Magazine* , June 1995.
6. Hung JY. Torque ripple minimization for variable reluctance motors. *Mechatronics*, 4(8), pp.785- 98, 1994.
7. Reay DS, Toud MM, Green TC, Williams BW, Switched reluctance motor control via fuzzy adaptive systems. *IEEE Control Systems Magazine*, 15(3), pp.8-15, 1995.
8. Hofmann W, Krause M. Fuzzy logic based control of flux and torque in AC-drives. *In: Marks RJ, editor. Fuzzy logic technology and pplications. IEEE Technical Activities Board*, p.p 190-5, 1994.
9. Lee TH, Nie JH, Lee MW., A fuzzy controller with decoupling for multivariable nonlinear servomechanisms, with applications to real-time control of a passive line-of-sight stabilization system. *Mechatronics,* 7(1), pp.83-104, 1994.
10. Lawrenson PJ, Stephenson JM, Blenkinsop PT, Corda J, Fulton NN. Variable-speed switched reluctance motors. *IEE Proc, Part B* , 127(4), pp.253-65, 1980.
11. Ilic-Spong M, Marino R, Peresada SM, Taylor DG. Feedback linearizing control of switched reluctance motors. *IEEE Trans Automat Control*, 32(5), pp.371-9, 1987.

Generating Random Orthogonal Polygons[*]

Ana Paula Tomás[1] and António Leslie Bajuelos[2]

[1] DCC-FC & LIACC, University of Porto, Portugal
apt@ncc.up.pt
[2] Department of Mathematics / R&D Unit "Mathematics and Applications"
University of Aveiro, Portugal
leslie@mat.ua.pt

Abstract. We propose two different methods for generating random orthogonal polygons with a given number of vertices. One is a polynomial time algorithm and it is supported by a technique we developed to obtain polygons with an increasing number of vertices starting from a unit square. The other follows a constraint programming approach and gives great control on the generated polygons. In particular, it may be used to find all n-vertex orthogonal polygons with no collinear edges that can be drawn in an $\frac{n}{2} \times \frac{n}{2}$ grid, for small n, with symmetries broken.

1 Introduction

Besides being of theoretical interest, the generation of random geometric objects has applications that include the testing and verification of time complexity for computational geometry algorithms, as observed by Zhu et al. in [15] and Auer and Held in [2]. This has also been a major motivation for us. In particular, we needed a sufficiently large number of varied orthogonal polygons to carry out an experimental evaluation of the algorithm proposed in [13] for solving the MINIMUM VERTEX GUARD problem for arbitrary polygons. This problem is that of finding a minimum set G of vertices of the given polygon P such that each point in the interior of P is visible from at least a vertex in G, belonging to the *Art Gallery problems* [8, 16].

Polygons are one of the fundamental building blocks in geometric modelling and they are used to represent a wide variety of shapes and figures in computer graphics, vision, pattern recognition, robotics and other computational fields. Some recent publications address uniform random generation of simple polygons with *given vertices*, in the sense that a polygon will be generated with probability $\frac{1}{T}$ if there exist a total of T simple polygons with such vertices [2, 15]. Since no polynomial time algorithm is known to solve the problem, researchers either try to use heuristics [2] or restrict the problem to certain classes of polygons such as monotone [15] or star-shaped [11].

[*] This work has been partially supported by funds granted to LIACC through *Programa de Financiamento Plurianual, Fundação para a Ciência e Tecnologia (FCT)* and *Programa POSI*, and by R&D Unit "Mathematics and Applications" (Univ. of Aveiro) through *Programa POCTI, FCT, co-financed by EC fund FEDER*.

R. Conejo et al. (Eds.): CAEPIA-TTIA 2003, LNAI 3040, pp. 364–373, 2004.
© Springer-Verlag Berlin Heidelberg 2004

Programs for generating random orthogonal polygons have been developed in LISP by O'Rourke et al. to perform experimental tests in the context of [10] and independently by M. Filgueiras in Tcl/Tk (personal communication, 2003). Recently, O'Rourke kindly made available his program to us. The main idea behind it is to construct such a polygon via growth from a seed *cell* (i.e., unit square) in a board, gluing together a given number of cells that are selected randomly using some heuristics. Filgueiras' method shares a similar idea though it glues rectangles of larger areas and allows them to overlap. O'Rourke observed that there is no easy way to control the final number of vertices of the polygon with his program and that what is controlled directly is the area of the polygon, i.e., the number of cells used. However the number of cells may change because the program transforms the generated polygon when it has (non-overlapping) collinear edges to remove such collinearity.

Our Contribution. We propose two different methods for generating random orthogonal polygons with *a given number of vertices*. The first one is a polynomial time algorithm. It is supported by a result we prove in this paper that every orthogonal polygon may be obtained from the unit cell by employing a sequence of INFLATE-CUT transformations. The other method follows a constraint programming approach, and explores the fact that the generation problem may be modelled naturally as a constraint satisfaction problem in finite domains (CSP). It gives control on other characteristics of polygons, though it is computationally much more expensive. We have not yet tried to classify the degree of randomness of the polygons constructed by our methods.

The paper is structured as follows. In section 2, we introduce basic concepts and results about simple polygons and we describe how to obtain generic orthogonal polygons from standardized orthogonal polygons (that we call grid n-ogons). Then, in sections 3 and 4, we present our two methods for generating grid n-ogons. We conclude giving some implementation details and empirical results in section 5.

2 Background and Terminology

A *simple polygon* P is a region of a plane enclosed by a finite collection of straight line segments forming a simple cycle. Non-adjacent segments do not intersect and two adjacent segments intersect only in their common endpoint. These intersection points are the *vertices* of P and the line segments are the *edges* of P. This paper deals only with simple polygons, so that we call them just polygons, in the sequel. A vertex is called *convex* if the interior angle between its two incident edges is at most π; otherwise it is called *reflex* (or *concave*). We use r to represent the number of reflex vertices of P. A polygon is called *orthogonal* (or *rectilinear*) if its edges are either horizontal or vertical (i.e., if edges meet at right angles). O'Rourke [9] has shown that $n = 2r + 4$ for every n-vertex orthogonal polygon (*n-ogon*, for short). So, orthogonal polygons have an even number of vertices.

Every n-vertex polygon P is well defined by the sequence of its vertices $v_1, \ldots, v_n$, given in counterclockwise (CCW) order. P will be locally to the left of any edge e_i traversed from v_i to v_{i+1}. All index arithmetic will be modulo n, though we shall use n instead of 0, and $e_i = \overline{v_i v_{i+1}}$.

We shall now describe how to obtain generic orthogonal polygons from standardized orthogonal polygons, that we call grid n-ogons.

2.1   Classes of Orthogonal Polygons

Definition 1. *We say that an n-ogon P is in general position iff every horizontal and vertical line contains at most one edge of P, i.e., iff P has no collinear edges. For short, we call "grid n-ogon" each n-ogon in general position defined in a $\frac{n}{2} \times \frac{n}{2}$ square grid.*

Lemma 1. *Each grid n-ogon has exactly one edge in every line of the grid.*

Each n-ogon not in general position may be mapped to an n-ogon in general position by ϵ-perturbations, for a sufficiently small constant $\epsilon > 0$. Consequently, we may restrict generation to n-ogons in general position.

Every n-ogon P in general position may be identified with a unique grid n-ogon, as follows. We consider that the northwest point of the grid has coordinates $(1, 1)$. We order the horizontal edges of P by top-to-bottom sweeping and we order its vertical edges by left-to-right sweeping. If we then assign to each edge its order number, P gets identified with a single grid n-ogon, as shown in Fig. 1. If $\mathcal{V}_{i-1}$ and $\mathcal{H}_i$ are the numbers given to the vertical edge e_{i-1} and to

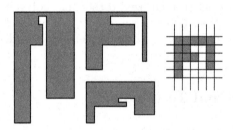

Fig. 1. Identifying three n-ogons with a single grid n-ogon, for $n = 12$.

its consecutive horizontal edge e_i, then $(\mathcal{V}_{i-1}, \mathcal{H}_i)$ is the vertex that corresponds to vertex v_i in the grid n-ogon. Each grid n-ogon identifies a class of n-ogons. Given a grid n-ogon we may create an n-ogon that is an instance of its class by randomly spacing the grid lines though preserving their ordering. When we analysed the program by O'Rourke, we found that this idea was already there. The number of classes may be further reduced if we group grid n-ogons that are identical under symmetries of the square. In this way, the grid n-ogons in Fig. 2 represent the same class. We shall come back to this issue in sections 4 and 5.

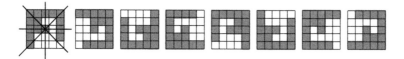

Fig. 2. Eight grid n-ogons that are identical under symmetries of the square. From left to right, we see images by clockwise rotations of 90°, 180° and 270°, by flips wrt horizontal and vertical axes and flips wrt positive and negative diagonals.

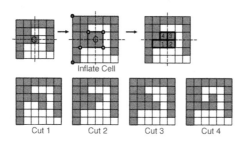

Fig. 3. Illustrating INFLATE-CUT transformation. The two rectangles defined by the center of C and the vertices of the leftmost vertical edge $((1,1),(1,7))$ cannot be cut, so that there remain the four possibilities shown.

3   The Inflate-Cut Algorithm

Fig. 3 illustrates a technique we developed to obtain grid $(n+2)$-ogons from a given grid n-ogon, that we called INFLATE-CUT. The idea is that INFLATE grows the area of the grid n-ogon P constructed up to a given step and then CUT removes a rectangle from it to create a new grid ogon, with $n+2$ vertices (i.e., with exactly one more reflex vertex). So, let $v_i = (x_i, y_i)$, for $i = 1, \ldots, n$ be the vertices of P and C be a unit cell in its interior. Let (p, q) be the coordinates of the northwest corner of C.

The INFLATE *Transformation.* The result of applying INFLATE to P using C is a new n-vertex orthogonal polygon $\tilde{P}$ with vertices $\tilde{v}_i = (\tilde{x}_i, \tilde{y}_i)$ given by $\tilde{x}_i = x_i$ if $x_i \leq p$ and $\tilde{x}_i = x_i + 1$ if $x_i > p$, and $\tilde{y}_i = y_i$ if $y_i \leq q$ and $\tilde{y}_i = y_i + 1$ if $y_i > q$, for $i = 1, \ldots, n$. Two lines will be free in the new grid, namely $x = p+1$ and $y = q+1$. They intersect in the center of inflated C, that will be the new reflex vertex, when the CUT transformation is as we establish now.

The CUT *Transformation.* Let $\tilde{v}_C = (p+1, q+1)$. Compute the four intersection points defined by the straight lines $x = p+1$ and $y = q+1$ and the boundary of $\tilde{P}$ (i.e., the points where the four horizontal and vertical rays that start at $\tilde{v}_C$ first intersect the boundary of $\tilde{P}$). Select one of these intersection points at random, and call it $\tilde{s}$. Let $\tilde{v}_m$ be one of the two vertices on the edge of $\tilde{P}$ that contains $\tilde{s}$. The rectangle defined by $\tilde{v}_C$ and $\tilde{v}_m$ may be cut if and only if it contains no vertex of $\tilde{P}$ except $\tilde{v}_m$. If the rectangle may be cut, let $\tilde{s}'$ be $\tilde{v}_C + (\tilde{v}_m - \tilde{s})$, and remove $\tilde{v}_m$ from $\tilde{P}$ inserting instead $\tilde{s}$, $\tilde{v}_C$, $\tilde{s}'$ if this sequence in CCW order (or $\tilde{s}'$, $\tilde{v}_C$, $\tilde{s}$, otherwise). If the rectangle cannot be cut, try to use in a similar way either the other extreme of the edge that contains $\tilde{s}$ or the remaining intersection points. CUT fails for C when no rectangle may be cut, as shown in Fig. 4.

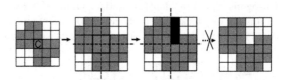

Fig. 4. CUT fails for cell C. We get a grid ogon if we remove the black rectangle, but this cut violates the preconditions of CUT, since the rectangle has two vertices of P.

Input: *The number of vertices n (must be even and $\geq$ 4).*
Output: *A random grid n-ogon P.*

$r := n/2\text{-}2;$
$P := \{(1,1),(1,2),(2,2),(2,1)\};$ /* *(i.e., the unit square)* */
while *r > 0* **do**
    repeat
        Select one grid cell C in the interior of P (at random);
        Apply INFLATE *using C to obtain $\tilde{P}$;*
        Apply CUT *to remove a rectangle (at random) from $\tilde{P}$;*
    while CUT *fails for C;*
    $P := \tilde{P};\ \ r := r\text{-}1;$
end

Fig. 5. The INFLATE-CUT algorithm.

The INFLATE-CUT algorithm, given in Fig. 5 generates a random grid n-ogon from the unit square (i.e., from the 4-ogon) using INFLATE and CUT. The random selections of C and of rectangles must avoid loops. There is always one cell that may be inflated to continue the process. In fact, CUT never fails when the unit cell C has an edge that is part of an edge of P.

The INFLATE-CUT algorithm may be adapted to generate all grid n-ogons, for a given n, instead of one at random. Proposition 1 states the completeness of INFLATE-CUT. Its proof is not immediate, as indicated by the example in Fig. 6.

Proposition 1. *For each grid $(n+2)$-ogon, there is a grid n-ogon that yields it by* INFLATE-CUT, *for all even $n \geq 4$.*

The major ideas of our proofs are illustrated in Fig. 7. They were inspired by work about convexification of simple polygons, and, in particular, by a recent paper by O. Aichholzer et al. [1]. This topic was introduced by Paul Erdös [4] who conjectured that a nonconvex polygon would become convex by repeatedly reflecting all its *pockets* simultaneously across their *lids*. This conjecture was

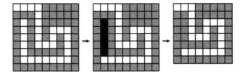

Fig. 6. The inverse of INFLATE-CUT transformation: finding a grid n-ogon that yields a given grid $(n+2)$-ogon. The rightmost polygon is the unique grid 16-ogon that gives rise to this 18-ogon, if we employ INFLATE-CUT.

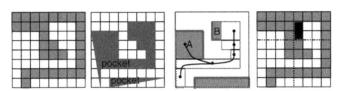

Fig. 7. The two leftmost grids show a grid 18-ogon and its pockets. The shaded rectangles A and B are either leaves or contained in leaves of the tree associated to the horizontal partitioning of the largest pocket. The rightmost polygon is an inflated grid 16-ogon that yields the represented grid 18-ogon, if CUT removes rectangle B.

later corrected by Nagy [12], who showed the Erdös-Nagy theorem that requires that pockets be flipped one by one.

Any nonconvex polygon P has at least one concavity, or *pocket*. A pocket is a maximal sequence of edges of P disjoint from its convex hull except at the endpoints. The pocket's *lid* is the line segment joining its endpoints. Pockets of n-ogons, together with their lids, define simple polygons that are almost orthogonal except for an edge. We may render them orthogonal by introducing artificial edges, as shown in Fig. 7. Given such a pocket Q, let Π be the partition of Q into rectangles obtained by extending the horizontal edges incident to its reflex vertices until they hit the boundary. Let us consider the *dual graph* of Π. It captures the adjacency relation between pieces of Π. Its nodes are the pieces of Π and its edges connect adjacent pieces. Such a graph is always a tree and every leaf that does not contain the artificial horizontal edge contains (or is itself) a rectangle that might have been removed by CUT. Now, at most one leaf contains the artificial horizontal edge. Moreover, if the tree consists of a single node (rectangle), it trivially satisfies the conditions of CUT. Though, this proof shares ideas of a proof of Meisters' *Two-Ears Theorem* [7] by O'Rourke, we were not aware of this when we wrote it.

Another concept – *mouth* – helped us refine CUT and reduce the number of possible ways of generating a given $(n+2)$-ogon.

Definition 2. *(Toussaint [14]) A vertex v_i of P is said to be a principal vertex provided that no vertex of P lies in the interior of the triangle (v_{i-1}, v_i, v_{i+1}) or in the interior of the diagonal (v_{i-1}, v_{i+1}). A principal vertex v_i of a simple polygon P is called mouth if the diagonal (v_{i-1}, v_{i+1}) is an external diagonal, i.e., the interior of (v_{i-1}, v_{i+1}) lies in the exterior of P.*

We are not aware of any work that uses this concept as we do. Nevertheless, INFLATE-CUT is somehow doing the reverse of an algorithm given by Toussaint in [14] that computes the convex hull of a polygon globbing-up mouths to successively remove its concavities. For orthogonal polygons, we would rather define *rectangular mouths*, saying that a reflex vertex v_i is a rectangular mouth of P iff the interior of the rectangle defined by (v_{i-1}, v_i, v_{i+1}) is contained in the exterior of P and contains no other vertices of P. To justify the correction of our technique, we observe that when we apply CUT to obtain a grid $(n+2)$-ogon, the vertex $\tilde{v}_C$ (that was the center the inflated grid cell C) is always a rectangular mouth of the resulting $(n+2)$-ogon. In sum, we may rephrase the *One-Mouth Theorem* by Toussaint [14] and show Proposition 2.

Proposition 2. *Each grid n-ogon has at least one rectangular mouth, for $n \geq 6$.*

4   A Constraint Programming Approach

The method we have described can be easily adapted to generate all grid n-ogons, for small values of n. For instance, by applying INFLATE-CUT to all cells in the polygon and considering all possibilities of cutting rectangles, for each cell. It is difficult to see how to eliminate symmetric solutions, or even if that is possible. Clearly, we would like to eliminate the possibility of generating them. The number of grid n-ogons grows exponentially with n, so that it does not make sense the comparison of solutions to filter out symmetric ones. To make matters worse, the same n-ogon may be generated from a unit square by performing similar transformations, though in a different order. It is easy to locally detect and break some symmetries: if a given n-ogon is symmetric, then we would possibly not apply INFLATE-CUT to cells that are in symmetric positions.

A major advantage of the following approach is the ability to control the generated polygons by imposing constraints in addition to a basic core that translates the notion of grid n-ogon. In particular, it is possible to completely break symmetry during search through constraints. Several approaches and techniques have been proposed (e.g, [5, 6]) for similar purposes, in recent years.

For certain applications, as for example, to check conjectures, it is also important to restrict the generated polygons (e.g., to constrain their area, the number of consecutive reflex vertices, the length of their edges, etc). This second approach gives this kind of control.

4.1   A Simple Constraint Satisfaction Model

Let us define a grid n-ogon by giving the sequence

$$(X_1, Y_1), (X_1, Y_2), (X_2, Y_2), (X_2, Y_3), (X_3, Y_3), \ldots, (X_k, Y_k), (X_k, Y_1)$$

of its vertices, for example, in CCW order, with $k = \frac{n}{2}$. So, to generate grid n-ogons we have to find ordered sequences $X_1, X_2, \ldots, X_k$ and $Y_1, Y_2, \ldots, Y_k$, such that $Y_i \in 1..k$, $X_i \in 1..k$, for all i, with all X_i's and Y_i's distinct (for the polygon to be in general position). Additional constraints must be imposed to guarantee that non-adjacent edges will not intersect. As there is a single edge per line, we just have to avoid intersections between each vertical edge and all horizontal edges that are non-adjacent to it. When the vertices are ordered as above, $e_{1+2j} = \overline{(X_{1+j}, Y_{1+j}), (X_{1+j}, Y_{2+j})}$ and $e_{2+2j} = \overline{(X_{1+j}, Y_{2+j}), (X_{2+j}, Y_{2+j})}$ define the polygon's edges, for $j = 0, \ldots, k-1$, being $k+1 \equiv 1$. For all j, the vertical edge e_{1+2j} does not intersect any non-adjacent horizontal edge $e_{2+2j'}$ if and only if (1) holds for $j' \in \{0, \ldots, k-1\} \setminus \{j-1, j\}$,

$$\frac{X_{1+j} - X_{1+j'}}{X_{2+j'} - X_{1+j'}} \notin [0,1] \quad \vee \quad \frac{Y_{2+j'} - Y_{1+j}}{Y_{2+j} - Y_{1+j}} \notin [0,1] \tag{1}$$

To encode these constraints as finite domain constraints, we get more disjunctive constraints

$$\frac{A-B}{C-B} \notin [0,1] \equiv (C > B \wedge (A \leq B \vee A \geq C)) \vee (C < B \wedge (A \geq B \vee A \leq C))$$

the model being actually declaratively simple but computationally too complex.

5   Experimental Evaluation

We have developed prototype implementations of the INFLATE-CUT method and of this constraint programming model. For INFLATE-CUT, we may show that our implementation (in the C language) uses linear space in the number of vertices and runs in quadratic time in average. Fig. 8 shows some empirical results. To

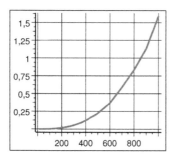

Fig. 8. Average time performance of our implementation of INFLATE-CUT. It yields a random grid 1000-ogon in 1.6 seconds in average (AMD Athlon Processor at 900 MHz).

achieve this, it keeps the vertices of P in a circular doubly linked list, its area (i.e., the number of cells) and the total number of cells of P in each horizontal grid line, this also in a linked list. To compute the coordinates (p, q) that identify cell C, it first uses these counters to find row q and then left-to-right and top-to-bottom sweeping techniques to find column p and the four delimiting edges.

Moreover, it first checks whether CUT will succeed for C and performs explicitly INFLATE only if it does. To check whether a rectangle may be cut it performs a rotational sweep of the vertices of P.

As concerns the second method, we developed a prototype implementation using CLP(FD) [3] for SICStus Prolog together with a simple graphical interface written in Tcl/Tk to output the generated polygons and interact with the generator. This program may be used to generate either an n-ogon at random or all n-ogons by backtracking, for very small n.

To break symmetries we added additional constraints to the CSP model described above. First we required that $X_1 = 1$. This means that amongst all sequences that are circular permutations of $v_1, \ldots, v_n$, we choose the one that defines v_1 as the highest vertex in the leftmost vertical edge of P. Then, we require that $P \preceq_{LEX} \sigma(P)$, for all $\sigma \in D_4$, where D_4 is the group defined by the eight symmetries of the square grid and $\preceq_{LEX}$ is the lexicographic order. If we refer back to Fig. 2, this means that only the second polygon there would be generated. On the other hand, if we add $P = \sigma(P)$, for all σ in a subgroup S of D_4, the generator yields polygons that exhibit all the symmetries in S. Our implementation has been mainly used by us to test some conjectures about orthogonal polygons (for $n < 20$) and to construct symmetrical n-ogons (for $n < 90$). Global constraints were used to implement this ordering constraint and those preventing intersections of non-adjacent edges. Nevertheless, we think that efficiency could still be improved by exploring geometric features of the solutions to the problem and adding redundant constraints to reduce the search.

Since the number of polygons grows exponentially with n, and we need polygons with a larger number of vertices, the empirical results indicate that it may be impractical to use our second method to produce a relevant tests set to the algorithm described in [13]. So, INFLATE-CUT algorithm has some important advantages.

6   Conclusions

Two different methods were proposed for generating random orthogonal polygons with a given number of vertices. One allows for great control on the form of polygons, but is computationally too expensive. The other is a polynomial time algorithm and seems more adequate for the generation of random polygons, provided no special features are sought, apart from the desired number of vertices. Similar ideas may be explored to generate random simple polygons.

Acknowledgement

We would like to thank Domingos Cardoso for detecting a flaw in our former proof of Proposition 1.

References

1. Aichholzer, O., Cortés, C., Demaine, E. D., Dujmovic, V., Erickson, J., Meijer, H., Overmars, M., Palop, B., Ramaswawi, S., Toussaint, G. T.: Flipturning polygons. Discrete & Computational Geometry **28** (2002), 231–253.
2. Auer, T., Held, M.: Heuristics for the generation of random polygons. In Fiala, F., Kranakis, E., Sack, J.-R. (Eds), Proc. of 8th Canadian Conf. Computational Geometry (CCCG'96), Carleton University Press (1996) 38–44.
3. Carlsson M., Ottosson G., Carlson B.: An open-ended finite domain constraint solver. In Proc. of PLILP'97, LNCS 1292, 191-206, Springer-Verlag, 1997.
4. Erdös, P.: Problem number 3763. American Mathematical Monthly **42** (1935) 627.
5. Gent, I. P. , Harvey, W., Kelsey, T.: Groups and constraints – symmetry breaking during search. In P. Van Hentenryck (Ed.), Proc. of CP'02, LNCS 2470, Springer-Verlag (2002) 415-430.
6. McDonald, I., Smith, B.: Partial symmetry breaking. In P. Van Hentenryck (Ed.), Proc. of CP'02 LNCS 2470, Springer-Verlag (2002) 431-445.
7. Meisters, G. H.: Polygons have ears. American Mathematical Monthly **82** (1975) 648-651.
8. O'Rourke, J.: Art gallery theorems and algorithms. Oxford University Press (1987).
9. O'Rourke, J.: An alternate proof of the rectilinear art gallery theorem. J. of Geometry **21** (1983) 118–130.
10. O'Rourke, J., Pashchenko, I., Tewari, G.: Partitioning orthogonal polygons into fat rectangles. In Proc. 13th Canadian Conference on Computational Geometry (CCCG'01) (2001) 133-136.
11. Sohler, C.: Generating random star-shaped polygons. In Proc. 11th Canadian Conference on Computational Geometry (CCCG'99) (1999) 174–177.
12. Sz.-Nagy, B.: Solution of problem 3763. American Mathematical Monthly **46** (1939) 176–177.
13. Tomás, A. P., Bajuelos, A. L., Marques, F.: Approximation algorithms to minimum vertex cover problems on polygons and terrains. In P.M.A Sloot et al. (Eds): Proc. of ICCS 2003, LNCS 2657, Springer-Verlag (2003) 869-878.
14. Toussaint, G. T.: Polygons are anthropomorphic. American Mathematical Monthly **122** (1991) 31–35.
15. Zhu, G., Sundaram, G., Snoeyink, J., Mitchell, J.: Generating random polygons with given vertices. Computational Geom. Theory and Appl. **6**(5) (1996) 277–290.
16. Urrutia, J.: Art gallery and illumination problems. In J.-R. Sack and J. Urrutia, editors, Handbook on Computational Geometry. Elsevier (2000).

Genetic Programming for Automatic Generation of Image Processing Algorithms on the CNN Neuroprocessing Architecture

Víctor M. Preciado[1], Miguel A. Preciado[2], and Miguel A. Jaramillo[1]

[1] Departamento de Electrónica e Ingeniería Electromecánica
Universidad de Extremadura, E-06071 Badajoz, Spain
{vmpreciado@ieee.org, miguel@unex.es}
[2] Dept. de Ingeniería de Sistemas y Automática, Universidad de Sevilla
Paseo de los Descubrimientos, s/n, 41092 Sevilla, Spain

Abstract. The Cellular Neural Network Universal Machine (CNN-UM) is a novel neuroprocessor algorithmically programmable having real time and supercomputer power implemented in a single VLSI chip. The local CNN connectivity provides an useful computation paradigm when the problem can be reformulated as a well-defined task where the signal values are placed on a regular 2-D grid (i.e., image processing), and the direct interaction between signal values are limited within a *local neighborhood*. This paper introduces a Genetic Programming technique to evolve both the structure and parameters of visual algorithms on this architecture. This is accomplished by defining a set of node functions and terminals to implement the basic operations commonly used. Lastly, the procedures involved in the use of the algorithm are illustrated by several applications.

1 Introduction

The Cellular Neural Network Universal Machine (CNN-UM) is a programmable neuroprocessor having real-time power implemented in a single VLSI chip [1]. This neurocomputer is a massive aggregate of regularly spaced nonlinear analog cells which communicate with each other only through their nearest neighbors. This fact makes the CNN an useful computation paradigm when the problem can be reformulated as a task where the signal values are placed on a regular 2-D grid, and the direct interaction between signal values are limited within a finite local neighborhood [2]. This cellular structure and the local interconnection topology not only resemble the anatomy of the retina, indeed, they are very close to the operation of the eye [3], especially when photosensors are placed over each tiny analog processor.

Local interaction facilitates the implemetation of this kind of networks as efficient and robust full-custom mixed-signal chip which embeds distributed optical signal acquisition in a 0.5 μm standard CMOS technology [4]. The chip is capable to complete complex spatio-temporal image processing tasks within short

R. Conejo et al. (Eds.): CAEPIA-TTIA 2003, LNAI 3040, pp. 374–383, 2004.

computation time ($< 300ns$ for linear convolutions) but, in contrast, programming in the framework of this novel architecture is not a trivial matter. Manifold nonlinear phenomena – from nonlinear waves to chaotic oscillations – may appear while designing the topology and weights of this dynamic network. In this direction, several works has been presented to yield a programming methodology when the operator is restricted to binary output and the stability of the network is assumed.

In this paper we propose a stochastic optimization technique based on Genetic Programming to automatically generate image processing programs in this neurocomputing architecture. In contrast with previous algebraic design techniques, this input-output approach offers a flexible description of CNN's and makes possible to learn propagating and grey-scale-output templates. On the other hand, the resulting cost function is difficult to minimize. Due to complex dynamic phenomena in the network, the energy function to be minimized is noisy when chaos or sustained oscillations appear in the network, and non-differentiable when catastrophes, bifurcations or multistability ocurrs.

The paper is organized as follows. In Section 2, the cellular neural network mathematical model and the architecture of the CNN-Universal Machine prototyping system is introduced. The optimization technique based on a GP algorithm, as well as implemented software tools, are described in Section 3. Experimental applications to automatic algorithm design, and the summary of the experiences are our main results presented here.

2 CNN-Based Neuromorphic Architecture

The CNN Universal Machine (CNN-UM) architecture [1] is an *analogic* spatio-temporal array computer wherein analog spatio-temporal dynamics and logic operations are combined in a programmable framework. Elementary instructions and algorithmic techniques are absolutely different from any digital computers because elementary operators (denominated *templates*) perform complex spatio-temporal nonlinear dynamics phenomena by varying the local interconnection pattern in the array.

2.1 CNN Dynamical Model

The simplest CNN cell consists in a single capacitor which is coupled to neighbouring cells through nonlinear controlled sources. The dynamic of the array can be described by the following set of differential equations

$$\frac{d}{dt}x_{i,j}(t) = -x_{i,j}(t) + \sum_{k,l \in N_r} A_{k,l} y_{i+k,j+k}(t) + \sum_{k,l \in N_r} B_{k,l} u_{i+k,j+k}(t) + I \quad (1)$$

with output nonlinearity

$$y(x) = \frac{1}{2} \left[|x - 1| - |x + 1| \right] \quad (2)$$

The input,state and output, represented by $u_{i,j}, x_{i,j}$ and $y_{i,j}$.

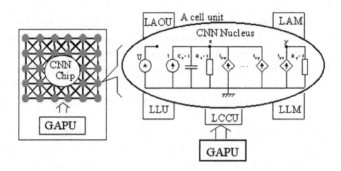

Fig. 1. Schematic architecture of the Cellular Neural Network-Universal Machine.

2.2 CNN-Univeral Machine Architecture

The elementary image processing tasks performed on the input data by a single template can be combined to obtain more sophisticated operation mode on the CNN Universal Machine (CNN-UM) [1]. The machine uses the simple CNN dynamics (1) in a time multiplexed way by controlling the template weights and the source of the data inputs for each operation. The machine supplies memory and register transfers at each cell that allow the outputs of simple CNN operations to be combined and/or supplied to the inputs of the next operation.

The architecture of the CNN-UM is shown in Fig. 1. As it can be seen, the CNN-UM is an array computer with a dynamic CNN core, called CNN nucleus. The CNN-UM extends this core in two main parts: *(i)* the array of extended CNN cells and *(ii)* the Global Analogic Programming Unit (GAPU).

An *extended CNN cell* has the following extra elements added to the CNN nucleus (core cell):

- *Local Analog Memory (LAM)*; a few continuous (analog) values are stored in the LAM in each cell,
- *Local Logic Memory (LLM)*; several binary (logic) values are stored in the LLM in each cell,
- *Local Logic Unit (LLU)*; a simple programmable multi input/single output logic operation is executed, the input and output is stored in the LAM,
- *Local Analog Operation Unit (LAOU)*; analog operations between input images are executed. The input and output is stored in the LAM,
- *Local Comunication and Control Unit (LCCU)* which receives the messages from the central (global) "commander", the GAPU, and programs the extended cells accordingly.

Due to implementability concerns, the template neighborhood radius is generally restricted to be as small as possible, and templates are applied in a space-invariant manner (*A* and *B* are the same for every cell). The actual ACE4k visual microprocessor [4] is an array of 64×64 CNN cells that occupies an area of $9145 \times 9548 \ \mu m^2$ packaged in a 120 Pin Grid Array using a low power budget ($< 1.2W$ for the complete chip).

3 Genetic Programming Approach

Genetic programming, as is common with other evolutionary approaches, applies
the principles of Darwinian selection to a population of parametric solutions to
a given optimization problem [8]. Evolutionary processes begin with the generation of an initial population of random candidate solutions. The population
is then iteratively modified by reproduction operators that selectively replicate
the most promising solutions and by genetic operators that randomly alter their
representation to generate novel search points in the search space. The structure
and variable size of the individuals evolved make genetic programming ideally
suited to implement classifiers, controllers and black-box models by means of
supervised learning approaches. Given a set of model input/output pairs (col-
lectively describing correct classifications or the response of the system under
analysis to a known set of stimuli), an evolving population of programs is usually
able to infer computational rules that map inputs onto outputs. In this paper,
GP is used to perform automatic generation of visual algorithms on the CNN-
UM neuroprocessor. It can be found in the literature several related approaches
which illustrate the application of GP in the synthesis of low-level image filters
[5] or feature detectors [6]. For sake of clarity, several concepts related with the
proposed algorithm are defined below.

Definition 1 (Terminal and Function Set). *In this work, as is common in
this kind of optimization problems, the structure used to codify the individuals are
the tree. Tree nodes are classified in functions or terminals. Functions represent
intermediate tree nodes corresponding to an elemental image processing operation. In the CNN computing environment, functions are related to a particular
connectivity pattern and the associated nonlinear dynamics. On the other hand,
terminals are final tree nodes representing a potential input image. Similarly,
we can define a* function set *as a subgroup of templates selected from a previously determined template library. To conclude our definitions, a* terminal set *is
the group of images which are available to be the input of the visual algorithms.
Consequently, the terminal and function sets are building blocks which must be
carefully selected to efficiently reach a feasible solution.*

Next, particular features of our GP approach are commented.

- **Codification:** As it is usual in GP, Lukasiewicz prefix notation is used to
  codify each tree into a sequence of nodes. From a software implementation
  point of view, each obtained sequence is codified in a binary string according
  to a code which establish a univocal correspondence between each terminal
  a string of bits.
- **Initial Generation:** The performance of the following three different methods have been previously proved in [7]:
  - *Full Generation* in which trees are generated with a previously defined
    branch generation depth. This means that every branch in the tree reach
    this fixed depth.

- In the *Grow technique,* the codified trees (in prefix notation) are generated connecting terminals and functions to a root node according to a predetermined probability. In our approach, every branch is limited in depth, thus if this limit is achieved terminal nodes are automatically added until the end of the branch.
- The *Ramped Half & Half* technique is an hybrid method between the *Full Generation* and *Grow Technique.* In this case, a half of the initial population is generated by the full method, and the other half by a modified grow technique in which the branch depth is modified from 2 to a maximum value along the individuals of the initial population.

3.1   Fitness Function

A well-defined fitness or cost function, which compares the desired output to the result of the transient in the neural network, is an essential matter for obtaining succesfull GP results. While the proposed methodology has to tackle with many different problems, several fitness functions has been proved. It is responsability of the user to properly choose the most adequate cost function based on the *a priori* information about the problem. In this work we have implemented the following functions:

- **Correlation-Based Fitness:** A correlation operator between desired and output image is applied as usually defined in signal processing theory. This kind of cost function is specially interesting when the desired output is a grey-scale image.

$$f_{corr}(\boldsymbol{p}) \triangleq \frac{\sum_{i\in\mathbf{I}}\left(y_i^d \cdot y_i(\infty)\right)}{k^2\sqrt{\sum_{i\in\mathbf{I}}\left(y_i^d\right)^2 \cdot \sum_{i\in\mathbf{I}}\left(y_i(\infty)\right)^2}} \tag{3}$$

where $\boldsymbol{p}$ denotes the parameter vector, $\mathbf{I}$ is the whole set of pixels in the image, k is the size of the network, y_i^d is the value of the ith pixel of the desired output and $y_i(\infty)$ stands for the corresponding pixel of the settled output.
- **Absolute Difference:** It is exclusively defined to measure the distance between binary images. It used a simple first-order norm between pixels in both desired and output images in the following format. The result is normalized taking into account the size of the images.

$$f_{abs}(\boldsymbol{p}) \triangleq \frac{\sum_{i=1}^{k}\left(\left|y_i^d\right| - |y_i(\infty)|\right)}{k} \tag{4}$$

- **Special Difference:** The special difference fitness function allows a *fuzzy* definition of the desired image. It is defined in the space of binary images as follows

$$f_{spc}(\boldsymbol{p}) \triangleq \frac{1}{s\left(\mathbf{Z}\right)}\sum_{i\in\mathbf{Z}}\left(\left|y_i^d\right| - |y_i(\infty)|\right) + \frac{1}{s\left(\bar{\mathbf{Z}}\right)}\sum_{i\in\bar{\mathbf{Z}}}y_i^d\left(1 - |y_i(\infty)|\right), \tag{5}$$

$$\mathbf{Z} \equiv \left\{i\in\mathbf{I} : y_i^d = 0\right\} \text{ and } \bar{\mathbf{Z}} \equiv \left\{i\in\mathbf{I} : y_i^d \neq 0\right\}. \tag{6}$$

where the function s denotes the size in pixels of the set used as argument. Therefore, this method gives a different treatment to zero and non-zero values in the image, relying a greater emphasis on black pixels in the output.

Several secondary components are included in the fitness function to avoid several non-feasible individuals. These are a *penalty all-black/all-white* used to avoid individuals consisting in a uniform black or white image which can yield a high fitness evaluation in several problems, and a *number-of-operations penalty* which gives a handicap to huge trees.

3.2 Genetic Operators

Genetic operators used in this work are similar to those used in standard GP algorithms [8]. Thus, we briefly enumerate the kinds of operators implemented and experimentally proved in our software tool.

- **Selection.** Four different selection methods have been developed: μ, λ (from nu individual, lamda sons are generated, from which best nu individuals are chosen), $\mu + \lambda$ (from nu individual, lamda sons are generated, and from all nu+lambda individuals, nu individuals are chosen), *ranking* and *tournament* as usually defined in Evolutionary Optimization theory.
- **Mutation.** As in the selection operator, four different kinds of operators have been developed: the *Subtree mutation* – in which a subtree is stochastically selected and substituted for another stochastically generated tree –, the *Node operator* which stochastically modifies a tree node, the *Hoist method* which substitutes an individual tree with a stochastically extracted subtree, and *Collapse mutation* which stochastically extracts a subtree and substitutes it for a stochastically generated terminal node.

Once the theoretical details have been exposed, we presents a software tool implemented to prove, in a friendly GUI, the manifold posibilities presented by the GP algorithm under study.

4   Numerical Results

A complete software package has been programmed to numerically implement the GP algorithm herein studied. Two programs outlight in this package: the *CNN Visual Algorithm Simulator* and the *GP-based Generator of CNN Visual Algorithm*. Both have been programmed in Borland C++ Builder, and are specifically designed to handle individuals represented by means of a tree structure.

The *GP-based Generator of CNN Visual Algorithm* implements the GP searching algorithm discussed in this paper, and allows the user to define all search parameters previously commented. The *CNN Visual Algorithm Simulator* permits the simulation of user-defined algorithms and single templates. It can be used to verify or refine any solution algorithm obtained by GP optimization. Both programs use a template library which can be arbitrarily modified by the user to include interesting templates.

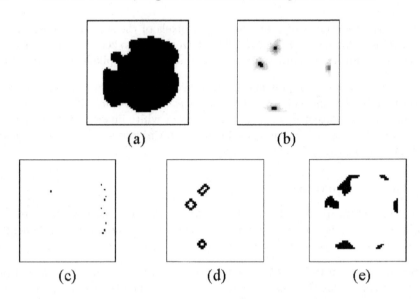

Fig. 2. Automatic generation of a visual algorithm for roughness measurement. The paremeters used in the GP algorithm are: population=200, crossover probability=0.8. The mutation probabilities are: subtree=0.02, node: 0.03, collapse=0.005, hoist=0.01. Parameters used in the generation of the first population: generation type=Ramped half and half, terminal probability=0.07, generation depth=6. Selection parameters: selection type=Ranking, probabilities range (0.5, 1). Fitness evaluation: image evaluation type=special difference, number of functions penalty=ON.

In the following, some examples of GP searching application are shown in order to illustrate the performance of the implemented software package for the automatic generation of image processing algorithms on the CNN-UM.

Example 1 (Roughness Measurement).
In this example, the desired algorithm takes a binary input image that contains a black figure over a white background, and make a measure of its roughness by the detection of concavities in the boundary of the black object. Both the desired and output images are shown in Fig. 2, and GP parameters are specified in the label of the figure.

Successive automatically obtained solutions are represented in Fig. 2 (c)-(e). It can be seen how the first solutions don´t accomplish with a minimum quality requirement. This is due to the stochastic nature of our optimization algorithm. After 396 generations, the solution which fulfill our minimum requirement is the one showed in Fig. 2 (e). The automatically generated algorithm is represented as a tree in Fig. 4 (a), where discontinuous line box marks an *intron* – a redundant piece of code that usually appears in GP individuals.

Example 2 (Depth Estimator).
In this example, we are looking for a simple program which estimate the depth of a concrete object in a scene. The depth estimator algorithm searched needs four

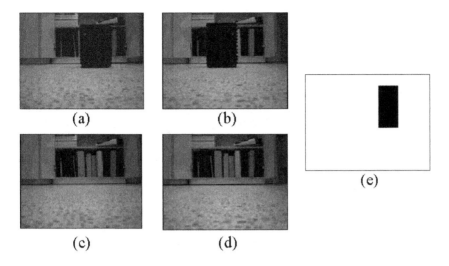

Fig. 3. Automatic generation of a visual algorithm for 3D depth estimation. The paremeters used in the GP algorithm are: population=200, crossover probability=0.8. Mutation probabilities: subtree=0.02, node=0.03, collapse=0.005, hoist=0.01. Generation parameters: generation type=Ramped half and half, terminal probability=0.07, generation depth=8. Selection parameters: selection type=Ranking, probabilities range=(0.5, 1). Fitness evaluation: image evaluation type=correlation, number of functions evaluation=ON.

input images represented in Fig. 3: two of them representing the right and left images of a stereoscopically captured scene including the object (the black box), Fig. 3 (a)-(b), and the other two representing the scene without the object, Fig. 3 (c)-(d). From a GP point of view, these four images constitute the terminal set. The desired algorithm makes a estimation of the depth map of the scene. The result is based in disparity, in such a way that, in the output image, each object disparity is shown by horizontal segments.

After 204 generations, the obtained solution can be seen in Fig. 3 (e), fulfills our minimum requirement. The automatically generated algorithm is represented as a tree in Figure 4 (b).

5 Conclusions

In this paper, a new learning machine for automatic design of CNN visual algorithms was described. The novel neurocomputng architecture based on the Cellular Neural Network-Universal Machine has been briefly presented. Complex dynamics in this nonlinear networks provides us with a powerful tool for real-time image processing. On the other hand, there is only specific methodologies to design a very reduced set of image processing operators, almost all of them based on an extension of classical LTI filters [9]. In this paper, we propose a general design approach consisting in using the stochastic optimization technique

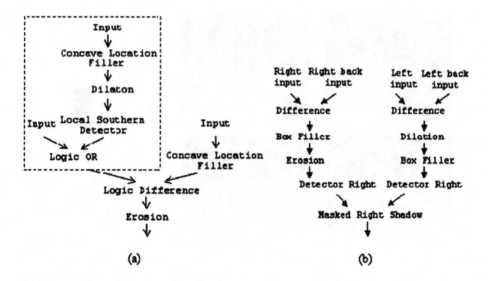

Fig. 4. Automatically generated visual algorithms for roughness measuremente (a), and depth estimation (b). The appearance of introns in the first algorithms can be observed in the framed subtree.

called Genetic Programming for automatic generation of visual algorithms. We have briefly presented nonlinear dynamics of the CNN and the associated computational infrastructure which yields the CNN-UM. Next, we have presented a GP-based methodology to accomplish an automatic design of image algorithms.

It is important to note that the objective of this methodology isn't the elimination of the hands of the expert from the design process, but provide an useful tool to the expert designer in order to facilitate his work in the framework of programming this neuroprocessor. From this point of view, it is worth noting that a basic knowledge about how the GP works is essential for the user to properly configure the manifold parameters needed for a correct performance of the algorithms.

As correct GP configuration is essential for an effective searching, several rules have been observed to provide acceptable results:

(i) The set of terminals and the desired image must be representative enough to appropriately orient the search process, and shouldn't be too complex to slow it down.

(ii) The set of functions should include every neccesary operator for the solution to be fulfilled, but not too numerous to retard the searching.

(iii) When the problem involves binary output images, the special difference fitness is recommended because it permits a fuzzy definition of the desired image, which results very interesting in finding unknown algorithms. It is also recommended to include a penalty for big trees, because it is usual the appearance of introns to protects individuals from the destructive effects of mutation and crossover, making higher its probability of standing for generations.

(iv) The ramped half-and-half is an efficient method to yield a more diverse and heterogeneous initial population.

(v) The ranking method of selection produce an interesting equilibrium between searching orientation and diversity standing, which benefits the searching process.

(vi) Each mutation operator produces a different effect over the searching: the hoist operator tends to impoverish population diversity, the subtree operator provoke increasing individual trees size – thus parsimony pressure must be increased –, node operator enrich population diversity, and secondary effects haven't been detected, and collapse operator tends to decrease individuals size, therefore it must be used moderately.

References

1. T. Roska, A. Zarandy, S. Zold, P. Foldesy, and P. Szolgay, "The computational infrastructure of the analogic CNN computing - Part I: The CNN-UM Chip prototyping system", *IEEE Trans. Circuits Syst.*, vol. 46, no. 1, pp. 261-268, 1999.
2. L. O. Chua, and L. Yang. "Cellular neural networks: Theory". *IEEE Trans. Circuits Syst.*,vol. 35, no. 10. pp. 1257-1272, 1988.
3. F. Werblin, T. Roska, and L. O. Chua," The analogic cellular neural network as a bionic eye," *Int. J. circuit Theory Appl.*, vol. 23, no. 6, pp. 541-549, 1995.
4. G. Liñán, S. Espejo, R. Domínguez-Castro, and A. Rodríguez-Vázquez, "The CN-NUC3: an Analog I/O 64 x 64 CNN Universal Machine with 7-bit Analog Accuracy", in Proc. IEEE Int. Workshop on Cellular Neural Networks and their Applications (CNNA'2000), pp. 201-206, 2000.
5. M. Ebner, "On the evolution of interest operators using genetic programming", in *First European Workshop on Genetic Programming*, pp. 6-10, 1998.
6. R. Poli, "Genetic Programming for Feature Detection and Image Segmentation," in: Evolutionary Computing. Lecture Notes in Computer Science, vol. 1143. Springer, Berlin, pp. 110-125, 1996.
7. V.M. Preciado, D. Guinea, J. Vicente, M.C. Garcia-Alegre, and A. Ribeiro," Automatic CNN Multitemplate Tree Generation", in *Proc. IEEE Int. Workshop on Cellular Neural Networks and their Applications (CNNA'2000)*, pp. 327-332, 2000.
8. J. Koza, Genetic Programming, MIT Press, Cambridge MA, 1992.
9. K.R. Crounse and L.O. Chua, "Methods for image processing and pattern formation in cellular neural networks: A tutorial," *IEEE Trans. Circuits Syst.*, Vol. 42, no. 10, pp. 583-601, 1995.

Heuristic Based Sampling in Estimation of Distribution Algorithms: An Initial Approach

Luis de la Ossa, José A. Gámez, and José M. Puerta

Computer Science Department / $i^3\mathcal{A}$
Castilla-La Mancha University
Campus Universitario s/n
Albacete, 02071
{ldelaossa,jgamez,jpuerta}@info-ab.uclm.es

Abstract. Estimation of Distribution Algorithms (EDAs) are a kind of evolutionary algorithms where classical genetic operators are replaced by the estimation of a probabilistic model and its simulation in order to generate the next population. With this work we tackle, in a preliminary way, how to incorporate specific heuristic knowledge in the sampling phase. We propose two ways to do it and evaluate them experimentally through the classical knapsack problem.

1   Introduction

On the last few years, researchers have been working on a new family of evolutionary algorithms called *Estimation of Distribution Algorithms* (EDAs) [11]. As well as genetic algorithms [12], EDAs are based on populations, but the transition from a generation to another has been modified. Unlike GAs, there are neither crossover nor mutation operators on EDAs. Instead, the new population of individuals is sampled from a probability distribution which is estimated from a database formed by individuals of the former generations. Whereas in GAs interrelations among different variables involved on individuals representation are generally not considered, on EDAs these interrelations are implicitly expressed on the joint probability distribution associated to selected individuals on each iteration. Since joint probability distribution is not manageable even for small problems (with few variables), the idea is to estimate a model $\mathcal{M}$ that is a simplification of such distribution.

Figure 1 shows the scheme of a generic EDA. As can be seen, it starts from an initial population of m individuals randomly generated (in most cases), as it happens with most generational algorithms. On the second step, a number s ($s \leq m$) of individuals is selected (normally those whose values are better relating to evaluation function) as database for the model estimation.

After that, a probabilistic n-dimensional model, the one that better reflects the interdependences among the variables, is induced, and an auxiliary population is obtained from the model through sampling. Lastly, the new population D_i is obtained from the former population D_{i-1} and the auxiliary population. This selection is generally carried out by using elitism.

R. Conejo et al. (Eds.): CAEPIA-TTIA 2003, LNAI 3040, pp. 384–393, 2004.

EDA Approach

1. $D_0 \leftarrow$ Generate initial population (m individuals)
2. Evaluate population D_0
3. $k = 1$
4. Repeat until stop condition
   (a) $D_{k-1}^{S_e} \leftarrow$ Select $s \leq m$ individuals from D_{k-1}
   (b) Estimate a new model $\mathcal{M}$ from $D_{k-1}^{S_e}$
   (c) $D_{k-1}^m \leftarrow$ Sample m individuals from $\mathcal{M}$
   (d) Evaluate D_{k-1}^m
   (e) $D_k \leftarrow$ Select m individuals from $D_{k-1} \cup D_{k-1}^m$
   (f) $k = k + 1$

Fig. 1. General scheme of an EDA

The main problem when dealing with EDAs is related to estimation of the model $\mathcal{M}$, since the more complex $\mathcal{M}$ is, the richer it becomes, but it also increases the effort dedicated to the model estimation.

Due to the fact that a new model must be built for each generation, proposals concerning to the way that the model is estimated are an important issue of research. However, sampling from the obtained probabilistic model (step 4.(c) of the algorithm described in 1) hasn't received any interest from research community yet.

In this work we make an initial proposal about the use of heuristic knowledge during the sampling phase. This fact is used by other evolutionary algorithms such as those based in *ants colonies* [7].

In order to do that, the work is organized into five sections besides this introduction. Section 2 describes the most commonly used families of EDAs. Next, we study the weight of the sampling in the algorithm and we formulate our proposals on section 3. In section 4 we described experiments that have been carried out and, finally, sections 5 and 6 are dedicated to discussion of the results and conclusions.

2   Estimation of Distribution Algorithms (EDAs)

In the literature, we can find different approaches for the estimation phase . The used models are *univariate* [1, 14], *bivariate* [3] and *n-variate* [10].

We give a brief description of them below.

2.1   Univariate Models

They are the simplest models and they do not consider any dependences among variables. Thus, n-dimensional joint probability distribution is factorized as the product of n independent and univariate probability distributions.

$$P(x_1, x_2, \ldots, x_n) = \prod_{i=1}^{n} P(x_i)$$

The two main approaches are the UMDA algorithm [14] and the PBIL algorithm [1] which, despite belonging to another paradigm, can be also considered as an EDA.

In UMDA algorithm, the parameter estimation for each variable is done by using marginal counts that are present on the s cases considered on (D_{k-1}^{Se}).

In opposition to what happens with UMDA, PBIL does not estimate a new model on each generation, but it refines the current one by considering s cases from D_{k-1}^{Se}. The importance of the estimated model $\mathcal{M}^e$ when updating the current one is controlled by a parameter $\alpha \in (0, 1]$ known as *learning rate*.

Concretely, if P_{k-1} is the current model, then the new one P_k is given by:

$$P_k(X_i) = (1 - \alpha)P_{k-1}(X_i) + \alpha\mathcal{M}^e(X_i)$$

Notice that, if $\alpha = 1$, then PBIL algorithm is equivalent to UMDA.

2.2 Bivariate Models

Bivariate models allow dependences between pairs of variables. If we visualize the model as a directed graph, this implies that each variable can have, at most, one parent[1]. Thus, there are some variables now whose "apriori" probability must be estimated and some others whose probability is conditioned to its *parent* variable: $P(X_i|X_j)$. Moreover, the problem is double now, because we must learn the structure (the dependences) as well as the parameters (probability tables).

Structural learning is the really complex phase, since once the structure is known, the estimation of the parameters basically consist on a calculus of frequencies from the database. The most outstanding bivariate models (by its use) in literature are those whose resulting graphical structure is a chain [6] or a tree [3]. In order to get a tree structure, COMIT algorithm [3] uses the well known Chow and Liu method [5], which is based on the concept of mutual information.

2.3 N-Variate Models

These models allow the use of statistics of order n. Most common are those that allow estimating a Bayesian Network [9]. This can give rise to a huge family of algorithms depending on the learning algorithm used, the metrics, the constraints, the kind of variables, etc. (see [11] chapter 3 for a revision). Lastly, notice that, for all of the models described in this section, it is very usual to smooth the maximum likelihood estimates (MLE) by using, for instance, the Laplace correction.

---

[1] Notice that this graph would be completely unconnected for univariate models since there would be no edges at all.

3   Introducing Heuristic Knowledge on the Sampling Phase

Once a model is estimated, it becomes necessary to generate a population of m individuals from it. This is done by sampling the probability distribution codified by such model. The most commonly used technique is the *Probabilistic Logic Sampling* (PLS), proposed by Henrion [8] to allow approximate propagation over Bayesian networks. The idea is to sample a variable s once that the values of its parents $(pa(x_i))$ have already been sampled. Figure 2 shows pseudo code for PLS.

PLS Algorithm

---

1. Establish an order σ of the variables on the net such that no variable appears before its parents.
2. From $k = 1$ until number of samples do
   (a) From $i = 1$ until $|\sigma|$ do
      i. $X_j = \sigma(i)$
      ii. Obtain a value for X_j by sampling the marginal distribution $P^*(X_j) = P(X_j|\mathbf{c})$, where $\mathbf{c}$ is the configuration of values already obtained for $pa(X_j)$.

Fig. 2. Description of Henrion's Probabilistic Logic Sampling: PLS

3.1   Integrating Heuristic Knowledge

The use of knowledge has recently been proposed for different stages of EDAs such as the generation of initial population or model estimation. Thus, in [4] knowledge is used to generate the initial population so that it establishes a good starting point for the search. Another option is the proposed in [2], where the authors use domain knowledge to restrict the possible dependence relations among variables, therefore they speed up the structural learning process and obtain, moreover, better results. Also in [2] it's proposed the use of only local optima as individuals of the population, the same way as *Memetic algorithms* [13].

However, up to now, knowledge hasn't been used for the sampling phase. Our intention in this work is to face this task through the addition of heuristic knowledge, as well as it is done with other evolutionary computation techniques such as *ant colonies* (ACs) [7]. On ACs, given a certain state i, the next one j is chosen by sampling the distribution $k \cdot [\tau_{ij}]^\alpha \cdot [\eta_{ij}]^\beta$ where τ represents the memoristic information, η is the heuristic information about the domain, k is a normalization constant and α and β are two control parameters to tune the importance of each component.

Inspired on this way of proceeding, but also considering that the solution is locally built in ACs whereas it is done in a global way in EDAs, we have designed the next two approaches to incorporate heuristic knowledge to the sampling phase. In both cases we suppose that our problem is a maximization one, and the existence of a vector $I(X_i)$ which contains the local heuristic information for each value x_i^j of the variable X_i.

Mode A.- The goal is to introduce the heuristic value $I(\cdot)$ into the distribution that must be sampled. However, since the intensive use of heuristic could drive the process to local optima, we consider the use of a value $\beta \in [0, 1]$ to adjust the influence of heuristic knowledge. We define the next probability distribution:

$$P_h(X_i) = k \cdot P^*(X_i) \cdot I(X_i)$$

where k is a normalization constant. Now, we substitute the step 2.a.ii on the PLS algorithm by the following pseudo-code:

if $(r = uniform[0, 1]) \leq \beta$
then   obtain the value of X_i sampling $P_h(X_i)$
else   obtain the value of X_i sampling $P^*(X_i)$

Mode B.- In this second proposal, the goal is to always sample the same distribution and, therefore, the influence of the heuristic is directly controlled on the definition of P_h through the β parameter. We define $P_h(\cdot)$ as a convex combination between $P^*(\cdot)$ and $I(\cdot)$:

$$P_h(X_i) = \beta \cdot k \cdot I(X_i) + (1 - \beta) \cdot P^*(X_i)$$

where again, k is a normalization constant. Now, on the step 2.a.ii of the PLS algorithm we use P_h as the distribution to be sampled.

As can be seen in both cases, if we set $\beta = 0$ we obtain the PLS and with $\beta = 1$ we would obtain a sample which always makes use of the heuristic value.

4   Experimental Study

To carry out a preliminary experimental study of the behavior of the algorithms proposed in this work, we have considered the classical binary knapsack problem: given a finite set of objects $\{O_1, \ldots, O_n\}$ where each object O_i has an associated weight p_i and a known value (profit) v_i, the goal is to select the subset of objects whose value is best and whose sum of weights do not exceeds the capacity of the knapsack. This problem has been successfully approached with EDAs [11], so we want to remark that our goal here is to compare between PLS and heuristic based PLS, and not to test the goodness of EDAs when applied to the knapsack problem.

Representation of each solution s_j for the problem is made by a binary vector of dimension n, that is: $s_j[1..n]$. The i-th object is selected to enter into the knapsack if $s_j[i] = 1$, otherwise $(s_j[i] = 0)$, it is not selected.

If c is the total capacity of the knapsack, formally, the optimum solution to the binary knapsack problem is a vector s^* such that:

$$s^* = \arg\max_{s \in \Omega_s} \sum_{i=1}^{n} v_i s[i] \quad \text{constrained to} \quad \left(\sum_{i=1}^{n} p_i s[i] \right) \leq c$$

The evaluation of each solution s_j is made by obtaining the sum of the values of every object contained in the knapsack, but penalizing the solutions which are not valid, that is, those which violate the constraints of the problem. We concretely use the following function:

$$f(s_j) = \begin{cases} \sum_{i=1}^{n} v_i s_j[i] & \text{if } \sum_{i=1}^{n} p_i s_j[i] \leq c \\ K \cdot \left(\sum_{i=1}^{n} p_i - \sum_{i=1}^{n} p_i s_j[i] \right) & \text{if } \sum_{i=1}^{n} p_i s_j[i] > c \end{cases}$$

Where K is a positive number such as for each s_j that exceeds the capacity c, we have $K \cdot (\sum_{i=1}^{n} p_i - \sum_{i=1}^{n} p_i s_j[i]) \leq \min(v_1, \ldots, v_n)$. This last expression means that each selection that surpasses the capacity c will obtain a worst evaluation than each valid solution (which doesn't surpasses the capacity c). The chosen value for K is $K = \min(p_i)/((\sum_{i=1}^{n} p_i) - c)$.

Probabilistic models are defined over n binary variables $\{X_1, \ldots, X_n\}$. For the EDAs designed to solve this problem, each variable X_i corresponds with the object O_i and, therefore, with the position $s_j[i]$ of the feasible solutions.

We can see the main design aspects of these algorithms below:

Heuristic Component Used: Heuristic information chosen for the problem has frequently been used in the literature for the solution of this problem when using greedy methods.

For the inclusion of the heuristic information we must define $I(X_i)$ for each variable. In this case, since variables are binaries, we must define $I(X_i = x_i^1)$ and $I(X_i = x_i^0)$, that is, the information we have about including the object represented by X_i on the solution and the contrary (not including it). Concretely, we define $I(X_i)$ as:

$$I(X_i) = \begin{cases} I(X_i = x_i^1) = v_i \\ I(X_i = x_i^0) = ((\sum_{j=1, j \neq i}^{n} v_j/p_j)/(n-1))p_i \end{cases}$$

That is, the ratio between profit and weight is used for the decision of including a certain object and the average of all these ratios will be used to calculate the probability of not including it to the solution. We must consider that these two amounts will be related when making a decision for a certain object i on the way of: *How much up the average profits the inclusion of an object i.*

This heuristic information has been used as it was exposed on section 3.1 during the sampling phase. We have considered $\beta = 0.5$ for generality, giving therefore the same importance to heuristics and to the learnt distribution. This information has been used to initialize the population in some of the experiments as well.

Concretely, initial population can be generated in a totally at random(using a uniform distribution for all of the variables) or by means of the next distribution:

$$P(X_1, \ldots, X_n) = \prod_{i=1}^{n} (k \cdot I(X_i))$$

where k is a normalization constant. We refer to this second initialization as *informed initialization*.

Description of Parameters: For the accomplished experimentation we have generated 12 cases of 500 objects with the generator proposed in [15].

We have tried 4 different problems with different capacities. Besides, we have used for all of them a parameter that can take values 1, 2 and 3 depending on whether values and weights are not correlated, weakly correlated or strongly correlated.

In all of the experiments the size of the population has been fixed as the number of variables in the problem. As stop criterion, we establish a maximum number of iterations (100) that were not reached by previous experiments, although the algorithm also stops if the best solution up to the moment is not improved during 25 consecutive iterations.

Half of population is selected (by elitism) for model estimation. Next population is obtained from previous one and the sampled individuals by selecting those with best fitness.

Implemented Algorithms: We have implemented the two kind of univariate models formerly described: UMDA and PBIL (using $\alpha = 0.5$).

For the experimentation we have executed UMDA and PBIL algorithms with the three kind of sampling: PLS, PLS-modeA and PLS-modeB. Populations have been generated randomly, repairing each individual by eliminating objects at random until the weight don't exceed the capacity of the knapsack.

Each experiment has been repeated 20 times and average ($\pm$ deviation) results are shown in table 1: value of the objective function, number of generations transcurred until the best value is found and number of different individuals evaluated. In this case number of different individuals is smaller than evaluation becouse a hash table has been used. Any case, the number of evaluations can be computed as the product between population size and number of generations.

Results are analyzed on the next section.

5   Discussion

Analysis and Discussion of the Results. From the study of experimental results (table 1)it's worth pointing out that, for each of the algorithms, every time that one of the proposed samplings is used, either mode A or mode B, a better result is obtained and, moreover, a lower number of evaluations is needed until the moment when the best individual is found. If we consider that we also need a lower number of generations to find the best result, we can conclude that, new samplings speed up convergence of the algorithm. We have also obtained results with an initial population of twice the number of variables in the problem, noticing that the behavior of heuristic samplings with respect to PLS are similar.

Table 1. Results using random initialization and reparing individuals. Average and deviation over 20 runs. The first line shows the value of evaluation function, the second the number of generations elapsed until the best solution is found and the third one the number of different individuals evaluated

Caso / Mode:	UMDA			PBIL		
	MLP	ModeA	ModeB	MLP	ModeA	ModeB
Problem 1:	193.8±3.02	197.35 ± 1.39	197 ±1.45	194.15±3.28	197.4 ±1.39	197.6 ± 1.05
	33.3 ±3.42	19.45 ±3.02	18.65 ±2.72	52.5±4.45	26 ±2.36	24.65 ± 4.07
Correlation :1	16447.1 ± 1271	9922.5 ± 1463.85	9513.6 ± 1366.32	25300.55±1449.38	13196.3 ± 1206.07	12.521 ± 2013.23
Problem 1:	43.15 ± 1.09	44.25 ± 0.72	44.45 ± 0.6	13.6 ±0.68	44.25 ±0.64	44.4 ±0.5
	63.95 ±5.55	37.25 ± 4.99	38.2 ± 5.29	78.4 ±7.13	50.5 ± 8.4	51.65 ± 5.9
Correlation :2	31.951 ± 2737.32	18710.8 ± 2393.33	19245.25±2536.74	39006.75 ±3555.22	25131.4 ±3957.34	25737.95 ±2877.34
Problem 1:	297 ± 0	297 ±0	297 ± 0	297±0	297 ± 0	297 ± 0
	26.3 ± 1.72	7.75 ± 0.85	7.85 ± 0.99	39±2.45	13.15 ± 0.75	13.2 ± 1.36
Correlation :3	13358.5 ±902.46	4100.25 ± 478.94	4068.25 ±520.44	19659.5±1212.49	6751.7 ±353.12	6766.45 ± 626.16
Problem 2:	624.45 ±10.55	642.1 ±3.95	642.6 ± 3.76	633±7.89	642.7 ±4.65	643.15 ± 2.94
	43.5 ±5.57	26 ±6.97	25.1 ± 3.74	69.05±8.12	32.55 ± 4.15	33.2 ± 6.05
Correlation :1	19900 ±1171.7	12767.65 ±2486.61	12641.15± 1701.41	31273±1413.8	16326.25 ±1980.87	16666.05 ± 2858.31
Problem 2:	102.95 ±1.5	105.9± 1.45	105.75 ± 1.52	103.2 ± 2.04	106 ±1.08	106.35 ± 2.09
	85.5 ±7.39	44.5 ± 5.43	42.8 ± 7.22	93.5 ±4.51	58.7 ± 4.32	61.4 ± 6.09
Correlation :2	41546.2 ±2984.44	22280.9 ± 2528.74	21335.4 ± 3123.95	46589.15 ±2211	29299.65 ±2157.61	30676.5 ±2792.58
Problem 2:	449 ±10.46	463±0	462 ± 3.08	456 ±8.01	461.5 ± 3.66	462.5±2.24
	48.15 ±7.48	16.25 ±2.43	14.95 ± 1.76	71.1 ±8.53	26.2 ±3.69	25.95 ±3.25
Correlation :3	24252.4 ± 3597.32	8313.75 ±1244.1	7676.65 ± 905.83	35562.85 ± 4071.78	13321.45 ±1859.86	13151.1 ± 1665.61
Problem 3:	873.3 ± 0.98	874.85 ± 0.49	875 ± 0	868.4 ± 1.67	875 ± 0	874.95±0.22
	91 ± 6.06	43.45 ±3.44	45.35 ±4.17	97.45 ± 2.67	68.45 ± 6.68	66 ± 7.85
Correlation :1	45575.5 ± 2860.84	21984.9±1704.17	22886.65±1997.19	48986.6 ±1367.25	34433.05 ± 1862.37	33207.25 ± 3903.33
Problem 3:	342.85 ± 1.27	357.35 ± 0.67	357.35 ± 0.67	337.45±1.5	354.9 ± 0.91	355.05 ± 0.83
	96.25 ±4.06	95.6 ± 3.41	93.45 ± 5.13	95.25 ±4.42	95.95 ± 3.38	94.65 ±5.59
Correlation :2	48434.9±2035.98	48101.1±1677.58	46997.45 ± 2536.4	47827.8 ±2201.08	48260.45 ± 1682.97	47545 ± 2769.94
Problem 3:	1679.0± 0	1679 ± 0	1679 ± 0	1662 ± 5.79	1679.0 ± 0	1679±0
	76 ±3.39	25.5 ±1.85	25.2±1.7	97.7 ± 2.11	45.3 ± 2.05	45.7 ±1.66
Correlation :3	38199.9 ± 1686.66	12969.6 ± 925.39	12831.7± 832.32	49120.7 ±1057.99	22876.6 ±1049.33	23026.1 ±891.98
Problem 4:	2393.7± 3.83	2397.6 ± 0.5	2397.3 ±1.34	2381.7 ± 3.44	2397.75 ± 0.44	2397.75 ±0.44
	85.05±6.01	39.2 ± 6.21	39.55 ± 7.27	97.45 ±2.8	63.3 ± 7.54	65.9 ±8.3
Correlation :1	42127.45±2526.77	18825.15 ± 1812.9	18812.65 ± 1858.57	48920 ± 1631.35	30736.35 ± 2365.6	31533 ± 2511.72
Problem 4:	738.6 ± 3.47	765.5 ± 1.28	766.1 ± 1.52	729.45 ± 1.99	761.15 ± 1.63	761.5 ±2.21
	97.6 ± 3.17	94.75 ± 3.58	95.65 ± 4.3	96.6 ±4.44	95.85 ± 2.46	96.6 ± 2.68
Correlation :2	49.008.4 ± 1575.72	47658.32 ± 1796.98	48071 ± 2177.3	48622.65 ±2227.35	48237.85 ±1241.06	48497.4 ± 1342.1
Problem 4:	2171 ± 5.03	2186 ± 3.08	2186 ± 3.08	2102.85 ± 10.87	2179.45 ±4.36	2179 ± 4.27
	93.55 ±3.59	71.15 ±6.67	72.15 ±8.12	98.85 ±1.35	88.55 ± 6.24	87.15 ±6.41
Correlation :3	47058.2± 1801.48	35838.1 ±3290.61	36258.55 ±4030.73	49700.45 ±672.05	44444.55 ± 3119.97	43864.6 ±3185.91

Heuristic Information. In this work, we have considered that heuristic information $I(X_i)$ is static and can be calculated a priori. However, there are some problems where information $I(X_i)$ depends on the partial solution currently sampled, that is, we have some information of the type $I(X_i|\mathbf{c})$, where $\mathbf{c}$ is the partial configuration obtained until that moment[2].

We will denominate that heuristic information as *dynamic* and it may cause that the ancestral order proposed by PLS cannot be used, however, we can utilize other kind of sampling where we basically use propagation techniques in Bayesian networks to, in each step, calculate the sampling distribution $P^*(X_i)$ as $P(X_i|\mathbf{c})$. Besides, in propagation we would use $\mathbf{c}$ as evidence, regardless of the inclusion or not of the parents of X_i in $\mathbf{c}$. Obviously, this process would be more costly than the proposed in this work, although this inconvenient can be alleviated by using approximate propagation techniques.

---

[2] For example, in the traveling salesman problem, represented as a permutation, the inclusion of a city j on the partial route obtained will depend on the city i from which we depart and the cities already visited.

Relation with Other Techniques. Beyond the differences and similarities existing between EDAs and ACs, it is evident that it exists some relation between the proposal of sampling presented in this work and the one used by ACs. However, we must enphasize that, the focus used in this work may explode dependence relationships further of the use of a univariate model as it could also be seen on the memoristic component in AC.

6   Conclusions

In this work, we have proposed two ways to incorporate specific heuristic knowledge on the sampling phase of EDAs. Developed algorithms have been tested experimentally by solving the classical optimization problem of the binary knapsack, verifying that, including this kind of knowledge helps to find a better solution and doing it faster, with a lower number of evaluations.

As future work, we plan to make a more rigorous study in order to validate our proposals, as well as introduce new ways of incorporating heuristic knowledge either on the sampling phase or in the estimation of the EDAs. Moreover, due to the fact that less individuals are evaluated, we believe that the proposed sampling processes are very interesting for problems where evaluation of an individual is very costly as it happens with machine learning problems.

Acknowledgments

This work has been partially supported by the Consejería de Ciencia y Tecnología (JCCM) under project PBC-02-002.

References

1. S. Baluja. Population-based incremental learning: A method for integrating genetic search based function optimization and competitive learning. Technical Report CMU-CS-94-163, Computer Science Department, Carnegie Mellon University, 1994.
2. S. Baluja. Using a priori knowledge to create probabilistic models for optimization. *International Journal of Approximate Reasoning*, 31:193–220, 2002.
3. S. Baluja and S. Davies. Combining multiple optimization runs with optimal dependecy trees. Technical Report CMU-CS-97-157, Computer Science Department, Carnegie Mellon University, 1997.
4. R. Blanco and B. Sierra P. Larrañaga, I. Inza. Selection of highly accurate genes for cancer classification by estimation of distribution. In *Workshop of Bayesian Models in Medicine (held within AIME 2001)*, pages 29–34, 2001.
5. C. Chow and C. Liu. Approximating discrete probability distributions with dependence trees. *IEEE Trans. on Information Theory*, 14:462–467, 1968.
6. J.S. de Bonet, C. L. Isbell, and P. Viola. Mimic: Finding optima by estimating probability densities. *Advances in Neural Information Processing Systems*, Vol. 9, 1997.

7. M. Dorigo and L.M. Gambardella. Ant Colony System: a Cooperative Learning Approach to the Traveling Salesman Problem. *IEEE Transactions on Evolutionary Computation*, 1:53–66, 1997.
8. M. Henrion. Propagating uncertainty in Bayesian networks by probabilistic logic sampling. In J.F. Lemmer and L.N. Kanal, editors, *Uncertainty in Artificial Intelligence 2*, pages 149–163. North Holland, 1988.
9. F.V. Jensen. *Bayesian Networks and Decision Graphs*. Springer Verlag, 2001.
10. P. Larrañaga, R. Etxeberria, J.A. Lozano, and J.M. Peña. Combinatorial optimization by learning and simulation of Bayesian. In *Uncertainty in Artificial Intelligence: Proceedings of the Sixteenth Conference (UAI-2000)*, pages 343–352. Morgan Kaufmann Publishers, 2000.
11. P. Larrañaga and J.A. Lozano. *Estimation of distribution algorithms. A new tool for evolutionary computation*. Kluwer Academic Publishers, 2001.
12. Z. Michalewicz. *Genetic Algorithms + Data Structures = Evolution Programs*. Springer-Verlag, 1996.
13. P. Moscato. Memetic algorithms: A short introduction. *New Ideas in Optimizacion*, pages 219–234, 1999.
14. H. Mühlenbein. The equation for response to selection and its use for prediction. *Evolutionary Computation*, 5:303–346, 1998.
15. D. Pisinger. Core problems in knapsack algorithms. *Operations Research*, 47:570–575, 1994.

Heuristic Rules and Genetic Algorithms for Open Shop Scheduling Problem

Jorge Puente, Helio R. Díez, Ramiro Varela,
Camino R. Vela, and Luis P. Hidalgo

Centro de Inteligencia Artificial,
Universidad de Oviedo, Campus de Viesques, E-33271 Gijón,
{puente,ramiro,camino}@aic.uniovi.es
http:\\www.aic.uniovi.es

Abstract. Open Shop Scheduling is a meaningful paradigm of constraint satisfaction problems. In this paper, a method combining heuristic rules and evolutionary algorithms is proposed to solve this problem. Firstly, we consider several dispatching rules taken from literature that produce semi-optimal solutions in polinomial time. From these rules we have designed probabilistic algorithms to generate heuristic chromosomes that are inserted in the initial population of a conventional genetic algorithm. The experimental results show that the initial populations generated by the proposed method exhibits a high quality, in terms of both solutions cost and diversity. This way the genetic algorithm converges to much better solutions than when it starts from a ramdom population.

1 Introduction

In this paper we approach the Open Shop Scheduling (OSS) problem by means of a hybrid strategy that consists of combining dispatching rules together with a conventional genetic algorithm. The idea is to transform a deterministic dispatching rule into a probabilistic algorithm which generates a set of heuristic solutions with an acceptable degree of diversity. These heuristic solutions are then inserted into the initial population of the genetic algorithm. The experimental results show that the combined method is more effective than each one separately.

The remainder of this paper is organized as follows. In section 2 we formulate the OSS problem. In section 3 we introduce the DS/LTRP and DS/RANDOM dispatching rules; both of them are in fact greedy algorithms that produce solutions within a subspace of feasible schedules called the space of dense schedules. We also indicate how probabilistic algorithms can be designed from these rules. In section 4 we describe the subspace of active schedules. This is a subspace of feasible schedules that contains dense schedules and that includes at least one optimal solution. We also indicate how the heuristics used in the former rules can be exploited to generate schedules in this space. Section 5 briefly describes the main components of the genetic algorithm we have used in this work. In section 6 we formalize the proposed method to build up heuristic chromosomes. Section 7 reports results from an experimental study carried out on problems taken from common repositories. Finally, section 8 summarizes the main conclusions of this work and proposes some ideas for future work.

R. Conejo et al. (Eds.): CAEPIA-TTIA 2003, LNAI 3040, pp. 394–403, 2004.
© Springer-Verlag Berlin Heidelberg 2004

Algorithm DS/LTRP

> **while** *there are unscheduled tasks* **do**
>
>> 1. *Select the machine M_j with the earliest possible starting time from the partial schedule built up to now, let t_{ini} be the earliest initial time for M_j.*
>> *(*) Ties are solved by selecting the machine with longest remaining processing time.*
>>
>> 2. *(**) Select among the available tasks of the machine M_j at t_{ini} the one belonging to the job J_i with the largest remaining processing time, and assign t_{ini} as its starting time.*
>
> **endwhile;**
> **end.**

Fig. 1. DS/LTRP scheduling algorithm.

2 Problem Formulation

The Open Shop Scheduling problem (OSS) can be formulated as follows: we have a set of m machines $\{M_j, 1 \leq j \leq m\}$, a set of n jobs $\{J_i, 1 \leq i \leq n\}$ and a set of $n \times m$ tasks $\{T_{ij}, 1 \leq i \leq n, 1 \leq j \leq m\}$. The task T_{ij} belongs to job J_i and has to be processed without preemption over the machine M_j during t_{ij} time units. There is not a-priori ordering on the tasks within a job and different tasks of the same job cannot simultaneously be processed on different machines. In addition, a machine cannot process two different tasks at the same time. The objective is to select a starting time to every task so that every constraint is satisfied and the total time from the beginning of the first task to the completion of the last one, the makespan, is minimized. This problem is usually identified in the literature by the tag O//Cmax. When $m \geq 3$ the problem is NP-hard, as proven in [3].

3 Dispatching Rules DS/LTPR and DS/RANDOM

One of the most common strategies to solve Scheduling problems are dispatching rules. They are usually greedy algorithms that make decisions by means of a criterion of local optimization. In the literature we can find a wide variety of this type of heuristic strategies for the OSS problem [5,6,8]. In this paper we first consider the DS/LTRP rule and then its variant called DS/RANDOM which have been proposed in [6], even though they are inspired by previous proposals. Both of these two rules are characterized by the fact that they generate dense schedules (this is the meaning of the DS label, *Dense Scheduling*). A schedule is dense if it is never the case that a machine is idle while a task is available for this machine. A task is considered available when no other task of the same job is being processed. The label LTRP stands from the rule "Longest Total Remaining Processing first" proposed in [8].

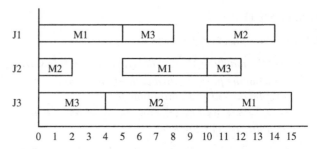

Fig. 2. An optimal solution of a 3 jobs and 3 machines problem. It is active but not dense.

The main advantage of constraining the search to the space of dense schedules is that, in average, they tend to have lower values of makespan than random feasible schedules. However there is no guarantee of this space to contain some optimal schedule.

Figure 1 shows the algorithm of the DS/LTRP rule. The algorithm has two sources of non determinism (* and **), which are solved by a criterion that gives priority to the machines and jobs with the longest remaining processing time. The DS/ RANDOM rule is a variant of the previous one where situations of non determinism are solved at random.

4   Active Schedules

As we have pointed out in the previous section, the main problem of dense schedules is that it is not guaranteed that they include some optimal solution. However there is another subset of the set of feasible schedules that includes at least one optimal solution: the space of active schedules. A schedule is active if to start earlier any operation, at least another one must be delayed. Figure 2 shows an optimal solution (by means of a Gantt diagram) to a problem with 3 jobs and 3 machines. It is active but not dense since, as we can observe, machine M_3 is idle along the time interval [4,5] while at the same time one of the tasks of the job J_1 is available.

Here we consider the well-known G&T algorithm proposed by Giffler and Thomson in [4] to get active schedules. Figure 3 shows a concretion of this algorithm where it is combined with the dispatching rule LTRP. One of the most interesting features of the G&T algorithm is its ability to further reduce the search space by means of a parameter δ. When the value of this parameter is 1 the search is performed over the whole space of active schedules; as long as the parameter is reduced the search space gets narrowed to a subset of the space of active schedules so that it might no longer contain any optimal schedule. At the limit value $\delta=0$ the search is constrained to non-delay schedules.

5   A Genetic Algorithm for the OSS

Genetic Algorithms are among the most outstanding techniques to solve scheduling problems. Even though basic GAs produce in general rather moderate results, they

Algorithm AS/LTRP

while *there are unscheduled tasks* **do**

1. *Select the unscheduled task T_{ij} with the earliest completion time if it is scheduled at this stage. Let t_{end} be the completion time of this task if it is scheduled at this stage.*
   (*) Ties are broken by selecting the task T_{ij} such that

$$max\big(RT(J_i), RT(M_j)\big) = \max_{T_{kl}\ unscheduled} \big(max(RT(J_k), RT(M_l))\big)$$

2. *Select among the available tasks for the machine M_j and the unscheduled tasks of the job J_i those that can start at a time lower than t_{end}, let B be this set, and t_{ini} the earliest init time for the tasks of B at this stage.*

3. *Reduce the set B to those tasks that can start in the interval*

$$\big[t_{ini}, t_{ini} + \delta(t_{end} - t_{ini})\big]$$

   where δ is a parameter with a value in the interval [0..1].

4. *(**) Select the task T_{pq} from the set B such that*

$$max\big(RT(J_p), RT(M_q)\big) = \max_{T_{kl}\in B}\big(max(RT(J_k), RT(M_l))\big)$$

   and schedule at its earliest starting time

endwhile;

end.

Fig. 3. AS/LTRP scheduling algorithm. *RT(J)* and *RT(M)* refers respectively to the remaining processing time of the job *J* and the machine *M* at this stage.

perform much better when hybridized with other techniques such as tabu search, simulated annealing or any domain specific heuristic. In this section we first describe the main components of a conventional GA for the OSS problem taken from [7]. There, this GA in hybridized by means of a tabu local search that produces good results. However in this work we only consider the basic GA and propose a method to seed the initial population with heuristic chromosomes. As we have mentioned this method is inspired on the dispatching rules described in section 3.

Chromosome Encoding
A suitable chromosome encoding for the OSS problem is a permutation of the whole set of its tasks. Such a permutation should be understood to express partial orders among each subset of tasks belonging to each one of the jobs as well as each subset of tasks requiring the same machine. It is clear that in general some of these partial orderings might not be compatible each one to the others, due to it might express cyclic precedence among a subset of tasks. Hence the evaluation function should include any kind of repair method in order to guarantee feasibility.

Chromosome Evaluation

In order to evaluate chromosomes we use the following strategy, as done in [7]: tasks are visited according to the order in which they appear in the chromosome from first to last. Then the starting time for a given task is selected in such a way that it is the lowest possible taking into account the starting times selected for previously visited tasks. It is easy to prove that this strategy builds up active schedules.

A common alternative is to exploit the G&T algorithm. In this case to solve the situations of non determinism of the algorithm the task of set *B* that is placed the leftmost in the chromosome is chosen to be scheduled next. Moreover, this alternative seems to be more flexible due to the fact that it allows for narrowing the search space to a subspace of the active schedules. This search space reduction might be effective for big problem instances, as it is in similar problems, for example the Job Shop Scheduling, as shown in [7].

Evolution Strategy and Genetic Operators

As evolution strategy we adopt a variant of the method reported in [7] which produced in our experiments slightly better results. First the best solution of the population is passed without any change to the next generation. Then all chromosomes are randomly distributed into pairs. To each one of these pairs the genetic operators crossover and mutation are applied (according to the crossover and mutation probabilities) to obtain two offsprings. Finally, these offsprings are put together with their parents and the best two out of the four are selected, with different makespan if possible, until the next generation is full.

The crossover operator is LOX (Linear Order Crossover): given two parents a substring is selected from the first one. This substring is placed into the offspring in the same position as in the first parent. Then the remaining genes are placed according to their relative ordering in the second parent.

To mutate chromosomes we consider two possibilities: insertion mutation and swap mutation. The first one selects one operation at random and then insert it at a random position. The second one selects two positions at random and then swaps the operations in these positions.

6   Building Heuristic Chromosomes

As we have pointed out, one of the possibilities of improving the performance of a GA is seeding the initial population with heuristic chromosomes instead of random ones. If this is the case, it is expected that the GA gets finally better solutions than when starting from a random population. However it is also well known that biasing the initial population with non random chromosomes have the risk of premature convergence, hence directing the search towards suboptimal solutions. In order to avoid such an abnormal convergence what we have to do is to ensure an acceptable degree of diversity.

The methodology we use in this work has a precedent in a previous work about the Job Shop Scheduling problem [10], where we exploited a family of probability-based heuristics for variable and value ordering. Now we exploit the dispatching rules described in figures 1 and 3. The idea is to translate deterministic decisions into probabilistic ones. Hence, from all possible choices at each stage of the search we make a selection according to a probability that depends on the reliance assigned to each choice by the LTRP heuristic. This reliance is estimated for each task T of the set B by the expression

$$\frac{RPT(T)}{\sum_{T' \in B} RPT(T')},$$

where $RPT(T')$ stands for the remaining processing time of the job the task T' belongs to. In this way it is expected to get both enough diversity and better initial solutions than in the random case.

Table 1. Results from the set of problems of size 10×10 proposed by Taillard. LB is the lower bound calculated as proposed by Taillard. The third column is the result of the deterministic rule DS/LTRP while the fourth column represents the best solution found in a heuristic population of 500 chromosomes. The last four columns show the results of applying the GA a number of 20 times for each of the problems with crossover probability 0,8; mutation probability 0,2; 150 generations and population size of 500 chromosomes. In every case the cost of the best solution found in all the 20 experiment and the mean values of the best solution reached in each one are showed.

Prob	LB	DS/LTRP rule	Best HIP	GA HIP Best	GA HIP Mean	GA RIP Best	GA RIP Mean
1	637	671	647	640	640,5	680	696,9
2	588	631	594	589	591,2	610	626,1
3	598	659	607	601	606,3	634	646,1
4	577	591	578	578	578,0	590	607,7
5	640	653	647	643	643,9	664	690,4
6	538	576	538	538	538,0	564	578,7
7	616	672	626	617	624,4	640	660,0
8	595	623	604	598	598,8	622	640,0
9	595	618	604	602	602,4	618	640,8
10	596	615	603	598	599,9	627	639,2

7   Computational Study

Two sets of test problems were considered for experimental study. First the set of problems proposed by E. Taillard which are available at the OR-library. Currently these problems are considered to be easy to solve, so that recently a new set has been proposed by J. Hurink et al. in [2]. This is a set of small size problems but much more difficult to solve than Taillard's, which have been used in recent works like for example [2], [5] and [7].

Tables 1 and 2 summarize the results from the Taillard problems of size 10×10 and 20×20 respectively. As we can observe, in every case the basic GA does not produce good results. However we have got quite good solutions with the heuristic populations. Moreover, the best solution within the heuristic population is always much better than the one produced by the deterministic DS/LTRP rule. Even in a number of

Table 2. Comparison of populations generated at random and by means of the probabilistic methods DS/RANDOM and DS/LTRP. Every population has 1000 chromosomes.

	RANDOM			DS/RANDOM			DS/LTRP		
Prob	Best	Mean	SD	Best	Mean	SD	Best	Mean	SD
1	749	871	44,4	649	693	18,1	646	686	17,3
2	680	794	46,0	595	633	18,5	589	627	15,7
3	701	819	45,0	608	651	17,6	613	646	16,1
4	660	773	44,8	583	620	17,2	581	614	15,5
5	752	863	46,9	646	692	19,0	643	684	17,4
6	638	734	42,4	540	573	14,9	538	571	14,6
7	710	830	45,8	625	671	20,1	624	660	17,2
8	696	809	45,2	604	652	20,2	603	643	17,9
9	703	807	45,3	606	645	18,8	602	640	17,5
10	685	806	44,9	602	648	18,8	603	640	16,9

Table 3. Results from the 20×20 Taillard's problems. The meaning of each column is the same as in Table 1.

				GA with HIP	
Prob	LB	DS/LTRP rule	Best HIP	Best	Mean
1	1155	1163	1157	1155	1156,3
2	1241	1252	1245	1245	1245,0
3	1257	1299	1257	1257	1257,0
4	1248	1261	1248	1248	1248,0
5	1256	1275	1259	1256	1257,3
6	1204	1208	1204	1204	1204,0
7	1294	1298	1296	1296	1296,0
8	1169	1197	1179	1174	1178,2
9	1289	1311	1290	1289	1289,9
10	1241	1254	1241	1241	1241,0

experiments the optimal solution appears within the heuristic population. Regarding execution times, for the GA this time is about 7,1 secs. for a problem of size 10×10 and about 42 secs. for a problem of size 20×20. On the other hand, execution times to generate heuristic populations are almost null with respect to the execution times of the GA. These values are obtained over a AMD Duron processor at 800 Mhz.

From these experiments we can observe that in general the heuristic populations are much better for problems of size 20×20 than for small problems of size 10×10. In particular an optimal schedule appears a greater number of times for the largest problems. This fact suggests us that the smaller the problem the lower the probability of finding an optimal schedule within the search space of dense schedules. Consequently it would be interesting to restrict the search of heuristic schedules to a subspace of the active schedules larger than the dense schedules. This could be achieved by means of the algorithm of figure 3 by setting the parameter δ to a value greater than 0.

Table 4. Results from Hurink problems.

Prob	Opt.	DS/LTRP	Heuristic Population			Genetic Algorithm	
			Best	Mean	SD	Best	Mean
5×5							
1	1042	1138	1081	1230,6	102,5	1050	1050,0
2	1054	1219	1081	1230,4	101,5	1054	1054,2
3	1063	1101	1065	1108,1	37,7	1065	1084,1
4	1004	1255	1051	1177,5	47,0	1004	1013,1
5	1002	1177	1008	1172,8	47,0	1002	1007,1
6	1006	1144	1042	1136,9	46,7	1006	1006,4
7	1000	1111	1027	1132,9	59,9	1000	1003,4
8	1000	1177	1000	1129,7	76,4	1000	1000,0
9	1012	1139	1037	1127,8	55,9	1012	1012,0
6×6							
1	1056	1162	1085	1188,5	43,2	1066	1083,2
2	1045	1328	1072	1213,1	55,4	1047	1062,3
3	1063	1178	1080	1215,3	46,1	1074	1079,7
4	1005	1255	1057	1154,7	40,8	1022	1033,9
5	1021	1215	1053	1166,0	43,5	1027	1031,2
6	1012	1160	1032	1157.9	52.5	1012	1012,4
7	1000	1360	1025	1120.3	39.0	1012	1022,1
8	1000	1151	1005	1142,4	54,4	1004	1004,8
9	1000	1084	1003	1115,2	44,6	1002	1002,9
7×7							
1	1048[a]	1180	1097	1194,7	36,4	1083	1094,9
2	1055	1254	1106	1203,2	43,8	1083	1100,4
3	1056	1199	1099	1201,5	40,8	1072	1081,9
4	1013[a]	1152	1065	1161,9	38,2	1049	1061,5
5	1000	1103	1023	1140,2	39,2	1000	1005,4
6	1011	1148	1060	1149,2	36,4	1043	1044,6
7	1000	1084	1001	1085,9	38,5	1000	1000,0
8	1005	1082	1029	1142,3	44,4	1023	1038,3
9	1003	1183	1054	1143,9	45,8	1027	1033,2
8×8							
1	1074[b]	1142	1093	1202,6	38,3	1074	1083,9
2	1087[b]	1169	1108	1204,0	39,3	1087	1090,6
3	1072[b]	1169	1101	1199,4	38,7	1072	1076,0
4	1103[b]	1169	1118	1199,9	37,2	1103	1108,4
5	1080[b]	1169	1097	1198,4	36,9	1080	1080,2
6	1000	1113	1032	1118,2	35,2	1021	1038,0
7	1000	1169	1101	1198,2	36,5	1099	1099,1
8	1095[b]	1169	1095	1199,2	37,2	1095	1106,2

[a] The best solution known. [b] The best solution of our experiments

Regarding quality and diversity of the heuristic populations, we report in table 3 results from experiments on 10×10 Taillard's problems. In this case we compare random populations against populations generated by the probabilistic DS/LTRP and DS/RAMDOM rules. As we can observe the quality of solutions clearly improves when the former two rules are used, being the DS/LTRP the best one as expected. Here is important to observe that the larger the degree of diversity the lower the quality of solutions. This is often the case when the initial solutions are biased by means of any heuristic knowledge. In such situations what we have to do is to keep a degree of diversity beyond a threshold that prevents premature convergence to suboptimal solutions. Unfortunately this threshold can only be determined by experiments. In our experiments premature converge is not found as shown in table 1.

Table 4 reports results from the Hurink problems. In this case we show the quality of initial populations, given by the best and mean values of the heuristic populations, as well as the degree of diversity given by the standard deviation.

8 Conclusions

The reported experimental results show that our proposed approach to the OSS problem exhibits both efficiency and efficacy enough to be compared against recent approaches. For example, in [2] Brucker et al. propose a branch and bound algorithm that finds out optimal solutions for many of the problems proposed by themselves, but the amount of execution time is prohibitive for problems of size 8×8. In [7] Liaw proposed a GA hybridized by means of a tabu local search that is able to solve to optimality the 6×6 and lower problems, but the GA is only capable to solve 1 out of the 8 7×7 problems, while results for 8×8 problems are not reported. Regarding dispatching rules proposed by Guéret and Prins in [5], the results are worse than ours, but the execution time is much lower as expected from their greedy and polynomial nature.

As future work we plan to implement a new strategy to build up heuristic chromosomes following the algorithm AS/LTRP of figure 3. We also plan to exploit the tabu search proposed in [7] together with our heuristic seeding methods and at the same time constrain the search to subsets of active schedules by means of the G&T algorithm.

References

1. Bierwirth, C. A Generalized Permutation Approach to Jobshop Scheduling with Genetic Algorithms. OR Spectrum, Vol. 17 (1995) 87-92.
2. Brucker, P., Hurink, J., Jurish, B. and Wostmann, B., A branch and bound algorithm for the open-shop problem, Discrete Applied Mathematics 76 (1997) 43-59.
3. Gonzales, T. and Sahni, S. Open shop scheduling to minimize finish time, Journal of the Association of Computing Machinery 23 (4) (1976) 665-679.
4. Giffler, B. Thomson, G. L.: Algorithms for Solving Production Scheduling Problems. Operations Reseach 8 (1960) 487-503.

5. Guéret, Ch. and Prins, Ch., Classical and new heuristics for the open-shop problem: A computational study. European Journal of Operational Research 107 (1998) 306-314.
6. Liaw, Ch-F., An iterative improvement approach for the nonpreemtive open shop scheuling problem, European Journal of Operational Research 111 (1998) 509-517.
7. Liaw, Ch-F., A hybrid genetic algorithm for the open shop scheduling problem, European Journal of Operational Research 124 (2000) 28-52.
8. Pinedo, M., Scheduling: Theory, Algorithms, and Systems. Prentice-Hall, Enblewoodd Cliffs, NJ. (1995).
9. Taillard, E.: Bechmarks for basic scheduling problems. European Journal of Operational Research, Vol 64 (1993) 278-285.
10. Varela, R., Vela, C. R., Puente, J., Gómez A.: A knowledge-based evolutionary strategy for scheduling problems with bottlenecks. European Journal of Operational Research, Vol 145 (2003) 57-71.

Hybrid Approach Based on Temporal Representation and Classification Techniques Used to Determine Unstable Conditions in a Blast Furnace

Juan Mora[1], Joan Colomer[2], Joaquím Meléndez[2],
Francisco Gamero[2], and Peter Warren[3]

[1] Universidad Tecnológica de Pereira
La Julita, Pereira, Colombia
jjmora@utp.edu.co
[2] Universidad de Girona
Campus Montilivi EPS Building P4, Girona, Spain
{colomer,quimmel,gamero}@eia.udg.es
[3] Corus Group
30 Millbank, London SW1P 4WY, UK
Peter.Warren@corusgroup.com

Abstract. This paper discusses the analysis of differential pressure signals in a blast furnace stack, by a hybrid approach based on temporal representation of process trends and classification techniques. The objective is to determine whether these can be used to predict unstable conditions (slips). First, episode analysis is performed on each individual trend. Next, using the obtained episodes and variable magnitudes, the classification tool is trained to predict and detect the fault in a blast furnace. The proposed approach has been selected in this application, due to the best results obtained using the qualitative representations of process variables instead of only raw data.

1 Introduction

Industries have spent large sums of money on sensors and logging devices to measure process signals. These data are usually stored in data bases to be analysed by the process experts, but as the amount of data stored increases, the task of extracting useful information becomes more complex and difficult.

In order to provide an adequate supervisory system, which assists the process experts, it is necessary to provide powerful tools to analyse the process variables. Two Artificial Intelligence (AI) techniques working together are proposed as strategy, to deal with the signal and to perform classification tasks respectively.

First, the strategy proposes qualitative and quantitative representations of signal trends useful in supervision, especially in fault detection and diagnosis. One of these techniques is the representation of signals by episodes as it is proposed in [6] and [9]. The proposed approach has been selected in this application case due to the best results obtained using the qualitative representations instead of only raw data of process variables.

R. Conejo et al. (Eds.): CAEPIA-TTIA 2003, LNAI 3040, pp. 404–414, 2004.

Second, and having obtained episode-based information of each process variable, a fuzzy classification method is proposed to obtain classes [2] [8]. These classes are related to functional states of the process under analysis. By using the combination of the here-proposed techniques (one to extract qualitative/quantitative information of a single variable, and the other one aimed at analysing the behaviour of several process variables), it is possible to develop a decision support system applied to industrial process. The application of the proposed approach to the Redcar blast furnace, operated by Corus, is presented in this paper.

In the following section, the process description is given. Next in section 3, the episode-based representation of process variables is defined. In 4, the fuzzy classification method is presented. Later on in 5, the episode approach used in this specific case and the model of data arrangement used to obtain the training data are explained. In 6 the test results are analysed and finally the conclusions of this work are presented.

2 Process Description

In the blast furnace process, iron oxide is reduced to metallic iron, which is then melted prior to tapping at 1500 deg C. Liquid slag is also removed, the slag being formed from the non-ferrous components of the iron ore (predominantly lime, silica, magnesia and alumina).

The blast furnace itself is a water-cooled vessel, of circular cross-section, about 30m tall. Layers of coke and prepared iron ore (burden) are alternately charged into the top in a controlled manner. Air at approximately 1100 deg C (hot blast) is blown into the bottom of the furnace through copper water-cooled tuyeres. The air reacts with the coke, and supplementary injected oil, to generate both heat to melt the iron and slag, and to form a reducing gas of CO and H2. The burden takes about 7 hours to reduce and melt as it descends the furnace stack; the residence time of the ascending reduction gases is in the order of seconds. The furnace is kept full by charging a fresh batch of burden as soon as the level drops in the top. Burden descent is usually steady at about 5 meters/hour. The liquid iron and slag collect in the furnace hearth, built from carbon bricks, and are periodically removed by opening a clay-lined taphole.

Redcar blast furnace is the largest in the UK, producing 64000 tonnes of liquid iron per week. Each hour requires the charging of over 5 batches of prepared ore, each at 120 tonnes, and the same number of batches of coke, each of 30 tonnes. Heat is removed at the wall through large water-cooled panels, called staves, installed over 13 rows. These are made from copper in rows 7 to 10, the region of highest heat load, and cast iron above and below these levels.

The Redcar plant has 4 columns of pressure tappings. The pressure is measured at each stave row between row 6 and row 13 in each quadrant. Fig. 1a shows the furnace cross section.

Under normal state, the pressure should reduce gradually between the bottom (row 6) and the top (row 11) of the section of furnace stack under examination. It has been noticed that trends in differential pressure (pressure drop) between the lower and middle part of the stack can be a good indication that the furnace process will become unstable. The differential pressures found most responsive are the pressure measured at row 6 minus the pressure measured in row 9, for each quadrant individually.

An 'unstable' event is where the material in the furnace stack suddenly 'slips' rather than descend steadily. Such an event can be detected by a suddenly change in differential pressure values over the 4 columns of pressure tappings. In fig. 1b, differential pressure trends are recorded at a frequency of one sample/min. over a 10-hour period. In this figure, it is possible to locate three different unstable conditions (slips) as highlight by the doted lines.

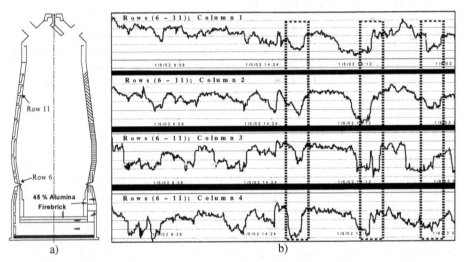

Fig. 1. a) Transverse section of blast furnace. b) Fault determined by pressure differentials.

3   Representation of Signals Using Episodes

Signal representation by means of episodes provide a good tool for situation assessment. On the one hand, uncertainty, incompleteness and heterogeneity of process data make the qualitative reasoning a useful tool. On the other hand, reasoning not only with instantaneous information, but with historic behaviour of processes is necessary. Moreover, since a great deal of process data is available for the supervisory systems, to abstract and use only the most significant information is required. The representation of signals by means of episodes provides an adequate response to these necessities.

The general concept of episode in the field of qualitative reasoning was defined as a set of two elements: a time interval, named temporal extent and a qualitative context, providing the temporal extension with significance [4].

The qualitative representation of process trends is a general formalism for the representations of signals by means of episodes [3]. This formal approach introduces the concept of trend as a sequence of episodes characterised by the signs of the first and the second derivative. It has a practical extension in the triangular and trapezoidal representations.

Later on, in [5] a qualitative description of signals consisting of primitives, episodes, trends and profiles is proposed. Primitives are based on the sign of first and second derivatives (positive, zero or negative). Thus, nine basic types compose the set of primitives. The trend of a signal consists of a series of episodes, and a profile is obtained by adding quantitative information.

In [6] previous formalisms are extended to both qualitative and numerical context in order to be more general. It means that it is possible to build episodes according to any feature extracted from variables. According to this formalism, new representations can be generated to describe signal trends depending on the second derivative that can be computed by means of a band-limited FIR differentiator. The qualified first derivative at the beginning and end of each episode is used in order to obtain a more significant representation. Then, a set of 13 types of episodes is obtained. Finally, as this formalism proposes, it has been enlarged in order to consider any function of the signal as basis representation. Examples of these functions are the own signal, the first derivative, second derivative, its integral, etc. These functions even could be consider simultaneously when are needed for to describe all the interesting variable characteristics offering a richer representation. Therefore, the functions must be chosen according to the signal and process behaviour and supervisory system objectives. According with this formalism an episode Ek is a set of numerical and qualitative values, including the time instants that determine the temporal extension of episodes, the qualitative state (QS) obtained from the extracted features and auxiliary characteristics, which can be any quantitative or qualitative data as it is presented in (1).

$$Ek = <tlk, QSk, \{ \text{ Auxiliary characteristics } \}, trk > \qquad (1)$$

In section 5.1, the episode-based representation used in this process is presented.

4   Classification Method

To analyze the variables previously represented by episodes, the Learning Algorithm for Multivariable Data Analysis (LAMDA), has been used to classification purpose. This algorithm was proposed by Joseph Aguilar [2]. Recently some other authors have been working in this original classification technique as it is presented in [1] and [8].

This methodology proposes to abstract significant information from the set of variables under classification (four differential pressures). This information, so called "*descriptors*", is obtaining by means of an extraction technique (in this case, episodes). The set of variables conforms the so called "*object*". LAMDA represents the object in a set of "*classes*" by means of the logic connection of the descriptors available. Class (c_k) is defined as the universe of descriptors, which characterize one set objects (differential pressures).

Learning in LAMDA is performed in two steps as it is depicted in figure 2. First (Learning-1), the parameters used to construct the knowledge are updated using training data and its pre-assigned classes. These classes are result of an expert definition (supervised-learning); or a definite number of allowable classes due to a self-learning process (unsupervised learning). The classes and updated learning parameters are the output of this initial learning stage. On the second stage (Learning-2), the output classes are analyzed by an expert to establish a relationship to states. States are defined by a set of classes, which has a special meaning for the operators. This is an

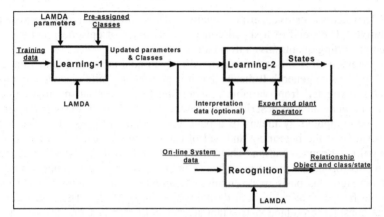

Fig. 2. Detailed functionality of LAMDA classification algorithm.

optional stage and is accomplished specially if a self-learning process is performed. Two learning step (Learning-1 and Learning-2) are accomplished off-line, but the option of learn online is also available in this methodology.

The recognition process is performed using updated learning parameters, classes and states generated in previous stages. In this stage, as presented in the fig 3, every object is assigned to a class. Recognition is performed according to similarity criteria computed in two stages: MAD and GAD calculation.

MAD (Marginal Adequacy Degree) is a term related to how similar is one object descriptor to the same descriptor of a given class, while GAD (Global Adequacy Degree) is defined as the pertinence degree of one object to a given class [1].

First MAD to each existing class is computed for each descriptor of an object. The implementation of LAMDA includes a possibility function to estimate the descriptors distribution based on a "fuzzification" of the binomial probability function computed as (2). This approach has been used in this work, but other implementation, frequently

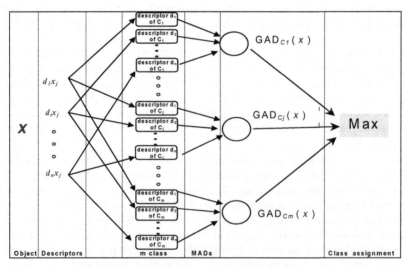

Fig. 3. Basic LAMDA recognition methodology.

used when the volume of the observed data is important, it is very likely to follow a Gaussian or semi-Gaussian distribution [8]

$$MAD(d_i x_j / \rho_{(i/k)}) = \rho_{(i/k)}^{d_i x_j} \left(1 - \rho_{(i/k)}\right)^{\left(1 - d_i x_j\right)} \tag{2}$$

Where: $d_i x_j =$ Descriptor i of the object j

$\rho_{(i/k)} =$ Prototype parameter for the descriptor i of the class c_k

Second, these partial results are aggregated to get a GAD of an individual to a class. GAD computation was performed as an interpolation between a t-norm and a t-conorm by means of the β parameter (β = 1 represents the intersection and β = 0 means the union).

$$GAD = \beta T(MAD) + (1 - \beta) S(MAD) \tag{3}$$

The used t-norm and s-conorm are minimun/maximun as presented in (4). In addition, some connectors used for GAD computation are presented in [8].

$$t - norm = \min\{x_1, x_2, ... x_n\} \qquad s - conorm = \max\{x_1, x_2, ... x_n\} \tag{4}$$

This classification algorithm has been used to relate the set of four differential pressures with the pre-fault and the fault states (slips).

5 Proposed Strategy

The strategy approach proposes two techniques working together, to deal with the signal and to perform data mining tasks respectively. First the episode-based representation of process variables is used to extract quantitative and qualitative information of pressure differentials. Next a procedure to construct the objects used as inputs for the classification method is applied. As a result, the object matrix based on episodes is conformed. Then, a fuzzy classification method is proposed to create classes. These classes are related to functional states of the process under analysis.

The episode based representation and the object conformation for the pressure differentials of the Redcar blast furnace is presented in the next subsections.

5.1 Episode Based Representation

Using the first derivate to obtain the episode, it is possible to have a useful representation of the signal. This simple representation, however, offers enough information to characterize signals of the analyzed process to slip detection.

\	F: fall	—	Gm: steady trend, medium value
/	H: rise	⌄	Gl: steady trend, low value
⌐	A: rapid fall	⌃	Gh: steady trend, high value
⌐	L: rapid rise		

Fig. 4. Useful set of episodes.

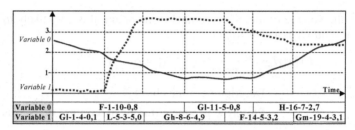

Fig. 5. Episode representation of process variables.

Due of the use of the first derivative, only five basic types were used in this approach: A, F, G, H, and L. However, since the previous state to a slip is a fall in pressure followed by a steady trend at low level, a differentiation has been introduced among the episodes of stability state according to the value of the signal. So G episode was subdivided in High (Gh), Medium (Gm) and Low (Gl) as presented in figure 4. This representation has been adopted to represent symptoms of blast furnace instability. An example of this representation for two variables is shown in Fig. 5.

Process variables presented in figure 5 are represented by episodes as shown in table 1.

Table 1. Episode based representation of the process variables (variable 0 and variable 1), depicted in figure 5.

Episode description of variables							
Variable 0				Variable 1			
Type	Starting time	Duration	End value	Type	Starting time	Duration	End value
F	1	10	0,8	Gl	1	4	0,1
Gl	11	5	0,8	L	5	3	5,0
H	16	7	2,7	Gh	8	6	4,9
				F	14	5	3,2
				Gm	19	4	3,1

5.2 Object Conformation

Taking into account the fact that the episodes are asynchronous by nature, it is necessary to develop a strategy to conform the set of objects used for the classification stage. The formed objects are synchronized to the change instants of each one of the four differential pressures used to detect the instability state of the blast furnace (slip).

The procedure applied to conform each object is presented as follows. (In brackets an example is presented for variables in fig 5).

- Step one: Detect the instant t_{vc} in which one new episode starts in any variable V_c. ($t_{v1}=19$. $V_c=Variable\ 1$.)
- Step two: Identify the type of the new episode (current) and save the type of the previous one in the same variable. (*By Variable 1, new episode type = Gm and previous episode type = F.*)
- Step three: Recover the previous and current episodes of all analysed variables. (*By Variable 0, current episode type = H and previous episode type = Gl.*)

Variable 0		F-1-10-0,8						Gl-11-5-0,8					H-16-7-2,7							
Variable 1	Gl-1-4-0,1		L-5-3-5,0			Gh-8-6-4,9					F-14-5-3,2				Gm-19-4-3,1					
Time-line	1	2	3	4	5	6	7	8	9	10	11	12	13	14	15	16	17	18	19	20 21 22

	Variable 0				Variable 1			
	Current episode	Previous episode	Current duration	Current value	Current episode	Previous episode	Current duration	Current value
	H	Gl	3	1.50	Gm	F	0	3.20

Fig. 6. Object conformation of process variables.

- Step four: Compute the time between t_c and the time which the current episode starts in all variables. It corresponds to the duration of the current episode.(*Time between* t_{v1} *and* t_{v0} = *19-16=3.*)
- Step five: Measure the current value Cv of each process variable.($Cv_0=1.5$, $Cv_1=3.2$.)
- Step six: Conform the object using the obtained data. (*The object is presented in figure 6.*)

As a result of the previous procedure application a set of synchronized objects based on the episode representation are obtained as it is presented in table 2. The value is directly taken from the rough data and corresponds to the value of each variable at the time given by the time line column.

The episode variable description presented in table 2 contains the data, which conform the training files used in the learning phase of the fuzzy method. For the first object, the previous type of episodes is supposed to be equal to the current one.

The obtained results of applying the proposed strategy to four variables are presented in the next section. Each variable consist of a differential between the pressures measured in row 6 and row 9, in the four columns of the blast furnace.

6   Classification Tests and Results

Several test were performed in order to identify clearly the fault and mainly the pre-fault stage in the Redcar blast furnace. Using data taken directly from the process and presented in the two first columns of table 3, it was possible to select a set of files for training and recognition.

Table 2. Object matrix obtained from the episode based representation of the process variables in table 1.

Time line	Variable 0				Variable 1			
	Current episode	Previous episode	Current duration	Current value	Current episode	Previous episode	Current duration	Current value
1	F	F	0	2.50	Gl	Gl	0	0.20
5	F	F	4	2.00	L	Gl	0	0.18
8	F	F	7	1.30	Gh	L	0	4.90
11	Gl	F	0	0.80	Gh	L	3	4.80
14	Gl	F	3	0.70	F	Gh	0	4.90
16	H	Gl	0	0.80	F	Gh	2	4.00
19	H	Gl	3	1.50	Gm	F	0	3.20

The descriptors used to detect the pre-fault and the fault states are eight: The type of the current episode (qualitative), and the value of the pressures differential (quantitative), for each furnace column when a new episode appears in any variable. These descriptors were selected according to the results obtained in the recognition stage. Using these descriptors extracted by the files Data set N. 1, 3, 6, and 10 the classification tool was trained. The files not used by training were used in the recognition stage. The results of the recognition process are presented in of table 3.

Table 3. Results of the LAMDA recognition stage in prediction (pre-fault) and detection (fault) of slips in a blast furnace.

File Name	Depth of slip	Recognition stage	
		Pre-fault	Fault
Data set N.1	2.0m	Yes	Yes
Data set N.2	2.0m	Yes	Yes
Data set N.3	1.5m	Yes	Yes
Data set N.4	1.5m	Yes	Yes
Data set N.5	1.5m	Not	Not
Data set N.6	1m	Yes	Yes
Data set N.7	1m	Yes	Yes
Data set N.8	1m	Yes	Yes
Data set N.9	1m	Yes	Not
Data set N.10	1.5m (partial)	Not	Yes
Data set N.11	1.5m (partial)	Not	Not
Data set N.12	1.5m (partial)	Not	Not
Data set N.13	No slips	N/A	N/A
Data set N.14	No slips	N/A	N/A

According to of table 3, in most of the files used in training process it is possible to recognize the pre-fault and also the fault state. Not in data set 10 for pre-fault state. In addition, it is also possible to detect the pre-fault ad fault states using different sets of data. This last result is used to test the capability of the proposed approach, to detect faulty situations on the supervised process.

As an example of the presented on of table 3, a situation to detect the fault and the pre-fault stage is presented in Fig 7. It is possible to see that class 9 is related to the pre-fault state while class 5 is related to the fault state (Slip). The remaining classes are not related to those two states, but they are related to different operative states of the process.

7   Conclusions

In this work, a new methodology based in the combination of two techniques has been used as complementary strategies to supervise a process. The paper shows the use of the episode representations in the field of diagnosis as it is proposed in the CHEM project.

The proposed approach has been selected in this application case, due to the best results obtained using the qualitative representations instead of only raw data of process variables. This representation satisfies the necessities of control system diagnosis regarding to temporal and qualitative reasoning.

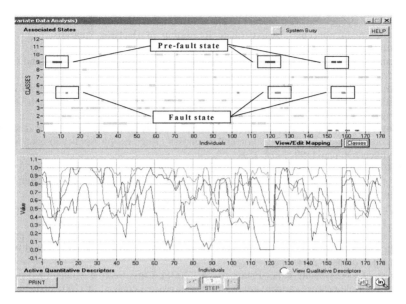

Fig. 7. Examples of pre-fault and fault detection. Slip prediction in Redcar blast furnace.

The object conformation approach, gives an object matrix of qualitative and quantitative data used as input of the classification method. This method, after the initial training stage, helps to determine classes, close related to specific process states at each instant when an object is conformed. This approach reduces the computation time, because the recognition stage is only performed when the type of episode in any variable changes. In addition this approach takes advantage of the qualitative data provided by episodes instead of only use raw data.

As a result, the previous situations at the fault stage were detected, given an efficient approach to the slip prediction in blast furnaces. In addition, the fault situation is also detected using both episode type and rough data, as inputs for the classification system.

Acknowledgments

This work is partially supported by the projects "Advanced Decision Support Systems for Chemical/Petrochemical manufacturing processes – CHEM" within the (EC IST program: IST-2000-61200) and CICYT DPI SECSE. DPI2001-2198 (Supervision Experta de la Calidad de Servicio Eléctrico) within the CICYT program from the Spanish government.

References

1. Aguado, J.C. "A Mixed Qualitative-Quantitative Self-Learning Classification Technique Applied to Situation Assessment in Industrial Process Control". PhD. Thesis Universitat Politècnica de Catalunya, (1998).

2. Aguilar J., López N. "The process of classification and learning the meaning of linguistic descriptors of concepts". Approximate Reasoning in Decision Analysis, pag 165-175. North Holland. (1982).
3. Cheung, J. T., Stephanopoulos G. "Representation of Process Trends, parts I and II. Computers" Chemical Engineering 14, (1990) pag. 495-540.
4. Dash, S., Rengaswamy, R., Venkatasubramanian, V. (2001). A Novel Interval-Halving Algorithm for Process Trend Identification", 4th IFAC Workshop on On-Line Fault Detection &Supervision in the CPI, Seoul, Korea, (2001).
5. Janusz, M. and Venkatasubramanian, V. "Automatic generation of qualitative description of process trends for fault detection and diagnosis". Engineering Applications of Artificial Intelligence 4, pag. (1991) 329-339.
6. Meléndez, J.; Colomer, J. "Episodes representation for supervision. Application to diagnosis of a level control system". Workshop on Principles of Diagnosis DX'01, (2001) Sansicario (Italy).
7. Moore, K. "Using neural nets to analyze qualitative data". A Marketing Research, vol. 7, n°1, (1995) pag.35-39.
8. Waissman J. "Construction d'un modele comportemental pour la supervisión de procedes: Aplication a une station de traitement des eaux" Doctoral thesis - Institut National Politechnique de Tolouse. (2000). pag. 17-28.
9. Wong, J.C; McDonald, K.A.; Palazoglu, A. (2001). Classification of abnormal operation using multiple process variable trends. Journal of process control, 11 (2001). pag. 409-418.

Kernel Functions over Orders
of Magnitude Spaces by Means of Usual Kernels.
Application to Measure Financial Credit Risk

Mónica Sánchez[1], Francesc Prats[1], Núria Agell[2], and Xari Rovira[2]

[1] MA2, Universitat Politècnica de Catalunya Pau Gargallo
5 08028 Barcelona, Spain
{monica.sanchez,francesc.prats}@upc.es
[2] ESADE, Universitat Ramon Llull Av. Pedralbe
62 08034 Barcelona, Spain
{agell,rovira}@esade.edu

Abstract. This paper lies within the domain of learning algorithms based on kernel functions, as in the case of Support Vector Machines. These algorithms provide good results in classification problems where the input data are not linearly separable. A kernel is constructed over the discrete structure of absolute orders of magnitude spaces. This kernel will be applied to measure firms' financial credit quality. A simple example that allows the kernel to be interpreted in terms of proximity of the patterns is presented.

1 Introduction

The construction of machines able to learn to classify patterns, that is to assign them a class among a finite set of possibilities, is one of the main goals of Artificial Intelligence. Lately, different learning machines based on kernels, such as Support Vector Machines (SVM), have been developed and studied in depth because of their numerous applications and their efficiency in the learning process.

Support Vector Machines are learning systems, which use linear functions in a feature space of higher dimension as classification functions by using several kernels [7] and [15]. One of the most important steps in the construction of Support Vector Machines is the development of kernels adapted to the different structures of the data in real world problems [4], [6], [8]. The main usefulness of Support Vector Machines is the classification of non linearly separable data by using kernel functions. There are two cases in which this tool is used. First, when data are not linearly separable, in spite of belonging to a euclidian space. In this case, by means of the kernel function , from an implicit non-linear mapping, the input data are imbedded into a space named feature space, potentially of higher dimension, in which the separability of the data can be obtained in a linear manner.A library of the most usual kernel functions (gaussian, polynomial, ...)is available. Second, when the input space does not have an inner product, the kernel function is used to represent data in a euclidian space to be classified.

R. Conejo et al. (Eds.): CAEPIA-TTIA 2003, LNAI 3040, pp. 415–424, 2004.
© Springer-Verlag Berlin Heidelberg 2004

This representation is obtained via an explicit mapping from the input space into a euclidian feature space, where the methodology described for the first case can be applied.

A key factor in situations in which one has to obtain some conclusions from imprecise data, is to be able to use variables described via orders of magnitude. One of the goals of Qualitative Reasoning is just to tackle problems in such a way that the principle of relevance is preserved [9]; that is to say, each variable involved in a real problem is valued with the required level of precision.

In classification processes the situation in which the numerical values of some of the data are unknown, and only their qualitative descriptions are available - given by their absolute orders of magnitude - is not unusual. In other situations, the numerical values, even though they might be available, are not relevant for solving the proposed problem. This paper starts from absolute orders of magnitude models, [13]and [14], which work with a finite set of symbols or qualitative labels obtained via a partition of the real line, where any element of the partition is a basic label. These models provide a mathematical structure which unifies sign algebra and interval algebra . This mathematical structure, the Qualitative Algebras or Q-Algebras, have been studied in depth [1], [14].

This work is framed in the development of the MERITO (Analysis and Development of Innovative Soft-Computing Techniques with Expert Knowledge Integration. An Application to Financial Credit Risk Measurement) project, in which different AI tools for the measurement of the financial credit risk are analyzed.The main goal is to develop tools able to be used in situations in which numerical data and qualitatively described data simultaneously appear.

The processes employed by specialized rating agencies are highly complex. Decision technologies involved are not based on purely numeric models. On the one hand, the information given by the financial data is used, and the different values included in the problem are also influential. On the other hand, they also analyze the industry and the country or countries where the firm operates, they forecast the possibilities of the firm's growth, and its competitive position. Finally, they use an abstract global evaluation based on their own expertise to determine the rating. In general, experts agree that the existing functionality between numerical data of the firm and its default probability is less relevant than the existing relation between data orders of magnitude and its final classification.

It has to be pointed out that in the 60's some economists made qualitative modelisations of economic systems and proved that these models (induced by sign algebra) can lead to significant conclusions. More recently, different AI techniques have been applied to business, finance and economics [2], [3], [10] and [12].

In this work, a methodology for the construction of kernel functions in absolute orders of magnitude spaces is presented in two steps. First, an explicit function over qualitative labels with values in a feature space of n-tuples of real numbers is defined. Second, a known kernel function that will allow the classification via a Support Vector Machine is utilized.

In Section 2 the absolute orders of magnitude model with granularity n, OM(n), constructed via a symmetric partition of the real line into 2n+1 classes, is presented. Section 3 gives the basic concepts of Support Vector Machines and the importance of kernels for these kinds of learning algorithms. In Section 4 the methodology for the construction of a kernel to be able to work in spaces OM(n) is presented. This methodology is based on the composition an explicit function from the quantity space into a euclidian space with a given kernel. In Section 5, an example in which two of these kernel functions are built over pairs of firms is given. The firms are represented by the parameters that affect their credit quality, belonging to different orders of magnitude models, and the results are interpreted in terms of "proximity" between their risks. Finally, in Section 6, several conclusions and some proposals for future research are outlined.

2   The Absolute Orders of Magnitude Model

In this section the absolute orders of magnitude qualitative model is described [1]. The absolute orders of magnitude model considered in this work is a generalization of the model introduced in [14]. The number of labels chosen for describing a given real problem depends on the characteristics of each problem.

The absolute orders of magnitude model of granularity n, OM(n), is constructed from a symmetric partition of the real line in 2n+1 classes:

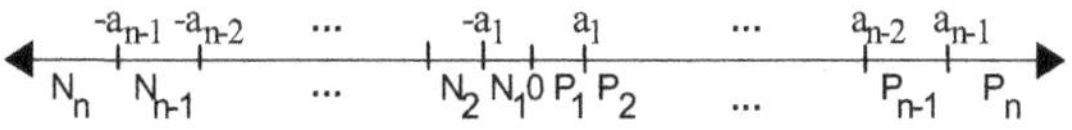

Fig. 1. Partition of the real line

where $N_i=[-a_i,-a_{i-1})$, $0 = \{0\}$ and $P_i=(a_{i-1},a_i]$.

Each class is named basic description or basic element and is represented by a label of the set S_1:

$$S_1 = \{N_n, N_{n-1}, ..., N_1, 0, P_1, ..., P_{n-1}, P_n\}.$$

The quantity space S is defined as the extension of S_1 with the set of labels in the following form:

For all $X, Y \in S_1$, with $X < Y$ (i.e., $x < y$ for all $x \in X, y \in Y$) the label [X,Y] is defined as:

$$[X,Y] = \begin{cases} X, & \text{if } Y = 0 \\ Y, & \text{if } X = 0 \\ \text{the minimum interval with respect to} \\ \text{the inclusion that contains } X \text{ and } Y & \text{if } X \neq 0 \text{ and } Y \neq 0 \end{cases}$$

An order relation P is defined in S: given $X, Y \in S$, X is more precise than Y ($X \leq_P Y$) if $X \subseteq Y$.

For all $X \in S - 0$, the *basis of* X is the set $B_X = \{B \in S_1 - 0 : B \leq_P X\}$; and for all $X \in S$, *the extended basis of* X is the set $B_X^* = \{B \in S_1 : B \leq_P X\}$.

It is also considered a qualitative equality: given $X, Y \in S$, they are q-equal, $X \approx Y$, if there exists $Z \in S$ such that $Z \leq_P X$ and $Z \leq_P Y$. This means that they have a common basic element, i.e., $B_X^* \cap B_Y^* \neq \oslash$. The pair $(S, \approx)$ is called a qualitative space of absolute orders of magnitude; and, taking into account that it has 2n+1 basic elements, it is said that $(S, \approx)$ has granularity n.

The qualitative expression of a set A in the real line, denoted by $[A]$, is the minimum element of S, with respect to the inclusion, that contains A.

Given a basic label $U \in S_1$ the U-expansion X_U of any label $X \in S$ is the element in S that results from its expansion until obtaining one qualitatively equal to the basic given (this is the generalization of the concept introduced in [1] in the particular case of zero-expansion):

$$X_U = \text{Min} \{Y \in S : X \leq_P Y \text{ and } U \leq_P Y\} = [X \cup U]$$

Then X_U is the smallest interval with respect to the inclusion containing X and U. Therefore $X = X_U$ if and only if $X \approx U$ (i.e. $U \subset X$), and always $X \approx X_U$ and $U \approx X_U$.

The U-expansion X_U of any label $X \in S$ does not depend on the values of the landmarks taken to determine the basic labels.

This model is specially suitable for problems in which it is intended to obtain the magnitude of a result from the qualitative description of the variables involved. Qualitative descriptions are used because either numerical values are unknown or only orders of magnitude are considered by experts.

In the case of the credit quality evaluation, the goal is to obtain its order of magnitude from the absolute orders of magnitude of the variables involved.

3   Kernels and Support Vector Machines

In this work a methodology that allows SVM to be used when the patterns are described by their absolute orders of magnitude is proposed.

Before the construction of a suitable kernel for this kind of discrete spaces, the basic concepts of SVM and kernel functions are reviewed. SVM were introduced by Vapnik and their co-authors in 1992 [5] and described with detail in [16].

The SVM are used in learning problems, where the input data are not linearly separable. From a non-linear mapping the input data are imbedded into a space named feature space, potentially of higher dimension, in which the separability of the data can be obtained in a linear manner. In Figure 2 a scheme of this process can be observed.

Noting the input space by X and the feature space by F, a machine of non-linear classification is built in two steps. First, a non-linear mapping $\Phi : X \to F$ transports the input data to the feature space, and afterwards an algorithm of linear separation is used in this new space.

An important characteristic of the learning process of a SVM is the fact that only a few elements of the training set are meaningful for the classification. These elements, named support vectors (SV), are the closest to the separator hyperplane ones. In Figure 3 the support vectors are doubly marked.

Let T be the set of input-output training data pairs:

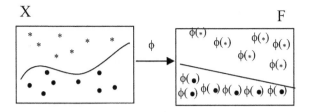

Fig. 2. Mapping from the initial space to characteristic space

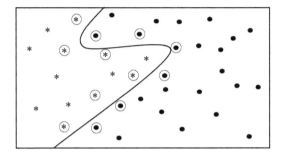

Fig. 3. Binary classification of non linearly separable patterns by means of SVM

$$T = (xi, yi), xi \in X, yi = -1, +1,$$

where labels +1 and -1 represent the two different classes of patterns to classify.

If the training set is linearly separable by a hyperplane then the decision function can be written as:

$$f(x) = \text{sign} \left(\sum_{x_i \in \text{SV}} \alpha_i y_i (x_i \cdot x) + b \right)$$

where α_i and b are the hyperplane coefficients and x_i are the elements in T which have been chosen as support vectors in the learning process.

When data are non-linearly separable, the decision function turns out to be a non-linear function which appears by substituting the inner product in X by an inner product in the feature space F, given by a function K defined from the map $\Phi : X \rightarrow F$ as:

$$K(x_i, x_j) = < \Phi(x_i), \Phi(x_j) > .$$

Such a function K is called a kernel. The name kernel is derived from Integral Operation Theory, and a characterization of this kind of functions is given by Mercer's theorem [15].

The decision function thus has the form:

$$f(x) = \text{sign} \left(\sum_{x_i \in \text{SV}} \alpha_i y_i K(x_i, x) + b \right)$$

An important advantage of this methodology is that it is not necessary to have an input space with a euclidian distance. Suitable kernels are used to work with many different kinds of patterns (text words, images, genetic information, protein chains) mapping them into vectors in a feature space F, which is a euclidean space. Different applications can be found in [8] and [11].

4   Construction of Kernels in a $[OM(n)]^k$ Space

With the objective to construct kernel functions in the space of k-tuples of qualitative labels S^k, a function Φ from S^k into a subset of $\mathbb{R}^{(2n+1)k}$ is defined. Then a kernel will be obtained from the composition of this function with one of most usual kernels. The present work is one step in the development of a machine learning that allows us to assign a category to each company according to its level of risk, by means of quantitative and qualitative values describing their financial situation.

This process begins with the introduction of the "positioning" concept of a label with respect to a basic element. This is defined by using the concept of U-expansion introduced in section 2.

Given a basic element $U \in S_1$, the "remoteness with sign" of a label $X \in S$ with respect to U is defined as:

$$as_U(X) = \begin{cases} \text{card}\,(B^*_{X_U}) - \text{card}\,(B^*_X) & \text{if } U < B \quad \forall B \in B^*_X \\ \text{card}\,(B^*_X) - \text{card}\,(B^*_{X_U}) & \text{if } U > B \quad \forall B \in B^*_X \\ 0 & \text{if } U \in B^*_X \end{cases}$$

where X_U is the U-expansion of X, and the relation ¡ is induced by the usual order in the real line; $U < B$ means that $x < y \quad \forall x \in U \, \forall y \in B$. The further $X \in S$ is from the basic U, the greater the absolute value of $as_U(X)$, and it is positive when X is on the right of U, negative when it is on the left of U and 0 when X and U are qualitatively equal.

The map "positioning" ϕ that captures the remoteness of all labels with respect to the basic ones is defined:

$$\phi : S \longrightarrow \mathbb{R}^{2n+1}$$
$$X \longrightarrow (as_{N_n}(X), \cdots, as_{N_1}(X), as_0(X), as_{P_1}(X), \cdots, as_{P_n}(X))$$

Finally, it is considered as the map from S^k to $\mathbb{R}^{(2n+1)k}$ whose components are the positioning functions:

$$\Phi : \qquad S^k \qquad \longrightarrow \mathbb{R}^{(2n+1)k}$$
$$(X_1, \cdots, X_k) \longrightarrow (\phi(X_1), \cdots, \phi(X_k))$$

This function Φ reflects the "global positioning" of the components of the vector of labels $\mathbf{X}$.

The following proposition allows us to construct new kernels in $[OM(n)]^k$, combining the function Φ defined above with a suitable kernel from the available ones in real spaces.

Proposition. Let $\Phi : A \longrightarrow B$ be a function and $K : \Phi(A) \times \Phi(A) \longrightarrow \mathbb{R}$ a kernel defined over $\Phi(A)$. Then the composition $K' = K \circ (\phi \times \phi)$ is a kernel on A.

Demonstration: being that K is a kernel over $\Phi(A)$, there exists an application α from $\Phi(A)$ to a feature space $(F, <, >)$ such that $K(\Phi(x), \Phi(z)) = < \alpha(\Phi(x)), \alpha(\Phi(z)) >$, for all $x, z \in A$ [15].

Taking $\beta = \alpha \circ \Phi : A \longrightarrow F$, it is possible to write:

$$
\begin{aligned}
K'(x, z) &= (K \circ (\phi \times \phi))(x, z) \\
&= K(\phi(x), \phi(z)) \\
&= < \alpha(\Phi(x)), \alpha(\Phi(z)) > \\
&= < \beta(x), \beta(z) >
\end{aligned}
$$

and, consequently, K' is a kernel defined over A.

The above proposition ensures the possibility of obtaining kernels over the space of qualitative k-tuples by the composition of gaussian kernels and polynomial kernels with the global positioning function $\Phi : S^k \longrightarrow \mathbb{R}^{(2n+1)k}$. For instance, if it is considered a gaussian kernel $\mathrm{Gauss}(x, z) = e^{-\|x-z\|^2/c}$, with $c > 0$, then, for any $\mathbf{X}, \mathbf{Y} \in S^k$:

$$
K'(\mathbf{X}, \mathbf{Y}) = \mathrm{Gauss}(\Phi(\mathbf{X}), \Phi(\mathbf{Y})) = \exp\left[- \| \Phi(\mathbf{X}) - \Phi(\mathbf{Y}) \|^2 / c \right] =
$$

$$
\exp\left[- \frac{(as_{N_n}(X_1) - as_{N_n}(Y_1))^2 + \cdots + (as_{P_n}(X_1) - as_{P_n}(Y_1))^2}{c} \right]
$$

And if we consider a polynomial kernel $\mathrm{Poly}\,(x, z) = [< x, z > + \theta]^d$, then:

$$
K''(\mathbf{X}, \mathbf{Y}) = \mathrm{Poly}\,(\Phi(\mathbf{X}), \Phi(\mathbf{Y})) = [< \Phi(\mathbf{X}), \Phi(\mathbf{Y}) > + \theta]^d =
$$

$$
\left[\sum_{j=1}^k \left(\sum_{i=1}^n as_{N_i}(X_j) \cdot as_{N_i}(Y_j) + as_0(X_j) \cdot as_0(Y_j) + \sum_{i=1}^n as_{P_i}(X_j) \cdot as_{P_i}(Y_j) \right) + \theta \right]^d
$$

Next an example of a real calculation of these kernels in a particular case is given, and the results obtained are interpreted in terms of "proximity".

5   Example

The example presented below is framed in the development of the MERITO project, which sets out to adapt Soft-Computing techniques, in particular Support Vector Machines (SVM), to the measurement of the financial risk using qualitative orders of magnitude models. The use of these models will allow us to incorporate expert knowledge.

In particular, a qualitative system based on an absolute orders of magnitude model is considered to represent some of the factors that are relevant in computing credit risk. Three of these factors are considered to compare firms, as a previous step to their classification according to their level of risk.

As a first step, the approach will be applied using just the three accounting ratios: leverage (L), return on capital (ROC), and market value (MV). According to the experts' knowledge, the variability ranges and the most relevant landmarks presented in table 1 are considered for those variables.

Table 1. Company descriptors

Variable	Variability range	Landmarks
$V_1 = L$	$[0, +100]$	$\{25, 50, 75\}$
$V_2 = ROC$	$[-100, +100]$	$\{I, 2I, 5I\}$
$V_3 = MV$	$[0, +20]$	$\{0.5, 1, 1.5\}$

Each one of the variables has different range and landmarks. The first variable V_1, the leverage of the firm, always takes positive values. It is accepted that a firm's leverage is very low when it is under 25, low when it is between 25 and 50, normal when it is between 50 and 75, and high when it is over this value The second variable V_2, return on capital, is defined as the profit on the capital plus debt, and it is qualitatively measured by comparing it with the interest without risk I of the country in which the firm operates. In the case of a multinational company, the interest paid in the headquarters' country is used. A firm's ROC is bad when it is under I, normal when it is between I and $2I$, good between $2I$ and $5I$, and very good over $5I$. Finally, the variable MV represents the firm's market value in relative terms, i.e. with respect to the average size of the sector's firms. The landmarks 0.5, 1 and 1.5 define labels for MV, which are low, normal, high and very high. Firms with values out of the intervals given in the table are not considered.

Once their variability ranges have been decided, a translation to transform the central landmark to zero is applied to each variable. All of them take values in a $OM(2)$ space, although the discretizations of the real line that give rise to their orders of magnitude are different. For each company the new variables V_1', V_2', V_3' will take values in the same orders of magnitude space, with basic labels $\{NG, NP, 0, PP, PG\}$.

We consider, for instance, three firms **X**, **Y**, **Z** defined by the labels:

X=(PP,[NG,NP],[NP,PG]), **Y**=([PP,PG],NP,0) and **Z**=(NG,PP,[NG,NP]).

As we can see, **X**'s leverage is high, its ROC is bad and it is quite a large firm, **Y**'s leverage is very high, its ROC is bad and it is medium sized, and finally **Z**'s leverage is very low, its ROC is good and it is small. It can easily be appraised that **Z** is a company clearly different from the other two, and this fact will be shown in the results of the kernel.

To obtain the vectors $\Phi(\mathbf{X})$, $\Phi(\mathbf{Y})$ and $\Phi(\mathbf{Z})$, table 2 with the remoteness with sign of the different labels with respect to all basic elements is used: We obtain:

$\Phi(X) = (3, 2, 1, 0, -1, 0, 0, -2, -2, -3, 1, 0, 0, 0, 0),$
$\Phi(Y) = (3, 2, 2, 0, 0, 1, 0, -1, -2, -3, 2, 1, 0, -1, -2)$ and
$\Phi(Z) = (0, -1, -2, -3, -4, 3, 2, 1, 0, -1, 0, 0, -2, -2, -3).$

Table 2. Remoteness with sign

$X \setminus U$	NG	NP	0	PP	PG
NG	0	−1	−2	−3	−4
NP	1	0	−1	−2	−3
0	2	1	0	−1	−2
PP	3	2	1	0	−1
PG	4	3	2	1	0
$[NG, NP]$	0	0	−2	−2	−3
$[NP, PP]$	1	0	0	0	−1
$[PP, PG]$	3	2	2	0	0
$[NG, PP]$	0	0	0	0	−1
$[NP, PG]$	1	0	0	0	0
$?$	0	0	0	0	0

Considering the gaussian kernel K':
$$K'(X, Y) = \exp\left[- \parallel \varPhi(X) - \varPhi(Y) \parallel^2 /c\right] = \exp[-11/c]$$
$$K'(X, Z) = \exp\left[- \parallel \varPhi(X) - \varPhi(Z) \parallel^2 /c\right] = \exp[-93/c]$$
$$K'(Y, Z) = \exp\left[- \parallel \varPhi(Y) - \varPhi(Z) \parallel^2 /c\right] = \exp[-90/c]$$
And in the case of the polynomial kernel K":
$$K''(X, Y) = [< \varPhi(X), \varPhi(Y) > +\theta]^d = (32 + \theta)^d,$$
$$K''(X, Z) = [< \varPhi(X), \varPhi(Z) > +\theta]^d = (1 + \theta)^d,$$
$$K''(Y, Z) = [< \varPhi(Y), \varPhi(Z) > +\theta]^d = (7 + \theta)^d,$$

In both cases, and as commented at the beginning of the section, it is observed that the nearer the qualitative values of the variables are, the greater the values of the kernel are. That is , greater results correspond to more similar patterns. This suggests that the selected representation will be suitable to be used in the later classification of firms according to their credit quality.

6   Conclusions and Future Research

The present work belongs to a wider project, which aims at motivating, defining and analyzing the viability of the use of learning machines in structures defined by orders of magnitude spaces.

The focus of this paper is the construction of kernel functions to be used in problems for which the input variables are described in terms of their ordered qualitative labels. These kernel functions have been built beginning with the concept of global positioning that allows as to capture the idea of remoteness and proximity between qualitative values.

Although this paper has focused on a classification problem by using Support Vector Machines, the methodological aspects considered and given can be used in any learning system based on kernels.

As a future work, the given method to be applied in problems of classification and multi-classification will be implemented. Concretely, and within the MER-ITO project, the results obtained by using input variables defined over orders of magnitude spaces will be compared with the ones obtained by using numerical values.

Applying the described methodology, we will also work simultaneously with quantitative and qualitative data, using positioning vectors to represent qualitative values, and combining them with quantitative ones.

References

1. Agell, N.: Estructures matemàtiques per al model qualitatiu d'ordres de magnitud absoluts. Ph. D. Thesis Universitat Politècnica de Catalunya (1998).
2. Agell, N., Ansotegui, C., Prats F., Rovira, X., and Sánchez, M.: Homogenising References in Orders of Magnitude Spaces: An Application to Credit Risk Prediction. Paper accepted at the 14th International Workshop on Qualitative Reasoning. Morelia, Mexico (2000).
3. P. Alpar, W. Dilger. Market share analysis and prognosis using qualitative reasoning. Decision Support Systems. vol. 15, núm. 2, pàg. 133-146 (1995).
4. Angulo, C. Aprendizaje con màquina núcleo en entornos de multiclasificación. Ph. D. Thesis Universitat Politècnica de Catalunya (2001).
5. Boser, B.E., Guyon, I.M. and Vapnik, V.N. A Training Algorithm for Optimal Margin Classifiers. In D. Haussler, ed, Proc. of the 5th Annual ACM Workshop on Computational Learning Theory. pp 144-152. ACM Press (1992).
6. Burges, C. A tutorial on support vector machines for pattern recognition, Data Mining and Knowledge Discovery, 2 (1998), 1-47.
7. Cortes, C; Vapnik,V. Support vector networks, Machine Learning, 20 (1995), 273-297.
8. Cristianini, N.; Shawe-Taylor, J. An Introduction to Support Vector Machines and other Kernel-based learning methods. Cambridge University Press (2000).
9. Forbus, K. D. Commonsense physics. A: Annals Revue of Computer Science (1988) 197-232.
10. S. Goonatilake y Ph. Treleaven. Intelligent Systems for Finance and Business. John Wiley & Sons (1996).
11. Lodhi, H; Saunders, C; Sahwe-Taylor, J;Cristianini, N.; Watkins, C. Text Classification Using String Kernels. Journal of MachineLearning Research, (2): 419-444 (2002).
12. J.J. Maher y T.K. Sen. Predicting Bond Ratings Using Neural Networks: A Comparison with Logistic Regression. Intelligent Systems in Accounting Finance & Management, vol 6, 59-72 (1997).
13. Piera, N. Current Trends in Qualitative Reasoning and Applications. Monograph CIMNE, núm. 33. International Center for Numerical Methods in Engineering (1995).
14. Travé-Massuyès, L.; Dague, P.; Guerrin, F. Le Raisonnement Qualitatif pour les Sciences de l'Ingenieur. Hermès (1997).
15. Vapnik, V. The nature of statistical learning theory, Springer Verlag New York (1995).
16. Vapnik, V. Statistical Learning Theory, Wiley (1998).

Negotiation Support
in Highly-Constrained Trading Scenarios

Juan A. Rodríguez-Aguilar[1,2], Antonio Reyes-Moro[1], Andrea Giovanucci[1],
Jesús Cerquides[1], and Francesc X. Noria[1]

[1] iSOCOLab
Intelligent Software Components, S. A.
Edificio Testa, C/ Alcalde Barnils, 64-68 A
08190 Sant Cugat del Vallès, Barcelona, Spain
{jar,toni,andrea,cerquide,fxn}@isoco.com
http://www.isoco.com
[2] Artificial Intelligence Research Institute, IIIA
Spanish Council for Scientific Research, CSIC
08193 Bellaterra, Barcelona, Spain
jar@iiia.csic.es
http://www.iiia.csic.es

Abstract. Negotiation events in industrial procurement involving multiple, highly customisable goods pose serious challenges to buyers when trying to determine the best set of providers' offers. Typically, a buyer's decision involves a large variety of constraints that may involve attributes of a very same item as well as attributes of different, multiple items. In this paper we present the winner determination capabilities of *iBundler*[10], an agent-aware decision support service offered to buyers to help them determine the optimal bundle of received offers based on their constraints and preferences. In this way, buyers are relieved with the burden of solving too hard a problem, and thus concentrate on strategic issues. *iBundler* is intended as a negotiation service for buying agents and as a winner determination service for reverse combinatorial auctions with side constraints.

1 Introduction

One particular, key procurement activity carried out daily by all companies concerns the negotiation of both direct and indirect goods and services. Throughout negotiations the decision-making of buyers and providers appears as highly challenging and intricate because of an inherently high degree of uncertainty and the large number of parameters, variables, and constraints to take into account.

Consider the problem faced by a buyer when negotiating with providing agents. In a negotiation event involving multiple, highly customisable goods, buyers need to express relations and constraints between attributes of different items. On the other hand, it is common practice to buy different quantities of the very same product from different providers, either for safety reasons or because

R. Conejo et al. (Eds.): CAEPIA-TTIA 2003, LNAI 3040, pp. 425–434, 2004.

offer aggregation is needed to cope with high-volume demands. This introduces the need to express business constraints on the number of suppliers and the amount of business assigned to each of them. Not forgetting the provider side, suppliers may also impose constraints or conditions over their offers. Offers may be only valid if certain configurable attributes (f.i. quantity bought, delivery days) fall within some minimum/maximum values, and assembly or packing constraints need to be considered. Once the buyer collects offers, he is faced with the burden of determining the winning offers. The problem is essentially an extension of the combinatorial auction (CA) problem, which can be proven to be NP[11]. It would be desirable to relieve buyers from solving such a problem.

We have tried to make headway in this direction by deploying *iBundler*[10], a decision support service acting as a combinatorial negotiation solver (solving the winner determination problem) for both multi-attribute, multi-item, multi-unit negotiations and auctions. Thus, the service can be employed by both buyers and auctioneers in combinatorial negotiations and combinatorial reverse auctions [13] respectively. In this paper we introduce the formal model and the computational realisation of the decision problem solved by *iBundler*.

The paper is organised as follows. Section 2 introduces the market scenario where buyers and traders are to negotiate, along with the requirements and constraints they may need. Next, a formal model capturing such requirements is put forward to set the foundations for the decision problem. The actual computational realisation of our decision support for negotiations is thoroughly detailed in section 4. Finally, section 5 provides some hints on the expected performance of the service.

2   Market Scenario

Although the application of combinatorial auctions (CA) to e-procurement scenarios (particularly reverse auctions) may be thought as straightforward, the fact is that there are multiple new elements that need to be taken into consideration. These are new requirements explained by the nature of the process itself. While in direct auctions, the items that are going to be sold are physically concrete (they do not allow configuration), in a negotiation event involving highly customisable goods, buyers need to express relations and constraints between attributes of different items. On the other hand, it is common practice to buy different quantities of the very same product from different providers, either for safety reasons or because offer aggregation is needed to cope with high-volume demands. This introduces the need to express constraints on the number of providers and the amount of business assigned to each of them. Not forgetting the provider side, providers may also impose constraints or conditions over their bids/offers. Offers may be only valid if certain configurable attributes (f.i. quantity bought, delivery days) fall within some minimum/maximum values, and assembly or packing constraints need to be considered.

Current CA reviewed do not model these features with the exception of[3, 12], where coordination and procurement constraints can be modelled. The rest of work focuses more on computational issues (CA is an NP-complete problem[11]) than in practical applications to e-procurement. Suppose that we are willing to buy 200 chairs (any colour/model is fine) for the opening of a new restaurant, and at that aim we employ an e-procurement solution that launches a reverse auction. If we employ a state-of-the-art CA solver, a possible resolution might be to buy 199 chairs from provider A and 1 chair from provider B, simply because it is 0.1% cheaper and it was not possible to specify that in case of buying from more than one provider a minimum of 20 chairs purchase is required. On the other hand the optimum solution might tell us to buy 50 blue chairs from provider A and 50 pink chairs from provider B. Why? Because although we had no preference over the chairs' colour, we could not specify that regarding the colour chosen all chairs must be of the same colour. Although simple, this example shows that without means of modeling these natural constraints, solutions obtained are seen as mathematically optimal, but unrealistic and with a lack of common sense, thus obscuring the power of decision support tools, and preventing the adoption of these technologies in actual-world settings.

Next we detail the capabilities required by buyers in the kind of negotiation scenario outlined above. The requirements below are intended to capture buyers' constraints and preferences and outline a powerful providers' bidding language:

Negotiate over Multiple Items. A negotiation event is usually started with the preparation of a request for proposal (RFQ) form. The RFQ form describes in detail the requirements (including attribute-values such as volume, quality specifications, dates as well as drawings and technical documentation) for the list of items (goods or services) defined by the negotiation event.

Offer Aggregation. A specific item of the RFQ can be acquired from several providers simultaneously, either because not a single provider can provide with the requested quantity at requested conditions or because buyers explicit constraints (see below).

Business Sharing Constraints. Buyers might be interested to restrict the number of providers that will finally trade for a specific item of the RFQ, either for security or strategical reasons. It is also of usual practice to define the minimum amount of business that a provider may gain per item.

Constraints over Single Items. Every single item within an RFQ is described by a list of negotiable attributes. Since: a) there exists a degree of flexibility in specifying each of these attributes (i.e. several values are acceptable) and b) multiple offers referring the very same item can be finally accepted; buyers need to impose constraints over attribute values. An example of this can be the following: suppose that the deadline for the reception of certain item A is two weeks time. However, although items may arrive any day within two weeks, once the first units arrive, the rest of units might be required to arrive in no more than 2 days after.

Constraints over Multiple Items. In daily industrial procurement, it is common that accepting certain configuration for one item affects the configuration of a different item, for example, when dealing with product compatibilities. Also, buyers need to express constraints and relationship between attributes of different items of the RFQ.

Specification of Providers' Capacities. Buyers cannot risk to award contracts to providers whose production/servicing capabilities prevent them to deliver over-committed offers. At this aim, they must require to have providers' capacities per item declared. Analogously, next we detail the expressiveness of the bidding language required by providers. The features of the language below are intended to capture providing agents' constraints and preferences.

Multiple Bids over Each Item. Providers might be interested in offering alternate conditions/configurations for a same good, i.e., offering alternatives for a same request. A common situation is to offer volume-based discounts. This means that a provider submits several offers and each offer only applies for a minimum (maximum) number of units.

Combinatorial Offers. Economy efficiency is enhanced if providers are allowed to offer (bid on) combination of goods. They might lower the price, or improve service assets if they achieve to get more business.

Multi-unit Offering. Each provider specifies the minimum (maximum) amount of units to be accepted in a contract.

Homogeneous Combinatorial Offers. Combinatorial offering may produce inefficiencies when combined with multi-unit offering. Thus a provider may wind up with an award of a small number of units for a certain item, and a large number of units for a different item, being both part of the very same offer (e.g. 10 chairs and 200 tables). It is desirable for providers to be able to specify homogeneity with respect to the number of units for complementary items.

Packing Constraints. Packing units are also a constraint, in the sense that it is not possible to serve an arbitrary number of units (e.g. a provider cannot sell 27 units to a buyer because.his items come in 25-unit packages). Thus providers require to be capable of specifying the size of packing units.

Complementary and Exclusive Offers. Providers usually submit XOR bids, i.e., exclusive offers that cannot be simultaneously accepted. Also, there may exist the need that an offer is selected only if another offer is also selected. We refer to this situation as an AND bid. This type of bids allows to express volume-based discounts. For example, when pricing is expressed as a combination of base price and volume-based price (e.g. first 1000 units at $2.5 p.u. and then $2 each).

Obviously, many more constraints regarding pricing and quantity can be considered here. But we believe these faithfully address the nature of the problem. Actually, *iBundler* has been applied to scenarios where some of these constraints do not apply while additional constraints needed to be considered. This was the case of a virtual shopping assistant, an agent that was able to aggregate several on-line supermarkets and optimize the shopping basket. To do so, it was necessary to model the fact that delivery cost depends on the amount of money spent at each supermarket.

3   Formal Model

In this section we provide a formal model of the problem faced by the buyer (auctioneer) based on the description in section 2. Prior to the formal definition, some definitions are in place.

Definition 1 (Items). *The buyer (auctioneer) has a vector of items $\Lambda = \langle \lambda_1, \ldots, \lambda_m \rangle$ that he wishes to obtain. He specifies how many units of each item he wants $U = \langle u_1, \ldots, u_m \rangle, u_i \in \mathbb{R}^+$. He also specifies the minimum percentage of units of each item $M = \langle m_1, \ldots, m_m \rangle, m_i \in [0,1]$, and the maximum percentage of units of each item $\bar{M} = \langle \bar{m}_1, \ldots, \bar{m}_m \rangle, \bar{m}_i \in [0,1], \bar{m}_i \geq m_i$, that can be allocated to a single seller. Furthermore, he specifies the minimum number of sellers $S = \langle s_1, \ldots, s_m \rangle, s_i \in \mathbb{N}$, and the maximum number of sellers $\bar{S} = \langle \bar{s}_1, \ldots, \bar{s}_m \rangle, \bar{s}_i \in \mathbb{N}, \bar{s}_i \geq s_i$, that can have simultaneously allocated each item. Finally, a tuple of weights $W = \langle w_1, \ldots, w_m \rangle, 0 \leq w_i \leq 1$, contains the degree of importance assigned by the buyer to each item.*

Definition 2 (Item Attributes). *Given an item $\lambda_i \in \Lambda$, let $\langle a_{i_1}, \ldots, a_{i_k} \rangle$ denote its attributes.*

Definition 3 (Sellers' Capacities). *Let $\Pi = \langle \pi_1, \ldots, \pi_r \rangle$ be a tuple of providers. Given a provider $\pi_i \in \Pi$ the tuple $C^i = \langle c_1^i, \ldots, c_m^i \rangle$ stands for the minimum capacity of the seller, namely the minimum number of units of each item that the seller is capable of serving. Analogously, the tuple $\bar{C}^i = \langle \bar{c}_1^i, \ldots, \bar{c}_m^i \rangle$ stands for the maximum capacity of the seller, i.e. the maximum number of units of each item that the seller is capable of providing.*

Definition 4 (Bid). *The providers in Π submit a tuple of bids $B = \langle B^1, \ldots, B^n \rangle$. A bid is a tuple $B^j = \langle \Delta^j, P^j, M^j, \bar{M}^j, D^j \rangle$ where $\Delta^j = \langle \Delta_1^j, \ldots, \Delta_m^j \rangle$ are tuples of bid values per item, where $\Delta_i^j = \langle \delta_{i_1}^j, \ldots, \delta_{i_k}^j \rangle \in \mathbb{R}^k, 1 \leq i \leq m$, assigns values to the attributes of item λ_i; $P^j = \langle p_1^j, \ldots, p_m^j \rangle, p_i^j \in \mathbb{R}^+$, are the unitary prices per item; $M^j = \langle m_1^j, \ldots, m_m^j \rangle, m_i^j \in \mathbb{R}^+$, is the minimum number of units per item offered by the bid; $\bar{M}^j = \langle \bar{m}_1^j, \ldots, \bar{m}_m^j \rangle, \bar{m}_i^j \mathbb{R}^+, \bar{m}_i^j \geq m_i^j$, is the maximum number of units of each item offered by the bid; and $D^j = \langle d_1^j, \ldots, d_m^j \rangle$ are the* bucket *or* batch *increments in units for each item ranging from the minimum number of units offered up to the maximum number of units.*

Given a bid $B^j \in B$, we say that B^j does not offer item $\lambda_i \in \Lambda$ iff $m_i^j = \bar{m}_i^j = 0$.

In order to model homogeneity constraints, we define a function $h : B \to 2^\Lambda$. Given a bid $B^j \in B$, $h(B^j) = \{\lambda_{j_1}, \ldots, \lambda_{j_k}\}$ indicates that the bid is homogeneous with respect to the items in $h(B^j)$. In other words, if the buyer (auctioneer) picks up bid B^j the number of units allocated for the items in $h(B^j)$ must be equal.

Furthermore, in order to relate sellers to their bids we define function $\rho : \Pi \times B \to \{0,1\}$ such that $\rho(\pi_i, B^j) = 1$ indicates that seller π_i is the owner of bid B^j. This function satisfies the following properties:

- $\forall B^j \in B \ \exists \pi_i \in \Pi$ such that $\rho(\pi_i, B^j) = 1$; and
- given a bid $B^j \in B$ if $\exists \pi_i, \pi_k \in \Pi$ such that $\rho(\pi_i, B^j) = 1$ and $\rho(\pi_k, B^j) = 1$ then $\pi_i = \pi_k$.

The conditions above impose that each bid belongs to a single seller.

Definition 5 (XOR Bids). *Let* $xor : 2^B \to \{0,1\}$ *be a function that defines whether a subset of bids must be considered as an XOR bid. Only bids owned by the very same seller can be part of an XOR bid. More formally* $xor(\mathcal{B}) = 1 \Rightarrow \exists! \ \pi \in \Pi$ *such that* $\rho(\pi, B^i) = \rho(\pi, B^j) = 1 \ \forall B^i, B^j \in \mathcal{B}, B^i \neq B^j$. *Thus, f.i. if* $\exists B^j, B^k \in B \ xor(\{B^j, B^k\}) = 1$ *both bids are mutually exclusive, and thus cannot be simultaneously selected by the buyer.*

Definition 6 (AND Bids). *Let* $and : \cup_{i=1}^n B^i \to \{0,1\}$ *be a function that defines whether an ordered tuple of bids must be considered as an AND bid. Thus, given an ordered tuple of bids* $\langle B^{j_1}, \ldots, B^{j_k} \rangle$ *such that* $and(\langle B^{j_1} \ldots B^{j_k} \rangle) = 1$ *then the buyer can only select a bid* $B^{j_i}, 1 < i \geq k$, *whenever* $B^{j_1}, \ldots, B^{j_{i-1}}$ *are also selected. Furthermore, all bids in an AND bid belong to the very same seller. Put formally,* $and(\mathcal{B}) = 1 \Rightarrow \exists! \ \pi \in \Pi$ *such that* $\rho(\pi, B^i) = \rho(\pi, B^j) = 1 \ \forall B^i, B^j \in \mathcal{B}, B^i \neq B^j$.

AND bids are intended to provide the means for the buyer to express volume-based discounts. However, they should be regarded as a generalisation of bidding via price-quantity graphs.

Based on the definitions above we can formally introduce the decision problem to be solved to provide support to the buyer (auctioneer):

Definition 7 (Multi-attribute, Multi-unit Combinatorial Reverse Auction). *The multi-attribute, multi-unit combinatorial reverse auction winner determination problem (MMCRAWDP) accounts to the maximisation of the following expression:*

$$\sum_{j=1}^n y_j \cdot \sum_{i=1}^m w_i \cdot V_i(q_i^j, p_i^j, \Delta_i^j)$$

subject to the following constraints:

1. $q_i^j \in 0 \cup [m_i^j, \bar{m}_i^j]$
2. $q_i^j \ mod \ d_i^j = 0$
3. $\sum_{j=1}^n q_i^j = u_i$ [1]
4. $\forall \pi_k \in \Pi \quad q_i^j \cdot \rho(\pi_k, B^j) \in \{0\} \cup [c_i^k, \bar{c}_i^k]$
5. $\forall \pi_k \in \Pi \quad q_i^j \cdot \rho(\pi_k, B^j) \in \{0\} \cup [m_i \cdot u_i, \bar{m}_i \cdot u_i]$
6. $\forall \lambda_{j_t}, t \in h(B^j) \quad q_i^j = q_t^j$
7. $\forall \lambda_i \in \Lambda \quad \sum_{k=1}^r x_i^k \in [s_i, \bar{s}_i]$
8. $and(\langle B^{j_1}, \ldots, B^{j_k} \rangle) = 1 \Rightarrow y^{j_1} \geq \ldots \geq y^{j_k}$
9. $\forall B' \subseteq B$ such that $xor(B') = 1 \quad \sum_{B^j \in B'} y^j \leq 1$

---

[1] We assume here that there is no free disposal, i.e. sellers are not willing to keep any units of their winning bids, and the buyer is not willing to take any extra units.

10. $a \cdot v_{i,l} + b \geq \delta^j_{i,l} \geq a' \cdot v_{i,l} + b'$ where $a, b, a', b' \in I\!R$
11. $c \cdot v_{i,l} + d \geq v_{j,k} \geq c' \cdot v_{i,l} + d'$ where $c, d, c', d' \in I\!R$

where

- $y_j \in \{0, 1\}, 1 \leq j \leq n$, *are decision variables for the bids in* B;
- $x^k_i \in \{0, 1\}, 1 \leq i \leq m, 1 \leq k \leq r$, *are decision variables to decide whether seller* π_k *is selected for item* λ_i;
- $q^j_i \in I\!N \cup \{0\}, 1 \leq j \leq n, 1 \leq i \leq m$, *are decision variables on the number of units to select from* B^j *for item* λ_i;
- $V_i : I\!R^+ \times I\!R^+ \times I\!R^{i_k} \rightarrow I\!R, 1 \leq i \leq m$, *are the bid valuation functions for each item; and*
- $v_{i,l}$ *stands for a decision variable for the value of attribute* a_l *of item* λ_i.
- $a, b, a', b', c, c', d, d'$ *are buyer-defined constant values.*

Next, we detail the semantics of the restrictions above:

1. This constraint forces that when bid B^j is selected as a winning bid, the allocated number of units of each item q^j_i has to fit between the minimum and maximum number of units offered by the seller.
2. The number of allocated units q^j_i to a bid B^j for item λ_i must be a multiple of the batch d^j_i specified by the bid.
3. The total number of units allocated for each item must equal the number of units requested by the buyer.
4. For each item, the number of units allocated to a seller cannot exceed his capacities.
5. The total number of units allocated per seller cannot exceed or be below the maximum and minimum percentages that can be allocated per seller specified by the buyer.
6. For homogeneous bids, the number of units allocated to the items declared homogeneous must be the same.
7. The number of sellers to be awarded each item cannot exceed or be below the maximum and minimum number of total sellers specified by the buyer.
8. Bids being part of an AND bid can only be selected if the bids preceding them in the AND bid are selected too.
9. XOR bids cannot be jointly selected.
10. Intra-item constraints are modelled through this expression. It indicates that only those bids whose value for the attribute item related to the decision variable that satisfy the expression can be selected.
11. Inter-item constraints are modelled through this expression. It puts into relation decision variables of attributes belonging to different items.

There are several aspects that make our model differ from related work. Firstly, traditionally all combinatorial auction models assume that the buyer (auctioneer) equally prefers all items. Such constraint is not considered in our model, allowing the buyer to express his preferences over items. Secondly, multi-attribute auctions and combinatorial auctions with side constraints have been separately dealt with. On the one hand, Bichler [2] extensively deals with multi-attribute auctions, including a rich bidding language. On the other hand, Sand-holm et al. [13] focus on multi-item, multi-unit combinatorial auctions with side constraints where items are not multi-attribute. We have attempted at formu-lating a model which unites both. Lastly, to the best of our knowledge neither inter-item nor intra-item constraints have been dealt with in the literature at the attribute level [7] though they help us better cope with multiple sourcing.

4   Implementation

The problem of choosing the optimal set of offers sent over by providing agents taking into account the features of the negotiation scenario described in section 2 is essentially an extension of the combinatorial auction (CA) problem in the sense that it implements a larger number of constraints and supports richer bidding models. The CA problem is known to be NP-complete, and consequently solving methods are of crucial importance. In general, we identify three main approaches that have been followed in the literture to fight the complexity of this problem:

- As reported in [8], attempts to make the combinatorial auction design prob-lem tractable through specific restrictions on the bidding mechanism have taken the approach of considering specialised structures that are amenable to analysis. But such restrictions violate the principle of allowing arbitrary bidding, and thus may lead to reductions in the economic outcome.
- A second approach sacrifices optimality by employing approximate algo-rithms [6]. However, and due of the intended actual-world usage of our ser-vice, it is difficult to accept the notion of sub-optimality.
- A third approach consists in employing an exact or complete algorithm that guarantees the global optimal solution if this exists. Although theoretically impractical, the fact is that effective complete algorithms for the CA problem have been developed .

Many of the works reviewed in the literature adopt global optimal algorithms as a solution to the CA because of the drawbacks pointed out for incomplete methods. Basically two approaches have been followed: traditional Operations Research (OR) algorithms and new problem specific algorithms[4]. It is always an interesting exercise to study the nature of the problem in order to develop problem specific algorithms that exploit problem features to achieve effective search reduction. However, the fact is that the CA problem is an instance of the multi-dimensional knapsack problem MDKP (as indicated in [5]), a mixed integer program well studied by the operation research literature. It is not surprising, as reported in [1], that many of the main features of these problem specific new algorithms are rediscoveries of traditional methods in the operations research community. In fact, our formulation of the problem can be regarded as similar to the binary multi-unit combinatorial reverse auction winner determination problem in [13] with side constraints[12]. Besides, expressing the problem as a mixed integer programming problem with side constraints enables its resolution

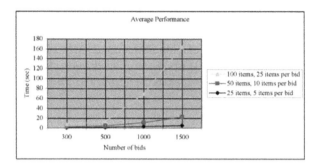

Fig. 1. Average performance of iBundler

by standard algorithms and commercially available, thoroughly debugged and optimised software which have shown to perform satisfactorily for large instances of the CA problem.

With these considerations in mind, the core of our service has been modelled and implemented as a mixed integer programming problem. We have implemented two versions: a version using ILOG CPLEX 7.1 in combination with SOLVER 5.2; and another version using using iSOCO's Java MIP modeller that integrates the GLPK library [9]. In both cases it takes the shape of a software component. Hereafter we shall refer to this component as the *iBundler* solver.

5   Validation and Performance

After the above-described implementation two major issues arose. On the one hand, unitary tests were needed in order to guarantee that *iBundler*'s behaviour is sound or, in other words, that *iBundler* produces the optimal solution taking into account the variety of constraints and bidding expressivenes described in section 2. On the other hand, since combinatorial auction solvers are computationally intensive, a major issue is whether our service was to behave satisfactorily in highly-demanding trading scenarios.

At this aim, we devised a customisable generator of data sets targeted at serving for the two purposes above. Our generator artificially created negotiation problems for *iBundler* by wrapping an optimal solution with noisy bids. Thus *iBundler* is fed by the generator with an RFQ, plus a buyer's constraints, plus a set of bids of varying features (single, combinatorial, AND, and XOR). The generator constructs the artificial negotiation problem based on several parameters, namely: number of providers, number of items, number of bids per provider (mean and variance), number of items per bid (mean and variance), offer price per item (mean and variance). In this way, not only were we able to measure the performance of *iBundler* but also to automatically verify its sound behaviour.

Figure 1 shows how *iBundler* behaves when solving negotiation problems as the number of bids, the number of items, and the items per bid increase.

The results show that *iBundler* can be employed to conduct real-time decision-making in actual-world negotiation scenarios. It is hard to imagine a negotiation event in which several hundreds of bids are concurrently submitted by a given set of providers to compete for RFQs containing dozens of items. Nonetheless *iBundler* performs well even in such extreme scenarios. Therefore, its scalability is also ensured.

References

1. A. Andersson, M. Tenhunen, and F. Ygge. Integer programming for combinatorial auction winner determination. In *Proceedings of the Fourth International Conference on Multi-Agent Systems (ICMAS)*, pages 39–46, Boston, MA, 2000.
2. Martin Bichler and Jayant Kalagnanam. Bidding languages and winner determination in multi-attribute auctions. *European Journal of Operation Research.* (to appear).
3. J. Collins and M. Gini. An integer programming formulation of the bid evaluation problem for coordinated tasks. In R. V. Dietrich, B.and Vohra, editor, *Mathematics of the Internet: E-Auction and Markets*, volume 127 of *IMA Volumes in Mathematics and its Applications*, pages 59–74. Springer-Verlag, 2001.
4. Y. Fujishima, K. Leyton-Brown, and Y. Shoham. Taming the computational complexity of combinatorial auctions: Optimal and approximate approaches. In *Proceeding of the Sixteenth International Joint Conference on Artificial Intelligence (IJCAI'99)*, pages 548–553, August 1999.
5. R. C. Holte. Combinatorial auctions, knapsack problems, and hill-climbing search. In *Lecture Notes in Computer Science*, volume 2056. Springer-Verlag, Heidelberg, 2001.
6. H. H. Hoos and C. Boutilier. Solving combinatorial auctions using stochastic local search. In *Proceedings of AAAI-2000*, 2000.
7. Jayant Kalagnanam and David C. Parkes. *Supply Chain Analysis in the eBusiness Era*, chapter Auctions, Bidding and Exchange Design. 2003. forthcoming.
8. Frank Kelly and Richard Steinberg. A combinatorial auction with multiple winners for universal service. *Management Science*, 46:586–596, 2000.
9. A. Makhorin. Glpk – gnu linear programming toolkit. http://www.gnu.org/ directory/GNU/glpk.html, 2001.
10. Juan A. Rodríguez-Aguilar, Andrea Giovanucci, Antonio Reyes-Moro, Francesc X. Noria, and Jesús Cerquides. Agent-based decision support for actual-world procurement scenarios. In *2003 IEEE/WIC International Conference on Intelligent Agent Technology*, Halifax, Canada, October 2003.
11. M. H. Rothkopt, A. Pekec, and R. M. Harstad. Computationally manageable combinatorial auctions. *Management Science*, 8(44):1131–11147, 1995.
12. T. Sandholm and S. Suri. Side constraints and non-price attributes in markets. In *International Joint Conference on Artificial Intelligence (IJCAI)*, Seattle, WA, 2001. Workshop on Distributed Constraint Reasoning.
13. T. Sandholm, S. Suri, A. Gilpin, and D. Levine. Winner determination in combinatorial auction generalizations. In *First Joint Conference on Autonomous Agents and Multiagent Systems (AAMAS'02)*, pages 69–76, Bologna, Italy, July 2002.

Normalized Cyclic Edit Distances: An Efficient Algorithm[*]

Andrés Marzal and Guillermo Peris

Universitat Jaume I (Castelló), Spain
{amarzal,peris}@lsi.uji.es

Abstract. Cyclic strings are sequences with no beginning or end, which are useful for modelling different objects in pattern recognition. For instance, in digital image analysis, strings can represent contours of 2D objects. Several methods have been described to compute the dissimilarity of two cyclic strings such as the cyclic edit distance. However, no method has been provided that takes into account the normalization of the cyclic edit distance. In this paper, we propose an algorithm to compute normalized cyclic edit distances, and illustrate the performance of the method in practice.

1 Introduction

Measuring distances between strings is a fundamental problem in pattern recognition, with applications to several fields such as artificial vision, computational biology, image and text processing, error correction, information retrieval, etc [6]. Formally, the edit distance between a string X with length m and a string Y with length n, is defined as the minimum weighted number of edit operations needed to transform X into Y, and can be computed in $\mathcal{O}(mn)$ time [13].

Cyclic strings (see [2] for a review) are a special kind of strings where the beginning (or end) of the sequence is not defined, and they naturally arise in numerous applications; for instance, in modelling the closed contours of objects [10] (Figure 1). There is a trivial algorithm to compute the cyclic edit distance in $\mathcal{O}(m^2n)$ time, which is based on comparing one string with all the possible rotations of the other. Maes [11] proposed a divide and conquer algorithm that reduces the computational cost to $\mathcal{O}(mn\log(m))$ time. Marzal and Barrachina [3] formulated a *branch and bound* algorithm for the Levenshtein cyclic edit distance which significantly speeds up computation while maintaining the worst-case complexity. Peris and Marzal [8, 9] extended this algorithm to different cost functions. However, none of the methods described above takes the length of the strings into account. This leads to some paradoxical behaviour: for instance, 9 errors when comparing 10 character cyclic strings lead to a lower distance than 10 errors in the comparison of cyclic strings of length 100, whereas it is to be expected that the last pair of strings should be considered more similar.

[*] This work has been supported by the the Spanish Ministerio de Ciencia y Tecnología and FEDER under grant TIC2002-02684.

R. Conejo et al. (Eds.): CAEPIA-TTIA 2003, LNAI 3040, pp. 435–444, 2004.

2 = 0000766455707444443111012445421

Fig. 1. 2D contour representation using 8-directions chain codes.

The normalized edit distance was introduced by Marzal and Vidal [1] and is defined as the sequence of edit operations that minimizes the ratio of the weight and length of the sequence. These authors described an algorithm to compute the normalized edit distance in $\mathcal{O}(mn^2)$ time. Later, Vidal, Marzal, and Aibar [7] introduced a fractional programming algorithm that, in practice, reduces the computational cost to $\mathcal{O}(smn)$, where s is the number of iterations. Experiments with typical applications showed that s usually ranges from 2 to 4 when a good approximation of the solution is used to initialize the process. Arslan and Eğecioğlu [4, 5] derived an algorithm based on a technique by Megiddo for the optimization of objective functions, with a time complexity $\mathcal{O}(mn \log n)$, though no experimental results were provided.

In this paper, we define the normalized cyclic edit distance, extending the algorithms for normalized edit distance to cyclic strings, and we study the performance of this distance by its application in some experiments. The outline of the paper is as follows: in sections 2 and 3, cyclic edit distance and normalization of edit distances are reviewed, respectively. In section 4, the normalized cyclic edit distance is introduced and the results of experiments with an OCR application are shown in section 5. Finally, the conclusions are presented in section 6.

2   Cyclic Edit Distance

Let Σ be an alphabet of symbols, let $X = x_1 x_2 \ldots x_m$ and $Y = y_1 y_2 \ldots y_n$ be strings in Σ^* and let λ be the empty string. The edit distance between strings X and Y is the minimum weighted number of edit operations needed to transform X into Y. An edit operation is a pair $(a, b) \neq (\lambda, \lambda)$, also denoted by $a \to b$. Four edit operations are usually defined: insertion ($\lambda \to b$), deletion ($a \to \lambda$), substitution ($a \to b$, where $a \neq b$) and matching ($a \to a$). These operations are weighted by a set of values $\gamma = (\gamma_I, \gamma_D, \gamma_S, \gamma_M)$. We will denote a general edit operation as e and $\gamma(e)$ will be its cost.

A string X can be transformed into a string Y with a sequence of edit operations $E = e_1 e_2 \ldots e_l$, with an associated cost

$$\Gamma(E) = \sum_{i=1}^{l} \gamma(e_i). \tag{1}$$

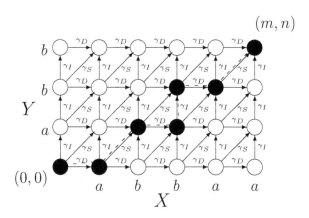

Fig. 2. Edit graph for strings $X = abbaa$ and $Y = abb$. An edit path is represented.

The edit distance between X and Y for a cost function γ is defined as the minimum sequence of edit operations that transforms X into Y:

$$ED(X, Y, \gamma) = \min_{E \in \mathcal{E}_{XY}} \Gamma(E), \tag{2}$$

where $\mathcal{E}_{XY}$ is the set of sequences of edit operations that transform X into Y.

The so-called *edit graph* (see Figure 2) is a directed acyclic graph with $(m + 1) \times (n + 1)$ nodes, where each arc represents an edit operation: horizontal arcs correspond to deletions, vertical arcs to insertions, and diagonal arcs to substitutions or matchings. Computing a minimum sequence of edit operations is equivalent to finding an optimal path from node $(0, 0)$ to node (m, n). This computation can be achieved in $\mathcal{O}(mn)$ time by dynamic programming.

A cyclic string $[X]$ is defined as the set $\{\sigma_k(X) : 0 \leq k < |X|\}$, where $\sigma_k(X) = x_{k+1} \ldots x_m x_1 \ldots x_k$ is known as the k-rotation of string X. The *cyclic edit distance* between $[X]$ and $[Y]$, written as $CED([X], [Y], \gamma)$, is defined as $\min_{X \in [X]}(\min_{Y \in [Y]} ED(X, Y, \gamma))$, where $ED(X, Y, \gamma)$ is the edit distance between (non-cyclic) strings. A trivial algorithm computes $CED([X], [Y], \gamma)$ in $\mathcal{O}(m^2 n)$, since

$$CED([X], [Y], \gamma) = \min_{X \in [X]} \left(\min_{Y \in [Y]} ED(X, Y, \gamma) \right) = \min_{X \in [X]} ED(X, Y, \gamma). \tag{3}$$

An $\mathcal{O}(mn \log n)$ *divide and conquer* algorithm, due to Maes [11], is based on a property of optimal paths in the edit graph, namely, that optimal paths associated to different rotations of string X cannot cross each other on an extended edit graph underlying the comparison of $X \cdot X$ and Y (Figure 3).

The Branch and Bound (BB) method introduced by Marzal, Barrachina, and Peris [3, 8, 9] has the same worst case computational complexity as Maes' algorithm, but is more efficient in practice because it explores only the rotations that may actually lead to an optimal path in the extended edit graph. For that

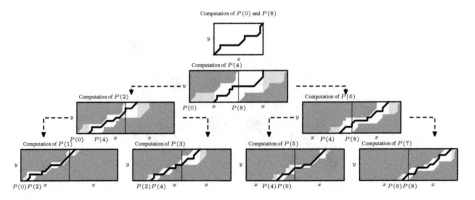

Fig. 3. Search space for the computation of the cyclic edit distance. Each frame represents an edit graph. Dark shaded regions in each frame are not visited when computing optimal paths. Optimal edit paths are drawn with thick lines.

purpose, it computes a lower bound of the edit distance for a set of rotations and prunes all rotations that have a lower bound greater than the best distance computed at each step of the algorithm.

Both Maes' and the BB algorithms are exact methods. But the cyclic edit distance can be computed approximately with suboptimal methods, such as the Bunke-Bühler method [10], with a cost $\mathcal{O}(mn)$. Recently, Mollineda, Vidal, and Casacuberta [2, 12] introduced a new, more accurate approximate algorithm based on the Bunke-Bühler method that requires some training on cyclic strings obtained for the application.

3   Normalization of Edit Distances

The normalized edit distance between strings X and Y is defined as

$$NED(X, Y, \gamma) = \min_{E \in \mathcal{E}_{XY}} \frac{\Gamma(E)}{L(E)}, \tag{4}$$

where $L(E)$ (length of E) is the number of edit operations in the sequence E. It must be noted that this normalized distance cannot be obtained by first obtaining $ED(X, Y, \gamma)$ and then dividing its value by the length of the corresponding path, as was shown in [1] (see Figure 4).

3.1   Basic Algorithm

In [1], Marzal and Vidal introduced an algorithm for computing NED based on dynamic programming. This algorithm is based on the fact that the length $L(E)$ of any edit path E is bounded as $\max(m, n) \leq L(E) \leq m + n$. So, the number of different lengths of optimal paths between X and Y is $N = \min(m, n) + 1$. To compute NED, we just have to save, for each node in the edit graph, the best

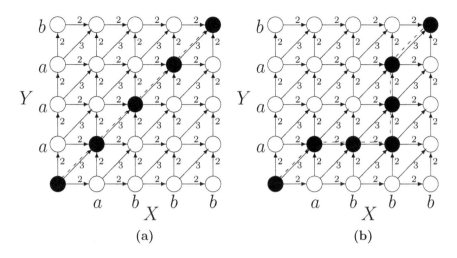

Fig. 4. (a) Optimal path between strings $X = abbb$ and $Y = aaab$, with $\gamma = (2, 2, 3, 0)$; (b) Optimal path for normalized edit distance. Note that $NED(X, Y, \gamma) = 1.33$ is lower than the post-normalized edit distance, $\frac{ED(X,Y,\gamma)}{4} = 1.5$.

distance for every possible length from the initial node. This leads to an $\mathcal{O}(m^2n)$ dynamic programming algorithm.

3.2   Fractional Programming

In [7], Vidal *et al.* developed a new algorithm based on fractional programming. This method is applicable to optimization problems involving ratios of linear functions. In the normalized edit distance, the problem to be solved is

Problem A:

$$\hat{d} = \min_{E \in \mathcal{E}} \frac{\Gamma(E)}{L(E)}, \qquad \Gamma, L : \mathcal{E} \to \mathbb{R}; \quad L(E) > 0, \forall E \in \mathcal{E}. \tag{5}$$

Dinkelbach's algorithm [14] solves problem A by means of problem $A(\lambda)$:

Problem A(λ):

$$\hat{d}(\lambda) = \min_{E \in \mathcal{E}}(\Gamma(E) - \lambda L(E)), \qquad \Gamma, L : \mathcal{E} \to \mathbb{R}; \quad L(E) > 0, \forall E \in \mathcal{E}. \tag{6}$$

Dinkelbach's algorithm begins with an initial guess for λ (in [7] the post-normalized edit distance is proposed as the initial guess), and problem $A(\lambda)$ is solved, thus obtaining an optimal path $\hat{E}$. With this value of $\hat{E}$, a new λ is computed with $\Gamma(E)/L(E)$, and the procedure is repeated until convergence. This algorithm is shown in Figure 5 (a). It can be shown that the computation of problem $\min_{E \in \mathcal{E}}(\Gamma(E) - \lambda' L(E))$ can be formulated in terms of the edit distance problem using a different cost function:

Algorithm FP
$\hat{E} := arbitrary\_path(\mathcal{E})$
$\hat{\lambda} := \Gamma(\hat{E})/L(\hat{E})$
repeat
  $\lambda' := \hat{\lambda}$
  $\hat{E} := arg\min_{E \in \mathcal{E}}(\Gamma(E) - \lambda' L(E))$
  $\hat{\lambda} := \Gamma(\hat{E})/L(\hat{E})$
until $\hat{\lambda} := \lambda'$
return $(\hat{E}, \hat{\lambda})$
End FP

(a)

Algorithm Megiddo(X, Y, γ)
$Q = \{\Gamma(E)/L(E) \mid E \in \mathcal{E}_{XY}\}$
repeat
  $\lambda := \text{median}(Q)$
  $\gamma' := (\gamma_I, \gamma_D, \gamma_S + \lambda, \gamma_M + \lambda)$
  $v := ED(X, Y, \gamma')$
  if $v = 0$ **then**
    return λ
  else if $v < 0$ **then**
    $Q := Q - \{q \mid q \geq \lambda\}$
  else
    $Q := Q - \{q \mid q \leq \lambda\}$
End Megiddo

(b)

Fig. 5. Algorithm for the Normalized Edit Distance based on (a) fractional programming, (b) Megiddo's algorithm.

$$\min_{E \in \mathcal{E}}(\Gamma(E) - \lambda' L(E)) = ED(X, Y, \gamma') - \lambda'(m + n), \qquad (7)$$

with $\gamma' = (\gamma_I, \gamma_D, \gamma_S + \lambda', \gamma_M + \lambda')$.

This algorithm has a computational cost of $\mathcal{O}(smn)$, s being the number of iterations. As noted in [7], the value of s is usually between 2 and 4.

3.3   Megiddo's Algorithm

Recently, Arslan and Eğecioğlu [4, 5] developed a new method to compute the normalized edit distance based on a technique by Megiddo for the optimization of rational objective functions. First, a set Q is generated with all the possible values for the NED (considering all possible edit paths), and then the median of this set, $\hat{\lambda}$, is used to compute $\min_{E \in \mathcal{E}}(\Gamma(E) - \hat{\lambda}L(E))$ according to (7). If the minimum obtained is zero, then $NED(X, Y, \gamma) = \hat{\lambda}$; if the minimum is negative, then we continue the procedure with the set of values greater than $\hat{\lambda}$, otherwise, the lower set is taken. Though this algorithm (shown in Figure 5 (b)) computes the NED in $\mathcal{O}(mn \log n)$ time, no experiments were provided by Arslan and Eğecioğlu to compare this approach with the fractional programming technique.

4   Normalization of Cyclic Edit Distances

Extending the definition of normalized edit distance to cyclic strings, we define the normalized cyclic edit distance (NCED) between the cyclic strings $[X]$ and $[Y]$ as

$$NCED([X], [Y], \gamma) = \min_{X \in [X]} NED(X, Y, \gamma) = \min_{X \in [X]} \min_{E \in \mathcal{E}_{XY}} \frac{\Gamma(E)}{L(E)}. \qquad (8)$$

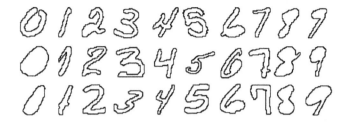

Fig. 6. Sample of 8-direction contours of handwritten digits.

Both fractional programming and Megiddo's algorithm can be extended to solve NCED, but now the problems involved are:

Problem A:

$$\hat{d} = \min_{X \in [X]} \min_{E \in \mathcal{E}_{XY}} \frac{\Gamma(E)}{L(E)}, \qquad \Gamma, L : \mathcal{E} \to \mathbb{R}; \quad L(E) > 0, \forall E \in \mathcal{E}. \qquad (9)$$

Problem A(λ):

$$\hat{d}(\lambda) = \min_{X \in [X]} \min_{E \in \mathcal{E}_{XY}} (\Gamma(E) - \lambda L(E)), \qquad \Gamma, L : \mathcal{E} \to \mathbb{R}; \quad L(E) > 0, \forall E \in \mathcal{E}.$$
$$(10)$$

Therefore, the same techniques used for NED can be used for NCED, by just substituting the standard ED computation with a CED. The computational costs are $\mathcal{O}(smn\log(n))$ and $\mathcal{O}(mn(\log(n))^2)$ for fractional programming and Megiddo's algorithm, respectively, using either Maes or BB to compute the CED.

5   Experiments

In order to test the performance of the normalized cyclic edit distance for both time efficiency and classification rates, a set of experiments were carried out on a handwritten digits recognition task. The outer contour of 100 instances of each digit was represented using 8-directions chain codes (see Figure 6). The strings were extracted from images at three different resolutions, so that the resulting average string lengths were 50, 150 and 300. These cyclic strings were converted to non-cyclic strings by heuristically choosing the leftmost pixel of the highest row in the image as the starting point. All the experiments were performed on a Pentium III at 850MHz running under Linux 2.2.

The methods compared in these experiments were the ordinary edit distance (ED), the cyclic edit distance (CED), the normalized edit distance (NED) and the normalized cyclic edit distance (NCED). For both CED and NCED, Maes and Branch and Bound algorithms were used and, for normalization, both Fractional Programming (FP-NCED) and Megiddo (M-NCED) techniques were employed. Finally, the Levenshtein edit weights, $\gamma = (1, 1, 1, 0)$, were used in all the experiments.

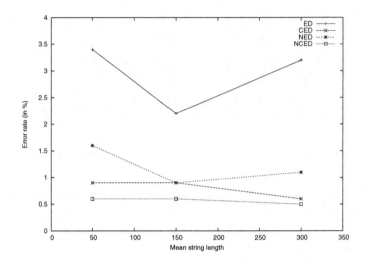

Fig. 7. Error rate for standard and cyclic edit distance, both normalized and unnormalized.

5.1   Classification Rate

The classification experiments were performed with the 3 Nearest Neighbours rule, and the error rate was estimated with a ten-fold cross-validation procedure by taking 10 prototypes and 90 test samples for each class.

The results for the classification error rates are shown in Figure 7. Both CED and NED reduce the error rate, but the best result is obtained when both techniques are used altogether. For instance, for strings of length 300, the error rates are 3.2% (ED), 1.1% (NED), 0.6% (CED) and 0.5% (NCED).

Furthermore, it can be observed that, in this experiment, the error rate for NCED does not depend on the string length, that is, the classification result does not almost change with the image resolution.

5.2   Time Performance

Some experiments were performed in order to compare Megiddo's algorithm and fractional programming for the computation of NCED. For this comparison, we define the number of iterations in Megiddo's algorithm as the number of standard edition distances computed in the binary search. In Table 1, the average number of iteration and maximum iterations are compared for both implementations of NCED. It can be seen that the average number of iterations of FP-NCED hardly changes with the string length, with a maximum number of 3 iterations. However, M-NCED needs far more iterations and this number is strongly dependent on the string size.

Results for time performance are shown in Figure 8, measured as the number of dynamic programming (DP) operations, that is, the number of visited nodes in

Table 1. Comparison of mean (maximum) number of iterations for different normalization methods.

Average length	FP-NCED	M-NCED
50	2.50 (3)	9.13 (13)
150	2.53 (3)	11.55 (15)
300	2.58 (3)	13.19 (17)

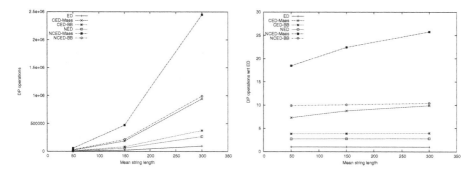

Fig. 8. Performance of different methods, both normalized and unnormalized, measured as the number of dynamic operations and relative to standard edit distance values.

the edit graph when computing an optimal edit path. Normalization was carried out with the fractional programming technique.

It can be seen that the normalization of cyclic and non-cyclic edit distances approximately doubles the cost of the corresponding unnormalized method. Furthermore, the NCED computational cost corresponds to about eight times that of the ED cost, both in time and in number of dynamic programming operations. This relationship is independent of the string size.

It is interesting to point out that, as the error rate for NCED is almost independent of the image resolution, using strings with average length of 50 the computational cost can be reduced by a factor of 30, with respect to strings with average length of 300, and no significant loss of performance.

6 Conclusions

In this paper, we have defined the normalized cyclic edit distance, and have proposed several methods for computing it efficiently. When using NCED, the error rate for a handwritten digits recognition task is significantly reduced. Furthermore, best execution time is obtained by combining the Fractional Programming method and the branch and bound technique, which outperforms both Megiddo's and Maes' algorithm.

Furthermore, the error rate obtained using NCED is stable when changing the image resolution and, therefore, that the computational cost can be greatly reduced with no significant loss of classification performance.

References

1. A. Marzal and E. Vidal. Computation of normalized edit distances and applications. *IEEE Transactions on Pattern Analysis and Machine Intelligence*, 15(9): 926–932, 1993.
2. A. Marzal, R. Mollineda, G. Peris, and E. Vidal. *Pattern Recognition and String Matching*. Kluwer Academic, 2002.
3. A. Marzal and S. Barrachina. Speeding up the computation of the edit distance for cyclic strings. *International Conference on Pattern Recognition*, pages 271–280, 2000.
4. A.N. Arslan and O. Egecioglu. An efficient uniform-cost normalized edit distance algorithm. In *IEEE computer Society*, Proc. 6-th String Processing and Information Retrieval Conference (SPIRE '99), pages 8–15, 1999.
5. A.N. Arslan and O. Egecioglu. Efficient Algorithms for Normalized Edit Distance. *Journal of Discrete Algorithms*, 1(1):1, 2000.
6. D. Sankoff and J. Kruskal, editors. *Time Warps, String Edits, and Macromolecules: The Theory and Practice of Sequence Comparison*. Addison-Wesley, Reading, MA, 1983.
7. E. Vidal, A. Marzal, and P. Aibar. Fast computation of normalized edit distance. *IEEE Transactions on Pattern Analysis and Machine Intelligence*, 17(9):899–902, 1995.
8. G. Peris and A. Marzal. Fast Computation of Cyclic Edit Distances: Dependence on the Cost Functions. *Proceedings del IX Symposium Nacional de Reconocimiento de Formas y Análisis de Imágenes, AERFAI*, 1, 2001.
9. G. Peris and A. Marzal. Fast Cyclic Edit Distance Computation with Weighted Edit Costs in Classification. *Proc. of the International Conference on Pattern Recognition, ICPR'02*, 4, 2002.
10. H. Bunke and H. Bühler. Applications of Approximate String Matching to 2D Shape Recognition. *Pattern Recognition*, 26(12):1797–1812, 1993.
11. M. Maes. On a cyclic string-to-string correction problem. *Information Processing Letters*, 35:73–78, 1990.
12. R. A. Mollineda, E. Vidal, and F. Casacuberta. *Efficient techniques for a very accurate measurement of dissimilarities between cyclic patterns*, volume 1876, pages 121–126. Springer, 2000.
13. R.A. Wagner and M.J. Fischer. The string-to-string correction problem. *Journal of ACM*, 21(1):168–173, 1974.
14. W. Dinkelbach. On nonlinear fractional programming. *Management Science*, 18(7): 492–498, 1967.

On the Heuristic Performance
of Perimeter Search Algorithms

Carlos Linares López

Deimos Space
Ground Segment Systems Division
Ronda de Poniente, 19
Edificio Fiteni VI, Portal 2
28760 Tres Cantos, Madrid, Spain
carlos.linares@deimos-space.com
http://www.deimos-space.com

Abstract. Whilst creating a perimeter around the goal node has led to very good results in some domains, it has been demonstrated that the performance decreases dramatically in other domains. This paper introduces a mathematical model which explains this phenomenon. Its purpose is twofold: firstly to analyze the performance of the heuristic function employed in perimeter search algorithms with any perimeter depth, $h_{p_d}(\cdot)$, and secondly to compare it with the performance of its unidirectional counterpart, $h(\cdot)$. The model introduced herein will be used for deriving other very important properties of the perimeter heuristic function such as the cross-over point where one heuristic function is preferable to the other.

1 Introduction

Most of the ideas introduced in the specialized bibliography for improving the performance of the heuristic functions that guide search algorithms towards the goal node, t, from a start node, s, tend to sacrifice the optimality of the solutions turning the original heuristic function, $h(\cdot)$, into a non-admissible one. However, these new heuristic functions avoid the generation of many nodes [1]. Other ideas that do not sacrifice the admissibility of the resulting heuristic functions are: criticizing relaxed models [2–4] of the original heuristic functions; automatic learning methods of new and more accurate heuristic values [5–8] and, lastly, the perimeter search algorithms that are the subject of this paper.

Perimeter search algorithms where simultaneously and independently introduced by Manzini [9] and Dillenburg and Nelson [10]. They consist of two stages:

First, creation of a perimeter (denoted as P_{p_d}) around the goal node t which contains all the nodes whose cost for reaching t is equal to a predefined value p_d, known as the perimeter depth, and whose children have costs strictly bigger than p_d. This perimeter can be created using a brute-force search algorithm such as depth-first search.

R. Conejo et al. (Eds.): CAEPIA-TTIA 2003, LNAI 3040, pp. 445–456, 2004.
© Springer-Verlag Berlin Heidelberg 2004

Second, search from the start node s using a single-agent search algorithm guided by the heuristic function $h_{p_d}(\cdot)$, defined as:

$$h_{p_d} = \min_{m \in P_{p_d}} \{h(n, m) + h^*(m, t)\}$$

that forces the forward search to approach the perimeter nodes instead of the target node t from any node n outside the perimeter. In the preceding formula, $h^*(m, t)$ is the optimal cost from the perimeter node m to the target node t and that will be lower than or equal to the perimeter depth p_d, and $h(n, m)$ is the heuristic distance from the node n to the node m.

The authors proved that the new heuristic function $h_{p_d}(\cdot)$ preserves the admissibility of the original heuristic function, $h(\cdot)$. They also proved $h_{p_d}(\cdot)$ is more informed than $h(\cdot)$, this is $h_{p_d}(n) \geq h(n)$ for any node n [2]. Moreover, in spite of the fact that the evaluation of $h_{p_d}(\cdot)$ may imply a large number of evaluations of $h(\cdot)$, Manzini demonstrated that this number decreases with the search depth.

Hermann Kaindl and Gerhard Kainz [6] have proved empirically that while the perimeter idea improves dramatically the performance of the unidirectional search for solving the Korf's test suite of the 15-Puzzle, the improvement for solving mazes is not that spectacular though it is still feasible [11]. On the other hand, Carlos Linares [12] has shown that in the shortest-path problem with costs that follow a continuous distribution, the perimeter idea does not improve the performance of its unidirectional counterpart at all.

Since Hermann Kaindl and Gerhard Kainz recognized that they were not able to explain mathematically the differences among these results [6], almost no mathematical analysis have been devised for characterizing this phenomenon. Carlos Linares and Andreas Junghanns [13] derived a mathematical expression that predicts how the number of evaluations of $h(\cdot)$ decreases in the evaluation of $h_{p_d}(\cdot)$ with the search depth and they established a mathematical relation of the time spent by any unidirectional search algorithm when using a perimeter depth, p_d, or not.

This paper introduces a mathematical model which aims at characterizing the difference in the accuracy between the original heuristic function, $h(\cdot)$ and the perimeter heuristic function, $h_{p_d}(\cdot)$. Therefore, it is not a study of the performance of the perimeter search algorithms and its unidirectional counterparts but an analysis of the conditions under which one heuristic function is preferable to the other. Section 2 introduces the mathematical model that characterizes both functions. Section 3 ends the paper with some relevant conclusions.

2   Mathematical Model

This section introduces the mathematical model used for modelling the performance of $h_{p_d}(\cdot)$. It consists of a function Ω which estimates the probability that $h_{p_d}(\cdot)$ will improve the accuracy of $h(\cdot)$.

2.1 Preconditions

This analysis is restricted to domains which meet the following requirements:

- The cost of all arcs, $c(n, n_i)$, with n_i being a successor of n, is always equal to 1: $c(n, n_i) = c(n_i, n) = 1$.
- The only allowed changes of the heuristic function $h(\cdot)$ from node n to node n_i are $\{-1, +1\}$, when estimating its distance to the same node m: $|h(n, m) - h(n_i, m)| = 1$, where node n_i is a successor of node n, i.e., $n_i \in$ SCS(n).

Examples are domains like the N-Puzzle when guided by the Manhattan distance, or the problem of finding the shortest path in a maze with obstacles when guided by the sum of the difference of the coordinates x and y.

2.2 Characterization of $h(\cdot)$

The mathematical model makes use of the following *domain-independent* conditional distribution functions:

$$\alpha_i = p(h(n_j, t) = i + 1 | h(n, t) = i), n_j \in \text{SCS}(n)$$

$$\beta_i = p(h(n_j, t) = i - 1 | h(n, t) = i), n_j \in \text{SCS}(n)$$

such that:

$$\alpha_i + \beta_i = 1, \forall i, 0 \le i \le h_{\max} \tag{1}$$

where $h_{\max}$ is the maximum heuristic distance from any node n of the state space to the goal node t. In other words, α_i is the probability that a node n randomly sampled outside of the perimeter that has a heuristic distance to the target node t equal to i has one descendant whose heuristic distance to the target node t is $i + 1$. Similarly, β_i is the probability that a node n randomly sampled outside of the perimeter that has a heuristic distance to the target node t equal to i has one descendant whose heuristic distance to the target node t is $i - 1$.

These distributions can either be easily sampled or they can be derived from the total density function introduced by Richard E. Korf and Michael Reid [14], $f(x) = p(h(n, t) = x)$, i.e., the likelihood that the distance from any node n randomly sampled to the goal node t will be exactly equal to x.

As a matter of fact, taking into account the second precondition mentioned above, it turns out that:

$$f(i) = \alpha_{i-1} f(i - 1) + \beta_{i+1} f(i + 1) \tag{2}$$

Now, considering the minimum distance, 0 (which is, by default, the distance from the target node t to itself), we find that: $\alpha_0 = 1$ and $\beta_0 = 0$. As 0 is the minimum distance, there will be no α_{-1}, so that equation (2) can simplify to $\beta_1 f(1) = f(0)$ so that:

$$\beta_1 = \frac{f(0)}{f(1)}$$

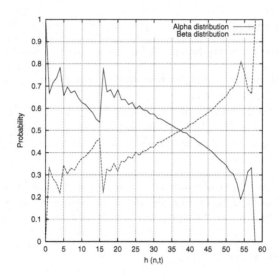

Fig. 1. Marginal distributions α and β for the 15-Puzzle

and $\alpha_1 = 1 - \beta_1$ according to equation (1). From these values it is possible to derive the marginal distributions α_i and β_i from the values of $f(i)$ solving β_{i+1} from equation (2):

$$\beta_{i+1} = \frac{f(i) - \alpha_{i-1}f(i-1)}{f(i+1)} \qquad (3)$$

from which α_{i+1} can be easily derived according to equation (1):

$$\alpha_{i+1} = 1 - \beta_{i+1} \qquad (4)$$

Therefore, it is proven that distributions α and β can be computed from $f(x)$.

Figure 1 shows the distributions α and β of the Manhattan distance computed with the sampling of 10^6 solvable instances of the 15-Puzzle.

2.3 Calculation of the performance of $h_{p_d}(\cdot)$

Let us denote the probability $p(h_{p_d}(n,t) = h_0 + \delta + p_d | h(n,t) = h_0)$ as $\Omega^{h_0, \delta}(p_d)$. This is the probability that h_{p_d} will improve the original heuristic estimation $h_0 = h(n,t)$ in $\delta + p_d$ units so that $h_{p_d} = h_0 + \delta + p_d$ for any node n outside of the perimeter. Thus, the purpose of this analysis is to characterize Ω for any feasible combination of h_0, δ and p_d. Note δ takes values from the interval $[-p_d, +p_d]$ in steps of two units because of the restrictions introduced in section 2.1.

Fortunately, function Ω can be expressed in terms of simpler events: the number of perimeter nodes generated at depth p_d from the target node t that have a heuristic distance equal to $h_0 + \delta$ to an arbitrary node n outside the perimeter whose heuristic distance to the target node t is h_0. Let us denote this event as $\Gamma^{h_0, \delta}(p_d)$.

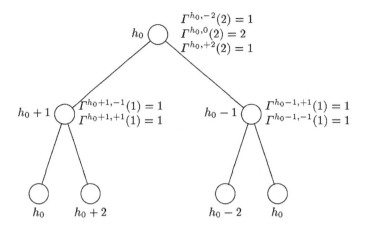

Fig. 2. An example of Γ

Figure 2 shows a plausible case where the perimeter nodes (or terminal nodes) generated at depth $p_d = 2$ from the target node t (the root of the tree) have different heuristic distances to the node n (shown to the left of internal nodes and below the leaves) expressed with different variations of the original heuristic distance $h_0 = h(n, t)$. For example, the number of perimeter nodes with a heuristic distance equal to $h_0 + 0 = h_0$ from the target node t to the node n under consideration is 2 since the first immediate successor of the root has a descendant meeting this property and the second immediate successor of the root adds another one. In other words: $\Gamma^{h_0,0}(2) = 2$ because for the first successor $\Gamma^{h_0+1,-1}(1) = 1$ and for the second successor $\Gamma^{h_0-1,+1}(1) = 1$. Note how the values δ of the immediate successors of the root have changed their value in order to ensure a final alteration $\delta = 0$ in the root node.

Lemma 1. *The following relationships are always true, i.e., they are axioms of the mathematical model proposed:*

$$
\begin{aligned}
&p(\Gamma^{h_0,0}(0) = 1) = 1 \\
&p(\Gamma^{h_0,0}(0) = x) = 0, \forall x \neq 1 \\
&p(\Gamma^{h_0,\delta}(0) = 0) = 1, \forall \delta \neq 0 \\
&p(\Gamma^{h_0,\delta}(0) = x) = 0, \forall \delta \neq 0, \forall x \neq 0 \\
&p(\Gamma^{h_0,\delta}(p_d) = 0) = 1, \forall \delta > p_d \\
&p(\Gamma^{h_0,\delta}(p_d) = x) = 0, \forall \delta > p_d, \forall x \neq 0
\end{aligned}
\tag{5}
$$

Proof. They are in fact very easy to understand. They only represent trivial relationships of the cases that have to be taken into account when computing the function Γ. The first four mean that no change δ other than 0 of the original heuristic estimation h_0 can be obtained with a null perimeter depth. The last two establish that it is not feasible to alter the original heuristic estimation h_0 in an amount greater than the perimeter depth.   □

Theorem 1. *Let $T(2, p_d)$ denote a uniform tree search rooted at the target node t generated with a brute branching factor $b = 2$ and depth p_d. Assuming that the target node t has a heuristic distance equal to h_0 to an arbitrary node n outside the perimeter, $h(n, t) = h_0$, the probability that $T(2, p_d)$ has exactly x terminal nodes whose heuristic distance to the node n is $h_0 + \delta$ is:*

$$p(\Gamma^{h_0, \delta}(p_d) = x) = \sum_{i=0}^{x} \left(\alpha_{h_0} \cdot p(\Gamma^{h_0+1, \delta-1}(p_d - 1) = i) + \right.$$
$$\beta_{h_0} \cdot p(\Gamma^{h_0-1, \delta+1}(p_d - 1) = i)) \times \qquad (6)$$
$$(\alpha_{h_0} \cdot p(\Gamma^{h_0+1, \delta-1}(p_d - 1) = x - i) +$$
$$\left. \beta_{h_0} \cdot p(\Gamma^{h_0-1, \delta+1}(p_d - 1) = x - i) \right)$$

Proof. Equation (6) assumes that the probability of one node having $i + (x - i) = x$ terminal nodes satisfying one condition can be split into two *independent* events: the first successor having i terminal nodes satisfying the condition and the second child having $x - i$ leaves satisfying the same condition; so that its probability can be computed as the product of both probabilities. On the other hand, every factor results from the total probability theorem which states that when an arbitrary event A can be represented as the union of N *mutually exclusive* events B_i, its probability can be computed as:

$$P(A) = \sum_{i=1}^{N} P(A|B_i) \times P(B_i)$$

The mutually exclusive events result from considering that every successor will either increment the heuristic distance of its parent or decrement it. The conditional probability of the former is α_{h_0} and the conditional probability of the latter is β_{h_0}.

Finally, the sum of equation (6) embraces the $x + 1$ different combinations to distribute two non-negative values less than or equal to i whose sum is equal to i.   □

Figure 3 shows the density function of two Γ distributions computed with a perimeter depth equal to 4 units and all the plausible values of δ with two different original heuristic distances, 25 and 50, in the 15-Puzzle. Both distributions have been obtained using the α and β distributions shown in figure 1 – hence, using the Manhattan distance. The values obtained are expected to be very accurate since the branching factor considered $b = 2$ is very close to the branching factor computed by S. Edelkamp and Richard E. Korf [15] $b = 2.13$.

The following result is a generalization of the first theorem for an arbitrary branching factor.

Theorem 2. *Let $T(b, p_d)$ denote a uniform tree search rooted at the target node t generated with a brute branching factor b and depth p_d. Assuming that the target node t has a heuristic distance equal to h_0 to an arbitrary node n outside the perimeter, $h(n, t) = h_0$, the probability that $T(b, p_d)$ has exactly x terminal nodes whose heuristic distance to the node n is $h_0 + \delta$ is:*

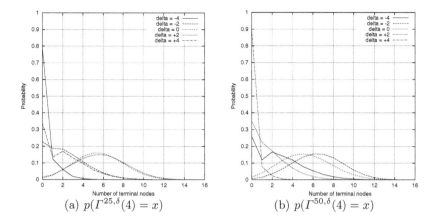

Fig. 3. Sample distributions of $p(\Gamma^{h_0,\delta}(4) = x)$

$$p(\Gamma^{h_0,\delta}(p_d) = x) = \sum_{i_1=0}^{x} \sum_{i_2=0}^{x-i_1} \cdots \sum_{i_{(b-1)}=0}^{x-\sum_{j=0}^{b-2} j} (\rho(h_0, \delta, p_d - 1, x - \sum_{j=0}^{b-1} i_j) \times \tag{7}$$
$$\prod_{j=0}^{b-1} \rho(h_0, \delta, p_d - 1, i_j))$$

where ρ is defined as:

$$\rho(h_0, \delta, p_d, x) = (\alpha_{h_0} \cdot p(\Gamma^{h_0+1,\delta-1}(p_d - 1) = x) + \tag{8}$$
$$\beta_{h_0} \cdot p(\Gamma^{h_0-1,\delta+1}(p_d - 1) = x))$$

Proof. As in the previous theorem, equation (7) assumes that the probability of one node having x terminal nodes satisfying one condition can be decomposed into b *independent* events such that its probability can be computed as the product of the probabilities of those events. Also, as in the previous theorem, every factor results from the total probability theorem where the *mutually exclusive* events consist of either incrementing the heuristic distance of its parent (according to the α distribution) or decrementing it – according to the β distribution.

Besides, the sum shown in equation (7) represents all the different combinations of having x terminal nodes satisfying one condition considering separately the contributions of every successor:

$$\binom{x+b-1}{x} = \frac{(x+b-1)!}{x!(b-1)!}$$

$\square$

The function Ω can now be derived for an arbitrary brute branching factor b thanks to the definition of $p(\Gamma^{h_0,\delta}(p_d) = x)$.

Theorem 3. *Let $T(b, p_d)$ denote a uniform tree search rooted at the target node t generated with a brute branching factor b and depth p_d. Assuming the target* *node t has a heuristic distance equal to h_0 to an arbitrary node n outside the perimeter, $h(n,t) = h_0$, the probability that $h_{p_d}(n,t) = h_0 + \delta + p_d$ is:*

$$\Omega^{h_0,2k-p_d}(p_d) = \left(\prod_{i=0}^{k-1} p(\Gamma^{h_0,2i-p_d}(p_d) = 0)\right) \times (1 - p(\Gamma^{h_0,2k-p_d}(p_d) = 0)),$$

$$0 \le k < p_d$$

$$\Omega^{h_0,+p_d}(p_d) = \prod_{i=0}^{p_d-1} p(\Gamma^{h_0,2i-p_d}(p_d) = 0) \quad (9)$$

Proof. Since $h_{p_d}(\cdot)$ is defined as the minimum of the sum of the heuristic evaluations to the perimeter nodes plus the perimeter depth p_d, the probability that $h_{p_d}(\cdot)$ is $h_0 + (-p_d) + p_d = h_0$ equals:

$$\Omega^{h_0,-p_d}(p_d) = 1 - p(\Gamma^{h_0,-p_d}(p_d) = 0)$$

because if for any perimeter node the heuristic distance is $-p_d$, $h_{p_d}(\cdot)$ will yield $(-p_d) + p_d$ since $-p_d$ is the minimum allowed heuristic distance.

Considering now the next allowed value $\delta = -p_d + 2$, the probability that $h_{p_d}(\cdot)$ is $h_0 + (-p_d + 2) + p_d = h_0 + 2$ equals:

$$\Omega^{h_0,2-p_d}(p_d) = p(\Gamma^{h_0,-p_d}(p_d) = 0) \times (1 - p(\Gamma^{h_0,2-p_d}(p_d) = 0))$$

This formula assumes that the events $\Gamma^{h_0,-p_d}(p_d) = 0$ and $\Gamma^{h_0,2-p_d}(p_d) = 0$ are *independent* so that the probability of Ω can be computed as their product. The first event states that no perimeter node shall exist such that the heuristic distance to the node n is $h_0 - p_d$ and the second event means that at least one perimeter node shall have a heuristic distance to the node n equal to $h_0 - p_d + 2$. Under these conditions, $h_0 - p_d + 2$ is the least heuristic distance to the node n so that it shall be chosen by $h_{p_d}(\cdot)$ yielding a value equal to $h_0 + (-p_d + 2) + p_d = h_0 + 2$. The first expression of equation (9) is derived by reasoning like this successively. The second expression results simply from the observation that all perimeter nodes shall have a heuristic distance to the node n under consideration equal to $h_0 + p_d$ in order for $h_{p_d}(\cdot)$ to choose this value, yielding $h_0 + p_d + p_d = h_0 + 2p_d$ which is the upper allowed value of $h_{p_d}(\cdot)$.

Finally, it is very easy to demonstrate that the sum of all the values of $\Omega^{h_0,\delta}(p_d)$ for the same combination of h_0 and p_d is exactly equal to 1.   □

Figure 4 shows a couple of Ω distributions, namely $\Omega^{25,\delta}(4)$ and $\Omega^{50,\delta}(4)$ computed from $p(\Gamma^{h_0,\delta}(4) = x)$ as shown in figure 3. As can be seen, the most likely value of $\Omega^{25,\delta}(4)$ is $\Omega^{25,-2}(4)$, i.e., with a perimeter generated at depth 4, the perimeter idea is likely to improve a heuristic estimation of 25 units in $4 + (-2) = 2$ units. However, it is very likely that a perimeter generated at depth 4 will not improve the heuristic estimations of the Manhattan distance with an original heuristic estimation of 50 units since the most likely value of $\Omega^{50,\delta}(4)$ is $\Omega^{50,-4}(4)$ which represents a benefit of $4 + (-4) = 0$ units.

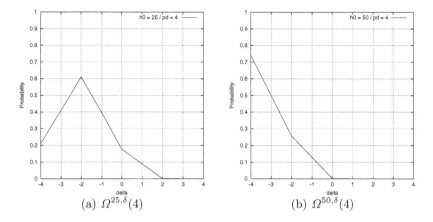

(a) $\Omega^{25,\delta}(4)$ (b) $\Omega^{50,\delta}(4)$

Fig. 4. Ω distributions for a perimeter depth equal to 4 units

2.4 Asymptotic Performance of $h_{p_d}(\cdot)$

This section proves that the benefits of the perimeter idea are asymptotically bounded. Considering the α distribution is constant, this is, that α_i is always equal to a constant value generically denoted as α and introducing the expressions $p(\Gamma^{h_0,\delta}(p_d) = x)$ shown in equation (6) (this is, for a constant brute branching factor $b = 2$) in the equation (9) it is very easy to note that the following relationships always hold:

$$
\begin{aligned}
p(\Gamma^{h_0,-1}(1) = 0) &= \alpha^2 \\
p(\Gamma^{h_0,-2}(2) = 0) &= (\alpha + \alpha^2(1 - \alpha))^2 \\
&= (\alpha + p(\Gamma^{h_0,-1}(1) = 0)(1 - \alpha))^2 \\
p(\Gamma^{h_0,-3}(3) = 0) &= (\alpha + (\alpha + \alpha^2(1 - \alpha))^2(1 - \alpha))^2 \\
&= (\alpha + p(\Gamma^{h_0,-2}(2) = 0)(1 - \alpha))^2
\end{aligned}
\tag{10}
$$

so that for any perimeter depth p_d and for a brute branching factor $b = 2$:

$$
p(\Gamma^{h_0,-p_d}(p_d) = 0) = (\alpha + p(\Gamma^{h_0,-p_d+1}(p_d - 1) = 0)(1 - \alpha))^2
\tag{11}
$$

It is easily noticeable that when $\alpha = 0$, $p(\Gamma^{h_0,-p_d}(p_d) = 0) = 0$ and according to equation (9) it follows $\Omega^{h_0,-p_d}(p_d) = 1$. In other words, if $\alpha = 0$ it is not expected that $h_{p_d}(\cdot)$ will ever improve the heuristic estimations of $h(\cdot)$. Analogously, if $\alpha = 1$ it follows that $p(\Gamma^{h_0,-p_d}(p_d) = 0) = 1$ and once again in virtue of equation (9), $\Omega^{h_0,-p_d}(p_d) = 0$. Therefore, if $\alpha = 1$, it is expected that $h_{p_d}(\cdot)$ will always improve the heuristic estimations of $h(\cdot)$. Thus, the greater α, the more likely it is that $h_{p_d}(\cdot)$ will improve the performance of $h(\cdot)$. The last outstanding step is to prove that $p(\Gamma^{h_0,-p_d}(p_d) = 0)$ is a strictly increasing function in the interval $[0,1]$. To do so, it is enough to realize that this function has a positive derivative in the interval $[0,1]$ for all the allowed values of p_d.

Figure 5 shows the probability that $h_{p_d}(\cdot)$ does not improve the performance of $h(\cdot)$ (equation (11)) for different perimeter depths ranging from 1 (the rightmost curve) to 10 – the leftmost curve. As it can be seen, these probabilities are

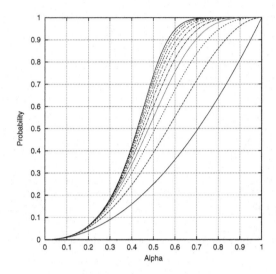

Fig. 5. $p(\Gamma^{ho,-d}(d) = 0)$ for different values of p_d, $0 < p_d \leq 10$

asymptotically bounded, which is especially important since it neccessarily implies that the benefit of the perimeter idea is asymptotically bounded. Therefore, the following *domain-independent* result is especially relevant:

Theorem 4. *The relative performance of the perimeter heuristic function $h_{p_d}(\cdot)$ when being compared to $h(\cdot)$ drops below $\alpha = (\sqrt{2} - 1)$ for a brute branching factor $b = 2$.*

Proof. We are interested in the value of α which has a probability equal to $\frac{1}{2}$ in the figure 5 since this is the value for which it is not decidable whether $h_{p_d}(\cdot)$ will perform better than $h(\cdot)$ or not. Therefore, we are seeking the asymptotic cut point of the functions shown in equation (11) and the straight line $y = \frac{1}{2}$.

In order to simplify the exposition, let us simplify the nomenclature with the following rule $f_i^2(\alpha) = p(\Gamma^{ho,-i}(i) = 0)$. Now, the expressions (10) can be rewritten like this:

$$f_1^2(\alpha) = \alpha^2$$
$$f_i^2(\alpha) = (\alpha + f_{i-1}^2(1 - \alpha))^2, i > 1 \tag{12}$$

In the limit $f_i^2(\alpha) = f_{i+1}^2(\alpha)$ such that $f_i(\alpha) = (\alpha + f_i^2(1 - \alpha))$. Solving this equation it turns out that the only solution in the interval $[0, 1]$ is $(\sqrt{2} - 1)$. □

3 Conclusions

A mathematical tool for comparing the performance of the perimeter heuristic function $h_{p_d}(\cdot)$ and the original heuristic function $h(\cdot)$ has been introduced. Based on the preceding analysis some conclusions can be drawn:

- The marginal distributions α and β are interchangeable with the total density functions introduced by Richard E. Korf and Michael Reid [14], $f(x)$. Henceforth, these distributions are useful not only for studying the performance of the perimeter heuristic functions, but even for the performance of any unidirectional search algorithm.
- It has been proven that the performance of the perimeter heuristic function $h_{p_d}(\cdot)$ drops below $\alpha = (\sqrt{2} - 1)$ in any domain with a brute branching factor $b = 2$.
  It can be seen in figure 1 that $\alpha(h_0 = 45) \simeq (\sqrt{2} - 1)$ so that perimeter heuristic functions are not likely to improve the heuristic estimations of the Manhattan distance for values greater than 45.
- The most relevant conclusion is that the performance of $h_{p_d}(\cdot)$ is explained in terms of the distribution of the original heuristic function $h(\cdot)$ with the aid of the marginal distributions α and β. That is, this analysis is *domain-independent*.

Acknowledgments

This paper benefited from discussions with Andreas Junghanns who provided many comments.

To Antonio Gutierrez from Deimos Space S. L., who derived the asymptotic point where the performance of $h_{p_d}(\cdot)$ drops. To Mike Rennie from Deimos Space S. L. also, who reviewed the translation into english.

To the referees, who have improved the quality and contents of this paper with their comments.

References

1. Pohl, I.: First results on the effect of error in heuristic search. In Meltzer, B., Michie, D., eds.: Machine Intelligence. Volume 5. American Elsevier, New York (1970)
2. Pearl, J.: Heuristics. Addison-Wesley, Reading MA (1984)
3. Hansson, O., Mayer, A., Yung, M.: Criticizing solutions to relaxed models yields powerful admissible heuristics. Information Sciences 63 (1992) 207–222
4. Korf, R.E., Taylor, L.A.: Finding optimal solutions to the twenty-four puzzle. In: Proceedings AAAI-96. (1996) 1202–1207
5. Kainz, G., Kaindl, H.: Dynamic improvements of heuristic evaluations during search. In: AAAI-96. (1996) 311–317
6. Kaindl, H., Kainz, G.: Bidirectional heuristic search reconsidered. Journal of Artificial Intelligence Research 7 (1997) 283–317
7. Culberson, J.C., Schaeffer, J.: Efficiently searching the 15-puzzle. Technical Report TR 94-08, University of Alberta (1994)
8. Culberson, J.C., Schaeffer, J.: Searching with pattern databases. In: Advances in Artificial Intelligence. Springer-Verlag (1996) 402–416
9. Manzini, G.: BIDA*: an improved perimeter search algorithm. Artificial Intelligence 75 (1995) 347–360

10. Dillenburg, J.F., Nelson, P.C.: Perimeter search. Artificial Intelligence **65** (1994) 165–178

11. Korf, R.E.: Depth-first iterative-deepening: An optimal admissible tree search. Artificial Intelligence **27** (1985) 97–109

12. Linares, C.: Caracterización de los modelos de búsqueda de un agente con descripciones generalizadas de los nodos origen y destino. PhD thesis, Facultad de Informática. Universidad Politécnica de Madrid (2001)

13. Linares, C., Junghanns, A.: Perimeter search performance. In: Proceedings of the 3rd International Conference on Computers and Games (CG'2002), Edmonton, Canada (2002)

14. Korf, R.E., Reid, M.: Complexity analysis of admissible heuristic search. In: Proceedings AAAI-98. (1998) 305–310

15. Edelkamp, S., Korf, R.E.: The branching factor of regular search spaces. In: AAAI-98. (1998) 299–304

Plug & *Play* Object Oriented Bayesian Networks

Olav Bangsø[1], M. Julia Flores[2], and Finn V. Jensen[1]

[1] Aalborg University, Department of Computer Science
Frederik Bajers Vej 7E, DK-9220 Aalborg Øst, Denmark
{bangsy,fvj}@cs.auc.dk
[2] University of Castilla-La Mancha, Department of Computer Science
Campus Universitario s/n, 02071 Albacete, Spain
julia@info-ab.uclm.es

Abstract. Object oriented Bayesian networks have proven themselves useful in recent years. The idea of applying an object oriented approach to Bayesian networks has extended their scope to larger domains that can be divided into autonomous but interrelated entities. Object oriented Bayesian networks have been shown to be quite suitable for dynamic domains as well. However, processing object oriented Bayesian networks in practice does not take advantage of their modular structure. Normally, the object oriented Bayesian network is transformed into a Bayesian network, and inference is performed by constructing a junction tree from this network. In this paper we propose a method for translating directly from object oriented Bayesian networks to junction trees, avoiding the intermediate transformation. We pursue two main purposes: firstly, to maintain the original structure organized in an instance tree and secondly, to gain efficiency during modification of an object oriented Bayesian network. To accomplish these two goals we have exploited a mechanism allowing local triangulation of instances to develop a method for updating the junction trees associated with object oriented Bayesian networks in highly dynamic domains. The communication needed between instances is achieved by means of a fill-in propagation scheme.

1 Introduction

Object Oriented Bayesian Networks (OOBNs) [4, 2] have proven themselves useful for modeling large and complex domains. The idea of modularity is, obviously, also applicable to highly dynamic domains, where the system is under time constraints; instances of classes are added or removed to reflect the changes in the domain. The classes of OOBNs allow automatic generation of a model from sensor data. This can e.g. be applied in tracking: whenever sensors indicate a new object in the domain, an instance of an appropriate class can be added to the domain. The class hierarchy of OOBNs allows refining of the instances when sensor readings give additional information on an object. The problem remaining is that whenever the model is changed, it requires a re-compilation of the entire network, which may be a time consuming task, especially triangulation is computationally expensive. However no attempt has been made at exploiting the structure of instances induced by the OOBN framework for belief propagation.

R. Conejo et al. (Eds.): CAEPIA-TTIA 2003, LNAI 3040, pp. 457–467, 2004.
© Springer-Verlag Berlin Heidelberg 2004

In this paper we will present a triangulation method for OOBNs where the structure of the OOBN is maintained and triangulation is performed locally in the instances. The global triangulation will be ensured by propagating fill-ins in a scheme similar to that described for multiply sectioned Bayesian networks in [12]. This method will translate each class into a junction tree, and whenever an instance of a class is added, the junction tree for that class will be plugged into the system.

We will also present a scheme for updating the junction tree whenever some class has been modified using Incremental Compilation (IC) [3]; it seems reasonable that after a series of local changes, only some parts of the network will need to be re-compiled. IC focuses on re-compiling only the necessary parts.

2   Object Oriented Bayesian Networks

Dividing a large network into smaller pieces has been proposed in several different places in the literature [8, 10, 5, 4]. In this section we will briefly describe the OOBN framework of [1] through an example.

In the object oriented paradigm, the basic component is an object, an entity with identity, state and behavior. Each object is assigned to a class, which is a description of a set of objects with the same structure, behavior and attributes. Whenever an object of a class is needed, an instance of that class is created. Note that each instance has a unique encapsulating class, the class in which they are instantiated[1].

In [1] nodes that constitute an entity are grouped into an instance, which has a label (identity) and a fixed structure (state and behavior). A class in an OOBN is defined as a BN fragment containing three sets of nodes:

- O: the set of output nodes; nodes that can be parents of nodes outside instances of the class.
- I: the set of input nodes; represents nodes that are not in the class, but are used as parents of nodes inside instances of the class. Input nodes cannot have parents in the class.
- P: the set of protected nodes; nodes that can only have parents and children inside the class.

The input and output nodes constitute the *interface*; the part of instances of a class that interfaces with the surroundings of the instance. In the example a farmer has two cows and wants a model describing how the fodder influences his income[2]. The two cows can be modeled by class, and it is shown in Fig. 1. The output nodes are shaded, the input nodes are dotted. The input nodes represent nodes that are not part of this class but are parents of nodes inside. The output nodes are those that can be parents of nodes outside instances.

---

[1] The outermost class has no encapsulating class, and is viewed as both a class and an instance.

[2] This example should not be seen as an attempt at modeling cows, but only as an illustration of concepts.

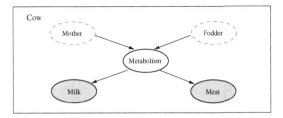

Fig. 1. A class modeling OMDs cows.

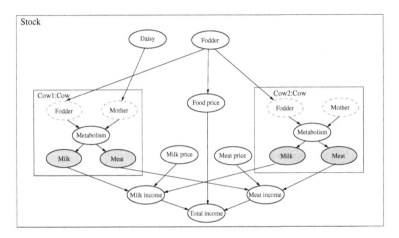

Fig. 2. Two instances of the **Cow** class joined to the **Stock** class through regular and reference links. Note that in [1] and [2] reference links are represented by double arrows, but here we will use single arrows.

When an instance of a class is created, it is plugged on to one class, its encapsulating class, and it can then be linked to the rest of the network through the interface. To do this, a new type of link needs to be defined; the reference link. The child node in a reference link must be an input node and the parent node is used as a parent of the children of this input node. The two nodes linked by a reference link must have the same number of states. In Fig. 2 two instances of the **Cow** class have been created and linked to the encapsulating class, **Stock**, using the interfaces of the instances and reference links. For example, *Daisy* will be a parent of *Cow*1.*Metabolism* via the input node *Cow*1.*Mother* and the reference link from *Daisy* to it. Note that only the interface nodes of the instances are accessible from **Stock**. The interface nodes of an instance are viewed as part of the instance, and as part of the encapsulating class of instance. This entails that all links connect nodes from the same instance. For example, the link from *Cow*1.*Milk* to *Milk income* in Fig. 2 is specified in the encapsulating class (the **Stock** class).

To allow the presence of input nodes without a parent, a default potential is introduced; a probability distribution over the states of the input node, used

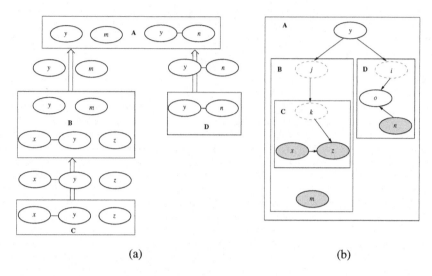

(a)   (b)

Fig. 3. (a) An IT where the fill-in messages can be seen. Note that y is in both **A**'s interface to **B** and to **D**. (b) An OOBN inducing the IT. Note that the input nodes are not in the IT, as they are overwritten by y.

to create a regular node if the input node is not a child in a reference link. *Cow2.Mother* in Fig. 2 is such a node.

The way OOBNs are built, with instances of classes inside a unique encapsulating class, ensures that a tree of instances can be constructed. We will term such a tree an Instance Tree (IT). The IT will have the outermost class as the root, and each instance inside this class will define a subtree with that instance as the root. An example of an IT, and the structure of an OOBN inducing it can be seen in Fig. 3 with the encapsulating class **A** as the root instance.

We define the interface between a node, X, in the IT and its parent in the IT as the output nodes of X and the parents of reference links to input nodes in X. It is worth noting that the interface nodes are part of both the instance where they are defined and the class encapsulating the instance, and hence in both the IT nodes for the instance and the encapsulating class. All communication between instances will take place via nodes in the interface. In Fig. 3a the interface between **A** and **B** consists of y and m. If two instances are supposed to communicate, the communication will follow the path in the tree connecting them. As can be seen from this tree structure, any OOBN can be translated into a multiply sectioned Bayesian Network [11]. The difference being that OOBNs have classes and a class hierarchy, so modifying a class may affect several nodes in the IT.

3   Triangulating the Instance Tree

An OOBN can be translated into a Bayesian network, and a Junction Tree (JT) is then constructed from this. We wish to accomplish a JT construction keeping the natural partitioning into a set of instances offered by OOBNs. To do this we need to come up with a compilation method for OOBNs and especially to deal with the triangulation step[3]. To keep the partitioning we must ensure that all links connect two nodes from the same instance, that is:

1. No links or moralizations exist between variables not in the same instance.
2. No fill-ins between variables not in the same instance are added during triangulation.

The first is true by construction, all parents of a node will be inside the same instance. Any link between two variables in two different instances must be between interface nodes, and these interface nodes will jointly be in at least one of the instances.

To ensure the second we will take outset in the IT. We propose a method to maintain this *modular* structure when triangulating. This method consists of two steps:

1. Propagating fill-ins between instances in the IT.
2. Triangulating the instances in the IT.

3.1   Propagation of Fill-ins

Since the interface sets between two instances in the IT d-separate them, we can apply fill-in propagation as explained in [12]. Note that we will only propagate fill-ins, moral links, and regular links between interface nodes (for ease of exposition we will call them all fill-ins). We fix the root of the tree to be the root instance of the IT, and only a collect of fill-ins will be performed.

Any elimination order for the leaves of the IT can be used, with the constraint that the interface nodes are not eliminated. Looking at Fig. 3 again, the nodes x, y and z are not eliminated from the instance C. As the fill-ins between nodes not yet eliminated will be the same no matter the sequence so far [9], any order will suffice in this step. This sequence yields a set of fill-ins and those involving two interface nodes are propagated upwards in the IT. In the example, the fill-in between x and y is propagated to $\mathbf{B}$. This process is repeated recursively until the root node has received fill-ins from all its descendants. Using this kind of fill-in propagation we obtain a valid triangulation [12]. This method of triangulation ensures that there are no fill-ins between variables not in the same instance as any fill-in propagated will be between interface nodes contained in the sending as well as the receiving instance in the IT.

Once fill-ins have been properly collected, we can triangulate each instance separately as the interfaces d-separate an instance from the instances in the IT above it. The only requirement is that the interface to the parent in the IT is eliminated last. Effort may be spent on finding an optimal triangulation of each instance in the IT under this constraint. Optimal triangulation of the instances will, however, not guarantee an optimal global triangulation. Instead the re-triangulation task if changes occur in the OOBN can be reduced.

---

[3] Once the triangulation is completed a JT is easily obtainable.

3.2   Using IC for Local Triangulation

If a BN is compiled into a JT, and some modifications are made to the BN, the changes will require a new compilation process of the entire BN in order to obtain the resulting JT. This re-compilation will, in many cases, take more effort than necessary. It seems quite logical to assume that, if only few changes have been made, most of the processing needed to obtain the JT is redundant.

Fig. 4 illustrates the main idea behind IC. At the upper left side the initial BN, **N**, is shown detailing only the relevant portion for this example. The rest of the network will not play any role and that is what IC takes advantage of. If we compile **N** we will obtain the JT, **T**, just below. At the upper right side, the initial BN has been modified, producing **N'**. A way of obtaining the new **T'** will be to compile the entire BN **N'**. Nevertheless, from this simple example it is apparent that only a small part of **N'** needs to be re-compiled.

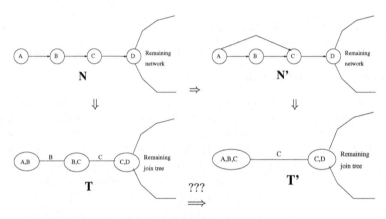

Fig. 4. Incremental Compilation reaches the resulting JT avoiding a full re-compilation.

The Maximal Prime Subgraph Decomposition (MPSD) is the key to accomplishing the step **T** → **T'** without compiling **N'**. As shown in [7], Maximal Prime Subgraphs (MPSs) can be triangulated independently of each other. The MPSD is unique for a BN and easy to construct from any JT if it has been constructed using a triangulation where there are no redundant fill-ins. The MPSD is obtained by aggregating pairs of cliques whose common separator is not complete in the moral graph. Fig. 5 shows the decomposition for the well-known Asia example from [6]. For every modification, the affected MPSs are detected. The nodes contained in these and the links between them will be re-compiled (and therefore, re-triangulated), ignoring the rest of the network. This partial compilation yields a tree that will substitute the corresponding *old* part in the JT.

In [3] four possible modifications affecting the tree structure are studied: removal of an arc/node and addition of an arc/node. In this context we also need to consider the addition or removal of a fill-in (between two interface nodes), as messages along the IT contain this kind of information.

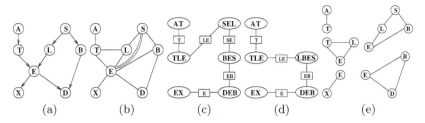

Fig. 5. (a) The Asia network. (b) Moral and triangulated graph for Asia. (c) A JT for Asia. (d) Maximal Prime Subgraph Tree for Asia. (e) Maximal Prime Subgraph Decomposition for Asia.

To perform fill-in addition or removal operations we have extended the original IC procedure by using the same method for adding or removing a fill-in $A - B$ as [3] does for processing a link $A \rightarrow B$. In the following, we give some examples to illustrate the method.

Suppose that an instance represents the Asia network structure, and it receives a fill-in between X and D (Fig. 6.a). This modification will mark the MPSs $[EX]$ and $[DEB]$ (see Fig. 5.d). So, it is sufficient to only consider the four nodes E, X, D and B and the links between them (Fig. 6.b). Compilation yields the JT for this small graph (Fig. 6.c). This JT will replace the old part and has to be connected to the rest of the JT. Fig. 6.d and Fig. 6.e show the old tree **T** and the new one **T'**, where the shaded areas represent the modified parts.

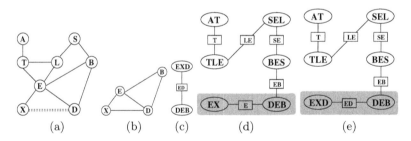

Fig. 6. MPSD-based incremental compilation of Asia when adding fill-in $X - D$.

The reverse operation may happen as well: we previously had a fill-in between X and D and we receive the message that it is absent. This situation is illustrated in Fig. 7.

As this example is quite simple, we shall give a more complex one (Fig. 8.a). We assume we have received a new fill-in, A-S. Now, there is an MPS ($[TLE]$) in the tree path from the MPS containing the family of S, $[LBES]$, and the one containing A, $[AT]$. So, the affected subgraph of this modification contains the nodes A, T, L, E, S and B. Fig. 8.b shows this together with a re-triangulation. Fig. 8.c presents the corresponding JT and Fig. 8.d and 8.e depict the old and new JTs with the affected parts shaded. The reverse operation is very similar.

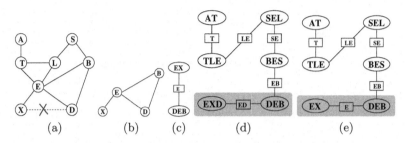

Fig. 7. MPSD-based incremental compilation of Asia when removing the fill-in $X - D$.

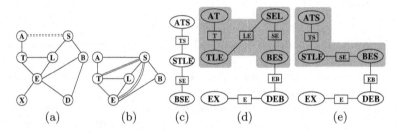

Fig. 8. MPSD-based incremental compilation of Asia when adding fill-in $A - S$.

4   OOBNs in Highly Dynamic Domains

In highly dynamic domains, e.g. tracking, lots of changes to the network happen while in use. Typically, reference links and instances come and go as objects appear and disappear. This means that there might not be sufficient time for a complete recompilation of the network each time a change has occurred. The goal is to re-triangulate only the necessary parts of the network. We will do this by applying the two-step triangulation method described previously. In the following we will show how the method can be used for fast re-triangulation, making it a useful tool in highly dynamic domains. There are nine (four) different changes that can be made, the first eight (three) can only occur in the outermost class, otherwise it will fall under the last:

1. Adding/removing a regular link/node.
2. Adding/removing a reference link.
3. Adding/removing an instance.
4. Changing a class specification.

Note that fill-in propagation only occurs in 4., as the others take place in the root instance of the IT, and fill-ins are only propagated upwards in the IT. We let all interface nodes be both in their instance and in the encapsulating class.

Adding/removing a link/node will force a re-triangulation of the root instance, but using IC, only the relevant subset of the graph will be re-triangulated. This will not change the triangulation of instances plugged to the root instance, as they can be triangulated independently of the rest of the network due to the

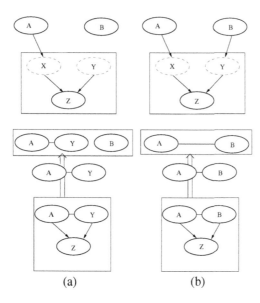

(a)   (b)

Fig. 9. (a) An OOBN and the triangulated IT achieved from it. (b) A reference has been added and the triangulation of the IT has changed.

fill-in propagation scheme. If moralizations or fill-ins between interface nodes of an instance appear/disappear, they will only be relevant for the root instance.

Adding/removing a reference link will not affect the triangulation of the instance where the child of the link is defined. The triangulation of all instances of a class are identical, except for names of reference nodes[4]. If a reference link is added, the child of the reference link will have its name changed, and the default potential for that node, which was used previously, will be removed from the JT. If a reference link is removed, the name of the child will also change, and the default potential will be added to the JT. None of this changes the triangulation.

However, the interface to the parent in the IT will change, and hence the message sent upwards during fill-in propagation may change. Adding a reference link will add the parent of the link to the interface to the instance of the child and remove the child. Removing a reference link will remove the parent from the interface and add the input node of the instance that was the child of the link. If a fill-in including the child of the reference link was sent by the instance during propagate fill-ins, the message is changed, as this fill-in now includes a different node. A re-triangulation of the root instance using IC will be triggered. Again, only the relevant part of the root instance will be re-triangulated.

In Fig. 9.a an example of an OOBN is shown on top of the triangulation of the IT and the fill-ins propagated. The JT for this OOBN will have potentials over A, B, Y and Z. If a reference link from B to Y is added the name of Y will change to B in the instance, B will replace Y in the interface to the root instance of the IT. This changes the message to be sent, so the new message will

---

[4] The class of an instance is compiled independently of the uses of the instances.

be propagated, and the root re-triangulated (Fig. 9.b). If the reference from B to Y is removed, the situation will return to that in Fig. 9.a.

Adding/removing an instance will not affect the local triangulation of the instance, as all classes will be triangulated when specification of them is done.

Adding an instance with no links will not induce any fill-ins in other instances in the IT, as the instance will be separated from the rest of the network until regular links and reference links are added. So adding an instance will not require any fill-in propagation or re-triangulation as this will be handled when links are added to or from the instance. The IT will be updated with the new sub-tree, and the overall JT will have the JT for the instance added, and in effect become a forest.

Removing an instance will be handled by removing the sub-tree for the instance from the IT, and removing the JT associated with it from the overall JT. The root instance will be re-triangulated without the fill-ins received from the removed instance using IC.

Changing a class specification can include any of the previously mentioned actions any number of times, so to avoid fill-in propagation more than once, propagation will not occur before modification of the class is completed. The changes to the class are handled by viewing the class as the root instance of its own local IT and using the techniques described above.

Once modification of the class is finished, the fill-ins between the interface nodes are found. The class will already be triangulated and the JT found by this triangulation will substitute the JT part associated with each instance of the class in the overall JT. Note that some names may be changed in the various instances, through reference links, this should be handled when substituting the JT part.

All that remains now is to propagate the fill-ins by a collect fill-ins initiated by the root instance, and re-triangulate the classes where changes has occured, either through new fill-ins or manual changes. The OOBN is triangulated again, using only local operations.

In this scheme it is worth noting that all the information needed to re-triangulate any instance will be available locally in each instance after propagation of fill-ins has been done. A class can be precompiled, and the JT obtained hereby can easily be incorporated into a JT for an OOBN.

It may be expedient to only have the interface nodes that are linked to the encapsulating class be represented there. This will require that all instances of a class are triangulated separately, and re-triangulated whenever the links to the interface nodes changes instead of just using the triangulation of the class for all instances. The best method will be a question of time spent on re-triangulation versus the quality of the triangulation.

5   Conclusion

We have presented a way of performing a global triangulation over an OOBN efficiently keeping the structure of instances induced by the OOBN. For that purpose we have used the instance tree of the OOBN. For modifications to OOBNs we have taken advantage of incremental compilation, enhancing it to handle fill-ins. These contributions enable us to precompile classes and "plug" the JT for a class into already existing JTs, whenever an instance of it is added. This provides an environment suited for dealing with dynamic domains.

Acknowledgements

The author M. Julia Flores has collaborated in this paper during a stay as a research fellow visitor at the Decision Support Systems Group of Aalborg University, and her work has been partially supported by the Spanish Ministerio de Ciencia y Tecnología (MCyT), under project TIC2001-2973-C05-05.

References

1. O. Bangsø and P.-H. Wuillemin. Object oriented Bayesian networks, a framework for top-down specification of large Bayesian networks with repetitive structures. Technical report, Department of Computer Science, Aalborg University, Denmark, 2000.
2. O. Bangsø and P.-H. Wuillemin. Top-down construction and repetitive structures representation in Bayesian networks. In *Proceedings of the Thirteenth International FLAIRS Conference*, Florida, USA, 2000.
3. M. J. Flores, J. A. Gámez, and K. G. Olesen. Incremental compilation of a Bayesian network. pages 233–240. Morgan Kaufmann Publishers, 2003. Proceedings of the Fifteenth Conference on Uncertainty in Artificial Intelligence (UAI-03).
4. D. Koller and A. Pfeffer. Object-oriented Bayesian networks. In Dan Geiger and Prakash P. Shenoy, editors, *Proceedings of the Thirteenth Conference on Uncertainty in Artificial Intelligence*, pages 302–313, San Francisco, 1997. Morgan Kaufmann Publishers, San Francisco.
5. K. B. Laskey and S. M. Mahoney. Network fragments: Representing knowledge for constructing probabilistic models. In Dan Geiger and Prakash P. Shenoy, editors, *Proceedings of the Thirteenth Conference on Uncertainty in Artificial Intelligence*, pages 302–313, San Francisco, 1997. Morgan Kaufmann Publishers, San Francisco.
6. S. L. Lauritzen and D. J. Spiegelhalter. Local computations with probabilities on graphical structures and their application to expert systems. 50:157–224, 1988.
7. K. G. Olesen and A. Madsen. Maximal prime subgraph decomposition of bayesian networks. Part B. bf 32:1:21–31, 2002.
8. M. Pradhan, G. Prova, B. Middleton, and M. Henrion. Knowledge engineering for large belief networks. 1994.
9. D. J. Rose. Triangulated graphs and the elimination process. 32:597–609, 1970.
10. S. Srinivas. A probabilistic approach to hierarchical model-based diagnosis. 1994.
11. Y. Xiang. *Probabilistic Reasoning in Multiagent Systems. A graphical models approach*. Cambridge University Press, Cambridge, UK, 2002.
12. Y. Xiang and F. V. Jensen. Inference in Multiply Sectioned Bayesian networks with extended Shafer-Shenoy and lazy propagation. In *Proceedings of the Fifteenth Conference on Uncertainty in Artificial Intelligence (UAI-99)*, pages 680–687. Morgan Kaufmann Publishers, San Francisco, 1999.

Real-Time Extensions in Multi-agent Communication

Jose Soler, Vicente Julián, Ana García-Fornes, and Vicente Botti

Departamento de Sistemas Informáticos y Computación, Spain
{jsoler,vinglada,agarcia,vbotti}@dsic.upv.es
http://www.dsic.upv.es/users/ia

Abstract. The agent and multi-agent system paradigm has changed the development process of certain software systems. The technologies employed in multi-agent systems must be adapted for their correct utilization in real-time environments. The main deficiencies detected for the correct integration of these systems are examined in this article. The paper proposes a solution for the specification of some temporal restrictions in the system interactions. The article shows an approximation allowing the incorporation of time in the agent communication process for real-time environments. The article also presents an example that illustrates the applicability of the proposal.

1 Introduction

Communication among agents constitutes one of the most important aspects in the multi-agent system area (MAS). Several works related to the communication problem have been developed in the last few years. Among the principal advances in this area we can highlight the specification of standard communication languages [5] [4] and content languages [7][8] as well as the development of interaction protocols that permit the performance of complex negotiation processes [6]. Different multi-agent systems have been successfully implemented in numerous areas. In these systems, the agents are capable of interacting with each other using the existing languages and protocols.

Nevertheless, the current approaches have certain deficiencies in certain environments; specifically, the applicability of multi-agent systems to real-time environments requires specific functionalities that are not currently available. In environments of this type, is necessary an appropriate time management in the communicative processes. This management includes the control of the message level and the content level. Moreover, agents that work in these environments must fulfil specific temporal restrictions, which imply the use of specific real-time agent architectures.

The basic requirements that must be satisfied in order to develop real-time MAS are identified in this article. The fulfilment of these requirements would allow the use of high-level communication mechanisms in real-time environments. These systems would be more flexible and adaptable. One of these requirements refers to the need for temporal restrictions on the communicative acts, or on the actions associated with them. To solve this problem, this article shows how to incorporate the concept of time into the communication processes among agents, expressing the most common temporal conditions.

R. Conejo et al. (Eds.): CAEPIA-TTIA 2003, LNAI 3040, pp. 468–477, 2004.

The rest of the article is structured as follows: in section 2, the requirements that a real-time MAS must satisfy are identified, in section 3 a proposal for the incorporation of temporal restrictions in the agent messages is described. These restrictions are related to the reception of messages and to the execution of associated actions. The proposal is presented as a set of extensions over FIPA SL. Section 4 shows an example of real-time MAS, where the extensions explained in the previous section are employed. Finally in section 5, some conclusions are explained.

2 Requirements of a Real-Time MAS

The real-time MAS area is still in a premature state of development which is why we don't have clear and consolidated definitions. Nevertheless, we can perform a characterization of the basic requirements of real-time systems and of real-time distributed systems [10], and we can try to move them to platform agents in order to be able to develop MAS that has real-time extensions. The requirements that should be met are:

Time Representation in the Communication Process. To be able to reason over the temporal instant at which an event is produced, it is necessary to integrate the time concept inside the information transmitted among the different entities that make up a distributed system. The agent communication language FIPA ACL was not developed with these features in mind. It will be necessary to add the mechanisms that facilitate the integration of the time concept without having to resort to ad-hoc solutions that differ between applications and that endanger the system interoperability.

Global Time Management. In real-time distributed systems it is absolutely necessary to have a common global time for all the elements that make up the system. There are several strategies that manage and synchronize the clocks of each computer. Different levels of precision are obtained with each of them. The Network Time Protocol (NTP) [11] for Internet or Cristian's algorithm for intranet [2] are some of the most important algorithms. Platform Agents must provide this global time service, so that the agents can be synchronized. Platform agents should also be adapted to have a global time for the agents of diverse platforms that want to interact.

Real-Time Communication. In real-time distributed systems, it is necessary be able to assure the communication. This supposes communication protocols with a low and restricted latency[1], as well as fault detection. One example is the CAN protocol [13]. Usually, the problem where it is feasible to use the MAS paradigm does not need such strict restrictions for communication. However, there is no doubt about the need for efficient protocols to assure a maximal delivery message time to the developed applications.

Hard Resource Management. The execution of tasks in real-time systems is assured, by exercising a strict control on the available resources. There is a planning

---

[1] Latency: interval between the sending of a message and its reception.

algorithm that assures the task execution and the coherent use of resources. The agent platforms must implement hard resource management. This is very important when facilitating agent mobility among platforms.

Fault Tolerant Execution. Real-time systems are considered to be predictable. However, it is also indispensable for them to develop fault tolerant systems. This is fundamental since the systems that are controlled are usually critical and a system fall would be catastrophic. A relevant work in this area is [3]. The fault tolerance in MAS must be twofold. First, the execution of the agents must be assured after an internal failure, as well as after a failure in the communication process. Platform agents must be capable of assuring certain requirements in order to offer communication mechanisms and strategies that permit agent execution recovery.

3 Time Representation in FIPA

It is important to highlight that agent languages as FIPA ACL are languages that focus on the asynchronous communication among agents. This means that an agent sends a message and it does not get blocked waiting for a response. There are several basic points about the communication among agents in which it would be useful to introduce the time element.

First, an agent with temporal restrictions may need to have a response within a specific time. If this is not possible, the agent must be able to develop some alternative actions. The agent should indicate in its message what the maximum time for waiting the response message is.

Secondly, an agent requests other agents to perform an action. These actions can be characterized by the time; for example, to begin an action at a specific time or to complete an action before a deadline, etc. On the other hand there exists the need to specify interaction protocols that have time as a determinant factor which extends the current FIPA functionalities. For example: the request for periodic actions. The different cases are described in the following points.

3.1 Maximum Time of Message Response

A FIPA ACL message contains the *reply-by* field which allows us to represent the maximum time for a message response. An example of this temporal restriction is shown in Figure 1. The figure shows a request interaction where the need to receive an answer before 3 seconds is expressed.

The value indicated in the *reply-by* field can be a global time or a relative time which begins at message reception. The following message shows a query using a relative time of 3 seconds:

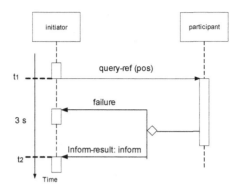

Fig. 1. AUML Scheme of a query interaction with a deadline of 3 seconds.

```
( query
 :sender initator
 :receiver responder
 :language fipa-sl
 :protocol fipa-query
 :reply-to prueba1
 :reply-by +00000000T000003000
 :content ( .... )                    )
```

3.2 Time in Message Content

The structure of the FIPA ACL message should not be modified, because it is considered to be a standard. Therefore, it will be necessary to introduce temporal restrictions into the message content. To do this, one of the different time representations that are already in the literature can be used. A review of these can be seen in [14].

The required temporal restrictions for MAS are usually related to the agent action execution. For example, an agent can request an action that must be finished before a deadline or an action that must be initiated at a specific time. This paper presents a set of extensions for FIPA SL content language [7] in order to represent these temporal restrictions. These extensions permit an explicit representation of point-based time [14]. The added temporal restrictions are exclusively associated to action executions. *After, before* and *at* are the atomic operators that we have adopted in order to provide the needed expressiveness. The following grammatical rules define the terms that extend FIPA SL:

```
ActionExpression    =  "(" "action"  Agent   TermOrIE
                              TemporalExpression ")"
                    | "(" "action"  Agent   TermOrIE ")"
                    | "(" "|"  ActionExpression
                              ActionExpression    ")"
                    | "(" ";"  ActioExpression
                              ActionExpression    ")"
```

```
TemporalExpression     = IntervalExpresion
                       | IntervalExpression   PeriodicTerm
                       | DurationExpression
                       | DurationExpression   PeriodicTerm

IntervalExpression     =  "(" "begin"   TemporalTerm ")"
                       |  "(" "end"     TemporalTerm ")"
                       |  "(" "begin"   TemporalTerm
                              "end"     TemporalTerm ")"

DurationExpression     =  "(" "during"
                              "begin"   TemporalPTerm
                              "end"     TemporalPTerm ")"

TemporalTerm           =  TemporalPTerm
                       |  "(" "after"  DateTime ")"
                       |  "(" "before" DateTime ")"

TemporalPTerm          =  "(" "at"      DateTime ")"
                       |  "(" "at"      DateTime
                              "duration"  DateTime* ")"

PeriodicTerm           =  "(" "every" DateTime*
                              "during"  DateTime* ")"
```

The term DateTime* denotes a duration. It is an expression that begins with "+".

With the extensions proposed for FIPA SL, we can express the following temporal restrictions over the actions:

1. Restrictions at the beginning of an action by means of the expression `begin`: it is possible to specify a specific time (t) within which the action has to begin (at t), or an interval of time [t + ε] in which it has to be initiated (at t duration 10), where t is a specific time, and ε is a relative value. Also, a temporal limit can be expressed for the beginning of the action using the expressions (before t) and (after t). For example: (begin (before 20020505T103503000))

2. Restrictions for the end of an action can be expressed by means of the expression `end`: the same restrictions expressed above can be used in this case. For example: (end (before +0000000T000003000))

3. Restrictions on the execution interval of the action by means of the expression `begin` - `end`. For example: (begin (after 20030206T150503000)) end (before 20030206T150506000))

4. Restrictions on the periodic execution of actions by means of the expression `every` - `until`: we will represent the periodic execution of an action up to a certain instant. The period will always be indicated by means of a temporary relative value. For example: (begin (before 20030206T150500000) (every +0000000T000030000 during +0000000T010000000)). In this case, the receiver should start the action before 15:05, and the action must be repeated every 30 seconds for 1 hour.

5. Restrictions on the action duration by means of `during` `begin` - `end`: this allows us to indicate the duration of the action execution. For example:

```
(to_move)  (during begin (at 20030107T050300000) end (at
20030107T050320000)).
```
In this case, a robot should begin to move at 5:03:00 and it should finish at exactly 5:03:20.

When an agent receives a message with one of these temporal restrictions, it must be capable of interpreting the message. Therefore, the agent must know whether it is capable of executing the action with its restrictions.

An example of the desired expressiveness is shown in Figure 2. In this case, Robot 1 sends a request so that Robot 2 moves itself a specific distance by means of the action *to_move*. The instant at which it must begin to move is determined in t1. In this case, it must be later than t1.

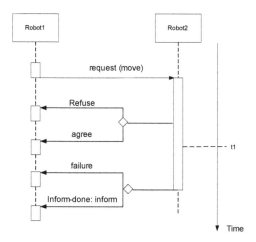

Fig. 2. Request interaction with a temporal restriction.

In this case, the message generated to initiate the interaction is the following:

```
( request
  :sender robot1
  :receiver robot2
  :language extended-fipa-sl
  :ontology robot
  :protocol fipa-request
  :reply-to test2
  :content ( action  robot2 ( move( :x 10 :y 50))
           ( begin ( after 20030610T150003000 )) ) )
```

3.3   Time Synchronization

Some authors have used the NTP algorithm where the sending and receiving of messages is done by means of ACL messages [9]. This solution can serve to synchronize clocks in some e-commerce transactions but it cannot be employed in real-time systems. In these systems, a more precise synchronization is necessary. In an agent platform with real-time characteristics, this time synchronization might be a platform service.

3.4 Integration in an Agent Platform

The extensions over FIPA described above are not sufficient to develop real-time MAS. An agent architecture that efficiently supports and manages the temporal restrictions represented in messages is required. The proposed extensions have been successfully joined in SIMBA platform [12]. SIMBA allows us to build real-time MAS in accordance with the considerations presented in section 2. The agents in this platform not only understand the expressed restrictions, but they are capable of assuring the fulfilment of these restrictions. An agent in SIMBA understands the time representation in the communicative processes which permits the internal management of tasks and resources and gives support to a controlled agent execution. A SIMBA platform is made up of a set of real-time agents, which are based on ARTIS agent architecture [1], and a special agent (Manager Platform Agent -MPA-), which is in charge of FIPA platform management services.

4 Application Example

The example consists of developing a system that manages different autonomous robots that are placed in a closed environment. These robots accept orders from an interface agent in order to jointly move an object from an initial position to a final position. The required functionality of the system can be summarized in the following sequence of phases (shown in Figure 3):

1. The object movement action is introduced into the system through an interface agent.
2. The robot team is created to move the object (the team can be formed by more than 2 robots).
3. The planning for positioning the robots is done.
4. The robots move to the initial positions.
5. The object is moved by the robots.
6. The movement is monitored to be able to take corrective action if necessary.

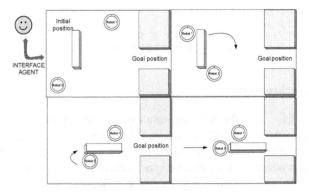

Fig. 3. A possible scenario.

In this example, the platform is comprised of a set of autonomous robots, implemented as real-time agents, and the interface agent. The robot agents have two roles, depending on whether the robot is the team boss or just a member. The team boss is in charge of planning the tasks and, then, communicating these tasks to the rest of the team.

The possible identified interactions are the following:

1. Make a request (I1). The interface agent makes a movement request to a robot agent of the system.
2. Create a team (I2). Once there is a movement goal, the robot team must be created. This process must be started by the robot that receives the request from the interface. This agent assumes the boss role of the team.
3. Request position (I3). On some occasions, a robot agent can request positions from other robot agents.
4. Request state (I4). The robot agent that has the boss role requests what another robot is currently doing.
5. Send orders (I5). The boss robot will interact with the rest of the robot agents by sending action orders to accomplish the system goal.

The I5 interaction is shown in Figure 1. In this case, the boss robot sends a movement order to the subordinate robot. This order implies that the receiver must start its movement to a specific position at a time expressed in the temporal constraint.

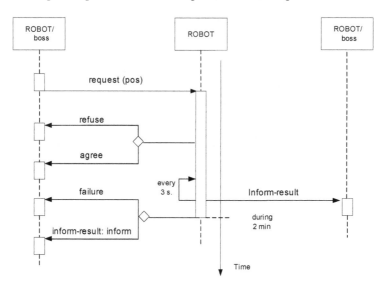

Fig. 4. AUML diagram for I3 interaction.

In another temporally restricted interaction, Figure 4 shows the design of the I3 interaction. In this interaction, we use the request protocol incorporating a periodic action. This action is another communicative act (an inform message), which indicates the robot position. The period for the action is 3 seconds, and the action must be performed until the maximum time is reached.

The message sent by the boss robot to ask for a position is the following:

```
( request
  :sender robot_1
  :receiver robot_2
  :language extended-fipa-sl
  :ontology robot
  :protocol request
  :reply-by +00000000T000003000
  :reply-to posicion1
  :content ( action robot_2
             (inform-ref
              :sender robot_2
              :receiver robot_1
              :content "((iota (sequence ?x ?y ?th)
                      (robot :id knijo :pos
                             (posicion (punto ?x ?y)?th ))))"
          (at 20030605T143003000 (every +0000000T000003000
                                 during +00000000T000200000 ))))
```

5 Conclusions

The incorporation of the time concept into the interactions of a multi-agent system is an important feature to be able to use systems of this type in environments with temporal restrictions. This article has described how to add temporal information to communicative processes by means of an extension of the FIPA SL content language. This temporal information must be understood and validated by the agents that receive the messages. They can then decide whether the restrictions are feasible or not. This is one of the reasons for the need for specific architectures for environments of this kind. In our proposal, we employ the SIMBA platform, which is a specific multi-agent platform for real-time environments. We are currently working on the example presented in the previous section. The use of the temporal extensions in messages allows us to express certain behaviours in the interaction processes that were previously impossible to specify without these extensions.

Acknowledgements

This work has been funded by grant number DPI2002-04434-C04-02 of the Spanish government and by grant number CTIDIB/2002/61 of the Generalitat Valenciana.

References

1. Botti, V., Carrascosa, C., Julian, V., and Soler, J. (1999). Modelling agents in hard real-time environments. In MAAMAW'99, volume 1647 of LNAI, Springer-Verlag. 63–76
2. Cristian, F., Fetzer, C.: Probabilistic Internal Clock Synchronization. In Proc. of 12th Symposium on Reliable Distributed Systems. IEEE Computer Society Press.(1994) 22–31

3. Cristian, F.: Understanding Fault-Tolerant Distributed Systems. Comm. ACM, Vol 34 (2). (1991) 57-78

4. Finin, T; Fritzson, R; Mckay, D; McEntire, R. "KQML as an Agent Communication Language". Proc 3rd Int. Conf. On Information and Knowledge Management, 1994.

5. FIPA: FIPA ACL Message Structure Specification. Technical Report SC00061G, http://www.fipa.org/specs/fipa00061/

6. FIPA: FIPA Interaction Protocol Library Specification. Technical Report, http://www.fipa.org/specs/fipa00025/

7. FIPA: FIPA SL Content Language Specification. Technical Report SC00008G, http://www.fipa.org/specs/fipa00008/

8. Genesereth, M. R., Fikes, R.: *Knowledge Interchange Format.*- Report Logic-92-1. Stanford:, 1992.- Manual de referencia, versión 3.0.

9. Jennings B., Brennan R., Gustavsson R., Feldt R., Pitt J., Prouskas K., Quantz J., FIPA-compliant Agents for Real-time Control of Intelligent Network Traffic, *Computer Networks,* 31, 2017-2036, (1999).

10. Kopetz, H.: REAL TIME SYSTEMS: Design Principles for Distributed Embedded Applications. Kluwer Academic Publisher (1997)

11. Mills, D.: Improved Algorithms for Synchronizing Computer Network Clocks. In: IEEE Transactions Networks, June (1995) 245–254

12. Soler, J., Julian, V., Rebollo, M., Carrascosa, C., and Botti, V. Towards a real-time MAS architecture. In Proc. of Challenges in Open Agent Systems. AAMAS'02, Bolonia (2002).

13. Tindell, K. Burns, A.: Guaranteeing message latencies on Control Area Network (CAN). Proc of the 1st International CAN Conference (1994).

14. Vila, L.: On temporal representation and reasoning in knowledge-based systems. Monografies de l'IIIA. Consell Superior d'Invetigacions Científiques. 1995

Representing Canonical Models
as Probability Trees

José del Sagrado[1] and Antonio Salmerón[2]

[1] Dept. of Languages and Computation
[2] Dept. of Statistics and Applied Mathematics
University of Almería
Almería, 04120, Spain

Abstract. Canonical models are useful because they simplify the construction of probabilistic models exploiting causal patterns. In this paper we study the relationships between canonical models and their representation and computation using probability trees, placing special emphasis on the approximation of very large canonical models.

1 Introduction

One of the major problems in building a probabilistic network model of a domain is to provide a full set of conditional probabilities $P(y|\mathbf{x})$ relating each possible value y of each variable Y to every set of possible values $\mathbf{x}$ of the set of variables $\mathbf{X}$ which have been identified as the direct causes of Y. Thus for a variable Y, with domain $\{y_1, y_2, y_3\}$, which has two direct causes X_1 and X_2 whose domains are $\{x_{11}, x_{12}, x_{13}\}$ and $\{x_{21}, x_{22}, x_{23}\}$, respectively, it is necessary to provide estimates of $p(y_1|x_{11}, x_{21})$, $p(y_1|x_{11}, x_{22})$, $\cdots$, $p(y_3|x_{13}, x_{23})$. This is a considerable task that is complicated by the fact that the various causes often point to disparate frames of knowledge whose only connection is that they have a common consequence [10]. Canonical models of interaction between multiple causes provide a means of computing the necessary set of conditional probabilities by specifying only the conditional probabilities of the cause given a single effect.

The first model suggested was the Noisy OR [9, 10], based on a form of disjunctive interaction in which any member of a set of causes can make a particular event likely to occur, and this likelihood is not diminished by the occurrence of several causes simultaneously. Pearl's model only admits binary variables and has subsequently been adapted and generalised by several authors. Henrion [7] extended the model allowing the occurrence of the event, even when all the direct causes identified by the model are absent, by including a "leak" probability. Díez [5] generalises the model to take account of multi-valued events. Finally, Srinivas [12] completes the generalisation, by allowing multi-valued causes and permitting the combination of the effect of the causes to be calculated by any discrete function. Recently, a general framework for canonical models has been proposed [6]. The main advantage of this general framework is that can be easily used to generate other canonical models.

R. Conejo et al. (Eds.): CAEPIA-TTIA 2003, LNAI 3040, pp. 478–487, 2004.

Though specific algorithms for inference in Bayesian networks with canonical models have been developed, the most general approach consists of transforming the canonical model into a probability distribution and then use a standard inference algorithm. Probability distributions are usually represented as tables of real numbers. This representation is exponential in the number of variables in the distribution. A more compact representation is based on probability trees [1]. They are particularly useful when there are regularities in the probability distributions represented. The probability distributions resulting from canonical models contain many regularities, what suggests that the joint use of canonical models and probability trees can be highly beneficial.

Our proposal is to combine the use of canonical models and probability trees in order to represent the conditional probabilities needed to define a probabilistic network model. The paper is structured as follows. In Section 2 we briefly describe the general framework for canonical models. Section 3 studies the basic use of probability trees. In Section 4 we face to the problem of representing and computing canonical models using probability trees. The paper ends with conclusions in Section 5.

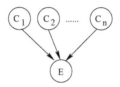

Fig. 1. Basic structure of a canonical model.

2   Canonical Models

The basic structure of a canonical model is depicted in Figure 1. A canonical model represents a probabilistic relationship among a finite number of variables. We will consider a variable E which is influenced by its parents $\{C_1, C_2, \cdots, C_n\}$, where all the variables involved in the models are discrete and have a finite number of values. Although canonical models can describe different types of causal interactions (E can be seen as the effect and $\{C_1, C_2, \cdots, C_n\}$ as its set of causes), they can be considered just as particular probabilistic relationships, leaving out any causal interpretation.

Díez and Druzdzel [6] provide a classification for canonical models, distinguishing among three categories:

1. *Deterministic models.* When E is a function of the C_i's, $e = f(c_1, \cdots, c_n)$. Then, the conditional probability $P(e|\mathbf{c})$ is given by

$$P(e|\mathbf{c}) = \begin{cases} 1 \text{ if } e = f(\mathbf{c}), \\ 0 \text{ otherwise,} \end{cases} \tag{1}$$

where f describes the type of interaction between $\{C_1, \cdots, C_n\}$ and E. Usually, f is a logical operator such as OR, AND, XOR or NEG, but also it can be a function as MAX or MIN. Function f also induces the valid domains of the variables involved in the model. For instance, if f is a logical operator all the variables have to be binary, but in the case of MAX and MIN we can use ordinal variables. The name of the model is taken from function f.

2. *Noisy models*. They indicate that E is the result of a combination of intermediate events Z_i which are caused by C_i. This situation is depicted in Figure 2, which corresponds to a general noisy model. In this case, we have a conditional distribution $P(z_i|c_i)$ representing the relationship between C_i and Z_i and a deterministic model representing the relationship between the Z_i's and E. Variables Z_i can be eliminated from the model by marginalisation and the conditional probability $P(e|\mathbf{c})$ for all noisy models is given by [6]

$$P(e|\mathbf{c}) = \sum_{\mathbf{z}|f(\mathbf{z})=e} \prod_i P(z_i|c_i). \tag{2}$$

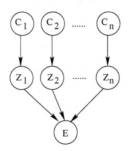

Fig. 2. General structure of noisy models.

3. *Leaky models*. They cover situations in which it is unfeasible to identify all the variables that have a direct influence over E. Including a "leak" probability, $P(e|\neg c_1, \cdots, \neg c_n)$, variable E in question may occur even when $\neg\{C_1, \cdots, C_n\}$. Díez and Druzdzel [6] show how to incorporate this "leak" probability to a general noisy model, obtaining the conditional probability $P(e|\mathbf{c})$ as

$$P(e|\mathbf{c}) = \sum_{\mathbf{z}} \left(\prod_i P(z_i|c_i) \right) \cdot \left(\sum_{e_L|f(\mathbf{z},e_L)} P(e_L) \right), \tag{3}$$

where $P(e_L)$ is a (vectorial) parameter that represents the leak probability. Usually, in real situations, $P(e_L)$ is given by

$$\begin{cases} P(e_L) = P(e|\neg c_1, \cdots, \neg c_n) \\ P(\neg e_L) = 1 - P(e|\neg c_1, \cdots, \neg c_n) \end{cases} \tag{4}$$

The main advantage of canonical models is the reduction, from an exponential to a linear order of magnitude, of the number of parameters necessary to specify the conditional probability distribution $P(e|\mathbf{c})$. Also, the parameters in canonical models lend themselves to more intuitive interpretations, simplifying the construction of a probabilistic network model.

3   Probability Trees

Once the model has been specified, in order to carry out inference tasks, it must be represented using a data structure compatible with inference algorithms. Traditionally, probability distributions have been represented as tables of real numbers, but recently probability trees [1–3] have been used rather than tables, since they provide a more compact and flexible representation. Actually, probability represent not only probability distributions, but any non-negative function (also called potentials).

A *probability tree* is a directed labeled tree, where each internal node represents a variable and each leaf node represents a probability value. Each internal node has one outgoing arc for each state of the variable associated with that node. Each leaf contains a non-negative real number. The *size* of a tree $\mathcal{T}$, denoted as $size(\mathcal{T})$, is defined as its number of leaves.

A probability tree $\mathcal{T}$ on variables $\mathbf{X}$ represents a potential $\phi : \Omega_{\mathbf{X}} \to \mathbb{R}_0^+$ if for each $\mathbf{x} \in \Omega_{\mathbf{X}}$ the value $\phi(\mathbf{x})$ is the number stored in the leaf node that is reached by starting from the root node and selecting the child corresponding to coordinate x_i for each internal node labeled with $X_i \in \mathbf{X}$.

A probability tree is usually more a compact representation of a potential than a table. This fact is illustrated in Figure 3, which displays a potential ϕ and its representation using a probability tree. The tree contains the same information as the table, but using five values instead of eight. Furthermore, trees allow to obtain even more compact representations in exchange of loosing accuracy, what is specially interesting when inference must be carried out under limited resources (memory or CPU). This is achieved by pruning some leaves and replacing them by the average value, as shown in the second tree in Fig. (3).

In the worst case the size of a tree will be equal to the size of the corresponding probability table, but usually the presence of regularities will reduce the size of the probability tree, achieving a more efficient inference.

Propagation algorithms require two basic operations over potentials: *combination* and *marginalisation*. Both can be carried out directly over probability trees (see [3] for more details). The combination of two trees $\mathcal{T}_1$ and $\mathcal{T}_2$ associated with potentials ϕ_1 and ϕ_2, respectively is denoted by $\mathcal{T}_1 \otimes \mathcal{T}_2$, and is a tree representing the pointwise multiplication of $\phi_1 \cdot \phi_2$. Given a tree $\mathcal{T}$ associated with a potential ϕ defined over $\mathbf{X}$, $\mathcal{T}^{\downarrow \mathbf{Y}}$ is its marginal over $\mathbf{Y} \subset \mathbf{X}$.

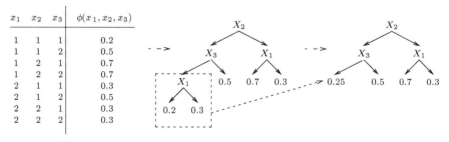

x_1	x_2	x_3	$\phi(x_1, x_2, x_3)$
1	1	1	0.2
1	1	2	0.5
1	2	1	0.7
1	2	2	0.7
2	1	1	0.3
2	1	2	0.5
2	2	1	0.3
2	2	2	0.3

Fig. 3. A potential ϕ, a probability tree representing it and an approximation of it after pruning some branches.

4   Representation and Computation of Canonical Models Using Probability Trees

Our first proposal is to use probability trees in order to improve the representation of canonical models. Once this goal has been achieved, we will show what are the benefits of using this representation when we carry out exact and approximate probability propagation.

4.1   Canonical Models as Probability Trees

Constructing a tree $\mathcal{T}$ representing a potential ϕ for a set of variables $\mathbf{X}$, without any other additional restriction is rather straightforward: the tree will contain one branch for every configuration $\mathbf{x}$ of $\mathbf{X}$, and one leaf for every value $\phi(x)$. So, in the case of canonical models we could simply apply this procedure. However, this procedure can lead to unnecessarily big trees, as pointed out in [11], where an efficient method for constructing a probability tree from a given potential is given. The idea is to build the tree incrementally, by selecting the most informative variable as label for each interior node. The information is measured as the difference of the Kullback-Leibler distance of the partial tree before and after branching to the complete potential.

Let us focus on the task of constructing a probability tree that represents the conditional probability $P(E|\mathbf{C})$ provided by any of the canonical models. In the case of deterministic canonical models all the variables in $\mathbf{C}$ are more informative than the objective variable E, because the value of E is obtained as a function f of the values of $\mathbf{C}$. So, the variables in $\mathbf{C}$ must be placed closer to the root than E and the values stored in the leaves correspond to those returned by f. If $p_0 = 0$, Figure 4.(a) depicts a discrete OR model and we can observe how the disposition of variables influences on the size of the tree if we exploit the regularities imposed by f. It is important to point out that the size of the probability tree representing an OR model is linear in the number of variables involved in the model. In fact, taking as reference Figure 4.(a), it can be seen that only the left branch of the tree grows as the number of variables increases, remaining the right sub-tree of each variable in that branch equal to $\{0, 1\}$. The same reasoning can be applied to AND models. Furthermore, with this kind of representation, specifying probabilities may be easier for a user. In fact, the user need not be aware of what a canonical model is, but simply represent all the potentials as probability trees and in a natural way the canonical model arises.

The construction of a probability tree $\mathcal{T}$ that represents the conditional probability $P(E|\mathbf{C})$ estimated by noisy or leaky models is more complicated, because this estimation is performed by combinations and marginalizations over probability distributions. However, as we mentioned before, these types of operations can be carried out over probability trees. So, we can look for a way of constructing a tree that represent these canonical models combining trees.

In the case of noisy models, we need a tree $\mathcal{T}_f$ representing the model of interaction between variables imposed by f, i.e. a deterministic model between the auxiliary Z_i's and the objective variable E. And also, we need trees T_i representing the parameters from which the canonical model is computed, i.e. the conditional probability distributions $P(Z_i|C_i)$. Now, we can combine all of these trees following equation 2 as

$$T = \left\{ T_f \otimes \prod_i T_i \right\}^{\downarrow\{E,C_1,\cdots,C_n\}} \qquad (5)$$

obtaining a tree T that represents any noisy canonical model.

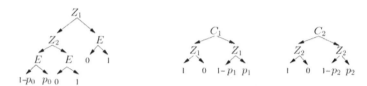

a) Discrete OR with leak probability p_0.   b) Trees specifying the model's parameters.

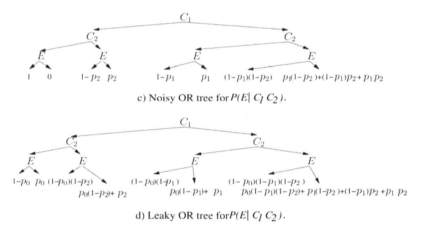

c) Noisy OR tree for $P(E|C_1\,C_2)$.

d) Leaky OR tree for $P(E|C_1\,C_2)$.

Fig. 4. Canonical OR models represented as probability trees.

For example, the tree in Fig. 4.(c) represents a noisy OR model and can be computed combining T_f in Fig. 4.(a), in which $p_0 = 0$, and the T_i trees depicted in Fig. 4.(b). Also, note how the restriction $P(z_i|\neg c_i) = 0$ imposed by the noisy OR model is reflected in the T_i trees.

In the case of leaky models, a "leak" probability $p_0 = P(e|\neg c_1,\cdots,\neg c_n)$ is incorporated to extend the noisy models. So, we can consider constructing their representation as probability trees taking as basis the combination of trees found in equation 5 and somehow adding the leak probability. This can be easily attained if we substitute $P(e|\neg z_1,\cdots,\neg z_n)$ by p_0 in the tree T_f that represents the discrete canonical model which is being applied. For example, Fig. 4.(a) shows a leak probability tree for a discrete OR model. If the interaction between the variables in the model is given by a more sophisticated function that allows ordinal variables, a set of leak probabilities must be provided, $\{p_{01}, p_{02}, \cdots, p_{0k}\}$, indicating the probability that the objetive variable E takes a value different of that assigned to its inactivity when all the others explicit variables, $C_1, \cdots, C_n$, are known to be absent, i.e. $p_{0i} = P(E = e_i|\neg c_1, \cdots, \neg c_n)$ where $e_i \neq \neg e$. These leak probabilities will be included into the tree $\mathcal{T}_f$. Once $\mathcal{T}_f$ has been modified, the probability tree representation for the leaky model is obtained following the tree combination proposed in equation (5).

4.2   Max Models

The models in the OR/MAX family are specially interesting from the point of view of knowledge engineering. We will show now how these models can be managed with probability trees. The MAX model assumes that a certain gradded effect E can be produced by different causes $\{C_1, \cdots, C_n\}$ which act independently. The degree reached by E would be the maximum of the degrees produced by each cause if it were acting independently from the others. We will start describing the representation of MAX models in its deterministic version, and then the noisy and leaky models. The variables involved in a *deterministic MAX model* are ordinal with identical domain, and the value of E is computed as

$$e = f(\mathbf{c}) = \max\{c_1, \cdots, c_n\}. \tag{6}$$

A probability tree $\mathcal{T}_{\max}$ representing a deterministic MAX model is constructed plaxing variables C_i closer to the root than E, since they are more informative. Figure 5.(a) shows the representation as a probability tree of a deterministic MAX model for $P(E|Z_1Z_2)$, where $dom(E) = dom(Z_1) = dom(Z_2) = \{0, 1, 2\}$, if $p_{01} = p_{02} = 0$.

Following the general structure of a noisy model introduced in Section 2, the tree representation of a *noisy MAX model* is constructed combining a tree $\mathcal{T}_{\max}$ representing the deterministic MAX relationship between E and the auxiliary variables Z_i's, with the product of the trees $\mathcal{T}_i$ representing the model's parameters, following Eq. (5). Each tree $\mathcal{T}_i$ defines a probability distribution $P(Z_i|C_i)$, standing for the probability that C_i, when taking a value c_i, raises E to value e_i. So, the noisy MAX model allows that the domains of the C_is be different from that of E, while $dom(Z_i) = dom(E)$. If there is not any additional restriction over the values of the model's parameters, the probability tree obtained after the combination corresponds to a *generalised noisy MAX*. The tree representation for the *standard noisy MAX* is obtained imposing the restrictions $P(Z_i = \neg e|\neg c_i) = 1$. In other words, if E represents an anomaly with normality state $\neg e$ (the absence of that anomaly) and the C_i's are causes that can produce E independently, then E will reach, for sure, its normality state once we know that C_i has reached its own normality state $\neg c_i$. For example, Fig. 5.(b) shows the tree representation of the model's parameters for a generalised noisy MAX, where the domains of the variables are $dom(C_1) = \{1, 2\}$, $dom(C_2) = \{0, 1\}$, and $dom(E) = dom(Z_1) = dom(Z_2) = \{0, 1, 2\}$.

In situations where some of the causes of an effect E may be implicit in the model these causes can be captured by a leak probability vector. Each leak probability $p_{0i} = P(E = e_i | \neg c_1, \cdots, \neg c_n)$ has to be included into the $\mathcal{T}_{MAX}$ as the values of the leaves for configurations $(e_i, \neg z_1, \cdots, \neg z_n)$. This situation is depicted in Fig. 5.(a), where p_{0i}, $i = 1, 2$, is the leak probability $P(E = e_i | \neg z_1, \neg z_2)$. Once $\mathcal{T}_{MAX}$ has been modified, the tree representation for the leaky MAX is obtained by combining the trees applying Eq. (5).

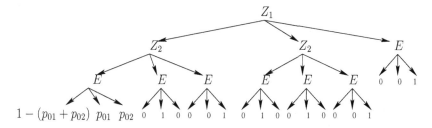

a) Discrete MAX tree with leak probabilities p_{01} p_{02}

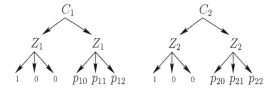

b) Trees specifiying the model's parameters.

Fig. 5. Canonical MAX models represented as probability trees.

Finally, observe that the tree representation of noisy MAX, leaky OR and noisy OR models are particular cases of the leaky MAX, if we apply the necessary restrictions to each of them.

4.3   Probability Propagation

Perhaps the most important advantage of representing canonical models by means of probability trees is that standar propagation algorithms can be used. The maximum benefit is attained if the propagation algorithm is able to take advantage of the factorisation of the model described in Eq. (5), as the Lazy [8] and Lazy-penniless [4] propagation algorithms. It means that no special effort or distinction is necessary when dealing with canonical models from the point of view of propagation if we adopt the framework presented in this paper.

This feature enlarges the class of solvable problems, since it is possible to apply approximate algorithms that take advantage of the probability tree representation. If eventually any of the potentials corresponding to canonical models is too large, it can be approximated by a probabilty tree in which some branches are pruned, as in Penniless propagation [3].

Another benefit comes from the fact that usually many branches in a probability tree representing a canonical model are equal to zero. Algorithms as Penniless propagation take advantages of this, since the potentials involved in the propagation process (messages over a join tree) do not grow by the branches marked with zero after a combination operation. Probability tables cannot take advantage of this fact.

5   Experimental Results

Table 1 shows the experimental results obtained using the proposed representation of canonical models as probability trees. All the networks were generated randomly. Each node has five parents and two values in average. Most of the distributions were specified in the noisy-or interaction models. The experimets realized consists in the transformation of the original network changing the representation of all of the noisy-or interaction models to probability tables or trees.

Table 1. Time expended computing a representation of noisy-or models as probability tables or trees and size used.

Nodes	Tables (secs.)	Table sizes	Trees (secs.)	Tree sizes
50	5,968	566	5,485	556
150	20,766	2010	20,281	1968
250	45,157	3286	41,922	3248
350	67,578	4432	64,953	4380
450	63,297	5448	57,297	5352

As show in the table, the time expended in the transformation from noisy-or models to probability trees, as well as the storage needs are less than that of transforming them to probability tables, as were expected.

6   Conclusions

In this paper we have studied the representation of the three categories of canonical models (deterministic, noisy and leaky) in terms of probability trees. All the restrictions that can be applied to canonical models have been incorporated to the tree representation, showing that probability trees are a compact and sound representation tool. Also, we have paid special attention to the representation of the OR/MAX family of models analasing the influence of its properties into the proposed representation. Our proposed representation of canonical models has proven beneficial in saving of storage requirements. In the case of discrete canonical models the size of the tree grows linearly, instead of exponentially, with the number of variables. Only, in extreme situations, for example in the MAX models when all the causes have different domains the size of the tree will be that of the conditional probability table.

Besides, probability trees have been used in algorithms to perform exact and approximate probability propagation in Bayesian networks. Actually, networks with canonical models can be used with any standard propagation algorithm, which means that these models can be tackled without need of implementing new software.

In the future we will investigate the performance of the proposed representation against the standard computation of canonical models and specific algorithms to carry out probability propagation with canonical models in Bayesian networks.

Acknowledgments

This work has been supported by the Spanish Ministry of Science and Technology, through project TIC2001-2973-C05-02.

References

1. C. Boutilier, N. Friedman, M. Goldszmidt and D. Koller: Context-Specific Independence in Bayesian Networks. Proceedings of the 12th Conference on Uncertainty in Artificial Intelligence,, Morgan Kaufman, San Mateo, CA (1996) 115–123
2. A. Cano and S. Moral: Propagación exacta y aproximada mediante árboles de probabilidad en redes causales. VII Conferencia de la Asociación Española para la Inteligencia Artificial (CAEPIA'97), Málaga (1997) 635–644
3. A. Cano, S. Moral and A. Salmerón: Penniless propagation in join trees. International Journal of Intelligent Systems **15** (2000) 1027–1059
4. A. Cano and S. Moral and A. Salmerón: Lazy evaluation in Penniless propagation over join trees. Networks **39** (2002) 175–185
5. F.J. Díez: Parameter adjustment in Bayes networks. The generalized noisy OR–gate. Proceedings of the 9th Conference on Uncertainty in Artificial Intelligence, Morgan Kaufman, San Mateo, CA (1993) 99–105
6. F.J. Díez and M.J. Druzdel: Fundamentals of canonical models. IX Conf. de la Asociación Española para la I.A. (CAEPIA'2001), Vol. II, Gijón (2001) 1125–1134
7. M. Henrion: Some practical issues in constructing belief networks. Uncertainty in Artificial Intelligence 3, L. N. Kanal, T.S. Levitt and J.F. Lemmer (eds.), Elsevier Science Publishers, Amsterdam (1989) 161–173
8. A.L. Madsen and F.V. Jensen: Lazy propagation: a junction tree inference algorithm based on lazy evaluation. Artificial Intelligence **113** (1999) 203–245
9. J. Pearl: Fusion, propagation and structuring in belief networks. Artificial Intelligence **29** (1986) 241–288
10. J. Pearl: Probabilistic reasoning in intelligent systems: networks of plausible inference. Morgan Kaufman (1988)
11. A. Salmerón, A. Cano and S. Moral: Importance sampling in Bayesian networks using probability trees. Comput. Statistics and Data Analisys **34** (2000) 387–413
12. S. Srinivas: A generalization of the noisy-OR model. Procs. of the 9th Conf. on Uncertainty in Artif. Intelligence, Morgan Kaufman, San Mateo, CA (1993) 208–215

Robust Aggregation of Expert Opinions
Based on Conflict Analysis and Resolution*

Miguel Angel Garcia and Domènec Puig

Intelligent Robotics and Computer Vision Group
Department of Computer Science and Mathematics
Rovira i Virgili University
Av. Països Catalans 26, 43007 Tarragona, Spain
{magarcia,dpuig}@etse.urv.es

Abstract. This paper presents a new technique for combining the opinions given by a team of independent experts. Each opinion is associated with a confidence level that represents the expert's conviction on its own judgement. The proposed technique first measures the conflict level introduced by every expert by taking into account the similarity between both its opinion and confidence, and those of the other experts within the team. An expert who disagrees with the majority of other experts with a similar confidence level is assumed to be conflicting (an "outlier" expert). Based on those conflict levels, an arbitration mechanism determines the reliability associated with each expert, by considering that a reliable expert is the one which is both confident and non-conflicting. Finally, the aggregated opinion is obtained as a weighted average (linear opinion pool) of the original expert opinions, with the weights being the reliability levels determined before. The proposed technique has been applied to texture image classification, leading to significantly better results than commonly-used opinion integration approaches.

1 Introduction

Given a set of alternatives that may represent possible solutions to a certain problem of interest, *group decision making* consists of first scoring every alternative based on the *opinions* (beliefs) given by a group of independent experts, and then choosing the alternative with the largest score. We assume that each expert opinion is represented as a probability and may be associated with a *confidence level* that expresses the conviction of the corresponding expert on its own judgement [11]. Confidence levels will be assumed to range between zero and one.

A key issue in group decision making is how to obtain a final opinion by integrating the different expert opinions and their confidences. A wide variety of techniques have been proposed for integrating multiple opinions in many different fields, from engineering to social sciences. Recent comprehensive surveys are [1] and [9]. Among the different opinion integration techniques, three main approaches are commonly utilized in practice if the group decision making process is to be automated: selection, voting and aggregation.

---

* This work has been partially supported by the Government of Spain under the CICYT project DPI2001-2094-C03-02.

R. Conejo et al. (Eds.): CAEPIA-TTIA 2003, LNAI 3040, pp. 488–497, 2004.

Selection is the simplest opinion integration mechanism, as it merely chooses for each alternative the expert's opinion with the largest confidence. This solution is little robust as, in the end, it entirely relies on the opinion of a single individual. Therefore, in the presence of discordant experts that strongly disagree with the majority of other experts in the team, selection may produce highly biased opinions that will likely lead to wrong final decisions.

In *voting* techniques, each expert does not give an opinion on each available alternative, but directly chooses the alternative that considers the best. The group decision making process finally selects the alternative that has been supported by the majority of experts. This "democratic" solution typically assumes that all experts have the same confidence on their judgements. This may lead to decisions being wrongly made in case they are supported by many low-confident experts.

Aggregation techniques combine the available opinions and confidences in order to reach a single consensus opinion that may be acceptable by all parties. Hence, these techniques are generally considered to be more reliable than both selection and voting. The classical aggregation techniques are surveyed in [3] and [4]. Among them, the most utilized are the linear opinion pool, the logarithmic opinion pool and the supra Bayesian approach. Another popular aggregation technique is the ordered weighted averaging (OWA) operators [12].

A *linear opinion pool* [2] is just a weighted arithmetic mean of expert opinions. Although the original technique does not define how the weights are computed, a reasonable choice is to use the experts' confidence levels as weights after having being normalized such that they sum to one. The problem appears when there are "outlier" experts within the team, as they will erroneously bias the final opinion towards their beliefs (the arithmetic mean is not a robust estimator).

A *logarithmic opinion pool* is the geometric mean of expert opinions, with each opinion being raised to the power of a normalized weight. Since all opinions are multiplied, in case that one is close to zero, the aggregated opinion will also be small, irrespectively of the other opinions. Therefore, this technique is also prone to decision errors caused by "outlier" experts.

The *supra Bayesian* approach is a direct application of the Bayes' Theorem. Given a particular set of independent expert opinions on a certain alternative, it is first necessary to define the functions that represent the joint likelihood of having such a combination of opinions conditioned on every available alternative. Moreover, it is also necessary to define the prior probability corresponding to every alternative. With those joint likelihoods and prior probabilities, the Bayes' Theorem determines the posterior probability of each alternative conditioned on the given set of expert opinions. Each posterior probability represents the consensus belief of the team of experts on a single alternative, and can be directly used by the decision maker as the final score for that alternative.

However, the supra Bayesian approach has a few drawbacks. The first one is that the confidence level associated with each opinion is not utilized in the process. Moreover, the necessary joint likelihood functions are difficult to compute in practice. The simplest way of defining them is as a product of independent likelihoods (one likelihood function per expert opinion). Unfortunately in this case, this approach suffers from the same problem of sensitivity to outliers as the logarithmic opinion pool, since a single opinion with a very low likelihood will inevitably reduce the joint likelihood, affecting the whole decision process.

OWA operators sort out the available set of expert opinions in descending order and then associate every position in the sorted list with a specific weight that is calculated according to the chosen operator. Finally, the aggregated opinion is obtained as the weighted average of the individual expert opinions. *BADD-OWA* operators 13. have been chosen in this work since they compute the aforementioned weights based on the actual values of the given expert opinions: $w_i = b_i^\alpha / \sum b_j^\alpha, \alpha \geq 0$, with b_i being the opinion ranked in the *i*-th position of the sorted list.

Unfortunately, OWA operators are also sensitive to outliers, since, for example, an outlier expert with a very large opinion may be ranked in the first position of the sorted list and may thus receive the largest weight. Moreover, confidence levels associated with the expert opinions are not considered in the process.

Alternatively, this paper proposes a robust opinion aggregation technique that reduces the effect of outlier experts in a group decision making process. The proposed technique consists of a new formulation of the weights of a linear opinion pool aimed at reducing the influence of conflicting experts in the team (those who disagree with the majority of other experts with a similar strength).

The next section describes the proposed opinion aggregation technique. Section 3 validates this technique through a practical application to the problem of classifying the pixels of an image into a set of predefined texture models of interest (alternatives) based on the outcome of multiple texture feature extraction methods (experts). Experimental results show that the proposed aggregation approach leads to better classification results than when the aforementioned opinion integration techniques are utilized instead. Conclusions and further lines are finally given in section 4.

2   Robust Aggregation of Expert Opinions

This section presents a new technique for integrating the opinions formulated by a collaborative group of experts, in such a way that conflicts raised when different experts give discordant opinions with similar confidence are detected and solved. This leads to a significative reduction of the influence of outlier experts in the final decision making process.

The proposed technique first measures the conflict level between each expert and the others in the group by taking into account all the available opinions and their associated confidence levels. Then, the reliability of each expert is estimated based on those conflict levels. An expert is considered to be reliable if both it is confident in its opinions and does not conflict with the other experts. Finally, the aggregated opinion is obtained by applying a linear opinion pool in which the weights are the aforementioned reliabilities after being normalized. These stages are described in more detail below.

2.1   Conflict Analysis

Let $\mathbf{A} = \{a_j, j = 1...T\}$ be a set of *T* alternatives corresponding to a certain problem. *M* independent experts will express an opinion about each of those alternatives. Let $\mathbf{O} = \{o_{ij}, i = 1...M\}$, $o_{ij} \in [0, 1]$, represent the set of opinions given by the different experts regarding alternative a_j. Let W_j be the set of confidence levels associated with those opinions according to every expert: $\mathbf{W}_j = \{w_{ij}, i = 1...M\}$, $w_{ij} \in [0, 1]$.

Given a set of M probabilities: $\Psi_j = \{\psi_i, i = 1...M\}$, the *similarity* between one of the elements in Ψ and the others is defined as [10]:

$$\text{Sim}_i(\Psi) \equiv \text{Sim}(\psi_i, \Psi \setminus \{\psi_i\}) = 1 - \frac{1}{M-1} \sum_{k=1, k\neq i}^{M} |\Psi_i - \Psi_k| \qquad (1)$$

Taking (1) into account, we define the *conflict* raised by an expert according to both its opinion o_{ij} and associated conviction w_{ij}, considering alternative a_j:

$$\text{Conflict}_{ij} = \text{Sim}_i(\mathbf{W}_j)[1 - \text{Sim}_i(\mathbf{O}_j)] \qquad (2)$$

This conflict measure ranges between zero and one, with the maximum conflict occurring when the expert opinion completely differs from the other opinions, $\text{Sim}_i(\mathbf{O}_j) = 0$, but its conviction on that opinion is similar to the convictions of the other experts, $\text{Sim}_i(\mathbf{W}_j) = 1$. It is important to note that this formulation only penalizes discordant experts when their confidences are similar to those of the agreeing experts. Indeed, a discordant expert does not necessarily have to be a bad expert.

2.2 Aggregation with Conflict Resolution

Whenever different expert opinions are to be integrated, it is necessary to put in place a mechanism that solves potential conflicts within the group. To this end, we apply a simple arbitration mechanism that reduces the influence of the opinions given by conflicting experts.

First of all, we utilize the conflict measure introduced above in order to define the *reliability* r_{ij} associated with opinion o_{ij} and confidence w_{ij}:

$$r_{ij} = w_{ij} (1 - \text{Conflict}_{ij}) \qquad (3)$$

Therefore, an expert is considered reliable when it is both non-conflicting (low Conflict_{ij}) and confident (high w_{ij}). Alternatively, an expert is considered unreliable whenever it has either a low confidence level or a high conflict level.

The previous reliabilities are normalized and applied as weights in a linear opinion pool that finally determines the aggregated opinion o_j regarding alternative a_j:

$$o_j = \sum_{i=1}^{M} \overline{r}_{ij} o_{ij} \qquad \overline{r}_{ij} = r_{ij} / \sum_{k=1}^{M} r_{ij} \qquad (4)$$

Equation (4) acts as an arbitration mechanism that reduces or even eliminates the influence of highly conflicting experts in any subsequent decision making process.

3   Application Example: Texture Pixel Classification

This section illustrates the application of the proposed technique to the field of computer vision. In particular, it describes a pixel-based classifier that integrates multiple texture experts (*texture feature extraction methods* or *texture methods* in short) by applying the technique presented in section 2. This classifier is an evolution of the one presented in [6], which used a conventional linear opinion pool as expert integration mechanism.

Let $\{\tau_1, \dots, \tau_T\}$ be a set of T texture patterns of interest (*alternatives*). Every texture τ_j is described by a set of sample images. Let $\mathbf{I}$ be an input textured image. In order to classify a target pixel $\mathbf{I}(x, y)$ into one of the previous texture patterns (*problem of interest*), a feature vector $(\mu_1(x, y), \dots \mu_M(x, y))$ is computed. Each feature $\mu_1(x, y)$ is obtained by applying a texture method μ_1 (*expert*) to the pixels contained in a square window centered at $\mathbf{I}(x, y)$, whose size is experimentally set for each method. M texture methods are considered.

The classification algorithm consists of four stages described in the next subsections. The proposed opinion aggregation technique is applied in the second stage.

3.1 Supervised Training Stage

A set $M \times T$ of likelihood functions $P_i(\mathbf{I}(x, y)|\tau_j)$ are defined based on the probability distributions corresponding to the evaluation of every method μ_i over the pixels of the sample images corresponding to each texture τ_j. Each of those distributions is defined in the interval $[MIN_{ij}, MAX_{ij}]$:

$$P_i(\mathbf{I}(x, y)|\tau_j) = P_{ij}(\mu_i(x, y) \in [MIN_{ij}, MAX_{ij}]) \tag{5}$$

Given a texture method μ_i and a texture model τ_j, each $P_i(\mathbf{I}(x, y)|\tau_j)$ defined in (5) can be interpreted as the *opinion* of an expert about the likelihood that $\mathbf{I}(x, y)$ is within a region that belongs to texture pattern τ_j. Moreover, each expert is associated with a weight w_{ij} that represents the expert's *confidence* about that opinion. This weight is defined as follows.

The *Kullback J-divergence*, which measures the separability between two classes (texture models in this context) is defined as [5]:

$$KJ_i(\tau_a, \tau_b) = \int_0^1 (A - B) \log(A/B) \, du \tag{6}$$

with A and B being defined from the previous probability distributions:

$$A = P_{ia}(MAX_{ia} \, u + MIN_{ia}(1 - u)) \text{ and } B = P_{ib}(MAX_{ib} \, u + MIN_{ib}(1 - u)).$$

The weights w_{ij} are then computed as the normalized average of the *Kullback J-divergences* between τ_j and the other texture models:

$$w_{ij} = d_{ij} / \sum_{k=1}^{M} d_{kj} \qquad d_{ij} = \frac{1}{T-1} \sum_{k=1, k \neq j}^{T} KJ_i(\tau_j, \tau_k) \tag{7}$$

This formulation of the experts' confidences implies that an expert that has a similar response for the different texture models (the Kullback J-divergence is low as the probability distributions of its responses for the different models will be highly over-lapped), will have a low confidence, since in this case, the expert cannot really differentiate among the different texture models. On the other hand, an expert whose probability distributions for the different models have little overlap (the Kullback J-divergence is high), will be able to better discriminate each texture model from the others. Hence, its judgement will be more meaningful.

3.2 Robust Integration of Texture Experts with Conflict Resolution

Let $\mathbf{O}_j(x, y)$ represent the opinions of M experts regarding the membership of pixel $\mathbf{I}(x, y)$ to texture τ_j: $\mathbf{O}_j(x, y) = \{P_j \mathbf{I}(x, y)|\tau_j)\ i = 1...M\}$, with $P_j \mathbf{I}(x, y)|\tau_j)$ being defined as (5). Let represent the convictions associated with those opinions (7): $\mathbf{W}_j = \{w_{ij}, i = 1...M\}$.

Taking (1) and (2) into account, the *conflict* raised by an expert according to both its opinion $P_j \mathbf{I}(x, y)|\tau_j)$ and associated conviction w_{ij} is formulated as:

$$\text{Conflict}_{ij}(x, y) = \text{Sim}_i(\mathbf{W}_j)[1 - \text{Sim}_i(\mathbf{O}_j(x, y))] \tag{8}$$

According to (3), the reliability associated with opinion $P_j \mathbf{I}(x, y)|\tau_j)$ and conviction w_{ij} is defined as:

$$r_{ij}(x, y) = w_{ij}(1 - \text{Conflict}_{ij}(x, y)) \tag{9}$$

The final integration of expert opinions (combined likelihood functions) is formulated according to (4) as follows:

$$P(\mathbf{I}(x, y) \mid \tau_j) = \sum_{i=1}^{M} \overline{r_{ij}(x, y)} P_i(\mathbf{I}(x, y) \mid t_j) \tag{10}$$

with being $\overline{r_{ij}(x, y)}$ the normalized reliability (4).

3.3 Maximum a Posteriori Estimation

Given a set of T combined likelihood functions $P_j \mathbf{I}(x, y)|\tau_j)$ (10), T posterior probabilities are computed by applying the Bayes rule:

$$P(\tau_j|\mathbf{I}(x, y)) = \frac{P(\mathbf{I}(x, y) \mid \tau_j) P_{xy}(\tau_j)}{\sum_{k=1}^{T} P(\mathbf{I}(x, y) \mid \tau_k) P_{xy}(\tau_k)} \tag{11}$$

with the prior probabilities $P_{xy}(\tau_j)$ being defined as:

$$P_{xy}(\tau_j) = \sum_{i=1}^{M} r_{ij}(x, y) / \sum_{k=1}^{T} \sum_{i=1}^{M} r_{ik}(x, y) \tag{12}$$

$\mathbf{I}(x, y)$ is likely to belong to the texture model τ_j that leads to the maximum posterior probability $P(\tau_j|\mathbf{I}(x, y))$.

3.4 Significance Test

In order to finally classify pixel $I(x, y)$ as belonging to τ_j, its posterior probability must be above a *significance level* (probability threshold) λ_j defined according to two ratios commonly utilized to characterize the performance of classifiers: *sensitivity* (S_n) and *specificity* (S_p) [6]. Pixel $I(x, y)$ will be labelled as belonging to texture class τ_j iff $P(\tau_j | I(x, y)) > \lambda_j$. Otherwise, it will be classified as an unknown.

3.5 Experimental Results

The previous classifier has been evaluated on real outdoor images containing textured surfaces. A total of 61,504 separate opinion aggregation experiments are conducted for every image (one experiment per valid image pixel). Such extensive experimentation is considered to be sufficient to provide statistically sound results. Fig. 1(*first column*) shows two of the input images. Four texture patterns of interest have been considered: "sky", "forest", "ground" and "sea". A set of sample images representing each of those patterns was extracted from the image database and utilized as the training dataset for the tested classifiers.

Fig. 1 (*second column*) shows the ground-truth classification of the given input images by considering the four texture patterns of interest. Black areas represent image regions that do not belong to any of the sought texture patterns. Those regions are discarded for the computation of classification rates.

Several widely-used texture feature extraction methods have been chosen to be integrated with the proposed technique [7]: four *Laws filter masks (R5R5, E5L5, E5E5, R5S5)*, two *wavelet transforms (Daubechies-4, Haar)*, four *Gabor filters* with different wavelengths (8, 4) and orientations (0°, 45°, 90°, 135°), two *first-order statistics (variance, skewness)*, a *second-order statistic (homogeneity)* based on *cooccurrence matrices* and the *fractal dimension*. All those texture methods were evaluated over windows of 17x17 pixels.

The proposed aggregation technique has been compared to the integration schemes described in section 1 (*selection, voting, linear opinion pool, logarithmic opinion pool, supra Bayesian* and *BADD-OWA* with $\alpha = 1$). In all cases, equation (10), which is the point in the classifier where the actual integration of expert opinions takes place, was replaced according to each approach. The expert opinions were the likelihood functions defined in (5) and their associated confidence levels the weights defined in (7).

Table 1 shows the pixel classification rates and average sensitivities and specificities obtained with the described texture classifier fed with the various opinion integration techniques, by considering the images shown in Fig. 1 (*first column*). The first row corresponds to the proposed aggregation scheme. The last row of the table shows the classification rates obtained with the best texture classifier (Gabor filters plus 5-Nearest Neighbors) in MeasTex [8], a popular texture classification framework that implements different well-known texture classifiers.

Table 1. Classification rates (*CR*), mean sensitivities (*Sn*) and mean specificities (*Sp*) obtained for the test images shown in Fig. 1 with the described classifier endowed with different opinion integration techniques. The first row corresponds to the proposed technique. The last row shows the best results with MeasTex.

Integration Technique	Fig. 1(*left*)			Fig. 1(*right*)		
	CR	S_n	S_p	CR	S_n	S_p
Robust aggregation	78	70	89	75	75	84
Selection	57	52	43	50	58	43
Voting	58	51	75	47	47	61
Linear Opinion Pool	70	54	85	68	59	70
Logarithmic Opinion Pool	65	40	60	58	46	60
Supra Bayesian	68	48	87	60	47	67
BADD-OWA ($\alpha = 1$)	62	46	64	56	41	59
MeasTex (Gabor, 5-NN)	73	62	78	68	67	76

In all cases, the texture classifier endowed with the proposed aggregation technique produced the best classification rates. Moreover, the linear opinion pool performed better than the logarithmic opinion pool as expected. In turn, the BADDOWA operator and the supra Bayesian approach, the latter with joint likelihood functions computed as the product of the individual likelihoods defined in (5), performed in between. The worst opinion integrators were selection and voting.

On the other hand, qualitative results also show that the texture classifier endowed with the proposed robust integration mechanism is able to better identify the regions that belong to the sought texture patterns, Fig. 1(*third column*). The three best results obtained with the alternative integration approaches shown in Table 1 are presented in Fig. 2. Among them, the linear opinion pool produces the best qualitative results for the tested images.

4 Conclusions

A robust technique for aggregating the opinions given by a team of independent experts has been presented. Each opinion is associated with a confidence level that represents the experts's conviction on its own judgement. The proposed technique first measures the conflict level introduced by every expert by taking into account the similarity between both its opinion and confidence, and those of the other experts within the team. An expert who disagrees with the majority of other experts with a similar confidence level is assumed to be conflicting (an "outlier" expert).

Based on those conflict levels, an arbitration mechanism determines the reliability associated with every expert, by considering that a reliable expert is the one which is both confident and non-conflicting. The aggregated opinion is obtained as a weighted average (linear opinion pool) of the original expert opinions, with the weights being the reliability levels determined before. In this way, this conflict resolution scheme reduces or even cancels the negative influence of outlier experts.

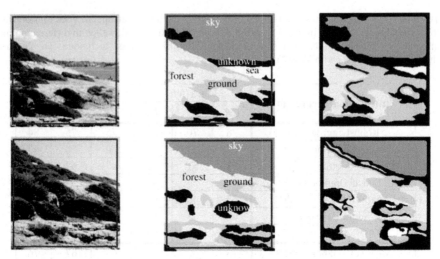

Fig. 1. (1st column) Test images. (2nd column) Associated ground-truth classification. (3rd column) Classification maps obtained with the proposed texture classifier and the aggregation scheme described in section 3 [78%, 75%]. Black regions in the ground-truth image are considered to belong to an unknown texture pattern. Each dark square encloses the image area in which 17x17 pixel evaluation windows can be fitted.

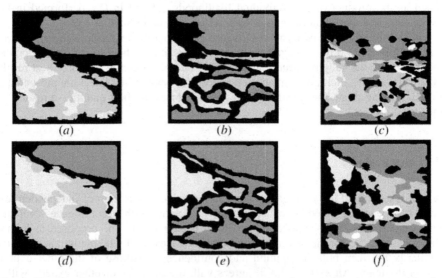

Fig. 2. Classification maps corresponding to the test images shown in Fig. 1 processed by the three best opinion integration techniques according to Table 1: (a,d) linear opinion pool [70%, 68%], (b,e) supra Bayesian [68%, 60%], (c,f) BADD-OWA ($\alpha = 1$) [62%, 56%].

The proposed technique has been evaluated in a real group decision making problem by embedding it into a texture image classifier that aims at identifying the texture pattern to which every pixel of an input image belongs. This classifier integrates multiple opinions given by a set of texture feature extraction methods from different families. Experimental results with real outdoor images show that the proposed aggregation technique leads to better quantitative and qualitative classification results than when it is replaced by other widely-used opinion integration schemes. Moreover, results are also superior to those obtained with traditional texture classifiers contained in MeasTex, a widely-recognized texture classification framework that integrates texture methods from the same family.

Further work will consist of studying the sensitivity of the proposed conflict resolution model to variations of the number of experts in the group. Another line consists of determining whether it is possible to use application-dependent knowledge and training procedures (e.g., reinforcement learning) in order to automatically select which experts provide the best opinions. Finally, the proposed aggregation scheme will be tested on other domains apart from computer vision.

References

1. Akter, T., Simonovic, S.S.: A General Overview of Multiple-objective Multiple-participant Decision Making for Flood Management. Research report, Facility for Intelligent Decision Support, University of Western Ontario, Canada (2002) (http://www.engga.uwo.ca/research/iclr/fids/Documents/MOMP_Report.pdf)
2. Berger, J.: Statistical Decision Theory and Bayesian Analysis. Springer (1985)
3. Clemen, R.T., Winkler, R.L.: Combining Probability Distributions from Experts in Risk Analysis. Risk Analysis, 19(2), (1999) 187-203
4. French, S.: Group Consensus Probability Distributions: A Critical Survey. In: Bernardo, J.M., DeGroot, M.H., Lindley, D.V., Smith, A.F.M. (eds.): Bayesian Statistics 2. Elsevier Science Publishers (1985) 183-202
5. Kittler, J.: Feature Selection and Extraction. In: Young, T.Y., Fu, K.S. (eds.): Handbook of Pattern Recog. and Image Proc. Academic Press (1986) 60-81
6. Puig, D., García, M.A.: Recognizing Specific Texture Patterns by Integration of Multiple Texture Methods. IEEE International Conference on Image Processing, Vol.1, Rochester, USA (2002) 125-128
7. Randen, T., Husoy, J.H.: Filtering for Texture Classification: A Comparative Study. IEEE Trans. PAMI, 21(4), (1999) 291-310
8. Smith, G., Burns, I.: Measuring Texture Classification Algorithms. Pattern Recognition Letters 18, (1997) 1495-1501. MeasTex Image Texture Database and Test Suite. Centre for Sensor Signal and Information Processing, University of Queensland, Australia, (http://www.cssip.uq.edu.au/staff/meastex/meastex.html)
9. Srisoepardani, K.P.: Evaluation of Group Decision Making Methods (Chapter 6). The Possibility Theorem for Group Decision Making, Ph. D. dissertation, Katz Graduate School of Business, University of Pittsburgh, USA (1996).
10. Theodoridis, S., Koutroumbas, K.: Pattern Recognition. Academic Press (1999)
11. Tubbs, J.D., Alltop, W.O.: Measures of Confidence Associated with Combining Classification Results. IEEE Trans. SMC, 21(3), (1991) 690-693
12. Yager, R.R.: On Ordered Weighted Averaging Aggregation Operators in Multicriteria Decision Making. IEEE Trans. SMC, 18(1), (1988) 183-190
13. Yager, R.R.: Families of OWA operators. Fuzzy Sets and Systems, 59 (1993) 125-148

Rotation-Based Ensembles[*]

Juan José Rodríguez[1] and Carlos J. Alonso[2]

[1] Lenguajes y Sistemas Informáticos
Universidad de Burgos, Spain
jjrodriguez@ubu.es
[2] Grupo de Sistemas Inteligentes
Departamento de Informática
Universidad de Valladolid, Spain
calonso@infor.uva.es

Abstract. A new method for ensemble generation is presented. It is based on grouping the attributes in different subgroups, and to apply, for each group, an axis rotation, using Principal Component Analysis. If the used method for the induction of the classifiers is not invariant to rotations in the data set, the generated classifier can be very different. Hence, once of the objectives aimed when generating ensembles is achieved, that the different classifiers were rather diverse. The majority of ensemble methods eliminate some information (e.g., instances or attributes) of the data set for obtaining this diversity. The proposed ensemble method transforms the data set in a way such as all the information is preserved. The experimental validation, using decision trees as base classifiers, is favorable to rotation based ensembles when comparing to *Bagging*, *Random Forests* and the most well-known version of *Boosting*.

1   Introduction

One of the research areas in Machine Learning is the generation of ensembles. The basic idea is to use more than one classifier, in the hope that the accuracy will be better. It is possible to combine heterogeneous classifiers, where each of the classifiers is obtained with a different method. Nevertheless, it is also possible to combine homogeneous classifiers. In this case all the classifiers have been obtained with the same method. In order to avoid identical classifiers, it is necessary to change something, at least the random seed.

There are methods that alter the data set. *Bagging* [3] obtains a new data set by resampling the original data set. An instance can be selected several times, so some instances will not be present in the new data set. The *Random Subspaces* [7] method obtains a new data set deleting some attributes. *Boosting* [10] is a family of methods. The most prominent member is AdaBoost. In this case the data set is modified depending on the classification errors of the previously generated base classifier. The bad classified examples are assigned a greater weight,

---

[*] This work has been supported by the Spanish MCyT project DPI2001-4404-E and the "Junta de Castilla y León" project VA101/01.

R. Conejo et al. (Eds.): CAEPIA-TTIA 2003, LNAI 3040, pp. 498–506, 2004.

so the next classifier will give more importance to those examples. Another possibility, instead of modifying the data set, is to modify the base learning method. For instance, in the *Random Forest* method [4], decision trees are constructed in a way such as the selected decision for a node is, to some extent, random. Comparatives among ensemble generation methods are presented in [1,5,8]

These method share the idea that it is necessary to modify the data set or the learning method in a way that the obtained classifiers will be, probably worst. None of the modifications would be considered if it was desired to obtain a unique classifier. The reason is that ensemble methods need diverse base classifiers.

This work proposes a method that transforms the data set, but in a way that all the present information is preserved. The idea is to group the attributes, and for each group to apply an axis rotation. Hence, all the available information (instance and attributes) in the data set is still available. Although there are a lot of learning methods that are invariant to rotations, one of the most used with ensembles, decision trees, are very sensitive to this kind of variations, because the generated decision surfaces are formed by parallels to the axis.

The rest of the work is organized as follow. The proposed method is described in 2. Section 3 includes the experimental validation. Some related works are presented in section 4. Finally, section 5 concludes.

2   The Method

It is based on transforming the data set, in a different way for each member of the ensemble. Then, the base learning method is used with the transformed data set. The results of the different classifiers are combined using majority vote.

The transformation process is based on Principal Component Analysis (PCA) [6]. These components are linear combinations of attributes. Normally, this technique is used for reducing the dimensionality of the data set, because the components are ordered according to their importance, so the last ones can be discarded. Nevertheless, we are going to consider all the components. In this case, the transformed data set has exactly the same information than the original one, with the only difference of axis rotation. This technique works with numeric attributes. If the data set has discrete attributes, they must be transformed to numeric.

One of the objectives in ensemble methods is that the combined classifiers were diverse, because nothing is gained if they are equal. Another objective, somewhat contradictory to the previous one, is that the combined classifiers were accurate. PCA is an adequate transformation for ensemble generation because, first, no information is loss, so the accuracy of the base classifiers should not be worsened, as happens with other ensemble methods. And second, because the model generated by the base classifier can be rather different, given that the method was not invariant to rotations.

Nevertheless, for a given data set, the result of PCA is unique. For generating different classifiers it is necessary to obtain several transformed data sets. The possibilities are:

- To apply PCA to a subset of the instances. Unless the number of instances were rather small, the results will be rather similar.
- To apply PCA to a subsets of the classes. In fact, this is a variant of the previous possibility, because when classes are selected, their instances are being selected. Nevertheless, the hope is that the results of the analysis will be more diverse.
- To apply PCA to a subset of the attributes. In this case only the selected attributes would be rotated. In order to modify all the attributes, it is possible to group the attributes in groups, and to apply PCA for each group.

The previous strategies are considered for the application of PCA, but once that the analysis has been obtained, then all the data set if reformulated using the components. If the previous strategies are combined, it is possible, except for very small data sets, to obtain a lot of different data sets.

The application of PCA to groups of attributes is another mechanism for diversification, but it also provides additional advantages. First, the execution time of the analysis depends mainly on the number of attributes, so is much quicker to do the analysis in groups that doing it with all the attributes.

Moreover, the storage requirements are considerably reduced. A component is a linear combination of the original attributes. If all the components are kept, then it is necessary a matrix for storing all the coefficients, so the space is quadratic in the number of attributes. If the analysis is done for groups, then the storage requirements are quadratic in the number of attributes per group, and linear in the total number of attributes.

Even more, the decisions that appear in the decision nodes of the trees compare the value of an attribute with a threshold. The new attributes are linear combinations of the original ones. If PCA is done in groups, the components are combinations of the attributes in the group, instead of all the attributes. Hence, the evaluation of the decision in a node is quicker.

Figure 1 shows the transformation process of the data set. A new additional parameter, c, is considered. It indicates the coefficient between the number of attributes in the transformed and original data sets. For instance, if $c = 0.5$, the transformed data set would have half the number of attributes than the original one.

3   Experimental Validation

The used method for constructing decision trees is one of the available in the WEKA library [12], named J48. It is a reimplementation of C4.5 [9]. The implementations of Bagging and AdaBoost.M1 are also from that library.

PCA is defined for numeric attributes. For the presented method, discrete attributes were converted to numeric ones, with as many attributes as possible values. This transformation was not applied for the methods used for comparison (bagging, boosting...) because they can deal directly with discrete attributes.

The used data sets appear in table 1. They are the ones available in the format of the WEKA library. All of them are form the UCI repository [2]. Some of the data sets were slightly modified. First, for the data sets "splice" and

Input:

- D: dat set
- s: integer (groups size)
- c: real (coefficient: final / original number of attributes)

Algorithm:

- $R \leftarrow$ empty data set
- $n \leftarrow$ attribute number in D (without the class)
- used$[1\ldots n] \leftarrow$ False
- $g \leftarrow \lceil c \times n/s \rceil$ (number of groups)
- For $i \leftarrow 1 \ldots g$ do
  - $A \leftarrow$ empty data set
  - For $j \leftarrow 1 \ldots s$ do
    * If there exists a k such as used$[k]$ is False
      · To select randomly a value for k such as used$[k]$ is False and the attribute a_k is not in A
    * Else
      · To select randomly a value for k such as the attribute a_k is not in A
    * $A \leftarrow A \cup \{a_k\}$
  - $P \leftarrow$ Principal Component Analysis of a subset of the instances in A
  - $A' \leftarrow A$ in the coordinates space defined by P
  - $R \leftarrow R \cup A'$
- $R \leftarrow R \cup \{C.\text{class}\}$

Output: R

Fig. 1. A description of the method for transforming the data set.

"zoo" an attribute was eliminated. They were instance identifiers. This kind of attributes are not useful for learning, and in the current implementation, they cause a considerably overhead, because continuous attributes are converted to numeric. Second, for the data set "vowel", there was an attribute indicating if the instance was for training or for testing. This attribute was eliminated. Moreover, this data set includes information of the speakers and their sex. We consider two versions, "vowel-c" and "vowel-n" using and not using this context information, because there are works that use and not use this information.

The experimental setting was the following. The number of classifiers to combine was 10. It is normal to see experimental settings with 100 base classifiers, but when using using full decision trees we think is not a very practical setting. For each data set and ensemble method, 10 10-fold cross validations were performed. The parameters of the different methods were the default ones. For rotation-based ensembles, the number of attributes is each group was 3, the coefficient value was 1 (the number of attributes in the original and transformed data set are nearly the same).

The obtained results for the different ensemble methods, using decision trees, are shown in table 2. For the 32 data sets, in 27 the accuracy result was better

Table 1. Characteristics of the used data sets.

data set	classes	examples	discrete	continuous
anneal	6	898	32	6
audiology	24	226	69	0
autos	7	205	10	16
balance-scale	3	625	0	4
breast-cancer	2	286	10	0
breast-w	2	699	0	9
colic	2	368	16	7
credit-a	2	690	9	6
credit-g	2	1000	13	7
diabetes	2	768	0	8
glass	7	214	0	9
heart-c	5	307	7	6
heart-h	5	294	7	6
heart-statlog	2	270	0	13
hepatitis	2	155	13	6
hypothyroid	4	3772	22	7
ionosphere	2	351	0	34
iris	3	150	0	4
labor	2	57	8	8
letter	26	20000	0	16
lymphography	4	148	15	3
primary-tumor	22	239	17	0
segment	7	2310	0	19
sonar	2	208	0	60
soybean	19	683	35	0
splice	3	3190	60	0
vehicle	4	846	0	18
vote	2	435	16	0
vowel-c	11	990	2	10
vowel-n	11	990	0	10
waveform	3	5000	0	40
zoo	7	101	16	2

for our method than for bagging, an also in 27 (but not the same ones) our method was better than AdaBoost.M1. This table also shows the cases where a significant difference was found, using a paired t-test with a significance level of 5%.

For some ensemble methods, when used in conjunction with decision trees, it is recommended not to apply the pruning process [1,5]. Hence, the experiments were repeated with this condition. The obtained results are shown in table 3. Now, it is also included the method Random Forests, because it does not use a pruning step. For this method the number of base classifiers was 20, because in [4] when this method is compared to boosting, it doubles the number of base classifiers. The reason is that is much quicker to generate a random tree that using the normal methods for constructing trees.

Table 2. Obtained results for the different data sets with different methods for generating ensembles. It shows the average value and the standard deviation of the accuracy. The base classifiers are pruned decision trees. The best value for each row is marked in **boldface**. The symbols $\sqrt{}$ and $\times$ indicate, respectively, a significant difference favorable and unfavorable to our method.

data set	Rotations	Bagging	AdaBoost.M1
anneal	99.19 ± 0.89	98.83 ± 0.90	**99.59** ± 0.70
audiology	80.31 ± 7.06	81.20 ± 7.42	× **84.75** ± 7.44
autos	83.30 ± 7.92	82.91 ± 7.16	**85.26** ± 7.06
balance-scale	**90.02** ± 2.64	$\sqrt{}$ 82.17 ± 3.26	$\sqrt{}$ 78.35 ± 3.78
breast-cancer	71.92 ± 6.36	**73.17** ± 5.55	66.89 ± 7.33
breast-w	**97.00** ± 1.90	$\sqrt{}$ 95.84 ± 2.24	96.08 ± 2.16
colic	84.02 ± 5.54	**85.15** ± 5.75	81.63 ± 6.20
credit-a	**86.10** ± 3.80	86.01 ± 3.82	84.01 ± 4.36
credit-g	**73.80** ± 3.48	73.45 ± 3.85	70.75 ± 3.82
diabetes	**76.24** ± 4.93	75.21 ± 4.62	$\sqrt{}$ 71.69 ± 4.80
glass	74.21 ± 9.60	**75.38** ± 9.38	75.25 ± 7.59
heart-c	**81.78** ± 6.68	78.40 ± 7.31	78.59 ± 6.97
heart-h	**80.25** ± 6.72	79.23 ± 6.89	78.84 ± 6.98
heart-statlog	**82.37** ± 6.74	80.74 ± 7.18	78.59 ± 7.15
hepatitis	**83.24** ± 8.77	81.95 ± 8.21	82.38 ± 8.01
hypothyroid	**99.68** ± 0.29	99.59 ± 0.31	99.65 ± 0.31
ionosphere	**93.51** ± 4.05	91.74 ± 4.59	93.05 ± 3.92
iris	**95.93** ± 4.73	94.53 ± 5.22	94.33 ± 5.22
labor	**90.37** ± 12.48	81.63 ± 16.89	87.17 ± 14.28
letter	**95.67** ± 0.41	$\sqrt{}$ 92.65 ± 0.58	95.53 ± 0.45
lymphography	**82.60** ± 8.92	77.80 ± 10.14	80.87 ± 8.63
primary-tumor	**45.49** ± 6.22	43.11 ± 6.85	41.65 ± 6.55
segment	**98.15** ± 0.97	$\sqrt{}$ 97.39 ± 1.10	98.12 ± 0.90
sonar	**82.99** ± 8.52	77.58 ± 8.82	79.13 ± 8.68
soybean	**94.36** ± 2.25	$\sqrt{}$ 92.66 ± 3.09	92.83 ± 2.85
splice	**95.38** ± 1.25	$\sqrt{}$ 94.44 ± 1.26	94.58 ± 1.16
vehicle	**76.89** ± 3.78	74.87 ± 4.00	75.59 ± 3.99
vote	**96.46** ± 2.54	96.32 ± 2.59	95.51 ± 3.05
vowel-c	**96.93** ± 1.90	$\sqrt{}$ 89.70 ± 3.47	$\sqrt{}$ 92.85 ± 2.69
vowel-n	**95.55** ± 2.16	$\sqrt{}$ 89.23 ± 3.59	$\sqrt{}$ 91.97 ± 2.87
waveform	**83.90** ± 1.69	$\sqrt{}$ 81.61 ± 1.79	$\sqrt{}$ 81.40 ± 1.88
zoo	92.69 ± 7.37	93.70 ± 7.20	**96.15** ± 6.11
Win - Loss		5 - 27	5 - 27

For the 32 data sets, rotation based ensembles are better than Bagging, Random Forest and Boosting, respectively, for 27, 25, and 24 data sets.

4   Related Works

The most similar work is [11], because it uses PCA as a mechanism for ensemble generation. For each class, it does the analysis, and then the less important

Table 3. Obtained results for the different data sets with different methods for generating ensembles. It shows the average value and the standard deviation of the accuracy. The base classifiers are unpruned decision trees. The best value for each row is marked in **boldface**. The symbol $\sqrt{}$ indicates a significant difference favorable to our method.

data set	Rotations	Bagging	R. Forest	AdaBoost.M1
anneal	99.21 ± 0.86	98.88 ± 0.92	99.45 ± 0.72	**99.53** ± 0.64
audiology	80.00 ± 7.62	81.07 ± 8.04	78.29 ± 7.21	**83.37** ± 7.38
autos	83.55 ± 8.01	83.45 ± 7.76	82.59 ± 7.92	**84.24** ± 8.00
balance-scale	**90.12** ± 2.63	$\sqrt{}$ 81.50 ± 3.46	$\sqrt{}$ 81.37 ± 3.40	$\sqrt{}$ 76.88 ± 4.15
breast-cancer	**71.47** ± 6.61	69.72 ± 7.39	68.79 ± 6.95	66.83 ± 8.08
breast-w	**96.97** ± 1.84	$\sqrt{}$ 95.82 ± 2.35	96.22 ± 2.22	96.01 ± 2.05
colic	83.64 ± 5.27	84.72 ± 5.80	**85.29** ± 5.58	81.14 ± 6.33
credit-a	**86.12** ± 3.83	85.13 ± 4.00	85.97 ± 3.50	84.13 ± 3.98
credit-g	73.71 ± 3.52	72.22 ± 3.96	**74.94** ± 3.54	71.75 ± 4.58
diabetes	**76.09** ± 4.83	75.35 ± 4.55	76.03 ± 4.21	72.47 ± 5.20
glass	73.84 ± 9.62	75.10 ± 9.14	**78.41** ± 8.72	75.72 ± 9.13
heart-c	**81.84** ± 6.63	77.88 ± 7.09	81.21 ± 6.91	78.49 ± 7.22
heart-h	79.60 ± 6.81	78.59 ± 7.84	**80.62** ± 6.64	79.02 ± 7.42
heart-statlog	**82.04** ± 6.54	80.33 ± 7.53	81.07 ± 6.86	79.48 ± 7.89
hepatitis	**83.45** ± 9.02	82.15 ± 8.47	83.36 ± 7.66	82.23 ± 8.20
hypothyroid	**99.67** ± 0.28	99.61 ± 0.33	$\sqrt{}$ 99.27 ± 0.47	99.65 ± 0.30
ionosphere	**93.51** ± 3.98	91.88 ± 4.49	93.17 ± 3.95	92.80 ± 3.89
iris	**96.13** ± 4.56	94.40 ± 5.34	94.53 ± 4.96	94.27 ± 5.10
labor	**90.53** ± 12.27	83.50 ± 16.91	88.23 ± 13.55	87.53 ± 14.39
letter	**95.72** ± 0.41	$\sqrt{}$ 92.80 ± 0.58	$\sqrt{}$ 95.39 ± 0.49	95.45 ± 0.49
lymphography	82.25 ± 9.03	78.54 ± 9.67	82.36 ± 9.13	**82.70** ± 10.17
primary-tumor	**44.81** ± 6.60	42.60 ± 6.44	43.19 ± 6.82	42.04 ± 6.99
segment	98.17 ± 0.97	$\sqrt{}$ 97.43 ± 1.10	97.86 ± 0.89	**98.27** ± 0.81
sonar	**83.04** ± 8.58	77.54 ± 8.58	82.56 ± 8.79	80.24 ± 9.85
soybean	**93.92** ± 2.45	$\sqrt{}$ 91.57 ± 3.16	92.82 ± 2.92	92.45 ± 2.68
splice	**95.37** ± 1.24	$\sqrt{}$ 94.22 ± 1.19	$\sqrt{}$ 93.44 ± 1.57	$\sqrt{}$ 94.05 ± 1.28
vehicle	**76.90** ± 3.69	75.02 ± 3.88	75.45 ± 4.08	76.66 ± 3.90
vote	96.39 ± 2.64	**96.57** ± 2.45	96.11 ± 2.67	95.05 ± 3.17
vowel-c	**96.96** ± 1.90	$\sqrt{}$ 91.04 ± 3.39	96.72 ± 1.99	$\sqrt{}$ 94.22 ± 2.45
vowel-n	**95.59** ± 2.16	$\sqrt{}$ 89.38 ± 3.54	94.56 ± 2.69	$\sqrt{}$ 91.96 ± 2.51
waveform	**83.94** ± 1.70	$\sqrt{}$ 81.61 ± 1.77	83.38 ± 1.72	$\sqrt{}$ 81.39 ± 1.74
zoo	93.00 ± 7.18	93.90 ± 7.10	96.55 ± 5.49	**96.75** ± 5.61
Win - Loss		5 - 27	7 - 25	8 - 24

components are discarded. The number of components to keep is a parameter of the method. Although the analysis has been done using only one of the classes, the transformed data set is used for obtaining a classifier that discriminates among all the classes. The number of classifiers in the ensemble is limited to the number of classes, but the base classifiers can also be ensembles.

The principal difference is that in our case, the PCA is done for groups of attributes, not for all the attributes. Another difference it that in that work PCA is used only for one of the classes, in our case it is done for a subset of the classes. In this way, if the number of classes is not very small, there are a lot more cases for our method.

The last difference is that we consider all the components, none is discarded *a priori* (although is the classification method performs feature selection, as is the case for decision trees, some could be discarded *a posteriori*). PCA was designed for dimensionality reduction, so it appears a bit strange to keep all the components. The reasons are that PCA is a not supervised method, the class of each instance is not considered in the analysis. Hence, the non principal components can be indispensable for discriminating the classes. The danger of discarding important components is even greater if PCA is applied to a subset of the classes.

5   Conclusions and Future Work

A novel method for generating ensembles of classifiers has been presented. It is relatively simple, it only consists on grouping the attributes of the data sets in subgroups and the application of axis rotations for each subgroup. In this way, a new data set is obtained.

The experimental results show the method superiority, when using decision trees as base classifiers, compared to Bagging, Random Forest and AdaBoost.M1. It is somewhat surprising that the results of the method were better than the results for boosting, because it appears to be rather more elaborated, and with a most solid theoretical basis. Nevertheless, it must be pointed out that there are a lot of Boosting variants, and the one used is one of the most well-known but also one of the oldest. The reason for using that version was that it was the one available in WEKA. One of the features of boosting, not present in neither our method nor Bagging is the ability of obtaining *strong* classifiers from *weak* ones, such as decision stumps. On the other hand, Bagging and our method allow the construction of the base classifiers in parallel.

Apart from the number of base classifiers, the presented method has two parameters. First, the number of attributes present in each group. Second, the coefficient between the final and the original number of attributes. For the reported experiments these parameters were fixed. The number of attributes in each group was 3 and the number of attributes was the same in the original and in the transformed data sets. These parameters could be optimized for each data set using cross validation, but this approach is computationally intensive. Hence, it would be useful some heuristic rule for assigning values to these parameters.

Moreover, if the number of attributes is not the same in the original and final data sets, then the method could be useful for those methods that are rotation-invariant, because if the number of attributes is different, the model generated by the classification method can be different.

The experimental validation has been limited to classification problems. Apparently, the method can be also used for regression problems, if the base regression method is not invariant to rotations, as is the case for regression trees.

The presented method is compatible with another ensemble methods. First, the base classifier for an ensemble method can be another ensemble method. For instance, it could be possible to use the presented method using bagging as base classifier. In this way, it could be possible to combine 100 decision trees, but applying the PCA procedure only 10 times. This can be useful because the PCA procedure is slower than resampling, the used strategy for Bagging.

Second, it is possible to apply several transformations to the original data set. For instance, resample and then the presented method. In this way, the two ensemble methods are not used hierarchically, but simultaneously. Then, it is necessary to study the possible usefulness of some of these combinations.

References

1. Eric Bauer and Ron Kohavi. An empirical comparison of voting classification algorithms: Bagging, boosting, and variants. *Machine Learning*, 36(1–2):105–139, 1999.
2. C.L. Blake and C.J. Merz. UCI repository of machine learning databases, 1998. http://www.ics.uci.edu/~mlearn/MLRepository.html.
3. Leo Breiman. Bagging predictors. *Machine Learning*, 24(2):123–140, 1996.
4. Leo Breiman. Random forests. *Machine Learning*, 45(1):5–32, 2001.
5. Thomas G. Dietterich. Ensemble methods in machine learning. In *Multiple Classifier Systems 2000*, pages 1–15, 2000.
6. Jiawei Han and Micheline Kamber. *Data Mining: Concepts and Techniques*. Morgan Kaufmann, 2001.
7. Tin Kam Ho. The random subspace method for constructing decision forests. *IEEE Transactions on Pattern Analysis and Machine Intelligence*, 20(8):832–844, 1998.
8. Tin Kam Ho. A data complexity analysis of comparative advantages of decision forest constructors. *Pattern Analysis and Applications*, 5:102–112, 2002.
9. J. Ross Quinlan. *C4.5: programs for machine learning*. Machine Learning. Morgan Kaufmann, San Mateo, California, 1993.
10. Robert E. Schapire. The boosting approach to machine learning: An overview. In *MSRI Workshop on Nonlinear Estimation and Classification*, 2002. http://www.cs.princeton.edu/~schapire/papers/msri.ps.gz.
11. Kafan Tumer and Nikunk C. Oza. Input decimated ensembles. *Pattern Anal Applic*, 6:65–77, 2003.
12. Ian H. Witten and Eibe Frank. *Data Mining: Practical Machine Learning Tools and Techniques with Java Implementations*. Morgan Kaufmann, 1999. http://www.cs.waikato.ac.nz/ml/weka.

SACEME:
An Authoring Tool for Knowledge Acquisition
Using Techniques of Programming by Examples

Miguel A. Redondo, José R. Sánchez, Crescencio Bravo,
Manuel Ortega, and José Bravo

Dpto. de Informática, Universidad de Castilla - La Mancha
Paseo de la Universidad, 4. 13071 Ciudad Real (Spain)
{Miguel.Redondo,Crescencio.Bravo,Manuel.Ortega,Jose.Bravo}@uclm.es

Abstract. Intelligent Tutoring Systems apply techniques which evolve from the Artificial Intelligence to the development of computer-assisted educational systems. In most cases these techniques are based on the use of expert knowledge whose acquisition can involve a weak point in its construction process. This aspect significantly hinders the generalization of its use. This article describes a tool named SACEME which has been developed to tackle with the previous problem and applied to a particular domain with a system which suffered from this lack.

Introduction

Intelligent Tutoring Systems (ITS) apply techniques of Artificial Intelligence to the development of computer-assisted learning systems. These systems incorporate the capacity of dynamic adaptation to the development of the student's learning process, analyzing the learner's behavior to determine and to apply the most appropriate instructional strategies at every moment [1].

One of the important aspects in the development of ITS is Planning [2]. Planning is necessary when structuring the domain to study. This means that it is necessary to provide the system with the means required to represent the knowledge in a clear way, thus avoiding any kind of ambiguity that can interfere in the learning process. The plan includes a series of instructional activities in order to get the previously established learning objectives.

In addition, collaborative learning environments commit the learners to realize the cognitive and metacognitive activities contributing this way to the shared development of all the members in the group. In these environments individual as well as social tasks are approached, in which it is also necessary to analyze the achievements reached to plan and to direct the learning process automatically [3].

In the last years the ITS have surpassed the status of laboratory prototypes and they are now installed in classrooms, work places, and even on the Internet. However, they are difficult and expensive to build, which is an obstacle to generalize their use [1]. In order to foster the installation of these systems it is necessary to build authoring tools to facilitate the development of ITS to people with no experience in Knowledge Engineering.

R. Conejo et al. (Eds.): CAEPIA-TTIA 2003, LNAI 3040, pp. 507–516, 2004.
© Springer-Verlag Berlin Heidelberg 2004

Researchers in the field of Programming by Examples have demonstrated that it is possible to obtain and to infer knowledge from diverse domains in order to build abstractions from the manipulation of objects [4,5]. We can mention the systems RIDES [6] and Demonstr8 [7] as actual examples of authoring tools that use techniques of Programming by Examples to infer general procedures from examples specified by the user.

In this article we describe some of the characteristics of a tool that we call SACE-ME and that has been developed to capture experts' procedural knowledge in the teaching of the design of installations for the integral automation of housings and buildings (Domotics). This knowledge is used to guide the work that groups of learners carry out in an environment of collaborative learning of design [8,9].

In the following section the domain and the learning context on which we place our investigation are introduced, and we describe the system that has been developed to improve the teaching and learning process. Subsequently, we describe the expert knowledge that this system uses and how it is represented. Next, the characteristics of the tool developed to capture this knowledge are described, and finally, some conclusions of this work are drawn.

Domotics and the Teaching of Domotical Design

The term Domotics (*Home Automation*) is associated to the set of elements that, installed, interconnected and automatically controlled at home, release the user from the routine of intervening in everyday actions and, at the same time, they provide optimized control over comfort, energetic consumption, security and communications.

In Spain, the current "Formación Profesional" (Technical Training) outlined in the LOGSE takes into account certain professional profiles where the learning of Domotics is considered a necessity. Some training cycles of Electricity and Electronics focus on the study of the design and maintenance of single installations and of the automation of buildings dedicated to housings, as well as of the design of systems of automatic control for housings and buildings. In this area, the learning of the design of domotical facilities acquires a remarkable complexity and has a fundamental role.

In this kind of training, the realization of practical works is very important. However, the material required to carry out these works is usually very expensive and in many cases its availability is low. This problem increases since it is difficult to bring the student to real situations, to reproduce accidents and to deal with chaotic situations which can happen in the real world and whose design should be taken into consideration.

In order to alleviate this problem a distributed environment of domotical design was developed providing support for collaborative distance learning. The system, named DomoSim-TPC, is used to the configuration, realization, search, analysis and storage of activities of collaborative learning. With the inclusion of this system in the teaching of Domotics in Secondary Education, the educational protocol followed has been slightly modified.

As Figure 1 shows, using the DomoSim-TPC system, the activities of practical learning of the domotical design are structured in three clearly differentiated stages. In each of them diverse cognitive exercises are carried out and approached, and repre-

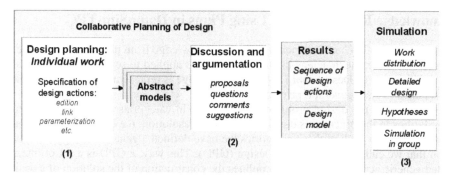

Fig. 1. Stages and tasks of domotic design learning carried out in an experience with Do-moSim-TPC.

sentations of expert knowledge are used. Next, these stages are described concisely and the most outstanding tasks carried out in each of them are pointed out:

1. Planning a design strategy. In this stage the learners, in an individual way, medi-tate, plan and define the steps that determine the strategy to follow to build the model that satisfies the requirements specified in the problem formulation. That is to say, they define the solution and the form of reaching it. In this process the user's actions can be driven by the system. For such purpose there is a tool named PlanEdit [10] which, by using an intermediate and abstract representation to specify the design and with expert knowledge represented in form of optimal plans of design, adapts to the learner's performance and advises them on which actions would be the best to approach at every moment. The justification of the tool used at this stage is due to the results obtained in diverse experiences car-ried out with real users [11].

2. Discussion, argumentation and search of agreement in the features of the design plans individually built. At this stage two cognitive practices are developed: de-signing and collaborating. The participants discuss on the solution, on their way and the steps taken to carry out in order to obtain it. This way, at this stage a proposal will be obtained, reflecting the view-point of each participant. Here the representations of knowledge used are the same as at the previous stage. This is done in order to determine whether the previous discussion derived from the models built is justified or, on the contrary, it does not lead to anything positive. That is to say, the system can intervene limiting the possibilities of participation in the dialogue process trying to lead the discussion. Both stages constitute what we call Collaborative Planning of Design [12].

3. Detailed design and simulation in group. Before checking the validity of the proposed model, the learners should detail and organize the attributes associated to the objects of the model. This task is carried out by means of a tool, which is also collaborative, based on the direct manipulation of the domain objects [13]. Later on, the students consider the hypotheses and simulation cases that should be check by means of the Collaborative Simulation of the behavior of this model.

Knowledge Representation Using Plans in DomoSim-TPC

The DomoSim-TPC environment uses expert knowledge from previous experience of some trainers and technicians in Domotics. This is applied to several tools, especially to the Planning of Design tool [10]. This knowledge is represented by means of plans associated to each general type of problem.

We classify the design problems in Domotics in categories depending on certain similarities in the procedures developed for their resolution, the elements required and the context. For each of these categories we have defined a general strategy of resolution that we call General Plan of Design (GPD). This way, a GPD is a set of interrelated generic actions of design that oulines the construction of the solution of a design problem. Some of these can only be obligatory, while others being optional, even some can be advisable regarding the quality of the final solution built. Among the actions of a GPD a precedence relationship imposing restrictions and obligations is set up. Before handling an action others should have been dealt with. Also, the fact of approaching an action could make others necessarily be carried out. For example, it is not possible to link two elements if one of them has not still been inserted. But if the connection could be established, then it is necessary to define its characteristics.

Thus, a GPD is a sequence of elements in the following way:

`<action>:<type>:<requirements>:<influences>`

`<action>` identifies an action, `<type>` indicates if it is obligatory, advisable or optional, `<requirements>` enunciates the actions that should be carried out to be able to approach this one in particular and `<influences>` makes reference to those actions that should be carried out as a consequence of the realization of the current action.

A problem, although it may be included in a certain category with an associate GPD, has a particular characterization that conditions its solution. These particularities are specially important if the system is aimed at following the user's performance to guide them in their work. Therefore, it is necessary to have a specific strategy relative to a particular problem and that can be obtained in a systematic way from the category in which the problem is framed. Therefore, we define the Optimal Plan of Design (OPD) as the sequences of actions that represent possible valid solutions to a particular problem. The OPD is obtained from the GPD and from the characteristics or parameters that make a problem specific. For this instantiation it is necessary to provide the GPD with a set of rules of the type:

`IF <parameter> THEN <modifyAction>`

Where `<parameter>` is one of the parameters specific to a problem, and `<modifyAction>` makes reference to a modification to apply some of the actions defined in the GPD. When applying these rules to a GPD, the OPD is obtained.

It is necessary to remark that we do not try to determine which the optimal solution to a design problem is. We simply register the expert's view-point, and therefore, we only want to represent what, according to his/her approach, it is the best way of solving the problem. This representation, in the form of a plan, can be studied and valued as a directed graph, where the nodes are actions, the arcs indicate precedence and the weight indicates the cost associated to the choice of an action, that is to say, the form in which the complexity of the solution increases [10].

We should remember that the purpose of this knowledge is to guide the learners while they are solving a proposed problem. The system does this by dynamically checking if the solution and its construction mechanism are valid. This is done by registering, in plan form, the actions that the user carries out. The learner's plan is compared with the OPD calculated for the problem and using the conclusions obtained, the system can show messages of mistake, suggestion or reinforcement help to direct the student towards a good solution [10]. The system even evaluate the solution that the student outlines, identifying it as one of the paths of the graph. Thus, the best solution is defined as the minimum cover tree of this graph.

With this position it is necessary to have an authoring tool to capture the experience of experts in the teaching of domotics design and to represent it as design plans, that is to say, to obtain the GPD for each generic problem and the particular aspects to automatically generate the OPD for a specific problem. Our decision has been to develop SACEME as a tool designed jointly with the participation of the final users (user-centred design to guarantee its usability) and based on ideas of the Programming by Examples paradigm. Next, we describe the most representative characteristics of SACEME.

Tool for the Automatic Acquisition of Design Plans

SACEME is proposed as a tool for facilitating the automatic acquisition of design plans, modelled as previously described. That is, to help the authors to express and to understand their knowledge and experience of the domain. Thus, the first premise is to have an important semantic wealth for the visualization of the knowledge. Therefore, the user interface will require an intensive design and programming work, trying to solve the lack of authoring tools in the construction process of a ITS [1]. According to this, the interface has been structured as a design environment close to the CAD[1] tools used in the industry. To this environment a graph representation of acquired knowledge has been included. This representation is named *graph of actions*.

Design Environment

This tool allows the experts to express to the actions they carry out in order to build the solution to a problem. Additionally, it verifies that the model built is coherent from the view-point of the problem formulation. For this purpose, implicit expert knowledge is used.

The implicit knowledge consists of rules obtained from the restrictions and necessities specified in the problem and from previous experiences. When the user carries out a design action (to insert or to eliminate an object, to link objects, etc.) the tool check that the established elementary restrictions are satisfied. Thus, we intend to make sure that the quality is kept. The tool uses mechanisms which check the information created to assure their accuracy, consistency, integrity and effectiveness. At the same time, certain flexibility is allowed in the strategy. The author can act freely, but the aforementioned restrictions have to accomplished. That is to say, a restricted flexibility is offered. This approach is used in other systems such as Expert-CML [14] or REDEEM [15]. The professionals who use SACEME are familiarized with CAD systems. This is the reason why the environment includes part of the functionality of a CAD tool. This can be seen in figure 2, which shows the user interface.

---

[1] Computer Assisted Design

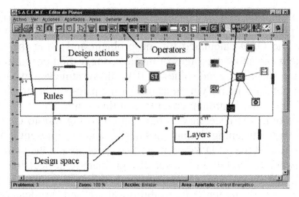

Fig. 2. User interface of the design environment.

Graph of Actions

In order to complete and refine the knowledge acquisition and, at the same time, to have a visualization of the actions carried out by the expert, a graph is used. This representation is generated automatically as a consequence of the actions carried out on the design environment. At least, all graphs of actions should have two nodes representing the actions of initialization and finalization of the design, and an arc linking both nodes. Starting from this minimum graph, new nodes and arcs will be added or eliminated, depending on the actions carried out on the design environment or directly interacting with the graph of actions. Each node represents a design action including information relative to the action type, to the object affected, to the scenario in which it is applied, etc. This information is represented on the node by using similar icons to those used in the design environment. The arcs indicate relationships and dependences among the design actions. When an action is carried out in the design environment, it will always be a continuation of other actions previously carried out, and it will be part of the requirements of such action. Then arcs will be created linking the action carried out to the nodes of the previous actions. In the same way, given an action and using implicit knowledge (implications of the action) the tool can determine the nodes directly depending on the preceding one. Thus, the graph of actions reflects the mechanisms and strategies inferred from observing the design that the expert directly carries out with the editor of the design environment.

An arc has information about its weight or cost. If from a node several arcs leave toward other nodes then each arc represents an alternative to continue with the design. In the expert's opinion it can have better and worse alternatives. The cost of the arc gives value to these alternatives. This way, the tool can determine which the best design strategy is. This strategy is the path starting from initial node to the final node, which is a minimum value for the sum of the cost of all the arcs.

All the design actions carried out using the design environment are automatically registered and dynamically reflected in the graph of actions, and vice versa. The tool shows the graph of actions and a partial view of the design environment (see figure 3). On the right, when a node of the graph is selected, the state of the design after approaching the action represented in this node is shown. This way, the author can obtain a historical vision of the design, allowing them to think about their work. In

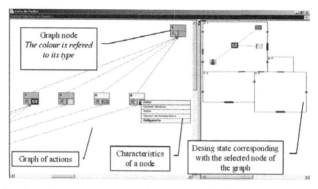

Fig. 3. Visualization of the graph of actions and its influences on the design.

addition, the author can propose other alternatives starting from the node selected (the currently represented state).

The nodes have an associated state defined as obligatory, advisable or optional. This state represents the character of the action associated to this node. By default, all nodes are obligatory, but the author can modify this state. It is necessary to define how the change of a node affects the rest of the nodes depending on it. For that purpose, we have defined a set of rules that spread the consequences of these changes along the whole graph of actions. For example, when changing a node from obligatory to optional, all the nodes depending on it will become optional, or when the change is from advisable to obligatory, the nodes depending on it as well as the nodes which it depends upon will become obligatory. This way, multiple strategies and alterations are defined. These alterations will always make reference to definitions and specific parameters of the problem to be solved.

Generating the Graph of Actions

The graph of actions is dynamically generated from observing the user's performance. This process is based on the definition of a set of generic design actions which we consider significant (insert, link, etc.). Our objective is to obtain different organizations of these actions, and also of the objects they affect.

A first organization is the sequence followed by the expert to make the design. But it constitutes a not very flexible sequence of actions. Another alternative consists in identifying the objects being inserted and in combining possible organizations of the generic design actions affecting them.

In order to determine possible organizations of the sequence of objects inserted, we identify subsystems as associations of objects and we consider that: (a) objects of a subsystem can be inserted in any order; (b) the subsystems are grouped in systems; (c) the tool can use information from the problem formulation to automatically extract restrictions about the order in which the design of each system should be carried out. Therefore, the method to generate the graph of actions is as follows: (1) to identify design patterns; (2) to determine the affected system and subsystem; and (3) to generate all possible alternatives as a result of determining the sequences of inserted objects and the valid sequences of generic design actions which can affect them.

Integrating into DomoSim-TPC

The objective pursued with SACEME is to acquire knowledge and represent it by using plans. These plans must be integrated in DomoSim-TPC to guide the learners when participating in learning activities based on problem solution.

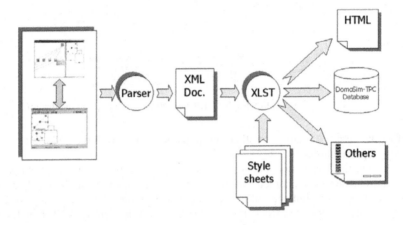

Fig. 4. Process of final representation of the knowledge acquired with SACEME.

In order to facilitate this integration we use XML and XLST technologies so that the acquired knowledge is processed and represented by using XML. Later, style sheets based on XLST are used to convert it into HTML. This way we can visualize it directly on any web browser. Also SACEME uses a style sheet to transfer the previous XML document into information that is directly integrated in the knowledge databases of DomoSim-TPC. These knowledge databases are supported by a relational database management system. Starting from the XML documents and using the appropriate styles, very diverse representations can be obtained. Thus, it is possible to integrate the knowledge acquired with other systems allowing the use of other techniques to visualize and present it in other devices with more restrictions in its user interface (see figure 4).

Conclusions

In this work we have approached the development of a tool for knowledge acquisition with the aim of integrating it in an environment of computer-supported collaborative learning of design. The knowledge is acquired by observing the performance of the experts in an environment that allows them to interact as they usually do. From this interaction information is obtained, organized and represented in form of a design plan. These plans are structured as graphs that can be visualized. They are even interactive, allowing the expert to realize the implications on the design of the changes carried out directly on the design plan (graph) and vice versa. Moreover, the graph displays the sequence of design actions carried out. The user can introduce other alternatives and evaluate them in terms of their quality. We have carried out an important effort in the visualization of the acquired knowledge and we offer the possibility to interact directly on this knowledge, adopting the metaphor of design actions carried out to build design plans. This approach can be adopted in systems that use cognitive representations in the form of plans for the teaching model and for the model of the domain. Especially, it is directly applicable to systems such as DomoSim-TPC which approach the teaching of design in any discipline, using a derived instruction model of the problem-based learning and a representation of the domain in the form of plans.

SACEME has been used to obtain over 30 plans (GPDs) for generic problems. These plans have been integrated directly in DomoSim-TPC. It has been installed in centers of profesional training for the realization of over 70 activities of collaborative learning of the design. These activities outlined the resolution of specific problems and their concrete solution strategies were generated (OPDs), with several valid alternatives and evaluated according to the opinion of the experts.

Currently, we are hoping to extend the representation of the GPDs and OPDs outlined so that, in the phase of the argumentative discussion with DomoSim-TPC, structures of social behavior and their implication on the ways to solve a design problem can be taken into consideration and evaluated. This extension should make us think about the technique to apply in order to automatically obtain this information relative to the form in which people work together to carry out a task (for example, to solve a complex problem of design).

Acknowledgments

This work has partially been supported by the Junta de Comunidades de Castilla – La Mancha and the Ministerio de Ciencia y Tecnología in the projects PBI-02-026 and TIC2002-01387.

References

1. Murray, T. (1999). Authoring Intelligent Tutoring Systems: An Analysis of the State of the Art. *Int. Journal of AIED*, 10(1), pp. 98-129.
2. Verdejo, M.F., (1992). A Framework for Instructional Planning and Discourse Modelling in Intelligent Tutoring Systems. In Costa, E. (Ed.), *New Directions for Intelligent Tutoring Systems*, vol 91. Berlin: NATO ASI Series, Springer-Verlag. pp. 147-170.
3. Redondo, M.A., Bravo, C., Bravo, J., Ortega, M., Organizing activities of problem based collaborative learning with the DomoSim-TPC system. In M. Llamaset al (Eds.), *Computers and Education: Towards a Lifelong Learning Society*. Kluwer Academic Publishers. (In Press).
4. Cypher, A., (1993) Watch What I Do: Programming by Demonstration. *The MIT Press*.
5. Myers,B.A.,(1988) Creating User Interfaces by Demonstration. *Academic Press*, San Diego.
6. Munro, A., Jonson, M.C., Pizzini, Q.A., Surmon, D.S., Towne, D.M., & Wogulis, J.L., (1997). Authoring simulation-centered tutors with RIDES. *Int. Journal of AIED*. Vol. 8, No. 3-4, pp.284-316.
7. Blessing, S.B., (1997) A programming by demonstration authoring tool for model tracing tutors. *Int. Journal of AIED*, Vol. 8, No. 3-4, pp. 233-261.

8. Bravo, C., Redondo, M.A., Bravo, J., & Ortega, M., (2000). DOMOSIM-COL: A Simulation Collaborative Environment for the Learning of Domotic Design. *Inroads - The SIGCSE Bulletin of ACM*, vol. 32, num. 2, pp.65-67.
9. Bravo, C., Bravo, J., Ortega, M., Redondo, M.A., (1999). A Simulation Distributed Cooperative Environment for the Domotic Design. Proc. of 4th Int. Workshop on CSCWD, Barthès, J.P., Lin, Z, Ramos, M., pp. 3-6. UTC Compiègne.
10. Redondo, M.A., Bravo, C., Ortega, M., & Verdejo, M.F., (2002). PlanEdit: and adaptive tool for design learning by problem solving. In P. De Bra et al (Eds.), Adaptive Hypermedia and Adaptive Web Based-Systems, LNCS 2347, pp. 560-563. Springer-Verlag.
11. Bravo, J., Ortega, M., & Verdejo, M.F., (1999). Planning in problem solving: a case study in Domotics. Proc. of Frontiers in Education. Kansas City (USA): IEEE Computer Society.
12. Redondo, M.A., (2002) Collaborative Planning of Design in simulation environments for distance learning. PhD Thesis. Dpto. Informática UCLM.
13. Bravo, C, Redondo, M.A., Ortega, M., Verdejo, M.F., Collaborative Discovery Learning of Model Design, In S. A. Cerri, G. Gourdères y F Paraguaçu (Eds.), Intelligent Tutoring Systems. LNCS 2363, pp. 671-680. Springer-Verlag, 2002.
14. Jones, M. & Wipond, K. (1991) Intelligent Environments for Curriculum and Course Development. In Goodyear (Ed.), *Teaching Knowledge and Intelligent Tutoring. Norwoord*, NJ: Ablex.
15. Major, N., Ainsworth, S. & Wood, D. (1997) REEDEM: Exploiting simbiosis between psychology and authoring environments. *Int. Journal of AIED*. Vol. 8, No. 3-4, pp. 317-340.

Scatter Search
for the Feature Selection Problem*

Félix C. García López, Miguel García Torres**,
José A. Moreno Pérez, and J. Marcos Moreno Vega

Departamento de E.I.O. and Computación
Escuela Técnica Superior de Ingeniería Informática
University of La Laguna, 38271 La Laguna
Santa Cruz de Tenerife, Spain
{fcgarcia,mgarciat,jamoreno,jmmoreno}@ull.es

Abstract. The feature selection problem in the field of classification consists of obtaining a subset of variables to optimally realize the task without taking into account the remainder variables. This work presents how the search for this subset is performed using the Scatter Search metaheuristic and is compared with two traditional strategies in the literature: the Forward Sequential Selection (FSS) and the Backward Sequential Selection (BSS). Promising results were obtained. We use the lazy learning strategy together with the nearest neighbour methodology (NN) also known as Instance-Based Learning Algorithm 1 (IB1).

1 Introduction

Instance-Based Learning (IBL) [1] is an inductive learning algorithm that generalizes tasks by storing available training instances in memory. The purpose of the classification problem, given a set of cases or instances of a known class, is to classify other cases of which only the features or variables are known. A similarity measure is needed between cases [11] for which the set of available features is used. However, not all of the variables that describe the instances provide the same quality of information; some of them do not significantly contribute and can even degrade the information.

The purpose of the feature selection problem is to obtain the subset of these features which optimally carry out the classification task. An appropriate feature selection affects efficiency, because is cheaper to measure only a subset of features, and accuracy, which might be improved by removing irrelevant features. This is of special interest in those problems with a large number of cases and features.

These problems are NP-hard [6]. Thus it is impossible to explore the whole solution space. The metaheuristics provide procedures for finding solutions with

---

* This work has been partially supported by the project TIC2002-04242-C03-01, 70% of which are FEDER founds.
** The work of the second author has been partially supported by CajaCanarias grant.

R. Conejo et al. (Eds.): CAEPIA-TTIA 2003, LNAI 3040, pp. 517–525, 2004.
© Springer-Verlag Berlin Heidelberg 2004

reasonable efficacy and efficiency. The application of evolutive procedures such as Genetic Algorithms [4] are described in the literature, but, to our knowledge, the Scatter Search (SS) has not been applied. In this work we analyse the SS metaheuristic in this problem, comparing its performance with two traditional strategies: the Forward Sequential Selection (FSS) and the Backward Sequential Selection (BSS).

In the next section we introduce the feature selection problem with a formal description of the problem and the most common solution strategies. In section 3 we describe the main elements of the Scatter Search metaheuristic in the application to this problem. The outcomes of the computational experience are shown in section 4 for several data sets and motivate our conclusions, shown in section 5.

2   The Feature Selection Problem

In the Feature Selection Problem there are two general approaches: the filter and the wrapper strategies. The first approach is characterized by the application of a different methodology in the training and test phases. The wrapper applies the same algorithm in the entire process. In the filter approach, the relevant algorithm FOCUS [3] examines the entire subset of features selecting those that minimize the number of features among those classifying correctly all of the training instances. Another relevant algorithm is *Relief*, which is a random algorithm that assigns a weight to each feature based on the two nearest cases.

The second approach consists of two traditional strategies: the FSS strategy and the BSS strategy. FSS starts with an empty subset of features and iteratively adds the best feature as it improves the solution. BSS starts with the whole set of features and iteratively removes the worst feature while it improves the solution. This last strategy provides less efficient procedures [6].

The formal description of the problem is as follows. Let A be a set of n cases (instances or objects) $A = \{a_i : i = 1, ..., n\}$ each one described by d features (or attributes) $\{X_j\}_{j=1...d}$ where each feature can be nominal or numeric. Each case is described by a vector $a_i = (a_{i1}, ..., a_{id})$ and a_{ij} corresponds to the value of feature X_j in the case a_i. Moreover, each case a_i belongs to a class labelled as $a_i(c)$. The purpose of the classification problem is to obtain the label of the instances using only a subset of features. Therefore the objective of our problem is to find the subset of features $S = \{X_{i_j} : j = 1 ... m\}$, $m \leq d$ that classifies best.

The classification task using the nearest neighbor approach is carried out by assuming the existence of a set of cases with known class labels (training set) and another set of cases with unknown class labels (test set). The information provided by the training set is used to find the optimal set of features $S = \{X_{i_j} : j = 1, ..., m\}$ to classify. To measure the quality of the classifier (subset of features and classification strategy) we consider the accuracy of the classification as the objective function, f. The associated optimization problem is to find the subset $S \subseteq \{X_j : j = 1, ..., d\}$ such that $f(S)$ is maximized.

Several methods can be considered when measuring accuracy of the algorithms when a set of classified cases is given. A method widely used in the literature is the k-fold cross validation that is described as follows. We consider a total set of cases T divided into k parts of the same size, $T_1, ..., T_k$ and k executions of the algorithm are performed. In the i-th execution the set T_i is taken as the test set and the union of the remainder subsets, $\cup_{j \neq i} T_j$, as training set. In [5] and [2] the method known as "5x2vc" is recommended, which consists in applying the cross validation with $k = 2$ for 5 different orderings of the data base. Such a procedure is also used in the training phase. The IB1 methodology is applied which implies classification by the class of the nearest neighbor [1].

The dissimilarity function between cases applied to determine the nearest neighbor is the distance function HEOM (Heterogenous Euclidean-Overlap Metric) [11]. The distance between two cases a_k and a_m, using the subset of features, $S \subseteq \{X_j : j = 1...d\}$, is defined as

$$d_{HEOM}(a_k, a_m) = \sum_{X_j \in S} d_j^2(a_k, a_m)$$

with

$$d_j(a_k, a_m) = \begin{cases} 1 & \text{if } a_{kj} \text{ or } a_{mj} \text{ are unknown} \\ d_s(a_{kj}, a_{mj}) & \text{if } X_j \text{ is nominal} \\ d_r(a_{kj}, a_{mj}) & \text{if } X_j \text{ is numeric} \end{cases}$$

where d_s is the overlap and d_r is the normalized rectilinear distance that is defined by:

$$d_s(a_{kj}, a_{mj}) = \begin{cases} 1 \text{ if } a_{kj} = a_{mj} \\ 0 \text{ otherwise} \end{cases}$$

and

$$d_r(a_{kj}, a_{mj}) = \frac{|a_{kj} - a_{mj}|}{max_j - min_j}$$

where max_j and min_j are the maximum and minimum values of the feature X_j observed in the training set.

The two traditional hill-climbing strategies, FSS and BSS, improve iteratively the selected subset but they differ in the initial set of features. The first strategy starts with an empty set and at each iteration it adds a feature in case of improvement. The second one starts with the whole set of features and at each iteration removes a feature if there is an improvement. The procedure is as follows:

- *Forward Subset Selection (FSS)*
  1. Initialize the set of features $S = \emptyset$.
  2. For each feature $X_j \notin S$, calculate $f(S \cup \{X_j\})$. Let j^* be such that $f(S \cup \{X_{j^*}\}) = \max_j\{S \cup \{X_j\})\}$ and $S^* = S \cup \{X_{j^*}\}$. If $f(S^*) > f(S)$, take $S = S \cup \{X_{j^*}\}$ and repeat step 2. Otherwise, stop.
- *Backward Subset Selection (BSS)*
  1. Initialize the set of features $S = \{X_j : j = 1, ..., d\}$.
  2. For each feature $X_j \in S$, compute $f(S \setminus \{X_j\})$. Let j^* be such that $f(S \setminus \{X_{j^*}\}) = \max_j\{S \setminus \{X_j\})\}$ and $S^* = S \setminus \{X_{j^*}\}$. If $f(S^*) > f(S)$, take $S = S \setminus \{X_{j^*}\}$ and repeat step 2. Otherwise, stop.

3   Scatter Search

The Scatter Search [8] is a recent evolutionary strategy that has been applied successfully to a wide range of optimisation problems. It starts with a population of solutions from which a subset of solutions are selected for the reference set *RefSet* that evolves by intensification and diversification mechanisms. The solutions of this set are combined to generate new solutions to update the reference set. The combination of the solution in the scatter search is guided and not random, unlike genetic algorithms. Another important difference is that the reference set that evolves in the scatter search is smaller in size than the usual populations in evolutive algorithms.

Figure 1 shows pseudocode of the scatter search.

---

procedure Scatter Search
begin
      GeneratePopulation(*InitPop*);
      GenerateReferenceSet(*RefSet*);
      repeat
          repeat
              SelectSubSet(*SubSet*);
              CombinationMethod(*SubSet, S*);
              ImprovingMethod(S, S^*);
          until (StoppingCriterion 1);
          UpdateReferenceSet(*RefSet*);
      until (StoppingCriterion 2);
end.

Fig. 1. Scatter Search Pseudocode

In order to generate the initial population we use a procedure similar to those used in the constructive phase of the GRASP (Greedy Randomize Adaptive Search Procedure) [12].

The elements of the scatter search in the application to feature selection problem are implemented in the following way:

1. *Generation of the population:*
   The initial population *InitPop* is constructed by generating solutions from the application of the following procedure until the previously fixed size is reached.
   (a) Do $S = \emptyset$.
   (b) For each feature $X_j \in X \setminus S$, calculate the accuracy with which $S_j = S \cup \{X_j\}$ classifies in the training set using the 5x2 cross validation.
   (c) The restricted candidate list, RCL, to the constructive phase of GRASP is constructed by cardinality and it is compounded by the $|RCL|$ best features according to the value $f(S_j)$.
   (d) Select randomly a feature in RCL. Let X_{j*} be such feature.
   (e) If by adding X_{j*} to S it improves the accuracy of the partial solution then do $S = S_{j*}$ and go to step (b). Otherwise, stop.

2. *Generation of the reference set:*
   The reference set, $RefSet$, is generated in two phases. The first phase includes the $\frac{1}{2}|RefSet|$ solutions of the population with the best values of the objective function f. Then the most diverse solutions with respect to the reference set are added, until the $|RefSet|$ size is reached, by using the following procedure in the second phase:
   (a) Let C be the set of all the features that belongs to any solution of the reference set.
   (b) For each solution S of the population that is not in the reference set, calculate the diversity degree $Div(S, C)$.
   (c) Let S^* be the solution with the highest diversity degree.
   (d) Add S^* to the reference set.
   The diversity degree between a solution S and the set of features C is defined as:
   $$Div(S, C) = |(S \cup C) \setminus (S \cap C)|$$

3. *Selection of the subset:*
   All subsets of two solutions of the reference set are selected (i.e., the inner loop of the pseudocode of Figure 1 is repeated for all the subsets with size 2 (stopping criterion 2)). The combination method is applied to each subset and is described in the next subsection. Note that in the first iteration it is necessary to apply the combination method to all the subsets. However, in later iterations it is only necessary to apply this method to the subsets not considered in previous iterations. This method increases efficiency.

4. *Combination Method:*
   Given two solutions S_1 and S_2, the combination method generates two new solutions, S_1' and S_2', as follows:
   (a) Include in S_1' and S_2' the features that are in S_1 and in S_2; i.e., $S_1' = S_2' = S_1 \cap S_2$. Let $C = (S_1 \cup S_2) \setminus (S_1 \cap S_2)$.
   (b) For each feature $X_j \in C$ calculate $f(S_1' \cup \{X_j\})$ and $f(S_2' \cup \{X_j\})$.
   (c) Let j_1^* and j_2^* be features such that $f(S_1' \cup \{X_{j_1^*}\}) = \max_j\{f(S_1' \cup \{X_j\})\}$ and $f(S_2' \cup \{X_{j_2^*}\}) = \max_j\{f(S_2' \cup \{X_j\})\}$ respectively.
   i. If $f(S_1' \cup \{X_{j_1^*}\}) > f(S_1')$ and $f(S_2' \cup \{X_{j_2^*}\}) > f(S_2')$ update the solution of which the feature X_{j^*} has an associated value of the objective function corresponding to $f = \max\{f(S_1' \cup \{X_{j_1^*}\}), f(S_2' \cup \{X_{j_2^*}\})\}$, do $C = C \setminus X_{j^*}$ and go to step (b). If $f_1^*(S_1' \cup \{X_{j_1^*}\}) = f_2^*(S_2' \cup \{X_{j_2^*}\})$, the feature is added to the partial solution with fewer features.
   ii. If only one of the solutions, S_1' or S_2', improves then add the corresponding feature, do $C = C \setminus X_{j^*}$ and go to step (b).
   iii. Otherwise, stop.

5. *Improving method:*
   We initially applied iteratively the FSS and BSS strategies as long as any improvement took place. However it was observed that it only slightly improved the solutions although a high computational effort was required. Therefore we decided to reject this method.

6. *Update of the reference set:*
The solution that improves the worst solution in the reference set is then added and replaces the worst one. Therefore, the outer loop in the pseudocode of figure 1 is repeated while the reference set is being updated (stopping criterion 2)

4   Computational Experience

For the computational experience, we considered standard databases from the U.C.I. repository [10]. To study the performance of the algorithms FSS, BSS and SS, we studied real and artificial databases independently. We also studied the small and average ones independently as well for real databases. The reason for doing this was that, for artificial data, the relevance of each feature is known, nevertheless this information is unknown for real databases. Furthermore a low number of instances can affect the undesirable overfitting effects.

Table 1. Characteristics of the Data Bases considered

Data Base	Name	Id	Features Total	Nom	Num	#Instances	#Classes
Small	Iris	Ir	4	0	4	150	3
	Echocardiogram	Ec	9	2	7	132	2
	Glass	Gl	9	0	9	214	7
	Bridges	Br	11	7	4	108	6
	Wine	Wi	13	0	13	178	3
	Heart(Long − Beach − Va)	HV	13	7	6	200	2
	Heart(Hungarian)	HH	13	7	6	294	2
	Heart(Cleveland)	HC	13	7	6	303	2
	Zoo	Zo	16	16	0	90	7
	SoybeanLarge	SbL	35	29	6	307	19
	Sonar	So	60	0	60	208	2
Average	PimaIndianDiabetes	Pm	8	0	8	768	2
	Vowel	Vw	10	0	10	528	11
	CreditScreening	Cx	15	9	6	690	2
	Anneal	An	38	29	9	798	5
Artificials	Monks − 1	Mo1	6	6	0	432	2
	Monks − 2	Mo2	6	6	0	432	2
	Monks − 3	Mo3	6	6	0	432	2

Table 1 shows the general characteristics of each database used for the experiments. The name is shown in the second column, and its label in the third one. Additional information is given about the total number of features and the number of nominal and numerical features. Finally the number of instances and the number of classes can be seen in the last two columns.

For the scatter search algorithm an initial population whose number depended on the number of features was considered. The number of solutions was fixed to half of the number of features describing the data. We considered $|LRC| = 3$ for the GRASP strategy to generate the initial population. A number smaller than 3 would make the GRASP strategy very similar to an FSS algorithm, and a larger number would be equivalent to a random initialization. The size of the reference set was set to $\frac{1}{2}|Pop|$, where Pop refers to the population.

Table 2. Accuracy and its standardad deviation in training

DB	#FS	FSS		BSS		SS	
Ir	4	96.09	±0.96	96.14	±0.94	96.08	±1.02
Ec	9	64.39	±4.80	65.61	±3.89	65.21	±4.82
Gl	9	69.88	±4.16	69.97	±3.60	70.49	±4.04
Br	11	59.22	±6.24	58.74	±6.84	60.41	±6.24
Wi	13	96.86	±2.07	97.04	±1.54	97.24	±1.56
HV	13	74.56	±2.92	75.56	±2.74	74.70	±3.83
HH	13	82.61	±3.22	82.15	±3.03	82.84	±3.20
HC	13	79.92	±3.93	80.16	±5.08	80.94	±3.42
Zo	16	91.81	±3.15	90.46	±2.41	93.21	±2.68
SbL	35	81.83	±2.61	81.38	±2.27	83.83	±2.10
So	60	85.04	±3.10	81.79	±3.10	90.40	±1.87
Pm	8	70.66	±1.23	70.53	±1.16	71.39	±0.90
Vw	10	82.07	±1.00	82.09	±1.03	82.14	±1.08
Cx	15	84.94	±1.68	83.22	±2.18	85.28	±1.73
An	38	96.00	±1.48	96.21	±0.86	96.34	±0.69
Mo1	6	81.13	±15.96	99.53	±0.35	96.22	±7.77
Mo2	6	62.25	±4.11	67.95	±1.83	65.03	±3.45
Mo3	6	97.55	±1.86	97.37	±2.17	96.27	±3.00

Table 3. Size of the optimal subset of features found and its standard deviation

DB	#FS	FSS		BSS		SS	
Ir	4	1.90	±1.10	2.80	±0.92	2.30	±1.16
Ec	9	3.10	±1.45	5.10	±1.37	3.20	±0.92
Gl	9	5.30	±1.42	5.70	±1.34	4.90	±1.10
Br	11	3.20	±1.14	7.60	±1.71	4.40	±0.70
Wi	13	5.50	±1.65	9.2	±1.40	6.20	±1.48
HV	13	2.90	±1.29	9.10	±1.20	3.10	±2.03
HH	13	4.60	±1.96	9.40	±1.96	4.30	±1.89
HC	13	4.90	±1.98	9.20	±1.32	6.10	±1.29
Zo	16	6.60	±2.12	13.90	±1.45	6.60	±0.70
SbL	35	17.20	±2.86	29.60	±1.78	18.60	±2.07
So	60	7.20	±1.87	53.70	±4.67	11.20	±2.39
Pm	8	3.40	±1.27	6.00	±1.25	3.50	±1.35
Vw	10	8.50	±1.18	9.30	±0.95	8.50	±1.18
Cx	15	2.20	±0.79	9.30	±1.34	2.80	±1.69
An	38	10.00	±1.41	27.60	±2.07	10.80	±1.75
Mo1	6	2.10	±0.88	3.00	±0.00	3.20	±0.42
Mo2	6	1.80	±1.69	5.00	±0.00	2.80	±1.93
Mo3	6	3.00	±0.00	3.00	±0.00	3.00	±0.00

This $RefSet$ was built with the $\frac{1}{2}|RefSet|$ best solution from Pop and with the same number of most diverse solutions.

Table 2 shows the cross-validation results obtained during the training. A 5x2cv was applied to validate the results and average outcomes are shown for each database. Average standard deviation is also given. Scatter Search found the best solution in most real databases.

The average number of features found for each database is given in Table 3. As we can see, the FSS is the algorithm with greater reduction capacity and the lowest reduction is performed by the BSS.

Outcomes during the test are given in Table 4. These outcomes can be compared with those from the base algorithm IB1. If we compare the results we notice that BSS is clearly different from the other algorithms. In small databases FSS performed better than SS but SS performed better in the most complicated problems (a large number of features). In average problems, SS obtained the

Table 4. Accuracy and its standardad deviation in testing

DB	IB1	#FS	FSS	BSS	SS
Ir	94.23	4	95.07 ±1.89	94.80 ±2.22	95.07 ±2.44
Ec	47.88	9	54.55 ±4.23	56.06 ±8.48	52.58 ±5.25
Gl	66.82	9	72.90 ±3.18	70.28 ±5.89	72.90 ±3.15
Br	58.70	11	59.44 ±4.49	58.52 ±7.62	59.26 ±5.45
Wi	94.61	13	94.83 ±2.38	95.28 ±2.94	95.06 ±2.61
HV	72.70	13	69.90 ±4.75	69.40 ±3.89	69.20 ±5.43
HH	78.43	13	80.82 ±3.55	78.23 ±2.42	79.66 ±3.84
HC	75.98	13	73.99 ±3.38	74.06 ±1.81	71.56 ±5.14
Zo	93.65	16	90.89 ±5.33	92.68 ±3.49	90.71 ±4.25
SbL	84.88	35	83.91 ±3.55	84.04 ±4.29	84.76 ±3.25
So	83.17	60	76.64 ±3.24	82.79 ±3.22	79.33 ±2.57
Pm	69.70	8	68.39 ±2.00	67.79 ±1.54	68.49 ±2.78
Vw	95.29	10	94.06 ±1.71	94.63 ±1.90	94.12 ±1.66
Cx	81.54	15	83.77 ±2.34	81.51 ±1.57	84.09 ±2.19
An	93.56	38	95.97 ±2.82	96.35 ±1.73	96.48 ±1.76
Mo1	78.34	6	81.91 ±15.97	100.0 ±0.00	97.84 ±6.83
Mo2	69.02	6	63.46 ±4.47	70.82 ±3.66	65.62 ±6.17
Mo3	81.88	6	97.91 ±1.57	98.20 ±0.83	96.82 ±3.08

Table 5. Capacity of reduction of each algorithm

DB	#FS	FSS	BSS	SS
Small	11.22	68.16%	20.77%	63.83%
Average	30.25	79.67%	56.86%	79.01%
Artificial	6.00	61.67%	38.33%	50.00%
Total	15.83	67.23%	23.33%	62.98%

best outcomes. This difference increased in the most complicated problems. The BSS algorithm performed best in artificial data.

Finally Table 5 shows the average reduction percentage for each algorithm. SS and FSS performed similarly in average problems and FSS has a higher reduction capacity in the rest of the problems. The BSS has the lowest reduction capacity.

5   Conclusions

The information contained in some features is not relevant enough for the classification problem; therefore the initial feature set can be reduced in order to obtain an optimal subset of features.

Scatter search in small databases is affected by overfitting due to the lack of number of instances; however it performs better if the number of features is large enough. In average data the results are similar except that, in problems with a small number of features, FSS and SS are similar although SS is slightly better.

In artificial data the BSS is the best algorithm because it is the most sensitive to the relevance of each feature among the strategies considered.

SS outcomes are promising. A deeper study of its methods is necessary. Future investigation will consider the application of this algorithm to other learning algorithms and the use of different objective functions.

References

1. D. W. Aha and D. Kibler and M. K. Albert. Instanced-based learning algorithms. Machine Learning, 6(37–66), 1991.
2. Ethem Alpaydin. Combined 5x2cv f-test for comparing supervised classification learning algorithms. IDIAP-RR 04, IDIAP, 1998.
3. J. R. Anderson and M. Matessa. Explorations of an incremental, bayesian algorithm for categorization. Machine Learning, 9(275–308), 1992.
4. J. Bala, K. Dejong, J. Huang, H. Vafaie, and H. Wechsler. Using learning to facilitate the evolution of features for recognizing visual concepts. Evolutionary Computation, 4(3):297–311, 1996.
5. Thomas G. Dietterich. Approximate statistical test for comparing supervised classification learning algorithms. Neural Computation, 10(7):1895–1923, 1998.
6. Ron Kohavi and George H. John. Wrappers for feature subset selection. Artificial Intelligence, 97(1-2):273–324, 1997.
7. K. Kira and L. Rendell. The feature selection problem: Traditional methods and a new algorithm. Tenth National Conference Conference on Artificial Intelligence (AAAI-92), pages 129–134. MIT, 1992.
8. M. Laguna and R. Martí. Scatter Search: Metodology and Implementations in C. Kluwer Academic Press, 2003.
9. M. Mitchell. An Introduction to Genetic Algorithms. Cambridge, MA: MIT Press, 1996.
10. P. M. Murphy and D. W. Aha. Uci repository of machine learning. Technical report, University of California, Department of Information and Computer Science, 1994.
11. D. R. Wilson and T. R. Matinez. Improved heterogeneous distance functions. Journal of Artificial Intelligence Research, 6:1–34, 1997.
12. M. G.C. Resende and C. C. Ribeiro. Greedy Randomized Adaptive Search Procedures. Handbook of Metaheuristics, F. Glover and G. G. Kochenberger (eds.). Kluwer Academic Publishers, 2003.
13. F. García-López and B. Melián B. and J. A. Moreno-Pérez and J. M. Moreno-Vega. Parallelization of the Scatter Search for the p-median problem. Parallel Computing, 29:575–589, 2003.
14. V. Campos and F. Glover and M. Laguna and R. Martí. An Experimental Evaluation of a Scatter Search for the Linear Ordering Problem. Journal of Global Optimization, 21:397–414, 2001.
15. J. P. Hamiez and J. K. Hao. Scatter Search for Graph Coloring Artificial Evolution, 168–179, 2001.

Social Analysis of Multi-agent Systems
with Activity Theory*

Rubén Fuentes, Jorge J. Gómez-Sanz, and Juan Pavón

Universidad Complutense Madrid, Dep. Sistemas Informáticos y Programación
28040 Madrid, Spain
{ruben,jjgomez,jpavon}@sip.ucm.es
http://grasia.fdi.ucm.es

Abstract. The development of software systems is a complex task that requires
support techniques to guide the process and solve inconsistencies in its products. In the agent paradigm, the use of social and intentional abstractions facilitates the application of these techniques in theories for the analysis of human
societies, such as the Activity Theory. The Activity Theory proposes patterns
that appear in human groups to explain their behaviour, and the study of their
internal contradictions to understand its evolution. These patterns can be translated to the agent paradigm to reason about the behaviour of multi-agent systems. To ease the use of such techniques, a partially automatized process is proposed. The aim is to create an assistant that helps developers in the specification
of their multi-agent systems. The use of this tool is evaluated through case studies specified with the INGENIAS notation.

1 Introduction

The development of ever more complex software systems requires the use of new
abstractions to facilitate their conception. Thus, the agent paradigm gives advantages
in the development of such systems over more traditional approaches based in the
system/subsystem decomposition [7]. However, developing Multi-Agent Systems
(MAS) is not a trivial task at all. The greater is the complexity of the system, the
greater is the number of elements involved in its description. That is why developers
need the support of assistant techniques that help them to manage the complexity of
developments [16]. Among these techniques can be considered those managing with
contradictions in models. *Contradiction* stands in this paper for an inconsistency,
ambiguity, vagueness, or uncompleteness in the specifications [14].

Developers usually check their models with the only support of their own experience and skills, complemented sometimes with the use of more or less formal techniques. Some illustrative examples of these techniques are the role-playing [6] and the
use of Petri Nets [1] or modal logics [15]. The more formal methods have the disadvantage of requiring skills that are not frequent among developers; the less formal
ones usually have problems of lack of scalability and guide for the process.

---

* This work has been developed in the project INGENIAS (TIC2002-04516-C03-03), which is
funded by Spanish Ministry of Science and Technology.

R. Conejo et al. (Eds.): CAEPIA-TTIA 2003, LNAI 3040, pp. 526–535, 2004.
© Springer-Verlag Berlin Heidelberg 2004

An alternative to the previous methods is translating specifications to other domains where detecting inconsistencies is easier. This translation pursues an adequate trade-off between usability and analysis capabilities. For some MAS approaches, this domain can be the Sociology: human societies and these MAS [10], [17] share a strong social and intentional component. This common foundation suggests that sociological theories can be applied to agents. Concretely, our approach proposes Activity Theory (AT) [9]. One key feature of AT is its capacity to provide analysis guidelines and to integrate contradictions as part of the system evolution. Its method of work consists in identifying the situation in a society, its possible conflicts, and the solutions adopted by the society to solve them. With this information, AT research identifies regular patterns, some of which correspond to contradictions. Then, AT uses these patterns as the basis to explain the behaviour and evolution of those human groups.

AT originally applies this method working in natural language and without support tools. Despite of the analytical instruments that it provides, the complexity of the considered software systems requires further assistance. That is why the process has to be complemented with applications that partly automate it and assist developers' use.

To satisfy the previous goal, this paper proposes a software agent that helps in the MAS design process. The agent detects contradictions that are depicted as patterns of AT. The detection is based in the transformation of model data with consecutive filters. The common features of the agent paradigm abstracted from the AT makes possible to apply the process to different MAS methodologies. The architecture isolates the components with this knowledge to minimize the impact of carrying it to new applications.

The rest of the paper is organized as follows. The section 2 explains the role of contradictions as an impeller of system development. Section 3 presents a brief overview of AT and explains why it can be used to check MAS specifications. In section 4, we show how to represent the contradictions of AT as structural patterns. Sections 5 and 6 detail the validation process based in these patterns and how to implement it with an agent architecture to help in MAS analysis respectively. Finally, conclusions discuss the applicability of AT and its method to the development of MAS taking into account the results of the experimentation.

2   Contradictions in Software Processes

Contradictions appear in the software process independently of the working approach [14]. The development of a system implies collaboration between customers and developers. The heterogeneity of these groups makes probable that the results of their work contain inconsistencies, ambiguities, vaguenesses, or omissions in the specifications. Besides, different components of the own system or its environment can have contradictory purposes what generates additional conflicts.

However, contradictions do not have to be seen just as problems to be removed. For an AT point of view [9], they can be the guiding principle of the development that determines how the evolution happens. For the software products, this means that new versions of the specification emerge as solutions to contradictions detected in previous stages.

3 Activity Theory with Multi-agent Systems

MAS are frequently described as social systems composed by intentional agents [10], [17]. In this kind of systems, global goals can only be satisfied through the interaction of system components. To understand the MAS in this way, it has to be considered as an organization, and not as a mere aggregation of elements [3]. Moreover, the components of MAS are intentional, in the sense that they follow the Rationality Principle [12]: Every action taken by an agent aims at achieving one of its goals.

Sociability and intentionality are also relevant features of the human societies. This common basis with MAS makes feasible applying sociological theories, Activity Theory in this work, for MAS analysis.

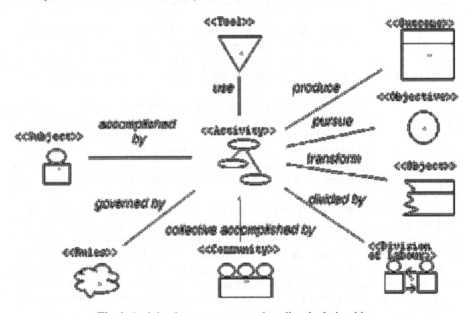

Fig. 1. Activity theory concepts and mediated relationships.

Activity Theory (AT) is a framework for the analysis of human organizations based in their practices. This analysis contemplates the social and temporal dimension of executed tasks and their evolution. Thus, the socio-cultural environment they belong to influences people; but people also modifies this environment actively, changing and creating its elements. This complex interaction of individuals and their environment has been called *activity* and is regarded as the fundamental unit of analysis. To ease their use, AT concepts applicable to MAS are depicted using UML [13] (see Fig. 1) and an icon code to distinguish the different stereotypes.

The *activity* [2] reflects a process. This process is carried out by a *subject* to satisfy one of its *objectives* thanks to the *outcome* obtained with transforming an *object*. The *subject* is the active element of the process and can be either an individual or a group. The *object* transformed by the *activity* can be an ideal or material one. The transformation process of the *object* into the *outcome* uses *tools*: *tools* always mediate *subject*'s processes over *objects* [18]. A *tool* can be anything used in the process, including both material tools (e.g. a computer) and tools for thinking (e.g. a plan). A fundamental feature of the *tool* is its dual quality in the *activity*: it provides the *subject* with the experience historically collected by his *community* and crystallised to it; at the same time, it also restricts the interaction to be from the perspective of that particular instrument, that is, the instrument does that other potential features of an *object* remain invisible to the *subject*.

The social level of the *activity* is characterized by three concepts: the *community*, the *rules*, and the *division of labour*. The *community* represents those *subjects* that share the same *object* [8]. An *activity* can involve several *subjects*, and each of them can play one or more roles and have multiple motives. *Rules* cover both explicit and implicit norms, conventions, and social relationships within the *community*. The *division of labour* refers to the organization of the *community* as related to the transformation process of the *object* into the *outcome*.

This vocabulary has been expanded with additional elements taken from i* [19] to represent contribution relationships. Contributions show how are the mutual influences between the *artifacts*, being an *artifact* whatever concept of AT. Added relationships for these contributions are: *contribute* (*positively*, *negatively* or undefined), *essential*, and *impede*.

4   AT Patterns

AT research [18], [9], [2], [8] identifies social patterns in human *activities*. These patterns are configurations of organizations described in terms of AT abstractions. Contradictions are a special kind of these patterns representing deviations of the norm in the society and carrying the seed of new forms of the *activity*. AT explains why societies behave as they do with these patterns, and with contradictions motivate their evolution.

Two of the most referenced contradictions in AT literature are the *Double bind* and the *Twofold meaning*. These contradictions can be described as patterns with the concepts and visual notation already seen.

A *double bind* (see Fig. 2) represents a situation in which every activity that the *subject* can carry out, affects negatively some of its goals. Since the *subject* follows the Rationality Principle [12], it should select an *activity* that aims to achieve one of its goals. However, whatever the chosen activity, it will also ills another of its goals at the same time. Therefore, no matter what the *subject* does because it cannot satisfy its needs.

Fig. 2. *Double Bind* contradiction.

A *double bind* can be solved sometimes through the decomposition of the original activity into others that minimize the negative effects but satisfy its *objectives*. In other occasions, a *double bind* call attention to contradictory responsibilities that should be split in roles that different *subjects* would play.

A *twofold meaning* situation (see Fig. 3) exists when an *artifact* has several different uses in an *activity*. The contradiction can appear if these uses harms mutually in the achievement of their goals.

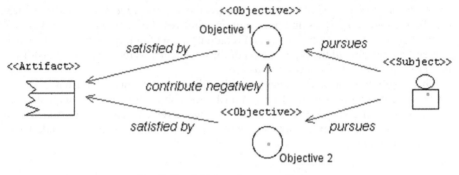

Fig. 3. *Twofold meaning* contradiction.

The *twofold meaning* can be caused by the lack of refinement in the contribution of the *artifact* to the *objectives*. If the *artifact* is not essential to satisfy at least one of the *objectives*, it can be removed from the system. In opposite case, its contribution to the *objective* has to be labelled as *essential* and its negative effect is unavoidable. This contradiction can also point out the need of commitment among several *objectives* of the system. When these goals are system requirements, this situation requires negotiation with the customer.

5   Model Validation Method

The patterns previously introduced are applied in the framework of a process to deal with contradictions in models (see Fig. 4). As a tool for validation, patterns do not show how to build a MAS, in the flavour of design patterns [4], but they call attention over conflictive configurations in the analysis and their possible solutions. Representing contradictions as structural patterns allows reducing the detection process of them to search for correspondences between patterns and the given models.

The process begins building the mappings between the vocabulary used in the MAS methodology and that of AT contradictions. Both of them model social and intentional systems and therefore, they have similar abstractions that can be put in correspondence. Thus, MAS and AT have intentional actors that pursue satisfying their goals through the execution of tasks in which they use resources. Fig. 5 shows the correspondence between the concepts of AT and the methodology of MAS development INGENIAS [5]. Developers only build once these mappings for a given MAS methodology. Then, they can be reused to translate models of the methodology to the language used in the contradiction patterns in other problems.

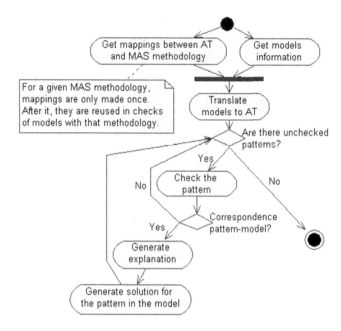

Fig. 4. Activity Diagram for the validation method with patterns.

For a given MAS, the method begins with a set of contradictions to check and the views that specify the system. Contradictions are described in terms of the AT language. The specification of the MAS should cover both functional and non-functional requirements.

The contradictions to be found are translated using the mappings with the language of the methodology. After that, models are traversed looking for structures of entities and relationships that fit with some pattern. If some of these groups is found, correspondences between terms allow giving an explanation of the contradiction based in the information present in the model.

Activity Theory	INGENIAS
Activity	Task, Workflow
Subject	Agent, Group, Organization
Object	Resource, Application, Fact
Outcome	Resource, Application, Fact
Objective	Goal
Tool	Resource, Application
Community	Group, Organization
Rules	Mental states
Division of Labour	Mental states

Fig. 5. Correspondence between AT and INGENIAS. Note that some concepts of AT have several possible translations in INGENIAS because they are more general.

Contradiction patterns have related solution patterns. These patterns express solutions to contradictions through the rearrangement and refinement of entities in the contradiction. Once that the correspondence between the problem and the views has been determined, it can be solved with a new configuration for the model. Some examples of these solutions appear in the section 4 of this paper.

The use of this method has to be complemented with conventional analysis techniques. It is help for MAS development that allows identifying potentially conflictive configurations in models. Sometimes, the pattern is not enough to know if there is a contradiction and the customer has to be asked about what to do.

6 Tool Architecture

The previous process has been implemented in a tool for developer's support in the INGENIAS IDE environment [5]. This tool consists in an agent with a rule-based system that contains the knowledge about the patterns and their application. The agent offers an interface for coordination with modelling tools of MAS methodologies. The resulting system is an interface agent similar to those proposed in [11].

The application design has considered three key goals: to ease the reuse with different methodologies, to allow personalization, and to evaluate the use of patterns for validation.

The reusability is based in the broad cover that abstractions extracted from AT provide for agent-based concepts: intentionality, social activity, and mediation in tasks. This knowledge builds a core that is applied over different methodologies and support tools thanks to the use of mappings. Besides, the architecture isolates those components specific for contradictions and methodologies with well-defined interfaces between them.

Personalization is needed to provide flexibility in the information management. Checking an analysis can provide a great number of possible contradictions. Determining what contradictions are significant depends on variable user's criteria that the tool should support.

Finally, to determine the usefulness of the validation, the system has metrics involving the number of analyzed elements, detected contradictions, and their quality.

The agent architecture (see Fig. 6) is organized in the following structural components:

1. *Vocabulary of the MAS Methodology.* It includes the primitives originally used to describe the system.
2. *MAS Description.* This is the specification of the system to check in terms of the vocabulary of the MAS methodology.
3. *Exporter.* This component is the tool that translates the original description of the system to a suitable format for the other components of the agent. This transformation does not change the vocabulary used in the specification.
4. *AT Vocabulary.* It gives the primitives to describe contradictions.
5. *Mappings Methodology-Contradictions.* The knowledge about how to translate the primitives that describe the system to those that describe contradictions is described through a set of mappings.

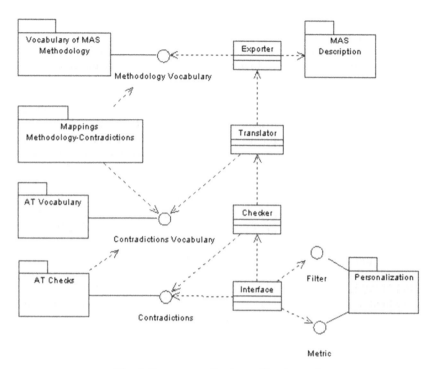

Fig. 6. Components for the verification tool.

6. *Translator.* It uses the mappings to transform the description of the MAS in terms of the vocabulary of the methodology to other based in the AT vocabulary.
7. *AT Checks.* These are the structural patterns that depict contradictions with the AT vocabulary.
8. *Checker.* This component searches correspondences with patterns in the system models.
9. *Personalization.* It contains filters, criteria for sorting, and quality metrics that can be applied over the list of contradictions obtained from models. This tailoring of the tool aims to ease the user's work with the obtained results.
10. *Interface.* This component applies the personalization criteria to the set of contradictions obtained checking the model.

7 Conclusions

This work is founded in the hypothesis that the contradictions detected by the AT sociological model can be translated to MAS models. The main results in this paper are what we have called AT contradiction patterns, methods for their disciplined use, and an implementation that shows its applicability. Contradiction patterns extracted from AT allow detecting conflictive configurations in models and suggesting evolutions to other less conflictive configurations. In this way, social contradictions in the

MAS are no longer just problems to remove but they are integrated in the development cycle as impellers of the refinement.

The method to check models is based in recognising contradictions using structural AT patterns. Models are traversed looking for groups that fit into the given structures. If correspondences are detected, the pattern and the elements that correspond with it explain the problem in terms of the model itself.

To ease the application of the method, we define an agent that can be plugged in modelling tools. The current prototype works with the INGENIAS IDE environment. The agent takes as input the mappings between the AT concepts and the specification language for MAS. This allows decoupling the knowledge about contradictions from the concrete MAS methodology. The management of contradictions by the user is done with filters and metrics that give their relevance.

The validation tool has been checked with several examples specified with the INGENIAS notation. *PSI3* describes a system for collaborative filtering in which users share recommendations in communities. Users are represented by *Personal Agents* and communities are managed by *Community Agents*. The other two examples try to model armies of tanks (*Robocode*) or *bots* teams (*Quake*) as MAS, essentially to study coordination capabilities. The specification of the first case studies made with the INGENIAS IDE can be found at *http://grasia.fdi.ucm.es/ingenias*.

In the future, the architecture of the support tool will be extended to have multiple agents for validation and verification tasks over specifications in the development environment. Thus, INGENIAS IDE will become a MAS where these agents interact between themselves to share the information obtained from the user or to suggest where to continue.

References

1. Cost, R. S., Chen, Y., Finin, T., Labrou, Y., Peng, Y.: *Using Colored Petri Nets for Conversation Modeling*. Issues in Agent Communication. Springer Verlag, (2000).
2. Engeström, Y.: *Learning by expanding*. Orientakonsultit, Helsinki, (1987).
3. Ferber, J.: *Multi-Agent Systems*. Addison-Wesley, (1999).
4. Gamma, E., Helm, R., Johnson, R., Vlissides, J.: *Design Patterns: Elements of Reusable Object-Oriented Software*. Addison Wesley Professional Computing Series, (1995).
5. Gómez-Sanz, J., Pavón J.: *Agent Oriented Software Engineering with INGENIAS*. In Proceedings of the CEEMAS 2003.
6. Jacobson, I., Rumbaugh, J., and Booch, G.: *The Unified Software Development Process*. Addison-Wesley, (1999).
7. Jennings, N. R., Wooldridge, M.: *Agent-Oriented Software Engineering*. In Handbook of Agent Technology, (ed. J. Bradshaw) AAAI/MIT Press, (2000).
8. Kuutti, K.: *Activity Theory as a potential framework for Human-computer interaction research*. In B.A. Nardi, (ed.), Context and Consciousness: Activity Theory and Human-Computer Interaction. Cambridge, MA: MIT press, (1996).
9. Aleksie Nikolaevich Leontiev: *Activity, Consciousness, and Personality*. Prentice-Hall, (1978).
10. Maes, P.: *Modeling Adaptive Autonomous Agents*. Artificial Life Journal, C. Langton, ed., Vol. 1, No. 1 & 2, MIT Press, (1994).
11. Maes, P.: *Agents that Reduces Work and Information Overload*. Readings in Intelligent User Interfaces Morgan Kauffman Publishers, (1998).
12. Newell, A.: *The knowledge level*. Artificial Intelligence, vol. 18 pp. 87-127, (1982).

13. OMG: *Unified Modeling Language Specification. Version 1.3.* http://www.omg.org
14. Pressman, R. S.: *Software Engineering: A Practitioner's Approach.* McGraw-Hill Series in Software Engineering and Technology. McGraw-Hill, Inc., (1982)
15. Rao, A. S., Georgeff, M. P.: *Modeling Rational Agents within a BDI-Architecture.* Proceedings of the 2nd International Conference on Principles of Knowledge Representation and Reasoning (KR'91).
16. Sommerville, I.: *Software Engineering.* Addison-Wesley International Computer Science Series. Addison-Wesley, (2001), 6th edition.
17. Sykara, K. P.: *Multiagent systems.* AI Magazine 19(2), (1998)
18. Vygotsky, L. S.: *Mind and Society.* Cambridge MA, Harvard University, (1978)
19. Yu, E. S. K.: *Towards Modelling and Reasoning Support for Early-Phase Requirements Engineering.* Proceedings of the 3rd IEEE Int. Symp. on Requirements Engineering (RE'97) Jan. 6-8, 1997, Washington D.C., USA. pp. 226-235.

SoftComputing Techniques
Applied to Catalytic Reactions

Soledad Valero[1], Estefanía Argente[1], Vicente Botti[1],
Jose Manuel Serra[2], and Avelino Corma[2]

[1] Departamento de Sistemas Informáticos y Computación
Universidad Politécnica de Valencia, 46020 Valencia, Spain
{eargente,svalero,onaindia}@dsic.upv.es
[2] Instituto de Tecnología Química, Universidad Politécnica de Valencia
46020 Valencia, Spain
{jsalfaro,acorma}@itq.upv.es

Abstract. Soft computing techniques have been applied to model and optimize the kinetics of catalytic reactions. Genetic algorithms have been combined with already trained neural networks to obtain new catalytic samples with relevant quality values. Thus, a suitable model of a genetic algorithm has been designed and implemented for this problem. In order to improve the results offered by this genetic algorithm, different combinations of its parameters have been studied. Moreover, this soft computing approach has been applied to some industrial reactions. Therefore, specific neural networks trained for each kind of reaction and the genetic algorithm have been joined together, getting successful results.

1 Introduction

Recently, the application of new techniques for rapid processing and fitting large amounts of experimental data has become an issue of great importance, specially in the field of high-throughput experimentation in organic chemistry and catalysis. Many efforts have being done in the development and optimization of artificial intelligent and data mining techniques [1] in combinatorial catalysis [2]. Those techniques should allow the extraction of information and knowledge from high-throughput experimentation raw data, establishing relationships and patterns between the input and output variables.

Soft computing is a collection of methodologies which aim to tolerance for imprecision, uncertainty and partial truth to achieve tractability, robustness and low solution cost [3]. The principal constituents of soft computing are fuzzy logic, neural computing, evolutionary computation, machine learning and probabilistic reasoning. What is particularly important about soft computing is that it facilitates the use of those techniques in combination, leading to the concept of hybrid intelligent systems.

In this paper, soft computing techniques for predicting and optimizing the kinetics of catalytic reactions using methods not based on fundamental knowledge have been studied. Specifically, artificial neural networks (ANNs) and genetic

R. Conejo et al. (Eds.): CAEPIA-TTIA 2003, LNAI 3040, pp. 536–545, 2004.

algorithms (GAs) are combined in order to discover the best kinetic values for several n-paraffin reactions inside an specific range of input values.

2   Aims of the Work

The conventional procedure for studying the kinetics of catalytic reactions implies analysing empirically each catalyst under different reaction conditions. Therefore, for the evaluation of the kinetics of a complex reaction it is required a large experimental effort with high temporal and financial costs, taking some weeks (even months). The application of ANNs and GAs in this field offers a new methodology for modelling without any prior assumption that could reduce the number of experimental samples required, so that the number of experiments in the reactor is reduced.

In this work, ANNs were applied to predict different catalytic parameters dealing with a relevant process such as the hydroisomerization of n-paraffins. This process has been widely studied by the Institute of Chemical Technology of the Polytechnic University of Valencia [4]. Different kinetic functions of this process are available at the Institute.

As regards the GA, it is an effective optimization technique because it is a stochastic algorithm. It relies on random elements in parts of its operations rather than being determined by specific rules. The genetic algorithm attempts to find the optimal solution to the problem by investigating many possible solutions simultaneously. The possible solution population is evaluated and the best solutions are selected to form next generations. Over a number of generations, goods traits dominate the population, resulting in an increase of the quality of the solutions. A genetic algorithm, to work effectively, requires a quick feedback of the fitness values of the samples. Hence the combination of GA with a NN seems suitable [5].

Genetic algorithms are a very powerful tool, but they could be dangerous if the problem codification is not appropriate. If the selected codification for the problem was wrong, it would be possible that the algorithm would solve a different optimization problem from the one under study. In the problem explained in this paper, each variable belongs to a continuous domain so it has been decided to adopt real-coded GAs to optimize the catalyst conditions. Therefore, each chromosome will be composed of a set of genes which will represent a variable of the problem. There are several studies that guarantee this kind of real codification [6],[7].

In this proposal (figure 1) each generation is tested by a neural network to obtain its fitness evaluation. This fitness evaluation (1) depends on the predictions of the conversion (X) and di-branched yield (Y_{di}) values. The quality of a catalyst is measured by means of equation (1), so the higger is the value of this equation, the better is the quality of the catalyst. Therefore, the GA obtains a quality rank of samples ordered from maximum to minimum.

$$F = (Y_{di}/X) * 100 . \tag{1}$$

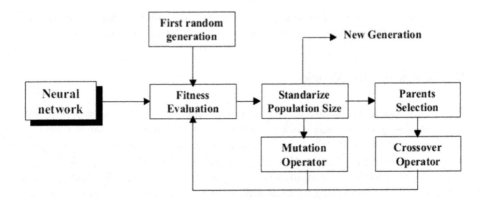

Fig. 1. Genetic Algorithm combined with Neural Networks

Afterwards, crossover and mutation operators are applied to the whole generation with a certain probability. Mutation operator would be able to alter genes with a new value, jumping randomly anywhere within the allowed domain. The number of genes to mutate in each individual is a parameter of the GA. Thus, the mutation is an explorer operator which looks for new solutions and prevents system to converge quickly on a local maximum, avoiding loss of genetic diversity.

On the other hand, a crossover operator is used based on confidence intervals [7]. This operator uses information from the best individuals in the population. Moreover, the crossover operator is associated with the capacity of interpolation (*exploitation*). This capacity is related to the belonging of a population parameter to a confidence interval. The crossover operator is also associated with the capacity of extrapolation (*exploration*), derived from its *not* belonging to the same confidence interval.

In order to select the suitable parents for the next generation, the *roulette wheel selection* method is used. This method consists of a random selection in which the best quality individuals have more possibilities to be selected. In this way, the explained operators create new individuals that are added to the population. In order to produce the next generation, that extended population is reduced to its original size by means of the *rank-space* method. This selection procedure links fitness to both quality rank and diversity rank. Thus, it promotes not only the survival of individuals which are extremely fit from the perspective of quality, but also the survival of those which are both quite fit and different from other, even more fit individuals. Summarizing, in each new generation all individuals are different. However, an individual can be present in more than one generation.

2.1   Framework of the Problem

The main objective of this work is to study the soft computing techniques explained above in the catalyst area. Therefore, a GA is combined with a NN that simulates the reaction process and allows to calculate the quality functions (1) used in the GA. We aim to find the best combination of the input values of a n-paraffin reaction that provides greater catalytic results. Input variables were: n-paraffin partial pressure, from 0.5 to 2 bar; hydrogen partial pressure, from 6 to 18 bar; reactor temperature, from 503 to 543K; and contact time, from 0.16 to 8h. Output values (predicted by the NN) were: n-paraffin conversion, and isomerization yields for mono- and di-branched products.

Several neural networks with the same structure were used. Each neural network had been trained with samples of a n-paraffin isomerization reaction, by means of a backpropagation training algorithm, so kinetic models of the reaction were obtained. Four different reactions were taken into account: n-octane (C8), n-heptane (C7), n-hexane (C6) and n-pentane (C5) isomerization reactions, all of them with a similar reaction scheme. All the training processes followed to determine the most suitable NN architecture and training algorithm to use are explained in [8]. In this work, we have focused on several points:

a) Analysis of the different parameters of the genetic algorithm (table 1). The aim of this study is to analyse the behaviour of the GA when its internal parameters are modified, in order to obtain a suitable GA model.
b) Analysis of the impact of the initial random generation on the GA. We analysed if a good or bad initial generation can affect in a relevant way the GA behaviour and its final results applied to our problem.
c) Soft computing model applied to different catalytic reactions. We studied the application of our proposal in the n-paraffin isomerization reactions mentioned above. In each case, the GA was combined with a NN specifically trained for each type of reaction.

Table 1. Values of the different parameters of GA taken into account

Study	Parameter	Values				
Mutation	Probability	5%	10%	15%	20%	
	Num. of genes	1	2	3	4	
Crossover	Probability	20%	40%	60%	80%	100%
	Best Quality	20%	30%	40%		
Population fit	α	0.3	0.5	0.7		
	Quality Surv.	10%	20%	30%	40%	

3 Results

All studies considered in previous section were carried out with successful results. Below we detail how the different experiments were made and the behaviour of the soft computing technique developed.

3.1 Analysis of the Parameters of the GA

The values of the GA parameters (table 1) determine its behaviour. Therefore, we studied them in order to obtain a GA model that provides high quality results.

Moreover each combination of the values of the GA parameters was tested four times. The population was set to 32 samples to simulate the reactor conditions (the reactor has a capacity of 32 samples).

In all studies, the GA was combined with a NN trained with 17000 samples of the n-octane isomerization reaction [8]. This NN provides a very precise model of the reaction.

Study of Mutation Parameters. It was pretended to determine the best parameters for the mutation process. The mutation probability (MP) and the number of genes to mutate were modified with the values shown in table 1. The rest of the parameters were fixed to: crossover probability=60%, α=0.5, selected best quality samples=30% and quality survival=20%.

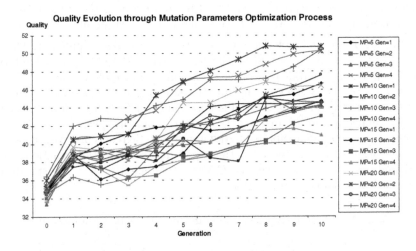

Fig. 2. Evolution of the quality average for each combination of the mutation parameters: mutation probability (MP) and number of genes to mutate (Gen)

The evolution of the mean quality of each generation for the different combinations of the mutation parameters is shown in figure 2. For each generation, the average of the qualities of the samples of the four tests is indicated. As it can be observed, the quality of samples is normally improved in each new generation. The best results were: (i) MP=10%, 1 gene to mutate; (ii) MP=5%, 4 genes to mutate; (iii) MP=10%, 3 genes to mutate. We determined that the first combination is the most suitable one as it allowed the GA to obtain a good evolution of the quality through all generations. Moreover, in few generations the GA obtained proper quality results. Furthermore, it provided the highest results at the final generation.

Study of Crossover Parameters. The crossover probability (CP) and the selected best quality samples (BQ) were modified with the values shown in ta-

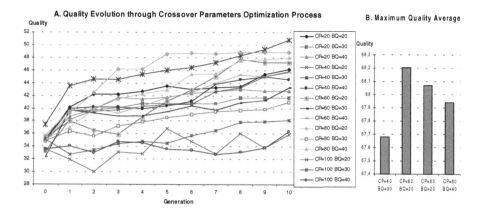

Fig. 3. A.Evolution of the quality average for each combination of the crossover parameters: crossover probability (CP) and selected best quality samples percentage (BQ). B.Maximum quality average obtained by best combinations

ble 1. The other parameters were set to: MP=10%, α=0.5, quality survival=20% and only one gene to mutate.

In figure 3.A, the evolution of the quality average for each combination of the crossover parameters is shown. As in the previous study, we indicate the quality average of all samples of each generation, for the four tests. The best combinations were: (i) CP=40%, BQ=30%; (ii) CP=80%, BQ=20%; (iii) CP=80%, BQ=40%; (iv) CP=60%, BQ=20%. In figure 3.B, the maximum quality average obtained by those four combinations is shown. We chose the second combination as it offered a good evolution of the quality through each generation, and one of the highest maximum qualities.

Study of General Parameters. In this case, two parameters were studied. The α parameter determines the size of the confidence interval used by the crossover operator. The QS parameter determines the size of the samples set selected only by quality criteria [7]. We modified α parameter and quality survival percentage (QS) with the values shown in table 1. The other parameters were set to: MP=10%, CP=80%, BQ=20% and one gene was mutated.

The evolution of the quality for the different combinations of the general parameters is shown in figure 4.A. The best values are: (i) α=0.5, QS=40%; (ii)α=0.7, QS=20%; (iii) α=0.7, QS=10%; (iv) α=0.7, QS=40%. As all combinations provided similar evolution results, we used the maximum quality results to determine which one to choose. In figure 4.B the maximum quality average obtained by those four combinations is shown. We selected the second combination as it provided the highest quality value.

To sum up, our GA model was parametrized with: probability mutation= 10%, crossover probability= 80%, best quality samples percentage=20%, α=0.7, quality survival=20% and only one random gene to mutate.

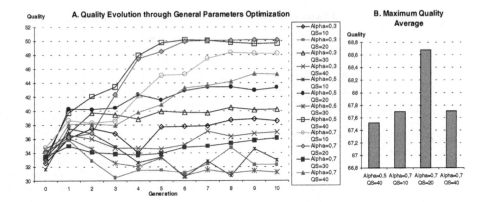

Fig. 4. A.Evolution of the quality average for each combination of the general parameters: α and quality survival percentage(QS). B.Maximum quality average obtained by best combinations)

3.2   Analysis of the Impact of the Initial Random Generation on the GA

Once the GA model was established, we studied whether the initial generation could influence in the behaviour of the genetic algorithm. Therefore, from all the previous tests, we chose the initial generation with the worst quality average and the one with the best quality average. Then, for both initial generations ten tests were made with our GA model and the NN described in previous section. Each test produced ten generations from the initial one. In table 2, the quality average of all tests for those ten generations is shown. Moreover, the average of the maximum quality obtained from the worst initial generation is 67.03, whereas from the best initial generation is 68.44. It can be observed that if the initial generation is really bad (i.e. has a very low quality), our GA model can hardly find generations with high quality.

3.3   Combination of GA and NN for Several N-Paraffin Isomerization Reactions

In previous studies we used a NN trained with a huge number of samples of n-octane isomerization, as we needed a very precise model of the reaction. However, the number of available samples is normally scarce for many reactions, as the process to obtain and test new samples is very costly. Therefore, we studied the combination of our GA model with NNs trained with fewer number of samples. As those NNs introduce more error to the predicted catalytic results, we analysed if our GA model still worked properly. Moreover, we applied our technique to other isomerization reactions, so we determined its suitability for other reactions.

Initially, we studied the combination of our GA model with four neural networks, trained with 85 samples of C8, C7, C6 and C5 respectively. Then, we

Table 2. Mean quality evolution obtained by the soft computing technique when the initial generation has a low quality (*worst initial generation*) versus a high quality (*best initial generation*)

Generation	Worst initial generation	Best initial generation
0	28.90	40.56
1	33.33	38.89
2	30.40	39.49
3	27.61	39.82
4	33.38	41.91
5	32.76	45.06
6	35.55	46.23
7	36.03	47.18
8	34.20	47.50
9	31.50	47.50
10	31.49	47.68

Table 3. Mean quality of the 15th generation and the average of the maximum quality obtained for all tests in each combination of GA and NN. Mean absolute errors of catalytic results (X, Y_{di}). Each NN was trained with 85 samples (*NN-85*) or 850 samples (*NN-850*) of a n-paraffin reaction: n-octane (*C8*), n-heptane (*C7*), n-hexane (*C6*) or n-heptane (*C5*), respectively

| | NN-85 | | | | NN-850 | | | |
Reaction	Mean Quality	Max Quality	X	Y_{di}	Mean Quality	Max Quality	X	Y_{di}
C8	59.95	74.13	0.050	0.081	60.68	68.55	0.013	0.029
C7	62.09	77.48	0.075	0.102	59.87	70.80	0.019	0.036
C6	64.30	87.79	0.142	0.188	65.32	82.85	0.025	0.047
C5	14.18	20.81	0.050	0.413	9.02	16.01	0.024	0.400

combined the GA with other four neural networks, trained with 850 samples of the same reactions respectively. Each combination was tested five times, reaching till 15 generations each time.

In table 3 the mean quality of the 15th generation and the average of the maximum quality obtained for all tests in each combination of GA and NN is shown. It can be observed that the soft computing technique applied offers suitable results for different reactions.

We can notice in table 3 that the combination of GA and a NN trained with 85 samples (NN-85) provides better mean qualities than the combination of GA and a NN trained with 850 samples (NN-850). This could be explained by the error introduced by the predictions of the neural network, which affects the calculation of the quality values.

In table 3 we indicate the mean absolute errors of the catalytic results (X, Y_{di}) predicted by those trained neural networks for 300 samples of each reaction.

Table 4. Quality values and sample number of the five best and five worst samples of last generation obtained by the GA using a NN trained with 85 samples (*NN-85*), versus quality values and ranking order obtained by this same generation tested by a NN trained with 850 samples (*NN-850*)

First Samples				Last Samples			
NN-85		NN-850		NN-85		NN-850	
Sample	Quality	Rank Order	Quality	Sample	Quality	Rank Order	Quality
1	70.62	1	67.87	28	51.62	28	45.11
2	69.95	2	68.33	29	36.96	29	35.64
3	69.70	4	67.33	30	36.12	30	33.31
4	69.66	5	67.11	31	32.07	31	28.51
5	69.40	6	66.73	32	12.24	32	12.63

It can be observed that NN-850 are more precise than NN-85. Therefore, NN-850 provide more accurate predictions than NN-85, i.e. more closer to real values.

Nonetheless, the sets of best and worst samples determined by the GA are nearly the same for both NN models. In table 4, the quality of the five best and five worst samples of n-octane reaction obtained by a GA combined with a NN-85 are shown. Those samples were also tested with a NN trained with 850 samples and then ordered by quality. It can be observed at table 4 that they practically obtain the same ranking order. Therefore, the GA and NN-85 combination could be used in the search and selection process of the most suitable samples to test, even if the predicted quality of those samples differs from the real one.

4   Conclusions

The conventional procedure for studying the kinetics of catalytic reactions implies analysing empirically each catalyst under different reaction conditions. Therefore, for the evaluation of the kinetics of a complex reaction it is required a large experimental effort with high temporal and financial costs, taking some weeks (even months).

The application of soft computing techniques to model, predict and optimize in the field of experimental catalysis offers a new methodology that can accelerate the development and optimization of new catalysts. Therefore, the combination of GAs and NNs provides a suitable tool to reduce the number of samples to analyse in the laboratory, decreasing the number of experiments needed. In addition, they can be applied to further catalyst scale up, process control and optimization. Thus, the total cost and time involved in the research of new materials can be reduced.

It should be pointed out that, in order to improve the behaviour of this soft computing technique an initial process should be carried out. This process would guarantee an initial generation having both diversity and quality enough to start with.

References

1. Gedeck, P., Willett, P.: Visual and computational analysis of structure activity relationships in high-throughput screening data. In: Current Opinion in Chemical Biology. 5 (2001) 389–395.
2. Corma, A., Serra, J.M., Argente, E., Botti, V., Valero, S.: Application of artificial neural networks to combinatorial catalysis: Modelling and prediction of ODHE catalysts. In: ChemPhysChem (2002) 939–945.
3. Zadeh, L.: Fuzzy Logic, Neural Networks and Soft Computing. In: Communications of the ACM. Vol. 37 (1994) 77–84.
4. Chica, A., Corma, A., Miquel, P.J.: Isomerization of C5-C7 n-alkanes on underctional large pore zeolites: activity, selectivity and adsorption features. In: Catalyst Today, Johns Hopkins University Press. Vol. 65 (2001) 101–110.
5. Rowe, R.C, Roberts, R.J.: Intelligent Software for Product Formulation. In: Taylor and Francis Ltd. London. (1998).
6. Herrera, F., Lozano, M., Verdegay, J.L.: Tackling real-coded genetic algorithms. Operators and tools for behavioural analysis. In: Artificial Intelligence Review. Vol. 12 (1998) 265–319.
7. Ortiz, D., Hervas, C., Muñoz, J.: Genetic algorithm with crossover based on confidence interval as an alternative to traditional nonlinear regression methods. In: ESANN'2001. Bruges, Belgium. (2001) 193–198.
8. Serra, J.M., Corma, A., Argente, E., Valero, S., Botti, V.: Neural networks for modelling of kinetic reaction data applicable to catalyst scale up and process control and optimization in the frame of combinatorial catalysis. In: Applied Catalysis (2003)(in press).

Sports Image Classification through Bayesian Classifier*

Youna Jung[1], Eenjun Hwang[1], and Wonil Kim[2]

[1] Graduate School of Information and Communication
Ajou University, Suwon, 442-749, Korea
{serazade,ehwang}@ajou.ac.kr
[2] College of Electronics Information Engineering
Sejong University, Seoul, 143-747, Korea
wikim@sejong.ac.kr
Phone: +82-2-3408-3785

Abstract. Most documents on the web today contain image as well as text data. So far, classification of images has been dependent on the annotation. For the more efficient and accurate classification, not only textual data but also image contents should be considered. In this paper, we propose a novel method for classifying specific image data; sports images. The proposed method is based on the Bayesian framework and employs four important color features to exploit the properties of sports images.

1 Introduction

Due to the explosive growth of documents on the Internet, new techniques and tools that can extract useful information or knowledge from those documents intelligently and automatically are needed [1]. Most documents on the web consist of text and image data. However, the importance of such image data has often been ignored. Even the manipulation of image data heavily depends on textual information such as annotation, ignoring the inherent characteristics of image data. Image mining could be used to obtain valuable information from raw image data.

Image mining is more than just an application of data mining to image domain. It is an interdisciplinary area that covers computer vision, image processing, image retrieval, data mining, machine learning, database, and artificial intelligence. Despite many applications and algorithms developed in those fields, image mining is still in its infancy.

One of the fundamental challenges to image mining is to determine how low-level, pixel representation contained in a raw image or image sequence can be efficiently and effectively processed to identify high-level spatial objects and their relationships. In other words, image mining deals with the extraction of implicit knowledge, image data relationships, and other patterns not explicitly stored in the image database.

---

* This research was supported by University IT Research Center Project.

R. Conejo et al. (Eds.): CAEPIA-TTIA 2003, LNAI 3040, pp. 546–555, 2004.
© Springer-Verlag Berlin Heidelberg 2004

In this paper, we propose a sports image classifier for sports image mining. It extracts low-level features of sports images such as color histogram, color coherence vector, edge direction histogram, and edge direction coherence vector, and then uses these extracted features and their combination to classify each image into one of predefined sports categories.

The rest of the paper is organized as follow. In Section 2, we first introduce several related works, especially image classification. In Section 3, we propose a sport image classifier based on the Bayesian framework. Then, in Section 4, we report on several experiments to evaluate performance of the proposed classifier. Finally, Section 5 is dedicated to discussion and then we conclude in section 6.

2 Related Work

2.1 Image Mining

Image mining is different from low-level computer vision and image processing in that image mining is focused on extracting patterns from large collection of images [3], whereas computer vision and image processing is focused on extracting specific features from a single image. Besides, image mining is also different from content-based retrieval. Although there seem to be some overlaps between them, image mining goes beyond the problem of retrieving relevant images. The goal of image mining is to discover image patterns that are significant in a large collection of images. In this paper, we focus on a specific image mining area called image classification.

2.2 Image Classification

Intellectual classification of content images is an important way to mine valuable information from a large image collection. The challenge in the image classification is how to group images into semantically meaningful categories based on low-level visual features. To achieve that, the most important task is to find characteristics of image features for discriminating one category from others. Such characteristics depend upon the application domain. For example, Maria-Luiza Antonie et.al. [2] distinguished the mammography of tumor from the normal mammography using features of medical images. A tumor in mammography is shown as a white hole. In the classification of tumor mammography, location and form of a white hole are important features. By the contrast, color and shape are more important than location or form in the classification of sports image, since most sports images have a unique pattern of color and/or shape appeared in the background (i.e. water, snow, and ground). In other words, features for classifying images are dependent upon the application domain. After defining domain-specific characteristics of images, we use several classification techniques to classify images. There are many data classification techniques such as decision tree, Bayesian classification, belief networks, neural network, case-based reasoning, genetic algorithms, rough sets, fuzzy logic techniques, K-nearest neighbor classification, and so on. Some of them work well in image classification. Their approaches to image data classification are discussed in detail.

Bayesian classification [5], a statistical technique, exhibits high accuracy and speed when applied to large database in contrast to decision tree, and neural network. However, in practice it is not always accurate. Because it makes assumption of class conditional independence, that is, given the class label of a training sample, the values of the attributes are conditionally independent to one another, but dependencies between features can exist. The binary Bayesian classifier [5] was used to perform hierarchical classification of vacation images into indoor and outdoor categories.

Bayesian belief network classification is also based on Bayes theorem. Unlike Bayesian technique, belief network classification reflects dependency of each other. To apply such dependency it employs two components. The first component is a directed acyclic graph, where each node represents a random attribute and each arc represents a probabilistic dependence. The second one is a conditional probability table. Hanchuan Peng and Fuhui Long [6] proposed an image mining algorithm to extract irregular feature. It based on belief network learning of pattern image pixels, each of which is regarded as a discrete variable with a limited number of states.

Classification by neural network has been less desired due to its long training time and poor interpretability. However, its high tolerance to noisy data makes neural network more useful. Recently, new algorithm is developed for extraction of rules from trained neural networks. However, sports image classification does not require high tolerance to noisy data. In addition, long training time of neural network classification technique imposes a heavy burden on the sports image classifier. Therefore, neural network classification is not suitable to sports image classifier.

Fuzzy set approach makes up for rule-based classification's defect involving sharp cutoffs for continuous attributes. It replaces "fuzzy" threshold cutoffs for continuous-valued attributes with degree of membership functions. Alejandro Jaimes and Shih-Fu Chang [7] suggested automatic classification combined with multiple fuzzy classifiers and machine learning techniques at multiple levels.

K-nearest neighbor classification stores all of the training images and then searches the closest pattern space to the new image for the k training images. Unlike decision tree, it assigns equal weight to each attribute and does not build a classifier until a new image needs to be classified. According to the later characteristic of K-nearest neighbor approach, it is called as lazy learner. Unfortunately, its computational cost can be expensive when the number of potential neighbor is great. Therefore, it commonly requires efficient indexing techniques. Theo Gevers et al. [8] studied a computational model to combine textual and image features for classification of images on Internet. This model used the K-nearest neighbor classifier to classify photographical and synthetic image. However, in sports image classification using color and shape features of raw image, its computational cost is expensive unless it employs an appropriate indexing technique. In addition, storing the entire sports images makes the classifier too heavy. Therefore, K-nearest neighbor classification technique is also not suitable to classify the sports images.

Among those techniques for image classification, we employed the Bayesian to classify sports image data on the Internet, because the Bayesian method in image classification has the following advantages.

1. It naturally allows for the integration of multiple features through the class conditional probability. Since sports image data have multiple features, Bayesian classifier is a good candidate for sport image classification.
2. It shows relatively low error rate in a huge database. Volume of image data on the Internet is enormous. In addition, the volume increases. Therefore, we need Bayesian classification technique having the high accuracy in huge volume to classify sports images on the Internet.

3   Sports Image Classification Using Bayesian Classifier

3.1   Bayesian Framework

We now review the Bayesian framework for image classification. Each data sample is represented by an n-dimensional feature vector, $X=(x_1, x_2, ..., x_n)$, depicting n measurements made on the image for n attributes, respectively, $A_1, A_2,..., A_n$. Suppose that there are m classes, $C_1, C_2,..., C_m$. Given an new image I, the Bayesian classifier calculates the posterior probability of each class, conditioned on I. The posterior probability is defined by Bayes theorem as follow [9]:

$$P(C_i \mid I) = \frac{P(I \mid C_i)P(C_i)}{P(I)} \tag{1}$$

To assign a new image I to a class, the classifier tries to find a class having the highest posterior probability. In equation (1), since $P(I)$ is constant for all classes, only $P(I|C_i) \cdot P(C_i)$ need be considered. The class prior probabilities may be estimated by $P(C_i) = \frac{s_i}{s}$, where s_i is the number of training images of class C_i, and s is the total number of training images. $P(I|C_i)$ is computed below the assumption of class conditional independence, presuming that there are no dependence relationships among the attributes. According to this assumption, $P(I|C_i)$ is defined as follows:

$$P(I \mid C_i) = \prod_{k=1}^{n} P(x_k \mid C_i) \tag{2}$$

The probabilities $P(x_1|C_i)$, $P(x_2|C_i)$,..., $P(x_n|C_i)$ can be estimated from the training samples, where

(i) If A_k is discrete-valued, then $P(x_k|C_i) = \frac{s_{ik}}{s_i}$, where s_{ik} is the number of training images of class C_i having the value x_k for A_k, and s_i is the number of training images belonging to C_i.

(ii) If A_k is continuous-valued, then the attribute is typically assumed to have a Gaussian distribution so that

$$P(x_k \mid C_i) = g(x_k, \mu_{c_i}, \sigma_{c_i}) = \frac{1}{\sqrt{2\pi}\sigma_{c_i}} e^{\frac{-(x_k - \mu_{c_i})^2}{2\sigma_{c_i}^2}}, \tag{3}$$

where $g(x_k, \mu_{c_i}, \sigma_{c_i})$ is the Gaussian (normal) density function for attribute A_k, while μ_c and σ_{c_i} are the mean and standard deviation, respectively, given the values for attribute A_k for training images of class C_i.

3.2 Bayesian Sports Image Classifie

In this paper, we propose a classification scheme for sports images using the Bayesian classifier. To do this, we capture high-level concepts (i.e. football/swimming/ skiing) from low-level image features (i.e. color, shape, and texture) through the training process.

Sports images can be distinguished exclusively since the differences between some sports images are noticeable. Such differences can be represented as differences between low-level features of a sports image. For example, images of water sports such as swimming and windsurfing have a large blue region by water, while images of snow sports have a white region. The proposed Bayesian sports image classifier uses four low-level features to classify the sports images. Each feature represents color or shape characteristic of the images.

This classifier assumes that each training image belongs to one of the classes. Semantic classes of the training image are illustrated in Fig. 1. The four low-level features used to depict an image are color histogram, color coherence vector, edge direction histogram, and edge direction coherence vector. We describe these features briefly from the viewpoint of sports image classification.

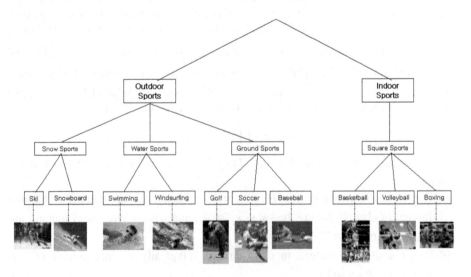

Fig. 1. Classes of sports images.

▪ Color histogram is a compact summary of an image in color dimension. In the Bayesian sports image classification, a value of color histogram identifies the characteristic of each sports image in color dimension. Color histograms are frequently used to compare images. Their use in multimedia applications includes scene break detection and objects identification. For a given image I, its color histogram is H_I. An image database can be queried to find the most similar image to I, and can return the image I' with the most similar color histogram $H_{I'}$. Typically, color histograms are compared using the sum of squared differences, called as L_2-distance, or the sum of absolute value of differences, called as L_1-distance. So the most similar image to I would be the image I' minimizing the L_2-distance or L_1-distance. Equation of L_1-distance (4) and L_2-distance (5) are as follows.

$$\| H_I - H_{I'} \| = \sum_{j=1}^{n} (H_I[j] - H_{I'}[j])^2 \tag{4}$$

$$| H_I - H_{I'} | = \sum_{j=1}^{n} | H_I[j] - H_{I'}[j] | , \tag{5}$$

where M is the number of pixels that an image has. We assumed that all images have the same number of pixels for the ease of explanation. $H(h_1, h_2, ..., h_n)$ is a vector, in which each component h_j is the number of pixels of color j in the image. n is the number of distinct (discredited) colors.

▪ Color coherence vector [12] is the degree to which pixels of that color are members of large similar colored regions. We refer to these regions as coherent regions. Our coherence measure classifies pixels as either coherent or incoherent. Coherent pixels are a part of some sizable contiguous region, while incoherent pixels are not. A color coherence vector (CCV) represents this classification for each color in the image. CCVs prevent coherent pixels in one image from matching incoherent pixels in another. This allows distinctions that cannot be made with color histograms. In the Bayesian sports image classification, CCVs help to find a sports image class having similar characteristic with input images in color dimension. At first, we blur the image slightly by replacing pixel values with the average value in a small local neighborhood (currently including the 8 adjacent pixels). This eliminates small variations between neighboring pixels. Then we discrete the color space, such that there are only n distinct colors in the image. The next step is to classify the pixels within a given color bucket as either coherent or incoherent. A coherent pixel is a part of a large group of pixels of the same color, while an incoherent pixel is not. We determine the pixel groups by computing connected components. We classify pixels as either coherent or incoherent depending on the size in pixels of its connected component(C). A pixel is coherent if the size of its connected component exceeds a fixed value T (e.g. 1% of number of pixels); otherwise, the pixel is incoherent. Color coherent vector (6) and equation for distance measure (7) of image I_a and I_b using the weighted Euclidean distance are as follows.

$$((a_1, b_1), \dots, (a_n, b_n)) \tag{6}$$

$$\sqrt{\frac{\sum_{j=1}^{n}((a_j - a_j')^2 + (b_j - b_j')^2)}{2n}}, \tag{7}$$

where a_j is (number of coherent pixels of the j's discretized color) / (total number of pixels in the image). b_j is (number of incoherent pixels of the j's discretized color) / (total number of pixels in the image)

- Edge direction histogram (EDH) [12] represents the global information of shape in an image. The edge direction information can be obtained by using the Canny edge detector [12]. In the Bayesian sports image classification, the EDH identifies the characteristic of each sports image in shape dimension. At first, we calculate Gaussian filter $S_{i,j}$ then compute the gradient along x-direction, $P_{i,j}$, and compute the gradient along y-direction, $Q_{i,j}$. Next, we compute the magnitude of the gradient to obtain an edge image, $M_{i,j}$, using $S_{i,j}$ and $P_{i,j}$. Finally, we compute edge direction histogram (8) as follow.

$$\theta = \arctan(\frac{Q_{i,j}}{P_{i,j}}) \tag{8}$$

- An edge direction coherence vector (EDCV) stores the number of coherent versus non-coherent edge pixels with the same directions (within a quantization of $5°$). A threshold on the size of every connected component of edges in a given direction is used to decide whether the region is coherent or not. Thus this feature is geared towards discriminating structured edges from arbitrary edge distributions when the edge direction histograms are matched. The EDCV helps the classifier to find sports image class having similar characteristic with input images in shape domain. The shape characteristic of images in the same sports class is similar by its background (i.e. ring or form of ground) or pose of player (i.e. shooting pose or almost fixed camera angle).

There are several differences between Bayesian classifier of textual data and that of image data. Images usually have various and complex attributes, which means image data, may be represented in high-dimension space. In addition, most of these attributes have continuous values. Accordingly, the Bayesian sports image classifier should reflect such characteristics of image data.

4   Experiments

Sports image is a good domain to show efficiency and accuracy of the proposed classifier because a sports image belongs to a single sports class. Moreover, sports images have unique characteristics, which can represent a sports category of an image. For instance, images of ground sports such as golf, soccer and baseball have a large green region by grass and indoor sports images such as basketball, volleyball and boxing have similar edge direction by ground line or ring.

For experiments, we used a sports image database composed of several sports classes such as ski, snowboard, swimming, windsurfing, golf, soccer, baseball, basketball, volleyball and boxing. We gather such sports images from Internet. Each sports class contains about 50 images. The total number of sports images in the database is 487.

First, we classified images using the proposed sports image classifier employing each single image feature. Image sets is classified into indoor/outdoor categories. Then images, belonging to the indoor category, are further divided into three categories, which are water sports, snow sports and ground sports. Images of water sports are classified into swimming images and windsurfing images. Images of snow sports are classified into ski images and snowboard images. Finally, images of ground sports are classified into golf, soccer and baseball categories. Secondly, the proposed sports image classifier uses the combinations of image features and performs classification. Accuracy of each classification is shown in Table 1 and Table 2.

Table 1. Accuracy of classification using each single image feature.

	CH	CCV	EDH	EDCV
indoor/outdoor	(260/487)53.4	(274/487)56.3	(302/487)62.0	(311/487)63.9
water/snow/ground	(256/344)75.0	(266/344)77.3	(238/344)69.2	(240/344)69.7
ski/snowboard	(67/97)69.1	(68/97)70.1	(69/97)71.1	(69/97)71.1
swim/windsurfing	(73/97)75.3	(71/97)73.2	(74/97)76.3	(75/97)77.3
golf/soccer/baseball	(105/150)70.0	(107/150)71.3	(108/150)72.0	(110/150)73.3
basket/volley/boxing	(88/143)61.5	(86/143)60.1	(99/143)69.2	(101/143)70.6

Table 2. Accuracy of classification using combinations of image features.

	CH& EDH	CH& EDCV	CCV& EDH	CCV& EDCV
indoor/outdoor	(314/487)64.5	(337/487)69.2	(312/487)64.1	(358/487)73.5
water/snow/ground	(278/344)80.8	(277/344)80.5	(286/344)83.1	(288/344)83.7
ski/snowboard	(70/97)72.2	(71/97)73.2	(70/97)72.2	(75/97)77.3
swim/windsurfing	(75/97)77.3	(76/97)78.3	(74/97)76.3	(77/97)79.3
golf/soccer/baseball	(107/150)71.3	(113/150)75.3	(110/150)73.3	(115/150)76.7
basket/volley/boxing	(98/143)68.5	(102/143)71.3	(102/143)71.3	(108/143)75.2

The classification using combinations of features is more accurate than the classification using a single feature. In the classification employing a single feature, the most effective feature is dependent on characteristic of the image. For example, a classification of sports images, which is dependent on color features such as water/snow/ground classification, has the best accuracy when it uses color features such as CH or CCV. By the contrast, sports image classification that is not based on color features such as swimming/windsurfing classification shows better accuracy when it uses edge features such as EDH or EDCV instead of color features.

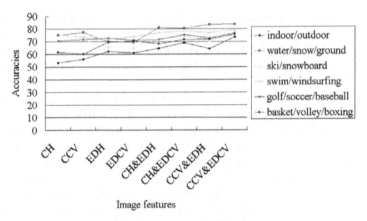

Image features

Fig. 2. Accuracy of classification.

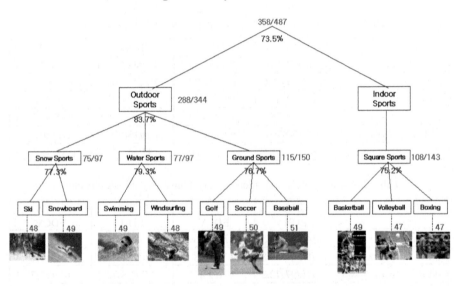

Fig. 3. Accuracy of classification using CCV&EDCV.

Most of the incorrectly classified images are close-up images or images taken in a long distant. An image of a swimmer's face does not have the characteristics from the swimming image class. It is just an image of human face. In the same manner, an image of soccer ground taken from the sky has no characteristics of the soccer image class.

5   Conclusion

Image data mining is a fast expanding field with many new issues. Specially, many researchers in various fields focus on image classification with deep interest in image mining. In this paper, we proposed a sport classifier based on the Bayesian framework. In processing sports images on the web, the proposed classifier can be more accurate by using annotated information of given image.

References

1. U.M. Fayyad, G. Piatetsky-Shapiro, P. Smyth, R. Uthurusamy: Advances in Knowledge Discovery and Data Mining. AAAI/MIT Press, (1996)
2. Maria Luiza Antoniek Osmar R. Zaiane, Alexandru Coman: Application of Data Mining Techniques for Medical Image Classification. In Proc. The 2nd Int. workshop Multimedia Data Mining (MDM/KDD), San Francisco, USA, August 26 (2001)
3. M. Datcu, K. Seidel: Image information mining: exploration of image content in large archives. IEEE Conf. On Aerospace, Vol. 3, (2000)
4. Ji Zhang, Wynne Hsu, Mong Li Lee: Image Mining: Issues, Frameworks and Techniques. In Proc. The 2nd Int. workshop Multimedia Data Mining (MDM/KDD), San Francisco, USA, August 26 (2001)
5. L. Bruzzone, D.F. Prieto: Unsupervised retraining of a maximum likelihood classifier for the analysis of multitemporal remote sensing image. IEEE Transactions on Geoscience and Resmote Sensing, Vol. 39, February (2001)
6. Alejandro Jaimes, Shih-Fu Chang: Model-Based Classification of Visual Information for Content-Based Retrieval. Storage and Retrieval for Image and Video Databases VII, IS&T/SPIE99, San Jose, CA, January (1999)
7. Theo Gevers et. al.: Classification of Image on Internet by Visual and Textual Information. Internet Imaging, SPIE, San Jose, January (2000.)
8. N. Vasconcelos, A. Lippman: Library-based coding: A representation for efficient video compression and retrieval. Data Compression Conf.'97, Snowbird, UT, (1997)
9. Jiawei Han, Micheline Kamber: Data Mining: concepts and techniques, Morgan Kaufmann press, p.296-303, (2001)
10. A.K. Jain, A. Vailaya: Image retrieval using color and shape, Pattern Recognition. 29(8):1233-1244, (1996)
11. J. Canny: A computational approach to edge detection. IEEE Transactions on Pattern Analysis and Machine Intelligence, PAMI-8(6):679-698, (1986)
12. Greg Pass, Ramin Zabih, J. Miller: Comparing images using color coherence vectors. In Proc. ACM Multimedia, 65-73, Boston, MA, November (1996)

Text Mining Using the Hierarchical Syntactical Structure of Documents

Roxana Danger[1], José Ruíz-Shulcloper[2], and Rafael Berlanga[3]

[1] Universidad de Oriente, Santiago de Cuba, Cuba
[2] Institute of Cybernetics, Mathematics and Physics, La Habana, Cuba
[3] Universitat Jaume I, Castellón, Spain

Abstract. One of the most important tasks for determining association rules consists of calculating all the maximal frequent itemsets. Specifically, some methods to obtain these itemsets have been developed in the context of both databases and text collections. In this work, the *hierarchical syntactical structure*'s concept is introduced, which supplies an unexplored dimension in the task of describing and analysing text collections. Based on this conceptual framework, we propose an efficient algorithm for calculating all the maximal frequent itemsets, which includes either the Feldman's or the Ahonen's concept of frequency depending on the practical application.

Keywords: Mining structured texts, Maximal co-occurrence, Association rules.

1 Introduction

Discovering association rules is a relevant problem in the field of Data Mining, which was initially introduced by Agrawal in [1]. The main solution to this problem consists in computing the frequent itemsets that appear in the database, and in constructing from them the interesting association rules (e.g. [7]).

Several works have demonstrated that some data mining algorithms developed for relational databases can be also applied to texts [2][3][5]. The problem of mining texts was firstly introduced in [3], which consisted in producing a set of association rules starting from the set of frequent terms of each document of the collection. In this work, the mining process is guided by a set of predefined predicates that state relevant semantic relationships between terms. In [2], a method to find out ordered maximal frequent itemsets in a document collection was presented. Here, the concept of frequent term differs from that of [3] in that a frequent term must be frequent throughout the collection, independently of its local frequency in each document.

The fast adoption of the standard XML (eXtended Markup Language) in the current open information systems has produced the emergence of a new kind of information warehouses where traditional structured data lives together with unstructured textual information. In this scenario, it seems urgent to define new text mining techniques that allow analysts to extract the useful knowledge that these warehouses contain.

Concerning to XML documents, few works in the literature has taken into account the document hierarchical structure for text mining purposes, and they are mainly

R. Conejo et al. (Eds.): CAEPIA-TTIA 2003, LNAI 3040, pp. 556–565, 2004.
© Springer-Verlag Berlin Heidelberg 2004

concerned with mining the structure but not the contents [6]. In our opinion, regarding the hierarchical structure of the documents can improve the interpretation of the extracted itemsets (and therefore the association rules), and it can allow analysts to focus on a particular level of the hierarchy to obtain different itemsets.

In this paper, we propose a new method to generate the maximal itemsets at any level of the hierarchical structure of the document collection (i.e. its XML-Schema or DTD). In this context, the concept of frequent term depends on the hierarchy level we are focusing on. Thus, if we focus on the top level of the hierarchy (the whole collection), the concept of frequent term corresponds to that of [2], whereas if we focus on the bottom level, the concept of frequent term corresponds to that of [3]. With our method, we can deal with any level of the structural hierarchy, providing in this way alternative itemsets, which can provide further knowledge of the application at hand.

The remainder of the paper is organised as follows. Section 2 introduces some preliminary concepts for the mining of hierarchical organised documents. Section 3 presents the proposed mining algorithm, which finds the itemsets depending on the selected hierarchical level. Section 4 presents the experimental results, and finally Section 5 gives some conclusions.

2 Preliminary Concepts

In the following paragraphs we introduce the necessary concepts to define the proposed mining algorithm. In this paper, we represent a document as a tree whose nodes are the XML elements and its leaves contain the texts we want to mine. We will denote each sub-tree of a document with T_{tag}, where *tag* is the root element of the sub-tree. Moreover, we will denote with $Terms(T_{tag})$ the set of textual terms appearing in the leaves of the tree T_{tag}. Finally, we will denote with MT_{tag} to the set of document sub-trees whose root is the element *tag*. Figure 2 shows an example of the structure of a document collection and different mining contexts (MT_{tag}).

Definition 1. Let T_{tag} be a document tree such that its leaves contains q terms, i.e. $|Terms(T_{tag})| = q$. A term $t \in Terms(T_{tag})$ is a frequent term of T_{tag} if and only if it appears at least $\delta(q)$ times in $Terms(T_{tag})$, where δ is the frequency threshold that depends on the number of terms q.

This definition corresponds to the usual concept of frequent term (i.e. keyword) as defined in [3], but applied to any level of the hierarchy. Thus, the term is said to be frequent for a given tree (e.g. a chapter, a section, etc.), if it sufficiently appears in it.

Definition 2. A term is said to be a frequent term in MT_{tag} if and only if it appears at least in $\delta_{MT_{tag}} (|MT_{tag}|)$ trees of MT_{tag}. Notice that the frequency threshold is a function that depends on the size of MT_{tag}.

This definition corresponds to the usual concept of frequent term but applied to any level of the document hierarchy.

Definition 3. A term is said to be a strongly frequent term in MT_{tag} if and only if it is a frequent term in at least in $\delta_{MT_{tag}} (|MT_{tag}|)$ trees of MT_{tag}.

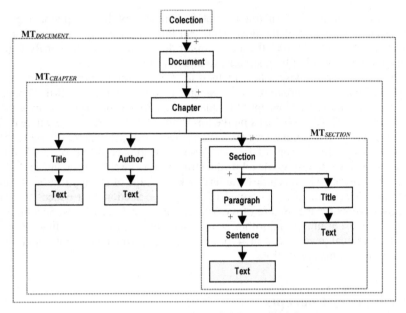

Fig. 1. Example of a document collection and mining contexts.

Definition 4. The set of terms $\{t_1, ..., t_m\}$, with $t_i \in \bigcup_{T_{tag} \in MT_{tag}} Terms(T_{tag})$ $(i \in \{1,..,m\})$ is a frequent itemset in MT_{tag} if its members co-occur at least $\delta_{tag}(q)$ times in T_{tag}.

Definition 5. A set of terms $\{t_1, ..., t_m\}$, with $t_i \in Terms(T_{tag})$ $(i \in \{1,.., m\})$ is a frequent itemset in MT_{tag} if its members co-occur at least $\delta_{MT_{tag}}(|MT_{tag}|)$ trees of MT_{tag}. Moreover, an itemset is said to be strongly frequent if it is a frequent itemset in at least $\delta_{MT_{tag}}(|MT_{tag}|)$ trees of MT_{tag}.

Definition 6. A (strongly) frequent itemset in MT_{tag} is said to be *maximal* if there not exists another (strongly) frequent itemset in MT_{tag} that is superset of it.

The problem of mining maximal (strongly) frequent itemsets in MT_{tag} consists of finding all the maximal (strongly) frequent itemsets in MT_{tag}. The solution to this problem requires as a previous step, the extraction of the (strongly) frequent terms in MT_{tag}, and to record the subsets (in which they are frequent) where they appear. This is because all the supersets of an infrequent itemset are also infrequent, and all the subsets of a frequent itemset are also frequent. The overall mining process is illustrated in the Figure 2.

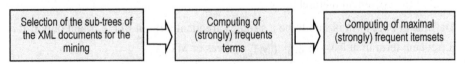

Fig. 2. Extracting the maximal frequent itemsets.

3 Finding Maximal Frequent Itemsets

The proposed mining algorithm basically extracts all the frequent terms (definitions 2 or 3) for a given structure element, and then it extends them to obtain the maximal itemsets. The lexicographical order between terms is used to incrementally extend the frequent sets. The algorithm takes as input the frequent terms at the MT_{tag} level, which are represented by the list F_w. Moreover, the algorithm uses a hash table T whose keys are the detected frequent terms and term pairs, and their values are the tree indexes of the MT_{tag} where each key occurs.

It is worth mentioning that the number of combinations between frequent terms to be explored during the extension of itemsets can be reduced if all the itemsets of cardinality 2 are pre-computed.

Algorithm GetMaximalItemsets(F_w, T, $\delta_{MT_{tag}}$, MaximalCo_Occs)

Objetive: Computing the maximal frequent itemsets
Input:
  F_w: Ordered set of frequent terms to be considered during the mining process.
  T: A hash table with the occurrences of frequent terms and term pairs.
  $\delta_{MT_{tag}}$: frequency threshold for the MT_{tag} level.

Output:
  MaximalCo_Ocs: Set of maximal frequent itemsets.

Method:
1. MaximalCo_Ocs =∅
2. forall p in F_w
3.   if p does not appear in a frequent pair then
4.   MaximalCo_Occs = MaximalCo_Occs ∪ {p}
5.   else
6.   TermsToUseForExt={p | ∃pair=(p, p⌐) ∈ T.keys()}
7.   Co_OccsToExtend = {CoOc | CoOc = (CoOcMax ∩ TermsToUseForExt) ∨ CoOc={p⌐} such that
          Co_OcMax∈ MaximalCo_Ocs, ∀CoOc⌐∈ Co_OccsToExtend, CoOc⊄CoOc⌐, p⌐∈ TermsToUse-
      ForExt }
8.   Extend({p},T[p], P$_f$, T, Co_OccsToExtend, $\delta_{MT_{tag}}$, MaximalCo_Occs)

Fig. 3. Algorithm to compute the maximal itemsets for a given structure element.

The maximal frequent itemsets are then obtained by taking each frequent term from F_w and then testing whether it is already included in a frequent pair (Figure 2, lines 3-4). If it does not occur, the unitary set formed by the frequent term is considered a maximal frequent co-occurrence. Otherwise, the frequent term can be extended to produce several maximal itemsets containing it. For this purpose, the algorithm takes all the already computed itemsets containing the term along with the terms with which it forms a frequent pair and they have not been included in the already computed itemsets. Then, it tries to extend the term as much as possible in order to obtain all the maximal frequent itemsets that contain it. (Figure 2, lines 6-8).

Figure 3 shows the algorithm that extends a given itemset *FreqSet* by using the already computed frequent itemsets, which are recorded in *Co_OccsToExtend*. In the case that *Co_OccsToExtend* has just one element, the extension of *FreqSet* with this element is then added to *MaximalCo_Occs* (Figure 3, lines 2-5). Otherwise, all the maximal frequent itemsets that contains *FreqSet* must be found (Figure 3, lines 7-36).

For this purpose, the algorithm takes each of the itemsets (*Co_Oc*) of *Co_OccsToExtend* (Figure 3, line 9) and it extends the frequent set *FreqSet* with it, generating a new frequent set *FreqSet'*. Then, the remaining itemsets (*Co_Oc'*) in *Co_OccsToExtend* are examined to know which of them can further extend *FreqSet'*:

1. If *FreqSet'* can be extended with *Co_Oc'*, then the following cases must be considered (Figure 3, lines 19-23):
   a. If the occurrences of *FreqSet'* are equal to those of *FreqSet*, the extension of *FreqSet* with *Co_Oc'* does not generate new itemsets different from those generated by *FreqSet'*. Therefore, this set should not be considered in the successive iterations (Figure 3, lines 19-21).
   b. If their occurrences are different, *Co_Oc'* must be recorded in order to find out all the possible combinations of maximal frequent itemsets generated from *FreqSet'*. This set is denoted with *Co_OccsToExtend'* (Figure 3, lines 22-23).

   The method *T.Hits(Itemset)* is here used to obtain the occurrences of a given itemset.

2. If *FreqSet'* cannot be extended with *Co_Oc'*, then the following cases must be regarded (Figure 3, lines 24-30):
   a. If *Co_Oc'* is a unitary set, then it is impossible to extend *FreqSet'* with *Co_Oc'*. Moreover, the term in *Co_Oc'* should not be considered in the successive iterations for the extension of *FreqSet'* (Figure 3, lines 24-25). Notice that those terms are discarded when the algorithm takes each itemset *Co_Oc'* (Figure 3, line 17).
   b. If *Co_Oc'* is not a unitary set, then *FreqSet* must be extended with all the pairs (*p, p'*) such that *p* is a member of *Co_Oc\Co_Oc'*, and *p'* is a member of the *Co_Oc'\Co_Oc* (Figure 3, lines 27-30). The itemsets that can be used to extend *FreqSet* ∪ {*p, p'*} are obtained by using the function *OthsFreqTerms*, which returns the terms with which *FreqSet* ∪ {*p, p'*} co-occurs.

Finally, the algorithm takes the other terms that can also extend *FreqSet'* but that were not included in any of the itemsets of *Co_OccsToExtend'* (Figure 3, line 32). Thus, *FreqSet'* is extended in turn by using a recursive call (Figure 3, line 33).

4   Results

To evaluate the obtained results we have taken two collections of news articles from the international section published in the Spanish newspaper "El País". The first collection comprises the news articles published during June 1999, which mainly reported about the Kosovo War. The other collection comprises news articles published during November 1999, which have a greater variety of topics. Before mining these collections, news articles are processed to reject stopwords (e.g. articles, prepositions and adverbs) and to extract the word lemmas (terms). We use as the *hierarchical syntactical structure* the following levels: the whole document collection, article, paragraph, sentences and terms. The characteristics of the document collection are summarised as follows:

Algorithm Extend(FreqSet, TCoinc, T, Co_OccsToExtend, $\delta_{MT_{tag}}$, MaximalCo_Occs)

Objetive: Add to MaximalCo_Ocs all the maximal frequent co-ocurrence sets that have its first term (following the lexicographical order) the first term of the frequent set FreqSet.

Input: FreqSet: Frequent set to be extended.
  TCoinc: Set of items of MT_{tag} in which the terms of FreqSet co-occur.
  T: The hash table containing the indexes of the elements of the MT_{tag}.
  Co_OccsToExtend: Frequent co-ocurrences to use for extending FreqSet (lexicographically ordered).
  $\delta_{MT_{tag}}$: frequency threshold for the MT_{tag} level.

Output: MaximalCo_Occs: Set of maximal frequent co-ocurrences.
Method:
1.   if |Co_OcsToExtend| ≤1 then
2.   if |Co_OcsToExtend| = 1 then
3.   CoOcMax = FreqSet ∪ Co_OcsToExtend[0]
4.   if CoOcMax ⊄ CoOcMax', ∀CoOcMax' in MaximalCo_Ocs then
5.   MaximalCo_Ocs.Add(CoOcMax)
6.   else
7.   NotConsider = ∅
8.   i = 0
9.   while i ≤ |Co_OcsToExtend|
10.   Co_Oc=Co_OcsToExtend [i]
11.   FreqSet'=FreqSet ∪ Co_Oc
12.   TCoinc'=TCoinc ∩ T.Hits(FreqSet ∪ Co_Oc)
13.   Co_OcsToExtend'=∅
14.   StopTerms=∅
15.   j = i + 1
16.   while j ≤ |Co_OcsToExtend |
17.   Co_Oc'=Co_OcsToExtend[j]
18.   TCoincs'=TCoinc' ∩ T.Hits(Co_Oc')
19.   if TCoincs'=TCoinc' then
20.   FreqSet'=FreqSet' ∪ {Co_Oc'}
21.   NotConsider=NotConsider ∪ {j}
22.   else If $|TCoincs'| \geq \delta_{MT_{tag}}$
23.   Co_OcsToExtend'=Co_OcsToExtend' ∪ {Co_Oc'}
24.   else If $|Co\_Oc'|$ =1 then
25.   StopTerms = StopTerms ∪ Co_Oc'
26.   else
27.   forall p,p'∈ F_w, (p, p')∈ T.keys( ), and p∈ Co_Oc\Co_Oc', p'∈ Co_Oc'\Co_Oc
28.   if $|$T.Hits(FreqSet ∪ {p,p'}) $| \geq \delta_{MT_{tag}}$ then
29.   CoOcsToExtend'= OthsFreqTerms (FreqSet ∪ {p,p'})
30.   Extend(FreqSet ∪ {p,p'}, T.Hits(FreqSet ∪ {p,p'}),
                                T, Co_OcsToExtend', $\delta_{MT_{tag}}$, MaximalCo_Ocs)
31.   j = j + 1
32.   Add to CoOcsToExtend' unitary set for each term in OthsFreqTerms ($\bigcup\limits_{\substack{p\in CoOc \ \vee \ p\in FreqSet, \\ CoOc\in CoOcsToExt\,end'}} p$)
33.   Extend (FreqSet', TCoincs', T, Co_OccsToExtend', $\delta_{MT_{tag}}$, MaximalCo_Occs)
34.   i=i + 1
35.   while i in NotConsider do
36.   i= i + 1

Fig. 4. Algorithm for the extension of the itemsets.

June 1999		November 1999	
Number of news articles:	530	Number of news articles:	456
Number of paragraph:	4549	Number of paragraph:	3542
Number of sentences:	10879	Number of sentences:	8853
Number of terms:	36342	Number of terms:	39568

We use as a function for the frequency threshold the percentage of the sub-trees included in each level (i.e. article, paragraph and sentence). In the experiments we only use the concept of maximal frequent itemset.

Regarding to the news of June, the optimal threshold for paragraphs and sentences is 0.44%, whereas for the article level is 5%. Table 1 presents the first 15 itemsets of

Table 1. Itemsets obtained for the collection of June 1999.

Sentence		Paragraph	
ItemSet	Relev.	ItemSet	Relev.
fuerza, internacional, kosovo	4.7594	augusto_pinochet, auto, baltasar_garz⊠n, caso, juez, procesamiento	19.6169
mill⊠n, peseta	3.7326	Baltasar_garz⊠n, genocidio, juez	7.6760
d⊠lar, mill⊠n	3.7181	fuerza, internacional, kfor, paz	6.7672
ej⊘rcito_de_liberaci⊠n_de_kosovo, elk	3.4240	alem⅌, canciller, gerhard_schr⊠der	6.6499
fuerza, kfor	2.5966	d⊠lar, mill⊠n, peseta	6.3618
fuerza, paz	2.1971	ej⊘rcito_de_liberaci⊠n_de_kosovo, elk, kosovo, serbio	6.1369
retirado, serbio	2.1507	fuerza, kfor, kosovo, paz	5.9906
bombardeo, otan	2.0738	fuerza, internacional, kfor, kosovo	5.9659
otan, yugoslavia	1.7932	fuerza, internacional, kosovo, tropa	5.7191
kosovo, tropa	1.7502	fuerza, internacional, kosovo, paz	5.6908
acuerdo, paz	1.7416	javier_solana, otan, secretario_general	5.5357
fuerzas, serbio	1.7335	fuerzas, kosovo, retirado, serbio	5.5248
otan, tropa	1.7075	iglesia, ortodoxo, serbio	5.4700
fuerzas, kosovo	1.6821	Augusto_pinochet, chile, general	5.3556
Albanokosovar, serbio	1.6099	Augusto_pinochet, general, juez	5.2107

Article	
ItemSet	Relev.
aliado, bombardeo, kosovo, militar, otan, serbio, yugoslavo	6.3607
belgrado, kosovo, otan, serbio, slobodan_milosevic, yugoslavia	5.8310
bombardeo, kosovo, otan, serbio, slobodan_milosevic, yugoslavia	5.8194
kosovo, otan, serbio, slobodan_milosevic, yugoslavia, yugoslavo	5.7143
belgrado, bombardeo, kosovo, otan, serbio, yugoslavo	5.6139
fuerza, fuerzas, kosovo, militar, otan, paz, serbio	5.5470
internacional, kosovo, otan, slobodan_milosevic, yugoslavia, yugoslavo	5.5410
fuerza, internacional, kosovo, militar, paz, serbio, tropa	5.5287
aliado, kosovo, otan, serbio, slobodan_milosevic, yugoslavo	5.5205
bombardeo, otan, presidente, serbio, slobodan_milosevic, yugoslavia	5.4877
internacional, kosovo, serbio, slobodan_milosevic, yugoslavia, yugoslavo	5.4733
belgrado, guerra, kosovo, otan, serbio, slobodan_milosevic	5.4313
bombardeo, kosovo, otan, serbio, yugoslavia, yugoslavo	5.4143
fuerza, fuerzas, internacional, kosovo, militar, paz, serbio	5.4079
Aliado, belgrado, kosovo, otan, serbio, yugoslavo	5.3703

each level ordered by the *mutual information function* [4], which calculates the information gain produced by each itemset.

Regarding to the news of November, the optimal thresholds for sentences and paragraphs is around 0.56%, and for articles is around 5%. Table 2 shows the first 15 itemsets obtained for each syntactical level.

From these experiments, we can notice that in the collection of June, many of the relevant itemsets refer to the Yugoslavian conflict. Nevertheless, the obtained itemsets for each syntactical level express different semantic relationships. Thus, the itemsets at the sentence and paragraph levels usually capture frequent linguistic relationships between terms (e.g. {force, international},{million, dollar}). However, at the article level, the itemsets use to describe the keywords that frequently co-occur in the collection. It can be also noticed that some topics that are not relevant at the article level (e.g. Pinochet's trial) become relevant at the paragraph level, since they are very frequent in the few news that involve these topics.

Table 2. Itemsets obtained for the collection of November 1999.

Sentence (0,56%)	
paz, proceso	2.7087
chechenia, ruso	2.5630
gobierno, presidente	0.9907
ministro, presidente	0.8301
político, presidente	0.4086

Paragraph (0,56%)		Article (5%)	
auto_de_la_audiencia_nacional, autorizar, baltasar_garzón, caso, españa, español, extradición, inglés, juez, prisión, procesamiento	39.1206	chechenia, guerra, rusia, ruso	5.0179
augusto_pinochet, baltasar_garzón, caso, españa, juez	12.857	chechenia, militar, rusia, ruso	4.8364
augusto_pinochet, baltasar_garzón, español, juez	9.6297	boris_yeltsin, presidente, rusia, ruso	4.5014
augusto_pinochet, españa, extradición	6.2376	chechenia, presidente, rusia, ruso	4.1045
augusto_pinochet, extradición, juez	6.0672	chechenia, moscú, rusia	3.8954
augusto_pinochet, españa, español	5.4386	chechenia, moscú, ruso	3.7847
checheno, militar, ruso	4.5265	moscú, rusia, ruso	3.6610
boris_yeltsin, presidente, ruso	4.2157	osce, rusia, ruso	3.6307
chechenia, guerra, ruso	4.0654	chechenia, guerra, ministro, ruso	3.6194
chechenia, militar, ruso	3.7521	chechenia, guerra, presidente, ruso	3.4346
caído, muro	3.6431	cumbre, rusia, ruso	2.9657
ira, sinn_fein	3.5347	caso, delito, juez	2.7741
derechos_humanos, violación	3.3849	ministro, presidente, rusia, ruso	2.6688
equipo, rescate	3.3774	chechenia, ministro, rusia	2.2832
chileno, dictador	3.3629	cuba, cubano	2.2520

It is worth mentioning that the mutual information function has the desired effects over the relevance of itemsets. Indeed, the frequent linguistic patterns used by the journalists obtain a low relevance with this function, whereas the itemsets with greater semantics obtain greater relevance values.

At the paragraph level, the itemsets with the greatest relevance are those that belong to little mentioned topics, which obtain significant differences with respect to the rest of the itemsets. On the other hand, the itemsets of the most mentioned topics have a relevance value between 7.0 and 5.0. At the article level, the function takes values in the same range as expected.

The collection of November has a similar behaviour, although the found frequent itemsets have lower relevance values. This is due to the greater number of mentioned topics.

As in the previous collection, we can also notice that the most relevant itemsets are always obtained at the paragraph level, and it is important to notice that those coincide with the most interesting itemsets.

5   Conclusions

In this work we have introduced a new text-mining algorithm based on the concept of *hierarchical syntactical structure*. It constitutes an unexplored approach for the description and analysis of structured document collections, ant it conceptually surpasses the previous text mining approaches in different aspects. Firstly, the number of meaningless item combinations is notably reduced when considering itemsets of the same hierarchical level. Additionally, the analysis of a collection can be performed from any of its different hierarchical levels.

We have also introduced an algorithm for computing the maximal frequent itemsets, in which the term frequency concept of Feldman and Ahonen is extended to any level of the syntactical hierarchy.

We have demonstrated that there are significant differences in the frequent itemsets found at the different syntactical levels. Moreover, we have shown that the mutual information function successfully expresses the relevance of these itemsets.

In the future, we are interested in comparing the obtained results with those generated by using the concept of maximal strongly frequent itemset.

Acknowledgements

This work has been partially funded by the research project CICYT (TIC2002-04586-C04-03).

References

1. Agrawal, R.; Imielinski, T.; Swami, A.: Mining Association Rules between Sets of Items in Large DataBases. In Proceeding of ACM SIGMOD Conference on Management of Data. Washington, DC. 1993. 207-216.

2. Ahonen-Myka, H.; Heinonen, O.; Klemettinen, M; Ikeri V, A.: Finding Co-occurring Text Phrases by Combining Sequence and Frequent Set Discovery. In Ronen Feldman, editor, Proceedings of Sixteenth International Joint Conference on Artificial Intelligence (IJCAI-99) Workshop on Text Mining: Foundations, Techniques and Applications, pp. 1–9, Stockholm, Sweden, 1999.
3. Feldman, R.; Dagan, I. : Knowledge Discovery in textual databases (KDT). In the Proceedings of the first International Conference on Data Mining and Knowledge Discovery, KDD'95, pp. 112-117, Montreal, August 1995.
4. Fano, R.: Transmission of Information, MIT Press, 1961.
5. Feldman, R.; Hirsh, H.: Mining Associations in Text in the presence of background knowledge. In Proceedings of the Second International Conference on Knowledge Discovery and Data Mining. 1996.
6. Termier, A., Rousset M. C., Sebag M.: TreeFinder: a First Step towards XML Data Mining. IEEE International Conference on Data Mining (ICDM 2002), pp. 450-457, 2002.
7. Toivonen, H.: Discovery of frequent patterns in large data collections. PhD Thesis, Report A-1996-5, University of Helsinki, Department of Computer Science, November 1996.

The Synergy of GA and Fuzzy Systems for Multidimensional Problem: Application to Time Series Prediction

Ignacio Rojas[1], Fernando Rojas[1], O. Valenzuela[2], and Alberto Prieto[1]

[1] Department of Architecture and Computer Technology, University of Granada, Spain
[2] Department of Mathematic, University of Granada, Spain

Abstract. The goal of this research is to design an optimal fuzzy system than can extract fuzzy rules and specify membership functions automatically by learning from examples. This method has the merits that it does not require both the precise mathematical modeling of fuzzy system and the human expert's help since the input-output characteristics of fuzzy system are approximated by learning the training examples. A multideme GA system is used in which various fuzzy systems with different numbers of input variables and structures are jointly optimized. We also propose coding by means of multidimensional matrices of the fuzzy rules such that the neighborhood properties are not destroyed by forcing it into a linear chromosome. We have applied the approach to two well-studied time series: sunspot and Mackey-Glass chaotic process. The results demonstrate that the approach is fairly effective and efficient in terms of relatively high prediction accuracy and fast learning speed.

1 Fuzzy Modeling by Genetic Algorithms

Two typical examples using the technique of learning from examples can be found by applying either neural networks or genetic algorithms in the design of the Fuzzy Systems and its Parameters (FP). The former approach has some drawbacks: 1) it can only use numerical data pairs; 2) it does not always guarantee the optimal system performance due to easy trapping to local minimum solution; and 3) it is not easy to interpret the created fuzzy rules due to its internal representation of weights. Designing the FP's based on the GAs has been widely attempted since it can provide more possibilities of finding an optimal (or near-optimal) solution due to the implicit parallelism of GAs.

Gas have the potential to be employed to evolve both the fuzzy rules and the corresponding fuzzy set parameters [12]. Some of the work of fuzzy systems and GAs concentrates exclusively on tuning of membership functions [9] or on selecting an optimal set of fuzzy rules [11], while others attempt to derive rules and membership functions together [5]. To obtain optimal rule sets and optimal sets of membership functions, it is preferable that both are acquired simultaneously [7]. To optimize the whole fuzzy system simultaneously, two structures will be used: one to encode the membership functions and the other for the fuzzy rules. Therefore, the structure of the chromosome is formed by two different matrix: the first one is an incomplete matrix

R. Conejo et al. (Eds.): CAEPIA-TTIA 2003, LNAI 3040, pp. 566–576, 2004.
© Springer-Verlag Berlin Heidelberg 2004

in which each row represents one of the variable of the system, and where the columns encode the parameters of the membership functions. The second one is a complete matrix in the form of a $n_1 \times ... \times n_n$ matrix, noting that n_m is the number of membership functions contained within each input variable. Note that each element of this second matrix is the conclusion of the fuzzy rules, and non-existent rules are encoded in the consequent with a Non A Number (NaN).

1.1 Membership Function Coding

The membership functions are encoded within an "incomplete" matrix in which each row represents one of the variables of the system, and where the columns encode the parameters of the membership functions. Because each of the input variables of the system has a different number of membership functions, the chromosome structure used to store the membership functions is not a "complete" matrix, as each of the m rows has a different number of columns n_m. As we have selected a triangular partition (TP), the only parameter that needs to be stored is the centre of the triangular function [15]. A fuzzy set X_m^i is defined by a linguistic function in the form:

$$
\mu_{X_m^i} = \begin{cases} \dfrac{x - c_m^{i-1}}{c_m^i - c_m^{i-1}} & if\ c_m^{i-1} < x \le c_m^i \\[2mm] \dfrac{c_m^{i+1} - x}{c_m^{i+1} - c_m^i} & if\ c_m^i < x \le c_m^{i+1} \\[2mm] 0 & otherwise \end{cases} \tag{1}
$$

where c_m^i represents the centre of the i membership function of the input variable *m*. Due to the membership function configurations selected, it is straightforward for a human operator to understand the final fuzzy system obtained. Because the number of membership functions is also optimized, it is possible for some of the input variables to be removed, and these would therefore have no membership function.

1.2 Fuzzy Rules Codification

In order to encode fuzzy rules, rather than a string or vector where the numerical consequents of the conclusions will appear, we carried out spatial encoding in the form of a $n_1 \times ... \times n_n$ matrix, noting that n_m is the number of membership functions contained within each input variable. By using string linear encoding, rules that are close together within the antecedent and which, when fuzzy inference is performed, are activated simultaneously, can be distantly encoded. Thus, in a planar structure, the neighborhood properties are destroyed when it is forced into a linear chromosome. According to the behaviour of GAs, it is preferable for fuzzy rules that are similar in the antecedent to be encoded as neighbors. Therefore, as it is implicit in encoding, rules that are neighbors in the rule table create interference with each other. Fig.1

shows the complete fuzzy systems codification. Note that the genetic operators described in the following section take into account the spatial structure of the fuzzy rules. Finally, as learning from examples is used, the training data might not cover the whole input domain. This would arise from the huge quantity of data that would be needed, and also from the physical impossibility of obtaining such data. In this case, an incomplete rule base is obtained, and the non-existent rules are encoded in the consequent with a Non A Number (NaN) and consequently are not taken into account in the fuzzy inference process.

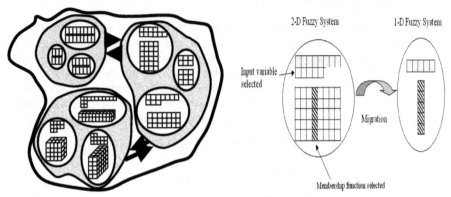

Fig. 1. Codification of a GA population with 3 demes

Fig. 2. Migration towards a fuzzy system with a lower dimensionality

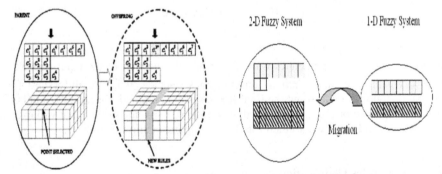

Fig. 3. Increasing the number of membership functions and rules

Fig. 4. Migration towards a fuzzy system with a higher dimensionality

1.3 Fitness Function

To evaluate the fuzzy system obtained, we have used the error approximation criterion. Nevertheless, in order to take into account the parsimony principle, that is, the number of parameters to be optimized in the system, we add a new term to describe the complexity of the derived fuzzy system. In the presented approach, GAs are used to search for an optimized subset of rules (both number of rules and the rule values) from a given knowledge base to achieve the goal of minimizing the number of rules used while maintaining the system performance. If we have various models based on the same set of examples, the most appropriate one is determined as that with the lowest description length. Another more flexible alternative is to define the fitness function as a linear combination of the error committed by the system and the number of parameters defining [6]:

$$fitness = W_E \cdot Error + W_C \cdot Complexity \qquad (2)$$

2   Multiple-Population or Multiple-Deme GA

The main issue of this article is that different structures of fuzzy systems may evolve and compete with each other, in such a way that even information obtained by fuzzy systems with different numbers of input variables may be shared. In general, for iden-tification purposes, *a priori* information about the structure of the fuzzy system is not always obtained. Even the number of inputs (for example, in time-series prediction problems) is not always known. For this purpose, a multiple-population (or multiple-deme) GA configuration is used [1], in which each deme has a different number of input variables. Within each deme there are fuzzy systems with different numbers of membership functions and rules. Basically, the configuration consists of the existence of several sub-populations which occasionally exchange individuals. Therefore it is necessary for them that exists intercommunication between the various demes that comprise the total genetic population. This exchange of individuals is called migra-tion and is controlled by several parameters. Multiple-deme GAs seem like a simple extension of the serial GA, in which few conventional (serial) GAs, run each of them on a node of a parallel computer (or simulated in one processor), and at some prede-termined times exchange a few individuals [1] .

2.1   Migration between Neighbour Demes

In this paper, two different situations of migration between demes are considered: the migration towards demes with a lower dimensionality and that towards those with a higher dimensionality. Fig.1 illustrates the case in which the exchange of individuals between demes only occurs between near neighbours, which is equivalent to say that the exchange occurs between fuzzy systems that differ by one in their input space dimensionality. The migration of a fuzzy system with a particular number of input variables towards a system with a lower dimensionality requires the previous, and random, selection of the variable to be suppressed (we term this variable m). The second step is to determine, again in random fashion, one of the membership func-tions of this variable (named j) and to construct the new, lower dimensionality, fuzzy system that only has the rules corresponding to the membership function j that has been selected (Fig.2). Thus, the set of membership functions of the new fuzzy system is identical to that of the donor system, except that the variable m has been removed. The rules are determined by the following expression:

$$R^{Offpring}_{i_1 i_2 \dots, i_{m-1}, i_{m+1} \dots, i_N} = R_{i_1 i_2 \dots i_{m-1}, j, i_{m+1} \dots, i_N} ; \, j \in \left[1, n_m \right] \qquad (3)$$

In the second case, the new fuzzy system (the new offspring) proceeds from a donor fuzzy system with a lower number of input variables (Fig.4). Here, it is not necessary to determine any donor system input variable, as in the migration described above, because the new offspring is created on the basis of the information obtained from the donor system, with the increase of a new variable; which is randomly selected from the set of variables in the higher dimensionality deme that are different to the deme with lower dimensionality. Initiallly, this new variable has a random number of homogeneously distributed membership functions, and its rules are an extension of the donor fuzzy system, taking the form:

$$R^{Offpring}_{i_1 i_2 \ldots, i_N, i_{N+1}} = R_{i_1 i_2 \ldots, i_N}$$
$$\forall i_{N+1}$$

3   Genetic Operators

To perform the crossover of the individuals within the same subsystem, we distinguish between the crossover of the membership functions and that of the rules.

3.1   Crossover of the Membership Functions

When two individuals have been selected (which could be designated i and i') within the same subsystem in order to perform the crossover of the membership functions, the following steps are taken:

1. One of the input variables of the system (for example, m) is randomly selected.

2. Let n^i_m and $n^{i'}_m$ be the number of membership functions of system i and i' for the randomly selected variable m. Assume that $n^i_m < n^{i'}_m$. Then from system i we randomly select two crossover points, p1 and p2, such that: $1 < p1 < p2 < n^i_m$. The membership functions that belong to the interval [p1,p2] of individual i are exchanged for the membership functions of individual i' that occupy the same position.

3.2   Crossover of the Rules

To achieve the crossover of the consequents of the membership functions, we substitute N-dimensional sub matrices within the two individuals selected to carry out the operation. One of the individuals is termed the receptor, R, whose matrix is going to be modified, and the other is the donor, D, which will provide a randomly selected sub matrix of itself. The crossover operation consists of selecting a sub matrix S from the rule matrix of the donor individual such that a matrix S^* of equal dimensions and located at the same place within the receptor individual is replaced by the new rules specified by matrix S. In other words, the new offspring O is equal to R, except in the sub matrix of the rules given by matrix S, located at the point vector $(A_1, A'_1, A_2, \ldots, A_N)$. Therefore, the following steps are taken:

1. Select two individuals R and D
2. In order to perform the (N+1) points crossover operator, select a vector $(A_1, A'_1, A_2,..., A_N)$, such as the sub matrices S and S^* fulfill $S \subset R$ and $S^* \subset D$.
3. Create an offspring interchanging the sub matrices S and S^* in R.

The crossover of the membership function and the crossover of the rules are applied in each generation.

3.3 Mutation

Regarding mutation, the parameters of the fuzzy system are altered in a different way from what occurs within a binary-coded system. As the individual is not represented by binary numbers, the random alteration of some of the system's bits does not occur. Instead of this, there are perturbations of the parameters that define the fuzzy system. Firstly, when the fuzzy system that will be mutated has been selected, a parameter defining the fuzzy system (membership functions or rules) is randomly selected with a probability of P_m. Secondly, the parameter is modified according to the following expression:

$$c_m^j = c_m^j + random(-\Delta c_m^{j-1}, \Delta c_m^{j+1})$$
$$R_{i_1 i_2 ... i_N} = R_{i_1 i_2 ... i_N} + random(-\Delta R, \Delta R) \tag{4}$$

where the values that perturb the membership functions are given by $\Delta c_m^{j-1} = \dfrac{c_m^j - c_m^{j-1}}{b}$

and $\Delta c_m^{j+1} = \dfrac{c_m^{j+1} - c_m^j}{b}$. The active radius '$b$' is the maximum variation distance and is used to guarantee that the order of the membership function locations remains unchanged (a typical value is $b=2$, meaning that, at most, a centre can be moved as far as the midpoint between it and its neighbour). The parameter ΔR is the maximum variation of the conclusion of the rules.

3.4 Increasing the Number of Membership Functions

This makes it possible for all of the information contained in the chromosomes of a fuzzy system to be transferred to another system with greater structural complexity, as the number of membership functions of a particular, randomly-selected, variable increases.

To achieve this, the first step is to select an input variable at random (for example, m) and within this variable to select a position of the membership functions, j, where $j \in [1, n_m]$. At this position j, a new membership function will be introduced, such that the order of the previously-defined functions remains unaltered. Thus, the new centre of this function is randomly selected but with the restriction: $c_m^j < c_m^* < c_m^{j+1}$. Thus the new distribution of membership functions for the variable m is now: { $X_m^1, X_m^2,...,$ $X_m^j, X_m^*, X_m^{j+1} ..., X_m^{n_m}$ }. In relation to the new rules that have been added, we perform a linear interpolation of the new rules with their immediate neighbours, adding a perturbation. Fig.4 represents the effects of this operator on a fuzzy system. This is expressed in mathematical terms as:

$$R^{Offpring}_{i_1 i_2 \dots i^j_m, \dots, i_N} = R_{i_1 i_2 \dots i_m, \dots, i_N}$$
$$j \in [1, n_m]; j \neq j^*$$

$$R^{Offpring}_{i_1 i_2 \dots i^j_{m}, \dots, i_N} = \left[\frac{R_{i_1 i_2 \dots i^j_m, \dots, i_N} + R_{i_1 i_2 \dots i^{j+1}_m, \dots, i_N}}{2} \right] + random(-\Delta R, \Delta R) \tag{5}$$

3.5 Decreasing the Number of Membership Functions

A reduction in the number of membership functions within a fuzzy system simply removes, at random, one of the membership functions from a variable that is also randomly selected. As well as the membership function, the rules associated with it are also removed.

4 Simulation Results

4.1 Synthetic Time Series

We will make use of time series generated from a differential of difference equation governed by determinism (in which, once the initial value is given, the subsequent states are all determined). This is the deterministic chaos of a dynamic system. The Mackey-Glass chaotic time series is generated from the following delay differential equation:

$$\frac{dx(t)}{dt} = \frac{ax(t-\tau)}{1+x^{10}(t-\tau)} - bx(t) \tag{6}$$

Prediction of this time series is recognized as a benchmark for testing various neural-network architectures [10]. When $\vartheta > 17$ (ϑ is the delay in equation (6)), the equation shows chaotic behaviour. Higher values of ϑ yield higher dimensional chaos. For the sake of comparison with earlier work, we have selected five input variables with a delay of 6 and the parameter ϑ in equation (6) equal to 17. The parameter values used in all simulation of the GA are presented in Table 1.

Table 1. GA parameters for Time Series Prediction

Crossover Probability	0.5
Mutation Probability	0.05
Number Of Generation	1000
Size Population In Each Deme	50
Type Of Selection	Elitist Roulette Wheel
Type Of Crossover	One-Point

We have considered five input candidates: x[t-24], x[t-18], x[t-12], x[t-6], x[t], to the system and the GAs have to find among them the more important inputs affecting the output x[t+6], taking into account the complexity of the final rule. Therefore, in this example N^max is equal to five. We employed 4 demes, with 2, 3, 4 and 5 input variables. As a result of predicting 6 steps ahead of the Mackey-Glass time series, the root mean square error and the correlation coefficient are 0.032 and 0.98. Fig.5.a shows the predicted and desired values (dashed and continuous lines respectively) for both training and checking data (which is indistinguishable from the time series here). As they are practically identical, the difference can only be seen on a finer scale (Fig.5.b). Table 2 compares the prediction accuracy of different computational paradigms presented in the bibliography for this benchmark problem (including our proposal), for various fuzzy system structures, neural systems and genetic algorithms.

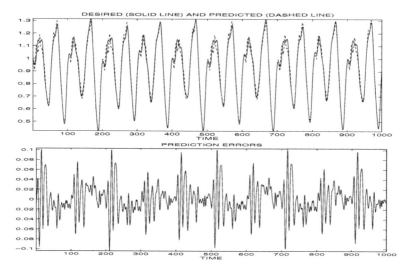

Fig. 5. a) Result of the original and predicted Mackey-Glass time series (which are indistinguishable). b) Prediction error

Table 2. Comparison Results Of The Prediction Error Of Different Methds For Prediction Step Equal To 6 (500 Training Data)

Method		Prediction Error (RMSE)
Auto Regressive Model		0.19
Cascade Correlation NN		0.06
Back-Prop. NN		0.02
Classical RBF (With 23 Neurons) [2]		0.0114
6th-Order Polynomial		0.04
Linear Predictive Method		0.55
Kim And Kim (Genetic Algorithm & Fuzzy System) [10]	5 Mfs	0.049
	7 Mfs	0.042
	9 Mfs	0.038
ANFIS & Fuzzy System [8]		0.007
Wang Et Al. [12]	Product T-Norm	0.0907
	Min T-Norm	0.0904
Our Approach, Using Only 3 Input Variables With 5, 6 And 8 Membership Functions		0.032

4.2 Real Time Series: Sunspot Series

Sunspot series is a record of the activity of the surface of the sun. The sunspot series is chaotic and is a well-known challenging task for time series analysis. The sunspot data set has long served as a benchmark and been well studied in the previous literature [3][4][13][14]. The data set consists of a total of 280 yearly averaged sunspots recorded from 1700 to 1979. In the experiment, the data points from 1700 to 1920 are used as the training set, those from 1921 to 1955 are used as the validation set, and the remaining data points from 1956 to 1979 are used as the test set. 12 previous sunspots are used as inputs to predict the current sunspot. As a result, there are a total of 209 data patterns in the training set, 35 data patterns in the validation set and 24 data patterns in the test set. Figure 6 shows the result of the original and predicted sunspot series, together with the error. Table 3 compares the prediction accuracy of classical ARMA method and percepton neural network presented in the bibliography for this benchmark problem [14] (including our proposal).

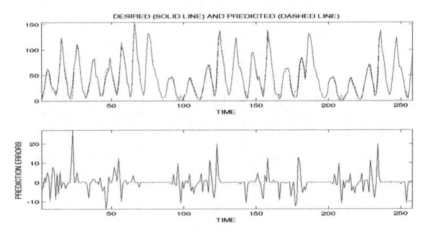

Fig. 6. Result of the original and predicted sunspot series and the error

Table 3. Comparison results of the prediction error of different methods for prediction the sunspot time series

Method	Prediction Error (MSE)
Perceptron Neural Network, Model: 2x11x1	160.8
Perceptron Neural Network, Model: 2x11x1	158.9
Perceptron Neural Network, Model: 2x11x1	157.8
Perceptron Neural Network, Model: 2x11x1	180.8
Perceptron Neural Network, Model: 2x11x1	180.4
ARMA(2,0)	177.3
Our approach, using 4 input variables with 5, 6,7 and 7 membership functions	15.91

5 Conclusions

While the bibliography describes many methods that have been developed for the adjustment or fine-tuning of the parameters of a fuzzy system with partially or totally known structures, few have been dedicated to achieving both simultaneous and joint structure and parameter adjustment. In this paper we propose a GA that is capable of simultaneously optimizing the structure of the system and tuning the parameters that define the fuzzy system. For this purpose, we applied the concept of multiple-deme GAs, in which several populations with different structures (number of input variables) evolve and compete with other. In each of these populations, the element also has a different number of membership functions in the input space and a different number of rules. In the proposed methodology, there is a big number of parameters to be optimized and therefore the computational cost is very high. Thanks to the use of multideme genetic algorithm, it is possible to perform the optimization using parallel platforms that can decrease the required time of calculation. Instead of the normal coding system employed to represent a fuzzy system, in which all the parameters are represented in vector form, we have performed coding by means of multidimensional matrices, in which the elements are real-valued numbers, rather than the traditional binary or Gray coding.

Acknowledgement

This work has been partially supported by the CICYT Spanish Project DPI2001-3219.

References

1. E. Cantú-Paz, "Topologies, migration rates, and multi-population parallel genetic algorithms". Proceedings of the Genetic and Evolutionary Computation Conference. San Francisco, CA: Morgan Kaufmann. pp. 91-98, 1999.
2. K.B. Cho, B.H.Wang "Radial basis function based adaptive fuzzy systems and their applications to system identification and prediction", Fuzzy Sets and Systems, vol.83, pp.325-339, 1995.
3. M.B. Cottrell, Y. Girard, M. Mangeas and C. Muller, Neural modeling for time series: a statistical stepwise method for weight elimination. IEEE Trans. Neural Networks 6 6 (1995), pp. 1355–1364.
4. C.D. Groot and D. Wurtz, Analysis of univariate time series with connectionist nets: a case study of two classical examples. Neurocomputing 3 (1991), pp. 177–192.
5. Homaifar, E. McCormick, "Simultaneous design of membership functions and rule sets for fuzzy controllers using genetic algorithms", IEEE Trans. Fuzzy Systems, 3, pp.129-139, 1995.
6. H. Ishibuchi, T. Murata, I.B. Türksen, "A genetic-algorithm-based approach to the selection of linguistic classification rules", Proc. EUFIT'95, Aachen, Germany, pp.1414-1419, 1995.
7. I. Jagielska, C. Matthews, T. Whitfort, "An investigation into the application of neural networks, fuzzy logic, genetic algorithms, and rough sets to automated knowledge acquisition for classification problems" *Neurocomputing*, vol.24 pp.37-54, 1999.

8. J.S.R. Jang, C.T. Sun, E. Mizutani, "Neuro-Fuzzy and soft computing", Prentice Hall, ISBN 0-13-261066-3, 1997.
9. C. Karr, E. Gentry, "Fuzzy control of pH using genetic algorithms", IEEE Trans. Fuzzy Systems, 1, pp.46-53, 1993
10. D.Kim, C. Kim, "Forecasting time series with genetic fuzzy predictor ensemble", IEEE Transactions on Fuzzy Systems, vol.5, no.4, pp.523-535, November 1997.
11. K. Kropp, U.G. Baitinger, "Optimization of fuzzy logic controller inference rules using a genetic algorithm", Proc. EUFIT'93, Aachen, Germany, pp.1090-1096, 1993.
12. J. Liska, S.S. Melsheimer, "Complete design of fuzzy logic systems using genetic algorithm", Proc. FUZZ-IEEE'94, pp.1377-1382, 1994.
13. S.J. Nowlan and G.E. Hinton, Simplifying neural networks by soft weight-sharing. *Neural Comput.* **4** (1992), pp. 473–493
14. Y.R. Park, T.J. Murray, C. Chen, "Predicting Sun Spots Using a Layered Perceptron Neural Networks", IEEE Transaction on Neural Networks, vol.7, no.2, March 1996, pp.501-505.
15. I. Rojas, J.J. Merelo, H. Pomares, A. Prieto "Genetic algorithms for optimum designing fuzzy controller", *Proceedings of the 2nd. Int. ICSC Symposium on Fuzzy Logic and Applications (ISFL'97), International Computer Science Conventions*, February 12-14, Zurich, ICSC Academic Press, Canada, ISBN 3-906454-03-7, pp. 165- 170, 1997.
16. L.X. Wang, J.M. Mendel, "Generating fuzzy rules by learning from examples", IEEE Trans. On Syst. Man and Cyber, vol.22, no.6, November/December, pp.1414-1427, 1992.

Time-Series Prediction: Application to the Short-Term Electric Energy Demand

Alicia Troncoso Lora[1],
Jesús Manuel Riquelme Santos[2], José Cristóbal Riquelme[1],
Antonio Gómez Expósito[2], and José Luís Martínez Ramos[2]

[1] Department of Languages and Systems, University of Sevilla, Spain
[2] Department of Electrical Engineering, University of Sevilla, Spain
{ali,riquelme}@lsi.us.es, {jsantos,age,camel}@us.es

Abstract. This paper describes a time-series prediction method based on the kNN technique. The proposed methodology is applied to the 24-hour load forecasting problem. Also, based on recorded data, an alternative model is developed by means of a conventional dynamic regression technique, where the parameters are estimated by solving a least squares problem. Finally, results obtained from the application of both techniques to the Spanish transmission system are compared in terms of maximum, average and minimum forecasting errors.

1 Introduction

Accurate prediction of the future electricity demand constitutes a vital task for the economic and secure operation of power systems. In the short, medium and long terms, generation scheduling comprises a set of interrelated optimization problems strongly relying on the accuracy of the forecasted load. The same happens in new competitive electricity markets, where the hourly bidding strategy of each partner is significantly conditioned by the expected demand. Consequently, it is crucial for the electric industry to develop appropriate forecasting techniques.

Existing forecasting methods for the estimation of electric demand can be broadly classified into two sets, namely: classical statistical methods [1, 2] and automated learning techniques. Statistical methods aim at estimating the future load from past values. The relationship between the load and other factors (temperature, etc) are used to determine the underlying model of the load time series. The main advantage of these methods lies in its simplicity. However, owing to the nonlinear nature of such a relationship, it is difficult to obtain accurate enough and realistic models for classical methods.

In the last few years, machine learning paradigms such as Artificial Neural Networks (ANN) [3–5] have been applied to one day-ahead load forecasting. The ANNs are trained to learn the relationships between the input variables (past demand, temperature, etc.) and historical load patterns. The main disadvantage of the ANN is the required learning time.

R. Conejo et al. (Eds.): CAEPIA-TTIA 2003, LNAI 3040, pp. 577–586, 2004.

Recently, classification techniques based on the k nearest neighbors (kNN), have been successfully applied in new environments outside traditional pattern recognition such as medical diagnosis tools, game theory expert systems or time series forecasting. Several papers have been published on the application of those techniques to forecast the electricity market price [6, 7], providing competitive results, but its application to the next-day load forecasting problem has not been yet tested.

This paper describes a time-series prediction method based on the kNN technique. The proposed methodology is applied to the 24-hour load forecasting problem, and the results obtained from its application to the Spanish case are analyzed. Then, based on available data, an alternative model is built up by a conventional dynamic regression technique. Finally, results obtained by both techniques are compared in terms of maximum, average and minimum forecasting errors.

2   Problem Statement

The one day-ahead load forecasting problem aims at predicting the load for the twenty-four hours of the next day. To solve this problem two schemes can be considered:

1. Iterated Scheme: This scheme forecasts the load for the next hour and the value obtained is used for the prediction of subsequent hours. The process is repeated until the 24-hour load forecasting is obtained. The iterated prediction has the disadvantage that the errors get accumulated particularly during the last hours of the prediction horizon.
2. Direct Scheme: Under this scheme, the load for the entire 24-hour period is forecasted from past input data. The direct prediction does not take into account the relationships between the load for one hour and the load for the next hour.

Test results have shown in average the same accuracy for both schemes. Thus, the direct scheme has been adopted.

2.1   Proposed Approach

In this section, a kNN approach [8] for next day hourly load forecasting is described. kNN algorithms are techniques for pattern classification based on the similarity of the individuals of a population. The members of a population are surrounded of individuals which have similar properties. This simple idea is the learning rule of the kNN classifier. Thus, the nearest neighbors decision rule assigns to an unclassified sample point the classification of the nearest of a set of previously classified points. Unlike most statistical methods, which elaborate a model from the information available in the data base, the kNN method considers the training set as the model itself. A kNN algorithm is characterized by issues such as number of neighbors, adopted distance, etc.

In the kNN method proposed in this paper, each individual is defined by the 24 demand values corresponding to a whole day. Thus, the kNN classifier tries to find the daily load curve which is "similar to" the load curve of previous days.

The basic algorithm for predicting the electric energy demand of a given day $d+1$ can be written as follows:

1. Calculate the distances between the load of day d, D_d, and that of preceding points $\{D_{d-1}, D_{d-2}, ...\}$. Let $v_1,...,v_k$ be the k nearest days to the day d, sorted by descending distance.
2. The prediction is:

$$\widehat{D}_{d+1} = \frac{1}{\alpha_1 + ... + \alpha_k} \sum_{l=1}^{l=k} \alpha_l \cdot D_{v_l+1} \tag{1}$$

where

$$\alpha_j = \frac{d_w(D_d, D_{v_k}) - d_w(D_d, D_{v_j})}{d_w(D_d, D_{v_k}) - d_w(D_d, D_{v_1})} \tag{2}$$

Notice that $0 \le \alpha_j \le 1$, i.e., the weight is null for the most distant day and is equal to one for the nearest day.

The two former steps are repeated for every day of the forecasting horizon, taking into account that true values replace forecasted ones for past days.

Therefore, the prediction aims at estimating the load for tomorrow from a linear combination of the loads corresponding to those days that follow the k nearest neighbors of today. The weights adopted for this averaging process reflect the relative similarity of the respective neighbor with the present day.

If the k nearest neighbors of D_d are $[D_{v_1}, ..., D_{v_k}]$, the set of points $[D_{v_1+1}, ..., D_{v_k+1}]$ will usually contain the k nearest neighbors of D_{d+1}, at least for noise-free time series.

Figure 1 geometrically illustrates the idea behind the kNN classifier when the considered number of neighbors is equal to one. Today's hourly load and tomorrow's unknown load are represented by circumferences. The four black

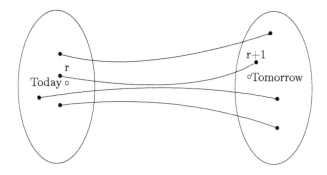

Fig. 1. kNN Learning Rule.

points are neighbors of today's load, point r being the nearest neighbor. Then, a possible estimation for tomorrow's load is the load of the day $r + 1$.

The classical kNN algorithm would resort to the actual nearest neighbors of day $d + 1$ for the prediction of D_{d+1}, but this is not possible because D_{d+1} is unknown in advance. The kNN proposed in this paper is a modification by which the k nearest neighbors of day d, whose demand is available, are adopted instead.

Some important parameters defining the kNN classifier are:

1. Choice of a metric: A time series Y can be considered as a point in a n-dimensional space. Given a sequence query, q, a sequence of Y, z, of the same length as q is searched, such that the distance between both sequences is minimum. The choice of the metric to measure the similarity between two time series depends mainly on the specific features of the considered series. The most common metric is the square of the Euclidean distance, although other metrics can be used [9, 10].
2. Number of neighbors: Accuracy of the forecasted load can be influenced by this parameter. In practice, the optimal value of k is usually small for noise-free time series, since a small number of different k values needs to be considered to find the optimal value. In this paper, k is determined by minimizing the relative, absolute and square mean errors for the training set.

2.2   Numerical Results

The kNN described in the previous section has been applied in several experiments to obtain the forecast of Spanish electric energy demand. The period January 2000-May 2001 has been used to determine the optimal number of neighbors and the best metric to measure the similarity between two curves.

The period June-November 2001 has been subsequently chosen as a test set to check the forecasting errors and to validate the proposed method.

Figures 2a) and 2b) show the influence of the number of neighbors on the relative, absolute and square mean errors for the considered training set, when the metric adopted to evaluate the similarity between a previous day and the historical data, is the Euclidean and Manhattan distance, respectively.

From these figures, the following can be stated for the particular time series under study:

1. The optimal number of neighbors is six using the Euclidean distance and thirteen using the Manhattan distance. Consequently, this number depends of the chosen distance.
2. This parameter is independent of the objective error function to minimize.

Test results have shown the same average error for the training set when both distances are considered. Thus, the Manhattan distance is the only one considered in the sequel.

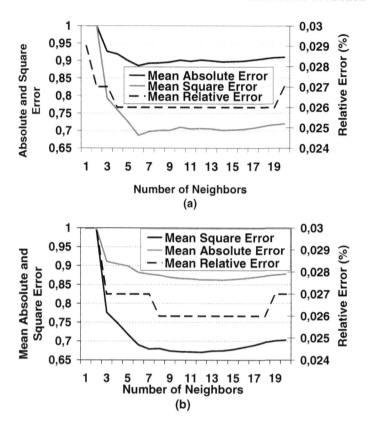

Fig. 2. Optimal No. of Neighbors with **a)** Euclidean distance, **b)** Manhattan Distance.

Figure 3a) shows the hourly average of both the actual and forecasted load for the working days from June 2001 to November 2001. The mean forecasting error, 2.3%, is of the same order as that of alternative techniques considered earlier, like ANNs [3–5].

Figure 3b) presents the hourly average absolute error of the forecasted load for the Autumn and Summer seasons. Note that the forecasting errors are larger during valley hours, i.e., hours with lower demand (1am-5am). However, it is more important to obtain a good prediction during peak hours (10am-2pm and 6pm-10pm) since the electric energy is more expensive at those periods.

Figure 4 presents the forecasted load on Monday August 6 and Thursday July 17, which are the days leading to the largest and smallest average relative errors respectively, along with the actual load for those days. It can be observed that the worst day corresponds with the first Monday of August, when most Spaniards start their Summer holidays.

Figure 5 presents the forecasted load for the two weeks leading to the largest and smallest average errors, along with the actual load for those weeks. Those weeks correspond with Tuesday September 11-Monday September 17 and Monday October 22- Friday October 26, respectively. Note that the week with higher

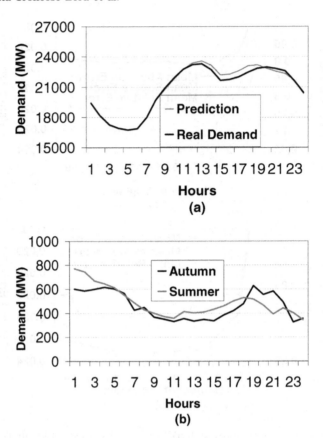

Fig. 3. a) Hourly average of forecasted and actual demand; **b)** Hourly average absolute error of the forecasted values.

Table 1. Daily Errors corresponding to the best and worst weekly Predictions.

	Daily errors (%)					Weekly error (%)
October 22 - October 26	3.13	1.25	1.11	0.08	0.07	1.4
September 11 - September 17	5.88	6.73	1.18	1.13	4.55	3.9

prediction errors is the one when the terrorist assault to the New York twin towers took place. Errors corresponding to September 12 arise as a consequence of the atypical behavior of the previous day.

The average errors for the five working days of the best and worst weeks appear in Table 1. The weekly mean errors are 1.4% and 4%, respectively.

3   Dynamic Regression

In this section a Dynamic Regression (DR) model is developed for the prediction of the hourly electricity demand. Under this approach, the demand at hour t,

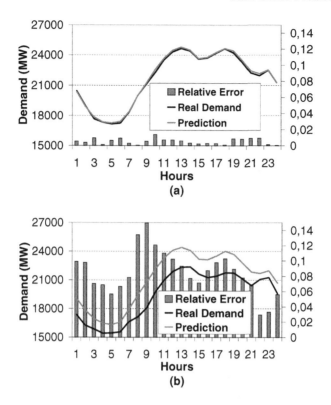

Fig. 4. a) Best Daily Prediction; **b)** Worst Daily Prediction.

D_t, is estimated from the demand at hours $t - 1$, $t - 2$,..., etc. First of all, a correlation study is performed on D_t, D_{t-1},... in order to determine which of the past demand values are most influential on the present demand.

Figure 6a) presents the average correlation coefficient between the present demand and past demand values for the period January 2000-May 2001. Notice that this coefficient presents a periodicity corresponding to a day. The main conclusion is that the highest correlation with the demand at a given hour takes place at the same hour of previous days. Furthermore, such a correlation decreases as the number of past hours increases.

In view of the conclusions obtained from the correlation study, the following model is proposed:

$$\widehat{D}_t = a_0 D_{t-1} + a_1 D_{t-24} + a_2 D_{t-48} + a_3 D_{t-72} + a_4 D_{t-96} + a_5 D_{t-120} \quad (3)$$

Experimental results suggest that it is not worth including extra terms like D_{t-23}, D_{t-25} in the model, as the average forecasting error for the tested period remains unaffected.

The model parameters a_i are obtained from the solution of the following least squares problem:

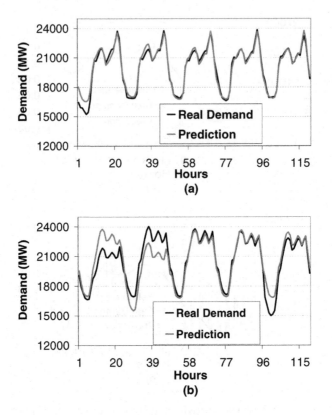

Fig. 5. a) Best weekly prediction; **b)** Worst weekly prediction.

$$\sum_t (D_t - \widehat{D}_t)^2 \tag{4}$$

where $\widehat{D}_t$ is defined by (3).

Those parameters can be computed only once, from the training set, or they can be updated daily.

3.1   Results

The regression model described above has been also applied to the load fore-casting problem in Spain. Working days between January 2000 and May 2001 have been employed to determine the model parameters, yielding $a_0 = 0.31$, $a_1 = 0.37$, $a_2 = 0.08$, $a_3 = 0.01$, $a_4 = -0.03$ y $a_5 = 0.25$. The small values of a_2, a_3 and a_4 suggest that, when predicting D_t, the most influential values are D_{t-1}, D_{t-24} and D_{t-120}, i.e., the previous hour, the same hour of the previous day and the same hour and same day of the previous week respectively.

Figure 6b) shows the evolution of the model parameters when they are up-dated every day for the period June-November 2001. It can be observed that

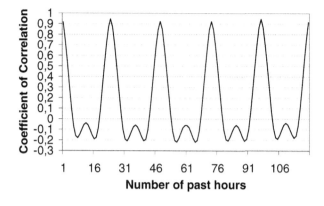

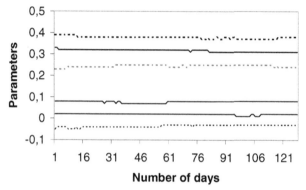

Fig. 6. a) Correlation Coefficients; b) Evolution of parameters a_i.

Table 2. Comparison of both methods.

	S.D.	Relative Error Mean (%)	Absolute Error Mean(MW)	Max. Error Daily (%)	Max. Error Hourly (%)
kNN	0.015	2.3	471	8.5	16.6
DR	0.019	2.82	572	9.2	19.3

these coefficients remain essentially constant, which means that no new demand patterns are added to the data base each time a day is included.

Finally, table 2 presents the standard deviation, the average absolute and relative forecasting errors, and the maximum daily and hourly errors obtained from the application of both the kNN method and the DR model to the period considered.

4   Conclusions

In this paper, a method based on the k Nearest Neighbors is proposed for the prediction of time series. The method is applied to the Spanish short-term electric load forecasting problem and the resulting errors for a six-month period are analyzed. Then a dynamic regression model whose parameters are obtained by solving a least squares problem is developed for the same application. Comparing the results provided by both approaches leads to the conclusion that the kNN classifier is more accurate for the load forecasting problem than the conventional regression method.

Acknowledgments

Thanks are due to the Spanish CICYT (TIC2001-1143-C03-02, DPI2001-2612) and Junta de Andalucía (ACC-1021-TIC-2002) for sponsoring this project.

References

1. A. D. Papalexopoulos and T. C. Hesterberg: A Regression-Based Approach to Short-Term System Load Forecasting. IEEE Trans. on Power System, Vol. 5, pp. 1535-1547. 1990.
2. F. J. Nogales, J. Contreras, A. J. Conejo and R. Spínola: Forecasting Next-Day Electricity Prices by Time Series Models. IEEE Trans. on Power System, Vol. 17, pp. 342-348. 2002.
3. A. S. Alfuhaid and M. A. El-Sayed: Cascaded Artificial Neural Network for Short-Term Load Forecasting. IEEE Trans. on Power System, Vol. 12, pp. 1524-1529. 1997.
4. J. Riquelme, J.L. Martínez, A. Gómez and D. Cros Goma: Load Pattern Recognition and Load Forecasting by Artificial Neural Networks. International Journal of Power and Energy Systems, Vol. 22, pp. 74-79. 2002.
5. R. Lamedica, A. Prudenzi, M. Sforna, M. Caciotta, V. Orsolini Cencellli: A Neural Network Based Technique for Short-Term Forecasting of Anomalous Load Periods. IEEE Transaction on Power Systems, Vol. 11, pp. 1749-1756. 1996.
6. A. Troncoso Lora, J. C. Riquelme Santos, J. M. Riquelme Santos, J. L. Martínez Ramos, A. Gómez Expósito: Electricity Market Price Forecasting: Neural Networks versus Weighted-Distance k Nearest Neighbours. DEXA Database Expert Systems and Applications, Aix Provence, 2002.
7. A. Troncoso Lora, J. M. Riquelme Santos, J. C. Riquelme Santos, A. Gómez Expósito, J. L. Martínez Ramos: Forecasting Next-Day Electricity Prices based on k Weighted Nearest Neighbours and Dynamic Regression. IDEAL Intelligent Data Engineering Autamitized Learning, Manchester, 2001.
8. B.V. Dasarathy : Nearest neighbour (NN) Norms: NN pattern classification techniques. IEEE Computer Society Press, 1991.
9. R. D. Short, K. Fukunaga: The Optimal Distance Measure for Nearest Neighbour Classification. IEEE Transaction on Information Theory, 1981.
10. K. Fukunaga, T. E. Flick: An Optimal Global Nearest Neighbour Metric. IEEE Transaction on Pattern Analysis and Machine Intelligence, 1984.

Towards a Clinical Practice Guideline Implementation for Asthma Treatment

Francisco Javier Sobrado[1], Juan Manuel Pikatza[1], Iker Unai Larburu[1],
Juan José Garcia[2], and Diego López de Ipiña[3]

[1] Department of Languages and Computer Systems, Faculty of Computer Science
The University of the Basque Country
{jibsootf,jippiacj,jiblaeni}@sc.ehu.es
[2] Wireless Systems Research Department, Avaya Labs Research, Basking Ridge, NJ, USA
jjga@avaya.com
[3] Consulting Department, 3G LAB, Cambridge, UK
dipina@3glab.com

Abstract. There is a tremendous amount of effort involved in the definition of
Clinical Practice Guidelines (CPG) by physicians. Because the quality of medical assistance is highly impacted by the use of CPG, and establishing their use
is difficult, we consider helpful to develop an effective solution that implements
CPG through Decision Support Systems (DSS). Among the many existing representation models for CPG, we have selected and applied GLIF. In addition,
we have created ontologies for the domains of asthma severity and Fuzzy Multicriteria Decision Aid approach (PROAFTN method). The results have been integrated into our DSS called Arnasa in order to provide support via Web to
asthmatic patients.

1 Introduction

Several CPG have been developed in the last years in order to reduce the unjustified
disparities in clinical practice, and therefore improve the quality of medical care while
decreasing costs [5]. Because of the importance of using CPG, medical institutions
should promote their implementation and deployment through computer systems, so
that physicians are provided with decision support.

Given that Telemedicine is considered a strategic priority in developed countries
[23], several studies [12] show that Clinical Decision Support Systems (CDSS) may
improve the fulfilment of CPG by physicians, as well as results on patients [9] [26], as
long as they are developed to provide specific decision support within the actuation
context. The development of CDSS has been proposed as a strategy to promote the
implementation of CPG [5] but it into faces the difficulty of translating the CPG narrative format an electronic format that is suitable as a Computer Interpretable Guideline (CIG). Moreover, we should not forget about integration to existing medical
records.

A possible solution to this problem is to develop a unique and standard representation model that allows sharing the guidelines among different medical institutions,
offers consistency while interpreting the guidelines, reduces costs, and puts together
the needed efforts for creating and improving model's quality and its tools.

R. Conejo et al. (Eds.): CAEPIA-TTIA 2003, LNAI 3040, pp. 587–596, 2004.
© Springer-Verlag Berlin Heidelberg 2004

On the other hand, the use of CIG in the medical environment offers decision aid, reduces ambiguities, assures the quality of medical care, and improves patients' education. Because of the appeal of this research direction, different representation models have been defined [29]. Some of them use ontologies [7] for specifying and reusing medical knowledge, and make use of frames for the representation [13].

For these models to be effective, they have to be integrated to existing medical records so that they procure particularized information for each patient, use a standard medical vocabulary, and are expressive enough.

In the decision nodes of a CPG, recommendations are offered to the user. They are calculated by means of Multicriteria Decision Aid (MCDA) methods [21].

We have planned the following goals for this present work:

1. Development of an ontology for representing the knowledge in the asthma domain.
2. Development of an ontology for representing the knowledge in the MCDA domain, which will be used by the CPG whenever making assignments is needed.
3. Representation of the asthma CPG and the Fuzzy Multicriteria Assignment Method (PROAFTN) through the GLIF model ontology, and integrating both representations with the previously developed domain ontologies.
4. Evaluation of tools for representing and executing processes.

Obtaining an effective solution to the real problem of asthma through the implementation of a CPG would improve the way this disease is treated and hence the patients' quality of life.

On the other hand, if we consider the management of asthma treatment to be similar to managing a process, the results of the present work could be reused for dealing with other domain processes without major additional efforts. Software development is a domain with a special interest for us, particularly the support to project management and the development stage. It would make significantly easier to build complex solutions in Telemedicine. We follow similar methods in both lines.

The present paper describes the work performed in order to implement the asthma CPG. This implementation includes the integration of an ontology for the asthma domain, and the MCDA method using the algorithm PROAFTN for multicriteria assignations. In the next section, we will introduce the work carried out in this area. In section 3, we will introduce the methods and resources employed; in section 4, the obtained results, and in the last one, the main conclusion gained from these results.

2   Background

After nine years of multidisciplinary work with medical staff from *Osakidetza – Basque Health Service* for research and development of DSS focused on the treatment of paediatrics chronic diseases [19][24], it is important to point out the importance of building safe and Web-accessible DSS that allow managing data and knowledge about CPG or processes.

Several representation models have been defined in the last couple of years [29]. These models offer the possibility to translate a CPG into a CIG. An abstract of the latest models is shown on Table 1.

Table 1. Different CPG representation models.

		Beginning year	Ending year
ArdenSyntax	[10]	1990	->
Asbru	[15]	1996	->
EON	[27]	1996	2003
GASTON	[2]	1998	->
GEM	[22]	1999	->
GLARE	[25]	1997	->
GLIF	[17]	1998	->
GUIDE	[20]	1998	2000
PRESTIGE	[9]	1996	1999
PRODIGY	[11]	1995	->
PROforma	[6]	1998	->
Siegfried	[14]	1996	->

A recent study about the Asbru, EON, GLIF, GUIDE, PRODIGY, and PROforma models was coordinated by Stanford University [18] to extract similarities and differences that would lead to standardise them in the future.

The decision aid following the guideline can be realized through justified recommendations based on a classification method, which can connect the problem data to a set of categories or alternatives.

There are different analysis than can be obtained for an alternative: 1) identify the best alternative, 2) order the alternatives from the best to the worst, 3) classify the alternatives in predetermined homogeneous sets, and 4) identify the distinctive attributes to describe them. We will focus on the first, applying the PROAFTN method due to its classificatory capacity in the current medical domain [1].

We will mention the asthma DSS developed by the Iowa University (USA)[26], because it follows a similar work line. It is a DSS implemented using CGI technology to evaluate asthma severity, and offers recommendations based on the information entered by the user.

3   Materials and Methods

Once we have examined all the existing methodologies [29], we chose GLIF as the model to implement the asthma CPG. There were several reasons for this decision. One of them is that its ontology (v. 3.5) is available, and includes examples and documentation. GLIF has been developed in agreement by several institutions. It supports multiple medical vocabularies and adds complementary specifications (Arden Syntax, HL7), which make it easy to be incorporated to medical environments. This formalism can work as the foundation for a standard one taking the best from other modelling methodologies [3].

To provide a solution for the diagnostics problem, different methods were used: statistics, pattern recognition, Artificial Intelligence, and neuronal networks. The multicriteria decision aid (MCDA) approach is another approximation that uses the preference relational system described by Roy [21] and Vincke [28], for the comparison between the individuals to classify and the prototypes or reference objects from categories. Among the advantages that this approach offers, it is important to point out that it prevents distance measures reclassification. It allows using both qualitative and quantitative criteria, which helps when data is expressed in different units. Moreover, it uses both inductive (from clinical data) and deductive (from available knowledge) learning. It differs from other classifiers that use knowledge based on actual cases, meaning they only use deductive learning. But the main advantage of MCDA, compared to traditional methods based on a single global criterion, is the use of both concordance and non-discordance principles (non-totally compensatory) to determine the relations of preference.

The recent application of the PROAFTN method to the diagnosis of acute leukaemia has obtained superior results than other methods like decision trees, production rules, K-NN, logistic regression, and multi-layer perceptrons [1].

In classification problems the PROAFTN method is capable of resolving multicriteria assignation issues. To begin with, we need a set of categories denoted by $\Omega = \{C^1,\ldots, C^k\}$, a prototype set $B^h = \{b^h{}_1, b^h{}_2,\ldots,b^h{}_{L_h}\}$ for each category and a set of attributes $F = \{g_1,\ldots.g_n\}$, where each g_j is defined by an interval $[S^1{}_j(b^h{}_i), S^2{}_j(b^h{}_i)]$, being $S^2{}_j(b^h{}_i) \geq S^1{}_j(b^h{}_i)$, for $j=1,..,n$, $h=1,..,k$ and $i=1,..,L_h$. With this information we can calculate the indifference indexes using (1), where $W^h{}_j$ is the positive coefficient that shows the relative importance assigned by experts to g_j from the C^h category. The addition of all coefficients $W^h{}_j$ is 1.

$$I(a, b_i^h) \quad = \quad (\overset{n}{\underset{j=1}{!}} \; (W_j^h x C_j(a, b_i^h)) x \prod_{j=1}^{n} (1 - D_j(a, b_i^h))^{w_j^h}) \tag{1}$$

Both the concordance $C_j(a, B^h{}_i)$ and the discordance $D_j(a, B^h{}_i)$ indexes are defined by the fuzzy sets from Fig 1. To get over the data inaccuracy the thresholds $d^+{}_j (B^h{}_i)$ and $d^-{}_j (B^h{}_i)$ are used. In order to indicate incompatibilities the $v^+{}_j (B^h{}_i)$ and $v^-{}_j (B^h{}_i)$ thresholds are used.

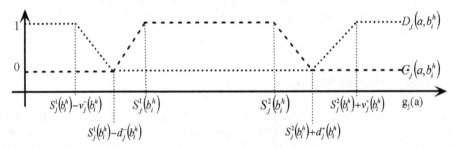

Fig. 1. Graphic for the partial indifference index between the object a and the prototype $b^h{}_i$, and the partial discordance index for that relation.

The fuzzy belonging degree for the object $d(a, C^h)$ from a category is evaluated through (2) using (3) to specifically assign an object to a category.

$$d(a, C^h) = max\{ I(a, B^h{}_1), I(a, B^h{}_2),\ldots, I(a, B^h{}_{L_h})\}, \; h=1,..,k \tag{2}$$

$$a \in Ch \Leftrightarrow d(a, Ch) = max\{ d(a, Cl)/ l \in I\{1,..,k\}\} \tag{3}$$

Using an intuitive way to explain how PROAFTN works, we provide the following example (Fig 2). Initially we have two categories, C1 and C2, which define the prototypes P1 and P2 respectively. Each one of these prototypes has the attributes g1, g2, and g3 with their corresponding concordance and discordance indices. On the other hand, we have the object we want to classify along with its attributes g1, g2 and g3.

We start by calculating (1)

$I(a, b1) > 0, \; I(a, b2)=0$

In this case we can see that $I(a,b2)$ is zero due to its total discordance with the attribute g3. Next, we calculate (2)

$$d(a, C1)=max\{I(a,b1)\}=I(a,b1)>0$$
$$d(a, C2)=max\{I(a,b2)\}=I(a,b2)=0$$

Finally, the object a is classified as C1 by applying (3).

3.1 Resources

For the implementation of the asthma CPG, the written guides from the National Asthma Education and Prevention Program (NAEPP) [16], along with interviews with medical staff from the Cruces Hospital of Barakaldo (Basque Country) were used as information sources.

The development process that we have followed for the CPG ontology is the one defined by METHONTO-LOGY [4], which is a methodology for ontology construction developed by the Polytechnic University of Madrid.

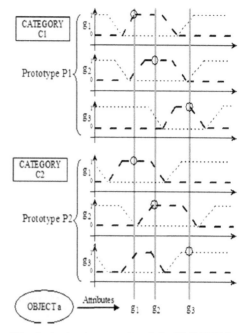

Fig. 2. A simple example of the PROAFTN's performance.

Regarding the tools we have used, we should at least mention the following ones. Protégé-2000 (v1.7) is a tool to build knowledge bases using frames that we have used as a development environment for ontologies. JESS (v 6.1) is an extensively known inference engine. FuzzyJESS (v 1.5) is an add-in for JESS that provided fuzzy logic capabilities. JessTab is a plug-in for Protégé that allows its connection to JESS.

4 Results

Our CPG implementation has been integrated into a DSS called Arnasa, which already has two previous releases built by ourselves, and is intended for monitoring asthma patients [24]. Its functionality is organized in several Web modules; each one specialized in a different area (e.g. security, visualisation of evolution data in 2/3D, consulting and localization of the user interface). For its implementation we have used J2EE technology (*Java 2 Platform, Enterprise Edition*).

The implementation of the CPG as a knowledge server (Fig.3) and its integration into the DSS provide full decision support capabilities. This knowledge server is composed by:

- Ontologies: a set of ontologies (asthma, CPG, MCDA, and PROAFTN).
- Protege-2000: a tool for ontology editing.
- Jess: an inference engine for executing the CPG.

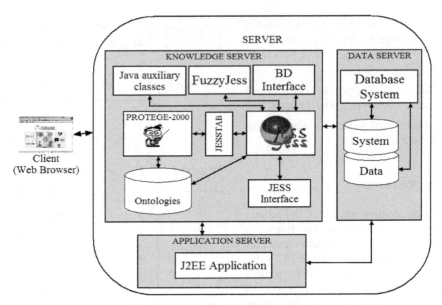

Fig. 3. DSS Arnasa v 3.0 Architecture.

- FuzzyJESS: a toolkit that provides fuzzy logic in Jess.
- JessTab plug-in: to link Jess and Protege-2000.
- Jess Interface: to control the CPG performance from the J2EE application.
- BD Interface: management of transactions between Jess and the DB.
- Java auxiliary classes: auxiliary functions used in Jess.

We have developed ontologies for the asthma domain and the multicriteria fuzzy assignment (PROAFTN method) that define a knowledge base. These ontologies (Fig.4) are accessible through Protege-2000 and Jess. Both in the development of the asthma ontology and in the CPG implementation, the application scope has been the evaluation of sickness severity. We expect to extend this scope in future releases (medication assignment, management of asthmatic crisis, etc).

GLIF has been used to represent the PROAFTN method and the asthma CPG, at the same time integrating those representations with their corresponding domain ontologies.

The PROAFTN method has been used inside the CPG to diagnose level of asthma severity in patients. In order to achieve it, we have used a fuzzy criteria set (Table 2), which is linked to the attributes of the three aspects to look at for each prototype:

- Diurnal symptoms
- Nightly symptoms
- Pulmonary function

The different categories to be assigned to a patient are the severity levels:

1. Mild Intermittent
2. Mild Persistent
3. Moderate Persistent
4. Severe Persistent

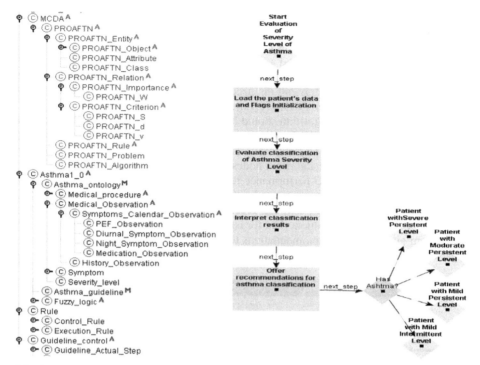

Fig. 4. View of the developed ontologies with Protege-2000.

Fig. 5. GLIF representation of a CPG asthma algorithm.

Table 2. Symptoms of each prototype, attributes and criteria for each asthma level for the severity diagnosis.

Symptoms	Attributes	1. Mild I.	2. Mild P.	3. Mod. P.	4. Severe P.
Diurnal	Emergency dep. visits	Short	Occasional	Moderate	Frequent
	Bronchodilator doses	Short	Occasional	Frequent	Daily
	Coughing	Weekly	Several-days	Daily	Continual
	Phlegm	Weekly	Several-days	Daily	Continual
	Fatigue	Absence	Occasional	Frequent	Continual
	Fatigue with exercise	Absence	Occasional	Frequent	Continual
	Missed school	Absence	Occasional	Frequent	Continual
	More inhaled steroids	Absence	Occasional	Frequent	Frequent
	Oral/nasal steroids	Absence	Occasional	Continual	Continual
Nightly	Coughing	Monthly	Fortnightly	Weekly	Daily
	Awakened with fatigue	Monthly	Fortnightly	Weekly	Daily
	Bronchodilator doses	Monthly	Fortnightly	Weekly	Daily
Pulmonary function (PBF) and variability	Morning before medic.	High, Low	High, Middle	Middle, High	Low, High
	Morning after medic	High, Low	High, Middle	Middle, High	Low, High
	Night before medic	High, Low	High, Middle	Middle, High	Low, High
	Night after medic	High, Low	High, Middle	Middle, High	Low, High

As it is common in MCDA, some attributes have more weight than others when determining a category. For example: "the patient attends to emergency room".

With the purpose of having the entire knowledge contained inside the KB, a set of rules has been added to the previously developed ontologies (Fig.4). These rules allow the execution and control of the different PROAFTN and CPG algorithms (processes) by JESS. It includes the creation of the *Rule* class and its subclasses (Fig.4), and the implementation of the rules as instances of those classes. On the other hand, to complete the PROAFTN method assignation process, we need a set of fuzzy rules. We have created for this purpose the class *PROAFTN_Rule* (Fig.4) and added it to the PROAFTN ontology. Therefore, all the needed knowledge for the representation and execution of the CPG and the PROAFTN method is part of the ontologies.

The follow up of each algorithm should be possible. The results of each execution should be available in a justified and reasoned way for the user. In order to attain it, we have created the *Guideline_Control* classes and it subclasses. Their instances hold the status information of the algorithm nodes used in each execution.

In order to show the CPG performance results, the physician receives a page containing information about the performed evaluation of the severity level. An example can be seen in Fig.6. It displays the results obtained after the application of the PROAFTN method to the patient data for each severity level. Based on those results, the system gives several recommendations to help the physician to classify the severity level of the patient. Finally, the system waits for the physician decision.

	Diurnal symptoms		Night symptoms		PEF	
Severe Persistent	Continual symptoms	60%	Frequent symptoms	50%	FEV1/PEF <= 60% predicted	0%
	Limitations in the physical activity	20%			PEF Variability >= 30%	0%
	Frequent exacerbations	20%				
Moderate Persistent	Daily symptoms	100%	> once a week	100%	60% < FEV1/PEF =< 80 % predicted	100%
	Daily use of short-acting inhaled beta2-agonist	90%			PEF Variability >30%	100%
	The exacerbations affect to the activity	90%				
	exacerbations > twice a week; may continue several days	90%				
Mild Persistent	Symptoms >twice a week, while < once a day	100%	> twice a month	100%	FEV1/PEF >=80% predicted	0%
	Exacerbations may alter the activity	100%			PEF Variability=20-30 %	0%
Mild Intermittent	Symptoms =< twice a week	0%	=< twice a month	0%	FEV1/PEF >= 80% predicted	0%
	Asyntomatic and normal PEF among exacerbations	20%			PEF Variability <20%	0%
	Short exacerbations	20%				

RECOMMENDATIONS: It is recommended to classify the patient inside the MODERATE PERSISTENT level [Explanations]

In what level will classify the patient?   ⊙ Severe Persistent   ⊙ Moderate Persistent   ⊙ Mild Persistent   ⊙ Mild Intermittent   [Classify]

Fig. 6. Severity evaluation results according to the PROAFTN method.

5   Conclusions

An effective CPG implementation can be achieved by means of the formalism GLIF, the application of ontologies, and support tools for their edition and execution. Physicians can easily understand the CPG representation through Prótegé-2000. The complexity of the domain information, including both the asthma treatment and the MCDA, recommends using domain ontologies that later will be integrated into the processes represented by GLIF.

Determining recommendations can bring different classification problems up for every decision node of the CPG. Because each determination is based on multiple fuzzy criteria, the implementation of additional MCDA or Soft-Computing methods is needed. This can be achieved in an effective and maintainable way by defining their classification processes with the method proposed in this work. When determining the asthma severity level, the PROAFTN implementation is effective on the Web.

Our solution is better than the Iowa proposal because: 1) We use Java technology, which is more powerful than the CGI technology they use. 2) The recommendations are based on the information extracted from the medical records of patients instead of entered manually by the user. 3) The knowledge representation is based on domain ontologies and a specific formalism to represent a CPG, such as GLIF, instead of decision trees.

In conclusion, the effectiveness of the CPG implementation through both GLIF and the utilisation of efficient classification methods make it applicable to the real world when it is integrated into a Web-based DSS. It provides recommendations for the physicians that helps them in the decision making process.

Acknowledgments

This job has been carried out with funding received from the Department of Economy and Tourism from the Guipuzkoa Council [OF-151/2002] with sponsorship from the European Union, and partial funding from the Ministry of Science and Technology [MCYT – TIC2001-1143-C03-01].

References

1. Belacel N, Boulasse MR. Multicriteria fuzzy assignment method: a useful tool to assist medical diagnosis. Artificial Intelligence in Medicine, 21 (2001), 201-207.
2. de Clercq PA, Hasman A. et al. Design and implementation of a framework to support the development of clinical guidelines. Int J Med Inform 2001; 64 285-318.
3. Elkin PL, Peleg M. et al. Toward Standardization of Electronic Guideline Representation, MD Computing, 2000, Vol. 17(6):39-44.
4. Fernandez M, Gomez-Perez A. et al. METHONTOLOGY: From ontological Art towards ontological engineering. Proc AAAI-97 Spring Symposium Series on Ontological Engineering, Stanford, USA, pages 33-40.
5. Field MJ, Lohr KN. Guidelines for Clinical Practice: From development to use. Washington DC: Institute of Medicine, National Academy Press; 1992.
6. Fox J, Johns N. et al. Disseminating Medical Knowledge-The PROforma Approach. Artificial Intelligence in Medicine, 14, 1998, 157-181.
7. Gomez-Perez, A., & Benjamins, R., "Overview of Knowledge Sharing and Reuse Components: Ontologies and Problem-Solving Methods", in: Proceedings of the IJCAI-99 Workshop on Ontologies and Problem-Solving Methods (KRR5), MorganKaufmann (1999).
8. Gordon C, Veloso M. Guidelines in Healthcare: the experience of the Prestige project. Medical Informatics Europe 1999, Ljubljana, Slovenia; p. 733-738.

9. Grimshaw JM, Russell IT. Effect of clinical guidelines on medical practice: a systematic review of rigorous evaluations. Lancet. 1993; 342(8883):1317-22.
10. Hripcsak G, Ludemann P, et al. Rationale for the Arden Syntax. Computers and Biomedical Research 1994; 27:291-324.
11. Johnson PD, Tu S, et al. Using Scenarios in Chronic Disease Management Guidelines for Primary Care. Proc. AMIA Annual Symposium, 2000 p. 389-393.
12. Johnston ME, Langton KB, et al. Effects of computer-based clinical decision support systems on clinician performance and patient outcome. Ann Intern Med. 1994;120(2)135-42
13. Peter D. Karp, "The design space of frame knowledge representation systems", Technical Report 520, SRI International AI Center, 1992.
14. Lobach DF, Gadd CS, et al. Siegfried: System for Interactive Electronic Guidelines with Feedback and Resources for Instructional and Educational Development. Medinfo 1998; 9 Pt 2:827-31.
15. Miksch S, Shahar Y, et al. Asbru: A task-specific, intention-based, and time-oriented language for representing skeletal plans. Proc. Seventh Workshop on Knowledge Engineering Methods and Languages (KEML-97) (Milton Keynes, UK, 1997).
16. NIH. National Asthma Education and Prevention Program-II Report, 1997.
17. Ohno-Machado L, Gennari JH, et al. The GuideLine Interchange Format: A Model for Representing Guidelines. JAMIA 5(4):357-372, 1998.
18. Peleg M., Tu S, et al. Comparing Computer-Interpretable Guideline Models: A Case-Study Approach. JAMIA, vol. 10, No. 1, Jan-Feb 2003, pp. 52-68 2002.
19. Pikatza JM, Aldamiz-Echevarria L, et al. DIABETES-I: A Decision Support System for the attendance in the treatment of Diabetes Mellitus type I. Diabetes, Nutrition & Metabolism: Clinical and Experimental 11, 1, 72, 1998.
20. Quaglini S, Stefanelli M. et al. Managing Non-Compliance in Guideline-based Careflow Systems. Proc. AMIA Annual Symposium 2000.
21. Roy B., Multicriteria methodology for decision aiding. Kluwer Academic, 1996.
22. Shiffman RN, Karras BT, et al. GEM: A proposal for a more comprehensive guideline document model using XML. JAMIA 2000; 7(5):488-498.
23. Smith MJ, Nesbitt TS, et al. Telehealth & Telemedicine: Taking Distance Out of Caring.1996. http://www.netpros.net/TH-TM-REPORT/cont.html
24. Sobrado FJ, Pikatza JM, et al. Arnasa: una forma de desarrollo basado en el dominio en la construcción de un DSS para la gestión del proceso de tratamiento del asma vía Web, Proc VII Jornadas de Ingeniería del Software y Bases de Datos 2002.
25. Terenziani P, Montani S, et al. Supporting physicians in taking decisions in clinical guidelines: the GLARE "What if" Facility. Proc. AMIA Annual Symposium 2002.
26. Thomas KW, Dayton CS, et al. Evaluation of Internet-Based Clinical Decision Support Systems. Journal of Medical Internet Research 1999;1(2):e6.
27. Tu SW, Musen MA. Modeling Data and Knowledge in the EON Guideline Architecture. Proc. Medinfo 2001, London, UK, 280-284. 2001.
28. Vincke Ph. Multicriteria decision aid. J. Wiley, New York (1992).
29. Wang D, Peleg M, et al. Representation Primitives, Process Models and Patient Data in Computer-Interpretable Clinical Practice Guidelines: A Literature Review of Guideline Representation Models. International Journal of Medical Informatics, 2002.

Towards a Generic Multiagent Model for Decision Support: Two Case Studies[*]

Sascha Ossowski[1], José Luís Pérez de la Cruz[2], Josefa Z. Hernández[3],
José-Manuel Maseda[4], Alberto Fernández[1], María-Victoria Belmonte[2],
Ana García-Serrano[3], Juan-Manuel Serrano[1], Rafael León[2], and Francesco Carbone[3]

[1] Dpt. of Computer Science, Universidad Rey Juan Carlos, Calle Tulipán s/n,
28933 Móstoles (Madrid), Spain
{sossowski,al.fernandez,jserrano}@escet.urjc.es
[2] ETSI Informática, Univ. Málaga
Málaga, Spain
{perez,mavi,leon}@lcc.uma.es
[3] Dpt. of Artificial Intelligence, Technical Univ. of Madrid, Campus de Montegancedo s/n
28660 Boadilla del Monte (Madrid), Spain
{phernan,agarcia,fcarbone}@isys.dia.fi.upm.es
[4] LABEIN, Parque Tecnológico Edif. 101
48170 Zamudio (Vizcaya), Spain
jmaseda@labein.es

Abstract. This paper describes how agent and knowledge technology can be used to build advanced software systems that support operational decision-making in complex domains. In particular, we present an abstract architecture and design guidelines for agent-based decision support systems, illustrate its application to two real-world domains - road traffic and bus fleet management - and discuss the lessons learnt from this enterprise.

1 Introduction

Decision Support Systems (DSS) provide assistance to humans involved in complex decision-making processes. Early DSS were conceived as simple databases for storage and recovery of decision relevant information [23]. However, it soon became apparent that the key problem for a decision-maker (DM) is not to *access* pertinent data but rather to *understand* its significance. Modern DSS help decision-makers explore the implications of their judgements, so as to take decisions based on understanding [12].

Knowledge-based DSS are particularly relevant in domains where human operators have to take operational decisions regarding the management of complex industrial or environmental processes [13,14]. Due to the inherent (spatial, logical and/or

---

[*] Work supported by the Spanish Ministry of Science and Technology (MCyT) under grant TIC2000-1370-C04.

R. Conejo et al. (Eds.): CAEPIA-TTIA 2003, LNAI 3040, pp. 597–607, 2004.

physical) distribution of these domains, a distributed approach to the construction of DSS has become popular [1]. Decision-support *agents* are responsible for parts of the decision-making process in a (semi-)autonomous (individually) rational fashion: they collect and facilitate decision relevant data [23], but also provide advanced reasoning services to analyse the meaning of this information [19]. However, despite recent advances in the field of agent-oriented software engineering [15,17,24], a principled approach to the design of knowledge-based multiagent systems for decision support is still to come.

This paper reports on an attempt to overcome this shortcoming. Section 2 introduces an abstract multiagent DSS architecture, and outlines how it is used to guide the construction of agent-based DSS. Section 3, describes its application to a problem of road traffic management in the greater Bilbao area, as well as its use for bus fleet management scenarios pertinent to the town Malaga. We conclude this paper summarising the lessons learnt and pointing to future work.

2 Agent-Based Decision Support: The SKADS Approach

In this section we describe the *Social Knowledge Agents for Decision Support* (SKADS) approach for the design and application of DSS. In line with the Gaia methodology [25], SKADS first models agent-based DSS in terms of organisational concepts [8,26], that are then further refined, so as to give rise to an agent-centred model. SKADS is particularly concerned with issues of agent interoperability, so it follows closely the FIPA standard for agent systems [11], paying special attention to FIPA's Agent Communication Language (ACL) and its abstract architecture [9]. In the sequel, we first outline the social and communicative *roles* that need to be supported by a DSS so as to cope with typical decision support interactions. Then, classes of *agents* are identified that should be present in any knowledge-based DSS. Finally, we come up with an abstract multiagent *architecture* and outline support for its implementation as DSS for particular domains.

Organisational Model
The key point in modern DSS is to assist the DM in exploring the implications of her judgements, so we first analyse typical "exploratory dialogues" between DM and DSS. Based on their (macro-level) functionality, we have identified the following *types of social interaction* [22] involving DSS: *information exchange, explanation, advice, action performing*. In DSS with multiple DM, additional *brokering* and *negotiation* interactions are often present, which identify potential partners to solve a given problem, and establish the conditions under which a certain action is performed, respectively. *Roles* usually describe different types of (micro-level) functionalities for classes of agents [25], so we introduce the concept of *communicative rol* to describe the communicative competence of agents in social interactions [21]. Communicative roles are characterised by the Communicative Actions (CA) [1] that they can perform (e.g.: an *information seeker* role is characterised by the FIPA CAs *query-if*, *query-ref* and *subscribe*), and may take part in one or more interaction pro-

Table 1. Organizational Concepts for Decision Support.

Type of Social Interaction	Communicative Role	Protocol
Action performing	requester, requestee	FIPA-request-protocol
		FIPA-request-when- protocol
Information exchange	informer, informee	FIPA-query-protocol
		FIPA-subcribe-protocol
Explanation	explainer, explainee	Explanation-protocol
Advice	advisor, advisee	Advisory-protocol
Negotiation	negotiation. requester,	FIPA-Propose-protocol,
(or: action performing II)	negotiation requestee	FIPA-CNET-protocol,
		. . .
Brokering	Brokering requester,	FIPA-brokering-protocol
	broker	FIPA-recruiting-protocol

tocols. We have analysed FIPA ACL on the basis of these concepts, and determined the generic types of social interactions that it supports [22]. As Table 1 indicates, with respect to DSS there was only a need for extensions to *Advice* and *Explanation* interactions (and their respective communicative roles).

Still, roles in agent-based DSS require domain competence as well, so we specialise communicative roles into social roles based on the elements of a domain ontology of which they *inform*, or that they *explain*. A minimum domain competence of a DSS will be centred on the following concepts:

- *system problems*: identify situations with decision-making options (classification).
- *problem causes*: express system problems in terms of causal features of the situation (diagnosis).
- *control actions*: represent the various decision alternatives (action planning).
- *foreseeable problems*: simulate potential consequences of decisions (prediction).

Fig. 1 summarises our organisational analysis of knowledge-based multiagent DSS in UML notation.

Agent Model

Social roles need to be mapped onto types of agents that will eventually play these roles in the DSS. Especially for knowledge-based agent systems, it is important that this process adequately reflects the *a priori* distribution present in the particular DS domain [20]. Usually, both of the following cases are present:

a. *one role – several agents*: In complex domains, it is often necessary (or desirable), to let different agents play the same role, but in different "parts" of a system. In this way, the agent model may better reflect a human organization, reduce communication requirements, or simply decrease the complexity of the necessary reasoning processes.

b. *one agent – several roles*: Knowledge-oriented design approaches, such as KSM [4], suggest that some types of domain knowledge can serve a number of purposes, and therefore may be used by agents to play different roles. Obvi-

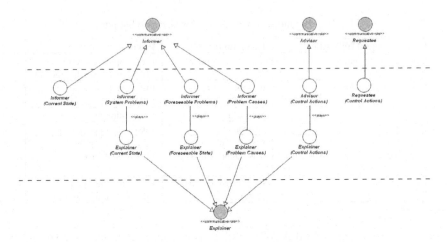

Fig. 1. Communicative and Social Roles in DSS.

ously, it would make no sense to replicate such knowledge bases among different agents.

Based on the social roles that we have identified previously, we have come up with the following agent types for DSS:

- *Data agents* (DA): DAs play the informer role with respect to the current state of a certain part of the system. As such, it is in charge of information retrieval from different information sources like sensors or databases, and its distribution.
- *Management Agents* (MA): MAs play the remaining *informer* roles as well as the *advisor* and *explainer* roles. By consequence, they need to be endowed with knowledge models that allow them to report on (and justify) problems, causes, potential future states etc, as well as to suggest potential management actions.
- *Action Implementation Agent* (AIA): these agents play the *requestee* role and are in charge of actually executing the actions that the DM has chosen to take.
- *User Interface Agent* (UIA): UIAs plays the remaining roles (*informee, requester*, etc.) on behalf of the user. Note that by conveniently sequencing and/or interleaving conversations, they are capable of answering a variety of questions (e.g., "What is happening in S?", "What may happen in S if event E occurs?", etc) [19]. Furthermore, notice that the finer the level of decomposition of social *informer* roles, the bigger the space of potential conversations that the UIA can engage in.

The SKADS approach requires at least one instance of these agent types to be presented in the DSS but, due to different *a priori* distributions in corresponding problem domain (see above), often several instances of the aforementioned agent types will coexist. In DSS that support multiple decision-makers, additional *Coordination Facilitators* (CF) may be present; these are agents providing negotiation and matchmaking (recruiting, brokering) support [7].

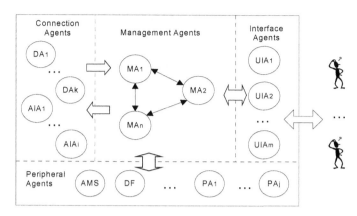

Fig. 2. SKADS abstract architecture.

SKADS Abstract Architecture and Platform

Fig. 2 shows the resulting abstract agent-based DSS architecture according to the SKADS approach. Notice that, depending on the level of detail in the definition of social roles (e.g. *informer* for *problems*, *diagnosis*, *prediction*, etc.) and their subsequent mapping to agent types, the MAs may be subdivided into several agents. Also note that the abstract architecture shown in Fig. 2 comprises a set of so-called peripheral agents: this includes Directory Facilitators (DF) and an Agent Management Systems (AMS) as required by the FIPA abstract architecture [7], but may also include third-party peripheral agents (PA) that supply added value services [10].

We provide support for implementations of agent-based DSS for particular domains through extensions of the FIPA-compliant JADE agent platform [1]. Respecting the communicative part of social roles that DSS agents play, we supply a set of software components that encapsulate the corresponding dialogical behaviour for its use by JADE agents [22]. Regarding domain reasoning, we have encapsulated many of the knowledge presentation and inference schemes of the KSM knowledge modelling environment [4] (so-called knowledge units), and made them available to JADE [18]. Finally, we aim at rendering support for the implementation of coordination matchmaking and decision-making based on the results of [3].

3   Case Studies

In this section we illustrate the instrumentation of our approach by two case studies in the domain of transportation management. The present research is the continuation of a long line of previous work in this field [4,6,10,13].

3.1   The Road Traffic Management Domain

We have used the SKADS architecture to develop a prototype DSS, aimed at assisting the operators at the Malmasin Traffic Control Centre in their task of managing traffic flows within the high-capacity road network of the Bilbao metropolitan area. Operators receive information about the current traffic state by means of loop detectors, and may decide to display messages on VMS panels above the road, so that drivers are warned about incidents and may avoid crossing congested areas.

When applying the SKADS approach to this problem, we had to take into account that operators conceive the road network in terms of so-called *problem areas*, defined according to geographical criteria and one-way sense of traffic. As a result, the relation between the abstract architecture and the actual structure of the DSS prototype is as follows:

- As many DAs as problem areas: Every DA is responsible for collecting the state information of the VMS panels and the data recorded by the loop detectors. It may complete and/or filter noisy data (e.g. due to transmission problems) making use of historical data series and transform the quantitative values observed into qualitative data (e.g. high speed, low occupancy).

- Two kinds of MAs: *problem detection agents* (PDAs) and *control agents* (CAs). PDAs are responsible for monitoring the traffic flow in a problem area, understanding the traffic behaviour and detecting problems. If a problematic situation is detected from the analysis of the data sent by the corresponding DA, the PDA requests a CA to solve it. Every CA is responsible for solving/minimising problems detected by one or several PDAs and with this aim it can communicate with other PDAs to get information about the state of their problem area and diagnose the congestion. From the information obtained in the areas surrounding the congestion, the CA generates control proposals. A control proposal consists of a collection of messages to be displayed on VMS panels with warnings or recommendations for alternative routes for drivers approaching the congestion. When several congestions are detected and two or more CAs compete for the use of the same VMS panels, the corresponding CAs communicate to reach an agreement on a consistent joint proposal.

- One UIA that interacts with the traffic operators in the control centre respecting traffic problems, control proposals etc.

- One AIA that executes the operators' decisions: once a traffic operator accepts a control proposal, the AIA displays the corresponding messages on the VMS.

The two types of Management Agents, PDAs and CAs, are the key components of our DSS for traffic management. They are endowed with knowledge bases that use either JESS rules or KSM frames [4]. In particular, PDAs require two kinds of knowledge:

- *Physical Structure*: knowledge representing both static and dynamic information about the network. The static information is a physical description of the problem area (nodes, sections, position of the sensors, etc.). The dynamic aspects allow the PDA to have abstract information derived from the basic data (e.g. traffic excess).

- *Traffic Problems*: knowledge about detection and diagnosis of the traffic state of the area. A problem is seen as an imbalance between capacity and traffic demand in a road, being the quantitative value of this imbalance the so-called traffic excess. The severity of the problem is a qualitative value obtained from traffic excess.

Each CA subscribes to certain PDAs, so as to be informed about the location and severity of traffic problems. It is endowed with the following four types of knowledge to generate coherent control proposals:

- *PDAs interdependence*. The causes of a congestion notified by a PDA can be related to the traffic state in surrounding problem areas that send the incoming flow to the congested section. The PDAs interdependence knowledge represents the relationship between problem areas and allows the CA to know which areas can be involved in the generation of the problem. Using this knowledge, the CA asks the corresponding PDAs for a description of the general state of their problem areas.
- *Control actions*. Once the control agent has received all the necessary information from the different PDAs, it generates control proposals. It uses its Control Actions knowledge base to determine coherent sets of VMS messages, and their expected impact on the drivers' behaviour. This makes it possible to rank alternative control proposal in terms of the estimated reduction of traffic excess in the problem area.
- *Conflict detection*. Each CA knows, for every VMS panel that it uses, which are the CAs it has to communicate with in order to agree on the use of the panel.
- *Conflict resolution*. Every CA involved in the agreement process sends and receives from the other CAs the panels they want to use and the severity of the different problems they are trying to solve. Conflict resolution rules assign priorities for the use of the panels based on the location and severity problems.

The road network of the Bilbao metropolitan area has been subdivided into 12 problem areas, so the prototype DSS application comprises 12 DAs and 12 PDAs. In addition, 5 CAs have been defined:

- Atena: solves problems for PDAs 2 and 6 and communicates with PDA 11
- Briseide: solves problems for PDAs 1, 4 and 8
- Cassandra: solves problems for PDAs 5, 7 and 10 and communicates with PDA 1

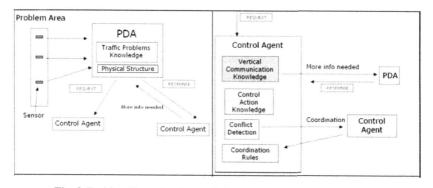

Fig. 3. Problem Detection Agent (left) and of a Control Agent (right).

- Demetra: solves problems for PDA 11 and communicates with PDAs 7 and 2
- Elena: solves problems for PDAs 3, 9 and 12 and communicates with PDA 7

Note that the association between PDAs and CAs is induced by both, topological and traffic behaviour criteria. Fig. 4 summarises the different Management Agents of our DSS prototype for traffic control, and outlines their interrelation.

3.2 The Bus Fleet Management Domain

In this section, we report on the use of the SKADS abstract architecture for the design and implementation of a prototype DSS for bus fleet management, an enterprise undertaken in collaboration with the Malaga urban bus company (EMT). EMT transportation services are structured into *lines*. There is a set of buses assigned to each line that are to deliver services according to a fixed schedule. Still, a variety of incidents can (and usually do) occur, so there is a *line inspector* for each line who takes decisions (in the main stop of the line) in order to adjust services to unforeseen circumstances, and a *control centre* where a *supervisor* is in charge of taking broader and more complex management decisions. Our prototype DSS aims at providing both, the inspectors and the supervisors, with the necessary information and recommendations to support their decision making processes.

The first stage in the definition of the prototype has been the identification of the required agents in terms of the SKADS abstract architecture:

- *Data Agents* (DA) provide information about the state of the buses: where and how are they? There will be one DA for each line.
- There is just one class of MAs in charge of the supervision of each line, so agents of this type are called *Line Management Agents* (LMA).
- *User Interface Agents* (UIA) display selected information to human operators on board or at the control centre (and also to line inspectors).
- Peripheral Agents are reused from other platforms and/or systems (yellow pages, etc.).

The generic communication model between these agents can be described as follows:

- LMAs subscribe to the information made available by the corresponding DAs;
- UIAs subscribe to incidents, problems, and recommendations detected by the UIA;
- LMAs may negotiate deals with each other respecting the exchange of vehicles.

In addition, the agents' basic capabilities can be described as follows:

- A DA *knows* about the state of a bus or a set of buses. It can *gather* information concerning the state of a bus.
- An LMA *knows* about the goals and constraints of the service and about the ways to fix the malfunctions. It can *identify* a problem, *diagnose* a problem, *plan* a set of actions and *predict* future behaviour of the line.

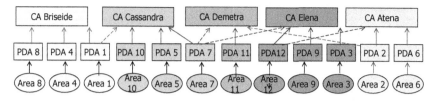

Fig. 4. MA agents for the road traffic management scenario.

The communication model has been implemented on top of the JADE platform, making use of FIPA concepts such as yellow and white pages, FIPA protocols, etc., as presented in section 2. Although in a final version the DSS will rely on DAs that use GPS to detect the position of the buses (and also other kinds of data sources to determine occupation, etc.), our prototype DAs have been implemented by means of simulators capable of generating location data that replicates the many problematic situations that may arise in a line.

LMA knowledge has been represented by means of sets of rules. The corresponding reasoning services are carried out by forward chaining inference engines. We have chosen CLIPS/JESS for these tasks. The ontology of the system, as shown in Fig. 5, has been modelled and instrumented by means of the PROTEGE-II tool.

These design decisions have been applied to a particular part of the EMT local transportation network. In particular, our prototype DSS is based on a faithful reproduction of the real operating conditions of three concrete lines (3, 12 and 15, which cover a sector in western Malaga) of the company EMT; in fact, several elicitation interviews have been performed in order to extract the knowledge and logs of real situations, and have been analysed in order to simulate and solve real problems.

The main window of our prototype is shown in Fig. 6. Line 12 has been selected for visualization: the schematic layout of this line appears on the left. Six buses are serving the line, which appear in the scheme together with their computed delays: in

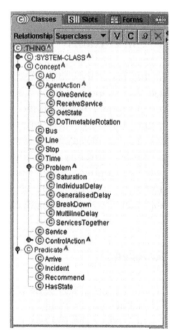

Fig. 5. BFM Ontology.

this case, five buses are delivering their service in time, while another one has suffered a breakdown. At the right of the window a decision support dialogue is shown: in the example, the DSS recommends to ask line 3 for a reserve vehicle. Finally, the bottom part of the window contains status information of the line and its simulator.

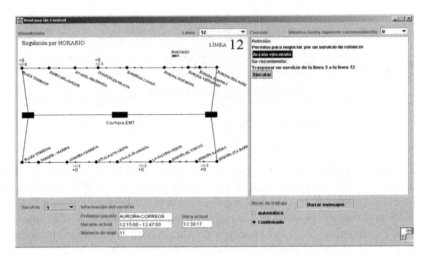

Fig. 6. Screenshot of the bus fleet management UIA.

4 Conclusions

In this paper we have presented the SKADS approach to the design of operational decision support systems based on agent and knowledge technology. Setting out from organisational and agent models, we have come up with an abstract multiagent architecture for DSS. The instrumentation of this architecture has been illustrated by two case studies in real-world transportation management domains.

We are currently proceeding with the implementation of the demonstrators for the two case studies. Despite initial problems with the integration of the different technologies, first results are encouraging. In the future, we are planning to extend our approach so as to cope with more open, large-scale service environments.

References

1. Austin, J.L. (1962): *How to do Things with Words*. Clarendom Press, Oxford.
2. Bellifemine, F.; Poggi, A.; Rimassa, G.; Turci, P. (2000): *An Object Oriented Framework to Realize Agent Systems*. Proc. WOA 2000 Workshop, 52–57.
3. Belmonte, M.V. (2002): *Formación de Coaliciones en Sistemas Multiagente – Una Aproximación Computacionalmente Tratable Basada en Teoría de Juegos*. Ph.D. Thesis, Univ. de Málaga.
4. Cuena J., Molina M. (1997): KSM – An Environment for Design of Structured Knowledge Models. *Knowledge-Based Systems* (Tzafestas, editor). World Scientific.
5. Cuena J., Ossowski S. (1999): Distributed Models for Decision Support. In: *Multi-Agent Systems — A Modern Approach to DAI* (Weiß, editor). MIT Press, 459–504.

6. Cuena, J.; Hernández, J.; Molina, M. (1996): Knowledge-Oriented Design of an Application for Real Time Traffic Management. In: *Proc. Europ. Conf. on Artificial Intelligence (ECAI-96)*, Wiley & Sons, 217–245.

7. Decker, K.; Sycara, K.; Williamson, M. (1997): Middle-agents for the internet. In: *Proc. Int. Joint Conf. on Artificial Intelligence (IJCAI)*, Morgan Kaufmann, 578–583.

8. Ferber, J.; Gutknecht, O.; Jonker, C.; Müller, J.P.; Treur, J. (2000): Organization Models and Behavioural Requirements Specification for Multi-Agent Systems. In: *Proc. ECAI 2000 Workshop on Modelling Artificial Societies and Hybrid Organizations*.

9. Fernández, A.; Ossowski, S. (2002): El estándar FIPA para sistemas inteligentes basados en agentes: una panorámica. *ALI Base Informática No 38*.

10. Fernández, A.; Ossowski, S.; Alonso, A. (2004): Multiagent service architecture for bus fleet management. *Int. Journal on Integrated Computer-Aided Engineering 10 (2)*.

11. FIPA - The Foundation for Intelligent Physical Agents. *http://www.fipa.org/*

12. French, S. (2000): *Decision Analysis and Decision Support*. John Wiley & Sons.

13. Hernández, J.; Ossowski, S.; García-Serrano, A. (2002): Multiagent Architectures for Intelligent Traffic Management Systems. *Transportation Research C 10 (5)*. Elsevier.

14. Hernández, J.; Serrano, J. (2000): Environmental Emergency Management Supported by Knowledge Modelling Techniques. *AI Communications 14 (1)*.

15. Iglesias, C.A.; Garijo Ayestarán, M.; González, J.C. (1999): A Survey of Agent-Oriented Methodologies. In: *Intelligent Agents V*. Springer-Verlag.

16. Klein, M.; Methlie, L. (1995): *Knowledge-Based Decision Support Systems*. John Wiley.

17. Hoa Dam, K.; and Winikoff, M. (2003): Comparing Agent-Oriented Methodologies. In: *Proc Workshop on Agent-Oriented Information Systems (AOIS-2003)*.

18. Ortíz Martín, R.; Saugar García, S. (2002): *Agentificación del entorno KSM*. Technical Report, Universidad Rey Juan Carlos de Madrid.

19. Ossowski, S.; Hernández, J.; Iglesias, C.A.; Fernández, A. (2002): Engineering Agent Systems for Decision Support. In: *Engineering Societies in an Agent World III* (Petta, Tolksdorf & Zambonelli, editores), Springer-Verlag.

20. Ossowski, S.; Omicini, A. (2003): Coordination Knowledge Engineering. *Knowledge Engineering Review 17 (4)*, Cambridge University Press.

21. Serrano, J.M. (2004): *La Pragmática de los Agentes Software – Análisis y Diseño de los Lenguages Artificiales de Comunicación Artificiales*. Ph.D. Thesis, Univ. Rey Juan Carlos.

22. Serrano, J.M.; Ossowski, S.; Fernández, A. (2003): The Pragmatics of Software Agents – Analysis and Design of Agent Communication Languages. *Intelligent Information Agents – An AgentLink Perspective* (Klusch et al., editores). LNAI 2586, Springer, p. 234–274.

23. Silver, M. (1991): *Systems that Support Decision Makers*. John Wiley & Sons.

24. Sturm, A.; Shehory, O. (2003): A Framework for Evaluating Agent-Oriented Methodologies. In: *Proc Workshop on Agent-Oriented Information Systems (AOIS-2003)*.

25. Wooldridge, M.; Jennings, N.; Kinny, D. (2000): The Gaia Methodology for Agent-oriented Analysis and Design. *Autonomous Agents and Multiagent Systems 3(3)*. Kluwer Academic Publishers, 285–312.

26. Zambonelli, F.; Jennings, N.R.; Wooldridge, M. (2000): Organizational Abstractions for the Analysis and Design of Multi-agent Systems. In: *Agent-Oriented Software Engineering* (Ciancarini y Wooldridge, editors), Springer-Verlag, 235 - 252.

Towards Biresiduated Multi-adjoint
Logic Programming

Jesús Medina[1], Manuel Ojeda-Aciego[1], Agustín Valverde[1], and Peter Vojtáš[2]

[1] Dept. Matemática Aplicada, Universidad de Málaga*
{jmedina,aciego,a_valverde}@ctima.uma.es
[2] Inst. of Computer Science, P.J. Šafárik University
vojtas@kosice.upjs.sk

Abstract. Multi-adjoint logic programs were recently proposed as a generalization of monotonic and residuated logic programs, in that simultaneous use of several implications in the rules and rather general connectives in the bodies are allowed. In this work, the need of biresiduated pairs is justified through the study of a very intuitive family of operators, which turn out to be not necessarily commutative and associative and, thus, might have two different residuated implications; finally, we introduce the framework of biresiduated multi-adjoint logic programming and sketch some considerations on its fixpoint semantics.

1 Introduction

A number of logics have been introduced in the recent years motivated by the problem of reasoning in situations where information may be vague or uncertain. Such type of reasoning has been called inexact or fuzzy or approximate reasoning. Here we propose a lattice-valued logic programming paradigm that we call *biresiduated* and *multi-adjoint*, which permits the articulation of vague concepts and generalizes several approaches to the extension of logic programming techniques to the fuzzy case.

Multi-adjoint logic programming was introduced in [7] as a refinement of both initial work in [12] and residuated logic programming [2]. It allows for very general connectives in the body of the rules and, in addition, sufficient conditions for the continuity of its semantics are known. Such an approach is interesting for applications in which connectives depend on different users preferences; or in which knowledge is described by a many-valued logic program where connectives can be general aggregation operators (conjunctors, disjunctors, arithmetic mean, weighted sum, ...), even different aggregators for different users and, moreover, the program is expected to adequately manage different implications for different purposes. The special features of multi-adjoint logic programs are the following:

1. A number of different implications are allowed in the bodies of the rules.
2. Sufficient conditions for continuity of its semantics are known.
3. The requirements on the lattice of truth-values are weaker that those for the residuated approach.

* Partially supported by Spanish DGI projects BFM2000-1054-C02-02, TIC2003-09001-C02-01 and Junta de Andalucía project TIC-115.

R. Conejo et al. (Eds.): CAEPIA-TTIA 2003, LNAI 3040, pp. 608–617, 2004.

It is important to recall that many different "and" and "or" operations have been proposed for use in fuzzy logic. It is therefore important to select, for each particular application, the operations which are the best for this particular application. Several papers discuss the optimal choice of "and" and "or" operations for fuzzy control, when the main criterion is to get the most stable control. In reasoning applications, however, it is more appropriate to select operations which are the best in reflecting human reasoning, i.e., operations which are "the most logical".

In this paper, we build on the fact that conjunctors in multi-adjoint logic programs need not be either commutative or associative and, thus, consider the possibility of including a further generalisation of the framework, allowing for *biresiduation*, in the sense of [11]. This way, each conjunctor in our multi-adjoint setting may potentially have two "lateral" residuated implications. This approach has been recently used by Morsi [9] to develop a formal system based on a biresiduation construction. Biresidua has also been used by Dunn [3] in the framework of substructural logics under the name of (partial) gaggles.

Yet another reason for introducing biresiduation is that fuzzy logic in a narrow sense [5] is still an open system and thus, new connectives can and should be introduced. Note that the concept of biresiduation used in this paper is not to be confused with the generalized biimplication, which is another usual meaning of this term as used in v.gr. [8]. A natural question then arises, whether the basic syntactico-semantical properties are not harmed by this generalisation.

The structure of the paper is as follows: In Section 2, the preliminary definitions are introduced; later, in Section 3, some motivating examples towards considering biresiduated implications are presented; in Section 4, the syntax and semantics of biresiduated multi-adjoint logic programs is given; finally, in Section 5, some concluding remarks and pointers to related works and ideas for future research are presented.

2 Preliminary Definitions

The main concept in the extension to logic programming to the fuzzy case is that of *adjoint pair*, firstly introduced in a logical context by Pavelka, who interpreted the poset structure of the set of truth-values as a category, and the relation between the connectives of implication and conjunction as functors in this category. The result turned out to be another example of the well-known concept of adjunction, introduced by Kan in the general setting of category theory in 1950.

Definition 1 (Adjoint pair). *Let $\langle P, \preceq \rangle$ be a partially ordered set and a pair $(\&, \leftarrow)$, of binary operations in P, such that:*

(a1) *Operation $\&$ is increasing in both arguments, i.e. if $x_1, x_2, y \in P$ and $x_1 \preceq x_2$, then $(x_1 \& y) \preceq (x_2 \& y)$ and $(y \& x_1) \preceq (y \& x_2)$;*

(a2) *Operation $\leftarrow$ is increasing in the first argument (the consequent) and decreasing in the second argument (the antecedent), i.e. if $x_1, x_2, y \in P$ and $x_1 \preceq x_2$, then $(x_1 \leftarrow y) \preceq (x_2 \leftarrow y)$ and $(y \leftarrow x_2) \preceq (y \leftarrow x_1)$;*

(a3) *For any $x, y, z \in P$, we have that $x \preceq (y \leftarrow z)$ holds if and only if $(x \& z) \preceq y$ holds.*

Then we say that $(\&, \leftarrow)$ forms an adjoint pair in $\langle P, \preceq \rangle$.

The need of the monotonicity of operators $\leftarrow$ and $\&$ is clear, if they are going to be interpreted as generalised implications and conjunctions. The third property in the definition corresponds to the categorical adjointness, and can be adequately interpreted in terms of multiple-valued inference as asserting both that the truth-value of $y \leftarrow z$ is the maximal x satisfying $x \& z \preceq y$, and also the validity of the following generalised modus ponens rule [5]:

> If x is a lower bound of $\psi \leftarrow \varphi$, and z is a lower bound of φ then a lower bound y of ψ is $x \& z$.

In addition to $(a1)$–$(a3)$ it will be necessary to assume the existence of bottom and top elements in the poset of truth-values (the zero and one elements), and the existence of joins (suprema) for every directed subset; that is, we will assume a structure of complete lattice, but nothing about associativity, commutativity and general boundary conditions of $\&$. In particular, the requirement that $(L, \&, \top)$ has to be a commutative monoid in a residuated lattice is too restrictive, in that commutativity needn't be required in the proofs of soundness and correctness.

Extending the results in [2, 12] to a more general setting, in which different implications (Łukasiewicz, Gödel, product) and thus, several modus ponens-like inference rules are used, naturally leads to considering several *adjoint pairs* in the lattice:

Definition 2 (Multi-Adjoint Lattice). *Let $\langle L, \preceq \rangle$ be a lattice. A multi-adjoint lattice $\mathcal{L}$ is a tuple $(L, \preceq, \leftarrow_1, \&_1, \ldots, \leftarrow_n, \&_n)$ satisfying the following items:*

(l1) $\langle L, \preceq \rangle$ *is bounded, i.e. it has bottom $(\bot)$ and top $(\top)$ elements;*
(l2) $(\&_i, \leftarrow_i)$ *is an adjoint pair in $\langle L, \preceq \rangle$ for $i = 1, \ldots, n$;*
(l3) $\top \&_i \vartheta = \vartheta \&_i \top = \vartheta$ *for all $\vartheta \in L$ for $i = 1, \ldots, n$.*

Remark 1. Note that residuated lattices are a special case of multi-adjoint lattice.

From the point of view of expressiveness, it is interesting to allow extra operators to be involved with the operators in the multi-adjoint lattice. The structure which captures this possibility is that of a multi-adjoint Ω-algebra, where Ω is the set of operators, which comprises the set of adjoint pairs and, possibly, other monotone operators such as *disjunctors* or *aggregators*.

3   Towards Biresiduation

In fuzzy logic there is a well developed theory of t-norms, t-conorms and residual implications. The objective of this section is to show some interesting non-standard connectives to motivate the consideration of a more general class of connectives in fuzzy logic. The motivation is the following:

When evaluating the relevance of answers to a given query it is common to use some subjective interpretation of human preferences in a granulated way. This is, fuzzy truth-values usually describe steps in the degree of perception (numerous advocations of this phenomenon have been pointed out by Zadeh). This is connected to the well-known fact that people can only distinguish finitely many degrees of quantity or quality (closeness, cheapness, etc.). Thus, in practice, although we used the product t-norm $x \&_p y = x \cdot y$, we would be actually working with a piece-wise constant approximation of it. In this generality, it is possible to work with approximations of t-norms and/or conjunctions learnt from data by a neural net.

Regarding the use of non-standard connectives, just consider that a variable represented by x can be observed with $m + 1$ different values, then surely we should be working with a regular partition of $[0, 1]$ into m pieces. This means that a given value x should be fitted to this "observation" scale as the least upper bound with the form k/m (analytically, this corresponds to $\lceil m \cdot x \rceil / m$ where $\lceil \_ \rceil$ is the ceiling function). A similar consideration can be applied to both, variable y and the resulting conjunction; furthermore, it might be possible that each variable has different granularity.

Formally, assume in x-axis we have a partition into n pieces, in y-axis into m pieces, and in z-axis into k pieces. Then the approximation of the product conjunction looks like the definition below

Definition 3. *Denote* $(z)_p = \dfrac{\lceil p \cdot z \rceil}{p}$ *and define, for naturals* $n, m, k > 0$

$$C_{n,m}^{k}(x, y) = \left((x)_n \cdot (y)_m \right)_k$$

Note that $C_{n,m}^{k}$ satisfies the properties of a general *conjunctor*, that is, it is monotone in both variables and generalizes the classical conjunction.

There are connectives of the form $C_{n,m}^{k}(x, y)$ which are non-associative and, there are connectives of the same form which are non-commutative as well. The following example shows some of them:

Example 1.

1. The connective $C = C_{10,10}^{10}$ is not associative.

$$C(0.7, C(0.7, 0.3)) = C(0.7, (0.21)_{10}) = C(0.7, 0.3) = (0.21)_{10} = 0.3$$
$$C(C(0.7, 0.7), 0.3) = C((0.49)_{10}, 0.3) = C(0.5, 0.3) = (0.15)_{10} = 0.2$$

2. The connective $C_{10,5}^{4}(x, y)$ is not commutative.

$$C_{10,5}^{4}(0.82, 0.79) = ((0.82)_{10} \cdot (0.79)_5)_4 = (0.9 \cdot 0.8)_4 = (0.72)_4 = 0.75$$
$$C_{10,5}^{4}(0.79, 0.82) = ((0.79)_{10} \cdot (0.82)_5)_4 = (0.8 \cdot 1)_4 = 1$$

□

Connectives as those in the example above can be reasonably justified as follows: If we are looking for a hotel which is close to downtown, with reasonable price and being a new building, then classical fuzzy approaches would assign a user "his" particular interpretation of "close", "reasonable" and "new". As, in practice, we can only recognize finitely many degrees of being close, reasonable, new, then the corresponding fuzzy sets have a stepwise shape. This motivates the lattice-valued approach we will assume in this paper: it is just a matter of representation that the outcome is done by means of intervals of granulation and/or indistinguishability.

Although the multi-adjoint approach to logic programming has been shown to be more general than the monotonic and residuated paradigms (which, in turn, generalizes annotated LP, possibilistic LP, probabilistic LP, etc), the discussion below introduces a context which cannot be easily accommodated under multi-adjointness.

On Operators $C_{n,m}^k$ and Biresidua

By using operators $C_{n,m}^k$, we study an example of adjoint pair which will motivate the need of biresiduation. Firstly, let us recall the well-known *residuum* construction, which has been extensively studied in the context of continuous t-norms, see [5, 6].

Definition 4. *Given* $C_{n,m}^k : [0,1] \times [0,1] \to [0,1]$, *we define the following operator:*

$$z \swarrow_{n,m}^k y = \sup\{x \in [0,1] \mid C_{n,m}^k(x,y) \leq z\}$$

for each $z, y \in [0,1]$, *which is called* r-adjoint implication of $C_{n,m}^k$.

As we have proved above, in general $C_{n,m}^k$ need not be commutative, therefore we have to show that the term *r-adjoint implication* makes sense: actually, the pair $(C_{n,m}^k, \swarrow_{n,m}^k)$ satisfies the properties of adjoint pair.

We will prove a slightly more general version of the statement: that the construction above leads to an adjoint pair assuming only that the supremum in the definition is indeed a maximum, but without assuming either commutativity or continuity of the conjunctor.

Proposition 1. *Consider a conjunctor* $\&: L \times L \to L$ *in a lattice, and assume that for all* $y, z \in L$ *there exists a maximum of the set* $\{x \in L \mid x \& y \preceq z\}$. *Then* $(\&, \swarrow)$ *is an adjoint pair.*

Proof. Let us prove that it is increasing in the first argument. Assume $z_1 \preceq z_2$, then

$$\{x \mid x \& y \preceq z_1\} \subseteq \{x \in L \mid x \& y \preceq z_2\}$$

therefore we have

$$z_1 \swarrow y = \sup\{x \in L \mid x \& y \preceq z_1\} \preceq \sup\{x \in L \mid x \& y \preceq z_2\} = z_2 \swarrow y$$

To show that $\swarrow$ decreases in the second argument, assume $y_1 \preceq y_2$. By monotonicity in the second argument, we have $x \& y_1 \preceq x \& y_2$ for all $x \in L$, which implies the following inclusion

$$\{x \in L \mid x \& y_2 \preceq z\} \subseteq \{x \in L \mid x \& y_1 \preceq z\}$$

therefore $z \swarrow y_2 \preceq z \swarrow y_1$.

For the adjoint property, consider $x, y, z \in L$ and assume $x \& y \preceq z$, then $x \in \{x' \mid x' \& y \preceq z\}$ and, therefore

$$x \preceq \sup\{x' \mid x' \& y \preceq z\} = z \swarrow y$$

For the converse, assume that $x \preceq z \swarrow y = \sup\{x' \mid x' \& y \preceq z\}$.

By the hypothesis, we have that the supremum is indeed a maximum; let us denote it by x_0. Then we have $x \preceq x_0$ and, by monotonicity in the first argument, we have

$$x \& y \preceq x_0 \& y \preceq z \qquad \square$$

The adjoint property might fail in the case that the supremum is not maximum, as the following example shows:

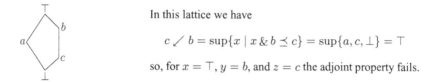

In this lattice we have

$$c \swarrow b = \sup\{x \mid x \,\&\, b \preceq c\} = \sup\{a, c, \bot\} = \top$$

so, for $x = \top$, $y = b$, and $z = c$ the adjoint property fails.

Fig. 1. Counterexample for Proposition 1.

Proposition 2. $(C_{n,m}^k, \swarrow_{n,m}^k)$ *is an adjoint pair.*

Proof. By the previous proposition, we have only to show that in the definition of the r-adjoint implication of $C_{n,m}^k$ the supremum is indeed a maximum.

Given $y, z \in [0, 1]$, let A denote the set $\{x \in [0, 1] \mid C_{n,m}^k(x, y) \leq z\}$. The result follows from the fact that if we have $x \in A$, then we also have $(x)_n \in A$ by the definition of $C_{n,m}^k$. Thus, the only possible values for the supremum are in the set $\{0, \frac{1}{n}, \frac{2}{n}, \dots, \frac{n-1}{n}, 1\}$, but suprema on a discrete subset of a linear order are always maxima. □

An interesting 'coherence' property that holds for continuous t-norms and their residua is that the truth-value of the consequent is greater or equal than the truth-value of the antecedent if and only if the truth-value of the implication is defined to be the top element. However, the property "if $z \geq y$, then $z \leftarrow y = \top$" does not hold for connectives $C_{n,m}^k$:

Example 2. If we consider the conjunctor $C_{4,5}^8 : [0, 1] \times [0, 1] \rightarrow [0, 1]$, we can check that $0.6 \geq 0.45$ and $0.6 \swarrow_{4,5}^8 0.45 \neq 1$. We have,

$$C_{4,5}^8(x, 0.45) = \frac{\left\lceil 8 \cdot \frac{[4 \cdot x]}{4} \cdot \frac{[5 \cdot 0.45]}{5} \right\rceil}{8} = \frac{\left\lceil 8 \cdot \frac{[4 \cdot x]}{4} \cdot 0.6 \right\rceil}{8}$$

and then

$$0.6 \swarrow_{4,5}^8 0.45 = \sup\{x \in [0, 1] \mid C_{4,5}^8(x, 0.45) \leq 0.6\} = 0.75 \neq 1 \qquad \square$$

In the following proposition, where we introduce a necessary and sufficient condition for the fulfillment of the coherence property for the connectives $C_{n,m}^k$, the notation $[0, 1]_n$ will be used to denote the discrete set $\{0, \frac{1}{n}, \frac{2}{n}, \dots, \frac{n-1}{n}, 1\}$.

Proposition 3. *Consider $z, y \in [0, 1]$ such that $z \geq y$ then $z \swarrow_{n,m}^k y = 1$ if and only if $y \in [0, 1]_k \cap [0, 1]_m$*

Proof. ($\Rightarrow$) Assume $z \swarrow_{n,m}^k y = 1$ for all $z \geq y$. In particular, for $z = y$ we have, from the hypothesis and the adjoint property, that $C_{n,m}^k(1, y) \leq y$. Moreover, we have the following chain of inequalities

$$y \leq \frac{\lceil m \cdot y \rceil}{m} \leq \frac{\left\lceil k \cdot \dfrac{\lceil m \cdot y \rceil}{m} \right\rceil}{k} = C_{n,m}^k(1, y) \leq y$$

Therefore, we actually have a chain of equalities. Now, considering the first equality we obtain $m \cdot y = \lceil m \cdot y \rceil$ which leads to $y \in [0,1]_m$. Similarly, one can obtain $y \in [0,1]_k$.

($\Leftarrow$) It is sufficient to show that $1 \in \{x \in [0,1] \mid C_{n,m}^k(x,y) \leq z\}$:

$$C_{n,m}^k(1, y) = \frac{\left\lceil k \cdot \dfrac{\lceil n \cdot 1 \rceil}{n} \cdot \dfrac{\lceil m \cdot y \rceil}{m} \right\rceil}{k} = \frac{\left\lceil k \cdot \dfrac{\lceil m \cdot y \rceil}{m} \right\rceil}{k} \overset{(i)}{=} \frac{\lceil k \cdot y \rceil}{k} \overset{(ii)}{=} y \leq z$$

where (i) and (ii) follow from $y \in [0,1]_m$ and $y \in [0,1]_k$ respectively. $\qquad\square$

Taking into account this result we obtain a condition for the fulfillment of the coherence property for the r-adjoint implication defined above in terms of the set of truth-values that can be attached to any given formula.

For example, consider that we are working on a multiple-valued logic, whose truth-values are taken on a regular partition of $[0,1]$, then the coherence property for the conjunctor $C_{n,m}^k$ automatically holds in any finitely-valued logics on a regular partition of $\gcd(k, m) + 1$ elements.

Consider for example that we need to work with the operator $C_{4,5}^8$ in our language. By the result above, the r-adjoint implication only fulfills the coherence property in the classical case, since $\gcd(8, 5) = 1$. Could we use another implication which turns out to be coherent in a multiple-valued logic? We have an obvious choice by using the non-commutativity of the operator. This leads to what we call the *l-adjoint implication* to the conjunctor.

Definition 5. *Given the conjunctor* $C_{n,m}^k : [0,1] \times [0,1] \to [0,1]$, *we define its* l-adjoint *implication as follows:*

$$z \diagdown_{n,m}^k y = \sup\{x \in [0,1] \mid C_{n,m}^k(y, x) \leq z\}$$

for each $z, y \in [0,1]$.

It is easy to prove a similar result to that of Proposition 3 and obtain that the l-adjoint implication to $C_{4,5}^8$ is coherent on a 5-valued logic, for $\gcd(8, 4) = 4$.

The biresiduated structure is obtained by allowing, for each adjoint conjunctor, two "sided" adjoint implications, as detailed in the following definition:

Definition 6. *Let* $\langle L, \preceq \rangle$ *be a lattice. A* biresiduated multi-adjoint lattice $\mathcal{L}$ *is a tuple* $(L, \preceq, \diagup^1, \diagdown_1, \&_1, \dots, \diagup^n, \diagdown_n, \&_n)$ *satisfying the following items:*

1. $\langle L, \preceq \rangle$ *is bounded, i.e. it has bottom and top elements;*
2. $(\&_i, \diagup^i, \diagdown_i)$ *satisfies the following properties, for all* $i = 1, \dots, n$; *i.e.*
   (a) *Operation* $\&_i$ *is increasing in both arguments,*
   (b) *Operations* $\diagup^i, \diagdown_i$ *are increasing in the first argument and decreasing in the second argument,*

(c) For any $x, y, z \in P$, we have that

$$
\begin{array}{llll}
1. & x \preceq y \diagup^i z & \text{if and only if} & x \,\&_i\, z \preceq y \\
2. & x \preceq y \diagdown_i z & \text{if and only if} & z \,\&_i\, x \preceq y
\end{array}
$$

The last conditions in (3c) make this algebraic structure a flexible and suitable tool for being used in a logical context, for they can be interpreted as a two possible multiple-valued *modus ponens*-like rules. From a categorical point of view, these conditions arise when considering the conjunctor as a bifunctor, and applying the adjointness either in its second or first argument, respectively. Also note that the requirements of the boundary conditions for the conjunctors are not necessary.

The proposition below introduces a characterization of the adjoint property for the pairs $(\&, \diagdown)$ and $(\&, \diagup)$.

Proposition 4. *Property (3c2) in the definition of biresiduated multi-adjoint lattice is equivalent to the following pair of conditions for all $x, y \in P$:*

$$
\begin{array}{ll}
(\mathbf{r1'})\ x \preceq ((y \,\&\, x) \diagdown y) & (\mathbf{r1''})\ x \preceq ((x \,\&\, y) \diagup y) \\
(\mathbf{r2'})\ (x \,\&(y \diagdown x)) \preceq y & (\mathbf{r2''})\ ((y \diagup x) \,\&\, x) \preceq y
\end{array}
$$

Remark 2. In the classical residuated case, conditions (r1) and (r2) are sometimes called $(\varPhi 2)$ and $(\varPhi 3)$, whereas (3b) is known as $(\varPhi 1)$, see e.g. [4].

4   Syntax and Semantics of Biresiduated Multi-adjoint Programs

Similarly to the (mono)-residuated multi-adjoint case, the structure which allows the possibility of using additional operators is that of a *biresiduated multi-adjoint Ω-algebra*. In this section we introduce the definition of the syntax and semantics of biresiduated multiadjoint logic programs. The programs are defined on a language $\mathfrak{F}$ constructed on a set of propositional symbol Π and the set of operators Ω and using a biresiduated multi-adjoint lattice $\mathcal{L}$ as the set of truth-values.

Definition 7. *A biresiduated multi-adjoint logic program (in short a program) on a language $\mathfrak{F}$ with values in $\mathcal{L}$ is a set $\mathbb{P}$ of rules of the form $\langle A \diagup^i B, \vartheta \rangle$ or $\langle A \diagdown_i B, \vartheta \rangle$ such that:*

1. *The head of the rule, A, is a propositional symbol of Π;*
2. *The body formula, B, is a formula of $\mathfrak{F}$ built from propositional symbols $B_1, \ldots, B_n$ $(n \geq 0)$ and monotone functions;*
3. *Facts are rules with empty body.*
4. *The weight ϑ is an element (a truth-value) of L.*

As usual, a query *(or goal) is a propositional symbol intended as a question ? A prompting the system.*

Let $\mathcal{I}_\mathcal{L}$ be the set of *interpretations*, that is, the unique recursive extensions of mappings $I : \Pi \to L$. The ordering $\preceq$ of the truth-values L can be easily extended to $\mathcal{I}_\mathcal{L}$, which also inherits the structure of complete lattice. The minimum element of the lattice $\mathcal{I}_\mathcal{L}$, which assigns $\bot$ to any propositional symbol, will be denoted $\triangle$.

A rule of a biresiduated multi-adjoint logic program is satisfied whenever its truth-value is greater or equal than the weight associated with the rule. The formal definition uses the following terminology: given an operator $\omega \in \Omega$, we will write $\dot{\omega}$ to denote its interpretation in $\mathcal{L}$.

Definition 8. *1. An interpretation $I \in \mathcal{I}_{\mathfrak{L}}$ satisfies $\langle A, \vartheta \rangle$ iff $\vartheta \preceq I(A)$.*

2. An interpretation $I \in \mathcal{I}_{\mathfrak{L}}$ satisfies $\langle A \swarrow^i B, \vartheta \rangle$ iff $\vartheta \mathbin{\dot{\&}_i} \hat{I}(B) \preceq I(A)$.

3. An interpretation $I \in \mathcal{I}_{\mathfrak{L}}$ satisfies $\langle A \nwarrow_i B, \vartheta \rangle$ iff $\hat{I}(B) \mathbin{\dot{\&}_i} \vartheta \preceq I(A)$.

4. An interpretation $I \in \mathcal{I}_{\mathfrak{L}}$ is a model *of a program $\mathbb{P}$ iff all weighted rules in $\mathbb{P}$ are satisfied by I.*

5. An element $\lambda \in L$ is a correct answer *for a query $?A$ and a program $\mathbb{P}$ if for any interpretation $I \in \mathcal{I}_{\mathfrak{L}}$ which is a model of $\mathbb{P}$ we have $\lambda \preceq I(A)$.*

Note that, for instance, $\perp$ is always a correct answer for any query and program.

The core of the Apt-van Emden-Kowalski semantics, the immediate consequences operator, can be easily generalised to biresiduated multi-adjoint logic programs.

Definition 9. *Let $\mathbb{P}$ be a program, the* immediate consequences operator $T_{\mathbb{P}}$ *maps interpretations to interpretations, and for an interpretation I and propositional variable A, $T_{\mathbb{P}}(I)(A)$ is defined as the supremum of the following set*

$$\{\vartheta \mathbin{\dot{\&}_i} \hat{I}(B) \mid \langle A \swarrow^i B, \vartheta \rangle \in \mathbb{P}\} \cup \{\hat{I}(B) \mathbin{\dot{\&}_i} \vartheta \mid \langle A \nwarrow_i B, \vartheta \rangle \in \mathbb{P}\} \cup \{\vartheta \mid \langle A, \vartheta \rangle \in \mathbb{P}\}$$

As usual, the semantics of a biresiduated multi-adjoint logic program is characterised by the post-fixpoints of $T_{\mathbb{P}}$; that is:

Theorem 1. *An interpretation I of $\mathcal{I}_{\mathfrak{L}}$ is a model of a biresiduated multi-adjoint logic program $\mathbb{P}$ iff $T_{\mathbb{P}}(I) \sqsubseteq I$.*

Note that the result is still true even without any further assumptions on conjunctors, which definitely need not be either commutative or associative or satisfy any boundary condition.

The monotonicity of the operator $T_{\mathbb{P}}$ for biresiduated multi-adjoint logic programming follows from the monotonicity of all the involved operators.

As a result of $T_{\mathbb{P}}$ being monotone, the semantics of a program $\mathbb{P}$ is given by its least model which, as shown by Knaster-Tarski's theorem, is exactly the least fixpoint of $T_{\mathbb{P}}$, which can be obtained by transfinitely iterating $T_{\mathbb{P}}$ from the least interpretation $\triangle$.

5   Related Work and Concluding Remarks

To the best of our knowledge, there is not much work done using biresidua in the sense considered in this paper. Recently, in [11] a study of the representability of biresiduated algebras was presented. This type of algebras were introduced in a purely algebraic context, and were studied for instance in [1] and in [3] in the framework of substructural logics. For instance, in [10] a structure of biresiduated algebra is defined together with a corresponding logical system regarding the use of fuzzy sets in the representation of multicriteria decision problems. On a different basis, Morsi [9] developed an axiom system based on a biresiduation construction and the completeness and soundness theorems were proved.

We have presented analytical evidence of reasonable non-commutative conjunctors which lead to the consideration of two biresiduated implications. Some properties have been obtained for these conjunctors and, finally, an application to the development of an extended logic programming paradigm has been presented, together with its fixpoint semantics. The introduction of a procedural semantics for the framework, together with the study of existence of a completeness theorem for the given semantics is on-going.

Although the central topics of this paper are mainly at the theoretical level, some practical applications are envisaged for the obtained results, such as the development of a generalized multiple-valued resolution. In a generalized context it is not possible to deal with Horn clauses and refutation, mainly due to the fact that $A \wedge \neg A$ can have strictly positive truth-value, but also to the fact that material implication (the truth value function of $\neg A \vee B$) has not commutative adjoint conjunctor. As our approach does not require adjoint conjunctors to be commutative, it would allow the development of a sound and complete graded resolution.

References

1. W. J. Blok and S. B. la Falce. Komori identities in algebraic logic. *Reports on Mathematical Logic*, 34:79–106, 2001.
2. C.V. Damásio and L. Moniz Pereira. Monotonic and residuated logic programs. In *Symbolic and Quantitative Approaches to Reasoning with Uncertainty, ECSQARU'01*, pages 748–759. Lect. Notes in Artificial Intelligence, 2143, 2001.
3. J. M. Dunn. Partial gaggles applied to logics with restricted structural rules. In K. Došen and P. Schroeder-Heister, editors, *Substructural Logics*, Studies in Logic and Computation, pages 63–108. Oxford University Press, 1993.
4. S. Gottwald. *Fuzzy Sets and Fuzzy Logic*. Vieweg, 1993.
5. P. Hájek. *Metamathematics of Fuzzy Logic*. Trends in Logic. Kluwer Academic, 1998.
6. E.P. Klement, R. Mesiar, and E. Pap. *Triangular norms*. Kluwer academic, 2000.
7. J. Medina, M. Ojeda-Aciego, and P. Vojtáš. Multi-adjoint logic programming with continuous semantics. In *Logic Programming and Non-Monotonic Reasoning, LPNMR'01*, pages 351–364. Lect. Notes in Artificial Intelligence 2173, 2001.
8. R. Mesiar and V. Novak. Operations fitting triangular-norm-based biresiduation. *Fuzzy Sets and Systems*, 104(1):77–84, 1999.
9. N.N. Morsi. Propositional calculus under adjointness. *Fuzzy Sets and Systems*, 132:91–106, 2002.
10. M. Sularia. A logical system for multicriteria decision analysis. *Studies in Informatics and Control*, 7(3), 1998.
11. C. J. van Alten. Representable biresiduated lattices. *Journal of Algebra*, 247:672–691, 2002.
12. P. Vojtáš. Fuzzy logic programming. *Fuzzy sets and systems*, 124(3):361–370, 2001.

Using the Geometrical Distribution
of Prototypes for Training Set Condensing⋆

María Teresa Lozano, José Salvador Sánchez, and Filiberto Pla

Dept. Lenguajes y Sistemas Informáticos, Universitat Jaume I
Campus Riu Sec, 12071 Castellón, Spain
{lozano,sanchez,pla}@uji.es

Abstract. In this paper, some new approaches to training set size reduction are presented. These schemes basically consist of defining a small
number of prototypes that represent all the original instances. Although
the ultimate aim of the algorithms proposed here is to obtain a strongly
reduced training set, the performance is empirically evaluated over nine
real datasets by comparing the reduction rate and the classification accuracy with those of other condensing techniques.

1 Introduction

Currently, in many domains (e.g., in multispectral images, text categorisation,
and retrieval of multimedia databases) the size of the datasets is so extremely
large that real-time systems cannot afford the time and storage requirements to
process them. Under these conditions, classifying, understanding or compressing
the available information can become a very problematic task. This problem is
specially dramatic in the case of using some distance-based learning algorithm,
such as the Nearest Neighbour (NN) rule [7]. The basic NN scheme must search
through all the available training instances (large memory requirements) to classify a new input sample (slow during classification). On the other hand, since
the NN rule stores every prototype in the training set (TS), noisy instances are
stored as well, which can considerably degrade the classification accuracy.

Among the many proposals to tackle this problem, a traditional method consists of removing some of the training prototypes. In the Pattern Recognition
literature, those methods leading to reduce the TS size are generally referred
to as *prototype selection* [9]. Two different families of prototype selection methods can be defined. First, the *editing* approaches eliminate erroneously labelled
prototypes from the original TS and "clean" possible overlapping among regions
from different classes. Second, the *condensing* algorithms aim at selecting a small
subset of prototypes without a significant degradation of classification accuracy.

Wilson introduced the first editing method [15]. Briefly, it consists of using
the k-NN rule to estimate the class of each prototype in the TS, and removing

---

⋆ This work has been supported by grants TIC2003-08496-C04-03 and CPI2001-2956-
C02-02 from CICYT MCT and projects IST-2001-37306 from the European Union
and P1-1B2002-07 from *Fundació Caixa Castelló-Bancaixa*.

R. Conejo et al. (Eds.): CAEPIA-TTIA 2003, LNAI 3040, pp. 618–627, 2004.

those whose class label does not agree with that of the majority of its k-NN. This algorithm tries to eliminate mislabelled prototypes from the TS as well as those close to the decision boundaries. Subsequently, many researchers have addressed the problem of editing by proposing alternative schemes [1, 7, 9, 16].

Within the condensing perspective, the many existing proposals can be categorised into two main groups. First, those schemes that merely select a subset of the original prototypes [1, 8, 10, 13, 14] and second, those that modify them [2, 3, 6]. One problem related with using the original instances is that there may not be any vector located at the precise point that would make the most accurate learning algorithm. Thus, prototypes can be artificially generated to exist exactly where they are needed.

This paper focuses on the problem of appropriately reducing the TS size by selecting a subset of prototypes. The primary aim of the proposal presented in this paper is to obtain a considerable size reduction rate, but without an important decrease in classification accuracy.

The structure of the rest of this paper is as follows. Section 2 briefly reviews a set of TS size reduction techniques. The condensing algorithms proposed here are introduced in Section 3. The databases used and the experiments carried out are described in Section 4. Results are shown and discussed in Section 5. Finally, the main conclusions along with further extensions are depicted in Section 6.

2   Prototype Selection

The problem of prototype selection is primarily related to prototype deletion as irrelevant and harmful prototypes are removed. This is the case, e.g., of Hart's condensing [10], Tomek's condensing [13], proximity graph-based condensing [14] and MCS scheme of Dasarathy [8], in which only critical prototypes are retained. Some other algorithms artificially generate prototypes in locations accurately determined in order to reduce the TS size. Within this category, we can find the algorithms presented by Chang [3] and by Chen and Józwik [6].

Hart's algorithm [10] is based on reducing the set size by eliminating prototypes. It is the earliest attempt at minimising the size set by retaining only a consistent subset. A consistent subset, S, of a TS, T, is a subset that correctly classifies every prototype in T using the 1-NN rule. The minimal consistent subset is the most interesting to minimise the cost of storage and the computing time. Hart's condensing does not guarantee finding the minimal subset.

Tomek's condensing [13] consists of Hart's condensing, adding an appropriate selection strategy. It consists of selecting a subset with the boundary prototypes (the closest to the decision boundaries). Some negative aspects are its computational cost $O(N^3)$ and that the boundary subset chosen is not consistent.

The Voronoi's condensing [14] is the only scheme able to obtain a reduced set that satisfies the consistency criteria with respect to a) the decision boundaries, and b) the TS. Despite this, the Voronoi condensing presents two important problems. First its high computational cost, since the calculation of the Voronoi Diagram associated to the prototypes set is required. And second, it deals with every representation space region in the same way.

In [14] an alternative similar to Voronoi condensing is proposed, with the aim of solving these two important drawbacks. This new alternative is based on two proximity graph models: the Gabriel Graph and the Relative Neighbourhood Graph. The main advantages of this algorithm are that a) it ignores the TS prototypes that maintain the decision boundaries out of the interest region, and b) it reduces the computational cost $(O(dN^2))$. Both condensed sets are not consistent with respect to the decision boundaries and therefore, they are not consistent with respect to the TS either.

Aha et al. [1] presented the incremental learning schemes *IB1-IB4*. In particular, *IB3* addresses the problem of keeping noisy prototypes by retaining only acceptable misclassified cases.

Within the group of condensing proposals that are based on generating new prototypes, Chang's algorithm [3] consists of repeatedly attempting to merge the nearest two existing prototypes into a new single one. Two prototypes p and q are merged only if they are from the same class and, after replacing them with prototype z, the consistency property can be guaranteed.

Chen and Józwik [6] proposed an algorithm which consists of dividing the TS into some subsets using the concept of *diameter of a set* (distance between the two farthest points). It starts by partitioning the TS into two subsets by the middle point between the two farthest cases. The next division is performed for the subset that contains prototypes from different classes. If more than one subset satisfies this condition, then that with the largest diameter is divided. The number of partitions will be equal to the number of instances initially defined. Finally, each resulting subset is replaced by its centroide, which will assume the same class label as the majority of instances in the corresponding subset.

Recently, Ainslie and Sánchez introduced the family of *IRSP* [2], which are based on the idea of Chen's algorithm. The main difference is that by Chen's any subset containing prototypes from different classes could be chosen to be divided. On the contrary, by *IRSP4*, the subset with the highest overlapping degree (ratio of the average distance between prototypes from different classes, and the average distance between instances from the same class) is split. Furthermore, with *IRSP4* the splitting process continues until every subset is homogeneous.

3   New Condensing Algorithms

The geometrical distribution among prototypes in a TS can become even more important than just the distance between them. In this sense, the *surrounding neighbourhood-based rules* [12] try to obtain more suitable information about prototypes in the TS and specially, for those being close to decision boundaries. This can be achieved by taking into account not only the proximity of prototypes to a given input sample but also their *symmetrical distribution* around it.

Chaudhuri [5] proposed a neighbourhood concept, the Nearest Centroide Neighbourhood (NCN), a particular realization of the surrounding neighbourhood. Let p be a given point whose k NCN should be found in a TS, $X = \{x_1, .., x_n\}$. These k neighbours can be searched for by an iterative procedure like the next:

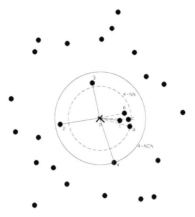

Fig. 1. Example of the NCN concept.

1. The first NCN of p corresponds to its NN, q_1.
2. The i-th NCN, q_i, $i \geq 2$, is such that the centroide of this and previously selected NCN, $q_1, .., q_i$ is the closest to p.

The neighbourhood obtained satisfies some interesting properties that can be used to reduce the TS size: the NCN search method is incremental and the prototypes around a given sample have a geometrical distribution that tends to surround the sample. It is also important to note that in general, the region of influence of the NCN results bigger than that of the NN, as can be seen in Fig. 1.

3.1   The Basic Algorithm

The TS size reduction technique here proposed rests upon the NCN algorithm. NCN search is used as an exploratory tool to bring out how prototypes in the data set are geometrically distributed. The use of the NCN of a given sample can provide local information about what is the shape of the probability class distribution depending on the nature and class of its NCN. The rationale behind it is that prototypes belonging to the same class are located in a neighbouring area and could be replaced by a single representative without significantly affecting the original boundaries. The main reason to use the NCN instead of the NN is to benefit from the aforementioned properties: that the NCN covers a bigger region, and that these neighbours are located in an area of influence around a given sample which is compensated in terms of their geometrical distribution.

The algorithm attempts to replace a group of neighbouring prototypes from the same class by a representative. In order to decide which group of prototypes is to be replaced, the NCN of each prototype p in the TS is computed until reaching a neighbour from a different class than that of p. The prototype with the largest number of neighbours is defined as the representative of its corresponding group, which lies in the area of influence defined by the NCN distribution and consequently, all its members can be now removed from the TS. Another possibility is to replace the group by its centroide. In this case, the reduction of the data set is done by introducing new samples. For each prototype remaining in the set, we update the number of its neighbours if some were previously eliminated as belonging to the group of an already chosen representative.

This is repeated until there is no group of prototypes to be replaced. The basic scheme has been named *MaxNCN*. A further extension consists of iterating the general process until no more prototypes are removed from the TS. The iterative version can be written as follows:

Algorithm 1 *IterativeMaxNCN*

---
  while *eliminated_prototypes* > 0 **do**
    for $i = eachprototype(TS)$ **do**
      $neighbours\_number[i] = 0$
      $neighbour = next\_neighbour(i)$
      while *neighbour.class* == *i.class* **do**
        $neighbours\_vector[i] = Id(neighbour)$
        $neighbours\_number[i] = neighbours\_number[i] + 1$
        $neighbour = next\_neighbour(i)$
      end while
    end for
    while $Max\_neighbours() > 0$ **do**
      $EliminateNeighbours(id\_Max\_neighbours)$
    end while
  end while

Apart from the basic *MaxNCN* and its iterative version, other alternatives have been implemented and tested: *IterativekNeighbours*, *Centroide* and *WeightedCentroide* among others. *IterativekNeighbours* is similar to Algorithm 1. The main difference relies on the number of neighbours allowed to be represented by a prototype: k. One of its main properties is that the limit of neighbours can be selected, depending on the TS size (here k is a percentage of the TS size).

In *Centroide*, the main difference to Algorithm 1 is that instead of using an original prototype as a representative, it computes the respective centroide of the NCN. The rationale behind this is that a new artificial prototype could represent better a neighbourhood because it can be placed in the best location.

WeightedCentroide uses the same idea, but each centroide is calculated weighting each prototype by the number of neighbours that it represents.

3.2   The Consistent Algorithm

Over the basic algorithm described in the previous subsection, we tried to do an important modification. The aim is to obtain a consistent condensed subset. The primary idea is that if the subset is consistent with the TS, a better classification should be obtained. Using the *MaxNCN* algorithm, some prototypes in the decision boundaries are removed because of the condensing order. We try to solve this problem by a new consistent approach. Other alternatives have been implemented. Two of them are presented here. The simplest one consists of applying *MaxNCN* and, after that, estimating the class of each prototype in the TS by NN, using the reduced set obtained. Every prototype misestimated is added to the reduced set. This algorithm has been here named *Consistent*.

Reconsistent is based on the same idea as *Consistent*. In this case, the new prototypes to be added will previously be condensed using as reference the original TS. Algorithmically, it can be written as it is shown in Algorithm 2.

Algorithm 2 *Reconsistent*

---
  for $i = eachprototype(TS)$ **do**
   $neighbours\_number[i] = 0$
   $neighbour = next\_neighbour(i)$
   while $neighbour.class == i.class$ **do**
     $neighbours\_vector[i] = Id(neighbour)$
     $neighbours\_number[i] = neighbours\_number[i] + 1$
     $neighbour = next\_neighbour(i)$
   end while
  end for
  while $Max\_neighbours() > 0$ **do**
   $EliminateNeighbours(id\_Max\_neighbours)$
  end while
  $count = 0$
  for $i = eachprototype(TS)$ **do**
   if $Classify(i)! = i.class$ **then**
     $count = count + 1$
     $incorrect\_class[count] = i$
   end if
  end for
  for $i = eachprototype(incorrect\_class[])$ **do**
   $neighbours\_number\_inc[i] = 0$
   $neighbour\_inc = next\_neighbour\_inc(i)$
   while $neighbour\_inc.class == i.class$ **do**
     $neighbours\_vector\_inc[i] = Id(neighbour\_inc)$
     $neighbours\_number\_inc[i] = neighbours\_number\_inc[i] + 1$
     $neighbour\_inc = next\_neighbour\_inc(i)$
   end while
  end for
  while $Max\_neighbours\_inc() > 0$ **do**
   $EliminateNeighbours\_inc(id\_Max\_neighbours\_inc)$
  end while
  $AddCondensedIncToCondensedTS()$

---

4   Description of Databases and Experiments

Nine real data sets (Table 1) have been taken from the UCI Repository [11] to assess the behaviour of the algorithms introduced in this paper. The experiments

Table 1. Data sets used in the experiments.

Data set	No. classes	No. features	TS size	Test set size
Cancer	2	9	546	137
Pima	2	6	615	153
Glass	6	9	174	40
Heart	2	13	216	54
Liver	2	6	276	69
Vehicle	4	18	678	168
Vowel	11	10	429	99
Wine	3	13	144	34
Phoneme	2	5	4324	1080

have been conducted to compare *MaxNCN*, *IterativeMaxNCN*, *IterativekNeighbours*, *Centroide*, *WeightedCentroide*, *Consistent* and *Reconsistent*, among other algorithms to Chen's scheme, *IRSP4* and Hart's condensing, in terms of both TS size reduction and classification accuracy (using 1-NN rule) for the condensed set.

The algorithms proposed in this paper, as in the case of Chen's, *IRSP4*, *MaxNCN* and *IterativeMaxNCN* need to be applied in practice to overlap-free (no overlapping among different class regions) data sets. Thus, as a general rule and according to previously published results [2, 16], the Wilson's editing has been considered to properly remove possible overlapping between classes. The parameter involved (k) has been obtained in our experiments by performing a five-fold cross-validation experiment using only the TS and computing the average classification accuracies for different values of k and comparing them with the "no editing" option. The best edited set (including the non-edited TS) is thus selected as input for the different condensing schemes.

5 Experimental Results and Discussion

Table 2 reports the 1-NN accuracy results obtained by using the best edited TS and the different condensed sets. Values in brackets correspond to the standard deviation. Analogously, the reduction rates with respect to the edited TS are provided in Table 3. The average values for each method are also included. Several comments can be made from the results in these tables. As expected, classification accuracy strongly depends on the condensed set size. Correspondingly, *IRSP4*, Hart's algorithm, *Consistent* and *Reconsistent* obtain the highest classification accuracy almost without exception for all the data sets, but they also retain more prototypes than Chen's scheme, *MaxNCN* and *IterativeMaxNCN*.

It is important to note that, in terms of reduction rate, *IterativeMaxNCN* is the best. Nevertheless, it also obtains the worst accuracy. On the contrary, *IRSP4* shows the highest accuracy but the lowest reduction rate. Thus, looking for a balance between accuracy and reduction, one can observe that the best options are Hart's, Chen's, the plain *MaxNCN* and the *Reconsistent* approach. In particular, *MaxNCN* provides an average accuracy of 69,52% (only 4 points less

Table 2. Experimental results: 1-NN classification accuracy.

	Edited	Chen	IRSP4	Hart	Iterat.	MaxNCN	Cons.	Recons.
Cancer	95.61	96.78	93,55	94,61	68,60	89,92	94,14	92,39
	(2.48)	(1.25)	(3,70)	(2,94)	(3,42)	(4,61)	(2,64)	(4,36)
Pima	67.32	73.64	72,01	73,31	53,26	67,71	73,05	71,74
	(4.64)	(2.85)	(4,52)	(3,69)	(5,80)	(5,45)	(3,62)	(5,93)
Glass	71.40	67.18	71,46	67,91	57,19	66,65	69,08	69,08
	(3.78)	(3.90)	(3,13)	(4,60)	(9,69)	(6,28)	(3,90)	(3,90)
Heart	58.17	61.93	63,01	62,87	58,16	59,92	63,96	63,59
	(5.93)	(5.22)	(5,11)	(4,27)	(7,26)	(5,53)	(6,87)	(5,98)
Liver	65.79	59.58	63,89	62,40	53,31	60,65	63,23	62,13
	(8.72)	(5.15)	(7,73)	(5,76)	(8,55)	(6,74)	(3,55)	(6,76)
Vehicle	64.41	58.56	63,47	62,17	55,20	59,33	62,76	62,65
	(2.11)	(2,46)	(1,96)	(2,16)	(4,42)	(2,17)	(1,04)	(1,88)
Vowel	97.90	60.16	96,02	90,74	78,63	90,73	94,93	94,73
	(1.23)	(9.27)	(1,77)	(2,30)	(5,18)	(1,78)	(1,63)	(1,53)
Wine	73.05	69.31	69,66	71,71	62,50	60,77	69,05	68,56
	(2.96)	(7.31)	(3,47)	(6,72)	(6,65)	(6,19)	(6,40)	(6,18)
Phoneme	70.26	70.03	71,60	71,04	65,06	70,00	72,17	70,96
	(7.52)	(9.14)	(8,74)	(7,90)	(7,57)	(8,05)	(7,72)	(7,13)
Average	73.77	68.57	73,85	72,97	61.32	69,52	73,60	72,87
	(4.38)	(5.17)	(4,46)	(4,48)	(9,95)	(5,20)	(4,15)	(4,85)

Table 3. Experimental results: set size reduction rate.

	Chen	IRSP4	Hart	Iterat.	MaxNCN	Cons.	Recons.
Cancer	98.79	93,72	93,09	99,11	96,10	86,91	94,09
Pima	90.61	70,03	79,04	95,99	85,35	73,01	80,19
Glass	67.58	32,71	51,33	73,13	62,15	47,43	50,00
Heart	85.18	55,80	67,22	92,53	78,35	64,18	69,59
Liver	82.97	45,41	63,20	91,21	74,83	57,85	65,65
Vehicle	65.79	35,60	45,98	74,85	56,59	40,28	44,71
Vowel	79.64	39,54	75,97	84,23	75,09	72,21	73,11
Wine	86.75	73,13	78,79	89,03	84,83	65,63	79,71
Phoneme	94.51	69,90	87,91	98,16	90,88	83,06	88,26
Average	83.54	57,32	71,39	88,69	78,24	65,62	71,70

than *IRSP4*, which is the best option in accuracy) with an average reduction of 78,24% (approximately 20 points higher than *IRSP4*). Results given by Chen's algorithm are similar to those of the *MaxNCN* procedure in accuracy, but 5 points higher in reduction percentage. The *Reconsistent* approach provides similar results to Hart's algorithm: an average accuracy of 72,87% (only 0,93 less than *IRSP4*) with an average reduction rate of 71,70% (around 14 points higher).

In order to assess the performance of these two competing goals simultaneously, Fig. 2 represents the normalised Euclidean distance between each pair (accuracy, reduction) and the ideal case (1, 1), in such a way that the "best" ap-

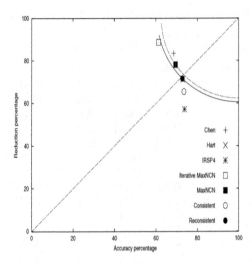

Fig. 2. Averaged accuracy and reduction rates.

proach can be deemed as the one that is nearer (1, 1). This technique is usually referred to as *Data Envelopment Analysis* [4] Among approaches with similar distances to (1, 1), the best ones are those nearer the diagonal, because they get a good balance between accuracy and reduction. Thus, it is possible to see that the proposed *Reconsistent*, along with *MaxNCN*, Hart's and Chen's algorithms represent a good trade-off between accuracy and reduction.

With respect to the other algorithms exposed here, as they are not considered so important as the ones compared until now, they are not drawn in Fig. 2, in order to obtain a more comprehensible representation. Anyway, their results are commented here. *IterativekNeighbours* obtains a good reduction rate but not the best accuracy rate (similar to *IterativeMaxNCN*). Anyway, comparing it to Hart, the positive difference in reduction is bigger than the negative difference in accuracy.

Centroide obtains more or less the same reduction as *IterativekNeighbours*, but its accuracy rate is a little bit higher. *WeightedCentroide* obtains more or less the same reduction rate as *IterativekNeighbours* and *Centroide*, and also a little bit higher accuracy rate than them.

Finally, it is to be noted that several alternatives to the algorithms here introduced have also been analysed, although some of them had a behaviour similar to that of *MaxNCN*. Other alternatives, as for example *MaxNN*, consisting of using the NN instead of the NCN, have a performance systematically worst.

Many algorithms have been tested. In Fig. 2 an imaginary curve formed by the results for some of them can be observed. It seems that when the classification accuracy increases, the reduction percentage decreases; and when the reduction percentage increases, the classification accuracy decreases. It makes sense because there should be some limit to the reduction. That is, a set can not be reduced as much as we want without influencing the classification accuracy.

6   Concluding Remarks

In this paper, some new approaches to TS size reduction have been introduced. These algorithms primarily consist of replacing a group of neighbouring prototypes that belong to a same class by a single representative. This group of prototypes is built by using the NCN, instead of the NN, of a given sample because in general, those cover a bigger region.

From the experiments carried out, it seems that *Reconsistent* and *MaxNCN* provide a well balanced trade-off between accuracy and TS size reduction rate.

References

1. D.W. Aha, D. Kibler, and M.K. Albert. Instance-based learning algorithms. *Machine Learning*, 6(1):37–66, 1991.
2. M.C. Ainslie and J.S. Sánchez. Space partitioning for instance reduction in lazy learning algorithms. In *2nd Workshop on Integration and Collaboration Aspects of Data Mining, Decision Support and Meta-Learning*, pages 13–18, 2002.
3. C.L. Chang. Finding prototypes for nearest neighbor classifiers. *IEEE Trans. on Computers*, 23:1179–1184, 1974.
4. A. Charnes, W. Cooper, and E. Rhodes. Measuring the efficiency of decision making units. *European Journal of Operational Research*, 2:429–444, 1978.
5. B.B. Chaudhuri. A new definition of neighbourhood of a point in multi-dimensional space. *Pattern Recognition Letters*, 17:11–17, 1996.
6. C.H. Chen and A. Józwik. A sample set condensation algorithm for the class sensitive artificial neural network. *Pattern Recognition Letters*, 17:819–823, 1996.
7. B.V. Dasarathy. *Nearest neighbor (NN) norms: NN pattern classification techniques*. IEEE Computer Society Press, Los Alamitos, CA, 1990.
8. B.V. Dasarathy. Minimal consistent subset (MCS) identification for optimal nearest neighbor decision systems design. *IEEE Trans. on Systems, Man, and Cybernetics*, 24:511–517, 1994.
9. P.A. Devijver and J. Kittler. *Pattern Recognition: A Statistical Approach*. Prentice Hall, Englewood Cliffs, NJ, 1982.
10. P. Hart. The condensed nearest neighbor rule. *IEEE Trans. on Information Theory*, 14:505–516, 1968.
11. C.J. Merz and P.M. Murphy. *UCI Repository of Machine Learning Databases*. Dept. of Information and Computer Science, U. of California, Irvine, CA, 1998.
12. J.S. Sánchez, F. Pla, and F.J. Ferri. On the use of neighbourhood-based non-parametric classifiers. *Pattern Recognition Letters*, 18:1179–1186, 1997.
13. I. Tomek. Two modifications of CNN. *IEEE Transactions on Systems, Man and Cybernetics, SMC-6*, pages 769–772, 1976.
14. G.T. Toussaint, B.K. Bhattacharya, and R.S. Poulsen. The application of Voronoi diagrams to nonparametric decision rules. In *Computer Science and Statistics: The Interface*. L. Billard, Elsevier Science, North-Holland, Amsterdam, 1985.
15. D.L. Wilson. Asymptotic properties of nearest neighbor rules using edited data sets. *IEEE Trans. on Systems, Man and Cybernetics*, 2:408–421, 1972.
16. D.R. Wilson and T.R. Martinez. Reduction techniques for instance-based learning algorithms. *Machine Learning*, 38:257–286, 2000.

X-Learn: An Intelligent Educational System Oriented towards the Net

Juan C. Burguillo and Ernesto Vázquez

E.T.S.I.T. Campus de Vigo, Universidad de Vigo, 36200 - Spain
J.C.Burguillo@det.uvigo.es
Phone: +34 986 813869

Abstract. Nowadays, there is a need for smart learning environments that offer personal services with capabilities to learn, reason, have autonomy and be totally dynamic. In this paper, we present X-Learn: a new e-learning environment we have designed to simplify the authoring and visualization of multimedia courses. X-Learn includes several intelligent assistants to help the teacher and the student during the learning process. These intelligent assistants improve the global performance and diminish some of the limitations of current e-learning environments.

1 Introduction

During last decade we have witnessed the success of the World Wide Web as a medium to deliver educational material. From the earlier Web-based educational systems to the present state of the art there has been an important evolution in a very short period of time. This evolution has taken advantage of improvements in the Web-based technology done during the last decade.

Nowadays, there is a need for smart learning environments that offer services to automate many of the time-consuming tasks that a teacher has to manage in a virtual course. On the other hand, students work should be supported and enhanced by the use of innovation techniques and new technologies. Artificial Intelligence techniques have a role to play in this new kind of learning systems. The first Intelligent Tutoring Systems (ITS) appear during the eighties to personalize the learning material to the student. Since that, a long path have been walked and presently, new e-learning systems try to adapt the contents to the students' skills, provide personalized evaluation and are oriented towards the net breaking the barriers of time and space.

This paper presents our current work centred on the environment X-Learn, which take advantage of the feedback gained from the last decade and includes the new paradigm of intelligent agents. X-Learn implements standardised educational notations to provide collaboration and interoperability among resources and tools developed in different institutions. Besides, X-Learn provides student intelligent tutoring and a teacher assistance. Taken all together, we think that the X-Learn environment presented in this paper is a new brick to improve the design of e-learning systems for the near future.

R. Conejo et al. (Eds.): CAEPIA-TTIA 2003, LNAI 3040, pp. 628–637, 2004.

The rest of the paper is organized as follows. Section 2 introduces the paradigm of intelligent educational systems (IES). Section 3 introduces X-Learn, an IES for e-learning we have developed. Section 4 describes the X-Tutor module of X-Learn, which provides intelligent tutoring. Finally, section 5 draws some conclusions.

2 Towards Intelligent Educational Systems

Nowadays, although a long path has been walked and new versions of e-learning environments include easy-to-use Web authoring tools, most of them still offer passive services. As a result, some instructors spend more time teaching and tutoring students in a distance-learning course than teaching the same course in a classroom setting. On the other hand, many tasks from the student point of view, can also be automatically managed by assistants to personalize the learning process: adapting the learning material to student's skills, searching on the Web and providing the teacher updated and accurate information about the student progress.

Therefore, presently there is a need for smart learning environments that offer personal services with capabilities to learn, reason, have autonomy, and be totally dynamic. The possibility to use Artificial Intelligence techniques to provide computer-aided support during the learning process appears from a practical point of view in the eighties, where the first Intelligent Tutoring Systems appear with the intention to adapt and personalize the learning material to the student [12]. Nevertheless, it is in the nineties with the Web apparition [5], the lower computer's cost, the multimedia support [9] and the Java language when arises with strength the paradigm of intelligent agents [15], the personal interfaces [10], the Intelligent Tutoring Systems [11], hypermedia systems [13] and collaborative systems [1][2]. An extended overview of artificial intelligent in education appears in [14].

These new set of Educational Systems are called to adapt the offered services to the multiple differences inherent to a global village audience. They have to be designed bearing in mind: didactical considerations (how to teach), characteristics of the different domains (what to teach) and personalized proposals according to the end user (to whom we teach). These new Intelligent Educational Systems (IES) are tools supporting learning at different levels whose capacity for adaptation qualify them as intelligent. The must be considered as a complementary tool to increase the quality of learning [14].

3 X-Learn: System Architecture

A clear drawback detected in the e-learning arena was the presence of too much heterogeneity among currently available systems. This means that there is no way to reuse the functionality implemented in a particular system by any other because every one of them has their own proprietary solutions. From the content point of view, it is also quite troublesome to embody those pedagogical elements that were thought to be

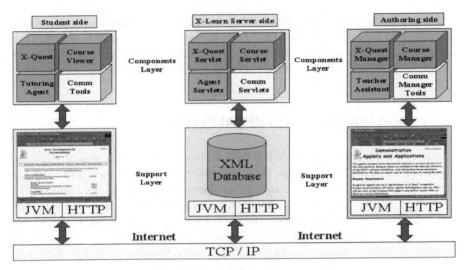

Fig. 1. X-Learn Architecture.

used in a particular system in any other different educational platform. We have designed X-Learn having this in mind and using standardized notations to describe course structure and course contents.

Figure 1 shows the X-Learn system architecture whose main modules follow the client/server model using the Java programming language as the basic building block to provide services independent from any chosen software platform. Course tutors, course designers and students access the different tools of X-Learn using any commercial browser.

From our previous experience developing distance learning environments [2] [4], we realise that it is very complex to maintain and update the changes in an environment with these features. Therefore, when designing the different modules we try to reduce their interactions using clearly specified interfaces in XML and following an engineering approach oriented to obtain a system composed by loosely-coupled components.

In the next paragraphs we describe the different X-Learn components that appear in figure 1. We provide an intuitive description organized around the components and their functions within X-Learn, instead of analysing the different roles (student side, server side and authoring side). In section 4, we will describe how the teacher and the student assistants interact with the rest of the system components and with the human users.

Course Authoring Tool. This tool is used to create the course structure and its contents. The course structure follows the IMS package model, where the courses have a hierarchical tree structure as it is described in [7]. This format simplifies the definition and inclusion of new thematic units inside the course. It is possible to specify different course structures with several difficulty levels and the visualization of each level can be personalized according to the instructor criteria. Every resource or content in a course can be described with a metadata structure using the Learning Object Metadata (LOM) [6] proposed by IEEE LTSC. The LOM format allows to reuse, classify and maintain the didactic resources, facilitating interoperability with other e-learning environments.

The Course Viewer. The learner may use the Course Viewer connecting to the X-Learn Web site. Once a course has been selected, a course tree structure is shown depending on the student skill level, together with the contents included in the selected resource. The learner can freely navigate in the course except when she desires to navigate through contents that have access requirements. In the X-Learn server side, there is a Java servlet, which manages student authentication and sends to its clients the course contents. At the same time, this servlet checks the access requirements. Another task performed by this servlet is to store the student traces and the questionnaire evaluation data in the XML database. Those traces provide information for assessment to the human tutor, the Teacher Assistant and the Student Assistant (the tutoring agent in fig. 1). This information can also be used to generate statistics concerning the most visited resources of the course, those ones that are more difficult to understand, etc.

Questionnaire Tool: X-Quest. We have developed a questionnaire tool named X-Quest [4] having different test types (true/false, multiple choice, multiple answer, fill blank and their combinations) and questionnaires may contain multimedia resources (audio, video, Java programs, Flash animations, etc). This evaluation tool allows the creation and maintenance of questionnaires to provide student evaluation. The resulting XML resources are compliant with the IMS specifications for evaluation purposes. All the information managed by X-Quest is stored in an XML database in the server side and shared with the other modules of X-Learn. Therefore, the Course Authoring Tool, the Course Viewer, the Teacher Assistant and the Student Assistant, may contact with a Java servlet that searches the information requested in the XML database.

General and Communication Tools. X-Learn have been benefited by the experience gained after developing the TeleMeeting system [2] and the Virtual Operating System [3], which managed on-line communications and off-line communications, respectively. Some of the applications designed and included in such systems has been adapted to X-Learn to provide support for groupware applications: general tools (agenda, calculator, ASCII map, etc), on-line communication tools (chat, telebrowsing, etc) and off-line communication tools (a shared file system, a forum and a votation tool).

X-Tutor: The Intelligent Tutoring System. The software assistants implemented in X-Learn are expert systems written in Java and we use JESS (Java Expert System Shell) [8] to analyse the input data and filter the information that is automatically managed. JESS is written in Java and strongly-oriented to support Java programs too, therefore it became an excellent candidate to support the function required.

The interconnection among Java and Jess is very efficient allowing the use of experts systems by Java-coded tools. At the same time, Jess code may access all the Java packages to handle and reason directly over Java objects.

The expert systems written in Jess use a knowledge base obtained by the definition of rules, functions and templates to produce facts as an output from the reasoning engine. The core of a system written in Jess is the inference engine (*jess.Rete*) that processes facts to produce new ones.

We decided to use Jess by several reasons: it is absolutely compatible with Java inheriting its advantages and the knowledge base is incremental (we can add more rules without modifying the code). Besides, the inference engine is rather fast (uses forward chaining) and this approach is the most appropriate within the context to be handled by X-Learn.

Architecturally speaking, we decided to locate the Jess support in a Java servlet on the server side. This makes processing more efficient as: users do not have to install any plugging to handle Jess classes; improves communication among the server and its clients, which can be light applets; and it is not necessary to send the student Jess data through the Internet.

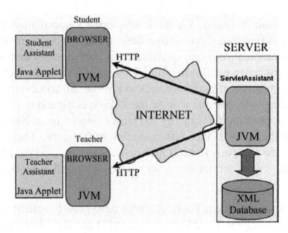

Fig. 2. X-Tutor Architecture.

Figure 2 presents the X-Tutor architecture composed by two applets, one used by the student (Student Assistant) and another one by the teacher (Teacher Assistant). Both applets connect with the Servlet Assistant, which handles their petitions and interact with the X-Learn database.

4   X-Learn Intelligent Assistants

In this section we introduce the interactions among the three system assistants: the Servlet Assistant, the Teacher Assistant and the Student Assistant. In X-Learn there is one Teacher Assistant per course, while there are multiple instances of the Student

Assistant to personalize the learning contents to every student. Besides, every Student Assistant is not always active, since students connect to the system at different times. Therefore, we decided to communicate all system assistants using an off-line scheme through the XML database.

Table 1. The XML definition of the KnowledgeBase contains definitions of templates, rules and functions needed by Jess.

```
<?xml version="1.0" encoding="ISO-8859-1"?>
<!DOCTYPE users SYSTEM "KnowledgeBase.dtd">
<KnowledgeBase>
  <!-- "Resource 'A' is a Course Resource" -->
  <Template>(deftemplate resource-of-course (slot re-
source)) </Template>
  <!-- "Resource 'A' needs Resource B" -->
  <Template>(deftemplate resource-require (slot re-
source) (slot resource-require))</Template>
  <!-- "..." MORE TEMPLATES -->

  <!-- "If Questionnaire 'A' Passed" => "Questionnaire
'A' Completed" -->
  <Rule>(defrule cuestionario-completado (aprobado
(resource ?x)) => (completado ?x) )</Rule>
  <!-- "..." MORE RULES -->

  <Function>(deffunction revision (?z) (call (fetch
list) add (new Consejo (fetch ?z) (new
java.lang.Integer 4) ) ))</Function>
  <Function>(deffunction pendiente (?x ?y) (call (fetch
list) add (new Consejo (fetch ?x) (fetch ?y) )
))</Function>
  <!-- "..." MORE FUNCTIONS -->

</KnowledgeBase>
```

4.1 Defining a Knowledge Base

Now, we describe briefly the knowledge base defined to be used by X-Tutor. This knowledge base uses XML to include the commands needed to describe the templates, the rules and the functions used by the inference engine.

Table 1 shows a partial description of the knowledge base, which contents the definitions needed to execute the inference engine over the set of facts generated by a student following a course. Every definition provides an intuitive syntax with real elements extracted from the real knowledge base we have coded. The real knowledge base contains presently about 40 templates, 20 rules and 10 functions.

4.2 Interaction between X-Tutor and X-Learn: The Servlet Assistant

X-Tutor assistants need information stored within the X-Learn database to generate advices. To get this information X-Tutor uses a set of servlets that appear in figure 3.

The student and the teacher assistants obtain user information from the *XML Users* database using the servlet *ServletUsers*. With the data obtained, X-Tutor can determine the course that a student is following and access to the needed information using a call to *ServletCourses*, which accesses to the course definition files created by the *Authoring Tool*.

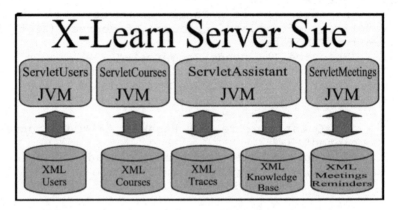

Fig. 3. Interaction among X-Tutor servlets and X-Learn databases.

The *ServletAssistant* is a servlet used to generate recommendations that will be displayed by the Student Assistant or by the Teacher Assistant. The *ServletAssistant* uses the student traces created by the *Course Viewer* and the *Questionnaire Tool* to insert them in the inference engine, starts the engine and, afterwards, obtains the new set of facts (advices) coming from the processing results.

The sequence followed by the Servlet Assistant to generate a recommendation list can be described as:

1. First, it is created an object to handle the inference engine (jess.Rete).
2. Read the rules, the templates and the functions needed to create the knowledge base.
3. Get information from courses and extract the facts produced by the Course Viewer (student traces) and X-Quest (questionnaire marks).
4. Get information from the student profile and filter personal data to obtain personal facts.
5. Execute the inference engine.
6. Get the list of facts (*student recommendations*) produced.
7. Send these recommendations to the Student Assistant applet.

4.3 The Teacher Assistant

The Teacher Assistant may be configured by its owner, the human instructor, in every course. This configuration could include, for instance, the agent's level of autonomy to send overdue notices to students on behalf of the instructor, the language used in the body of the e-mail, the teacher tasks that will be automatically managed by the agent: tracking the students results, participation, interaction, etc. The human instructor must be constantly and dynamically informed of students' participation in a course and assist a discouraged student before he or she drops out.

On the authoring side, the Teacher Assistant provides direct information to the instructor about the information recently obtained from the XML server-side database. When the Teacher Assistant is started, or any remarkable change happens in the XML database it informs the human teacher. Depending on the underlying expert system and the configuration introduced by the teacher, the Teacher Assistant automatically acts in three ways: modifying the XML database, using the Communication Tool Manager to send messages to the students or warning the instructor about new facts.

The action of modifying the XML database is the way to let permanent information to be used by the Student Assistant. The Teacher Assistant uses the Communication Tool Manager (and the servlet *ServletMeetings* of fig. 3) to send off-line messages to the students. Finally, the instructor is informed about data that can not be filtered and should be managed at a human level.

4.4 The Student Assistant

The Student Assistant helps and supervises the student during the learning process. This assistant gets input data from the student traces generated by the course viewer and the evaluation data stored by X-Quest. From this data and the predefined set of rules, the Student Assistant can influence the learner to concentrate on those didactic aspects that need further revision. Figure 4 presents a snapshot of this tool.

The Student Assistant interacts directly with the Teacher Assistant through the XML database storing data that should be processed on the authoring side. Besides, it assists students with specific learning needs, just like a human tutor or a classmate. It has some added features as, for instance, a smart search engine, finding specific resources to solve learning needs for a student.

5 Conclusions

In this paper we have introduced X-Learn: a new educational environment that has been designed to simplify the elaboration of multimedia educational resources and to provide an added value with the use of intelligent assistants. To solve the interoperability problem, X-Learn uses packages proposed by the IMS organization and metadata according to LOM (proposed by the IEEE LTSC). The use of standardized notation clearly enhances its interoperability and allows reusing the contents already designed.

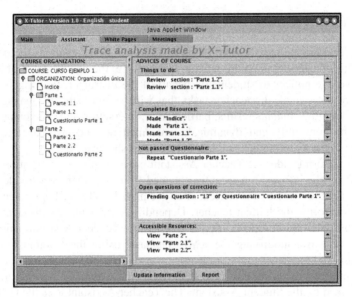

Fig. 4. A snapshot of the Student Assistant.

Furthermore, X-Learn provides a set of intelligent assistants to support both sides of the learning process. With the underlying support provided by JESS, X-Learn provides assistants to support both: the student and the teacher. The teacher can configure and automate many course ordinary tasks. On the other side, the student is continually supervised and oriented to improve the learning effectiveness.

All these features (interoperability, distributed artificial intelligence, authoring, course displaying and questionnaire evaluation) convert X-Learn in an Intelligent Educational System (IES) oriented towards the Internet.

The X-Learn modules described in this paper are fully operative and some of them (X-Quest mainly) have been already tested with students obtaining good results.

As further work, we plan to use all the system modules in real distance learning courses and we are also considering to expand the functionality of the system to provide a constructive and guided approach to solve practical exercises.

Acknowledgements

The first author wants to thank Ignacio Soto Campos for his valuable suggestions and expertise. The authors also want to thank the anonymous reviewers for their helpful comments.

References

1. Barros, B., Verdejo, F. Analysing student interaction processes in order to improve collaboration. The DEGREE approach. Int. Journal of Artificial Intelligence in Education 11, 221–241. (2000)

2. Burguillo J.C., Fernández, M.J., Llamas M. & Anido L. Improving Computer Support for Cooperative Applications over Internet. Lecture Notes on Computer Science, 1749, 305-310 (1999)
3. Burguillo, J.C., Pavón, P., Fernández, M.J. & Llamas, M. A Virtual Operating System for Internet Applications. 1st IFAC Conference on Telematics Applications in Automation and Robotics. Elsevier Publishers. Weingarten, Germany. (2001)
4. Burguillo, J.C, Santos, J.M., Rodríguez, D.A., Buendía, F., Benlloch, J.V. & Rodríguez, J. A Questionnaire-Authoring Tool to Support Computer Based Training through Distance Evaluation. EAEEIE' 01 Annual Conference on Education in Electrical and Information Engineering. May. Nancy. (2001)
5. Dillenbourg, P. Virtual Learning Environments. EUN Conference 2000, Learning in the new millennium. Building new education strategies for schools. (2000)
6. IEEE LTSC http://ltsc.ieee.org/
7. IMS Global Learning Consortium: Content Packaging Information Model (Version 1.1.2). Learning Resource Meta-Data Information Model (Version 1.2.1). Learning Resource Meta-Data XML Binding (Version 1.2.1). Final Specifications. http://www.imsproject.org/
8. JESS. The Java Expert System Shell. http://herzberg.ca.sandia.gov/jess/
9. Lustosa, L. Vers l'integration des Systemes Tutoriaux. Intelligents dans les Hypermedias: une etude bibliogra.que. Journal de la Formation Continue. (1993)
10. Maes, P. Intelligent Software. In Proceedings of Intelligent User Interfaces 1997. Orlando (Florida), USA. (1997)
11. Murray, T. Authoring Intelligent Tutoring Systems: An Analysis of the State of the Art. International Journal of Artificial Intelligence in Education 10 (1), 98-129. (1999)
12. B. Ohlsson, S. Some Principles of Intelligent Tutoring. Instructional Science 14, 293–326. (1986)
13. Stayanov S., Aroyo L., Kommers P. Intelligent Agent Instructional Design Tool for a Hypermedia Design Course. In Artificial Intelligence in Education (AI-ED'99). Lajoie S.P. & Vivet M. (Eds.), 101–108. (1999)
14. Urretavizcaya, M., Fernández, I. Artificial Intelligence and Education: an Overview. Upgrade, 3 (5), 53-58. (2002)
15. Wooldridge, M., Jennings, N. R. Intelligent Agents: Theory and Practice. The Knowledge Engineering Review 10 (2), 115-152. (1995)

A Neuro-fuzzy Decision Model
for Prognosis of Breast Cancer Relapse

José Manuel Jerez Aragonés[1], José Ignacio Peláez Sánchez[1],
J.M. Doña[1], and Enrique Alba[2]

[1] Depto. de Lenguajes y Ciencias de la Computación
Universidad de Málaga
Málaga 29071, España
{jja,jignacio}@lcc.uma.es
[2] Servicio de Oncología, Hospital Clínico Universitario
29071 Málaga, España

Abstract. The prediction of clinical outcome of patients after breast cancer surgery plays an important role in medical tasks like diagnosis and treatment planning. These kinds of estimations are currently performed by clinicians using non-numerical techniques. Artificial neural networks are shown to be a powerful tool for analyse data sets where there are complicated non-linear interactions between the input data and the information to be predicted, and fuzzy logic appears as an useful tool to perform decision making in real life problems. In this paper, we present an hybrid neuro-fuzzy prognosis system for the prediction of patients relapse probability using clinical-pathological data (tumor size, patient age, estrogens receptors, etc.) from the Medical Oncology Service of the Hospital Clinical University of Malaga. Results show the classification accuracy improvement obtained by the proposed model in comparison with an approach based on exclusively on artificial neural networks proposed in our previous work.

1 Introduction

Prediction tasks are among the most interesting areas in which to implement intelligent system. Precisely, prediction is an attempt to accurately forecast the outcome of a specific situation, using as input information obtained from a concrete set of variables that potentially describe the situation.

A problem often faced in clinical medicine is how to reach a conclusion about prognosis of cancer patients when presented with complex clinical and prognostic information, since specialists usually makes decision based on a simple dichotomization of variables into favourable and unfavourable classification [5, 9, 10].

In previous work [8], the decision making process existing when patients with primary breast cancer should receive a certain therapy to remove the primary tumor was analyzed, and a new system approach based on specific topologies of neural networks for different time intervals during the follow-up time of the patients was proposed, in order to make predictions over the patients outcome. The importance of different prognostic factors becoming significant predictors for overall survival was also analyzed. Some of these prognostic factor were discretized by the medical experts (i.e.,

R. Conejo et al. (Eds.): CAEPIA-TTIA 2003, LNAI 3040, pp. 638–645, 2004.
© Springer-Verlag Berlin Heidelberg 2004

[1,2,3] values for the grade of tumor; [1, 2] for estrogens receptors), although the loss of information taken place by this discretizing process could result very significant.

In this sense, fuzzy logic appears as a very appropriate tool for decision making problems in real life. Many of these decision making processes are performed with a lack of knowledge about the possible options to be chosen, as well of the consequences derived from a taken decision. In these cases, a lack of precision can arise implicit in the obtained results. The fuzzy logic [6, 7, 12] as well as the fuzzy sets theory applied to making decision process in group, lead to obtain results according to the human being behaviour and reasoning way [4]. Besides, it incorporates a higher consistence degree to different decision making models.

This works presents a new approach based on a fuzzy-neural networks system to process in an appropriate form these prognostic factors suspects of being significant in the prognosis of breast cancer relapse.

The paper is organized as follows: in section 2, we present a breast cancer overview; in section 3 the experimental material to be used is described; in section 4 we propose the fuzzy-neural networks system; in section 5 the experimental results are analyzed and compared to the previous work, and the final conclusions and future works are described in section 6.

2   Breast Cancer Overview

The most common types of breast cancer are called ductal carcinoma and lobular carcinoma, and for both types the cause is unknown. Recently two genes, BRC1 and BRC2 have been implicated in a certain type of breast cancer, and a number of other predisposing and prognosis factors have been identified including, for example, obesity, early menarche, pregnancies, numbers of estrogens receptors and size of tumor. Breast cancer can occur in men as well in women, but is much more common in women. The risk increases exponentially after age 30. In general, the rate of breast cancer is lower in underdeveloped countries and this rate is higher in more affluent countries.

As we enter the new millennium, treatment modalities exist for many solid tumour types and their use is well established. Nevertheless, an offset against this is the toxicity of some treatments. There is a real risk of mortality associated with treatment, so that it is vital to have the possibility to offer different therapies depending on the patients. In this sense the likelihood that the patient will suffer a recurrence of her disease is very important, so that the risks and expected benefits of specific therapies can be compared.

3   Experimental Data

Data from 1035 patients with breast cancer disease from the Medical Oncology Service of the Hospital Clinical University of Málaga, were collected and recorded during the period 1990-2000. Data corresponding to every patient were structured in 85 fields containing information about post surgical measurements, particulars and type of treatment. Ten independent input variables, selected from all these data fields, and essentially pointed out by medical experts as suspects of being risk factors for breast cancer prognosis, were incorporated to the model. All variables and their units or modes of representation, mean, standard deviation and median are shown in Table 1, where survival status appears as supervisory variable to be predicted by the prognosis system.

Table 1. Summary of patient data: range, mean, standard deviation and median.

Prognostic variables (Mnemonic)	Range	Mean	S.D.	Median
1 Age (Ag)	24-95	55,62	12,80	56
2 Menarchy age (Ma)	9-20	12,81	1,67	13
3 Menopause age (Mg)	27-70	48,74	4,99	50
4 First pregnancy age (Fp)	15-43	25,08	4,58	25
5 # Axillary lymph nodes (An)	0-34	2,42	4,16	1
6 Grade (Gr)	1, 2, 3	2,21	0,63	NA
7 Tumor size (Ts)	2-180	30,48	20,30	25
8 # Pregnancies (Pn)	0-18	2,98	2,11	3
9 Estrogen receptors (Er)	1, 2	1,53	0,49	NA
10 Progesteron receptors (Pr)	1, 2	1,39	0,48	NA
Supervisory variable				
Survival Status	0 (non-relapse) 1 (relapse)	0,21	0,41	NA

The prognostic factors in early breast cancer with adjuvant therapy after surgery, are time-dependent, that is, the strength of prognostic factor is not the same for different time intervals. Besides, the existence of a "peak" of recurrence in the distribution of relapse probability [1] demonstrates that the recurrence probability is not the same over time. In order to select the most important prognostic factors for predicting overall survival, the approach presented in this work trains neural networks with different set of input data for each time interval under study (Table 2).

A previous analysis of each variable characteristic with medical experts showed us that some of them fit well into fuzzy set conditions. Three prognostic factors were fuzzyfy: tumor size, number of axillary lymph nodes, and grade of tumor. This process gives the possibility of estimating, for example, whether the tumor size is 'small', 'median', 'large', ... depending on the interval time.

Table 2. Selected attributes (prognostic factors) and number of patients for every patients follow-up time intervals (in months).

Time interval	Selected attributes	# Patients
I_1 (0 – 10)	Ag, Ma, Fp, An, Ts, Pn	845
I_2 (10 – 20)	Ag, Ma, Fp, An, Ts, Mg, Gr	741
I_3 (20 – 30)	Ag, An, Ts, Gr	681
I_4 (30 – 40)	Ag, An, Ts, Gr, Er	600
I_5 (40 – 50)	Ag, Ma, Fp, An, Ts, Mg, Gr	520

4 The Proposed Model

A solution scheme is proposed based on specific topologies of neural networks combined with a fuzzy system for different time intervals during the follow-up time of the patients and a threshold unit to implement the decision making process (Figure 1). Selected inputs to the network are pre-processed by the fuzzy system and then computed by a back-propagation artificial neural network.

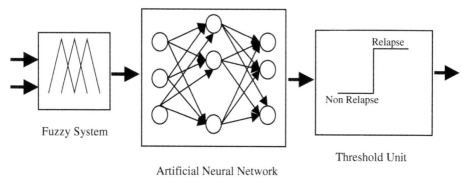

Fuzzy System

Artificial Neural Network

Threshold Unit

Fig. 1. The prognosis system.

4.1 Fuzzy System

The variables fuzzily process (size of tumor, grade of tumor and number of axillary nodes) implies the selection of data corresponding to every time interval under study. The goal is to perform an specific study of the variables ranges, developing a filter to eliminate the patients whose specified parameters in every corresponding time interval are not correct.

The patients just belonging to the time interval under study are chosen to construct the fuzzy sets, and their limits are estimated by means of intervals, taking into account that do not exist fixed bounds for them. These intervals were carried out using different percentiles that depend on the population. To notice, that the finishes percentile is 99, because, if it is 100, the finishes function takes the value 1 in the maximum interval.

These intervals will be using different percentile, which depend of the populations. Note, that the last percentile is 99, because if it is 100 the last function takes a value equal 1 in the maximum interval, and this occurrence can be casual.

To establish the membership function of the fuzzy sets, we calculate the mode of the interval in study to establish the interval with maximum ownership (membership function is equal to 1).

Triangular or trapezoidal ownership functions have not been used. Although they present a great simplicity and a good computational efficiency, they are composed of segments of right lines that are not soft in the points of the vertexes specified by the parameters. A valid option *is* the bell functions, which have a soft representation, but they don't allow specifying asymmetric ownership functions. For it is necessary the use of sigmoid functions which present the advantages of the type bell and, at the same time, the flexibility and simplicity of the triangular and trapezoidal functions.

We have implemented the extreme values for the first set with a zmf function and the one finishes with a 'smf' function, in this way the values that can be occur in some cases will belong at the first or the last group. The rest of functions is 'pimf', we use these functions because they are flexible and easy of using. Figure 2 shows the histogram corresponding to one of the fuzzy variables (size of tumor) for an specific time interval before the fuzzyfy process, and figure 3 presents the fuzzy sets resulting after the fuzzyfy process for the same interval time.

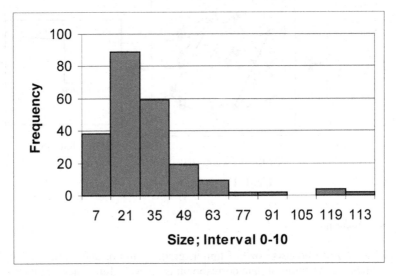

Fig. 2. Histogram of the variable 'size' of the tumor in the interval 0-10.

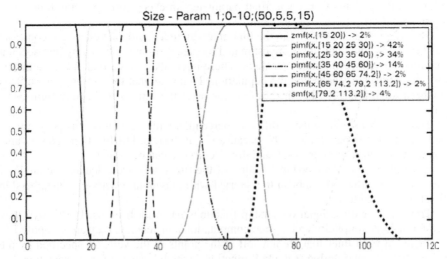

Fig. 3. Fuzzy sets resultants after the fuzzyfy process of the variable 'Size' of the tumor in the interval 0-10.

4.2 The Neural Networks System

The neural networks system computes attributes sets from fuzzy system giving a value corresponding to the posterior probability of relapse for the patient in study. The networks topology employed is multilayer perceptron with the Levenberg-Marquardt learning algorithm. This algorithm is more potent than the method of descent of the gradient although it requires more memory [11]. A function of minimum cost is used that provides a bigger guarantee of convergence of the network.

The input layer has so many elements as attributes suspicions of being risk factors for each time interval. The middle or hidden layers have 12, 17, 8, 11 and 16 elements respectively with hyperbolic tangent transfer functions. The output layers have one logistic element corresponding to the single dependent variable. The outputs elements predict the relapse probability by means of its numerical output (ranged from 0 to 1).

A crucial aspect of doing learning and prediction analysis with a neural network system is to split the database into two independent sets which will be used to train the neural network and to validate its predictive performance. During training the data vectors of the training set are repetitively presented to the network, that attempts to generate a 1 at the output unit when the survival status of the patient is relapse, and a 0 when the status is non-relapse.

In order to evaluate the proposed model, a standard technique of stratified 10-fold cross-validation was used [9]. This technique divides the patient data set into ten sets of approximately equal size and equal distribution of recurrent and non-recurrent patients. In each experiment a single set is used for testing the model that has been developed from the remaining nine sets. The evaluation statistics for each method is then assessed as an average of ten experiments.

4.3 Threshold Unit

The threshold unit outputs a class for survival status. In order to obtain an appropriate classification accuracy, which is expressed in percent of patients in the test set that were classified correctly, a cut-off prediction between 0 and 1 had to be chosen before any output of the network (ranged from 0 to 1) could be interpreted as a prediction of breast cancer relapse.

5 Results

In order to evaluate the correct classification probability of the proposed system and to establish a comparison with those results obtained in the previous work, the system was trained with and without pre-processing the input variables through the fuzzy subsystem, and the results, together with the a priori classification probability (PCP), have been simultaneously plotted in a diagram bar (Fig. 4).

The priori probabilities are the same ones for the two systems, due to we are working with the same patients in the two cases, the probability that a patient relapse in a given interval will be the same because it doesn't turn modified the field relapse in the fuzzy process.

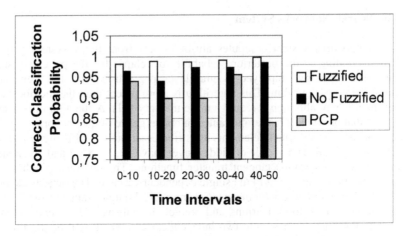

Fig. 4. Classification probability.

Two important results are observed in figure 4: (1) the proposed system always improves the non-fuzzy system. It is important to point out the difficult of this, given so high values of PCP for each time interval, and (2) this improvement is greater in the most critical interval during the follow-up time of the patients (interval I_2).

6 Conclusions and Future Work

Different topologies of feed-forward fuzzy-neural networks were used to obtain an optimal prediction accuracy for correct classification probability of patients relapse after breast cancer surgery using clinical-pathological data. During the study it has been proven how the importance of the prognosis factors varies in function of the time and of the used system.

The final prognosis system, based on a fuzzy block for pre-processing the system inputs, makes predictions about the relapse probability at different times of follow-up with a very little error ratio. The most important goal was to eliminated the subjective process performed by experts in the discretizing of three variables suspected of being risk factors for breast cancer prognosis. Other variables could not be fuzzyfy because of the lack of information to perform the discretizing process.

The obtained results encourage us to continue this line of research analyzing different possibilities to fuzzyfy other prognostic variables (re, rp) studying their relationships with other data presented in the patients database. Also new techniques, different to mode, for constructing the fuzzy sets could be proposed. On the other hand, we are actually working in designing a cooperative neuro-fuzzy system where the neural networks system and the fuzzy system interact between them in order to improve the prognosis system classification accuracy.

Acknowledgements

This work is supported by the projects TIC2002-04242-C03-02.

References

1. Alba E. 1999. Estructura del patrón de recurrencia en el cáncer de mama operable (CMO) tras el tratamiento primario. Implicaciones acerca del conocimiento de la historia natural de la enfermedad. 7° Congreso de la Sociedad Española de Oncología Médica, Sitges, Barcelona Abril 1999.
2. Carlos Andrés Peña Reyes, Moshe Sipper. A fuzzy genetic approach to breat cancer diagnosis. Artificial Intelligence in Medicine: 131-155, 1999.
3. Cox DR 1972. Regression Models and life tables. JR Stat Soc [B] 34:187 – 220, 1972.
4. Delgado D. Verdegay J. L. Vila M. A. 1993. On aggregation operations of lingüistic labels, Internat. J. Intelligent Systems 8. 351-370.
5. Duda RO, Hart PE. 1973. Pattern classification and scene analysis. New York. John Wiley and Sons, 1973.
6. Fodor J. and Roubens M. 1994. Fuzzy Preference Modelling and Multicriteria Decision Support. Kluwer Academic Publisher. Dordrecht.
7. Friedrich Steimann. On the use and usefulness of fuzzy sets in medical AI. Artificial Inteligence in medicine: 131-137, 2000.
8. Jerez, J.M., Gómez, J.A., Muñoz, J., Alba, E. A model for prognosis of early breast cancer. In Problems in Applied Mathematics and Computational Intelligence. ISBN: 960-8052-30-0, pp.165-170, 2001.
9. Kaplan SA, Meier, P 1958. Nonparametric estimation from incomplete observations. J. Am Stat Assoc, 53, 457 – 481, 1958.
10. McGuire W.L., Tandom A.T., Allred D.C., Chamnes G.C., Clark G.M., How to use prognostic factors in axillary node-negative breast cancer patients. J Natl Cancer Inst 82:1006-1015, 1990.
11. Patterson, D.W. Artificial Neural Network, Theory and Applications, Prentice Hall, 1996.
12. Peláez J.I. Doña J.M. MajorityAdditive-Ordered Weighting Averaging: A New Neat Ordered Weighting Averaging Operators Based on the Majority Process. International Journal of Intelligent Systems. Vol 18, 469-481. 2003.
13. White H. Learning in artificial neuronal network: a statistical approach. Neural computation 1: 425–464, 1989.

An Interactive Train Scheduling Tool for Solving and Plotting Running Maps*

Federico Barber[1], Miguel A. Salido[2], Laura Paola Ingolotti[1],
Monserrat Abril[1], Antonio Luis Lova[3], and María Pilar Tormos[3]

[1] DSIC, Universidad Politécnica de Valencia, Spain
{fbarber,lingolotti,mabril}@dsic.upv.es
[2] DCCIA, Universidad de Alicante, Spain msalido@dsic.upv.es
[3] DEIOAC, Universidad Politécnica de Valencia, Spain
{allova,ptormos}@eio.upv.es

Abstract. We present a tool for solving and plotting train schedules which has been developed in collaboration with the National Network of Spanish Railways (RENFE). This tool transforms railway problems into formal mathematical models that can be solved and then plots the best possible solution available. Due to the complexity of problems of this kind, the use of preprocessing steps and heuristics become necessary. The results are plotted and interactively filtered by the human user.

1 Introduction

Over the last few years, railway traffic have increased considerably, which has created the need to optimize the use of railway infrastructures. This is, however, a hard and difficult task. Thanks to developments in computer science and advances in the fields of optimization and intelligent resource management, railway managers can optimize the use of available infrastructures and obtain useful conclusions about their topology.

The overall goal of a long-term collaboration between our group at the Polytechnic University of Valencia (UPV) and the National Network of Spanish Railways (RENFE) is to offer assistance to help in the planning of train scheduling, to obtain conclusions about the maximum capacity of the network, to identify bottlenecks, to determine the consequences of changes, to provide support in the resolution of incidents, to provide alternative planning and real traffic control, etc. Besides of mathematical processes, a high level of interaction with railway experts is required to be able to take advantage of their experience.

Different models and mathematical formulations for train scheduling have been created by researchers [1–6], [8–10], etc. Several European companies are also working on similar systems. These systems include complex stations, rescheduling due to incidents, rail network capacities, etc. These are complex problems for which work in network topology and heuristic-dependent models can offer adequate solutions.

---

* This work has been supported by a join contract RENFE-UC/UPV and a visiting research fellow (Miguel A. Salido) from the Polytechnic University of Valencia, Spain.

In this paper, we describe a specific tool for solving and plotting optimized railway running maps. A running map contains information regarding the topology of the railways (stations, tracks, distances between stations, traffic control features, etc.) and the schedules of the trains that use this topology (arrival and departure times of trains at each station, frequency, stops, junctions, crossing, overtaking, etc,)(Figure 1). An optimized running map should combine user requirements with the existing constraints (railway infrastructures, user requirements and rules for traffic coordination, etc.). In our system, the railway running map problem is formulated as a Constraint Satisfaction Problem (CSP) to be optimized. Variables are frequencies, arrival and departure times of strains at stations. The parameters of the process are defined using user interfaces and database accesses. The problem formulation is then translated into a formal mathematical model to be solved for optimality by means of mixed integer programming techniques. Due to the dimensions of the problem and the complex nature of the mathematical models, several preprocesses and heuristic criteria are included in order to obtain good solutions in a reasonable time. The user can also modify the obtained timetable so that the system interactively guarantees the fulfillment of problem constraints by detecting whether a constraint or requirement is violated. Several reports can be obtained from the final timetable.

2   Problem Statement

A sample of a running map is shown in Figure 1, where several train crossings can be observed. On the left side of Figure 1, the names of the stations are presented and the vertical line represents the number of tracks between stations (one-way or two-way). The objective of the system is to obtain a correct and optimized running map taking into account: (i) the railway infrastructure topology, (ii) user requirements (parameters of trains to be scheduled), (iii) traffic rules, (iv) previously scheduled traffic on the same railway network, and (v) criteria for optimization.

A railway network is basically composed of stations and one-way or two-way tracks. A dependency can be:

– **Station:** Place for trains to park, stop or pass through. Each station is associated with a unique station identifier. There are two or more tracks in a station where crossings or overtaking can be performed.
– **Halt:** Place for trains to stop, pass through, but not park. Each halt is associated with a unique halt identifier.
– **Junction:** Place where two different tracks fork. There is no stop time.

In Figure 1, horizontal dotted lines represent halts or junctions, while continuous lines represent stations. On a rail network, the user needs to schedule the paths of n trains going in one direction and m trains going in the opposite direction, trains of a given type and at a desired scheduling frequency.

The type of trains to be scheduled determines the time assigned for travel between two locations on the path. The path selected by the user for a train trip

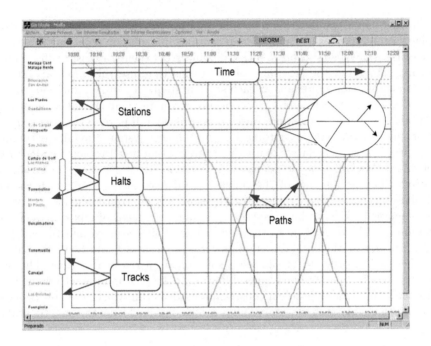

Fig. 1. A sample of a running map

determines which stations are used and the stop time required at each station for commercial purposes. New trains to be scheduled must be coordinated with previously scheduled trains. In order to perform crossing or overtaking in a section with a one-way track, one of the trains should wait in a station. This is called a *technical stop*. One of the trains is detoured from the main track so that the other train can cross or continue (Figure 2).

2.1 Railway Traffic Rules, Topological and Requirements Constraints

A valid running map must satisfy and optimize the set of existing constraints in the problem. Some of the main constraints to be considered are:

1. **Traffic rules** guarantee crossing and overtaking operations. The main rules to take into account are:
   - ***Crossing constraint***: Any two trains (T_i and T_j) going in opposite directions must not simultaneously use the same one-way track (A-B).

     $$T_i Arrives_A < T_j Departures_A \text{ or } T_j Arrives_B < T_i Departures_B$$

     The crossing of two trains can be performed only on two-way tracks and at stations, where one of the two trains has been detoured from the main track (Figure 2). Several crossings are shown in Figure 1.

– **Overtaking constraint**: Any two trains (T_i and T_j) going at different speeds in the same direction can only overtake each other at stations.

$$T_i Departures_A < T_j Departures_A \rightarrow T_i Arrives_B < T_j Arrives_B$$

The train being passed is detoured form the main track so that the faster train can pass the slower one (see Figure 2).

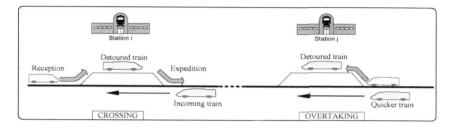

Fig. 2. Constraints related to crossing and overtaking in stations

– **Expedition time constraint**. There exists a given time to put a detoured train back on the main track and exit from a station.
– **Reception time constraint**. There exists a given time to detour a train from the main track so that crossing or overtaking can be performed.
– **Succession time constraint**. Any two trains traveling in the same direction must respect the safety headway between trains (even if speeds are different). This should be maintained at arrival times, departures times and along the entire path. The succession time constrain depends on the features of traffic control in each section between two locations (manual, automatic, etc.)

2. **User requirements**: The main constrains due to user requirements are:
   – **Type and Number of trains** going in each direction to be scheduled and **Travel time** between locations.
   – **Path of trains**: Locations used and **Stop time** for commercial purposed in each direction.
   – **Scheduling frequency**. The frequency requirements of the departure of trains in both directions This constraint is very restrictive, because, when crossing and overtaking are performed, trains must wait for a certain time interval at stations. This interval must be propagated to all trains going in the same direction in order to maintain the established scheduling frequency. The user can require a fixed frequency, a frequency within a minimum and maximum interval, or multiple frequencies.
   – **Time interval** for the departure of the first train going in one direction and the departure of the first train going in the opposite direction.
   – **Maximum slack**. This is the maximum time allowed to perform all the technical operations.

3. **Topological railways infrastructure and type of trains** to be scheduled give rise other constraints to be taken into account. Some of them are:

- Number of **tracks in stations** (to perform technical and/or commercial operations) and the number of tracks between two locations (one-way or two-way). No crossing or overtaking is allowed on a one-way track,
- **Closing times in the locations**, when no technical and /or commercial operations can be performed,
- Added **time for the stopping and starting** process of a train due to an unexpected/unscheduled technical stop.

In accordance with user requirements, the system should obtain the best solutions available so that all the above constraints are satisfied. Several criteria can exist to qualify the optimality of solutions: minimize duration and/or number of technical stops, minimize the total time of train trips (span) of the total schedule, giving priority to certain trains, etc.

2.2   General System Architecture

The general outline of our system is presented in figure 3. It shows several steps, some of which require the direct interaction with the human user to insert requirement parameters, parameterize the constraint solver for optimization, or modify a given schedule. First of all, the user should require the parameters of the railway network and the train type from the central database (Figure 4). This database stores the set of locations, lines, tracks, trains, etc. Normally, this information does not change, but authorized users may desire to change this information. With the data acquired from the database, the system carries out a *preprocessing step*, in which a linear constraint solver for optimization is used to solve a linearized problem in order to complete the formal mathematical model. In the *processing step*, the formal mathematical model is solved by a mixed-integer constraint solver for optimization, returning the running map data. If the mathematical model is not feasible, the user must modify the most restrictive problem parameters. If the running map is consistent, the graphic interface plots the scheduling (Figure 6). Afterwards, the user can graphically interact with the scheduling to modify the arrival or departure times. Each interaction is automatically checked by the constraint checker in order to guarantee the consistency of changes. The user can finally print out the scheduling, to obtain reports with the arrival and departure times of each train in each location, or graphically observe the complete scheduling topology.

3   Optimization Process: Preprocesses and Heuristics

The two main issues in our problem are (i) the specification of the model according to the existing constraints, and (ii) the constraint solver for optimization, which requires mathematical techniques, criteria and heuristics. This problem is more complex than job-shop scheduling [7], [10]. Here, two trains, traveling in opposite directions, as well as two trains traveling in the same direction use tracks between two locations for different durations, and these durations are

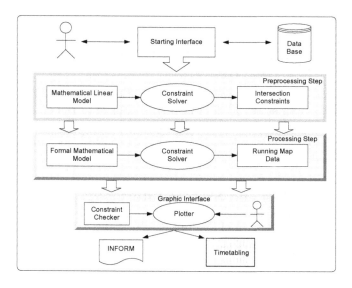

Fig. 3. General scheme of our tool

causally dependent on how the scheduling itself is done (ie: order of tasks), due to the stopping, and starting time for trains in a non-required technical stop, expedition, reception, succession times, etc. Some processes (detour from the main railway) may or may not be required for each train at each location. In our system, the problem is modeled as a CSP, where finite domain variables represent frequency and arrival and departure times of trains of locations. Relations on these variables permit the management of all the constraints due to the user requirements, topological constraints, traffic rules, commercial stops, technical operation, maximum slacks, etc. Hundred of trains, of different types and speeds, in different directions, along paths of dozens of stations have to be coordinated. Thus, many variables, and many and very complex constraints arise. The problem turns into a mixed-integer programming problem, in which thousands of inequalities have to be satisfied and a high number of variables take only integer values. As is well known, this type of model is far more difficult to solve than linear programming models. Depending on the problem size, some pre-processes are performed in the system in order to reduce the number of variables and the complexity of the complete mathematical model:

1. Topological and geometrical processes. Identification of bottlenecks, periodicity of running maps, possible wide-paths for trains, etc.
2. Linear programming approach, in order to identify potential crossing or overtaking. Important decisions in the linear problem are the probabilistic feasibility of stations where crossing or overtaking can be performed, optimal initial departure times to minimize intersections, frequency, etc.

Afterwards, the optimization process is performed in several ways according to the level of required solutions and the problem size:

1. Complete: The process is performed taking into account the entire problem.
2. Incremental: The process performs an incremental coordination of trains.
3. Iterative: The solution is obtained by replicating a pattern found in a previous process of a simpler problem.

In addition, several heuristics and prioritization criteria are applied. These pre-processes as well as the level of heuristics applied in the optimization process can be selected by the user (Figure 5). However, the system can also automatically recommend or select the appropriate choices depending on different parameters and the complexity of the problem.

4   Functionalities and System Interfaces

In this section, we make a brief description about the functionalities and some interfaces of the developed tool:

1. Specify a demand (Fig. 4). Through several interfaces, the user provides data about requirements of a demand: Number and type of trains to be scheduled, path, direction, frequency, commercial stops, time interval for the initial departure of the first train, maximum slacks, previous demands to be considered on the same network, etc.

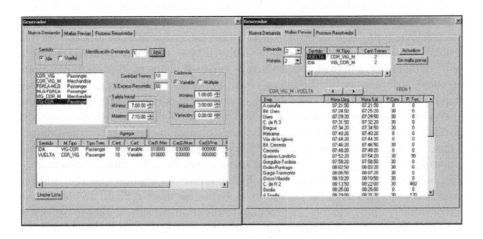

Fig. 4. Some user requirement interfaces

2. Parameterization of optimization process. (see Figure 5 left). The optimization process can be parameterized to bound the search space and/or the execution time, to perform an incremental search, etc. During the solving process, using mathematical optimization packages, its state is displayed (Figure 5 upper right), and when it ends, the information about its final state is shown. (Figure 5 lower right).

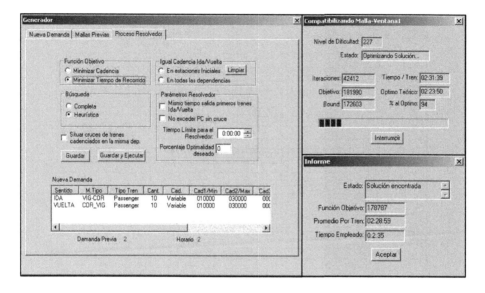

Fig. 5. Some interfaces for the optimization process

5   Evaluation

The application and performance of this system depends on several factors: Railway topology (locations, distances, tracks, etc.), number and type of trains (speeds, starting and stopping times, etc.), frequency ranges, initial departure interval times, maximum slacks, etc. Several running maps are shown in this section. Figure 6 shows the schedule obtained from a requirement for an established frequency of only one type of train, in both directions. Thus, only crossing problems appear in one-way track sections and are performed in adjacent stations. Time slacks for technical operations due to crossing are minimized. The running path shown is optimal for the given parameters.

The system allows the user interactively modify an obtained running map (see Figure 6 lower right). A range between any two stations can be selected, so the user can modify the arrival and departure times between them, the commercial and/or technical stops, etc. Interactively, the system checks these changes to assure constraint fulfillment, so that non-valid running maps that are not in accordance with traffic rules, topological and train constraints are allowed. This feature permits the user to adapt running maps to special circumstances and to try alternative scheduling, etc.

Figure 7 (left) displays a running map of two different types of trains. Thus, two different requirements should be coordinated on the same rail network. Each requirement specifies a given number and type of train, frequency, start times, paths, location stops, etc. More specifically, a new requirement is added to the running map in Figure 6, so that crossing and overtaking problems appear. Therefore, the system allows the user to add new requirements to a previous

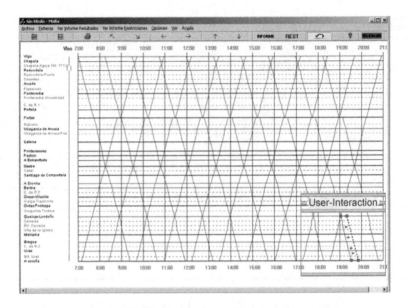

Fig. 6. A timetable with only one cadenced demand

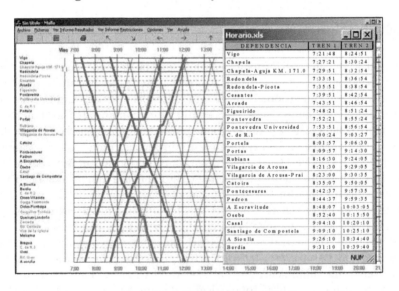

Fig. 7. A timetable with two demands

running map so that this previous running map can be modified or can be kept the same, depending on the user's needs. The different lines in Figure 6 and in Figure 7 correspond to the paths performed by each train, respectively, where each point of a line corresponds to the position of a train at a given time.

6   Conclusions

We have presented the main features of a flexible and useful tool for solving and plotting optimized train schedules in collaboration with the National Network of Spanish Railways (RENFE). No other equivalent system is known from authors. This tool transforms railway problems into formal mathematical models. The NP-Hard complexity of problems of this kind requires that several heuristic criteria and pre-process be parameterized by the user or automatically selected by the application. They are then added to the solving process in order to bound the search space and to obtain an optimal solution.

The main features of the proposed approach are: (i) the access to databases to obtain centralized data about the rail network, trains and required paths, (ii) the model specification for a complex problem, (iii) the various parameterizations, levels and approaches for search processes for optimization, (iv) the graphical interfaces and interactivity with the user. This tool, at a current stage of pre-integration, supposes the application of methodologies of Artificial Intelligence in a problem of great interest and will assist railways managers in optimizing the use of railway infrastructures and will help them in the resolution of complex scheduling problems.

References

1. Bussiecky, M.R., Winter, T., Zimmermann, U.T. *Discrete optimization in public rail transport*, Mathematical Programming 79(3), (1997), 415-444.
2. Bussiecky, M.R., Zimmermann, U.T. *Combinatorial Optimization Methods for Optimal Lines in Real-World Railway Systems*, Technical Report TR-95-03, (1996).
3. Caprara, A., Fischetti, M., Toth, P. *Modeling and Solving the Train Timetabling Problem*, Research Report OR/00/9 DEIS, (2000).
4. Caprara, A., Fischetti, M., Guida, P., Monaci, M., Sacco, G., Toth, P. *Solution of Real-World Train Timetabling Problems*, 34th Annual Hawaii International Conference on System Sciences (HICSS-34) **3** (2001).
5. Chiu, C.K., Chou, C.M., Lee, J.H.M., Leung, H.F., and Leung, Y.W., *A Constraint-Based Interactive Train Rescheduling Tool*, Constraints **7** (2002), 167–198.
6. Kaas, A.H., *Methods to Calculate Capacity of Railways*, Ph. Dissertation (1998).
7. Kreuger, P.; Carlsson, M.; Olsson, J.; Sjoland, T.; Astrom, E. *The TUFF train scheduler: Two duration trip scheduling on multi directional track networks*. Workshop on Tools and Environments for Constraint Logic Programming, (1997).
8. Lindner, T., *Train schedule optimization in public rail transport*, Ph. Dissertation, Technische Universitat Braunschweig, Germany, (2000).
9. Oliveira, E., Smith, B.M., *A Job-Shop Scheduling Model for the Single-Track Railway Scheduling Problem*, Research Report 2000.21, University of Leeds, (2000).
10. Zuidwijk, R.A., Kroon, L.G., *Integer Constraints for Train Series Connections*, Erasmus Research Institute of Management (ERIM), Discussion Paper. (2002).

Application of Evolutionary Computation Techniques to the Optimal Short-Term Scheduling of the Electrical Energy Production

Alicia Troncoso Lora[1], José Cristóbal Riquelme[1], José Luís Martínez Ramos[2], Jesús Manuel Riquelme Santos[2], and Antonio Gómez Expósito[2]

[1] Department of Languages and Systems, University of Sevilla, Spain
{ali,riquelme}@lsi.us.es
[2] Department of Electrical Engineering, University of Sevilla, Spain
{camel,jsantos,age}@us.es

Abstract. In this paper, an evolutionary technique applied to the optimal short-term scheduling (24 hours) of the electric energy production is presented. The equations that define the problem lead to a nonlinear mixed-integer programming problem with a high number of real and integer variables. Consequently, the resolution of the problem based on combinatorial methods is rather complex. The required heuristics, introduced to assure the feasibility of the constraints, are analyzed, along with a brief description of the proposed genetic algorithm. Finally, results from realistic cases based on the Spanish power system are reported, revealing the good performance of the proposed algorithm, taking into account the complexity and dimension of the problem.

Keywords: Genetic algorithms, scheduling, optimization, feasibility.

1 Introduction

The optimal short-term scheduling of the electrical energy production [1] aims at determining which generating units should be online and the corresponding optimal generation of thermal and hydro units along the scheduling period, usually 24 hours, in order to minimize the expected total cost satisfying the forecasted system load. The scheduling task leads to a nonlinear mixed-integer programming problem. Moreover, this problem is coupled in time by the maximum speed that generating units, specially thermal units, are able to change the produced energy (known as *up and down ramps*), and also by the topology of the hydro-electric power plants, with a delay in hours between the water of a reservoir being used and the availability of that water in the reservoirs downstream. A really large number of variables, both real and binary variables, is needed to properly model this problem. Many approaches have been proposed for the resolution of this optimization problem, ranging from *Dynamic Programming* to *Linear Mixed-Integer Programming* or *Lagrangian Relaxation* [2], the latter being the most widely used optimization method in commercial programs. *Genetic Algorithms* (GA) [3, 4], a general-purpose stochastic search method based on the

R. Conejo et al. (Eds.): CAEPIA-TTIA 2003, LNAI 3040, pp. 656–665, 2004.

mechanics of natural selection, have also been successfully applied to the Electrical Energy Scheduling problem since the adaptation is quite straightforward due to the combinatorial nature of this problem. In this paper, a GA applied to the optimal short-term (24 hours) electrical energy production scheduling is presented. The paper is organized as follows: Section 2 presents the equations used to model the scheduling problem, leading to a nonlinear mixed-integer programming problem with a large number of both real and integer variables. Section 3 briefly introduces the proposed GA, and several implementation issues that are crucial to obtain feasible solutions are discussed. Finally, Section 4 reports some results obtained from realistic cases based on the Spanish power system, and the main conclusions of the paper are outlined.

2   Formulation of the Problem

The objective of the scheduling problem is to determine the on/off state and the energy production of thermal and hydro units on each hour of the scheduling period, in order to minimize the total cost of the system satisfying the forecasted hourly demand and the technical constraints of thermal and hydro power plants.

2.1   Objective Function

The total energy production cost of the scheduling period is defined by

$$C_T = \sum_{t=1}^{n_t} \sum_{i=1}^{n_g} [C_i(P_{i,t}) + SU_i \cdot U_{i,t} \cdot (1 - U_{i,t-1}) + SD_i \cdot (1 - U_{i,t}) \cdot U_{i,t-1}] \quad (1)$$

where n_t is the number of hours of the scheduling period, n_g is the number of thermal units, each having a quadratic cost function, $C_i(P_{i,t})$, of the energy production, $P_{i,t}$; SU_i and SD_i are respectively the start-up and shut-down cost of thermal generator i, and $U_{i,t}$ is a binary variable representing the on/off state of the thermal generator i at hour t. It can be observed that the total production cost is a sum of quadratic functions of the energy of each thermal generator if the state of each generator was previously stated by the GA. This is the case of the proposed technique because the on/off states are managed by the GA. Notice that the production cost is only due to the production of thermal generators $P_{i,t}$, i.e., generators that produce energy by burning a fuel or by atomic means. Hydro units provide free-of-charge energy $PH_{h,t}$ that is only subject to the availability of water in the corresponding reservoirs.

2.2   Constraints

The minimization of the objective function is subject to technical constraints, water balance in hydroelectric power plants and the associated reservoirs, and to the system energy demand and reserve balances:

− Maximum and minimum limits on the hourly energy production of the thermal and hydro generators,

$$P_i^m \le P_{i,t} \le P_i^M \qquad i = 1, \dots, n_g \quad t = 1, \dots, n_t \qquad (2)$$
$$PH_h^m \le PH_{h,t} \le PH_h^M \qquad h = 1, \dots, n_h \quad t = 1, \dots, n_t \qquad (3)$$

where n_h is the number of hydro plants, $PH_{h,t}$ is the energy production of hydro plant h at hour t, and P_i^m, P_i^M, PH_h^m and PH_h^M are respectively the limits on the hourly energy production of the thermal unit i and hydro plant h.

The equation (2) cannot be fulfilled when thermal generators are either starting or stopping, starting and stopping periods begin respectively when the corresponding state changes to ON or OFF. In order to avoid this problem, this equation is modified for thermal units that are either being started-up or shut-down,

$$0 \le P_{i,t} \le P_i^M \qquad i = 1, \dots, n_g \quad t = 1, \dots, n_t \qquad (4)$$

Moreover, in order to penalize the power generated by thermal units during periods of shutting-down, energy that is out of the optimal commitment, penalty terms are added to the objective function as follows

$$C_T' = C_T + \sum_{t=1}^{n_t} \sum_{i=1}^{n_g} C_p \cdot P_{i,t} \cdot (1 - U_{i,t}) \qquad (5)$$

− Maximum up and down ramps of thermal units. The thermal units can not increase or decrease the production of energy at consecutive hours by more than a given maximum rate,

$$-RB_i \le P_{i,t} - P_{i,t-1} \le RS_i \qquad i = 1, \dots, n_g \quad t = 1, \dots, n_t \qquad (6)$$

where RS_i y RB_i are respectively the maximum up and down rates of the thermal generator i, usually known as *ramp limits*.
− Limits on the available water. The hydro units use water to generate electrical energy and water is a limited resource. Thus, the energy produced by a hydro unit is limited by the volumen of available water in the associated reservoir. In consequence, reservoir levels are subject to capacity limits,

$$VH_h^m \le VH_{h,t} \le VH_h^M \qquad h = 1, \dots, n_h \quad t = 1, \dots, n_t \qquad (7)$$

where $VH_{h,t}$ is the stored energy of reservoir h at hour t, corresponding to the hydro unit h; VH_h^m and VH_h^M are respectively the minimum and maximum limits on the stored energy imposed by the maximum and minimum possible water level of reservoir h.
− Hydraulic coupling between reservoirs. Time coupling exits due to cascaded reservoirs, since the water used to produce energy in a hydro unit will be

available later to the next hydraulic unit downstream with a certain delay, obviously when the water has arrived to the corresponding reservoir.

$$VH_{h,t} = VH_{h,t-1} - PH_{h,t} + \sum_{n(k)=h} PH_{k,t-d(k)} + W_h \qquad (8)$$

where $d(k)$ is the water delay time in hours between reservoir k and the next reservoir downstream, $n(k)$, that is supposed to be reservoir h, and W_h is the natural inflow of reservoir h.

- The total hourly energy production must be equal the total energy demand at that hour, D_t, which has been previously forecasted.

$$\sum_{i=1}^{n_g} P_{i,t} \cdot U_{i,t} + \sum_{h=1}^{n_h} PH_{h,t} = D_t \qquad t = 1, ..., n_t \qquad (9)$$

- The total energy that can be produced on each hour must exceed the forecasted demand by a specified amount, R_t, i.e., the generating capacity in reserve to be used if an unexpected event such as the failure of a plant or a large error on the forecasted demand happened.

$$\sum_{i=1}^{n_g} P_i^M \cdot U_{i,t} + \sum_{h=1}^{n_h} PH_h^M \geq D_t + R_t \qquad t = 1, ..., n_t \qquad (10)$$

- Minimum up and down times of thermal units. The minimum up time, UT_i, is the minimum number of hours that the unit i must be functioning after starting. Besides, the minimum down time, DT_i, is the minimum number of hours that the unit i must be shut-down after stopping.

$$\sum_{k=0}^{DT_i-1} (1 - U_{i,t+k}) \geq DT_i \quad \text{if unit } i \text{ is shut-down at hour } t \qquad (11)$$

$$\sum_{k=0}^{UT_i-1} U_{i,t+k} \geq UT_i \quad \text{if unit } i \text{ is started at hour } t \qquad (12)$$

Start-up and shut-down costs of realistic cases tend to reduce the number of shut-downs and start-ups to a minimum, making the minimum-time constraints useless in most cases. Moreover, the inclusion of hydraulic generation facilitates the fulfillment of the thermal unit constraints because the hydro units are faster in response and produce energy at no cost, i.e., the hydraulic energy will be strategically distributed among the hours of the scheduling horizon in order to avoid the starting of more thermal units than the strictly required.

As an example, Table 1 shows the number of constraints, binary and continuous variables of the above problem for a test system comprising 49 thermal units, 2 hydro units and the scheduling horizon embracing 24 hours.

Table 1. Dimension of the problem for a test system comprising 49 thermal units, 2 hydro units and 24 hours.

		Number of Variables	
Number of Constraints	Binary	Continuous	
$(2 \cdot n_g + 3 \cdot n_h + 2) \cdot n_t + 2 \cdot n_g$	$n_g \cdot n_t$	$(n_g + 2 \cdot n_h) \cdot n_t$	
2642	1176	1272	

3 The Proposed Genetic Algorithm

As presented in the previous section, the optimal scheduling of the electric energy production is a nonlinear, non-convex, combinatorial, mixed-integer and very large problem. Hence, there is no technique that would always lead to the optimal solution of the problem for realistic cases. In the last years, techniques based on heuristics, dynamic programming, linear mixed-integer programming and lagrangian relaxation have been applied to this particular problem. Techniques based on heuristics rely on simple rules that depends on the knowledge of power plant operators. Constraints of realistic problems are not properly modeled by dynamic programming approaches, and the number of required states increases exponentially, thus dealing to excessive computation times. Linear programming approaches cannot properly model neither the nonlinear objective function nor the nonlinear constraints, and crude approximations are required. Finally, the use of heuristic techniques is required by lagrangian relaxation approaches to calculate feasible solutions, deteriorating the quality of the obtained solutions. Consequently, new methods are still needed to obtain more optimal solutions to realistic problems. In this paper, a GA [5, 6] has been used to solve the scheduling problem due to its ability to deal with nonlinear functions and integer variables.

The proposed GA algorithm is used to compute the optimal on/off states of thermal units, i.e., the binary variables, while the optimal continuous variables, i.e., the hourly energy production of hydro and committed thermal units, are calculated solving a typical quadratic programming problem by a classical optimization algorithm in which the on/off states of thermal units are known.

Convergence characteristics of GA depend on several key implementation issues that are discussed in the rest of this section.

3.1 Codification of the Individuals

Each individual is represented by the on/off states of thermal generators during the scheduling period. Thus, individuals are represented by 0/1 matrices, with columns corresponding to time scheduling intervals and rows associated with thermal units. If element (i, j) is equal to one, the state of thermal unit i during time interval j is on. Similarly, if element (i, j) is equal to zero, the state of thermal unit i during time interval j is off.

3.2 Initial Population

Up and down ramp constraints of thermal units, equation (6), are a key factor in the convergence of the GA: if the initial population is strictly randomly selected, ramp constraints lead to many infeasible individuals in the initial generation, which makes successive generations suffer from poor diversity, and the GA may converge prematurely. To assure that the initial population contains an adequate percentage of feasible individuals, initial on/off schedulings are randomly selected but modified to account for the minimum start-up and shut-down times imposed by ramp constraints. For example, if generator g, with a maximum down ramp equal to 100 MWh, is on at hour 3 producing an energy of 400 MWh, this generator would require 4 hours to shut-down and, consequently, the generator at hours 4, 5 and 6 should be on. The state $U_{g,3}$ is strictly randomly generated but the states for the following hours, $U_{g,4}$, $U_{g,5}$ and $U_{g,6}$, are given by

$$U_{g,3} = 1 \Rightarrow U_{g,4} = U_{g,5} = U_{g,6} = 1 \tag{13}$$

3.3   Fitness Function

The fitness function evaluates the quality of an individual of the population. In this case, the function is the inverse of the total production cost of the individual. The total production cost is obtained solving a quadratic programming problem by using a nonlinear Interior Point method [7–9]. An extra-high-cost fictitious generator is included to satisfy the system demand, equation (9). This fictitious generator generates the necessary energy that the rest of generators cannot produce to satisfy the demand of the customers. A penalty term proportional to the deficit in reserve requirements is added in the cost function aiming at satisfying the reserve constraint. Penalty terms only apply to infeasible individuals, which are consequently eliminated throughout the evolutionary process.

3.4   Selection Operator

To produce a new generation, parents are randomly selected using a tournament selection technique that selects the best individuals for reproduction. The probability of a particular individual being selected is in proportion to its fitness function, taking into account that the total generation cost, including possible penalizations, is being minimized. The individuals chosen to be parents are included in the following generation.

3.5   Crossover Operator

Children are obtained by adding the binary strings that results from random partitions of each row, as shown in Figure 1a. A column-partitioning procedure may also be applied (Figure 1b). This crossover operator is a particular case of the multipoint crossover operator. As rows are associated with the thermal units, the first approach yields the infeasibility of new individuals in terms of minimum up and down times, equations (11) and (12), while the second approach affects to the constraint of the demand (9) and the reserve (10). The crossover probability has been set to one, i.e., two individuals that have been selected to be parents are always combined to obtain a new individual.

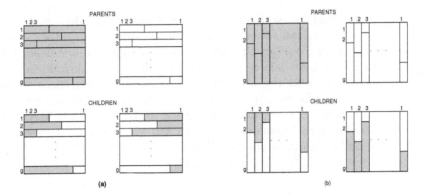

Fig. 1. Crossover Operator: a) random partitions of rows; b) random partitions of columns.

In the final version of the GA, the crossover by rows has been chosen because start-up and shut-down costs of realistic cases, along with the inclusion of hydraulic generation, tend to reduce the number of shut-downs and start-ups to a minimum, making the minimum-time constraints useless in most cases. All rows are always combined to obtain a new individual, though probabilities could have been used to determine which rows should be combined.

3.6 Mutation Operator

Following the crossover process, children are mutated to introduce some new genetic material according to a pre-defined mutation probability. The gene to be mutated is represented by a randomly selected generator and time interval, element (i, j) of the matrix representing a particular individual. The mutation implies changing the state on/off of the generator with some probability.

4   Test Results

The GA algorithm have been applied to several realistic cases based on the Spanish generation system, comprising 49 thermal units and one equivalent hydraulic generator, the scheduling horizon embracing 24 hours. Hourly system demand corresponds to a working day of 1998.

Table 2 shows the main parameters of the implemented GA.

Figure 2 shows the evolution of the fittest individual cost and the average cost of the generation throughout the evolutive process, with and without reserve requirements (figures 2a and 2b respectively). Obviously, reserve requirements lead to higher operating costs, both in the best solution (3152.71 and 3109.51 thousands of Euros, respectively) and in the average (3170.90 and 3132.02 thousands of Euros, respectively).

Figure 3 presents the optimal thermal and hydraulic generation, along with the evolution of the marginal cost during the scheduling period. The marginal

Table 2. Parameters of the proposed GA.

Maximum number of generations	Size of the population	Probability of crossover
5000	100	1
Number of children by reproduction	Number of mutations of the best individual	Probability of mutation
2	2	0.1

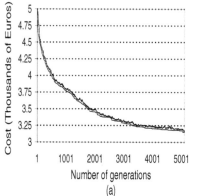

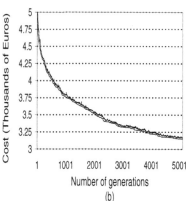

Fig. 2. Evolution of the best individual and average costs: a) reserve requirements considered; b) no reserve requirements considered.

cost represents the increment of cost when the system demand increases in one MWh, i.e., the hourly cost of the energy. Ramp constraints are only included in the second case (Figure 3b). Note that, when ramps are considered, a higher cost, fast-response generator is needed at hour 22 to satisfy a small peak of demand. As expected, the total operating cost is higher when ramps are included (3119.1 and 3109.5 thousands of Euros, respectively).

Figure 4 shows the optimal scheduling of a thermal generator, ignoring its ramp constraints (Figure 4a) and considering them (Figure 4b). Notice that ramps modify the optimal scheduling when the generator is starting and stopping. The penalty term imposed to the objective function when $U_{i,t} = 0$, forces the generator to adjust its output to the least possible value compatible with the ramp constraint (hours 15 and 16). Similar considerations apply when the generation is starting (hours 20 and 21).

Finally, Figure 5 shows the solution provided by the proposed GA applied to the optimal scheduling of 49 thermal units and two cascaded reservoirs with a delay of 10 hours and all the energy initially stored in the upstream reservoir. Note that the downstream reservoir 2 cannot start producing until water released by generator 1 arrives. The total available hydraulic energy cannot be used due to the hydraulic constraint and to the maximum power of generators.

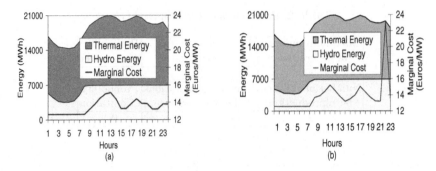

Fig. 3. Optimal thermal and hydraulic generation: a) no ramp constraints considered; b) ramp constraints considered.

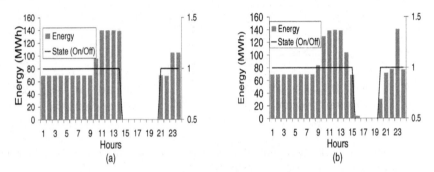

Fig. 4. Optimal scheduling of a thermal generator: a) no ramp constraints considered; b) ramp constraints considered.

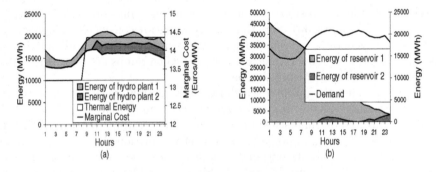

Fig. 5. Optimal thermal and hydraulic generation of a case with two cascaded reservoirs and all energy initially stored in the upstream reservoir.

5   Conclusions

In this paper an evolutionary technique applied to the optimal short-term (24 hours) electric energy production scheduling has been proposed. The equations defining the model of the problem have been presented leading to a nonlinear mixed-integer programming problem with a large number of real and integer variables. Some heuristics have been introduced to assure the feasibility of the solutions obtained by the GA, and key implementation issues have been discussed. Results from realistic cases based on the Spanish power system confirm the good convergence characteristics on the proposed GA.

Further research will be oriented to improve the modeling of realistic cases and to test other possible implementations of the selection, crossover and mutation operators.

Acknowledgments

The authors would like to acknowledge the financial support of the Spanish Ministry of Science and Technology, projects DPI2001-2612 and TIC2001-1143-C03-02, and of the Junta de Andalucía, project ACC-1021-TIC-2002.

References

1. A.J. Wood and B.F. Wollenberg, "Power Generation, Operation and Control", John Wiley & Sons Inc, 1996.
2. A.I. Cohen and V.R. Sherkat, "Optimization-Based Methods for Operations Scheduling", Proceedings of the IEEE, Vol. 75, No. 12, pp. 1574-1591, Decembber 1987.
3. N. Jiménez Redondo, A. Conejo y J. M. Arroyo, "Programación horaria de centrales térmicas mediante Algoritmos Genéticos de Punto Interior". Informática y Automática, Vol. 29-1, pp. 39-52. 1996.
4. S.A. Kazarlis, A.G. Bakirtzis and V. Petridis. "A Genetic algorithm Solution to the Unit Commitment Problem". IEEE Trans. on Power Systems, Vol. 11, No. 1, pp. 83-92. February 1996.
5. D. E. Goldberg. "Genetic Algorithms in Search". Optimization and Machine Learning. Addison-Wesley. Ready. Massachusetts, USA. 1989.
6. Z. Michalewicz "Genetic Algorithms + Data Structures = Evolution Programs". Third Edition, Springer-Verlag, Berlin, Germany. 1996.
7. Y. Wu, A.S. Debs and R.E. Marsten. "An Direct Nonlinear Predictor-Corrector Primal-Dual Interior Point Algorithm for Optimal Power Flow". IEEE Trans. on Power Systems, Vol. 9, pp. 876-883. 1994.
8. X. Yan and V. H. Quintana. "An efficient Predictor-Corrector Interior Point Algorithm for Security-Constrained Economic Dispatch". IEEE Trans. on Power Systems, Vol. 12, pp. 803-810. 1997.
9. J. Medina, V.H. Quintana, A. Conejo and F. Pérez Thoden. "A Comparison of Interior-Point Codes for Medium-Term Hydro-Thermal Coordination". PICA Conference, Columbus, Ohio. 1997.

Integration of a Generic Diagnostic Tool in Virtual Environments for Procedural Training

Alberto Lozano[1], Maite Urretavizcaya[2], Begoña Ferrero[2],
Isabel Fernández de Castro[2], Aritz Ustarroz[1], and Luis Matey[1]

[1] CEIT (Centro de Estudios e Investigaciones Técnicas de Gipuzkoa)
{alozano,austarroz,lmatey}@ceit.es
[2] Dpto. Lenguajes y Sistemas Informáticos, UPV-EHU
{maite,jipfemab,isabelfc}@si.ehu.es

Abstract. In this article we discuss the problems related to the process of integrating a generic diagnostic tool in virtual environments for training. Virtual environments are suitable applications for training procedural tasks; however, they usually lack the tools to provide an educational dimension to the training. In this research we propose the use of DETECTive, a generic diagnostic tool, in order to facilitate the development of virtual environments which maximise the educational value of the training. We consider that usability of the integrated system is a priority issue. Therefore, we seek a balance between the cost of knowledge acquisition and reliability in the diagnostic phase. The virtual reality system educationally improved during this research is VIRTOOL, a virtual learning environment for machine-tool processes.

1 Introduction

Earlier studies [1] show that virtual environments are very useful tools for learning procedural tasks (e.g. use of machine-tools), and there are many examples of commercial products that have been developed [2][3]. One of the advantages of virtual learning is that the problems caused by practical training in real environments – for example, the availability of resources or the risk of accidents – are eliminated. Nevertheless, in general, the main educational contribution of these systems is that the learner can repeat training sessions in the virtual environment in a realistic way. Moreover, multiple sessions do not imply additional costs. However, virtual training environments, in addition to trying to reproduce reality in the most realistic way technically possible, must include added educational functions [4].The educational capacity of the system may be improved by the use of intelligent tutoring techniques.

An Intelligent Tutoring System (ITS) is able to evaluate and guide students in their learning process. Thus, diagnosis of correct and erroneous knowledge acquired by the student becomes a key issue in order to obtain a suitable ITS behaviour. In declarative domains where only theoretical knowledge is assessed [5], the usual tests carried out are *multiple-choice*, *fill-gaps* and similar. On the other hand, in procedural domains, it is necessary to test the student's abilities when they confront with domain tasks. In this case, the correct assessment of the student's actions is entirely dependent on the degree of integration between the virtual environment and the ITS as it determines the quality of information about learner's actions that is used in the diagnosis phase.

R. Conejo et al. (Eds.): CAEPIA-TTIA 2003, LNAI 3040, pp. 666–675, 2004.

The implementation of a powerful diagnostic system able enough to diagnose the correctness of actions performed in a virtual environment is an arduous and complex task requiring a great deal of time. For this reason, this article focuses on the opportunities for adapting a generic diagnostic tool, which is able to provide information to an ITS, to the particular characteristics of a specific virtual reality system. Verifying the feasibility of this objective requires the actual problem to be analysed in two main ways:

- The design of the integrated architecture must allow students to interact with the diagnostic system, via the graphic environment. Appropriate monitoring and communication of the data handled must be the basis which guarantees the integration of the diagnostic module into other training systems.
- The usability of the system in the knowledge acquisition phase must be a priority issue. The intensive work involved in manually defining the domain represented in the virtual environment must be minimised. In addition, the proposed method to achieve it must be independent of the virtual environment.

The following sections 2 and 3 describe the principal characteristics of VIRTOOL and DETECTive, the tools used in this research. In section 4, we consider the problems related to the integration of both systems and the solutions devised. Some other applications are compared with our proposed method in section 5. Finally, in section 6, the conclusions reached are considered.

2   VIRTOOL

Within the framework of VIRTOOL project [6] a virtual learning environment has been designed and developed for machine tool processes (conventional and Computer Numeric Control) using interactive 3D graphics and Virtual Reality techniques. In addition to a simulator, the software integrates tools to help to define and generate new models of machinery and accessory libraries, as well as to prepare new learning resources for students in their learning process. VIRTOOL is the workbench used to facilitate the integration of DETECTive into a virtual environment.

Currently, the software is formed by four applications: Master, Generic, Case Generator and Machine. The first three applications are used in the pre-processing phase while Machine is the simulator that students use for training.

The generation of the virtual environments is performed in the pre-processing phase. Before the student can interact with Machine it is necessary to prepare and compile the data which will determine how the system subsequently behaves. The first step of the pre-processing phase in VIRTOOL involves the generation of new machine tool models (geometry and machine animations, functionality of handles, levers and buttons, configuration of machine parameters, etc.) The tool used in this step is **Master**.

The accessory libraries of the machine tools (previously constructed with Master) are defined in the second step using **Generic**. For example, some accessories are cutting tools, tool holders and assembly tools.

Finally, the teachers define the exercises using **Case Generator**. This application takes the data generated in the previous steps and helps the teacher (instructor) to define the objective and the solving plans of each exercise. The tool minimises the amount of data to be introduced by reusing procedures from its library. It is crucial to find a suitable balance between the quantity of data used and the accuracy in the diagnosis. An application capable of performing very accurate diagnoses, but which requires the definition of an excessive amount of data to achieve the desired function, would not be useful.

Once the pre-processing phase has been concluded, the student performs the assigned tasks on **Machine** (Fig. 1) by means of 2D and 3D methods.

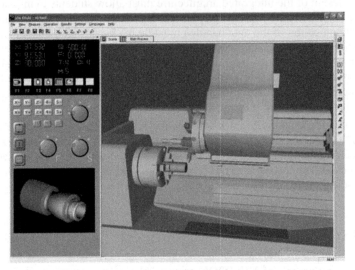

Fig. 1. Interface of Machine.

VIRTOOL includes a diagnostic module inspired in a simplified *plan recognition* technique [7][8]. It has been designed to verify progressively the feasibility of integrating the generic diagnostic tool into a virtual environment. The module checks whether the parameters and the execution order of the procedures performed by the student fit the teacher's definitions. Errors detected during the analysis will produce multimedia feedback, accompanied by didactic resources which may help the student to reach the task goals.

3   DETECTive

DETECTive [9] is a generic diagnostic tool, specially for procedural tasks, provided by a knowledge acquisition tool, KADI [10]. In addition, DETECTive can cooperate with an intelligent tutor. Thus, it has been embedded in IRIS-D [11] (an ITS authoring tool), and the development of ITS-based systems has been facilitated.

The kernel of DETECTive is responsible for the diagnosis and evaluation of the student's actions and analyses each procedure performed on the training environment. In order to accomplish this, the instructor must have previously defined the functional domain using KADI. This knowledge acquisition process has two phases:

- Definition of the performance domain: the instructor must define the set of objects represented in the virtual environment and the actions that students can perform. DETECTive has a meta-conceptual level with the necessary class-specifications to accomplish this,e.g., *concept, object, procedure,* etc.

- Definition of the procedural tasks: The instructor defines situations in which the performance domain components (objects, procedures, ...) have to be used in order to achieve an objective. These situations are represented by means of procedural exercises. The review of the exercise solving steps performed by the students provides information about their knowledge level. To facilitate this assessing process, the instructor must specify the solving knowledge which include most frequent solving plans, order deviations and typical errors.

DETECTive combines three diagnostic techniques (Fig. 2): plan recognition, plan adaptation and domain based diagnosis. Firstly, DETECTive tries to match the steps of the student's answer with the solving plans defined by the teacher in the knowledge acquisition process. When the student's actions do not fit the defined plans, these are adapted taking into account the order deviations. However, it is very likely that the steps performed by the student in the 3D environment do not fit into any of the solving plans (neither predefined by the instructor nor adapted by the system). In this last case, the diagnostic process is completed by analysing the current status of the performance domain, i.e., the current state of the domain objects and procedure preconditions. However, if the domain is complete and well defined, this last technique is better suited to a virtual environment in which the students play with freedom.

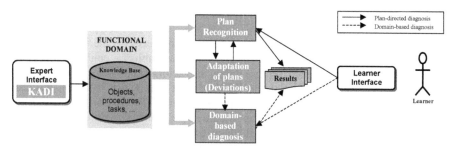

Fig. 2. DETECTive diagnostic process.

In general, when executing a domain based diagnosis, DETECTive cannot guarantee the accuracy of its results since they are not based on a teacher-defined plan and the functional domain may be incomplete. However, as the domain representation of the virtual environment implies implicit constraints, this effect is minimised and so reliable diagnostic results are obtained.

4   Integration Process

This section describes a proposal to integrate DETECTive and VIRTOOL. It offers a generic solution to the communication problem between the virtual environment and DETECTive, which can be adapted to other virtual environments.

Firstly, the problem of integrating DETECTive and VIRTOOL is addressed. Here, we discuss two main subjects: communication between the applications and interpretation of the actions performed in the virtual environment (in order to supply DETECTive with the information to diagnose the students' answers). Secondly, this section shows the basic features of the proposed design to unify the knowledge acquisition tools.

4.1 Integration Problems

The initial premise of the integration process corresponds to data sharing among subsystems: while VIRTOOL must be capable of simulating, for example, a milling machine, DETECTive must understand the data used in this simulation in order to be able to diagnose the actions performed by the student.

The success of the inter-application communication process mainly depends on two initial decisions: **what** is the most appropriate architecture for managing the shared data and **how** the flow of information produced during the training sessions is going to be managed.

The architecture designed to integrate the systems must avoid to limit to the control capabilities of the simulator. For this reason the data required by each system are kept separate and a communications protocol ensures data consistency is maintained. Protocol messages can initialise and monitor the training session, notify the execution of procedures at the simulator and report the results of the diagnostic process. In addition, the communications protocol is responsible for providing flexible communication channels so that DETECTive can transparently interact with the students via the virtual environment.

Another main issue to be solved by the integration process is the interpretation of actions in the virtual environment. It is necessary to establish a connection between natural language terms which represent the instructor's knowledge (the names of procedures used by DETECTive) and the data structures which represent the same concepts visually in the virtual environment (Machine). The reason is because DETECTive assumes that the simulator knows the name of the procedures performed by the student. However, it is often difficult to establish the relationship between the name of a procedure stored in DETECTive knowledge base and the visual event. The difficulty arises from the *procedure grain*, i.e., the quantity of data generated at the user interface that determines the name of a procedure. Intuitively, this difficulty is due to the fact that the instructor is able to describe actions of greater or lesser complexity by using a simple name. For example, the procedure "turn the crank" is a fine-grained procedure because it only comprises rotating the crank object (a very simple procedure to detect in VIRTOOL). However, the procedure "planing" is a coarse-grained procedure because this operation involves the manipulation of a concrete tool and several cranks in a specific way (a large number of variables must be verified in order to interpret the action). DETECTive does not specify the grain size. Therefore, the developer who integrates the systems must impose the procedure constraints in accordance with the technical possibilities of the 3D environment. Also, we should take into account that the finer the grain, the more refined the diagnostic will be.

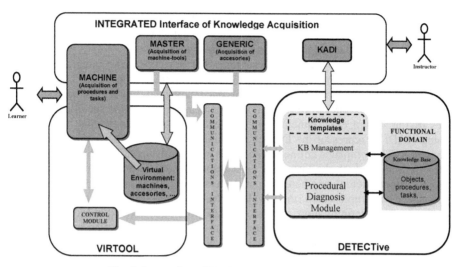

Fig. 3. Integration of DETECTive and VIRTOOL.

In a virtual environment integrating DETECTive, *"A procedure is the action performed on domain elements which is determined univocally from the state of a set of attributes"*. The control module designed (Fig. 3) determines the names of procedures using the state of the environment. Once the name of the procedure has been determined, it is transmitted to DETECTive for its diagnostic process.

VIRTOOL applications have been progressively modified in order to verify the viability of integrating DETECTive. VIRTOOL's original knowledge base was changed for reproducing the type of data handled by DETECTive, so that data communication requisites were common. These changes allowed to gradually evaluate DETECTive's architecture and to extrapolate results from the evaluation of VIRTOOL performed with students. This process revealed some improvements required by the diagnostic system. Primarily, the domain based diagnosis ought to be reinforced, in order to address better this aspect. Moreover, it is also necessary to add *spontaneous procedures* to identify changes in the virtual environment which have not been produced by student actions. Although they should not be directly analysed by DETECTive, they modify attributes which, in fact, are used to diagnose subsequent learner's actions.

4.2   Unification of the Knowledge Acquisition Tools

Experience says that instructors spend a large amount of time to complete the knowledge acquisition phase. Although existing tools facilitate this work, the manual definition of the functional domain for a virtual training system (order deviations, typical errors, solving plans, ...) is an arduous task which should be simplified. In this sense, DETECTive requires an extension of the functionalities provided by KADI.

The inherent complexity of a generic diagnostic system, which is, in addition, integrated into a virtual environment, increases the likelihood of designing incomplete domains. An incomplete domain is a common cause of later errors in the diagnostic process.

There are domain data generated in the VIRTOOL pre-processing phase (with Master and Generic) which are also necessary for DETECTive, so that the knowledge acquisition process would have to be performed twice.

To avoid the above mentioned problems, the developer who integrates DETEC-Tive with the virtual environment must achieve a previous process: the characteristics and constraints of the virtual environment, once they are defined, must be also defined in DETECTive in order to fit its representation capabilities to the specific characteristics of the virtual environment. So, the developer builds knowledge templates by using KADI to represent the DETECTive objects which can be manipulated on the simulator. The templates define the common characteristics of the objects and specify the constraints which the instructor must respect to define new elements. For example, to author a template where the parameters of a milling machine (e.g. power, cutting speed) are represented, the developer has to specify a constraint to prevent the instructor from defining more parameters than those ones defined in Machine.

Once the templates have been defined, the knowledge acquisition task that the instructor has to carry out is simplified as follows:

- Benefits in the acquisition of the performance domain (except for procedures): machines and tools are the elements of the VIRTOOL domain which the instructor has to represent in DETECTive. The definition of these elements are made, also in the pre-processing phase of VIRTOOL, using Master and Generic. These tools communicate with the DETECTive knowledge management system by using the communications module (the same Machine uses to communicate with the diagnostic module). In this way, the instructor's task is simplified by introducing data only once. In addition, the information the instructor has to provide is determined by the knowledge templates of DETECTive.

- Benefits in the acquisition of procedures and solving plans: the definition of new procedures and exercises will be achieved through the direct manipulation in the virtual environment by using Machine instead of Case Generator. The instructor performs actions in Machine and the control module tries to interpret them. If the procedure name of any executed action is not available, the teacher will define it explicitly. In order to acquire the solving plans of the exercise, the instructor performs an initial demonstration of its solution and refines it gradually adding order deviations, typical errors and so on. The interface of Machine must be extended for the acquisition of procedures and exercises in order to allow defining simple and compound procedures, order deviations, correct and erroneous solving plans, etc.

As a result of this knowledge acquisition process, we obtain two different views of the domain from an only task: the simulation knowledge used by VIRTOOL and the educational knowledge for DETECTive. The instructor can complete the domain definition by using KADI when it is needed.

The development of the acquisition system is still in an early stage. However, it has already been possible to draw some conclusions. The exercise acquisition system using demonstrations facilitates the definition of solving plans, but it must be improved to facilitate the acquisition of order deviations. However it may result simpler to define order deviations using KADI.

5 Educational Virtual Environments

This section contains a description of some of the educational tools used in the computer-assisted learning area that use similar techniques to the ones we propose. We focus on their procedural diagnostic capabilities, collaboration with 3D environments and knowledge acquisition methods.

RIDES and VIVIDS [12][13] are applications for authoring interactive graphical simulations with automatic support for diagnosing student actions. RIDES works with 2D graphics, while VIVIDS (an extended version of RIDES) can also use VISTA, a 3D virtual environment. In this environment, the autonomous agent STEVE interacts with the student and participates in the course of each training session. The authoring process with VIVIDS entails two main stages. Firstly, VIVIDS provides tools to build a prototype 2D model of the simulation. Then, it is gradually refined in coordination with the 3D browser. Synchronisation is performed using ToolTalk, an interapplication messaging system. VIVIDS manages the data necessary to simulate devices, whereas VISTA only displays them in the 3D environment. In our case, instead of creating object simulations, we share this responsibility with the virtual reality environment and focus on the integration of the generic diagnostic system. On the one hand, we try to take advantage of the diagnostic abilities in different domains and, on the other hand, to profit from the benefits of the simulation of different virtual environments. We consider that the RIDES and VIVIDS architecture could make difficult to reuse any of their components in other virtual reality systems, since low level control of the simulated devices may restrict the control capabilities of the simulator.

Diligent [14] is the system which learns procedural knowledge for the autonomous agent STEVE. Diligent uses the simulator itself to acquire this knowledge through a combination of programming by demonstration, autonomous experimentation and direct specification. The system assumes that the simulator can be externally controlled by sending commands to it in order to produce the same results as an instructor managing it in person. The knowledge acquisition task is greatly simplified, but we believe that requiring total control of the simulator via commands is a rigorous requirement in order to integrate different types of virtual environments.

It is also worth noting the authoring tool DEMONSTR8 [15], which builds model-tracing based tutors for arithmetic domains. In this respect, it resembles the original proposal of VIRTOOL. Although it is possible to use model-tracing in other domains, it is more appropriate to complement it with other techniques in order to obtain more accurate diagnoses.

IITSAT is an ITS authoring tool used for building training systems for different domains (military [16][17], flight training). The diagnostic system is dependent on training scenarios. Although this paper focuses on diagnosis, it is important to consider the experience of integrating IITSAT into graphical applications, some of which have been previously developed.

6 Conclusions and Future Work

The architecture presented in this article allows to employ DETECTive as a diagnostic kernel integrated in virtual environments. The developed communications module allows VIRTOOL and DETECTive to interact independently of their internal structures involved in the diagnostic process. The tests performed with students have been satisfactory; the generic nature of the knowledge base is maintained while the system interprets the actions of the students and links them to the elements defined in the knowledge acquisition phase. The procedures and exercises are defined through demonstrations in the virtual environment. The problem arises in defining deviations which may require a high number of demonstrations by the instructor. Referring that, we consider it is preferable that the definition of the functional domain be as complete as possible and the order deviations are built incrementally from results of task diagnostic– this is something already envisaged by DETECTive.

We have two current areas of study. The first one involves the evaluation of the real improvements offered by DETECTive in comparison with the original VIRTOOL system. In order to accomplish this, it will be necessary to analyse the DETECTive performance integrated in the virtual environment. Additionally, the time reduction in the knowledge acquisition phase will be evaluated, as well as the reliability of the acquired knowledge (novice users of the tool will have worse results). The interaction between the students and the tool (especially in the diagnostic process) will also be studied.

Acknowledgments

This research has been supported by the European Union (*VIRTOOL*, CRAFT-1999-70292), CICYT (*EDULAN*, TIC-2002-03141) and UPV-EHU (*ERAKUSLE*, 1/UPV 00141.226-T-13995/2001, 1/UPV 00141.226-T-14816/2002).

References

1. Stone, R.: Virtual reality for interactive training: an industrial practitioner's viewpoint. Int. J. Human - Computer Studies, 55 (2001) 699-711.
2. Tietronix Training Simulation. www.Tietronix.com
3. Fifth Dimension Technologies. www.5dt.com
4. Mellet d'Huart, D.: Virtual Environment for Training: An Art of Enhancing Reality. ITS 2002 Workshops (2002) 63-68.
5. Bloom, B.S., Engelhart, M.D., Murst, E.J., Hill, W.H. & Drathwohl, D.R.: Taxonomy of Educational Objectives. The cognitive Domain, Longmans. (1956).
6. Ustarroz, A., Lozano, A., Matey, L., Siemon, J., Klockmann, D., Berasategi, M.I.: VIRTOOL – Virtual Reality for Machine–Tool Training. Virtual Concept 2002. Biarritz (2002).
7. Kautz, H. & Allen, J.: Generalized Plan Recognition. Proceedings of the Fifth National Conference on Artificial Intelligence (1986) 32-37. Philadelphia. American Association for Artificial Intelligence.
8. Greer, J.E & Koehn, G.M.: The Peculiarities of Plan Recognition for Intelligent Tutoring Systems. Workshop on The Next Generation of Plan Recognition Systems: Challenges for and Insight from Related Areas of AI held in IJCAI 95.
9. Ferrero B., Fernández-Castro I., Urretavizcaya M. Diagnostic et évaluation dans les systèmes de «training» industriel. Diagnosis and assessment in industrial training systems. Simulation et formation professionnelle dans l'industrie 6(1) (1999) 189-217.

10. Martín, M.: Sistema de ayuda a la adquisición de conocimientos para el diagnóstico. Master Thesis in Computer Science, UPV/EHU (2002).
11. Ferrero, B., Arruarte, A., Fernández-Castro I., Urretavizcaya, M.: Herramientas de Autor para Enseñanza y Diagnóstico: IRIS-D. Inteligencia Artificial 12 (2001) 13-28.
12. Munro, A., Johnson, M.C., Pizzini, Q.A., Surmon, D.S., Towne, D.M., Wogulis, J.L.: Authoring Simulation-Centered Tutors with RIDES. Int. Journal of Artificial Intelligence in Education 8. (1997) 284-316.
13. Johnson, W., Rickle, J., Stiles, R., Munro, A.: Integrating Pedagogical Agents into Virtual Environments. Presence: Teleoperators and Virtual Environments 7(6) (1998) 523-546.
14. Angros Jr., R., Lewis Johnson, W., Rickel, J., Scholer, A.: Learning Domain Knowledge for Teaching Procedural Skills. AAMAS'02 (2002).
15. Blessing, S.B.: A Programming by Demonstration Authoring Tool for Model-Tracing Tutors. Int. Journal of Artificial Intelligence in Education 8 (1997) 233-261.
16. Stottler, R., Fu, D. Ramachandran, S., Jackson, T.: Applying a Generic Intelligent Tutoring System Authoring Tool to Specific Military Domains. Industry/Interservice, Training, Simulation & Education Conference (2001).
17. Stottler, R., Jensen, R.: Adding an Intelligent Tutoring System to an Existing Training Simulation. Industry/Interservice, Training, Simulation & Education Conference (2002).

TAPLI: An Adaptive Web-Based Learning Environment for Linear Programming

Eva Millán, Emilio García-Hervás, Eduardo Guzmán De los Riscos, Ángel Rueda, and José Luis Pérez de la Cruz

Departamento de Lenguajes y Ciencias de la Computación, ETSI Informática
Universidad de Málaga, Spain
eva@lcc.uma.es

Abstract. In this paper we present TAPLI, an adaptive web-based learning environment for Linear Programming. TAPLI is in fact a set of adaptive tools offered in a web-based learning environment: a) an adaptive hypermedia component, that is responsible of presenting the learning contents; b) a testing component, based on the SIETTE system (that implements *Computerized Adaptive Tests* using *Item Response Theory* as inference machine to estimate the student's knowledge level); and c) *a drill-and-practice component*, which generates exercises adapted to the student's knowledge level, and which coaches students while solving the problems posed by the system, offering guidance, support, help and feedback. The estimation of the student's knowledge level made by SIETTE is used by TAPLI as a basis to provide adaptation at all stages of the learning process: while learning the contents, while making tests, when being proposed an exercise and while solving it. Additionally the system provides an open student model that allows to inspect in detail the state of his/her knowledge at any time and to change the learning goals at any moment during the interaction with the system.

1 Introduction

The maturity and increasing availability of the Internet has presented new opportunities and challenges for the Education field. The development of adaptive web-based educational systems (AWES) can be of great help in the teaching and learning process, providing world-wide accessibility and timeless availability.

First efforts to develop web-based educational systems tried to move existing Intelligent Tutoring Systems (ITS) to the web [5] or to use authoring tools for developing adaptive hypermedia systems (AHS) [4]. Since then, dozens of web-based educational systems have been developed, like ELM-ART, an award-winning web-based learning system for LISP [18] or Activemath, a web-based system that generates adaptive mathematical courses [10]. Many of the technologies traditionally used in ITS and AHS have been implemented in the existing adaptive web-based educational systems [3], but also new adaptive techniques have been developed and successfully integrated into modern AWES.

The main goal in the research work presented here, was to use the web and adaptive technologies to create TAPLI[1]. It stands for *Tutorial Adaptativo de Programación*

---

[1] A short version of this paper was presented at ICWE'03 [12].

R. Conejo et al. (Eds.): CAEPIA-TTIA 2003, LNAI 3040, pp. 676–685, 2004.
© Springer-Verlag Berlin Heidelberg 2004

Lineal in Spanish, and it is available at http://www.lcc.uma.es/tapli. TAPLI is a web-based learning environment that can help students to learn Linear Programming. The most popular algorithm to solve Linear Programming problems is the Simplex algorithm (Dantzig, 1940), which is an iterative procedure that finds the optimum of a linear function subject to a number of linear constraints.

In adaptive hypermedia systems, adaptation is usually provided by two well-known techniques: *adaptive navigation support* (ANS), which helps students to find an optimal navigation path by using techniques like link annotation and disabling or direct guidance, and *adaptive presentation*, which adapts the page content to user's characteristics like knowledge, goals, experience, learning style, etc. Almost all web-based adaptive educational systems implement these techniques, which are also present in TAPLI, that, as explained in section 3.1, offers guidance (by means of the recommendations provided), link hiding and text hiding.

Other ways of adaptation provided in TAPLI, *adaptive testing* and *adaptive problem generation,* are not so common within adaptive educational systems. It is hard to find web-based systems that implement adaptive testing using psychometric theories like *Item Response Theory* (IRT) [15]. Examples of these kind of systems are Hypertutor [6], Hezinet [14] and some commercial tools like CATGlobal [13]. Other systems implement adaptive testing at a much more basic level (for example ELM-ART [18]). Adaptive problem generation is even harder to find (see [2] for a complete review of systems and issues).

This paper is structured as follows: in the next section we briefly present the history of TAPLI, which has been developed from our experience in other systems and tools. Section 3 is devoted to a complete presentation of the system. The paper finishes with some conclusions and future research directions.

2   Preliminaries and Tools

In the development of TAPLI, our previous research on Artificial Intelligence in Education has been of great help: namely, the lessons learned in the development of previous tools to assist in the teaching of Linear Programming, as EPLAR and ILESA; our studies about generation of problems in web-based tutors [2], and our experience in web-based adaptive testing [7].

The development of tools to assist in teaching Linear Programming has always been a focus of interest for some members of our research group that teach this subject in the University of Málaga. The first experience was EPLAR [11], which was just a problem solver that our students found quite useful because it allowed them to check the solutions of the exercises proposed during the course. However, we felt that much more could be done. The simplex algorithm has some characteristics that make it a specially suitable domain to be taught in a virtual environment: first, the learning of this domain is strongly based in acquiring problem solving skills; second, the procedure consists in a series of simple steps that have to be performed in certain order, feature that facilitates the model tracing task; third, the generation of problems at the right level of difficulty can be accomplished quite easily and finally, the different types of errors can be easily identified and corrected.

Our next step was the development of a web-based tool that provided *coached problem solving* [16], which has proven to be a very effective style for instruction.

This tool was called ILESA [9], and it was capable of coaching students while solving a problem and also to generate problems at the right level of difficulty based on the student model. The results obtained with ILESA were very encouraging, as the capability of generating problems was quite unique within web-based systems at the moment. Future researched aimed to the construction of a virtual environment that was not just a drill-and-practice tool, but also a place where the theoretical concepts could be acquired.

At the same time, other members of the group were involved in the development of the SIETTE system [7]. SIETTE is a web-based testing tool (available at http://www.lcc.uma.es/siette) that can be used by teachers (to edit tests for any subject domain) and students (to assess themselves on line). Tests generated by SIETTE are *Computerized Adaptive Tests* (CATs) [17] based on IRT. The operation mode of a CAT is the same used by a teacher: a question (named items in IRT) is posed to student. If it is answered correctly, a more difficult item is posed, else an easier item is presented. These adaptive techniques used in SIETTE result in shorter and more accurate tests, as shown in [8]. Test items can contain images, videos or java applets, making it a powerful tool that allows the use of tests to evaluate declarative and procedural domains. SIETTE can also be used as an autonomous tool or as a diagnosis module of other AWES.

It was then quite natural to use the SIETTE tool to define adaptive tests for the Linear Programming domain. In this way, a reliable and fast evaluation tool could easily be integrated in the web-based environment. The next challenge was to use the SIETTE system not only to evaluate the student with tests, but also to coach students during problem solving and to evaluate the results of the problem process. To this end, the possibility that SIETTE offers to define questions by means of java applets [1] has proven to be extremely useful. Java applets have been implemented for each of the steps of the simplex algorithm. These java applets are also capable of detecting student mistakes, offering feedback and help, and evaluating the problem solving process. The estimation of the student state of knowledge is always made by SIETTE, and based on this estimation the system is capable of generating problems at the right level of difficulty. How this is accomplished will be described in more detail in section 3.3.

3 The TAPLI System

The TAPLI system (Figure 1) is in fact a set of components that have been integrated in a single learning environment: a) an *adaptive hypermedia component*, that is responsible of presenting the theoretical concepts and examples; b) a *testing component*, that evaluates the student knowledge on each of the topics in which the domain has been decomposed, and c) a *drill-and practice component*, where students can solve problems while being coached by the system. Together, all these tools constitute a complete environment for learning Linear Programming. They are coordinated by an *instructional planner*, which is responsible of selecting the next component that will be used by the student in his learning process. The instructional planner uses the information provided by the *student model* to take this decision. The *student model* stores all the information obtained or inferred about the student. This information is stored in the *student models repository*. As a result, any time a student begins a learn-

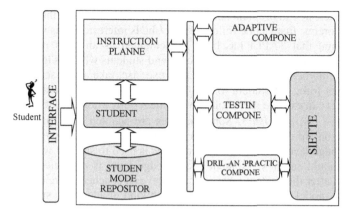

Fig. 1. The architecture of TAPLI.

ing session in TAPLI, the instructional planner will recover all data from his previous sessions. The remaining components of this architecture will be described in more detail in the next sections.

3.1 The Adaptive Hypermedia Component

This component has been designed so students that cannot attend lessons are able to learn the main concepts and techniques for Linear Programming. The curriculum has been organized into six topics.

TAPLI is an *adaptable* and *adaptive* system, because some characteristics are adapted according to information provided by the student while some others are adapted based on information gathered by the system during student's interactions. The information used to provide adaptation in TAPLI (student´s knowledge, learning goals, visited pages, etc.) is stored into the student model. Next we will describe which characteristics of TAPLI are adaptable and adaptive.

- *Adaptable characteristics.* When the student connects to TAPLI, he/she has to provide some information (name and password) so the system can create his/her student model . Also some personal learning characteristics are included in the model like topics of interest (learning goals[2]) within the domain of Linear Programming, and type of knowledge that wants to be acquired (theoretical and practical or only practical). According to this characteristics, the system will adapt to the student. Learning goals are used to adapt the suggested navigation structure (*i.e.*, the recommendations provided by the system), and also to hide links to tests that evaluate topics that are not learning goals. However, text pages related to topics that are not currently the focus of attention are not hidden. In this way, the student can take a look at them and change his/her learning goals accordingly. Strech-text techniques have been used so the system can adapt to the type of knowledge required by the student. In this way, the student that is

---

[2] The learning goals can be changed by the student at any time during the interaction with TAPLI

only interested in problem solving will only see links to the theoretical proofs of the theorems, that can be followed if he/she is interested. It is important to say at this point that TAPLI has been implemented as an open environment. This means that it has the ability to recommend students which is the best thing to do at each moment (read a page, solve an exercise, take a test, see an example) but does not force the student to follow the offered recommendations. In this way, students can explore the whole environment with whole freedom.

- *Adaptive characteristics.* Some features are adapted according to relevant information inferred by the system, as the list of visited pages and student's knowledge level. The list of visited pages is used to suggest which page the student should see next. Student's knowledge level is estimated by the SIETTE system after the student takes a test or solves a coached exercise, and kept in the student model. It is used to suggest which kind of action the student should take next (take a test/solve an exercise). Once the student has visited all the pages, the next page to be visited is selected according to the information contained in the student model (among those that the student is ready to learn and have not been visited yet).

As an example, we show in Figure 2 a snapshot of TAPLI interface during a session. The interface is divided into two different parts: on the right we have a frame that presents the curriculum and which also has a window where recommendations are offered and two informative buttons: *Tu conocimiento*, that allows students to inspect their student model and change his/her learning goals; and *Mapa del web*, which shows a statistics of the visited pages, as can be seen in the lower windows of the figure. For this particular student, the system offers two recommendations: what to *read* next (*Pasos del Simplex*, i.e. Simplex steps), which is based on the visited pages; and what to *do* next (*Test del método gráfico*, i.e., take a test about the graphic method), which is based on the current estimation of student's knowledge level. On the left side, the learning contents of the selected topic of the curriculum are shown.

3.2 The Testing Component

As explained in section 2, this component is based on the SIETTE system [7]. The testing component can be used at any time during the interaction with the system. The action *Take a test* is also recommended by the system whenever it is advisable. For example, for new students (to check their state of knowledge),whenever the student visits a page (to infer if the knowledge presented has been acquired), or when the student enters the drill-and-practice environment (to be able to generate problems at the required level of difficulty for student's level of knowledge).

Different tests have been defined for each of the six topics the subject has been divided into (see the second window in Figure 2 for a list of these topics). Each of these SIETTE tests classifies the student in $K=11$ classes (from 0 to 10). So for example in Figure 2 the student has taken tests about two topics obtaining a grade of 5 out of 10 in each of these two topics. After each topic is evaluated, a global grade is computed as a weighted average of the grades obtained in each topic.

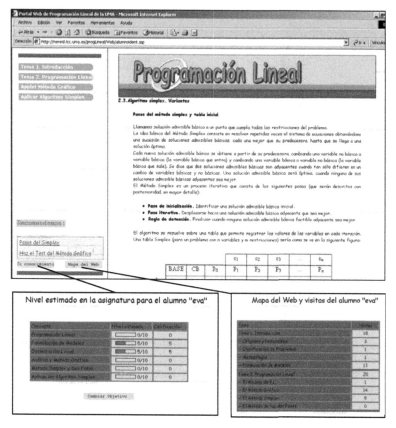

Fig. 2. Snapshot of TAPLI interface and windows for the estimated knowledge level (*Tu conocimiento*) and map of visited pages (*Mapa del web*).

The communication of this component with SIETTE is based on URL calls from one system to the other with the proper parameters. Initially, the testing component sends to SIETTE: a) the set of topics to be assessed; b) the current estimation of student's knowledge about these topics; c) the number of knowledge levels in which the student can be classified; d) the URL to which the results will be returned, and e) additional parameters to configure the test (item selection mechanism, finalization criteria, ...).

Once the evaluation has finished, SIETTE will invoke to the URL indicated, passing the new estimated knowledge levels of the student. With these data, TAPLI updates the student model, and uses this information to select the next best instructional actions to recommend.

3.3   The Drill-and-Practice Component

As explained in section 2, one of the major challenges in the development of TAPLI was to use the SIETTE system to allow coached problem solving in a

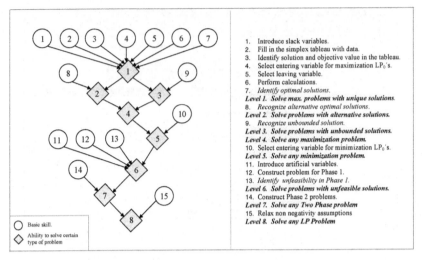

1. Introduce slack variables.
2. Fill in the simplex tableau with data.
3. Identify solution and objective value in the tableau.
4. Select entering variable for maximization LP$_0$'s.
5. Select leaving variable.
6. Perform calculations.
7. *Identify optimal solutions.*
Level 1. Solve max. problems with unique solutions.
8. *Recognize alternative optimal solutions.*
Level 2. Solve problems with alternative solutions.
9. *Recognize unbounded solution.*
Level 3. Solve problems with unbounded solutions.
Level 4. Solve any maximization problem.
10. Select entering variable for minimization LP$_0$'s.
Level 5. Solve any minimization problem.
11. Introduce artificial variables.
12. Construct problem for Phase 1.
13. *Identify unfeasibility in Phase 1.*
Level 6. Solve problems with unfeasible solutions.
14. Construct Phase 2 problems.
Level 7. Solve any Two Phase problem
15. Relax non negativity assumptions
Level 8. Solve any LP Problem

○ Basic skill.
◇ Ability to solve certain
   type of problem

Fig. 3. Learning strategy in TAPLI.

drill-and-practice environment. This has been accomplished by using one of the most powerful features of the SIETTE system, namely, the possibility to define questions by means of Java Applets.

Generation of problems for linear programming is an interesting issue that has already been discussed in [9] and [2]. The same techniques have been used here to generate problems at the right level of difficulty based on the current estimation of the student knowledge state.

In Figure 3 we can see the learning strategy used in TAPLI for acquiring problem-solving skills:

In this learning strategy we can see that the problem-solving procedure has been decomposed in basic skills (round nodes) and types of problems (square and shaded nodes). The graph show which skills are necessary for solving each of the eight different types of problems. For example, square node 1 shows that to be able to solve a maximization linear programming problem with unique solution, it is necessary to have skills 1 to 7. The levels are cumulative in the sense that each level of problems require also to be able to solve problems of all the preceding levels. So, for example, to be able to solve problems in node 6, it is necessary to have all skills required for problems 1 to 5, and also skills 11, 12 and 13. Therefore problems in level k are considered to be more difficult than problems in level k-1. In SIETTE, this corresponds to assigning increasing difficulty parameters to each level. Also, problem levels are used to estimate student's knowledge state by identifying it with the last problem level that the student is able to solve. Therefore, in this drill-and-practice component the number of classes K in which SIETTE classifies the students has been set to be K=8.

Different applets have been defined for each of the basic skills. The problem solving procedure is totally guided by a sequence of the adequate applets. As an example, we show in Figure 4 an applet where the student has to introduce basic variables in a problem which has been automatically generated by TAPLI according to his/her knowledge state.

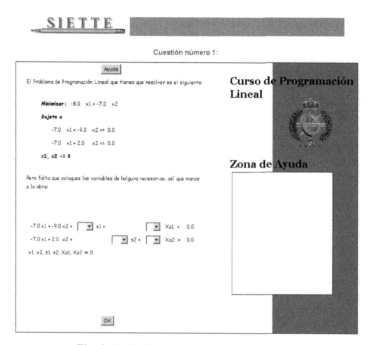

Fig. 4. Applet for introducing slack variables.

As it can be seen in Figure 4, there is a button *Ayuda* that the student can use to ask for help, which will be shown in the corresponding window (*Zona de ayuda*). Also, if the student makes a mistake the system will provide feedback to help in overcoming the impasse. It is important to say that both help and feedback are somewhat penalized by the system. If the student exceeds a maximum fixed number of help and feedback messages, the system will consider that he/she has not been able to solve the problem by himself/herself. Tough it certainly would be interesting to inform students that the use of help is penalized, we have not taken this option, mainly because we do want students to use feedback in this part of the system that is conceived as a practice environment and not as an evaluative component. Problems are evaluated by the applet itself: the student's problem solving procedure is classified as correct (if the correct solution has been achieved and the maximum number of required hints and feedback has not been reached), or incorrect (if the student was not able to solve the problem or needed too much help from the system), which also passes the result to SIETTE. In this way, for SIETTE, these exercises are just like any other test item, which is evaluated to be classified into one of the categories pre-established at the beginning of the test. Depending on the correctness of the solution, SIETTE will return information to update the student model. These data will be used to select the next best type of exercise to be posed next. Then another problem is automatically generated and posed.

This procedure has the advantage that SIETTE is totally responsible of updating the student model and of selecting the type of exercise to be posed next. This is very convenient because, as explained before, SIETTE uses theoretically sound methods (based on IRT) for both procedures.

4 Conclusions and Future Work

In this paper we have presented the TAPLI system, which is an adaptive web-based learning environment for Linear Programming. This system has three different educative components: an adaptive hypermedia component, where the learning contents are presented; a testing component, where students can be evaluated using CATs based on IRT; and a drill-and-practice component, where students can solve problems coached by the system. The two last components has been implemented reusing a well-founded assessment system (SIETTE).

The TAPLI system presents three different kinds of adaptation. First, the adaptive hypermedia component is able to provide adaptation in several ways: adaptive navigation support is achieved by direct guidance (recommendations) and by link hiding, while adaptive presentation is achieved by hiding parts of the text. Second, the test component offers adaptive tests to evaluate students. Finally, the generative capabilities of the system provide adaptation by problem generation and by personalized assistance during the problem solving process, which are indeed two innovative adaptation techniques for AWES.

A fully working version of TAPLI is currently available at http://www.lcc. uma.es/tapli. However, further work is needed in two different directions: First, there are certain improvements in the system that we would like to make, like to increase the range of adaptive techniques and using more elaborate student models. Once these enhancements are accomplished, it is indispensable to conduct formative evaluations with students, in order to see if TAPLI does indeed increase the rate of effective learning. To this end, a control group will use the system in their learning process while their classmates receive traditional teaching, and then the performance of both groups will be compared. Currently, students of Operations Research of the Computer Science School of the University of Málaga have been using the system through the web page[3] of the subject with satisfactory results, but we do need a carefully designed evaluation whose results can serve to guide us in the development of better versions of the system.

References

1. Arroyo, I., Conejo, R., Guzmán, E., & Woolf, B. P. (2001). An Adaptive Web-based Component for Cognitive Ability Estimation. Proceedings of the 9th World Conference of Artificial Intelligence and Education AIED'01 Amsterdam: IOS Press.
2. Belmonte, M. V., Guzmán, E., Mandow, L., Millán, E., & Pérez de la Cruz, J. L. (2002). Automatic generation of problems in web-based tutors. In L. Jain and R. Howlet: Virtual Environments for Teaching and Learning (pp. 237-277). World Scientific.
3. Brusilovsky, P. (1999). Adaptive and Intelligent Technology for Web-based Education. Special Issue on Intelligent Systems and Teleteaching, Künstliche Intelligenz, 4, 19-25.
4. Brusilovsky, P., Schwartz, E., & Weber, G. (1996). A Tool for Developing Hypermedia-based ITS on WWW. Proceedings of Workshop on Architectures and Methods for Designing Cost Effective and Reusable ITS at the 3rd International Conference on Intelligent Tutoring Systems.

---

[3] http://polaris.lcc.uma.es/~eva/asignaturas/tcio

5. Brusilovsky, P., Schwarz, E., & Weber, G. (1996). ELM-ART: an intelligent tutoring system on the World Wide Web. LNCS 1086, Springer Verlag.
6. Carro, J. A., Pérez, T. A., Gutiérrez, J., & Morlán, I. (1997). Planteamiento de ejercicios en un sistema hipermedia adaptativo. Novática, 125.
7. Conejo, R., Guzmán, E., Millán, E., Pérez, J. L., & Trella, M. (To appear). SIETTE: A WebBased Tool for Adaptive Testing. International Journal of Artificial Intelligence in Education.
8. Conejo, R., Millán, E., Pérez-de-la-Cruz, J. L., & Trella, M. (2000). An Empirical Approach to On-Line Learning in SIETTE. In roceedings of 3rd International Conference on Intelligent Tutoring Systems ITS''2000, LNCS 1839 (pp. 604-614). Springer Verlag.
9. López, J. M., Millán, E., Pérez J.L., & Triguero F. (1998). ILESA: A web-based Intelligent Learning Environment for the Simplex Algorithm. Proceedings of CALISCE'98 .
10. Melis, E., Andres, E., Budenbender, J., & Frischauf, A. (2001). ActiveMath: A Generic and Adaptive Web-Based Learning Environment . International Journal of Artificial Intelligence in Education , 12, 385-407.
11. Millán, E., Mandow, L., & Rey, L. (1999). EPLAR: Un entorno para la enseñanza de la Programación Lineal. En Desarrollo profesional y docencia universitaria: Proyecto de innovación en la Universidad. Servicio de Publicaciones de la Universidad de Málaga.
12. Millán, E., García, E., Guzmán, E., Rueda, A., & Pérez-de-la-Cruz, J. L. (2003). Adaptation and Generation in a Web-Based Tutor for Linear Programming. In Proceedings of 1st International Conference on Web Engineering (ICWE'03), LNCS 2722. Springer Verlag.
13. Promissor. (CATGlobal [Web Page]. URL http://www.catglobal.com
14. Pérez, T. A., Gabiola, K., Gutiérrez, J., López, R., González, A., & Carro, J. A. (1999). Hezinet: Interactive (Adaptive) Education Through Activities. Proceedings of ED-MEDIA'99.
15. Van der Linden, W., & Hambleton, R. (eds). (1997). Handbook of Modern Item Response Theory. New York: Springer Verlag.
16. VanLehn, K. (1996). Conceptual and Meta Learning during Coached Problem Solving. In Proceedings of 3rd International Conference ITS'96, LNCS Vol. 1086. (pp. 29-47). Springer Verlag.
17. Wainer, H. (ed.). (1990). Computerized Adaptive Testing: a Primer. Hillsdale, NJ: Lawrence Erlbaum Associates.
18. Weber, G., & Brusilovsky, P. (2001). ELM-ART: An Adaptive Versatile System for Web-based Instruction. International Journal of Artificial Intelligence in Education, 12, 351-384.

Author Index